AMERICAN CINEMATOGRAPHER MANUAL

TENTH EDITION

Volume II

REVISED 2014

EDITED BY

Michael Goi, ASC

THE ASC PRESS
HOLLYWOOD, CALIFORNIA

American Cinematographer Manual
Tenth Edition—Volume II

Copyright© 2013 by The ASC Press

Hollywood, California, USA
All Rights Reserved

ISBN 978-1-4675-6832-6

Cover design by Martha Winterhalter
Book design by Deeann j. Hoff
Production by Mark McDougal

Foreword

You hold in your hands the result of five years of thought, debate, and inspiration. When Stephen Burum, ASC, asked me to be the editor of this 10th edition of the venerable American Cinematographer Manual, the industry was in the birth throes of transition; digital intermediates were the exception and not the rule, we still used the term video rather than digital, and 4K as a viable production and post format was far beyond our reach. All these changes and many more came in rapid succession as we labored to bring this book to press. No sooner had we completed an article when it had to be updated due to sweeping advances in technology.

I am at heart a low-tech person. I like things simple. I questioned whether I was even the right person to be taking this book on. But in a strange way, it made sense. If I could design the manual in a manner that made sense to me, then the information it contained would be accesible to a wide spectrum of professional and prosumer image makers. Cinematographers today need to be closet scientists in order to decipher the tools they have at their disposal, but all those technologies need not be daunting; they can be fun to explore and exciting to utilize. Now more than ever, the dreams of a whole new generation can be made into real moving images. This edition contains some of the most comprehensive information on digital that you will find anywhere, but it doesn't leave behind the essential building blocks of film technology, which is at its highest level of development. Where we are now is really having the best of both worlds.

When you embark on a journey to a new world, it's best to take along a crew who know the territory. The contributors to this edition have proven to be the most helpful and dedicated group of scientists, artists and craftspeople one could possibly hope to assemble. Thanks go to Jim Branch, Curtis Clark, ASC; Richard Crudo, ASC; Dan Curry; Linwood G. Dunn, ASC; Richard Edlund, ASC; Jonathan Erland; Jon Fauer, ASC; Ray Feeney; Tom Fraser; Taz Goldstein; Colin Green and the Previsualization Society; Frieder Hochheim; Michael Hofstein; Bill Hogan; John Hora, ASC; Rob Hummel; Steve Irwin; Kent H. Jorgensen; Frank Kay; Glenn Kennel; Jon Kranhouse; Lou Levinson; Andy Maltz and the AMPAS Science and Technology Council; Vincent Matta; Tak Miyagishima; David Morin; M. David Mullen, ASC; Dennis Muren, ASC; Iain A. Neil; Marty Ollstein; Josh Pines; Steven Poster, ASC; Sarah Priestnall; David Reisner; Pete Romano, ASC; Andy Romanoff; Dr. Rod Ryan; Nic Sadler and Chemical Wedding; Bill Taylor, ASC; Ira Tiffen and Evans Wetmore.

Special thanks go to Iain Stasukevich for his assistance in research, Lowell Peterson, ASC, Jamie Anderson, ASC and King Greenspon for their proofreading skills, and Deeann Hoff and Mark McDougal for handling the layout of the book.

Extra special thanks go to Brett Grauman, general manager of the ASC, Patty Armacost, events coordinator, Delphine Figueras, my assistant when I was handling being ASC president while trying to finish this book, Saul Molina and Alex Lopez for their expertise in marketing and events management, Owen Roizman, ASC, who is the heart, soul and inspiration for the organization, George Spiro Dibie, ASC, my mentor and friend, Martha Winterhalter, whose knowledge of what we do and how to convey it to the world knows no bounds, and Gina Goi, my wife, for her love and support during my many twilight editing sessions.

Enjoy the Manual. Go make movies.

Michael Goi, ASC
Editor

Table of Contents

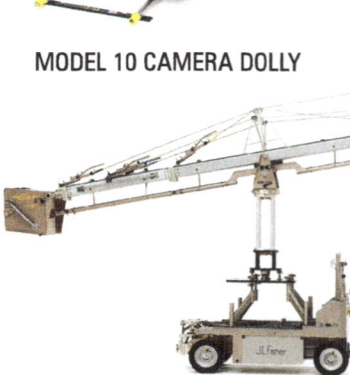

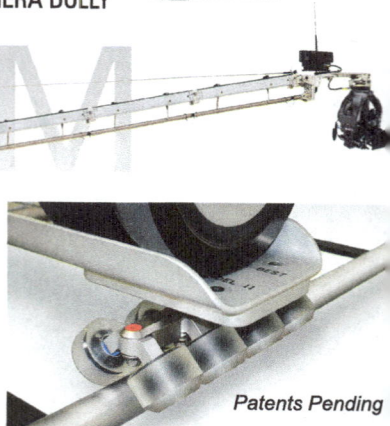

CAPTURE

PROCESS

ARCHIVE

SECURITY

MAKING YOUR WORK FLOW

codex

Gemini 4:4:4™

nano3D™

nanoFlash™

FlashXDR™

Engineering
the **NEXT** Revolution

Each of Convergent Design's recorders was a Revolution in digital video capture. When you choose a Convergent Design product, you can expect leading technology, field-proven resilience, and world class customer service.

convergent design

STAGE 12

STAGE 3

STAGE 26

STAGE 34

LE BABLOUSE

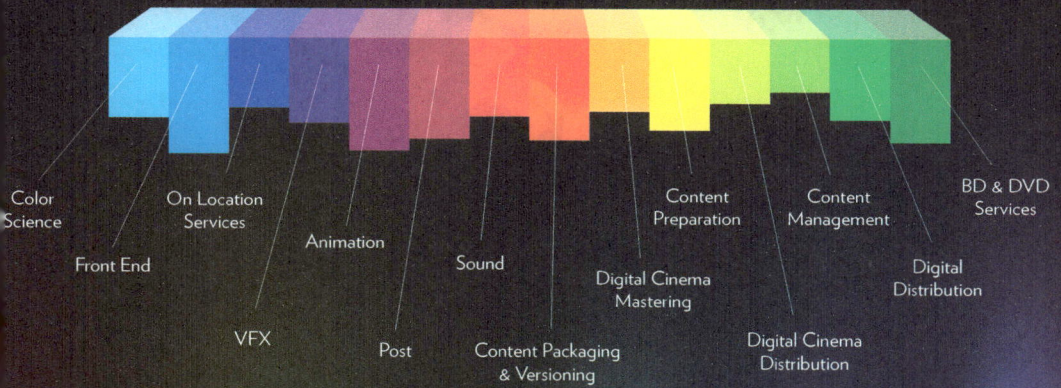

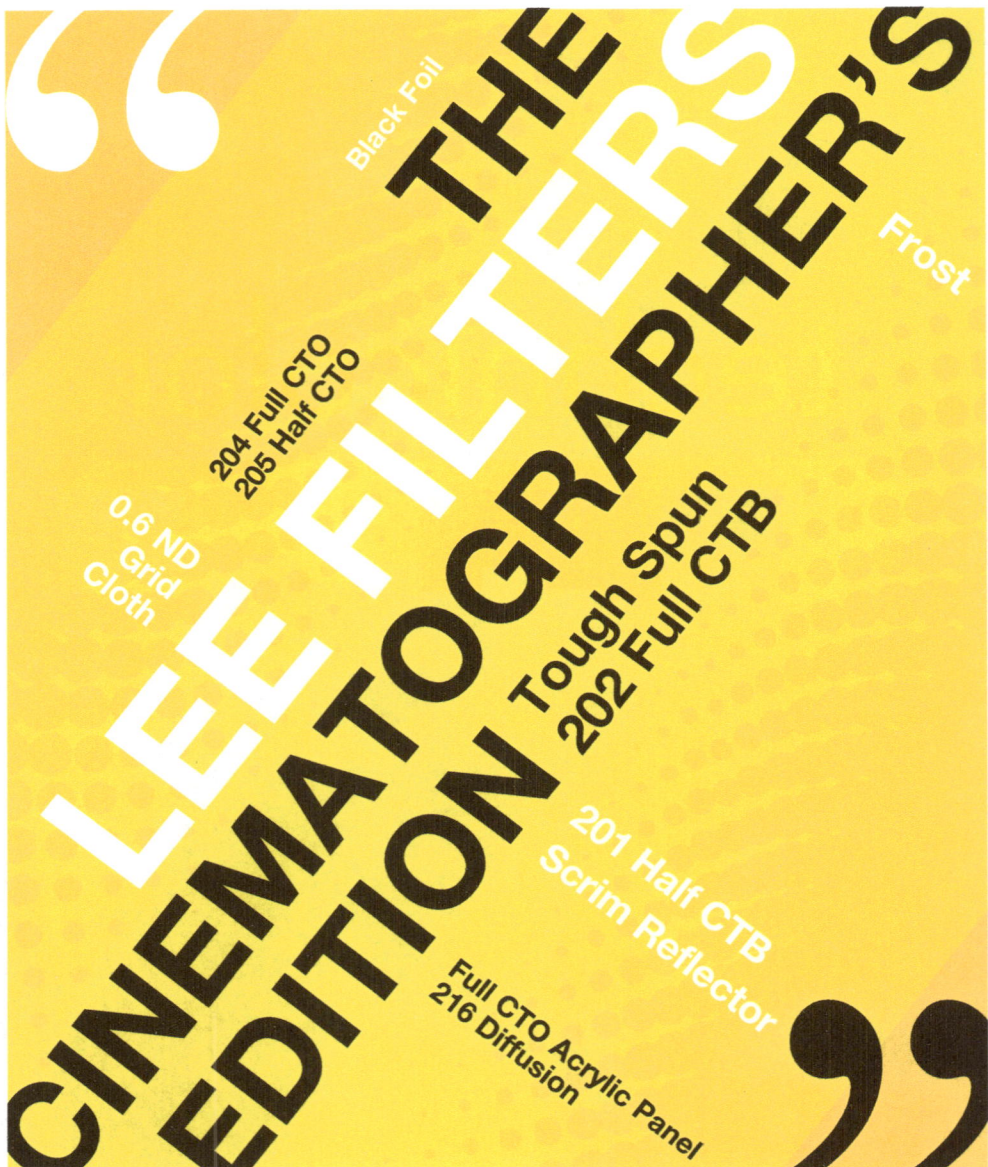

THE CLASSICS ARE
ALIVE

WHEN YOU CHOOSE TO ARCHIVE ON FILM, YOUR WORK LIVES ON.

Film is more than entertainment, it's history. Without it, countless classics would be lost.
Now, as digital storage becomes more seductive, modern classics could face extinction.
If it's worth shooting, it's worth saving. Protect your legacy on KODAK Asset Protection Films.

Find out more at www.kodak.com/go/archive

Kodak

DIGITAL CINEMA (RE)SOLUTION

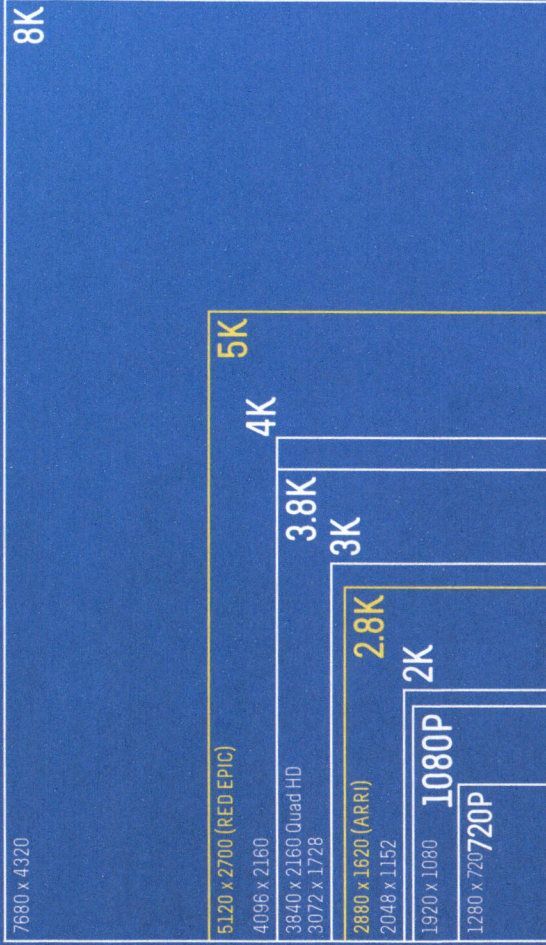

ARC
ADORAMA RENTAL CO

WE HAVE A SOLUTION
FOR YOUR RESOLUTION

ARC rents and supports the full
range of professional still & motion
equipment, including digital cinema
cameras, accessories, lenses,
lighting and grip.

8K
7680 x 4320

5K
5120 x 2700 (RED EPIC)

4K
4096 x 2160

3.8K
3840 x 2160 Quad HD
3072 x 1728

3K

2.8K
2880 x 1620 (ARRI)
2048 x 1152

2K
1920 x 1080 1080P

720P
1280 x 720

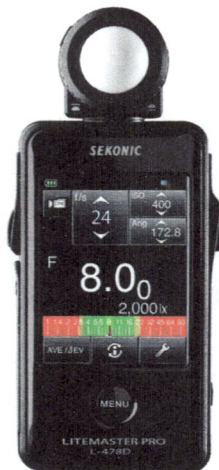

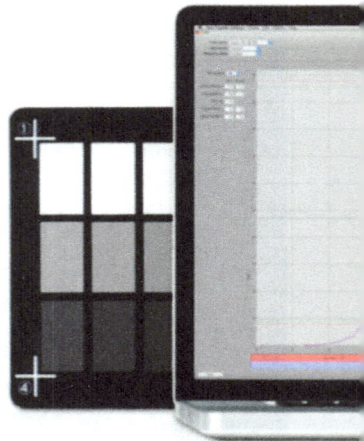

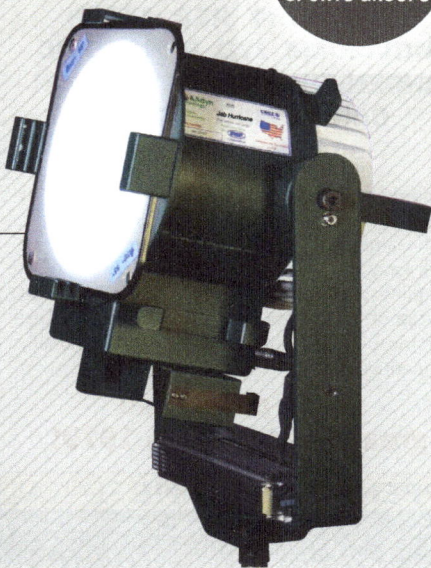

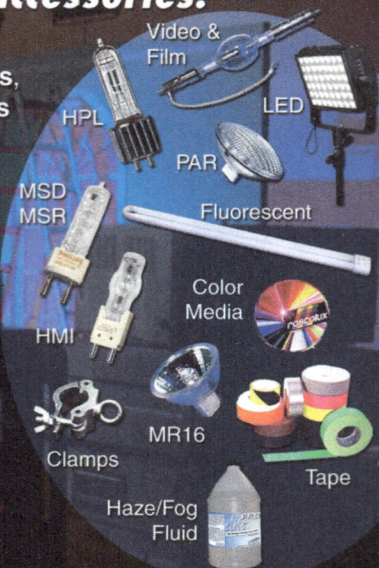

CINEMATOGRAPHERS PAINT THE MOOD
FOR MORE THAN 50 YEARS, PANAVISION HAS PROVIDED THE BRUSH

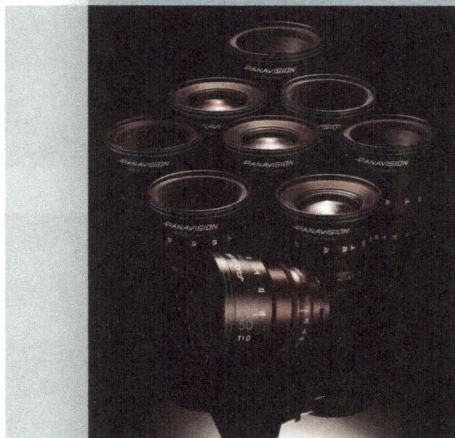

artistically
inspired

technically
advanced

PVINTAGE

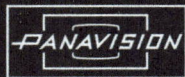

PANAVISION
www.panavision.com

ARTEMIS
DIRECTOR'S VIEWFINDER

- Completely updated engine
- Save images and notes to new internal image gallery
- Replicates popular motion picture cameras and lenses
- Add custom cameras for specific or exotic formats
- Available for iPhone, Android phones and the iPad

> I am working on a film called "Balls to the Walls" I use this app on every blocking rehearsal. I find the master and all the coverage and capture the frames and lens sizes in my photo library. Then I show the director. I can also start setting up the shot before the camera is in place. Great app and now an important tool for my work!
> **ROBERT REED ALTMAN**

> A lot easier and much more accurate than holding up your two hands to frame a shot. Much lighter than a heavy Director's Finder dangling from your neck. Every Director and DP should have this wonderful app.
> **FILM AND DIGITAL TIMES**

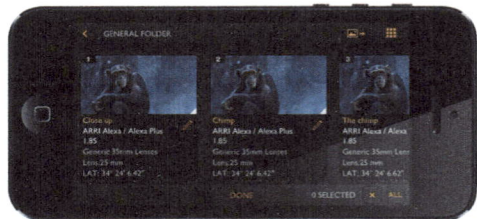

helios
sun position calculator

- Six tools to explore sun data
- Database of tens of thousands of locations around the world
- Email sun position data from within application
- Network connectivity not necessary for use

> I'm usually scouting for locations months before the DP comes on board and knowing precisely where the sun will be on the exact shoot date is essential. Helios is without doubt the best tool out there for DPs, production designers, location scouts and directors. Nothing comes even close.
> **RICHARD LONCRAINE**

> Simple. Elegant. Fast, Accurate... I love this!!!!
> **RUSSELL CARPENTER, ASC**

CHEMICAL WEDDING

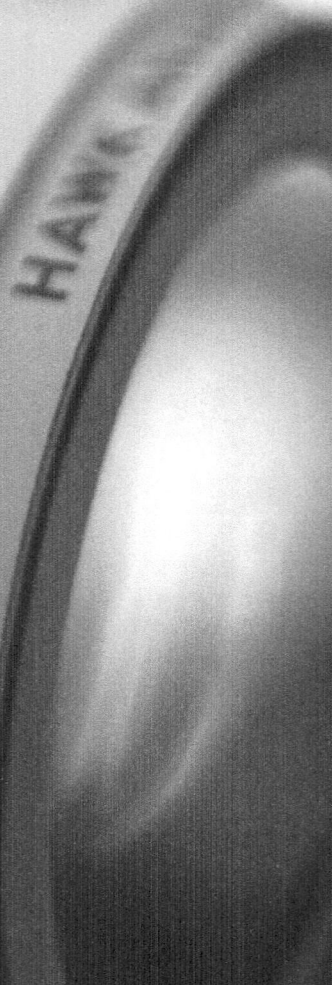

HAWK ®

THE FINEST ANAMORPHIC GLASS

Safety on the Set

by Kent H. Jorgensen and Vincent Matta

Safety plays a prominent role on any film and television set. It can be front and center, influencing decisions or a nagging annoyance, getting in the way of the creative process. Many people forget that the film and television industry is in fact, an industry. While it takes the artistic input of many different participants to make a film, the filmmaking process can place the cast and crew in situations that pose varying degrees of risk.

A production company's attitude is the starting place for dealing with the risks. Whether a union or a nonunion production, all the companies involved have a responsibility to see that their workers are trained and qualified to perform their specific job. Workers need to have their production's *Code of Safe Practices* communicated to them (sometimes also called *Polices and Procedures*), but many production people have little or no experience with issues of safety, or their productions may not operate with a Code of Safe Practices.

How can you help make a production safer?

Safety is an attitude. Make the conscious decision to not get hurt or sick or let anyone else get hurt or sick at work.

USE COMMON SENSE

Don't do things just to save time. If the camera is set up in the parking lane of a road and there are a number of people crowded into the lane, don't walk into traffic to get a lens or something to the camera. Drivers are not worried about you, and "cinematic immunity" doesn't protect you from their vehicles. Get the equipment to the camera as quickly but as safely as possible. (It's also part of the AD's job to help everyone get their jobs done quickly and safely on set.)

PLAN FOR THE JOB

During preproduction, on scouts, and any time shots are being discussed, make safety a part of the planning. Give qualified people all of the necessary parameters and listen to suggestions. Consider alternatives based on common sense, budget, schedule, and personal safety.

LEARN HOW TO DO YOUR JOB

Training to do a job safely and correctly is important. Simple things like learning to lift and carry equipment properly can save you from pain. Camera cases and other camera equipment are often heavy and can cause back and leg problems. Proper lifting techniques and carts will make your job easier, and will help you reach retirement without any lasting injuries.

LISTEN TO QUALIFIED PEOPLE

Sometimes a camera or lamp position has to be made safe before it can be used. If the setup wasn't planned for, it may take more time than is available. The qualified person should be able to say what it will take to do safely what was asked for. If the time or money isn't available, an alternative setup is needed.

INFORM EMPLOYER OF RISKS

Safety in the workplace is everyone's responsibility. Inform your employer of potential risks. It's okay to question the safety of doing something if there's the possibility of an imminent risk to the cast or crew. Have the employer address the issue so you can return to work.

MICROWAVE TRANSMITTERS

Many film and television productions use microwave transmitters to send video signals from the camera to remote monitors for viewing. A microwave transmitter is basically a radio at a high-frequency spectrum, and not a microwave oven. Even so, this equipment will pose a radiation hazard if improperly handled.

The average microwave transmitter is rated at 0.25W (+24dBm) nominal RF power output and is designated an intentional radiator. It can deliver video and audio signals over short ranges when used with a receiver and appropriate antennas in either fixed or mobile applications. When the transmitter is operating as an antenna, the system is emitting radio frequency energy, so safe operating procedures must be observed. On set, your microwave technician is the go-to individual for this information.

The microwave tech should know and be able to answer the following:
1. How much power is the system radiating?
2. What frequency is being transmitted?
3. How close of proximity is the system to your person?

EXPOSURE

Exposure is based upon the average amount of time spent within an electromagnetic field (RF energy) with a given intensity (field intensity in mW/cm2). There are two categories of exposure situations; occupational/controlled and general population/uncontrolled.

Occupational/controlled

These are situations in which persons are exposed as a consequence of their employment, provided those persons are fully aware of the potential for exposure and can exercise control over their exposure. These limits apply in situations when an individual is transient through a location where occupational/controlled limits apply provided the individual is made aware of the potential for exposure.

General population/uncontrolled

These are situations in which the general public may be exposed, or in which persons that are exposed as a consequence of their employment may not be fully aware of the potential for exposure or cannot exercise control over their exposure.

Exposure may be controlled by observing the FCC-compliant safe distances and remaining beyond those distances from the antenna at all times when the transmitter is operational. At no time should the user remain within a distance less than the indicated safe distance for a period greater than 30 minutes.

When setting cameras in an urban environment like New York City, Chicago, or Los Angeles, care should be taken in the placement of microwave transmitters and antennas. Many large cities use their rooftops to stage their repeaters for data and voice over IPs. Therefore, cameras should not be placed next to an active antenna stationed on these roofs. The production location manager should have this indicated on their surveys. Also, many rooftops will have warning signs posted.

Common sense should be factored into the use of microwave transmitters and antennas. FCC guidelines addressing a variety of frequencies can be accessed on the Internet at *http://www.fcc.gov.*

The industry has come a long way when it comes to safety. Today's training and procedures are changing to protect workers more than ever. The continuation of this trend takes a safe attitude. The work you're doing may be important, but is it worth getting hurt for?

Industrywide labor management safety bulletins may be found and downloaded from the Contract Services Administration Trust Fund at *www.csatf. org.*

Kent H. Jorgensen is the Safety Representative for IATSE Local 80 Grips Union
Vincent Matta is a Business Representative for the IATSE Local 600 Cinematographer's Guild

Preparation of Motion Picture Film Camera Equipment

by Marty Ollstein, Michael Hofstein and Tom "Frisby" Fraser

All motion picture camera equipment must be periodically inspected and maintained to ensure proper performance. Camera-rental facilities employ skilled technicians to service and repair equipment after each use. Once the equipment leaves the rental house, however, the camera crew must service that equipment throughout the production. The camera assistant must be prepared with the right knowledge, skills, tools and reference materials to properly maintain all equipment in the camera package.

The following is a list of procedures for the preparation of camera equipment needed to photograph a motion picture. It is the responsibility of the camera assistant to ascertain that all equipment and supplies needed and requested by the director of photography are present and in working order at the start of production.

INVENTORY

1. Basic equipment, from the ground up: spreader, hi-hat, tripods, tripod heads, camera bodies, batteries, all necessary cables, magazines (small and large), lenses and housings, zoom motor and control, follow-focus unit, matte boxes, filters and holders, changing tent or bag.

2. Additional accessories often requested by the director of photography: adapter plates (quick-release, dovetail/balance, riser, tilt), external speed and sync control (for use with monitors, computers, projectors or other required devices), specialty lenses, remote controls (for aperture, shutter angle and ramping), electronic focus tool or rangefinder, set of hard mattes, eyebrow, French flag, handheld accessories (matte box, follow-focus, shoulder pad, viewfinder, smaller magazines), viewfinder extender and leveler, barneys, rain shields, obie light, 'assistant' light, video tap, monitors (onboard picture, lens data display and free-standing), video recorder, time-code device.

3. Supplies to be purchased by the production company: raw stock, camera reports, film cores, empty film cans, black labpack bags, labels, cloth camera tape, paper tape, lens-cleaning cloths, tissues and fluid, cleaning swabs, orangewood sticks, camera oil, slate, spare camera fuses, rags,

air cans, felt markers, grease pencils, pens and pencils, chamois, chalk, disposable batteries, flash memory sticks.

4. Maintenance, measurement and repair tools, such as a device that tests steadiness (Steady Tester), back focus (Sharp Max or HD Collimator), flange gauge, crystal strobe gun.

5. For emergency service or replacement of equipment, keep the 24-hour phone number of the rental house available at all times. On remote locations where prompt service or replacement of defective or broken equipment is impractical, carry a backup camera body and set of cables.

INVOICE CHECK

When the equipment is first received, carefully examine the rental invoice to confirm that all equipment and supplies ordered by the director of photography and production company have indeed been delivered. Confirm that the serial numbers listed on the invoice match those engraved on the equipment. Make sure that all support accessories and supplies needed by the camera crew to perform their tasks are included.

Examine the rental invoice or work order and confirm that all equipment ordered by the director of photography is included. Make sure that all support accessories and supplies needed by the assistants to properly perform their tasks are also included. If items will not be needed until later in the production schedule, such as a high-speed camera or specialty lenses, notify and make arrangements with the rental house, camera crew and production company. This equipment should be prepped and picked up at least one day before it is needed in production. In an emergency, such as when a camera breaks down, a replacement camera body may be needed immediately. The new camera body will still need to be prepped prior to use in production, to insure it is technically sound.When the equipment is first received, and before removing the equipment from the rental facility, use the rental invoice to check that all equipment and supplies that have been ordered and billed for have indeed been delivered. Confirm that the serial numbers listed on the invoice match those engraved on the equipment.

Label each case with cloth tape and marker, or better, plastic tape printed by a handheld dispenser. List the contents of each case on its spine to facilitate finding an item during production. On a multiple-camera shoot, color code each camera and its respective accessories with colored electrical tape—Camera A/red, Camera B/blue, etc. When a case is in use, keep at least one latch locked after the needed items have been removed. This precaution indicates that an item is in use, and prevents the case from accidentally opening and spilling its contents, were it lifted or moved.

EQUIPMENT CHECKOUT

Set up and test each piece of equipment to determine it is in working order. Label each case with cloth tape and marker, or better, plastic tape printed by a handheld dispenser. When a case is being used, keep at least one latch locked to prevent accidentally spilling the contents.

Start from the ground up and build the camera system. Thoroughly check the entire package for completeness, compatibility and proper functioning. The equipment should be clean, free of dust and properly lubricated. Immediately return any piece of equipment that does not perform to your satisfaction.

The following list suggests standards by which to judge each piece of equipment.

The list describes the proper operating condition, position or setting required for each item, and suggests procedures to use in confirming its status. This guide is to be used in conjunction with the appropriate operation manual.

Some of the procedures described, such as measuring the flange focal depth, or testing the magazine clutch and brake tension, require specialized test equipment. If the required equipment is not available, or if you encounter any other problems or questions, speak to the camera technician who prepared the package at the rental house. It is likely that the technician has performed the tests himself and can give you the results.

1. **Spreader**
   a. Runners slide smoothly and lock in all positions.
   b. End receptacles accommodate the tripod points and spurs, and hold them securely.

2. **Tripods**
   a. Each leg extends smoothly and locks in all positions.
   b. Top casting accommodates the base of the tripod head (flat Mitchell, ball or other).
   c. Hinge bolts that attach each leg to the top casting are adjusted to proper tension. Each leg swings easily away from top casting and remains at selected angle.
   d. Wooden Tripods (baby, sawed-off, standard). Legs are solid and have no splits or breaks.
   e. Metal or Fiber Tripods (baby, standard, two-stage). Legs are straight and have no burrs or dents.

3. **Tripod Head**
   a. Base (Mitchell, ball or other) fits and locks into tripod top casting.
   b. Ball base (only) adjusts smoothly and locks securely in any position.

  c. Camera lockdown screw fits into camera body, dovetail base with balance plate, riser or tilt plate.

  d. Top plate of head includes a quick-release (touch-and-go) base, which accommodates a quick-release plate that bolts to camera body or any of the adapter plates.

  e. Eyepiece-leveler bracket and frontbox tripod head adapter on the head accommodates the leveler rod and frontbox being used.

  f. Friction or fluid head:

   1. Head balances to neutral position with camera attached. Balance springs engage and adjust properly.

   2. Pan and tilt movement is smooth.

   3. Both brake levers lock securely in all positions.

   4. Both drag knobs easily adjust the tension of movement from free movement to the tension required by the operator.

  g. Gear head:

   1. Head balances to neutral position with camera attached.

   2. Pan-and-tilt movement is smooth.

   3. Both brake levers engage properly. (Gears may move under stress.)

   4. Gears shift smoothly between each speed.

  h. Remote head:

   1. Head balances to neutral position with camera attached.

   2. Head responds immediately and smoothly to pan, tilt and roll operations.

   3. All camera functions are properly driven by remote controls provided, which may operate focus, iris, zoom, camera motor and ramping operations. Test that speed, direction and lag adjustments are accurate.

   4. Calibration of all controls is correct or can be adjusted properly. If not, calibrate as necessary,.

   5. Gears mesh properly (on certain heads).

   6. All required cables and connectors are present and operate properly.

   7. Wireless transmitter and receiver (on certain heads) operate properly.

   8. Head operation does not interfere with video tap signal or add video noise.

  i. Dutch head with third axis: Check all controls, drag knobs, locks, plates and attachments as with two-axis head.

  j. When transporting any type of tripod head, release all locks, and reduce the pan and tilt tension to 0 (no tension).

  k. Carry extra utlilty base plate to adapt to workbench in camera room or truck.

4. Camera Body

a. Accommodates and locks securely with camera lockdown screw to tripod head, balance plate, riser, tilt plate and shoulder pad.

b. All rollers in the film path move freely.

c. Camera interior is clean—no emulsion buildup, dust or film chips.

d. Camera oil and grease have been applied to lubrication points as recommended by camera manufacturer. Clean off any excess. (Frequency and amount of lubrication vary greatly with cameras. For 35mm, common practice is to lubricate every 15,000 feet or sooner if squeaking or rubbing noise is detected. High-speed cameras may require lubrication after each 1,000 feet.)

e. Flange focal depth is set to manufacturer's specifications. Confirm by measurement with depth gauge. *(See next section.)*

f. All fuses are intact and properly seated. Carry spare fuses.

g. Movement of the shutter, mirror, pull-down claw and registration pins are synchronized. Two tests for shutter sync:

    1. Carefully scribe a frame in the gate, then inch the motor back and forth manually. The film should remain stationary as long as the shutter stays open.

    2. Place a piece of film under the registration pin and inch the motor movement so that the pin presses against the film. Then inch the motor movement forward—the shutter should remain closed until the pin releases the film.

h. The "glow" that illuminates the ground glass is synchronized with the shutter—the light turns off before the shutter opens the gate. (Check only on certain cameras).

i. Camera speed holds a crystal speed at all speeds required for the production. Thoroughly test all external speed-control accessories being used in the camera package.

j. Shutter speed remains constant. Check by viewing shutter with crystal strobe gun.

k. External sync control device maintains camera sync with the external device(s) being used (monitor, computer, projector, or other camera).

l. Pitch and loop adjustments operate properly (certain cameras).

m. Buckle trip (certain cameras) stops camera movement.

n. Camera is quiet (except on MOS cameras). Decibel level is appropriate to camera used. Listen for abnormal noise while rolling test film through camera. Test with barney or blimp, if applicable.

o. Heating system operates properly; eyepiece does not fog.

p. All power ports operate and provide appropriate power.

q. Camera has correct configuration for chosen format (such as 3-perf,

Super 35mm, etc.). If the camera was adapted from another format (as from standard 35mm to Super 35mm), inquire how camera was modified. Some Arri cameras need only rotate the faceplate and mount; Panavision cameras require changing the face plate and lens mount, gate, and position of the movement.

Check the following on any body that has been adapted:

1. Lens covers full frame and aligns to proper center line.
2. Aperture plate or gate.
3. Camera movement.
4. Ground-glass markings—frame lines, center line.
5. Film-counter operation.
6. Zoom-lens tracking—lens coverage and alignment covers full frame and aligns to proper center line. For alignment, inquire how camera was adapted—whether by moving lens board (or mount) or adjusting zoom lens. Confirm by checking tracking.

5. Flange Focal Depth (Flange to Aperture-Plane Depth)

a. Flange depth can be sensitive to temperature variation.
b. Before measuring, rotate mirror and clear it entirely from aperture.
c. Measure with proper depth gauge and aperture-gauge plate.
d. If flange depth is outside tolerance, return to rental house technician.

6. Format—Movement, Aperture Plate, Lens Position, and Assist Monitor

(*Also see 4.q. above.*)

a. It once was a simple choice between three formats or aspect ratios: 1.33:1, 1.85:1 and 2.40.1. Currently there are many more alternatives, and the choice of equipment must be precisely coordinated to produce the intended result. (*For options see chapter on Cinematographic Systems.*)
b. Movement: The 4-perforation frame is standard for 35mm. If a 3-perf or 2-perf format is selected, the movement must have been modified by the rental facility for the chosen perforation advancement (2 or 3).
c. Correct gate/aperture plate is installed. Gate is clean and properly seated. Gate/aperture plate may include an aperture mask (format mask) and filter holder. Critical in determining regular or super formats. Regular formats use an 'Academy' or sound aperture that masks the analog sound area; super formats use a full (camera) or 'silent' aperture that exposes the soundtrack area. Variations of these two categories may be used to further define other aspect ratios, by masking off more of the image. Gate is clean and properly seated.

    d. Lens position: Lens should be positioned in the center of the frame, requiring different placement for regular and super formats. Some cameras can adjust position by simply rotating the lens mount—others require moving the entire lens board. Incorrect placement may cause vignetting and will affect the tracking of the zoom lenses. Alternate placement of lens may be requested.

    e. Video assist: Generated frame lines must align with ground-glass markings.

7. Ground Glass

    a. Choice must accommodate the chosen aspect ratio and may include a combination (as 1.85/TV), and creative preferences of the cinematographer (as 'common top' or shaded areas). Custom ground-glass markings may be ordered.

    b. Seated properly, focuses through viewfinder on grain or texture of glass. There is a 'ground' (textured) side and a smooth side. When correctly installed, the smooth surface faces the operator. (Remember: 'smooth operator.')

    c. Viewfinder glow properly displays ground-glass markings. On some cameras, the glow mask must be aligned to the ground-glass frame lines. Check brightness adjustment. If available, select desired color of glow.

    d. Test accuracy of framing and center lines. These tests insure that the lens plane, film plane and ground glass are properly installed, marked and aligned. Place SMPTE framing test film (RP40 for 35mm) in gate, then view through a 50mm lens or custom microscope attached mounted in lens port, and turn mirror back and forth to compare the frame lines and crosshairs on the film with those on the ground glass.

    e. Then shoot a film test of an accurate framing chart or rack leader chart. A useful rack-leader chart is 11" x 17", displays the frame lines with arrows pointing to the corners, Siemens stars (for focus), and the name of the production, producer, director and cinematographer. (It can be ordered, purchased or created.)

    f. Project film tests of framing to confirm framing accuracy. Compare test footage of rack-leader chart with SMPTE test film by superimposing or bipacking the two. Judge accuracy of framing and centering.

8. Batteries and Cables

    a. All batteries and cables in package are compatible—male pairs with female, the number of pins in connectors match. Connections are solid. Jiggle gently to confirm a snug fit.

    b. Batteries hold charge and cables conduct properly. Check with volt meter.

    c. Camera motor maintains desired speed while under the load of all other current-drawing accessories required for the production. These may include a zoom motor, assistant light, video tap, eyepiece heater and viewfinder glow. Check with each battery.

9. Lamps and LEDs

Lamps that require bulbs and LEDs may include an out-of-sync lamp, running lamp, flashing lamp, start-marking lamps (older cameras), time-code exposure LEDs, viewfinder glow LEDs, and others. All lamps must light at the proper time. Replace all defective bulbs and LEDs. Carry spares.

10. Variable Shutter

Mechanism operates through the full range of shutter-degree openings and locks in each position (certain cameras). Electronic adjustment (certain cameras) operates properly and locks at each angle required.

Set shutter at opening selected by the director of photography.

11. Viewfinder

    a. Ground glass is properly seated. Ground surface faces lens. Ground-glass focus is sharp. Check on focus chart at 2' with 25mm lens. If focus is soft, have it checked with portable collimator.

    b. The image is clear and clean. If necessary, remove ground glass and carefully clean with proper solvent and lint-free lens tissue. Then reseat properly (usually with audible 'click').

    c. Ground glass is marked for the aspect ratios requested by the director of photography.

    d. Eyepiece focuses easily to the eye of the operator. (Adjust diopter until the grains of the ground glass appear sharp.) Eyepiece focus for average vision should fall near the center of travel of the focus adjustment, leaving a range in either direction.

    e. Viewfinder extender fits properly between camera body and eyepiece. Magnifier and ND filter operate properly.

    f. Viewfinder extender leveling rod attaches securely to extender and to bracket on tripod head. Rod extends smoothly and locks in all positions.

    g. Viewfinder illumination, or glow, is synchronized with the shutter (certain cameras).

    h. Eyepiece heater warms to comfortable temperature.

12. Lenses

    a. Each lens and lens housing is compatible with—and seats securely in—the mount in the camera body.

   b. Front and rear elements are clear and clean, free of large chips and scratches, or any fingerprints or dirt. Blow off loose material with a blower bulb. Clean off grease with lint-free lens cloth or tissue moistened with proper lens-cleaning fluid.

   c. Iris leaves fall properly in place as they are closed from the full open position. Iris operates smoothly through the full range from wide open to the smallest aperture.

   d. Follow-focus assembly mounts properly. Focus gears align and mesh properly, easily and snugly to the lens gears. There is no delay, 'lost motion' or 'slop' when starting or changing direction of adjustment of focus or iris setting. Check both directions of adjustment. (Particularly important with standard geared or remote servo operation).

   e. Lens focus-distance markings are accurate. (*See Lens Focus Calibration Test below.*)

   f. Telephoto extenders and wide-angle adapters are adjusted to match and fit the lens intended for their use. If used with a zoom lens, check zoom back focus with the extender and/or adapter attached.

   g. Specialty lenses: Each lens properly performs the effect for which it was designed. Includes fisheye, periscope, swing/shift, slant focus, Lensbaby, and other lenses designed for specific uses.

   h. Remote focus and iris control:

     1. Gears mesh between lens barrel and motor.

     2. Focus and iris adjustment operate smoothly through their full range of motion.

     3. There is no 'lost motion' when starting or changing direction of focus or iris adjustment.

     4. Remote control maintains accurate calibration with lens barrel markings.

     5. All cables operate properly. Carry set of backup cables.

     6. 'Smart' lenses, such as the Arri LDS system and the Cooke/i system (send aperture, zoom and focus data to an onboard display and external devices and recorders): Confirm that the system precisely calibrates all devices to which it is connected and preserves all generated metadata.

13. Zoom Lens

   a. Zoom mechanism is aligned properly and tracks smoothly.

   b. Tracking test: The crosshairs on the ground glass remain centered on a point throughout the zoom.

   c. Lens focus-distance markings are accurate at all focal lengths. Focus is maintained throughout travel of zoom. Check at 7' and 12'. (*See Lens Focus Calibration Test.*)

    d. Back focus is sharp. Focus at full telephoto, then check focus at full wide.

14. Zoom Motor and Control
    a. Zoom Motor mounts securely and threads properly on the lens.
    b. Gears mesh properly between lens barrel and motor.
    c. Zoom control unit operates motor smoothly at all speeds in both directions. There is no 'lost motion' when starting or changing direction of zoom.
    d. Control unit maintains calibration with lens-barrel markings.
    e. All cables connecting the camera, zoom control, and zoom motor and camera operate properly.

15. Blimp Housing
    a. Housing fits snugly on lens and camera body.
    b. Distance and f-stop strips fit properly and match the markings on lens.
    c. Camera noise is adequately reduced.

16. Filters
    a. Both surfaces of each filter are clear, clean and free of major flaws.
    b. Filters are the proper size for lenses in package:
        1. Filters cover entire image area of each lens being used without vignetting.
        2. Filters cover entire front element of lens and allows the use of the full aperture of the lens.
        3. Filters fit properly into filter holders on lens, lens housing, matte box, filter tray or separate holder.
    c. Filter-mounting accessories accommodate all lenses used, and mount the number of filters on each lens required by director of photography without vignetting.
    d. The rotating filter stage used for polarizing filters turns smoothly and locks in any position.
    e. Sliding mount for graduated filters moves smoothly and locks in any position.
    f. Prepare labels for each filter (tape or Velcro) for display on the side of the matte box.
    g. Use a circular polarizer for cameras in which polarization can interfere with or darkens the viewing system or videotap. Ask technician and test viewing system with filter.

17. Matte Box
    a. Mounts securely to camera body (or lens), and when mounted on rods, extends smoothly along the supporting rods.

b. Test each lens with the correct matte box (4" x 4", 4" x 5.6", 6" x 6", etc.) to confirm there is no vignetting. If the lens barrel travels (extends) when focusing, the matte box must accommodate the extending lens.

c. No light passes between the matte box and the lens. If necessary, acquire additional rings, filter trays, rubber 'doughnuts' or an elastic 'skirt' to block light leaks.

18. Magazine

a. Fits snugly into the camera body.

b. Magazine doors fit and lock securely.

c. On coaxial magazines, label each 'Feed' and 'Take-up' door with tape.

d. Throat, film channels and interior are clean, clear of dust and film chips.

e. Loop adjustment operates properly (certain cameras).

f. Magazine gear timing is properly adjusted—film runs smoothly and quietly through the magazine.

g. Clutch tension and friction-brake tension have been measured with the proper tools and are correct.

h. Inspect magazine port seals (top and rear).

i. Magazine operation is quiet (except on MOS cameras). Use a barney to dampen sound if necessary.

19. Video Assist: Video Camera, Monitor and Recording Device

a. Video camera (or tap) mounts securely on the camera body.

b. All cables are compatible and operate the tap, monitor and recorder.

c. The iris, focus and gain controls adjust smoothly and produce a correct image on the monitor.

d. The image can be centered and sized properly on the monitor so that the entire film frame is visible and level.

e. The frame-line generator produces the proper aspect ratio on the monitor. The generated frame lines align with the ground-glass frame lines.

f. Color saturation and hue are acceptable. White-balance adjustment functions properly.

g. Confirm the tap is matched to and compatible with the camera. For instance, Arri has different HD-IVS taps for their respective camera models.

20. Time Code

a. Some systems currently in use include SMPTE code, Aaton code and the Arri in-camera slate. Confirm with the production company that the time code system ordered and installed is compatible with the postproduction plans (equipment and facilities).

b. LEDs light properly. Set film ASA for proper exposure on device. Carry spare bulbs.

c. LED and LCD displays read clearly.

d. Code maintains sync with each device being used.

e. Code records properly on film and can be used as needed in post. (*See Film Tests section.*)

21. Ramping

a. Frame-rate variation affects exposure. Ramping therefore requires exposure compensation. Determine whether exposure compensation will be accomplished by adjusting aperture, shutter angle or a combination of the two.

b. Confirm that the camera and ramping accessories provide the required functions. Fully test all ramping operations planned for the production.

c. Shoot film to insure consistent density exposure during ramping. (*See Film Tests section.*)

22. Accessories

a. Each accessory properly performs the function for which it was designed. All cables, power supplies and auxiliary support equipment are present and operational. Test and operate each device.

b. External speed control holds a crystal speed at all speeds required for the production.

c. External sync control maintains sync, or is properly driven by external device (monitor, computer, projector or another camera).

d. Rain gear protects camera from moisture.

e. Underwater housing seals properly and allows operation of all camera functions.

f. Camera heater takes proper period of time to warm up camera.

LENS FOCUS CALIBRATION

Methods to evaluate lens focus calibration:

1. Use camera to view charts directly through the lens. Use test procedure described below to evaluate lenses by checking focus through a range of distance.

2. Shoot film test of chart using suggested procedure, then process and project film.

   For more precise evaluation, when the equipment is available, the following two methods are recommended (camera rental facilities should have performed these tests on all their lenses):

3. Mount lens on projector and project reticle (transparency).

4. Examine lens on MTF machine.

TEST PROCEDURE

1. Prime Lenses
    a. 40mm or wider: Set camera lens at 3', 5' and 7' from focus chart. At each distance, check focus by eye through lens and focus lens visually; compare with lens-barrel distance markings. For more critical testing, shoot film tests of each lens.
    b. Longer than 40mm: Set camera lens at 7', 10' and 15' from focus chart. Focus lens lens visually, compare with lens distance markings.
    c. All lenses: Focus on distant object to test sharpness at infinity.
2. Zoom Lenses: Use calibration procedure (described for Prime Lenses) at minimum focus distance, 7', 12', and a distant object to test infinity. Test for several focal lengths, including full wide and full telephoto.
3. Note: Other lens-to-chart distances may be used, as long as the selected distance is engraved on the lens barrel. The chart should fill the frame as much as possible.
4. When the eye focus differs from the measured distance:
    a. If consistent from lens to lens:
        1. Check ground-glass seating. Reseat if necessary.
        2. Check lens mount.
        3. Check distance measurement technique and measuring device for accuracy.
        4. Have flange focal depth and ground-glass collimation checked.
    b. Single discrepancy:
        1. Return lens for collimation.
        2. If needed immediately, encircle lens barrel with chart tape, focus by eye, and mark the correct distances.

SCRATCH TEST

Run a scratch test for the camera and each magazine to determine whether there are any obstructions in the camera or magazine mechanism that might damage the film. Load a short end of virgin raw stock in the magazine and thread it through the camera. Turn on the camera motor and run the film through for several seconds. Turn off the motor. Remove the film from the take-up compartment of the magazine without unthreading the film from the camera. Examine the film with a bright light and magnifying glass. If any scratches or oil spots appear on the emulsion or base, mark the film (still threaded in the camera body) with a felt pen at the following points:

1. where it exits the magazine feed rollers
2. just before it enters the gate
3. just after it exits the gate
4. where it enters the magazine take-up rollers

Then carefully unthread the film and examine it to determine where the damage originates. Once the problem area has been identified, check that area for dust, film chips, emulsion buildup or burrs. Remove smooth burrs with emery paper, and remove obstructions with an orangewood stick.

Make periodic scratch tests on magazines and camera during production to avoid damage to the negative.

STEADINESS TEST

Test steadiness of camera movement by double-exposing a test image. Test at each speed required by the production.

1. Prepare chart, such as: Select a Target pattern to photograph:
   a. A simple grid or cross of narrow white tape on a black card.
   b. A target device, designed for this test. It mounts securely on a wall and can be rotated or shifted in place to create the desired offset.
   c. A 'steady tester' which mounts in the lens mount and provides an illuminated target locked to the camera body. A rotation of the unit creates the required offset.
2. Mark start frame in film gate with pen or paper punch. (Only necessary with cameras that do not run in reverse.)
3. Roll at least 30 seconds of the chart at 50% exposure.
4. Cap lens and rewind film in camera, or rewind film manually in dark room, and position the marked 'start' frame back in the film gate (so as to thread on the same perforation).
5. Offset chart by the width of the tape (a), rotate the dedicated target (b) or rotate the steady tester, and proceed to roll for another 30 seconds at 50% exposure (double-exposing the target).
6. Process and project the film to evaluate steadiness.
7. It is essential that both the camera and the chart target be rock-steady during exposure of the test.
8. With some cameras, an accessory is available to simplify this test. Called a 'steady tester,' it mounts in the lens mount and provides an illuminated target locked to the camera body. A rotation of the unit creates the offset needed.

DAILY PREPARATION FOR SHOOTING

1. Clean the aperture. Suggested methods:
   a. Pull aperture plate and pressure pad.
   b. Clean both with chamois, and if necessary, proper solvent.
   c. Remove hairs and dust from gate, channels and holes with an orangewood stick.
   d. Remove gels from filter holders and slots.
   e. Sight through lens to check gate. (Possible only with 40mm or longer.)

2. Clean dust and chips from film chamber. Avoid blowing material back into gate or into camera movement.
3. Warm up the camera:
    a. Run the camera for several minutes without film.
    b. In cold situations, run the camera for the amount of time it would take to run one full magazine through the camera at standard speed.
    c. Load proper film stock in magazines. Panavision offers a heater accessory that will warm up the camera in a few minutes.
4. Load correct film stock in magazine and label magazine with tape.
5. Prepare slate and camera reports.
6. Record and communicate instructions for telecine transfer regarding both format and 'look.'

FILM TESTS
(*See pages 289–312*).

Film tests are requested by the director of photography. Following is a list of tests that may be useful in preparation for a production. A standard gray scale and color chip chart are often used for such tests, as well as models that resemble the actors in the film to be photographed.

1. **Lens sharpness and color:** (This is particularly important if older lenses or lenses of different manufacturers are used on the same production.) Test each lens to insure consistent sharpness and color from lens to lens. Photograph the identical subject with each lens and compare on a one-light print.
2. **Film stock and emulsion batch:** Test each different film stock and emulsion batch to be used on the production for color balance, actual exposure index and exposure latitude.
3. **Laboratory processing:** normal, forced, flashed, bleach-bypass, etc. Test processing at same film laboratory selected to be used during the production. This is particularly important for determining the degree of forced processing, flashing or bleach-bypass effect that is desired.
4. **Flashing in-camera:** Evaluate levels of flashing for desired effect.
5. **Filters:** Test the effects of various filters on chosen representative subjects to facilitate the selection of filter types and grades for the production. For proper evaluation, use lenses and exposure values anticipated for the particular effect.
6. **Lighting:** Test the look of new lighting instruments, color gels and diffusion materials on selected subjects.
7. **Makeup:** Test makeup on actors under the lighting conditions planned for the production.
8. **Time-code sync:** Test sync with sound and any other other cameras planned to be used on the production. Process picture and sound, shoot

a film test, and have the production company process the picture and sound and send the footage through the entire planned postproduction workflow. Screen the result. This will insure that the time code used in production is compatible with all procedures, equipment and facilities used in post.

9. **External sync box:** Test sync with external device driving camera (monitor, computer, projector or other camera).

10. **Ramping:** Test ramping precision by shooting a solid even field (such as a cloudless sky or full-frame gray card) and performing all ramping operations. View test to evaluate consistency of film density—any shifts indicate exposure variation.

11. **Framing:** Shoot framing chart or rack-leader chart. Project test to evaluate framing accuracy.

TOOLS

A proper set of tools and supplies is essential to the preparation and maintenance of motion-picture equipment. Although the production company should provide the expendable supplies, a camera assistant's personal set of tools should include most of the following items:

Useful fluids:
- **Panchro Lens Fluid** – cleans lenses
- **Denatured alcohol** – cleans film path
- **Acetone** – cleans metal parts, lenses (does not streak or leave residue), but damages plastic and paint
- **Naptha or Lighter fluid** – removes adhesive residue
- **Camera oil** – acquire from respective camera manufacturer

Standard Tools:
- **blower bulb** – large (6")
- **lens brush** – camel's hair or soft sable (1")
  (use only for lenses, keep capped)
- **magazine brush** – stiff bristles (1"-2")
- **microfiber lens cloth**
- **lens tissue** – lint free
- **cotton swabs**
- **lens-cleaning solvent**
- **50' flexible cloth measuring tape**
- **lighter fluid**
- **scissors** – straight blade, blunt tip (2")
- **tweezers forceps** – curved dissecting forceps or hemostat
- **ground glass puller**

- **Arri SW2** – 2mm hex (for variable shutters)
- **magnifying glass**
- **small flashlight**
- **orangewood sticks**
- **tape** – cloth (1") black, white and colors; paper (½") white and colors; chart (¹⁄₁₆") white – for lens barrel markings; Velcro – (1") white, male and female
- **chalk** – thick, dustless
- **felt marking pens**
- **'write-on/wipe-off' pens** – for dry-erase plastic slates
- **powder puffs** – to clean rub-off slates
- **grease pencils** – black and white
- **pens and pencils**
- **film cores**
- **camera fuses**
- **multimeter**
- **soldering iron**
- **16-gauge solder**
- **solder wick de-soldering spool**
- **folding knife**
- **emery paper** – 600 grit – ferric-oxide coated
- **razor blades** – single-edge industrial
- **rope** – nylon line (⅛"-10' long)
- **camera oil** – per manufacturer
- **"camera grease"**
- **oil syringe and needle** – one fine, one wide
- **bubble level** – small, circular
- **ATG-924** (snot tape)
- **black cloth** – 2' square
- **set of jewelers screwdrivers**
- **set of hex wrenches** (¹⁄₃₂"-³⁄₁₆" and metric)
- **combination pliers** (6")
- **needlenose pliers** (6"), **miniature** (1")
- **crescent wrench** (6")
- **vice-grip pliers** (4")
- **diagonal cutters** (4")
- **wire strippers** (4")
- **screwdrivers** (⅛", ³⁄₁₆", ¼", ⁵⁄₁₆")
- **Phillips screwdrivers** (#0, #1, #2)
- **Arri screwdrivers** (#1, #2, #3)

Optional Items

Additional tools are often useful—each assistant collects his or her own personal set. Following is a list of optional items that many have found to be valuable:

▶ **insert slate**
▶ **color lily** (gray scale and color chip chart)
▶ **gray card**
▶ **electronic range finder**
▶ **angle finder**
▶ **electronic tablet or PDA** with camera-assistant software
▶ **electrical adapters**
▶ **U-ground plug adapter**
▶ **screw-in socket adapter**
▶ **WD-40 oil**
▶ **assistant light**
▶ **compass**
▶ **depth-of-field charts**
▶ **depth-of-field calculator**
▶ **footage calculator**
▶ **circle template** – for cutting gels
▶ **extra power cables**
▶ **magnetic screwdriver**
▶ **variable-width screwdriver**
▶ **wooden wedges** – to level camera
▶ **small mirror** – to create a highlight
▶ **dentist's mirror** – aid in cleaning
▶ **alligator clips**
▶ **graphite lubricant**
▶ **³⁄₈" x 16 bolt** – short and long
▶ **2 one-inch C-clamps**
▶ **black automotive weather stripping**
▶ **small wooden plank** – for mounting camera

THE CAMERA ASSISTANT

The position of camera assistant requires a person with a wide range of skills. The assistant must have technical knowledge of the camera, lenses and a myriad of support equipment. Production conditions have become more demanding, with tighter schedules, less rehearsal, faster lenses and smaller depths-of-field. He or she must be physically fit, capable of total concentration and able to retain a sense of humor under stressful conditions.

A feature cinematographer and director, Marty Ollstein conceived and developed Crystal Image software, which precisely emulates optical camera filter effects. He is a member of the ASC Technolgy Technology Committee, a SMPTE Fellow, and participated as a cinematographer in the ASC-PGA Camera Assessment Series (CAS) and Image Control Assessment Series (ICAS).

Michael Hofstein is a director of photography. He is a member of the International Cinematographers Guild and the Directors Guild of America.

A camera operator for 24 years, Tom Fraser is an active member of the Society of Camera Operators and a past member of their Board.

Preparation of Digital Camera Equipment

by Marty Ollstein

The "Preparation of Motion Picture Film Camera Equipment" chapter in this manual (page 427) has been used by generations of camera crews to guide and assist them in preparing equipment for production. As more productions elect to shoot with digital camera systems, camera crews accustomed to film cameras must learn to use the new equipment. Although some prep procedures are similar, digital cameras require new procedures and tools to properly prepare them for production. The following text will delineate the steps and alternatives involved in preparing a digital camera system for production.

PREP CREW RESPONSIBILITIES

This prep guide is intended for use by any member of the camera crew, from the cinematographer to the second assistant, as well as to those in new digital positions such as the digital-imaging technician (DIT). Each crew-member performs a different role in the preparation of the equipment, as they do on set during production, although some activities overlap.

The cinematographer has the responsibility for making the critical decisions—both creative and technical—that shape the camera preparation. The decisions determine what equipment is ordered, how the image is recorded, and how the look is achieved in production.

The cinematographer may participate in the prep, particularly on a smaller production, but it is usually the camera assistants and digital-imaging technician that actually do most of the work. As the position of digital-imaging technician is relatively new, the division of labor between the camera assistant and DIT may vary. The size of the production will also influence the allocation of tasks. Some crews may not include a DIT. The cinematographer should indicate his or her preferences as to how the work will be done.

The objective of this chapter is to support the camera crew in organizing and structuring the complex preparation process, so as to make sure that every critical issue is addressed. To this end, the workflow of digital-camera preparation is described in detail below in the chronological order of production:

A. Choices and Working Styles
B. Checkout

C. Testing
D. Daily Prep and Maintenance
E. Delivery of Elements

A. CHOICES AND WORKING STYLE

Every apsect of camera preparation depends upon the decsions made at the beginning of preproduction. When shooting film, the main decisions include gauge (16mm, 35mm, 65mm), film stock and camera. When shooting digital, there are many more questions to be answered and decisions to be made. For example, besides camera system, the cinematographer may have to choose the recording medium (tape, hard drive or solid state), the format (video or data, compressed or raw) and the color-sampling ratio (4:4:4 or 4:2:2). These decisions should be based on careful consideration of a series of factors associated with the production.

Another variable that affects the nature of the prep, as well as the workflow during production, is the choice of shooting style. This can range from a lean "film-style" shoot—with few, if any, large monitors and rare playback takes—to a full video-village setup, with a camera-control center and sophisticated color-correction capabilities. The shooting style can also eschew color correction of the recorded image while still using a look-management system—such as the ASC CDL (color decision list), display LUTs (look-up tables) and other metadata that can accompany the recorded image through post—to support the cinematographer's intent. The shooting style is usually determined by the cinematographer in conjunction with the director and producer.

In the video-village-style shoot, there may be a camera-control station that allows the DIT to carefully monitor many aspects of the digital recording and adjust levels as necessary. a typical system may include a small workstation dedicated to look management, equipped with image-processing software compatible with the ASC CDL, an additional device that records and transmits looks and display LUTs (such as Panavision's GDP or Technicolor's LUTher or DP LIghts), and a calibrated monitor. The role of the DIT in this working style is critical—the changes made can have a permanent effect on the recorded image.

Factors to Consider

The first and most universal factor to consider is the primary distribution venue intended for the production at the end of the process. If the production will be released theatrically and projected on large screens, certain standards and requirements should be met. The resolution of the image will be an important factor. However, if the release will be limited to a television broadcast, DVD or Blu-ray, or online distribution, the requirements are very different.

The postproduction workflow must also be considered. Each post facility has certain capabilities and preferences. Some cater to higher-resolution data workflows designed for digital cinema; others work with HD video workflows. This choice of workflow will influence camera, acessory and format selection. If the post workflow limits the production image to HD resolution, there may be no need to consider higher-resolution cameras or formats.

The physical parameters of a production have a natural effect on the operation of the camera department. Digital-camera studio rigs can be as imposing and heavy as studio film-camera rigs, yet other camera configurations can fit in the palm of your hand. Will the production be shot on studio stages or remote locations? If on location, is there ground floor/elevator roll-in access, or must the equipment be brought manually up narrow stairways? Will the set be well secured, or will the shooting be done on uncontrolled, crowded city streets? All of these issues inform the choices of camera, equipment and shooting style.

Of course, the creative look of the production should be a significant factor influencing all camera decisions. The look is decided by the cinematographer, in support of the director's vision, and in collaboration with the other creative department heads, including the production designer and visual-effects supervisor.

Last but not least, budget affects everything on a production, and camera is no exception. If the budget is modest but the director's vision is ambitious, the cinematographer must find a way to get the look the director wants without the equipment it might normally require. If the cinematographer understands the concepts and devices involved—what they do and how they do it—he or she will be better equipped to devise shortcuts, cut corners and improvise solutions without sacrificing quality or substance.

Look-Management Prep

The consistent use of a comphrehensive look-management system can keep the production process organized and insure that the look of the resulting image preseves the creative intent of the cinematographer and director. Defining the intended look is the first step, and a good strategy can be to create a series of "hero" frames based on scouting footage, screen tests of actors, or photography shot specifically for this purpose. Once converted into format compatible with the production's look-management system, the gathered images can be manipulated with the image-processing software to achieve the desired look; the resulting hero frames are then saved (along with the software recipe used to create them) in a format that can be shared with predictable quality. Calibrated displays and proper viewing environments are necessary for this process to work.

The choice of camera system may determine many issues associated with the look, but many other choices may remain, including the recording medium (tape, hard drive or solid state), color space and format, and recording bit depth and sampling ratio. Choices of aspect ratio, frame rate and shutter angle must also still be made. Each decsion narrows the selection of available equipment, and provides the crew with the information needed to do a thorough preparation.

B. CHECKOUT
Inventory - Master Production Equipment List
Once the decisions have all been made, the cinematographer develops the master list of equipment with the camera crew. Part of this list mirrors a film-shoot list, including items such as camera support (tripod, head, etc.), lenses, and many of the accessories and expendables. This makes sense, since some digital cameras (such as the Arri Alexa) are designed to be identical to a film camera on the front end—up to the sensor.

A generic digital camera inventory checklist:
1. **Camera system:** Camera body, videotape "magazines," onboard disk drives, onboard solid-state drives, all types of cables, EVF (electronic viewfinder), optical viewfinder (when available).
2. **Camera support:** Hi-hat, spreader, tripods, tripod heads, adapter plates, handheld rig.
3. **Lenses:** Lenses to cover (expose) the full area of the camera's sensor size.
4. **Camera accessories:** Matte boxes, follow-focus unit, "smart-lens" accessories, zoom motor, rods and adapters, filters, all remote controls.
5. **Power:** A/C adapter, batteries, power cables.
6. **Digital Support:** Monitors (onboard, handheld, viewing, reference, wireless), recorders (digital videotape, disk drive or solid state), backup systems (appropriate to medium), look-management tools (LUT box, color-correction console, workstation and software).
7. **Scopes:** Waveform, vectorscope, histogram, combination scopes.
8. **Media:** Enough digital tape cassettes of correct format (as HDCAM-SR), onboard hard-disk drives, onboard solid-state drives, flash memory cards or sticks.
9. **Expendables:** Supplies for assistant (varieties of adhesive tape, markers, camera reports, USB flash drives, etc.).
10. **Tools:** Portable collimator, Sharp Max, multimeter, monitor probe, light meter.
11. **Test charts:** Color chip chart (digital), gray scale, framing, resolution.
12. **Balls:** White ball with black hole (the "Stump" meter), set of balls for modeling lighting (mirrored, gray, white).

In-House Preparation

The staff at a rental house maintains, services, repairs and tests all equipment that passes through the facility. When a package is prepared for checkout, the items on the production's order are assembled, and final adjustments and settings are made before presenting the equipment to the client. All equipment delivered to a checkout bay should be in working order and perform according to technical specifications.

In the course of servicing equipment to prepare it for production, many measurements and tests are made by the engineers and prep techs. Some rental houses log the results of these tests and make them available to their clients. Otherwise, the camera crew may ask the prep tech about any measurement, setting, test or modification to confirm that it has been done, and if it has, request the exact results.

If a test needs to be made or repeated, the crew may ask the prep tech to have the rental house do it, or to assist them in performing the test in the prep area. Some diagnostic and preparation procedures require specialized test equipment.

Although many of the preparation steps listed below may have been performed by a rental-house technician, it is good practice for the crew to cover each step themselves, so as to thoroughly check and test the camera firsthand.

Crew Preparation

There are many aspects involved in a thorough prep of a digital camera system. This guide organizes the procedures into the following categories:
1. Universal Prep Procedures
2. Digital Camera Prep Steps
3. Setting up the Menu
   a. Format Settings
   b. Image and Color Settings—Scene Files and Looks

1. Universal Prep Procedures

Although there are many prep procedures exclusive to digital cameras, quite a few basic steps are the same as for film camera prep. Since the chapter "Preparation of Motion Picture Film Camera Equipment" (page 427) describes these steps in detail, they are listed here with only a brief summary description. As mentioned earlier, some digital cameras work just like a film camera on the front end.

Sections of "Preparation of Motion Picture Film Camera Equipment" that apply to digital prep:

▶ Invoice and serial number check, scheduling, labeling cases, color-coding multiple cameras (page 428)
▶ Equipment checkout procedure (pages 428-437)

1. Spreader: Arms open, hinge, slide and lock in all positions.
2. Tripods: Legs hinge, slide and lock in all positions.
3. Tripod head: All locks fully release and firmly lock, each spring tension position engages, pan and tilt tension adjustment operates smoothly and locks in detent positions).
4. Camera mount, plates: All plates are compatible, attach and lock snugly, release easily (quick-release), adjust and slide smoothly (for balance or tilt-angle adjustments).
5. Flange focal depth*: Depth is within recommended tolerance.
7. Ground glass*: Properly seated, focuses on grain, frame-line markings as ordered.
8. Batteries and cables: All supply full voltage, accept charge, cables connect firmly in ports and conduct current.
9. Lamps and LEDs: All light as expected; carry spares.
11. Optical viewfinder*: Check diopter, frame lines, glow and all other functions (magnification, ND, heater, etc.).
12. Lenses: Confirm collimation with focus tests, check color, calibrate remote controls.
    a. Follow-focus unit: Gears mesh snugly, have no play or delay.
13. Zoom lens: Confirm collimation, all rings operate smoothly, tracking stays centered.
14. Zoom motor and control: Smooth operation, adjusts through full range of speeds, no play or delay in gears.
16. Filters: Clean, correct size, fit holders and matte box.
17. Matte boxes: Mount properly, fit filters, do not vignette.

▶ **Lens focus calibration test**: Check lenses for proper collimation and correct witness marks (page 438).

2. Digital Camera Prep Steps

A. **Physical camera check:** Clean all surfaces, check all screws, switches, latches, locks, displays, lights.

B. **Pixel check:** Check for lit (white) or dead (black) pixels on the camera sensor, as well as on any monitors used for critical viewing.

Although most camera sensors and pixel arrays have some bad pixels, it is important to assess their number and confirm that they can be "covered" electronically. If there are too many, the image can be affected.

1. **Pixel check steps:**
   a. Fully warm up camera to normal operating temperature. 30 minutes is usually adequate. (Shooting in extreme temperatures may reveal more bad pixels.)

---

* Some differences from film camera prep.

    b. Set gain at 6db. Gain makes it easier to spot bad pixels.

    c. Warm up reference monitor. It must display the full resolution of the camera sensor, pixel for pixel.

    d. For lit (white) pixels:

        1. Cap lens.

        2. Reduce or eliminate ambient light in viewing environment.

        3. Examine displayed monitor image for a bright pixel.

    e. For dead (black) pixels:

        1. Frame an even bright field through the lens, such as the sky or a light.

        2. Search monitor display for a dark pixel.

    f. If lit or dead pixels are found, use the Auto Black Balance (ABB) of the camera to cover the problem pixels. The black balance function may need to be activated several times to cover all problem pixels—six times for sensors with RGB stripe patterns, such as the Genesis or F35.

    g. If ABB does not cover the problem pixels, return the camera to a rental-house technician. The rental house has the means to manually cover pixels, or it might choose to replace the camera.

    h. Once the camera has been checked, pixel check all monitors being used for critical viewing (including eyepiece viewfinder, onboard monitor and camera control reference monitor).

        1. Adjust, repair, or replace as necessary, *or:*

        2. Note exactly where bad pixels are located, so as to avoid concerns during production.

C. Clean "gate": Sensor, pre-filter or IR filter (filters may cover sensor) is clean, clear of any dust, hair, oil or smudge.

    Take extreme care. Use methods in the order listed below, as needed. Start with the safest. If unsuccessful, proceed to the slightly more aggressive methods described, then, if necessary, call in a technician.

    2. Sensor cleaning steps:

        a. Puff air with blower bulb (avoid canned air—it may spray propellant or force dust behind the filter onto sensor).

        b. Use clean, soft, fine brush to remove dust or hair (may use fine watercolor brush, washed in dishwashing fluid and thoroughly dried).

        c. Use cleaning swab (designed for sensors).

        d. Apply a drop of approved lens-cleaning fluid on swab (nonstreaking, residue-free, such as Panchro).

D. Equipment check:

1. Lens mount: Lens mount accommodates all lenses, releases and locks smoothly and firmly.

2. Follow-focus unit: Gears mesh easily and snugly. There is no lag or delay in operation.
3. Back focus: (*See "Back Focus Steps" below in "Daily Prep and Maintenance" section.*) Check back focus on each lens. Use portable collimator or focus chart and tape measure. Check each zoom throughout full focal range.

   Back focus rarely changes on single-chip production cameras, whereas it does vary with temperature on many ⅔" three-chip cameras. These cameras should be checked for back focus several times a day, and on each lens change.
4. Filtration (wheels, matte box):
   1. Filter wheels (ND and CC) rotate smoothly, set securely at each filter position, are clean, and match their label on the wheel.
   2. Matte boxes accommodate the appropriate lenses and filters (if multiple filter sizes), and do not vignette.
   3. Each filter is clean, unscratched, and matches the label on its pouch or slot in case.
5. Power: Cables, ports, connections, A/C adapter, onboard battery adapter and batteries produce expected voltage (12V or 24V), batteries accept charge, ports and cables all seat properly and conduct current.
6. Display functions: All displays (camera operation, smart lens, rangefinder) operate properly, are clear and easily read, have working backlight, and display running time code.
7. Camera switches and buttons
   a. All switches and buttons work properly – check each function with camera operation: on/off, gain, AWB, menu. (List varies with camera system.)
   b. Load assignable buttons as requested.
   c. Check record review function: It should play back a few seconds of the last take, then precisely reset camera to begin recording with no break in time code.
8. Auto black balance (ABB): auto black balance functions properly. Perform full black balance for all channels (may need to repeat several times to cover all pixels, depending on camera).
9. Remote-control functions – Remote control operates all necessary functions, smoothly and accurately.
10. Recording functions (make test recordings):
    a. Check on/off, record and playback switches.
    b. Confirm frame-rate display matches menu setting. Record at each frame rate to be used.
    c. Test each recording configuration: onboard tape magazine or solid-state deck (mounted both top and rear), as well as tethered remotely to a processor-recorder.

11. Viewfinder functions – EVF (electronic viewfinder):
    a. Eyepiece diopter adjusts smoothly and locks through full range.
    b. Optical path is clear and as bright as expected.
    c. Controls (contrast, brightness and chroma) adjust properly to make balanced image.
    d. Peaking adjusts smoothly and precisely. Set as requested by operator. (Peaking boosts the contrast of an edge or detail where lens is focused.)
    e. Zebra pattern turns on and off; activate levels adjust properly. Set levels as requested. (The zebra function provides a diagonal striped pattern that appears in the area of the frame where the light level reaches a specific, defined level. Many cameras offer two zebra patterns—one slanting left, the other right—to measure two different light levels. Levels can be selected within a range; common useful defaults are 70% and 100%.)
    f. Frameline markings are correct as ordered:
       1. Framelines are in the correct aspect ratio (aligned with the ground glass lines).
       2. Glow, shading and center lines are correct.
12. Camera accessories: All accessories, including remote controls, zoom motor and lights function properly. Test each device with operating camera.
13. Monitor check and calibration (*See "Field Calibration Steps" below in "Daily Maintenance" section*)
    a. Carefully test and adjust each monitor. Check all cables, ports and routing switcher. May include: EVF, onboard HD monitor, camera control reference monitor, video village viewing monitor
    b. Confirm frame lines have proper aspect ratio.
    c. Check image with superimposed menu text.
    d. Check calibration with SMPTE color bars; adjust as needed.
    e. Check color and density with color chip chart and waveform monitor.
    f. Match color and density of all monitors used on the set, as close as is practical.
       There are two types of calibration: technical calibration, which requires specialized equipment, and field calibration, which can be done on the set with standard monitor controls.
       Some rental facilities place a label on each monitor, stating the date it was calibrated in-house.
       A CRT monitor requires a dedicated 'probe' to perform proper calibration. High-end LCD monitors are calibrated with probes; others have internal circuits that perform calibration.
14. Scope calibration: Waveform, vectorscope, histogram. Confirm calibration of scopes (waveform, vectorscope, histogram, combination scopes). Use SMPTE bars and digital color chip chart.

15. Look-management hardware workstation, LUT boxes (GDP, LUTher, DP Lights), still camera.:
    a. All devices connect and operate properly.
    b. Fully test system:
       1. Record live test image.
       2. Ingest it into the system.
       3. Apply a look to the image with either an ASC CDL recipe or a saved LUT provided by the cinematographer.
       4. Check the image on a calibrated monitor to confirm transformation is appropriate to the look applied.
       5. Repeat with each ASC CDL and LUT provided by the cinematographer.

3. Setting up the Menus

The embedded menus play an integral part in digital-camera preparation.

Check operation of all menus, and all buttons, wheels and switches that operate them.

Confirm with prep tech that all menus are reset to the rental house reference standard. Backup standard setting to external flash memory card or stick.

Upload any scene files provided by cinematographer on memory stick or flash drive.

A. Format Settings

As discussed above, many choices must be made prior to equipment checkout. Based on the factors discussed, including distribution venue, post workflow, creative look, budget and physical conditions of the shooting, the key decisions are made. These decisions include the selection of the camera system and all other key choices that define how the camera will record the image.

Some cameras record in only one mode (one format). Others offer choices of modes, formats and settings. When there are choices, the camera menus must be set up to record in the chosen format. Setting up the menus is a fundamental part of the preparation for production.

Step through the menus, make the selections and adjust the settings as ordered by the cinematographer. The menus and options vary widely by camera system. The following list offers a brief description of each parameter that may need to be set.

1-2-3.: Select the color space, bit depth, and sampling ratio.

1. Color space (RGB, YUV or YCrCb):
   a. RGB provides full three-channel (red, green and blue) color information, comparable to three-layer emulsion film.

    b. YUV or YCrCb separates luminance (Y = light intensity or brightness) from chrominance (U and V = color information). This separation allows for color subsampling, in which luminance can be measured at a different frequency (more often) than chrominance. A color space is often associated with a particular bit-depth and sampling ratio.

2. Bit depth(8-bit, 10-bit, 12-bit): 10-bit depth provides more code values than 8-bit depth to use in representing light values. The 10-bit scale is 0–1023; the 8-bit scale is 0–255. The difference shows in tone subtlety. Higher bit depth comes at a cost—the additional tape, drive space or digital memory required to record and store the bits, and time in post to process them.

3. Sampling ratio (4:4:4, 4:2:2): The ratio of the frequency of the sampling (measurement) of luminance (the first integer) to chrominance (the second two integers) on odd and even scan lines. "4" represents full bandwidth—the maximum information that can be sampled.

4-5-6.: Set the frame rate, scan type, and resolution.

4. Frame Rate (23.976, 24, 25, 29.97, 30, 50, 59.94 and 60 the standard camera speeds): The choice of available frame rates varies among camera systems. Some provide a limited list, others allow a range of variable speed options. In the United States, the most common frame rates used in production are 23.976, 24, 29.97 and 30.

    Most current post facilities use the "fractional" rates (as 23.976, 29.97 and 59.94) for their workflows. For production footage shot in "integer" rates (24, 30, 60), a conversion is necessary. Opinions are split.

    a. Integer frame-rate advocates consider the conversion to be simple and to have little effect on the image. They shoot at 24 fps and convert in post.

    b. Fractional frame-rate advocates state that image quality is affected by the conversion. They shoot at 23.976, which can be used in video post without conversion.

    c. Productions that must record back to film for a theatrical release (at 24 fps in the United States) often use a 24P frame rate.

5. Scan type—Progressive (P), Interlace (I)

    a. Progressive scans all lines of pixels for each frame.

    b. Interlace scans every other line for each "field"—the odd lines for one field, then the even lines for the next field. Two consecutive fields together make up one full frame. Interlace scanning results in a higher shutter speed, which reduces motion blur.

6. **Resolution** (720 lines, 1080 lines, or 2K, 4K): High definition has been generally defined at 720 lines or greater. Most HD camera systems record 1080 lines. Some record raw data at 2K or 4K, recording more lines and greater definition. Frame rate, scan type (P or I) and resolution are often associated. The most common production frame rates are 23.976P, 24P, 25P, 29.97P, 30P, 50I and 59.94I.

7. **Test record on medium selected:**

    To accommodate the medium selected for the production, select an appropriate recording device and the configurations in which it will be used during the production. For instance, on the Genesis, HDCam-SR, tape recording can be accomplished either onboard or tethered by cable to a remote recorder.

    a. Recording medium (digital tape, hard drive, solid state):

    Depending upon the camera system and the format selected, different media are available for recording. Recording devices are available in different configurations for each medium, either onboard or tethered to a remote processor-recorder.

8. **Set up time code parameters in camera menu:**

    Set starting code according to selected time-code management strategy. Shoot tests with all devices involved in recording the time code (clockit, smart slate, time-code generator, sound recorder and camera).

    In cases where the image is recorded remotely from the camera by cable, check sync for processing latency—the image recording may be delayed and cause a sync problem.

Time code: Record run, continuous run, time of day, jam sync, genlock

There are several different strategies for recording time code on a digital camera. It is important to consult the post house and sound mixer to insure that the method selected is compatible with all systems that will be used on the production. To fully test the time-code system selected and confirm synchronization between camera and sound, the sound mixer should participate in a test using all sound and time-code hardware that will be used for the production. This may include a sound recorder, a clockit-type time-code generator and a smart slate that displays time code.

Some popular time code strategies:

a. Use the sound-recorder generator as the "master clock."

    1. Jam sync the clockit generator from the sound recorder.
    2. Jam sync the camera from the clockit.
    3. Mount the clockit on the camera, and feed continuous time code and genlock (tri-level sync) from the Clockit to the camera.

b. Jam sync the smart slate from the sound recorder (with audio time code). Record the image of the smart slate, running time code, at the head of each take. Sync the picture manually.

c. Record time code from the sound recorder onto one of the camera's audio tracks and a scratch production soundtrack onto another.

d. Generate code at the camera control station.

    1. Jam sync and feed time code to the camera through the fiber-optic master cable.

Timecode Types

▶ Record run—starts and stops at each roll of the camera.

▶ Time of day—runs continuously—is usually set for the time of day.

▶ Genlock—driven by an external source.

    The external time-code source driving the camera must be running code at the same frame rate as the camera.

B. Image and Color Settings: Looks and Scene Files

Some cameras feature extensive menus that allow a knowledgeable cinematographer or DIT to manipulate many digital parameters of the image. Looks can be by adjusting these settings, then saved for use as numbered scene files. These looks, however, will be "baked in" to the recorded image, so they should be made with care. Consultation with the post house and colorist is recommended.

Some cameras allow a limited number of scene files to be saved on the camera and recalled by number in scene-file slots; the saved scene files should also be saved to a flash memory card compatible with the camera. (The cinematographer may also provide the assistant with additional scene files on a flash card and ask to have them uploaded into the numbered slots on the camera.) Carefully log the location of each scene file, whether it is in a slot on the camera or on a numbered flash memory stick.

On the other hand, some cinematographers prefer to treat a digital camera more like a film camera, and just shoot with the standard menu setup provided by the rental house. This is often done with cameras that record raw data. When recording raw, settings made in camera menus are attached to the image as metadata, but are not baked in' to the recorded image. When the raw image data is later de-Bayered and rendered for viewing and processing, the attached metadata settings can be applied to create the look intended. But the metadata settings can also be ignored, or adjusted so as to achieve a completely different look. This workflow offers both flexibility and safety, but it requires good communication with the post house.

All cameras come from their manufacturer with factory presets for all menu items. For most cameras that offer a raw recording option, rental houses may make changes to the factory presets to optimize the recording for local production requirements. These settings then are considered the rental house's "standard" setup for the camera. The cinematographer may change these settings or use an in-camera function to reset to factory standard. The rental house may provide a backup copy of their rental house standard.

Some HD cameras offer extensive choices for "painting," or adjusting image characteristics such as gamma curves, knee point and slope, and sharpening and detail. These settings may determine what shadow and highlight detail is recorded or lost, what high frequency detail is included or obscured, and at what cost to image quality. The choice of a gamma curve can have a significant effect on the look of the image produced. A recommended strategy is to avoid any adjustment that will lend to the loss of image information that cannot be recaptured in post.

The cinematographer can set up different looks on the camera by making adjustments in the menu, then saving them to a scene file. Some cameras allow a limited number of scene files to be saved on the camera in scene file 'slots', which can be easily recalled by number. The saved scene files should also be saved to a flash memory card compatible with the camera. The cinematographer may provide the assistant with additional scene files on a flash card, and ask to have them loaded into numbered slots on the camera.

Carefully log which scene file (and the look it represents) is loaded into each numbered scene file slot on the camera. Also, keep a master log of scene file looks being used, and where to find them—such as, on which numbered flash memory stick they are saved.

A good way to keep track of all the different parameters in the menu is to use a spreadsheet that lists each menu page and the settings selected for each line item. If multiple scene files will be used on the production, the spreadsheet becomes even more useful. Each different scene file can have a column, or be assigned a unique color to identify its settings.

C. TESTING

Shooting tests with a digital camera is as necessary as it is with a film camera. However, the nature of digital video facilitates convenient monitoring and playback of any recorded test.

Useful targets:
▶ Color-chip chart designed for digital video.
▶ Focus chart with Siemens star, resolution line pairs.
▶ Rack-framing chart.
▶ Middle-gray card.
▶ Grayscale steps.
▶ Human models that resemble principal cast.

Useful tools:
▶ Waveform monitor.
▶ Vectorscope

❯ Histogram
❯ Light meter
❯ Test balls/spheres (middle gray, white, mirror, white with black hole).

1. Workflow

The most important test to perform in preproduction is a practical image test of the entire workflow—end to end, "scene to screen."

    a. Record images representative of the planned production photography. Include charts (color, focus, framing), models, motion, and lighting setups approximating the dynamic range anticipated.

    b. Use the same equipment (camera, lenses) and media ordered for production.

    c. Set up the camera and all supporting devices exactly as they will be set for production. If multiple configurations or settings are anticipated, shoot takes with each variation, clearly slating each one. This may include frame rates, scene files, recording configurations and any alternate looks achieved by changing menu settings.

    d. Record time code and audio as planned for production.

    e. Send the recorded material through the same workflow planned for the production. This may include transfers, conversions, processing by different software applications, and recording out to the final release medium. If the project is destined for a theatrical film release, this will require recording the material back to film.

    This test requires the full cooperation of the post facility. Most will welcome the opportunity to test and confirm a production's workflow before production begins. Just as the camera settings must be the same as planned for production, all settings, selections, devices and media used in the postproduction process must be the same as planned for the production.

    f. If the result of the test is unsatisfactory, the cause must be identified before proceeding to production.

2. Exposure/dynamic range

Just as a cinematographer tests a new film stock—or even a new batch number—for dynamic range, he or she should test a digital camera for its response to light. The result of this test can inform the cinematographer's lighting style. Knowing what happens to the image at certain levels of under- or overexposure allows the cinematographer to take full advantage of the camera's capabilities and push them to their limit.

    a. Use charts and a human model (the eye is most sensitive to exposure changes on a person's face).

    b. Shoot identical takes at 1-stop intervals, up to 5 stops under and 5 stops over the "normal" (middle gray) exposure setting. Add ½-stop intervals within 2 stops of normal, for more critical evaluation.

c. Clearly slate and log each take.

3. **Framing**

Shoot a rack-leader framing chart, with arrows pointing out to each corner of the frame. Align the eyepiece and ground-glass frame lines with the frame lines on the framing chart.

4. **Time code**

Record time code with all the same hardware planned for production—smart slate, Clockit, any other time-code generator, sound recorder (when available), and additional cameras. Confirm time code records properly, and all picture and sound stays in sync.

5. **Frame rates**

Record takes at each frame rate anticipated for production. For off-standard frame rates (slow or fast motion), send the footage through post processing, then view to evaluate the motion effects.

6. **Look management**

a. Load each of the shoot's planned looks into the system.

b. Record an appropriate scene for each of the respective looks.

c. Apply each look to the particular scene recorded for its use.

d. Evaluate the transformed scene on a calibrated monitor.

e. Create new scene files, ASC CDL recipes and LUTs as requested, using camera menus, image-processing software and LUT boxes, respectively.

7. **Traditional Visual Tests**

As for a film camera prep, shoot tests of all elements that require visual evaluation. (*See "Film Camera Prep," page 441.*)

a. All lenses and filters

b. Specialized lighting effects.

c. New lighting color gels and diffusion.

d. Makeup, sets and wardrobe as requested by production.

D) DAILY PREP AND MAINTENANCE

1. Set up camera package on the set for the first shot.

2. Power and warm-up camera and all hardware to proper operating temperature. If available and needed, use camera body and eyepiece heaters.

3. Examine sensor and clean as necessary.

   (*See "Sensor Cleaning Steps" section, page 453*)

4. Clean all lenses and filters as necessary.

5. Check for any lit or dead pixels.

   (*See "Pixel Check Steps" section, page 452*)

6. Run auto black balance (ABB) enough times to process all pixels on sensor.

7. Check for adequate supply of media (tapes, drives, cards) for the day's shooting. Prepare backup devices and media for use.
8. Check calibration on all monitors and adjust as necessary using field calibration procedures. (*See below.*)

    The calibration of a CRT is affected by the earth's magnetic field—it must be checked each time it is moved to a different location.

Field Calibration Setup Steps with SMPTE Bars

1. Place the monitor in the anticipated viewing environment on the set. (*See "Viewing Environment Guidelines."*)
2. Feed standard SMPTE bars to monitor.
3. Set monitor to display blue channel only.
4. Adjust chroma and hue controls to make the density of the four brighter vertical bars match the rectangular bar segments directly below each one, and match each other. Chroma will affect the outside bars; hue, the inner bars.
5. Reset monitor to view all three color channels.
6. Locate the three dark gray picture lineup generating equipment (PLUGE) bars below the sixth (red) bar.
7. Raise the brightness control until all 3 PLUGE bars are visible.
8. Reduce the brightness control until the middle bar blends into the darkest bar on the left.
9. Adjust contrast control so that the white reference square on the lower left is bright white, but not glowing into adjacent squares.
10. The contrast adjustment may affect the brightness adjustment. Adjust both so that the PLUGE bars and white reference square appear correct.
11. Set up a proper viewing environment on the set for the monitor(s) used for critical evaluation of the camera image. Human perception is very sensitive to ambient light. The color and intensity of the light surrounding a display will significantly affect any judgment made regarding density, contrast or color.

Viewing Environment Guidelines

SMPTE publishes recommended practices to create a viewing environment for the evaluation of color television images (SMPTE RP-166). It specifies standards for monitor setup, screen size, viewing distance, the color and brightness of surrounding surfaces, and the color and intensity of ambient light. The most critical factor is the color and brightness of the area immediately surrounding the monitor—what appears in the viewer's field of view.

It may be difficult to meet these standards on a practical set. A shaded corner (created with flags or a black "easy-up" with sides) and a gray cloth draped behind the monitor from a C-stand (illuminated by a light—approximately 6500°K—to set a neutral reference source) may be adequate. The surrounding ambient light should be substantially darker than the gray background—no more than 30% of the level of the background.

Check Back Focus on Lenses

▶ Back focus must be carefully monitored, particularly on many ⅔" three-chip cameras.

▶ Check back focus often: At beginning of the day, after shipping or changing locations, at each lens change, and whenever the temperature changes enough so that you need to remove or add clothing to stay comfortable.

▶ The adjustment is done on each lens by adjusting a ring at the back end of the lens. This ring brings the rear-element group mechanism farther or closer to the sensor.

Incorrect back focus does not affect focusing the lens by eye through the viewfinder—except at infinity. When the back focus is out of adjustment, the lens cannot be focused at infinity, and the distance witness marks on the lens cannot be used—they will not correspond to either eye or tape focus.

Back Focus Adjustment Steps

There are two methods to adjusting back focus:

1. Using a handheld collimator, such as a Sharp Max or HD collimator (both designed for this purpose).
2. Using a focus chart and tape measure.

A high-definition monitor is useful for both methods.

The camera should be at normal operating temperature—fully warmed up.

1. Using handheld collimator (Sharp Max, HD collimator):

a. Set lens distance ring at infinity.
b. Set aperture wide open.
c. If zoom lens, zoom in to maximum focal length.
d. Adjust eyepiece diopter.
e. Lower peaking circuit in viewfinder monitor.
f. Mount collimator: Slide its lens flange onto front of lens. Secure with locking screw.
g. Switch on the collimator's internal light.
h. View through camera eyepiece or on HD monitor.
i. Adjust collimator light fader for optimum viewing. If necessary, use camera ND filter to reduce brightness. Adjust light so that the circle of confusion at the center of the Siemens star stands out and is clearly defined from the surrounding star.
j. Loosen locking screw on lens back-focus ring.

k. Adjust the back-focus ring, racking back and forth through focus until the circle of confusion at the star's center is minimized both horizontally and vertically.

l. Tighten the back-focus locking screw.

m. On zoom lens, zoom out to widest focal length. Check back focus again—if off, adjust back focus ring. Then zoom back in to check. Repeat if necessary.

The back focus should now be correct. The lens will focus at infinity, and all witness marks should be accurate.

n. Remove the collimator.

o. Using a focus chart and tape measure, confirm back-focus adjustment. Check at infinity and a near distance by comparing eye focus with measured distance using lens witness marks. With zoom lenses, check focus at full telephoto, full wide, and in between. Confirm that the focus does not shift through the range of the zoom.

2. Using Focus chart (with Siemens star) or Pituro chart and tape measure

a. Set camera at such a distance that the chart fills (or nearly fills) the frame and the lens being checked has a witness mark for that distance.

c. If zoom lens, zoom in to maximum focal length.

d. Adjust eyepiece diopter.

e. Raise peaking circuit in viewfinder.

f. Set light intensity on chart for optimum viewing.

g. Adjust back focus with back-focus ring on lens (using steps j, k, l, m above).

E. DELIVERY OF ELEMENTS TO POST DAILIES, EDITORIAL, VFX AND DI

1. After consultation with production and postproduction personnel, decide which elements will be delivered to which location at the end of each production day.

2. Plan and schedule the daily delivery method, paying particular attention to the integrity and safety of the image media (avoiding unnecessary heat and movement).

3. Establish a clear labeling method, recognized by the postproduction personnel, that organizes the media and facilitates easy finding of requested items.

Have a happy prep!

A feature cinematographer and director, Marty Ollstein conceived and developed Crystal Image software, which precisely emulates optical camera filter effects. He is a member of the ASC Technology Committee, a SMPTE Fellow, and par-

ticipated as a cinematographer in the ASC-PGA Camera Assessment Series (CAS) and Image Control Assessment Series (ICAS).

Camera-Support Systems

by Andy Romanoff, ASC Associate Member
Frank Kay, ASC Associate Member
and Kent H. Jorgensen

New technologies offer the cinematographer more choices for moving the camera today. There are studio and location dollies, person-carrying cranes, remote-head-only cranes and telescopic cranes. The selection of remote heads includes two- three- and four-axis versions stabilized and unstabilized, heads and mounts qualified for helicopters and airplanes and a variety of body mounted stabilizers like the Steadicam.

DOLLIES WITH LIFTING ARMS

These dollies are characterized by lifting arms that swing up and down to raise and lower the camera. The design allows a significant amount of vertical travel (up to 48"), permitting most shots to be accomplished without reconfiguring the dolly. The design also makes it easy to place the camera next to walls and to arrange shots that look straight down. There are platforms and seats for the Steadicam operator to step off of which gives the cinematographer more options. These dollies come in different sizes and can support various weights including 3-D rigs.

DOLLIES WITH LIFTING CENTER POSTS

Post dollies raise and lower the camera using a column located directly under the camera. This design makes it easier for the operator to move around the dolly to follow action on shots that require long sweeping pans. Center-post dollies feature articulated legs which can be configured to allow the dolly to work in very constricted spaces. They can be either electric or hydraulic. The hydraulic lift is often referred to as a ped, pedestal, or single operator ped.

LOCATION/DOORWAY DOLLIES

A variety of dollies have been developed for operating in narrow spaces or to facilitate high speed or rough ground handheld chase work. These include both hydraulic or electric lift beams dollies along with no beam dollies.

TELESCOPIC CRANES

Telescopic cranes offer the ability to instantly adjust the size of the crane to the needs of the shot. They also offer the ability to change size during the shot, giving the director of photography great flexibility. The telescopic design permits a 30-foot crane to be moved around the set with the ease of a much smaller crane. Finally telescopic cranes can reach greater heights in smaller spaces than equivalent fixed length cranes.

REMOTE-HEAD-ONLY CRANES

These cranes feature modular construction which permits them to be built in various lengths. Many different models exist covering a range of 4 feet to 100 feet. The individual sections can usually be carried by two or three people, making it possible to bring the crane into a difficult location and then to build it on site.

REMOTE-HEAD OR PLATFORM CRANES

These cranes do double duty by carrying one or two people at lengths up to 30 feet and remote heads out to 50 feet. They are generally a little more bulky than remote-head-only cranes for a given length.

PLATFORM CRANES

Although a great deal of crane work is now done with remote heads, there are still advantages to the traditional person-carrying crane. Chief among them is the ability of the operator to see through the lens, as well as the uncomplicated setup of the camera.

REMOTE HEADS

Remote heads have revolutionized crane design as well as the shots that are made with them. The development of lightweight remote heads meant that crane arms could be built with a fraction of their original bulk, freeing the camera to move in space with great speed and freedom. The current generation of remote heads offers a wide variety of features and options, including three-axis operation, camera stabilization and automatic backpan compensation.

AIRPLANE AND HELICOPTER MOUNTS/HEADS

Aerial photography requires specialized mounts for optimum results. Mounts in this category have been certified for safe operation in various aircraft, and offer the ability to photograph scenes using extremely long lenses without shake or vibration.

REMOTE HAND WHEELS

Remote hand wheels are motor units that are attached to the pan and tilt shafts of gear heads so that the head may be operated at a distance. Although these units do not provide all the functionality of remote heads, they are quick and simple to set up and use.

CABLE RIGGED CAMERA SYSTEMS

These systems use a wire suspension rig to hang a remotely operated camera. The setup can be as simple as moving the camera between two points along a line, or as complicated as using a combination of trusses, I-beams, and winches to move the camera in three dimensional space. Many of these systems are computer operated, and can even be used for motion-controlled vfx work.

REMOTELY OPERATED TRACK SYSTEMS

Track systems, or "rail cameras" are capable of movements at high speeds over long distances. They can be rigged as a stand-alone system or be rigged to other support systems. Typically the dollies are fixed to the track, which allows them to be rigged right side up, upside down, horizontally, vertically, and diagonally. The versatility and speed of track systems allow them to do jobs which would be difficult or dangerous for a live crew member.

REMOTELY OPERATED ARMS

Borrowing from military stabilization technology, remotely operated arms allow for camera crane-like movement, but on a smaller scale. Like track systems, the arms can be used in situations where operation would be difficult or dangerous for a live crew member.

ELECTRIC OR GAS-POWERED DOLLIES

For years grips have used motors to speed up and reduce the effort needed to get a dolly shot. This has led to some dollies being custom-made from everything from gas-powered quad runners to electric utility carts. They can be rigged for cameras with operators, remote heads, or body-mounted stabilizers. Whether track-mounted or wheeled, these special-purpose dollies allow for camera movement with few restrictions.

SMALL JIBS AND SLIDERS

These pieces of equipment can cut a great deal of setup time. Their compact size allows for placement on a dolly or camera platform, and enables the operator to easily make small adjustments and moves. A dolly grip or operator who understands the equipment can maneuver big budget-looking shots using these small-budget solutions.

RADIO CONTROLLED VEHICLES

Radio controlled vehicles and aircraft are usually small in size and can create great opportunities for filmmakers. Their diminutive stature permits them access to places inaccessible by a human operator or by any other means (for instance, beneath cars).

Many of the above systems rely on radio technology to control the dolly, camera platform, and camera operation. As long as this technology—and the imagination of the filmmakers who use it—continues to mature, the movement of the camera will have no limits.

Andy Romanoff is president of Panavision Remote Systems
Frank Kay is marketing director, J.L. Fisher, Inc.
Kent H. Jorgensen is the safety representative for IATSE Local 80 Grips Union

KEY TO READING THE CRANE CHARTS		
	MANUFACTURER	
	CRANE MAKE/MODEL	
Minimum Length	SMALLEST USABLE LENGTH, CRANE CENTER PIVOT TO CENTER OF MITCHELL MOUNT	
Maximum Length	LONGEST USABLE LENGTH, CRANE CENTER PIVOT TO CENTER OF MITCHELL MOUNT	
Overall Length	LENGTH OF CRANE FROM NOSE TO TAIL AT MAXIMUM LENGTH	
Maximum Rise at Minimum Length	MEASURED FROM GROUND LEVEL TO THE MITCHELL MOUNT AT MAXIMUM EXTENSION	
Nose Load at Maximum Length	TOTAL WEIGHT OF CAMERA AND HEAD PACKAGE SUPPORTED BY THE CRANE AT MAXIMUM EXTENSION	
Min. Doorway Clearance (W x H)	THE WIDTH AND HEIGHT OF THE CRANE WHEN BUILT AT MAXIMUM EXTENSION	
All Up Weight in Max. Config.	DESCRIPTION OF ALL UP WEIGHT IN MAXIMUM CONFIGURATION	
Track Width	DESCRIPTION OF TRACK WIDTH	
Type	C=OPERATOR RIDING/REMOTE HEAD R=REMOTE HEADS ONLY F=FIXED LENGTH	O=OPERATOR ONLY T=TELESCOPIC

	AKELA	AEROCRANE		CHAPMAN		
	Akela	Super 30	Super 35	15' Hydrascope/ Ultra HY HY Base	20' Hydrascope/ Ultra HY HY Base	32' Hydrascope/ Ultra CS Base
Minimum Length	45' (13.7 m)	7'6" (2.2 m)	8'6" (2.6 m)	4'6" (1.37 m)	5'3.5" (1.6 m)	5'3.5" (1.6 m)
Maximum Length	85' (25.9 m)	28'6" (8.7 m)	34'6" (10.5 m)	13'10" (4.23 m)	19'2" (5.8 m)	32' (9.75 m)
Overall Length	96' (29.3 m)	35'10" (10.9 m)	42'10" (13 m)	18'3" (5.56 m)	19'7" (6 m)	39' (11.9 m) Overslung
Maximum Rise at Minimum Length	78' (23.3 m)	27'4" (8.3 m)	33'6" (10.2 m)	18'8" (5.68 m) Overslung	22'6" (6.86 m) Overslung	38' (11.6 m)
Nose Load at Maximum Length	100 lbs (45.4 kg)	125 lbs (57 kg)	125 lbs (57 kg)	250 lbs (113 kg)	200 lbs (90.9 kg)	250 lbs (113.6 kg)
Min. Doorway Clearance (W x H)	Ø	54" x 56" (1.3 m x 1.4 m)	54" x 56" (1.3 m x 1.4 m)	72" H x 36" W (2.2 m x 1.1 m)	72" H x 36" W (2.2 m x 1.1 m)	72" H x 48" W (1.3 m x 1.4 m)
All Up Weight in Max. Config.	8,000 lbs (3,629 kg)	2,700 lbs (1,225 kg)	3,200 lbs (1,452 kg)	1,700 lbs (774 kg)	2,110 lbs (959.09 kg)	2,709 lbs (1,231 kg)
Track Width	7'8" (2.3 m)	24.5"/32" (622/813 mm)	24.5"/32" (622/813 mm)	24" Center to Center	24" Center to Center	880 mm Center to Center
Type	R	C	C	Ø	Ø	Ø

CRANES

CHAPMAN

	73' Hydrascope on Ultra Base	Apollo/ Super Apollo	Electra/ Nike	Electra 14' Stage Crane	Lenny Arm Plus	Lenny Arm II
Minimum Length	10'6" (3.2 m)	12'9" (3.9 m)	9'6" (2 m)	Lens reach: 9'6" (2.9 m)	4'3" (1.6 m) w/24" camera plate	4'9" (1.5 m) w/24" camera plate
Maximum Length	72' (21.95 m)	18'9" (5.7 m) w/6' extension	12'6" (3.8 m) w/3' extension	Lens reach w/ extension: 12'6" (3.8 m)	34'1" (10.4 m) w/24" camera plate	38'9" (11.8 m) w/24" camera plate
Overall Length	85'10" (26.16 m)	28'8" (8.7 m)	16'9" (5.1 m) w/o extension	16'9" (5.1 m)	43'9" (13.3 m)	49'1" (15 m)
Maximum Rise at Minimum Length	75' (22.86 m) Underslung	15'11" (4.9 m)	10'6" (3.2 m)	8' (2.4 m)	33'2" (10.1 m)	37'4" (11.4 m)
Nose Load at Maximum Length	220 lb (106 kg)	2,740 lbs (1,245.5 kg)	1,400 lbs (636 kg)	1,400 lbs (636 kg)	168 lbs (76.4 kg)	346 lbs (157.3 kg)
Min. Doorway Clearance (W x H)	80"H X 50"W	7'7.5" x 8'4" (2.32 m x 2.54 m)	44" x 5'3.5" (1.12 x 1.61 m)	45.5"H X 63.5"W (1.2 x 1.6 m)	depends on dolly used	depends on dolly used
All Up Weight in Max. Config.	18,000 lbs (8,181.8 kg)	17,500 lbs (7,955 kg)	5,200 lbs (2,364 kg)	5,200 lbs (2,364 kg)	2,727 lbs (1,239.5 kg)	3,762 lbs (1,710 kg)
Track Width	Ø	6'4" (1.9 m)	39.88" (1 m)	39.88" (1 m)	depends on base	depends on base
Type	Ø	F	F	Ø	C	C

CRANES

CHAPMAN

	Lenny Arm II Plus	Lenny Arm III	Lenny Mini	Stinger Plus Jib Arm on Hustler IV	Super Apollo	Super Nova
Minimum Length	4'9" (1.5 m) w/24" camera plate	10'1" (3 m) w/24" camera plate	2'6" (.76 m) w/9" camera plate	60" (1.5 m)	12'9" (3.9 m)	17'3" (5.5 m)
Maximum Length	38'4" (11.7 m) w/24" camera plate	50'4" (15.3 m) w/24" camera plate	28'6" (8.6 m) w/9" camera plate	8' (2.4 m)	18'9" (5.7 m) w/6' extension	29'3" (8.8 m) w/12' extension
Overall Length	48'8" (14.8 m)	60'9" (18.5 m)	36'1" (10.9 m)	10' (3 m)	29'4" (8.9 m)	39'2" (11.9 m)
Maximum Rise at Minimum Length	37'4" (11.4 m)	43'3" (13.2 m)	28'2" (8.58 m)	13'1.25" (4 m)	19'5" (5.9 m)	30' (7.6 m) w/3' riser
Nose Load at Maximum Length	282 lbs (128.2 kg)	250 lbs (113.6 kg)	74 lbs (33.6 kg)	133 lbs (60.4 kg)	1,982 lbs (900.9 kg)	2,740 lbs (1,245.5 kg)
Min. Doorway Clearance (W x H)	depends on dolly used	depends on dolly used	depends on dolly used	42" x 27.5" (106 x 70 cm)	7'7.5" x 8'4" (2.3 x 2.5 m)	7'7.5" x 9'3" (2.3 x 2.8 m)
All Up Weight in Max. Config.	2,969 lbs (1,349.5 kg)	5,262 lbs (2,391 kg)	1,971 lbs (895.9 kg)	1,221 lbs (555 kg)	18,100 lbs (8,227 kg)	27,500 lbs (12,500 kg)
Track Width	depends on base	depends on base	depends on base	24.5" (62.2 cm) Center to Center	Ø	Ø
Type	C	C	R	Ø	Ø	F

	CRANES					
	CHAPMAN			**EGRIPMENT**		
	Titan II	Zeus	Zeus 16' Stage Crane	Javelin	Javelin Mark II	Piccolo
Minimum Length	17'3" (5.5 m)	11'6" (3.5 m)	Lens reach: 11'6" (3.5 m)	8' (2.4 m)	8' (2.4 m)	8'2" (2.4 m)
Maximum Length	29'3" (8.8 m) w/12' extension	14'6" (4.4 m) w/3' extension	Lens reach w/3' extension: 14'6" (4.4 m)	30' (9.1 m)	37.4' (11.4 m)	8'2" (2.4 m)
Overall Length	39'2" (11.9 m)	19'4.5" (5.9 m) w/o extension	19'4" (5.9 m)	39' (11.8 m)	45.3' (13.8 m)	15'4" (4.6 m)
Maximum Rise at Minimum Length	30' (7.6 m) w/3' riser	12'8" (3.9 m)	19'2" (5.8 m) w/3' riser	29'6" (8.9 m)	36.1' (11 m)	8'6" (2.5 m)
Nose Load at Maximum Length	2,500 lbs (1,136.3 kg)	1,300 lbs (591 kg)	1,300 lbs (591 kg)	143 lbs (65 kg)	88.2 lbs (40 kg)	550 lbs (249 kg)
Min. Doorway Clearance W x H	7'7.5" x 9'3" (2.3 m x 2.8 m)	4'3.25" x 5'9.25" (1.3 m x 1.7 m)	48" x 69.25" (1.2 m x 1.8 m)	48" x 7'6" (1.2 m x 2.2 m)	48" x 7'6" (1.2 m x 2.2 m)	36" (914 mm)
All Up Weight in Max. Config.	26,600 lbs (11,818 kg)	6,150 lbs (2,795 kg)	6,150 lbs (2,795.4 kg)	3,000 lbs (1,400 kg)	3,000 lbs (1,400 kg)	1,250 lbs (567 kg)
Track Width	Ø	43.875" (1.1 m) tread	43.875" (1.1 m)	32" (813 mm)	32" (813 mm)	24" (610 mm)
Type	F	F	Ø	R	R	C

CRANES

EGRIPMENT

	Scanner	Sky King	Super Maxi Jib	T12	Tulip/VIP	Xtreme T-12
Minimum Length	13'2" (4 m)	11'6" (3.5 m)	5'4" (1.6 m)	8'2" (2.4 m)	10'10" (3.3 m)	10'3" (3.1 m)
Maximum Length	17'6" (5.3 m)	40'8" (12.3 m)	15'4" (4.6 m)	32'10" (10 m)	31'4" (9.5 m)	33' (10 m)
Overall Length	23'4" (7.1 m)	50' (15.2 m)	22'4" (6.8 m)	39'5" (12 m)	38'4" (11.6 m)	43' (13 m)
Maximum Rise at Minimum Length	21' (6.4 m)	40' (12.1 m)	15'6" (4.7 m)	39'5" (12 m)	31'9" (9.6 m)	31.5" (9.5 m) lens height
Nose Load at Maximum Length	55 lbs (25 kg)	88 lbs (40 kg)	77 lbs (35 kg)	132 lbs (60 kg)	55 lbs (25 kg)	140 lbs (63.5 kg)
Min. Doorway Clearance W x H	28" x 5' (711 mm x 1.5 m)	48" x 7' (1.2 m x 2.1 m)	28" x 5' (711 mm x 1.5 m)	4'11" x 7'1" (1.4 m x 2.1 m)	48" x 7'6" (1.2 m x 2.2 m)	6'8"L x 5.5"W x 6'7.5"H
All Up Weight in Max. Config.	750 lbs (340 kg)	3,700 lbs (1,678 kg)	Ø	2,489 lbs (1,129 kg)	2,700 lbs (1,225 kg)	3,555 lbs (1,612 kg)
Track Width	24" (610 mm)	32" (813 mm)	24" (610 mm)	34" (95 cm)	32" (813 mm)	3'3" wide (990.6 mm)
Type	R	C	R	T	C	Ø

	GIRAFFE	GLIDE CAM	GRIP FACTORY MUNICH			
	Giraffe	GlideCam Vista Crane	GF-8	GF-8 Xten	GF-9	GF-10
Minimum Length	7'10" (2.3 m)	15' (4.5 m)	8'6" (2.53 m)		8'1" (242 cm)	10'7" (3.23 m)
Maximum Length	30' (9.1 m)	22' (6.7 m)	26'6" (8.1 m)		28'4" (842 cm)	39'10" (12.15 m)
Overall Length	38'6" (11.7 m)	23' (7 m)	33'8" (10.3 m)		33'9" (1,014 cm)	48'2" (14.71 m)
Maximum Rise at Minimum Length	29' (8.8 m)	30' (9.1 m)	26'2" (7.98 m)		47' (1,408 cm)	37'5" (11.42 m)
Nose Load at Maximum Length	220 lbs (100 kg)	40 lbs (18 kg)	110 lbs (50 kg)		55 lbs (25 kg)	110 lbs (50 kg)
Min. Doorway Clearance W x H	58" x 86" (1.4 m x 2.1 m)	53"W x 100"H (16.2 m x 30.5 m)	2'9" x 7'6" (.838 m x 2.2 m)		3'1" x 7'2" (94 x 216 cm)	Ø
All Up Weight in Max. Config.	2,515 lbs (1,141 kg)	Ø	1,797 lbs (815.1 kg)		985 lbs (448 kg)	3,016 lbs (1,368 kg)
Track Width	3'3" (1 m)	Ø	Ø		24.5" (622 mm)	Ø
Type	C	Ø	C		R	C

CRANES						
	GRIP FACTORY MUNICH	**J.L. FISHER**			**LOUMA**	**LOUMA SYSTEMS**
	GF-16	Model 20	Model 21	Model 22 &23	Louma	Louma 2
Minimum Length	11' (3.36 m)	41.5" (1.05 m)	58.5" (1.4 m)	89.5" (2.2 m)	3'6" (1 m)	8' (2 m 45)
Maximum Length	55'1" (16.81 m)	53.5" (1.3 m)	70.5" (1.7 m)	101.5" (2.5 m)	24'8" (7.5 m)	32' (9.75 m)
Overall Length	64'2" (19.59 m)	82" (2.08 m)	106.5" (2.7 m)	154.5" (3.9 m)	34'8" (10.5 m)	40' (12.2 m)
Maximum Rise at Minimum Length	50'2" (15.31 m)	10.5' (3.2 m) on model dolly	11.5" (292 mm) on model dolly	11' (3.3 m) on model dolly	27' (8.2 m)	33' (10 m) Underslung 137'6" (11.4 m 40) Overslung
Nose Load at Maximum Length	132 lbs (60 kg)	198 lbs (90 kg) w/optional weight set	180 lbs (82 kg)	190.5 lbs (86 kg)	155 lbs (70 kg)	198 lbs (90 kg)
Min. Doorway Clearance W x H	5'8" x 16'7" (1.77 m x 5 m)	27" x 48" (686 mm x 1.2 m)	27" x 48" (686 mm x 1.2 m)	27" x 60" (686 mm x 1.5 m)	7' x 28' (2.1 m x 8.5 m)	7'0.5"H (2.15 m)
All Up Weight in Max. Config.	5,306 lbs (approx.) (2,406.8 kg)	631 lbs (286 kg)	640 lbs (290 kg)	665 lbs (302 kg)	1,250 lbs (567 kg)	3,630 lbs (1,650 kg)
Track Width	Ø	24.5" (622 mm)	24.5" (62.2 mm)	24.5" (62.2 mm)	34.5" (876 mm)	3'3" (1 m)
Type	C	R	R	R	R	Ø

	CRANES					
	MOVIEBIRD				**MOVIE TECH**	
	MB 17	**MB 45**	**MB 30**	**MB 24**	**ABC Crane 120**	**Felix V**
Minimum Length	11'15" (3.4 m)	15'8" (4.83 m)	14'10" (4.5 m)	11'8" (3.6 m)	14'9" (4.4 m)	8' (2.4 m)
Maximum Length	16'5" (5 m)	45' (13.7 m)	30' (9.14 m)	23'9" (7.3 m)	39.5' (12 m)	17'4" (5.2 m)
Overall Length	2'3" (7 m)	53' (16.15 m)	38' (11.6 m)	53' (16.1 m)	44.5' (13.5 m)	22.5' (6.8 m)
Maximum Rise at Minimum Length	30'3" (9.25 m)	39'5" (12 m)	32'10" (10 m)	26'6" (8.1 m)	39' (11.8 m)	17'6" (5.3 m)
Nose Load at Maximum Length	165 lbs (70 kg)	121.3 lbs 955 kg)	165 lbs (70 kg)	165 lbs (70 kg)	50 lbs (23 kg)	132 lbs (60 kg)
Min. Doorway Clearance W x H	5'6" x 4'6" (1.7 m x 1.4 m)	6'6" x 4'11" (2 m x 1.5 m)	6'6" x 4'11" (2 m x 1.5 m)	6'6" x 4'8" (2 m x 1.43 m)	26" (660 mm) when used w/ ABC Crane dolly	39" x 70" (990 mm x 1.7 m)
All Up Weight in Max. Config.	1,735 lbs 787 kg	3,928 lbs 1,782 kg	2,775 lbs 1,259 kg	2,553 lbs 1,158 kg	420 lbs (191 kg)	1,331 lbs (604 kg)
Track Width	3'3.4'''	3'3.4" 1 m	3'3.4" 1 m	3'3.4" 1 m	24.5" (622 mm) when used w/ ABC Crane dolly	24.5" (622 mm)
Type	Ø	Ø	Ø	Ø	R	C

CRANES						
	MOVIE TECH		ORION		PANTHER	
	Phoenix	MT 400	Technocrane	Super Technocrane	Cine Jib	Foxy
Minimum Length	9'6" (2.8 m)	9.8' (3 m)	6'3" (1.9 m)	7'10" (2.3 m)	8' (2.4 m)	8' (2.5 m)
Maximum Length	39'5" (12 m)	36' (11 m)	20'2" (6.1 m)	30' (9.1 m)	8' (2.4 m)	28' (8.5 m)
Overall Length	47'10" (14.5 m)	42' (13 m)	26'5" (8 m)	38' (11.5 m)	13' (4 m)	33.5' (10.2 m)
Maximum Rise at Minimum Length	38'6" (11.7 m) euroadapter height	36' (11 m)	22' (6.7 m) small base 23'6" (7.2 m) large base & telescopic post	32' (9.7 m)	10' (3.1 m)	23' (7 m)
Nose Load at Maximum Length	159 lbs (72 kg)	99 lbs (45 kg)	180 lbs (82 kg)	180 lbs (82 kg)	570 lbs (260 kg)	110 lbs (50 kg)
Min. Doorway Clearance W x H	59.5" x 93.5" (1.5 m x 2.3 m)	102.3" x 46.8" 31.2 m x 14.3 m)	3'7" x 6'11" (1.1 x 2.1 m) small base 4'6" x 6'11" (1.4 x 2.1 m) large base & telescopic post	4'6" x 6'11" (1.3 x 2.1 m)	27" x 4' (70 x 130 cm)	3' x 7' (0.9 x 2.1 m)
All Up Weight in Max. Config.	3,744 lbs (1,698 kg)	1,710 lbs (776 kg)	1,870 lbs (848 kg) small base, 2,200 lbs (998 kg) large base & telescopic post	2,875 lbs (1,304 kg)	440 lbs (200 kg)	1,300 lbs (600 kg)
Track Width	39" (990 mm)	2.03' (62 cm)	24.5" (622 mm) small base 4'9" (1.4 m) large base & telescopic post	4'9" (1.4 m)	2'2" (62 cm)	2'1" (62 cm) or 3'3" (1 m)
Type	C	Ø	T, R	T, R	F	C

	CRANES					
	PANTHER				**SERVICE VISION**	
	Galaxy	Pegasus	Super Jib IIr	Swiss Jib	Mini Scorpio Crane	Super Scorpio Crane
Minimum Length	11' (3.3 m)	6.5' (2 m)	3'3" (1 m)	8' (2.5 m)	10.5' (3.2 m)	8.5' (2.6m)
Maximum Length	57' (17.3 m)	33' (10 m)	6.5' (2 m)	42.5' (13 m)	22' (6.7 m)	30' (9 m) or 37' (11 m)
Overall Length	67.5' (20.5 m)	41.5' (12.5 m)	11.5' (3.5 m)	50' (15.3 m)	27' (8.2 m)	45' (13,7 m) (in 37' configuration)
Maximum Rise at Minimum Length	50' (15 m)	33' (10 m)	10' (3 m)	34.5' (10.4 m)	22' (6.7 m)	30' (9 m) + configuration 37' (11 m) + configuration
Nose Load at Maximum Length	143 lbs (65 kg)	176 lbs (80 kg)	220 lbs (100 kg)	55 lbs (25 kg)	167 lbs (75.7 kg)	202 lbs @ 30' (91.6 kg @ 9 m)
Min. Doorway Clearance W x H	5' x 10' (1.6 m x 3 m)	5.2' x 7.8' (160 cm x 2.4 m)	27" x 5'3" (70 cm x 160 cm)	2'7" x 6' (70 cm x 180 m)	32.5" (0.8 m)	Ø
All Up Weight in Max. Config.	3,000 lbs (600 kg)	2,430 lbs (1,100 kg)	485 lbs (220 kg)	1,000 lbs (450 kg)	1,800 lbs (3.2 m)	3,300 lbs (1,497 kg)
Track Width	3'3" (1 m)	2'1" (62 cm) or 3'3" (1 m)	2'1" (62 cm)	2'1" (62 cm) or 3'3" (1 m)	dolly track & 1 m	3'3" 1 m track
Type	C	C	C	R	Ø	Ø

	STRADA	STRAIGHT SHOOT'R	SUPERTECHNO			
	Strada	Straight Shoot'r	Techno 15	Technodolly	Supertechno 22	Supertechno 30
Minimum Length	45' (13.7 m)	53" (1.4 m)	3'3" 1 m	3'3" 1 m	5'3" (1.6 m)	8'8" (2.64 m)
Maximum Length	100' (30.4 m)	77" (2 m)	13'9" 4.2 m	12'9.5" 3.9 m	22'4" (6.8 m)	22'7" (6.9 m)
Overall Length	112' (34.1 m)	110" (2.8 m)	19'8" 6 m	19'8" 6 m	29'6" (9 m)	31'2" (9.5 m)
Maximum Rise at Minimum Length	100' (30.4 m)	136" (3.5 m)	15'5" 4.7 m	14'9" 4.5 m	22'11" (7 m)	30'2" (9.2 m)
Nose Load at Maximum Length	85 lbs (39 kg) @ 100' (30.4 m) 200 lbs (91 kg) @ 72' (21.9 m)	100 lbs (43 kg)	77 lbs 35 kg	55 lbs 25 kg	77.2 lbs (35 kg)	77.2 lbs (35 kg)
Min. Doorway Clearance W x H	7'6" x 12'3" (2.3 m x 3.7 m)	depends on dolly used	7'3" 2.2 m	6'6' 2 m	8'2" (2.5 m)	8'2" (2.5 m)
All Up Weight in Max. Config.	8,500 lbs (3,856 kg)	350 lbs (159 kg) arm w/weights	1,146 lbs 520 kg	1,874 lbs 850 kg	1,433 lbs (650 kg)	2,646 lbs (1,200 kg)
Track Width	7' (2.1 m)	24" (610 mm)	2'10" 0.88 m	2'10" 0.88 m	Ø	4'9" (1.45 m)
Type	R	Ø	0	0	Ø	Ø

CRANES

	CRANES					
	SUPERTECHNO			**TECHNOCRANE S.R.O.**		
	Supertechno 50	Supertechno 100	New Technocrane	Techno 15	SuperTechno 20	SuperTechno 30
Minimum Length	11' (3.35 m)	15'9" (4.8 m)	(1.5 m)	4' (1.2 m)	6'3" (1.9 m)	7'10" (2.3 m)
Maximum Length	48'5" (14.75 m)	97'9" (29.8 m)	(6.3 m)	13'6" (4.1 m)	20'2" (6.1 m)	30' (9.1 m)
Overall Length	60'8" (18.5 m)	121'5" (37 m)	(8.3 m)	19'6" (5.9 m)	26'5" (8 m)	38' (11.5 m)
Maximum Rise at Minimum Length	49'2.5" (15 m)	104'11" (32 m)	(6.7 m)	15' (4.5 m)	22' (6.7 m) small base, 23'6" (7.2 m) & telescopic post	32' (9.7 m)
Nose Load at Maximum Length	77.2 lbs (35 kg)	77.2 lbs (35 kg)	(20 kg)	180 lbs (82 kg)	180 lbs (82 kg)	180 lbs (82 kg)
Min. Doorway Clearance W x H	8'2" (2.5 m)	18'0.5" (5.5 m)	(2.1 m)	2'7" x 6" (247 x 152 mm)	3'7" x 6'11" (1.1 x 2.1 m) small base, 4'6" x 6'11" (1.4 x 2.1 m) large base & telescopic post	4'6" x 6'11" (1.3 m x 2.1 m)
All Up Weight in Max. Config.	5,071 lbs (2,300 kg)	9,260 lbs (4,200 kg)	(350 kg)	1,270 lbs (576 kg)	1,870 lbs (848 kg) small base, 2,200 lbs (998 kg) large base & telescopic post	2,875 lbs (1,304 kg)
Track Width	6'7" (2.025 m)	Ø	(0.88 m)	34" (.863 m)	24.5" (622 mm) small base, 4'9" (1.4 m) large base & telescopic post	4'9" (1.4 m)
Type	Ø	Ø	Ø	T,R	T,R	T,R

CRANES				
	TECHNOCRANE S.R.O.		**TECHNOVISION**	
	SuperTechno 50	Technodolly	Technocrane	Supertechno
Minimum Length	11' (3.3 m)	5'3" (1.6 m)	6' (1.8 m)	8'2" (2.5 m)
Maximum Length	49' (14.9 m)	15'7" (4.6 m)	20' (6.5 m)	30' (9.1 m)
Overall Length	62' (18.8 m)	26'7" (8.1 m)	27' (8.4 m)	38'6" (11.7 m)
Maximum Rise at Minimum Length	50' (15.2 m)	24' (7.3 m)	22' (6.4 m)	32' (9.8 m)
Nose Load at Maximum Length	180 lbs (82 kg)	180 lbs (82 kg)	165 lbs (75 kg) excluding leveling head	165 lbs (75 kg)
Min. Doorway Clearance W x H	27" x 6" (685 x 1828 mm)	7'6" x 12'3" (2.2 m x 3.7 m)	4'2" x 7'4" (1.2 m x 2.1 m)	4'9" x 7' (1.5 m x 2.1 m)
All Up Weight in Max. Config.	5,534 lbs (2,510.2 kg)	2,600 lbs (1,179.3 kg)	2,000 lbs (850 kg)	3,000 lbs (1,361 kg)
Track Width	7' (2.1 m)	4'9" (1.4 m)	39" (1 m)	39" (1 m)
Type	T,R	T,R	T,R	T,R

KEY TO READING THE DOLLY CHARTS	
	MANUFACTURER
	DOLLY MAKE/MODEL
Minimum Boom Elevation	MINIMUM BOOM ELEVATION MEASURED AT THE TONGUE
Maximum Boom Elevation	MAXIMUM BOOM ELEVATION MEASURED AT THE TONGUE
Dolly Width	DOLLY WIDTH
Dolly Length	DOLLY LENGTH
Lifting Capacity	WEIGHT AT WHICH THE ARM OR POST CAN RAISE
Carrying Weight	THE TOTAL WEIGHT. INCLUDING OPERATOR, ASSISTANT, ETC., THE DOLLY CAN CARRY
Maximum Arm Lifts	MAXIMUM ARM LIFTS BEFORE RECHARGING
Track Width	TRACK WIDTH
Type	A= ARM P= POST

DOLLIES

CHAPMAN

	Hustler, II, III	Hustler IV	Hybrid, Hybrid II, Hybrid III	Pedolly	PeeWee, Super PeeWee, Super PeeWee II
Minimum Boom Elevation	19.5" (50 cm)	18" (48 cm)	15.25" (39 cm)	16.5" (42 cm)	24" (61 cm)
Maximum Boom Elevation	61" (1.6 m) w/o 12" riser	72" (1.8 m) w/12" camera	73" (1.9 m) w/12" camera	55.5" (1.4 m)	67" (1.7 m) w/12" camera
Dolly Width	27.5" (70 cm)	27½" (70 cm)	27" (69 cm)	22" (56 cm)	20" (51 cm)
Dolly Length	51" (1.3 m)	51" (1.3 m)	46" (1.2 m)	35.3125" (88 cm)	34.5" (88 cm)
Lifting Capacity	500 lbs (227 kg)	750 lbs (341 kg)	500 lbs (227 kg)	20 - 320 lbs (9 - 145 kg)	250 lbs (114 kg)
Carrying Weight	420 lbs (191 kg) no accesories	465 lbs (211 kg)	395 lbs (180 kg)	404 lbs (184 kg)	280 lbs (127 kg)
Maximum Arm Lifts	6 lifts	6 lifts	5 lifts	INFINITE	4 lifts
Track Width	24.5" (622 m)	24.5" (62.2 cm) Center to Center	24.5" (62.2 cm) Center to Center	24.5" (62.2 cm)	24.5" (62.2 cm) Center to Center
Type	A	Ø	A	A	A

DOLLIES				
	CHAPMAN			DOGGICAM	
	Super Pee-Wee III	Super PeeWee III+	Super PeeWee IV	Super Slide	Power Slide
Minimum Boom Elevation	15.75" (40 cm)	20.25" (51 cm)	17.25" (44 cm)	Ø	Ø
Maximum Boom Elevation	4.6' (1.4 m) w/o 12" riser	72.5" (1.84 m) w/12" Riser	71" (1.8 m) w/12" Riser	Ø	Ø
Dolly Width	20" to 32" (51 cm to 81 cm)	20" (51 cm)	20" (51 cm)	12" (3.6 m)	12" (3.6 m)
Dolly Length	34.5" to 43" (88 cm to 109 cm)	34.5" (88 cm)	34.5" (88 cm)	16" (4.8 m)	16" (4.8 m)
Lifting Capacity	300 lbs (136 kg) 1,100 lbs (500 kg) w/high post setup	4 lifts	350 lbs (159 kg)	Ø	Ø
Carrying Weight	295 lbs (131 kg) no accessories	295 lbs (134 kg)	295 lbs (131 kg)	45 lbs (20.4 kg)	45 lbs (20.4 kg)
Maximum Arm Lifts	4 lifts	4	5	Ø	Ø
Track Width	24.5" (62.2 cm)	24.5" (62.2 cm) Center to Center	24.5" (62.2 cm) Center to Center	10" (3 m)	10" (3 m)
Type	A	A	Ø	Ø	Ø

	DOLLIES				
	GRIP FACTORY MUNICH		**J.L. FISHER**		
	GF-Secondo Dolly	GF-Primo Dolly	Model 9	Model 10	Model 11
Minimum Boom Elevation	2'3" (0.7 m)	2'3" (0.7 m)	12.5" (31.75 cm)	13.75" (35 cm)	13.875" (35 cm)
Maximum Boom Elevation	4'6 (1.4 m)	4'6" (1.4 m)	61.7" (157 cm)	62.75" (159 cm)	51.25" (130 cm)
Dolly Width	31" (9.5 m)	31" (9.5 m)	30.25" (77 cm)	26.625" (68 cm)	20.5" (52 cm)
Dolly Length	31" (9.5 m)	39" (11.9 m)	68.5" (174 cm)	55.25" (140 cm)	40.0" (102 cm)
Lifting Capacity	550 lbs (249.5 kg)	550 lbs (249.5 kg)	500 lbs (227 kg)	500 lbs (227 kg)	200 lbs (90.72 kg)
Carrying Weight	550 lbs (249.5 kg)	550 lbs (249.5 kg)	445 lbs (202 kg)	435 lbs (197.7 kg)	307 lbs (139.25 kg)
Maximum Arm Lifts	200	200	5	7	7
Track Width	24" (7.3 m)	24" (7.3 m)	30.25" (77 cm)	26.625" & 32.00" (67.6 cm & 81.3 cm)	20.5" & 25.625" (52 cm & 65 cm)
Type	Ø	Ø	Ø	Ø	Ø

DOLLIES				
	MOVIETECH			**PANTHER**	
	Magnum Dolly	Rocker Dolly	Sprinter Dolly	Super Panther III	Panther Evolu-tion
Minimum Boom Elevation	2'7" (80 cm)	3" (91.44 cm)	11.4" (29 cm)	2'4" (70 cm)	26.5" (68 cm)
Maximum Boom Elevation	4'10" (80 cm)	Ø	Ø	4'8" (140 cm)	54.5" (138 cm)
Dolly Width	2'1" (64 cm)	20" (52 cm)	2'1" (79 cm)	18" or 2'4" (46 or 70 cm)	21" or 26" (53 or 68 cm)
Dolly Length	2'1" (64 cm)	28" (72 cm)	4'6" (137 cm)	34" or 2'4" (46 or 70 cm)	26" or 33" (68 or 84 cm)
Lifting Capacity	551 lbs (250 kg)	220 lbs (100 kg)	661 lbs (300 kg)	550 lbs (250 kg)	550 lbs (250 kg)
Carrying Weight	308 lbs (140 kg)	26 lbs (12 kg)	105 lbs (48 kg)	272 lbs (123 kg)	210 lbs (96 kg)
Maximum Arm Lifts	800	variable steering geometry	Ø	350 lifts	300 lifts
Track Width	2' (62 cm)	2' (62 cm)	2' (62 cm)	1'2" or 2'1" (36 or 62 cm)	1'2" or 2'1" (36 or 62 cm)
Type	P	Ø	Ø	P	P

KEY TO READING REMOTE HEADS AND HANDWHEEL CHARTS

	MANUFACTURER
	REMOTE HEAD MAKE/MODEL
Minimum Size W x D x H	THE SMALLEST USABLE CONFIGURATION WITH A SMALL 35MM FILM CAMERA PERMITTING 45° TILT UP OR DOWN
Maximum Size W x D x H	OVERALL DIMENSION WHEN SET UP TO PERMIT A 35MM STUDIO CAMERA WITH 1000' MAGAZINE AND ZOOM LENS TO POINT STRAIGHT DOWN
Camera Weight 2-axis	THE TOTAL WEIGHT OF THE CAMERA PACKAGE THE HEAD CAN CARRY
Camera Weight 3-axis	THE TOTAL WEIGHT OF THE CAMERA PACKAGE THE HEAD CAN CARRY
Unit Weight 2-axis	THE WEIGHT OF THE HEAD IN 2-AXIS MODE
Unit Weight 3-axis	THE WEIGHT OF THE HEAD IN 3-AXIS MODE
Type	CONVENTIONAL, STABILIZED OR UNDERWATER
For more information, contact the manufacturer	

REMOTE HANDWHEELS

	FX MOTION
	E-Gearing
Camera Weight 2-axis	120 lbs (60 kg)
Unit Weight 2-axis	50 lbs (25 kg) includes panahead

REMOTE HEADS

	A+C			AEROCRANE
	Power-Pod Classic	Pee-Pod 1600	Power-Pod 2000	Aerohead
Minimum Size W x D x H	19"x 19"x 12" (483 x 483 x 305 mm)	30"x 19"x 11.5" (483 x 483 x 292 mm)	25"x 24.5"x 7.75" (635 x 622 x 197 mm)	18"x 26" (457 x 660 mm)
Maximum Size W x D x H	31"x 19"x 12" (787 x 483 x 305 mm)	30"x 19"x 11.5" (762 x 483 x 292 mm)	40"x 24.5"x 7.75" (1,016 x 622 x 197 mm)	24"x 32" (610 x 813 mm)
Camera Weight 2-axis	85 lbs (39 kg)	60 lbs (27 kg)	200 lbs (91 kg)	60 lbs (27 kg)
Camera Weight 3-axis	Ø	45 lbs (20 kg)	150 lbs (68 kg)	60 lbs (27 kg)
Unit Weight 2-axis	75 lbs (34 kg)	35 lbs (16 kg)	70 lbs (32 kg)	61 lbs (28 kg)
Unit Weight 3-axis	Ø	50 lbs (23 kg)	125 lbs (57 kg)	72 lbs (33 kg)
Type	Conventional	Conventional & Stabilized	Conventional & Stabilized	Other

CHAPMAN

	Amphibian 2 or 3 Axis Waterproof	G-2 Gyro Stabilized	G-3 Gyro Stabilized	GSH
Minimum Size W x D x H	40"H x 21"W (101 x 53 cm)	30"H x 8"W x 36"D (75H x 20.3W x 91.5 cm)	30"H x 9"W x 36"D (75H x 22.9W x 91.5 cm)	2'6"x 1'9"x 3' (762 x 533 x 914 mm)
Maximum Size W x D x H	49"H x 28"W (124 x 71 cm)	30"H x 21"W x 36"D (75H x 53W x 91.5 cm)	30"H x 21"W x 36"D (76H x 53W x 91.5 cm)	Ø
Camera Weight 2-axis	114 lbs (51.8 kg)	200 lbs (90.9 kg)	Ø	Ø
Camera Weight 3-axis	114 lbs (51.8 kg)	Ø	250 lbs (113.6 kg)	150 lbs (68 kg)
Unit Weight 2-axis	68 lbs (31 kg)	70 lbs (31.8 kg)	Ø	Ø
Unit Weight 3-axis	110 lbs (50 kg)	Ø	90 lb (40.9 kg)	70 lbs (32 kg)
Type	Conventional	Stabilized	Stabilized	Stabilized

REMOTE HEADS

	DOGGICAM	EGRIPMENT		GEO LA
	Sparrow Head	Hot Head II	Scanner Head	SL Pod
Minimum Size W x D x H	12"W x 13"H (mini Sparrow Head)	27"x 15"x 11" (686 x 381 x 279 mm)	21"6"x 11" (533 x 152 x 711 mm)	15"H x 15"W x 7"D (381 x 381 x 178 mm)
Maximum Size W x D x H	12"W x 18"H (Sparrow Head 400)	33"x 18"x 11" (838 x 457 x 279 mm)	21"x 6"x 11" (533 x 152 x 711 mm)	15"H x 24"W x 7"D (381 x 609 x 178 mm)
Camera Weight 2-axis	35 lbs (16 kg)	154 lbs (70 kg)	35 lbs (16 kg)	60 lbs (27 kg)
Camera Weight 3-axis	Ø	Ø	Ø	Ø
Unit Weight 2-axis	16 lbs (7 kg)	51 lbs (23 kg)	19 lbs (9 kg)	20 lb (9 kg)
Unit Weight 3-axis	Ø	Ø	Ø	Ø
Type	Conventional	Conventional	Conventional	Conventional

	HYDROFLEX	KEY GRIP SYSTEMS	KEY HEAD	LIBRA
	Hydro Head	KEY HEAD	Key Head	Libra
Minimum Size W x D x H	16"x 6"x 28" (406 x 152 x 711 mm)	8.86"x 9.84"x 1'4.5" (225 x 250 x 420 mm)	16.5"x 11"x 6" (5 x 3.3 x 1.8 m)	20"x 20" (508 x 508 mm)
Maximum Size W x D x H	16"x 6"x 28" (406 x 152 x 711 mm)	8.86"x 1'1.66"x 1'4.75" (225 x 347 x 730 mm)	28.75"x 14"x 6" (8.7 x 4.3 x 1.8 m)	20"x 28" (508 x 711 mm)
Camera Weight 2-axis	52 lbs (24 kg)	66lbs (30 kg)	55 lbs (25 kg)	Ø
Camera Weight 3-axis	Ø	Ø	Ø	150 lbs (68 kg)
Unit Weight 2-axis	95 lbs (43 kg)	44 lbs (20 kg)	30 lbs (13.6 kg)	Ø
Unit Weight 3-axis	Ø	Ø	Ø	65 lbs (29 kg)
Type	Conventional & Underwater	Conventional	Conventional	Conventional & Stabilized

REMOTE HEADS

	LIBRA	LOUMA SYSTEMS	MEGAMOUNT	MO-SYS
	Liberated	Louma 2 Remote Head	Mega III	Lamda Head
Minimum Size W x D x H	30"x 20" (9 m x 6 m)	Ø	Ø	28"x 16"x 7" (8.5 x 4.8 x 2.1 m)
Maximum Size W x D x H	Ø	2'2"W x 3'H (66W x 92H cm)	36.9"x 30.75" (937 x 781 mm)	36"x 20"x 7" (11 x 6 x 2.1 m)
Camera Weight 2-axis	150 lbs (68 kg)	100 lbs (45 kg)	Ø	100 lbs (45 kg)
Camera Weight 3-axis	150 lbs (68 kg)	66 lbs (30 kg)	110 lbs (50 kg)	Ø
Unit Weight 2-axis	60 lbs (27 kg)	97 lbs (44 kg)	Ø	57 lbs (26 kg)
Unit Weight 3-axis	60 lbs (27 kg)	126 lbs (57 kg)	77 lbs (35 kg)	Ø
Type	Stabilized	Conventional	Conventional	Conventional

	MOVIEBIRD	MOVIETECH		
	Moviehead	P15	Alex Digital	Pele Digital
Minimum Size W x D x H	Ø	1'8.5"x 1'3" (520 x 380 mm)	1'2.77"x 1'4.14" (680 x 410 mm)	(740 x 720 mm)
Maximum Size W x D x H	Ø	1'8.5"x 1'3" (520 x 380 mm)	Ø	Ø
Camera Weight 2-axis	Ø	55 lbs (25 kg)	33 lbs (15 kg)	66 lbs (30 kg)
Camera Weight 3-axis	22 lbs (10 kg)	33 lbs (15 kg)	Ø	Ø
Unit Weight 2-axis	Ø	26 lbs (12 kg)	15 lbs (7 kg)	19.8 lbs (9 kg)
Unit Weight 3-axis	20 lbs (9 kg)	44 lbs (20 kg)	Ø	Ø
Type	Stabilized	Conventional	Conventional	Conventional

REMOTE HEADS

NETTMAN

	Cam-Remote	Compact	Mini-Mote	Snorkel
Minimum Size W x D x H	25.75"x 27.25" (654 x 692 mm)	23"x 23" (584 x 584 mm)	13.5"x 16" (343 x 406 mm)	36" (914 mm) vertical
Maximum Size W x D x H	30"x 42.5" (762 x 1,080 mm)	23"x 45" (584 x 1,143 mm)	43.5"x 45" (1,105 x 1,143 mm)	48" (1219 mm) vertical
Camera Weight 2-axis	180 lbs (82 kg)	Ø	60 lbs (27 kg) sm conf. 190 lbs (86 kg) lrg conf	Ø
Camera Weight 3-axis	180 lbs (82 kg)	70 lbs (32 kg)	75 lbs (34 kg)	160 lbs (73 kg)
Unit Weight 2-axis	70 lbs (32 kg)	Ø	63 lbs (29 kg)	Ø
Unit Weight 3-axis	117 lbs (53 kg)	80 lbs (36 kg)	105 lbs (48 kg)	125 lbs (57 kg)
Type	Conventional & Select Stabilization	Stabilized	Conventional	Conventional

	NETTMAN SYSTEMS	NETTMAN	PACE TECHNOLOGIES	PICTORVISION
	Stab-C	"Super G"	Aquahead	Pictorvision XR
Minimum Size W x D x H	27"x 36" (686 x 914 mm)	27"x 36" (686 x 914 mm)	33.75"x 8"x 33.625" (857 x 203 x 854 mm)	24" x 24" (7.3 x 7.3 m)
Maximum Size W x D x H	Ø	Ø	33.75"x 8"x 33.625" (857 x 203 x 854 mm)	44" x 44" (13.4 x 13.4 m)
Camera Weight 2-axis	Ø	Ø	100 lbs (45 kg)	150 lbs (68 kg)
Camera Weight 3-axis	120 lbs (54 kg)	120 lbs (54 kg)	Ø	150 lbs (68 kg)
Unit Weight 2-axis	Ø	Ø	68 lbs (31 kg)	85 lbs (38.5 kg)
Unit Weight 3-axis	115 lbs (52 kg)	160 lbs (72 kg)	Ø	110 lbs (50 kg) plus camera package
Type	Stabilized	Stabilized	Underwater	Stabilized

REMOTE HEADS

	POLECAM	POWERPOD		SALAMATI
	PT100 Head	Pee-Pod 500	Power Pod 2000	Hot Gears II
Minimum Size W x D x H	11" W x 12" H x 4.5" D (3.3 x 3.6 x 1.4 m)	1.04' x 0.9' (320 W x 300 mm H)	2.03' x 2.04' (621 H x 624 mm W)	19"x 19"x 8" (5.7 x 5.7 x 2.4 m)
Maximum Size W x D x H	11" W x 16" H x 4.5" D (3.3 x 4.8 x 1.4 m)	2' x 2.5' (614 W x 753 mm H)	3.9' x 2.7' (1200 H x 844 mm W)	36"x 27"x 8" (11 x 8.2 x 2.4 m)
Camera Weight 2-axis	81 lbs (37 kg)	66 lbs (30 kg)	198.4 lbs (90 kg)	100 lbs (45.3 kg)
Camera Weight 3-axis	81 lbs (37 kg)	66 lbs (30 kg)	150 lbs (68 kg)	80 lbs (36 kg)
Unit Weight 2-axis	4.8 lbs (2.1 kg) head only up to 12.8 lbs (5.8 kg) loaded	15 lbs (7 kg)	70.5 lbs (32 kg)	43 lbs (19.5 kg)
Unit Weight 3-axis	4.8 lbs (2.1 kg) head only up to 12.8 lbs (5.8 kg) loaded	24.2 lbs (11 kg)	123.4 lbs (56 kg)	63 lbs (28.5 kg)
Type	Conventional	Conventional	Conventional	Conventional

	SPACECAM		WESCAM	
	Spacecam	SpaceCam Aerial	Aerial System	Wescam XR
Minimum Size W x D x H	30"x 36" (762 x 914 mm)	36" DIA (10.9 m)	Ø	20"x 27"x 28" (508 x 686 x 711 mm)
Maximum Size W x D x H	30"x 36" (762 x 914 mm)	36" DIA (10.9 m)	36" (914 mm) diameter square	Ø
Camera Weight 2-axis	Ø	Ø	Ø	Ø
Camera Weight 3-axis	165 lbs (75 kg) 200 lbs (91 kg) w/dome	100 lb	Ø	150 lbs (68 kg)
Unit Weight 2-axis	Ø	Ø	Ø	Ø
Unit Weight 3-axis	165 or 200 lbs (75 or 91 kg) as above	210 lbs (95.2 kg)	200-250 lbs (91-113 kg) rigged depending on lens	90 lbs (41 kg)
Type	Stabilized	Stabilized	Stabilized	Stabilized

JIBS

	CAMMATE	CHAPMAN				GRIP FACTORY MUNICH
	CamMate 100	Lenny Mini Jib Arm/Hy Hy or CS Base	Lenny II Plus Jib Arm on CS Base	Lenny Arm III Jib on Ultra CS Base	Stinger II Jib on Hustler IV	GF-Multi Jib
Minimum Length	5'1" (1.5 m)	28" (71 cm)	4'9" (1.5 m)	7'3" (2.2 m)	7'4" (2.2 m)	3' (0.9 m)
Maximum Length	9'1" (2.7 m)	26'6" (8.08 m)	38'4" (11.7 m) on ultra base	55'4" (16.9 m)	12'4" (3.75 m)	16' (4.9 m)
Overall Length	12'5" (3.7 m)	82" (2 m)	50' (15.2 m)	64'4" (19.6 m)	17'6" (5.3 m)	20' (6 m)
Maximum Rise @ Maximum Length	15' (4.6 m)	25'7" (7.8 m)	37'4" (11.4 m)	47'3" (14.4 m)	9'4" (2.79 m)	15' (4.6 m)
Nose Load @ Max Length	75 lbs (34.1 kg)	143.5 lbs (62.1 kg)	282 lbs (128.2 kg)	147 lbs (66.7 kg)	131 lbs (59.5 kg)	80 lbs (36.2 kg)
Min. Doorway Clearance (W x H)	6'3"x 2'5" (1.8 m X 74 cm)	83.3"x 49.5" (2.1 x 1.3 m)	72"x 48" (1.8 x 1.2 m)	84"x 48" (2.1 x 1.2 m)	42"x 24.5" (106 x 70 cm)	depends on base
All Up Weight in Max Config.	258 lbs (117.3 kg)	1,935 lbs (879.5 lg)	3,709 lbs (1,683.6 kg)	Ø	1,316 lbs (598.1 kg)	250 lbs (113.4 kg) plus dolly base
Track Width	2' (61 cm)	34.5" (880 mm) center to center	34.5" (880 mm) center to center	34.5" (880 mm) center to center	24.5" (62.2 cm)	24' (7.3 m)
Type	Ø	Ø	Ø	Ø	Ø	Ø

	GRIP FACTORY MUNICH	J.L. FISHER				MOVIETECH
	GF-Jib	Model 20	Model 21	Model 22	Model 23	Master Jib
Minimum Length	4'6" (1.4 m)	41.5" (1.1 m)	58.5" (1.5 m)	89.5" (2.3 m)	60" (1.5 m)	44.5" (1,130 mm)
Maximum Length	6' (1.8 m)	53.5" (1.4 m)	70.5" (1.8 m)	101.5" (2.6 m)	21' (6.4 m)	142.9" (3,630 mm)
Overall Length	9' (2.7 m)	82.5" (2.14 m)	112" (2.85 m)	160.5" (4 m)	28'5" (8.5 m)	185.8" (4,720 mm)
Maximum Rise @ Maximum Length	8'4" (2.5 m)	7'6" (2.3 m)	8'6" (2.6 m)	10'7.9" (3.3 m)	20'7" (6.3 m)	174.8" (4,441 mm)
Nose Load @ Max Length	88 lbs (40 kg)	184 lbs (83 kg) w/opt. wgt. set	164 lbs (74 kg) w/opt. wgt. set	175 lbs (80 kg) w/opt. wgt. set	131 lbs (59 kg)	110 lbs (50 kg)
Min. Doorway Clearance (W x H)	depends on base	5'6" & 26.625" (1.7 m & 0.6 m)	5'6" & 26.625" (1.7 m & 0.6 m)	5'6" & 24.625" (1.7 m & 0.6 m)	7'2" (2.2 m)	39.3" x 178.7" (1 x 4.54 m)
All Up Weight in Max Config.	140 lbs (64 kg) plus base dolly	697 lbs (317 kg) w/Model 10 dolly & center mount	717 lbs (326 kg) w/Model 10 dolly & center mount	750 lbs (341 kg)	1,107 lbs (503 kg)	Ø
Track Width	24' (7.3 m)	24.5' (7.5 m)	24.5' (7.5 m)	24.5' (7.5 m)	24.5' (7.5 m)	Ø
Type	Ø	Ø	Ø	Ø	Ø	Ø

JIBS

	MOVIETECH	POLECAM		PORTAJIB	TECHNO JIB	
	MovieJib	Polecam SP Jib	Polecam PR 21	Porta-Jib Standard	Techno-Jib T24	Techno-Jib 15
Minimum Length	Ø	4' (1.2 m) hot head center to tripod mount	4' (1.2 m) hot head center to tripod mount	4'11" (1.5 m)	9' (2.7 m)	7' (2.1 m)
Maximum Length	84.6' (2150 mm)	20' (6 m) hot head center for tripod mount	28' (8.5 m) hot head center to tripod mount	7'8" (2.3 m)	24' (7.3 m)	16' (4.8 m)
Overall Length	724" (3,150 mm)	24' (7.3 kg) w/weight support fully extended	32' (9.7 kg) w/weight support fully extended	10'6" (3.2 m)	30'8" (9.3 m)	20'8" (6.3 m)
Maximum Rise @ Maximum Length	2,790 mm	18' (5.5 m)	25' (7.6 m)	varies with height of supporting tripod or dolly; average = 10'6" (3.2 m)	25' (7.6 m)	18' (5.5 m)
Nose Load @ Max Length	66 lbs (30 kg)	8 lbs (3.63 kg) camera weight	1.5 lbs (680 g) camera weight	45 lbs (20.4 kg)	55 lbs (25 kg)	70 lbs (31.7 kg)
Min. Doorway Clearance (W x H)	158" x 128.7" (1,480 x 730 mm)	2' x 3' (0.6 x 0.9 m) depending on tripod	2' x 3' (0.6 x 0.9 m) depending on tripod	6' x 3' (1.8 x 0.6 m) when on our tripod and 3 wheel base	68" x 49" (20.7 x 15 m)	68" x 35" (20.7 x 10.6 m)
All Up Weight in Max Config.	335 lbs (152 kg)	85 lbs (38.5 kg) with max head load	75 lbs (34 kg) with max head load	105 lbs (47.6 kg) excluding tripod support	1,575 lbs (714.4 kg)	1,375 lbs (624 kg)
Track Width	Ø	Ø works on any dolly/ tripod	Ø works on any dolly/ tripod	24.5" (7.5 m)	3.3' (1 m)	standard dolly track
Type	Ø	Ø	Ø	Ø	Ø	Ø

BODY-WORN SYSTEMS

	SACHTLER	TIFFEN
	Artemis Cine HD Pro	Steadicam
Minimum Size (W x D x H)	Ø	approx. 20"H x 4"W x 16"L, monitor 6"W sled model dimensions vary
Maximum Size (W x D x H)	Ø	approx. 27"H x 4"W x 16"L, monitor 6-8"W sled model dimensions vary
Camera Weight 2-axis	120 lbs (54.4 kg)	2-45 lbs (0.9-20.4 kg) depending on Steadicam model
Camera Weight 3-axis	120 lbs (54.4 kg)	2-45 lbs (0.9-20.4 kg) depending on Steadicam model
Unit Weight 2-axis	7.5 lbs (3.4 kg) w/o monitor and battery	5-33 lbs (2.3-15 kg) depending on Steadicam model (vest, arm & sled)
Unit Weight 3-axis	7.5 lbs (3.4 kg) w/o monitor and battery	5-33 lbs (2.3-15 kg) depending on Steadicam model (vest, arm & sled)
Type	Stabilized	Stabilized

SUSPENDED CAMERA SYSTEM

	PICTORVISION
	Eclipse
Minimum Size (W x D x H)	Ø
Maximum Size (W x D x H)	A 36" (0.9 m) ball that supports Arri 435 and Alexa, Imax, Iwerks, 3D rigs, and most digital cameras
Camera Weight 2-axis	Ø
Camera Weight 3-axis	80 lbs (36.3 kg)
Unit Weight 2-axis	Ø
Unit Weight 3-axis	275 lbs (125 kg)
Type	Stabilized

REMOTE CONTROLLED CAMERA

	VINTEN RADAMEC
	FHR-35 Remote Pan and Tilt
Minimum Size (W x D x H)	Ø
Maximum Size (W x D x H)	Ø
Camera Weight 2-axis	13 lbs (16 kg)
Camera Weight 3-axis	Ø
Unit Weight 2-axis	50 lbs (22.8 kg)
Unit Weight 3-axis	Ø
Type	Conventional

	TELESCOPIC CAMERA			
	MAT			
	Towercam XS	**Towercam**	**Towercam XL**	**Towercam FX**
Minimum Length	2.5' (0.762 m)	4.5' (1.4 m)	8' (2.7 m)	5.5' (1.7 m)
Maximum Length	4.5' (1.4 m)	14.5'. (4.4 m)	32.5' (10 m)	16' (4.9 m)
Travel Length	2.0' (0.6 m)	10' (3 m)	23.6'. (7.2 m)	10.5' (3.2 m)
Maximum Rise at Minimum Length	Ø	Ø	Ø	Ø
Nose Load at Maximum Length	132 lbs (60 kg)	132 lbs (60 kg)	100 lbs (45 kg)	132 lbs (60 kg)
Min. Doorway Clearance (W x H)	Ø	Ø	Ø	Ø
All Up Weight in Max. Config.	203 lbs (92 kg)	463 lbs (210 kg)	463 lbs (210 kg)	286 lbs (130 kg)
Track Width	24.5" (622 mm) by using with dolly	24.5" (622 mm) by using with dolly	39" (990 mm) by using with dolly	Ø
Type of column	Telescopic column	Telescopic column	Telescopic column	Telescopic column

Camera Section

compiled by Jon Fauer ASC
and M. David Mullen ASC

FILM CAMERAS

Information in this section is correct to the best of our knowledge. Including or omitting products does not signify endorsement or disapproval by the ASC. The ASC is not responsible for mistakes.

Listings are based on information supplied by manufacturers or distributors. As always, confirm doubts with film tests. Where possible, we tried to keep categories consistent, and tried to describe each camera with the following specifications:

Notes, Models: Facts, tidbits, iterations and modifications

Weight: English and Metric

Movement: Film transport—single or double pull-down claw, registration pins, adjustable pitch, 4-perforation, 3-perforation

FPS: Frame rate—fwd, reverse, speeds, sync.

Aperture: The "gate" in which each frame of film is exposed. The opening may be fixed or removable. Masks may define additional sizes and cropping. Information here includes format size and position, format masks, in-gate filters and gel slots. Among the aperture sizes are:

> **Full Silent Aperture** (variously called Full Aperture, Super 35, Full Frame, Full Frame Centered for TV, ANSI, Big TV) is .980" x .735" (24.89mm x 18.67mm).

> **European Silent Aperture** is 24mm x 18mm (.945" x .709")

> **Academy Aperture** (sometimes called Standard or Normal 35) is 22mm x 16mm (.868" x .630").

> **3-Perf Panaflex Camera Aperture** is .981" x .546" (style D) per SMPTE 59-1998.

dB: Operating Noise Level as measured by manufacturer, for sound cameras only.

Displays: Indicators/Readout

Lens: Lens Mount—things like PL, Panavision, BNC or bayonet. Also, how the mount is centered: Academy (Standard) or full-frame centered for TV (Super 35).

Shutter: fixed, variable (change while camera is running) or adjustable (change when camera is stopped). Mirror (reflex) shutter or beamsplitter.

Viewfinder: Eyepieces, finder extenders, levelers

Video: Video Assist

Viewing Screen: Ground glasses, fiber optic viewing screens, rangefinders. In addition to the ones offered by manufacturers, there are many permutations supplied by rental houses and custom suppliers. Note that there are two different SMPTE accepted Super 35 sizes: Panavision's is .945" wide x .394" height and ARRI/Clairmont/etc is .925" wide x .394" height.

Mags or Loads: Magazines and/or internal film loading. Core or daylight spools.

Accessories: Mechanical, mounting, matteboxes, rods, lens controls, follow focus, wireless, barneys, covers, and after-market add-ons.

Connections: Electrical and electronic accessories, inputs, outputs and connectors; time code.

Motors and Power: Power pin-out, operating voltage, camera motors, batteries

Misc: More information

Thanks to the following for additions, suggestions and proofing: Peter Abel, Bill Bennett, Denny Clairmont, Ron Dexter, Dave Kenig, Oli Laperal, Al Mayer, Jr., Tak Miyagishima, Nolan Murdock, George Schmidt, Juergen Schwinzer, Douglas Underdahl.

Credit really should go to all the people who have compiled past editions, upon which this is based.

35MM

Aaton 35-3P, 35-III, 35-II

Models: 35-3P (newest, optimized for quiet operation in 3-perf.); 35-III, 35-II (original)

Weight: 16 lbs/7 kg with 400' (122m) load and 12V DC onboard battery.

Movement: Single pull-down claw which is also the registration pin (steady to ½₀₀₀th of image height). Spring-loaded side pressure guides. Adjustable pitch. 3 or 4 perf.

FPS: 35-3P: Sync speeds: 24, 25, 29.97, 30 fps. Built-in var crystal control to 2 to 40 fps in 0.001 increments.

   35-III: 3–32 fps crystal-controlled adjustable in .001 fps increments via mini-jog wheel. 24, 25, 29.97, 30 fps sync speeds. Internal phase shift control for TV bar elimination

   35-II: 24, 25, and 29.97 or 30 fps. Variable speeds 6–32 fps. Maximum speed with external speed control is 32 fps, with 180° shutter only.

Aperture: .732" x .980" (18.59mm x 24.89mm).

dB: 4-perf 30dB. 3-perf 30dB. 26dB with barney. 35-3P: 3-Perf: 26dB. 4-Perf: 30/33dB

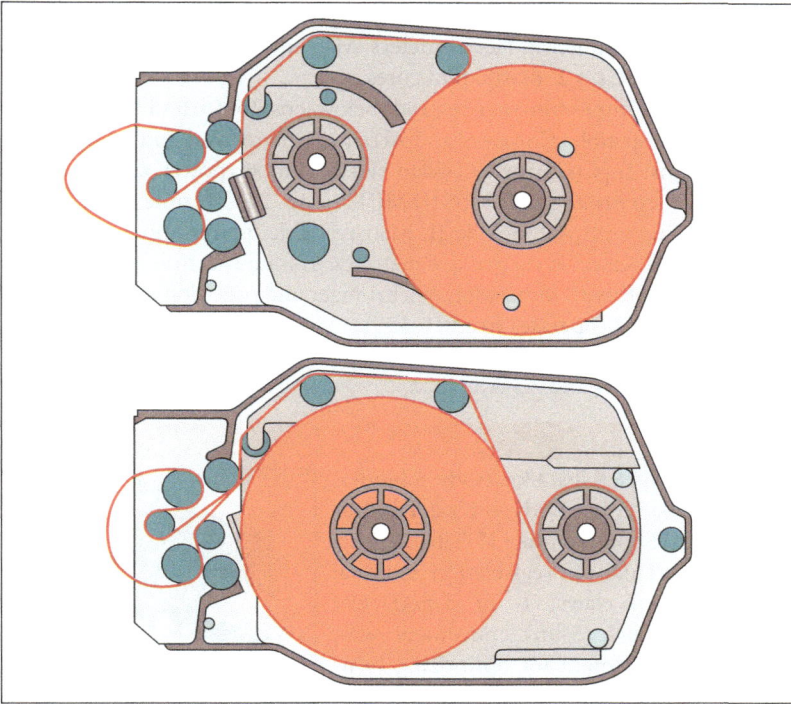

Aaton Magazine Diagrams

Figure 1a & 1b. Top: Position of film before exposure form 24-25 hole loop by placing a 2" core between front of magazine and film while lacing and make equal top and bottom loops. Bottom: Position of film after exposure. Film takes up emulsion side in

Displays: LCD Display, speed selection, remaining footage, ISO selection, battery voltage, time and date, full AatonCode readout via a single rotating jog wheel. Warning for speed discrepancy, misloading and low battery. Camera shutoff is automatic at end of roll.

Lens: Interchangeable Lens Mounts: Arri PL, Panavision, Nikon. User adjustable for Standard or Super 35.

Shutter: Mechanically adjustable mirror using shutter tool: 180°; 172.8°; 150°; 144°.

Viewfinder: Reflex Viewfinder. Eyepiece heater. Optional anamorphic viewing system.

Video: Integrated CCD Color Video Assist: NTSC or PAL; flicker-free at all camera speeds. Also black-and-white model with manual iris. Film camera time code, footage, on/off camera status are inserted in both windows and VITC lines. Built-in frameline generator.

Viewing Screen: Over 16 stock groundglasses; custom markings available. Aatonlite illuminated markings.

Mags: 400' (122m) active displacement mag (core spindles shift left to right) with LCD counter in feet or meters. Mag attaches by clipping onto rear of camera. Uses 2" plastic film cores.

Accessories: 15mm screw-in front rods below lens. 15mm and 19mm bridge-plate compatible. Chrosziel and Arri 4 x 5 matteboxes and follow focus.

Connections: Inputs: Amph9 (video sync), Lemo6 (power zoom), Lemo8 (phase controllers), Lemo5 (SMPTE and ASCII time code). Time recording with AatonCode II: Man-readable figures and SMPTE time code embedded in rugged dot matrices. ½ frame accuracy over 8 hours. Compatible with film-video synchronizer and precision speed control.

Power: 12 V DC (operates from 10-15v).

Motor: brushless, draws 1.4A with film at 25°C (77°F) Batteries: onboard 3.0 Ah NiMH and 2.5 Ah NiCd.

ARRICAM Lite

Weight: Body: 8.8 lbs/4 kg. Body + Finder: 11.7 lbs/5.3 kg. Body + Finder + 400' (122m) Shoulder Mag: 17.5 lbs/7.95 kg.

Movement: Dual-pin registration and dual pull-down claws, 4- or 3-Perf, low maintainance 5-link movement with pitch adjustment for optimizing camera quietness.

FPS: Forward 1–40 fps. Reverse 1–32 fps. All speeds crystal and can be set with $^{1}/_{1000th}$ precision

Aperture: Full frame with exchangeable format masks in gate. Gel holder in gate, very close to film plane. Aperture plate and spacer plate removable for cleaning.

dB: Less than 24dB(A). 3-Perf slightly noisier than 4.

Displays: (On camera left side) main display with adjustable brightness red LEDs for fps, shutter angle, footage exposed, or remaining raw stock. run/not ready LED. Extra display camera left and right (studio readout) with studio viewfinders.

Push-button controls for setting fps, shutter angle, display brightness, electronic inching, phase, footage counter reset.

Lens: 54mm stainless steel PL mount, switchable for standard or Super 35, with two sets of lens data system (LDS) contacts. LDS, when used with lens data box, provides lens data readout as text on video assist or shown on dedicated lens data display. Also simplifies ramps and wired and wireless lens control.

Shutter: 180° mirror shutter, electronically adjustable from 0°–180° in 0.1° increments. Closes fully (0°) for in-camera slating. Tiny motor in shaft

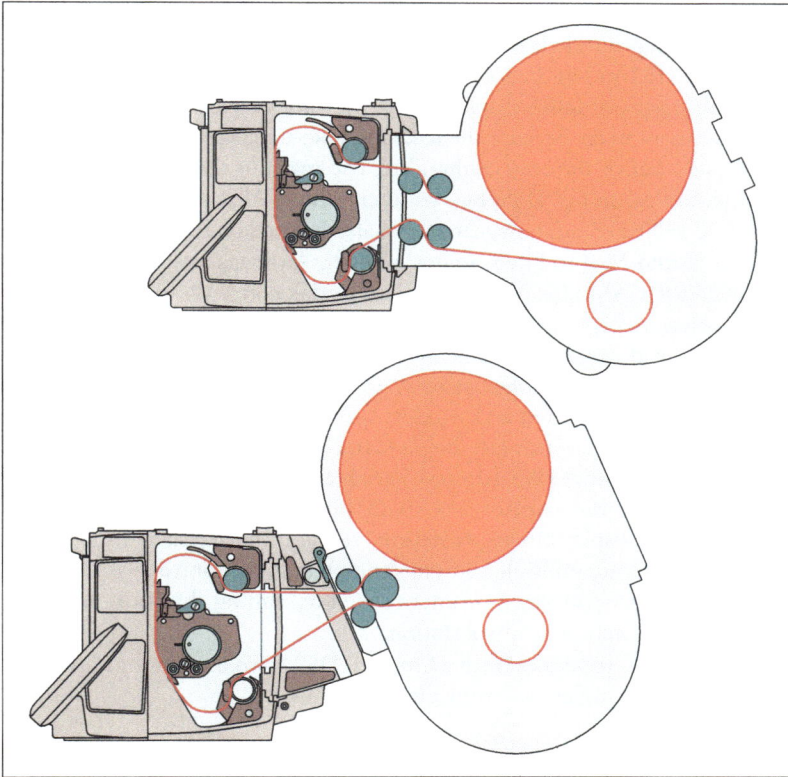

Arricam Lite Threading and Magazine Diagrams
Figure 2a & 2b. Top: LT shoulder. Bottom: LT/ST magazine. Film takes up emulsion side in.

controls shutter opening. Ramps range is 11.2°-180°.

Viewfinder: Four reflex viewfinders fit both cameras: Lite, Universal Lite, Studio, and Universal Studio. Universal finders can switch between spherical and anamorphic viewing. All swing to either side of camera and have contrast viewing filter, automatic or manual image orientation. Also available are Frameglows, various eyepiece extenders (with optical magnifier for critical focusing), 100 percent video tops, heated eyecup.

Video: ARRICAM Integrated Video System (IVS), color, flicker-free at all camera speeds, mechanical iris and electronic gain for exposure control, with frameline, camera status and lens (LDS) status inserter, image freeze and compare, color balance settings (auto, standard presets or manual), composite or S-VHS outputs. Video capture rate can be synchronized to film shutter for motion blur preview. Studio IVS fits on Studio viewfinders, Lite IVS fits on Lite viewfinders. 2" and 6" flat-panel onboard minimonitors.

Viewing Screen: Over 60 stock regular and Super 35 ground glasses. Custom rush ground glass design service via web.

Mags: 400' (122m) Lite Steadicam mag. 400' (122m) Lite shoulder magazine. Both mags are active displacement: they are smaller than standard displacement mags because the feed and take-up cores move left and right to stay out of the way of the film. The mags use torque motors, have mechanical and LCD footage counters, and. ARRICAM 400'(122m) and 1000' (300m) Studio magazines can also be used on the Lite camera with the Studio Mag to Lite Camera Adapter. All mags attach to the rear of the ARRICAM Lite. Accept standard Kodak cores. Wind emulsion *in*.

Accessories: Accepts the whole range of Arriflex matte boxes, 15mm or 19mm rod systems. Steadicam low-mode bracket, shoulder set, lens light and power bridge plate. Wired and wireless lens and camera control system, wired and wireless speed/shutter/iris ramping controls. Electronic accessories (see below) attached to Lite via cable or Remote Control Station, LDS Ultra and Variable Primes.

Connections: Speed control box (with built-in sync functions to shoot monitors, displays, rear-projection, etc. and master/slave function for phase accurate multiple camera shoots), manual control box, lens data box, lens data display, in-camera slate box, timing shift box, accessory power box, remote control station.

Power: 24V DC. (operates from 21 to 35 V DC). Two motors for movement and shutter; linked electronically.

ARRICAM Studio

Weight: Body: 12.3 lbs/5.6 kg.

Body+Finder: 17.8 lbs/8.1 kg. Body + Finder + 400' (122m) Studio Mag: 25.1 lbs/11.4 kg.

Movement: Low maintainance 5-link movement with dual pin registration and dual pull down claws, 4- or 3-perf, pitch adjustment for optimizing camera quietness.

Fps: 1–40 fps forward, 1–32 fps reverse, all speeds crystal and can be set with $\frac{1}{1000}$th precision.

Aperture: Full frame with exchangeable format masks in gate. Gel holder in gate, very close to film plane. Aperture plate and spacer plate removable for cleaning.

dB: Less than 20dB(A).

Displays: (On camera left side) main display with adjustable brightness red LEDs for fps, shutter angle, footage exposed, or remaining raw stock. run/not ready LED. Extra display camera left and right (Studio readout) with Studio viewfinders.

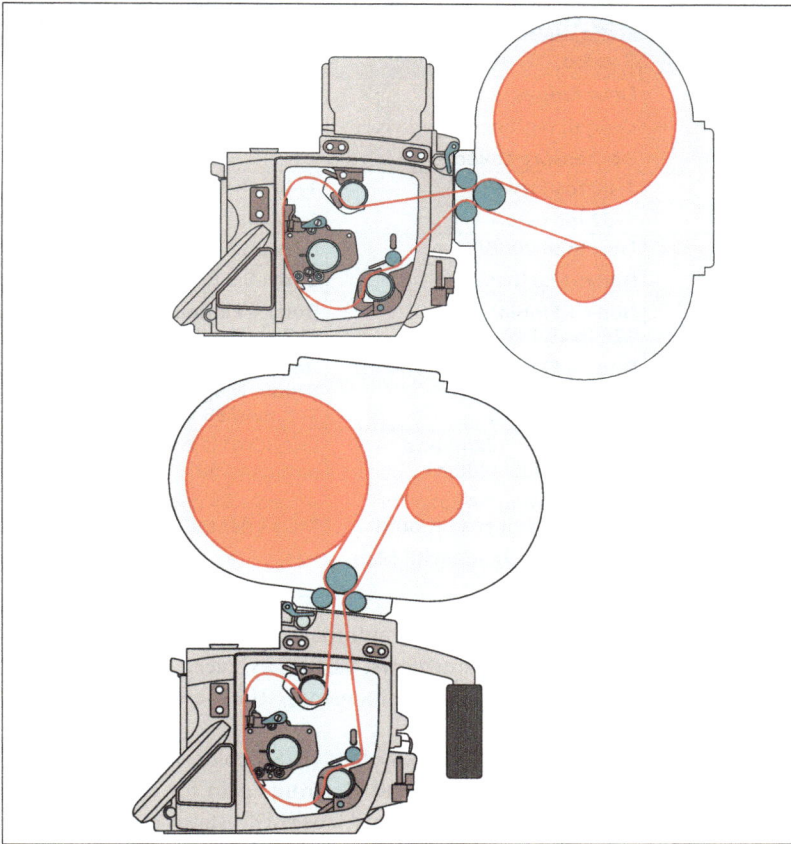

Arricam Studio Threading and Magazine Diagrams
Figures 3a & 3b. Top: St back load. Bottom: ST top load. Film takes up emulsion side in.

Push-button controls for setting fps, shutter angle, display brightness, electronic inching, phase, footage counter reset.

Lens: 54mm stainless steel PL mount, switchable for standard or Super 35, with two sets of lens data system (LDS) contacts. LDS, when used with lens data box, provides lens data readout as text on video assist or shown on dedicated lens data display. Also simplifies ramps and wired and wireless lens control.

Shutter: 180° miror shutter, electronically adjustable from 0°–180° in 0.1° increments. Closes fully (0°) for in-camera slating. For ramps, range is 11.2°–180°.

Viewfinder: Four reflex viewfinders fit both cameras: Lite, Universal Lite, Studio, and Universal Studio. Universal finders can switch between spherical and anamorphic viewing. All swing to either side of camera

ARRICAM Cameras Compared		
	Studio	**Light**
Physical	Door hinges at rear Longer, higher 3 accessory covers	Door hinges at front 2 accessory covers
fps	1–60 fps forward 1–32 fps reserve	1–40 fps forward 1–32 fps reverse
Noise Level	Less than 20dB(A)	Less than 24dB(A)
Weight	**Body:** 12.3 lbs/5.6 kg	**Body:** 8.8 lbs/4 kg
	Body + Finder: 17.8 lbs/8.1 kg	**Body + Finder:** 11.7 lbs/5.3 kg
	Body + Finder + 400' (122m) **Studio Mag:** 25.1 lbs/11.4 kg	**Body + Finder + 400' (122m)** **Studio Mag:** 17.5 lbs/7.95 kg
Mags	Studio 400' (122m) and Studio 1,000' (300m) Requires Mag Adapter for top, angles or read mount Accepts Lite mags with Mag Adapter	Lite 400' (122m) Steadicam and Lite 400' (122m) Shoulder Accepts Studio mags with Mag Adapter

and have a contrast viewing filter, automatic or manual image orientation. Also available are Frameglows, various eyepiece extenders (with an optical magnifier for critical focusing), 100 percent video tops, heated eyecup.

Video: ARRICAM Integrated Video System (IVS), color, flicker-free at all camera speeds, mechanical iris and electronic gain for exposure control, with frameline, camera status and lens (LDS) status inserter, image freeze and compare, color balance settings (auto, standard presets or manual), composite or S-VHS outputs. Video capture rate can be synchronized to film shutter for motion blur preview. Studio IVS fits on Studio viewfinders, Lite IVS fits on Lite viewfinders. 2" and 6" flat-panel onboard minimonitors.

Viewing Screen: Over 60 stock Regular and Super 35 ground glasses. Custom rush ground glass design service via web.

Mags: 400' (122m) and 1,000' (300m) Studio displacement magazines. Both mags use torque motors, have mechanical and LCD footage counters, and are standard displacement.

Lite 400' (122m) Steadicam and Lite 400' (122m) shoulder mags can be used with a Lite mag to studio camera adapter.

Studio mags attach to the top or rear of the camera with one of three mounts: top load adapter, dual port adapter, or back load adapter. Accept standard Kodak cores. Wind emulsion *in*.

Accessories: Accepts the whole range of Arriflex matte boxes, 15mm or 19mm rod systems. Steadicam low-mode bracket, shoulder set, lens light and power bridge plate. Wired and wireless lens and camera control system, wired and wireless speed/shutter/iris ramping controls. Electronic accessories (see below) can attached to Studio directly, via cable or remote control station. LDS ultra and variable primes.

Connections: Speed control box (with built-in sync functions to shoot monitors, displays, rear-projection, etc. and master/slave function for phase accurate multiple camera shoots), manual control box, lens data box, lens data display, in-camera slate box, timing shift box, accessory power box, remote control station.

Power: 24V DC. (operates from 21 to 35 V DC). Two motors for movement and shutter; linked electronically.

Arriflex 35-2C

Models: Over 17,000 were made, in various iterations; many still in use with numerous modifications—especially conversions from original 3 lens turret to PL mount and updated motors. The 35-2C/B has a three-lens turret, and an interchangeable motor drive system.

Weight: 5.3 lbs/2.5 kg (body only, no motor, PL mount)

   12 lbs./5.5 kg (camera w/200' (61m) mag, without film and lens.)

Movement: Single pull-down claw with extended dwell time to ensure accurate film positioning during exposure. Academy aperture is standard, with other formats available.

FPS: The most widely used motor is the Cinematography Electronics Crystal Base: 1–80 fps in 1-frame increments via push-buttons (1–36 fps with 12V battery; 1–80 with 2 12V batteries). It puts camera at standard lens height for rods.

   With ARRI handgrip motors: 20–80 fps with ARRI 32V DC high-speed handgrip motor (over 60 fps may be unsteady or may jam) 24/25 fps with 16V DC governor motor, 20–64 fps with 24–28V DC variable speed motor 8–32 fps with 16V DC variable speed motor Arri Sync Motors (120V) (240V) for blimps. (120S, 1000) (50/60 Hz)

Aperture: .866" x .630" (22mm x 16mm).

Displays: Dial tachometer on camera shows fps; footage indicated by analog gauge on magazines.

Lens: Originally made with three-lens turret with three Arri standard mounts (squeeze the tabs, push lens straight in). Later followed by tur-

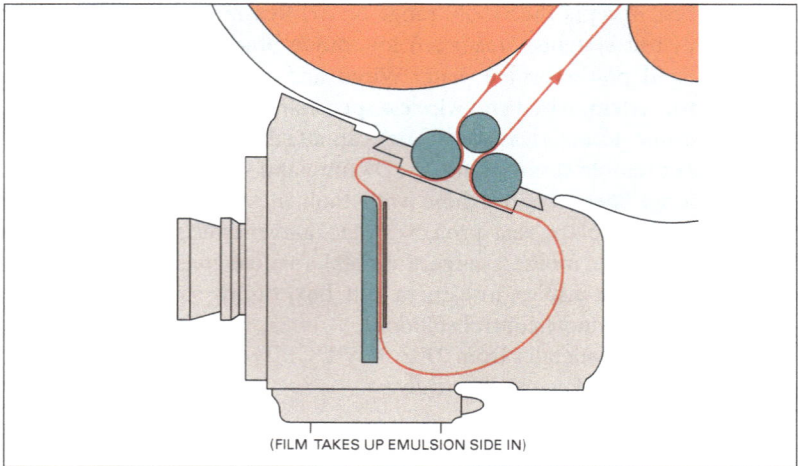

(FILM TAKES UP EMULSION SIDE IN)

Arriflex 35-2C Threading Diagram
Figure 4. Film takes up emulsion side in

ret with two standard mounts and one Arri bayonet mount (insert and twist). Hard-front PL mount modifications widely available.

Shutter: This is the camera that introduced the spinning mirror shutter with reflex viewing. Two segment (butterfly) mirror shutter, mechanically adjustable in 15° increments from 0°–165° when camera not running. Model 2C-BV fixed shutter of 165°. Exposure is $\frac{1}{52nd}$ of a second at 24 fps with a 165-degree shutter.

Viewfinder: 6.5X wide-angle eyepiece. Various camera doors with fixed, video, anamorphic and pivoting finders available.

Viewing Screen: Interchangeable for all aspect ratios.

Video: Aftermarket video assist with Jurgens Video Door among other companies.

Mags: Mags attach on top of camera. Accepts gear-driven, friction take-up, 2C, 35-3 and 435 magazines. 200' (61m) forward operation only, 400' (122m) forward or reverse, 1,000' (300m) not recommended. Mags are displacement and wind emulsion *in*. Some have collapsible cores. Others use 2" plastic cores .

Accessories: Matte Boxes, Bellows, clip-on, and lightweight versions. periscope finder; finder extender; and flat motor bases to mount on flat surface or inside blimp housing. Sound blimp: Model 120S for 400' (122m) magazines and model 1000 for 1,000' (300m) magazines. Aftermarket rain covers, splash housings, rain deflectors and underwater housings.

Connections: Cinematography Electronics 2C Crystal Motor Base. Norris intervalometer.

Power: 12, 16, 24, 32 V DC depending on motor.

Arriflex 35 II Models

Arriflex 35 II: 1946.

Arriflex 35 IIA: 1953. 180° shutter

Arriflex 35 IIB: 1960. New claw design, fixed 180° shutter

Arriflex 35 II BV: 1960. Variable shutter 0°–165°

Arriflex 35 II HS: 1960 high speed version (to 80fps)

Arriflex 35 II C: 1964. Improved viewing system; larger viewfinder optics to view full frame (anamorphic). Introduction of interchangeable ground glass system. Viewfinder door with de-anamorphoser. Interchangeable eyepieces.

Arriflex 35 II C/B: Three-port lens turret with one stainless steel bayonet mount and two ARRI standard mounts.

Arriflex 35 II CGS/B: Pilotone output and start marking

Arriflex 35 II CHS/B: High-speed model, 80fps maximum, specially pre-pared movement and 80fps tachometer. Uses 32V DC motor.

Arriflex 35 II CT/B: Techniscope™ format model. Uses 2-perf pull-down and half-height gate for widescreen aspect ratio of 2.35:1 with normal (not anamorphic) lenses, reducing film use by half.

ARRI 35IIC Medical Camera: 1964. Medical version of the 35-II used to shoot black and white 35mm film of moving X-ray images (used to di-agnose heart problems, for example). Medical cameras are usually gray, beige or light green. No lens turret; no viewfinder system. Sometimes equipped with ARRI standard lens mounts.

ARRITECHNO: 1970. Medical camera mounts to X-ray. No viewfinder or lens mount. Quick-change magazines snap on like a 16SR. These cam-eras require major modification to use for cinematography.

(courtesy of Jorge Diaz-Amador, Cinetechnic; Larry Barton, Cinematography Electronics)

Arriflex/SL-35 Mark III

Notes: A superlightweight camera for Steadicam, remote mounting, underwater and sports. Uses an Arri Medical 2C modified in a light-weight magnesium and delrin plastic body with custom camera electronics for Steadi-cam, handheld and rigging. Uses Arri 2C doors; 35-3 groundglasses; Super 35 gate. Stops with mirror in viewing position

Weight: 5.7 lbs/2.6kg without magazine.

Movement: Remanufactured Medical 2C high speed

FPS: 1–80 fps, forward and reverse; extra 50Hz speeds 33.333 and 16.666.

Aperture: Full aperture. Aperture plate: non-removable.

Power: Quartz-controlled DC motor, 24V; 5-pin #0 Lemo connector; camera on/off toggle and remote.

Displays: Red LED digital tach; red LED feet/meters digital footage/meters; red LED with reset and memory.

Lens: PL mount Standard or Super 35, Panavision and Panavision Super 35.

Shutter: 165° reflex mirror shutter.

Viewfinder: Works with Arri eyepiece and extender; also works with Jurgens door.

Video: Video only doors and finder/video doors

Viewing Screen: uses 35-3 groundglasses. Super 35 holder for Super 35 groundglass.

Mags: Accepts Arri 2-C and 35-3 style magazines. SL Cine makes lightweight magnesium low-profile (extended horizontal) and Steadicam (vertical) mags in 200' (61m) and 400' (122m) loads—to fit Arriflex 435, III series (35-3), II series (2-C) and SL-35 cameras.

Accessories: Low mode mount for Steadicam. Uses many existing 2C type accessories such as external speed controls, Arri- or Jurgens-2C doors and, with SL Cine lightweight riser, standard matte boxes and focus iris controls.

Connections: Two 11-pin Fisher connectors on back: 8.5 amp output at 12V DC. Two 24V Lemo connectors on front. Fischer 3-pin combi video and 12V power out; 5-pin Fischer remote on/off 12V.

Dimensions of body: 6"L x 5.5"H x 6"W

Arriflex 35-3C

Notes: A single PL mount evolution of the 2C design. About two dozen made.

Weight: 5.8 lbs/2.6 kg. (body only) 11.7 lbs/5.3 kg. (body, handgrip, 200' (61m) mag; no lens or film) 13.5 lbs/6.1 kg (body, handgrip, 400' (122m) mag, no lens or film.)

Movement: Same as 2C: single pin pull-down claw with extended dwell time to ensure accurate film positioning during exposure.

FPS: 24/25 fps crystal; 5–50 fps variable.

Aperture: .862" x .630" (22mm x 16mm).

Lens: 54mm diameter PL mount. Arri bayonet and standard mount lenses (41mm diameter) can be used with PL adapter. Flange focal distance of 52mm stays the same.) All zoom and telephoto lenses should be used with a special 3C bridge plate support system.

Shutter: Like the 2C, spinning reflex mirror shutter, adjustable from 0°–165°

in 15-degree increments while camera is stopped. Exposure is ¹⁄₅₂nd of a second at 24 fps with a 165-degree shutter.

Viewfinder: Three doors: fixed viewfinder, offset for handheld, pivoting finder. Three choices for fixed viewfinder door: regular, anamorphic and video tap. 6.5x super-wide-angle eyepiece.

Viewing Screen: 2C groundglasses.

Video: On fixed door.

Mags: Uses 2C, 35-3 and 435 mags. Some have collapsible cores. Others use 2" plastic cores .

Accessories: 2C, 35-3 and 435 accessories.

Power: Power input through a 4-pin connector. Pin 1 is negative; Pin 4 is +12V DC.

Arriflex/SL 35 Mark II

Notes: Earlier lightweight model, uses 2C groundglasses

Weight: 5.3 lbs/2.4kg without magazine.

Movement: Re-manufactured Arriflex Medical 2C

FPS: 1–80 fps, forward and reverse; extra 50Hz speeds 33.333 and 16.666.

Aperture: .862" x .630" (22mm x 16mm). Full aperture. Aperture Plate: Non-removable.

Power: Quartz-controlled DC motor, 24V; 3 pin #1 Lemo B connector; camera on/off toggle and remote.

Displays: Digital footage/meters; red LED with reset and memory.

Arriflex 35-3

Models: 3 generations of 35-3

Weight: 14.8 lbs./6.71 kg camera with 400' (122m) magazine (without film and lens).

Movement: One registration pin and dual-pin pulldown claw. Film channel incorporates a pressure pad at the back of aperture area. 3-perf available. Camera can run in reverse.

FPS: Quartz-controlled sync at 24/25/30 fps, 50/60Hz. An onboard variable-speed dial may be used to adjust camera speed from 4–50 fps at 12V DC. The camera is continuously variable from 4–100 fps (130 fps on the 35-3 130 fps camera) at 24V DC with a variable speed unit.

Aperture: .862 " x .630" (22mm x 16mm) full aperture, custom sizes available. Aperture plate removable for cleaning.

Motors, Power: 12/24V DC motor. Operating temperature range is -13°F to +122°F (-25°C to +50°C).

Displays: An electronic tachometer and footage counter. An external red

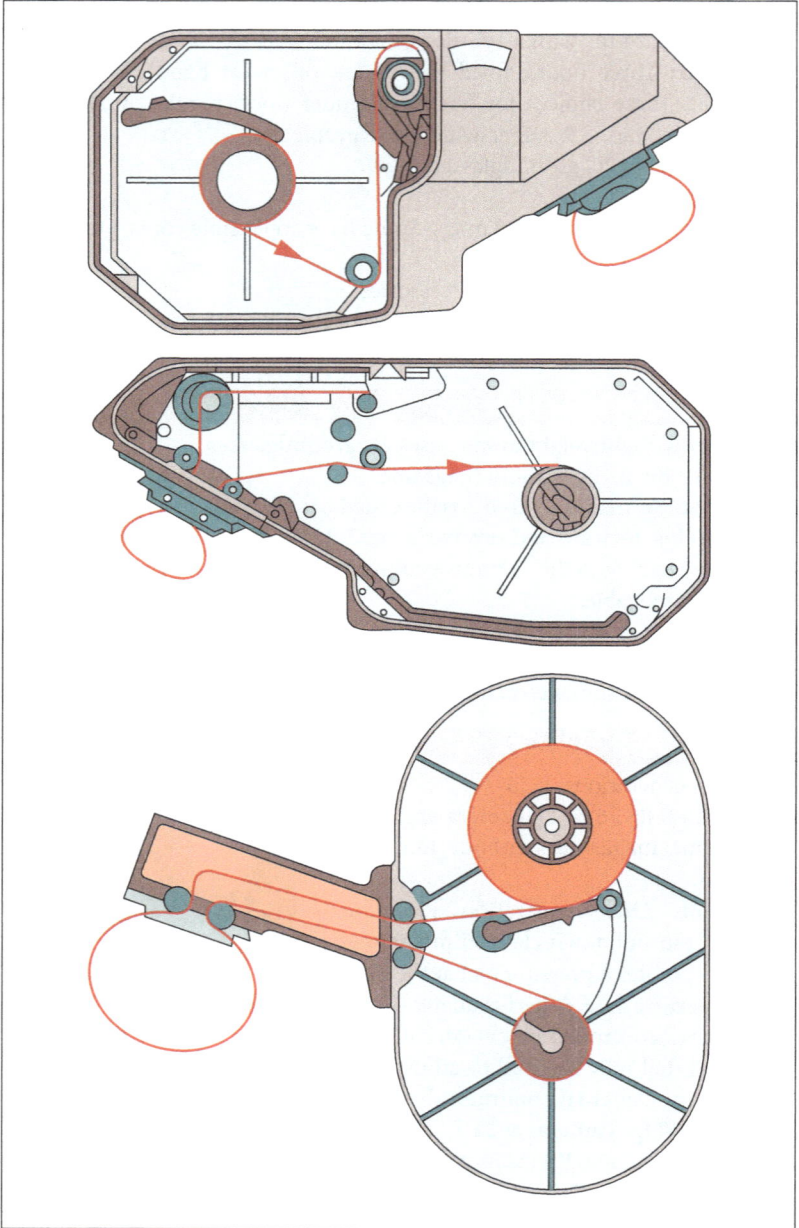

Arriflex 35-3 Shoulder and Steadicam Magazines
Figure 5a, 5b & 5c.Top: Shoulder magazine, feed side. Center: Shoulder magazine, take-up side. Bottom: Steadicam magazine. Film takes up emulsion side in.

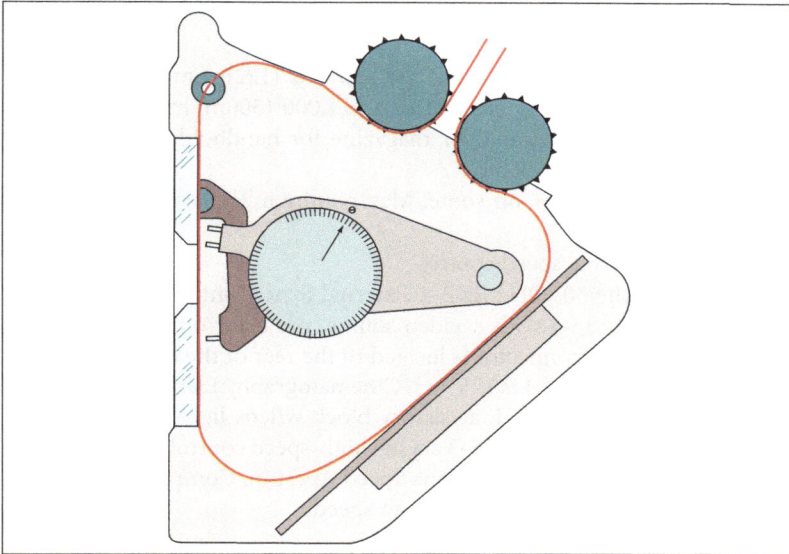

Arriflex 35-3 High Speed MOS Threading Diagram
Figure 5d. Film takes up emulsion side in.

LED located below the counter indicates when a low memory battery condition exists. A red LED to indicate an out-of-sync condition and a green LED to indicate variable speed mode are visible in the viewfinder.

Lens: 54mm diameter PL mount. Flange focal distance is 52mm. Super Speed and Standard lenses with PL mount, those with Arri Bayonet (41mm diameter) and Arri Standard lens mounts with PL adapter may be used. Aftermarket Nikon mounts.

Shutter: Rotating mirror shutter—three generations: first generation: 180° fixed shutter; second generation: 180°, 172.8°, 144° and 135°; third generation: 15°–135° in 15° increments, 144°, 172.8°, 180°

Second and third generations are mechanically adjustable with 2mm hex driver.

Viewfinder: Reflex Viewfinder: Four interchangeable doors with viewfinders are available: standard door with fixed viewfinder and mount for video tap; offset finder door for use with 400' (122m) coaxial shoulder magazine; pivoting finder door, pivots 210°; new pivoting finder door with optical adapter to attach video camera. All have adjustable super-wide-angle eyepiece with manual iris closure. Finder extenders available are 9" standard, 9" anamorphic, and 12.2" standard with ND.6 contrast viewing glass.

Video: Arri pivoting video door, Jurgens, Denz, P&S, JC&C, Boltersdorf, and other aftermarket video doors as well as CEI, Phillips and Sony taps.

Viewing Screen: Ground glasses for all aspect ratios are easily interchangeable.

Mags: Displacement type. 2C, 3C and 435 400' (122m) mags will fit. Top-mounted 200' (61m), 400' (122m), and 1,000' (300m) mags; 400' (122m) low-profile coaxial shoulder magazine for handholding. Aftermarket Steadicam mags available.

Cores: Collapsible cores on some. May require a 2" plastic core on other mags.

Accessories: external speed control

Connections: The 50/60Hz EXB-2 External Sync Control may be used to interlock the 35-3 with a video source, projector or another camera. A 4-pin power connector is located in the rear of the electronics housing. Pin 1 is (-); Pin 4 is 12V (+). Cinematography Electronics Precision Speed Control I and II, accessory block w/lens light, film/video synchronizing control, and 35-3 crystal high-speed control, intervalometer. Norris intervalometer, Preston's Speed Aperture Computer.

Power: 12V DC. Two batteries for high speed.

Arriflex 235

Notes: Small, lightweight MOS camera for handheld, rigs, underwater and crash housings. About half the weight and size of a 435.

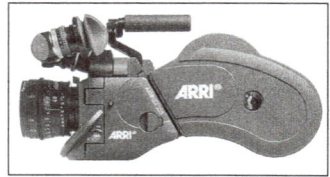

Weight: 3.5 kg/7.7 lbs. (body, viewfinder and eyepiece, without magazine)

Movement: Single pull down claw with two prongs; single registration pin. Registration pin in optical printer position (like 435). Camera available with 3- or 4-perf movements.

Frame Rate: 1–60 fps forward. 23.976, 24, 25, 29.97, 30 fps reverse (quartz accurate to .001 fps.).

Aperture: Super 35 (24.9 x 18.7mm) 0.98" x 0.74", same as ARRICAM ANSI S35 Silent 1.33 format mask). Fixed gap film gate.

Display: Operating buttons with an adjustable backlight

Lens: 54mm PL mount, adjustable for Normal or Super 35. Flange focal depth 51.98mm -0.01.

Shutter: Spinning, manually adjustable reflex mirror shutter. Mechanically adjustable with a 2mm hex driver at: 11.2°, 22.5°, 30°, 45°, 60°, 75°, 90°, 105°, 120°, 135°, 144°, 150°, 172.8° and 180°.

Viewfinder: Reflex viewfinder, can be rotated and extended like the 435. Automatic or manual image orientation in the viewfinder. Viewfinder and video assist are independent of each other, so switching to Steadicam or remote operation is done by simply removing the finder, leaving

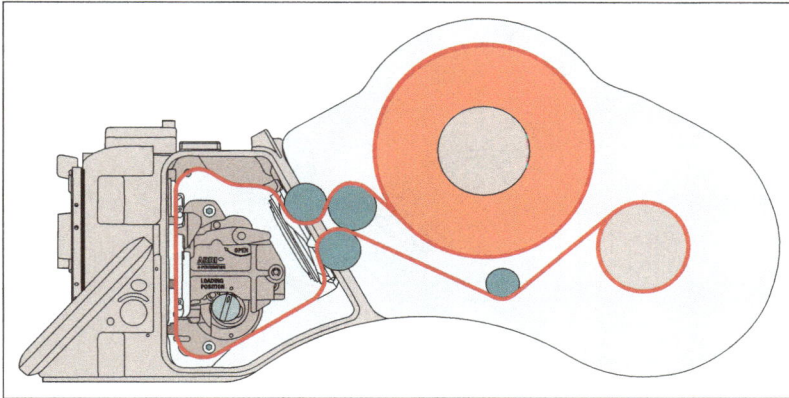

Arrilfex 235 Threading Diagram
Figure 6. Film takes up emulsion side in.

video assist on board. No need for a 100% video top. Optional medium finder extender.

Video: IVS color Integrated Video System

Viewing Screen: Interchangeable, uses 435 ground glasses.

Mags: New 200' (60m) shoulder magazine. Uses all existing 200' (60m) and 400' (122m) 2C, 3C, 35-3 and 435 displacement mags. Winds emulsion *in*. Cannot use 1000' (300m) magazines.

Connections: Power, mini monitor, remote accessory, 2x RS Remote Start. Uses most ARRI electronic accessories: RCU, WRC, ICU, ESU

Power: 24V DC (runs from 21V to 35V DC)

Misc.: Extra attachment points for rigging, reversible camera handle, extra low mode handle.

435 Advanced, 435 Extreme

Weight: 14.3 lbs/6.5kg without magazine.

Models: Usually called 435, it is probably the 435 ES model, (ES=Electronic Shutter). The basic 435 uses a mechanically adjustable shutter, but only a handful have been made. The newest model is the 435 Advanced, which has a more powerful shutter motor to enable shutter ramps 2.5 times faster. The Advanced does time lapse, motion control, the LCD is easier to read, LDS lens data contacts are built in. Extreme has many updated electronics.

Movement: Dual-pin registration conforming to optical printer standards, and dual pulldown claws. Can be replaced with a 3-perforation movement. Adjustable pitch control.

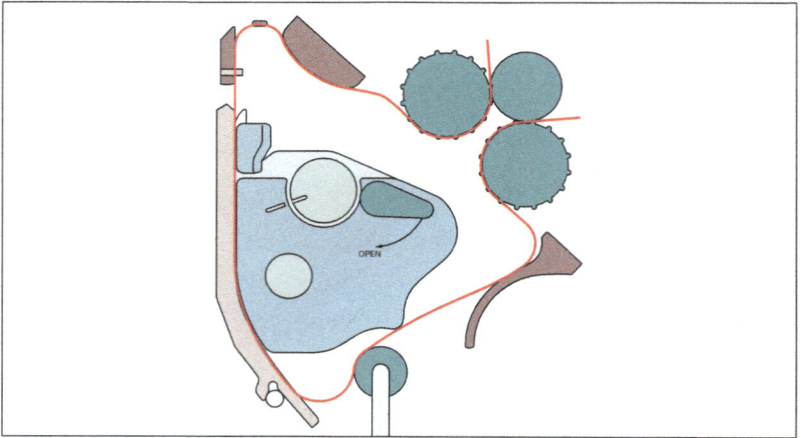

Arriflex 435 Threading Diagram
Figure 7. Film takes up emulsion side in.

Frame Rate: 1–150 fps, forward or reverse (quartz accurate to .001 fps.).

435 Advanced Model: 0.1–150fps ($\frac{1}{10}$ fps–150 fps)

Aperture: Interchangeable masks with full range of aspect ratios. Aperture Plate removable for cleaning.

Power: Quartz-controlled DC motors.

Display: Fps, forward and reverse run, film counter in feet and meters, shutter angle, time code (user bit and TC sensitivity). Warnings include incorrect movement position, asynchronous film speed, low battery voltage and film end.

Lens: 54mm PL mount, adjustable for Normal or Super 35.

Shutter: Spinning, adjustable reflex mirror shutter. The 435ES (Electronic Shutter) can be adjusted continuously from 11.2°–180° while camera is running. The plain 435 (non-ES) reflex mirror shutter is mechanically adjustable with a 2mm hex driver at: 11.2°, 15°, 22.5°, 30°, 45°, 60°, 75°, 90°, 105°, 120°, 135°, 144°, 172.8° and 180°. Both 435ES and 435 Advanced have these mechanical shutter angles as well; be sure not to activate electronic shutter at same time.

Viewfinder: Reflex viewfinder, the standard finder, which covers full aperture (Super 35), pivots to either side of the camera, with an adjustment knob to orient the image upright in any position. Adjustable in/out for left- or right-eyed viewing. ND.6 contrast filter flips in. The 435 uses 535 extension finders, eyepieces, ground glasses, field lenses and gate masks. An optional anamorphic viewfinder is also available for de-squeezing anamorphic lenses.

An optical tap with interchangeable beamsplitter ratio is integrated into the standard viewfinder, enabling the adaptation of the ½" video camera

CCD-2. The entire viewfinder module can be removed and replaced with a lightweight 100 percent video tap for Steadicam or remote filming.

Video: 435 Integrated Video System (IVS), color, flicker-free at all camera speeds, mechanical iris and electronic gain for exposure control, with frameline and camera status inserter, image freeze and compare, color balance settings (auto and standard presets), composite or S-VHS outputs. Video capture rate can by synchronized to film shutter for motion blur preview. IVS2 has additional features: ablility to turn flicker free off, manual color balancing, enhanced data display, etc.

Very early 435 cameras had a C mount for ½" CCD camera.

Viewing Screen: Interchangeable. ARRIGLOW.

Mags: Displacement, winds emulsion *in*. Uses all 2C, 3C, 35-3, as well as 435 magazines. Top-mounted 400' (122m) and 1000' (300m) magazine (435) 1000' (300m) mag torque motor driven. Also, a 400'(122m) Steadicam mag. Arri 35-3 and older magazines can be used but without time code.

Accessories: Accepts the whole range of Arriflex matte boxes, 15mm or 19mm rod systems. Steadicam low-mode bracket, shoulder set, lens light. Wired and wireless lens and camera control system, wired and wireless speed/shutter/iris ramping controls. Single-frame system, motion-control interfaces. For 435 Advanced: LDS Ultra and Variable Primes.

Connections: 24V DC, 3/5 amps and 12V, 3/5 amps. Most camera functions can be controlled via the remote-control unit (RCU-1) or Wireless Remote Control (WRC-1).

Electronic Sync Unit (ESU) provides synchronization with an external PAL or NTSC video signal (50/60Hz), another camera or a projector, or computer or video monitor via a monitor pick-up. It also contains a phase shifter, pilt tone generator, and selectable division ratio between an external source and the camera's frame rate.

Power: 28V to 30V "nominal" DC . The camera will start and run at speeds up to 129 fps as long as the battery voltage does not drop below 20.6V, high-speed running at speeds of 130 fps–150 fps requires that the camera voltage remain above 24V during camera startup. 35V is the absolute maximum, above which, the camera will not start.

Arriflex 535

Notes: The 535 came first, followed by the lighter 535B. There is no 535A—just the 535. Main difference is the viewfinder: the 535B is simpler and lighter. 535 has electronically controlled mirror shutter; 535B shutter is manual. 535 has 3-position beamsplitter.

Weight: Body only 21.6 lbs/9.82 kg. body + finder 29.4 lbs/14.19 kg., body + finder + mag (no film or lens) 36.4 lbs/16.55 kg.

Movement: Dual-pin registration conforming to optical printer standards, and dual pull-down claws. Can be replaced with a 3-perforation movement. Adjustable pitch control.

FPS: Quartz controlled 24/25/29.97/30 fps onboard; and

3–50 fps with external control such as Remote Unit (RU) or Variable Speed Unit (VSU). With external control, makes speed changes while camera is running, and runs at 24/25 fps in reverse. Pushing the phase button runs camera at 1 fps—but precise exposure not ensured at 1 fps.

Aperture: Universal aperture plate with interchangeable format masks provides full range of aspect ratios. Has a behind-the-lens gel filter holder. Gels are positioned very close to image plane, so they must be scrupulously clean and free of dust. Gate is easily removed for cleaning.

dB: 19dB.

Displays: In-finder displays use LEDs to allow the operator to monitor various camera functions, battery status, and programmable film-end warning. Digital LCD tachometer and footage displays: camera left/right; audible and visible out-of-sync warning; visible film jam; film end; error codes; improper movement position; improper magazine mounting; disengaged rear film guide indicators.

Lens: PL lens mount, 54mm diameter, with relocatable optical center for easy conversion to Super 35. Flange focal distance is 52mm.

Shutter: Microprocessor-controlled variable mirror shutter (535 only; the B is manual). Continuously adjustable from 11°–180° while running, in .01° increments, at any camera speed. The Arriflex 535 permits shutter angle changes while running at the camera or remotely. The 535's program also permits simultaneous frame rate/shutter angle effects, such as programmed speed changes with precise exposure compensation.

Viewfinder: Swing-over viewfinder enables viewing from either camera left or camera right, with constant image correction side to side and upright. A selectable beam splitter provides 80% viewfinder-20% video, 50-50 or video only. Programmable Arriglow for low-light filming. Nine preprogrammed illuminated formats, an optional customized format module, and fiber-optic focus screens. Switchable ND.3 and ND.6 contrast viewing glasses, a variety of in-finder information LEDs, and a 12"-15" variable finder.

Viewing Screen: Ground glasses and fiber-optic focus screens for all aspect ratios.

Video: Video Optics Module (VOM): provides flicker reduction and iris control.

Mags: Rear-mounted 400' (122m) and 1,000' (300m) coaxial, each with two microprocessor-controlled torque motors. Feed and take-up tension and all other functions are continuously adjusted by microprocessors. Mechanical and digital LCD footage counters built in.

Accessories: Variable Speed Unit (VSU) can attach to the 535 and permits camera speed changes between 3 and 50 fps, noncrystal.

Shutter Control Unit (SCU): mounts directly to the camera and permits camera shutter angle changes between 11° and 180° (535 only).

Remote Unit (RU): operational remotely from up to 60', provides a VSU/SCU (variable shutter/variable speed) combination. The RU links the SCU and VSU to permit manual adjustment of the frame rate while the 535's microprocessor varies the shutter angle—all to ensure a constant depth of field and exposure.

SMPTE time code module plugs in to utilize onboard time code generator, and provides full SMPTE 80-bit time code capability.

Electronic Sync Unit (ESU): Operational remotely from up to 60'; provides synchronization with an external PAL or NTSC video signal (50/60Hz), another camera or a projector, or computer or video monitor via a monitor pick-up. It also contains a phase shifter, Pilotone generator, and selectable division ratio between an external source and the camera's frame rate.

Camera Control Unit (CCU): provides integrated control over all electronic functions. External Sync Unit is designed for multicamera, video or projector interlock.

Laptop Camera Controller is software to control the camera via a serial cable.

Power: 24VDC. 3-pin XLR connector: Pin 1 is (-), and Pin 2 is +24V.

Arriflex 535 B

Notes: 535B is lighter than the 535.

Fps: same as 535—runs at crystal-controlled speeds from 3–60 fps. Has a manually adjustable mirror shutter, variable from 11° to 180° in 15-degree steps, and 144° and 172.8°. The 535B has a lightweight swing-over viewfinder. The entire finder is easily removed without tools and accepts a 100 percent video module for Steadicam use.

Weight: Body only 17 lbs/7.7 kg.; body + finder 22 lbs/10 kg.; body + finder + lightweight 400' (122m) mag; (no film or lens) 27.8 lbs/12.6 kg.

Movement: Same as 535. Same adjustable pitch control.

FPS: Crystal controlled onboard 24/25/29.97/30 fps forward and reverse ; and 3–60 fps with external control such as remote unit (RU) or Variable Speed Unit (VSU).

Aperture: Same as 535—Universal aperture plate with interchangeable format masks. Behind-the-lens gel filter holder.

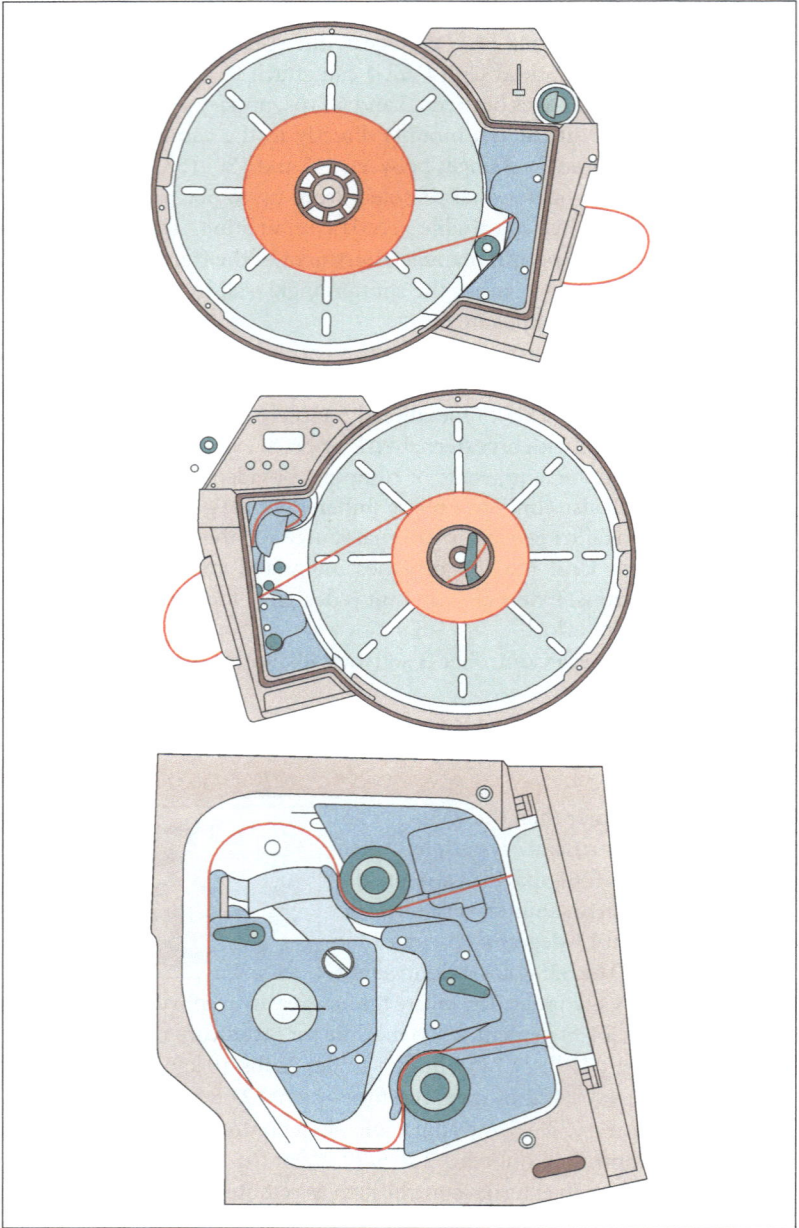

Arriflex 535 and 535B Magazine and Threading Diagrams
Figure 8a, 8b & 8c. Top: Magazine supply side. Center: Magazine take-up side.
Bottom: Threading diagram. Film takes up emulsion side in.

dB: 19dB.

Displays: LEDs in viewfinder displays ASY (out of sync), BAT (low battery), END (out of film). Digital LCD tachometer and footage displays: camera left/right; audible and visible out-of-sync warning; visible film jam; film end; error codes; improper movement position; improper magazine mounting; disengaged rear film guide indicators.

Lens: PL lens mount, 54mm diameter, converts from Standard to Super35.

Shutter: Mechanically adjustable from 15°–180° in 15° increments, along with 144° and 172.8° while camera is stopped

Viewfinder: Finder block with swing-over viewfinder enables viewing from either camera left or camera right, with constant image correction side to side and upright. Choice of beam splitters: 80% viewfinder-20% video or 50-50. Programmable Arriglow for low-light filming. Nine preprogrammed illuminated formats, an optional customized format module, and fiber-optic focus screens. ND.6 contrast viewing glass, a variety of in-finder information LEDs, and a 12"–15" variable finder. 535B finder block fits on 535. variously called a 535 A/B, 535B+ or 535A-.

Viewing Screens: Same as 535

Video: Video Optics Module (VOM): provides flicker reduction and iris control. Video only top or video only.

Mags: Same as 535. A lightweight displacement 400' (122m) mag was made for the 535B—it will fit the 535 as well.

　　Power and Accessories are same as 535.

　　535B threads the same as 535.

Arriflex 35BL

Notes: The Arriflex 35BL was conceived in 1966 as the first portable, dual pin registered, handheld, silent reflex motion picture camera. Its first significant production use was at the 1972 Olympic  Games, where it was employed for sync-sound, *cinéma vérité* and slow-motion filming at speeds to 100 fps. At the same time, its theatrical and television use began, especially for location work.

　　The camera evolved. The analog footage and frame rate indicators of the 35BL-1 were replaced by a digital readout on the 35BL-2. With the 35BL-3, the lens blimp was eliminated. The Arri 41mm bayonet mount was soon replaced by the larger 54mm diameter PL lens mount.

　　The 35BL-4 introduced a brighter eyepiece and illuminated groundglass. The 35BL-4s came out with a new, quieter, adjustable-pitch multilink compensating movement, new footage/meters counter, redesigned internal construction, and magazines with an external timing adjustment.

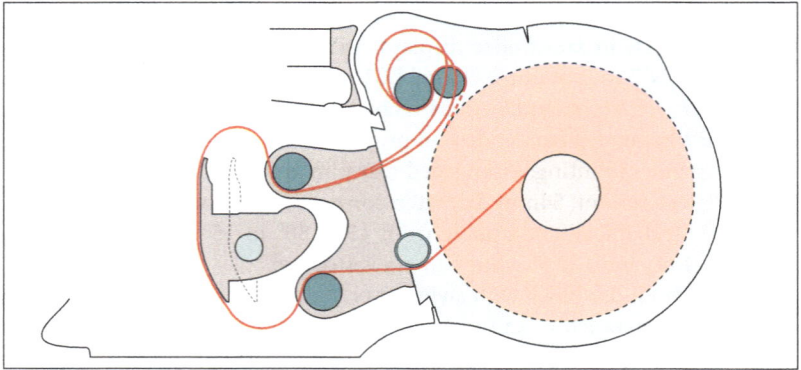

Arriflex BL-4s Threading and Magazine Diagram
Figure 9. Film takes up emulsion side in.

Movement: Industry standard dual pin registration. Two double pronged pull-down claws on early 35BL-1 cameras for high speed to 100 fps with special magazine roller arms. Two single prong pull-down claws on all other 35BL cameras.

35BL-4s movement has an adjustable pitch control.

Aperture: .862" x .630" (22mm x 16mm), custom sizes available. Aperture Plate is removable for cleaning.

35BL-3, 4 and 4s gates will fit 35BL-1 and 2 cameras, but not vice versa.

Displays: LED digital fps and footage readout on camera left. Audible out-of-sync warning. A red LED near the footage counter indicates low footage, memory, battery. BL-1 has mechanical readout.

Arriflex 35BL Camera Models				
Camera	Shutter Angles	Frame Rate	dB	Weight*
35BL-4s	180° 172.8° 144°	24, 25, 30 6-40	20	41.5 kg (31.9 lbs)
35BL-4	180° 172.8° 144°	24, 25 6-40	22	14 kg (30.9 lbs)
35BL-3	180° 172.8° 144°	24, 35 6-42	22	13 kg (28 lbs)
35BL-2	180°	24, 25 5-50	26	12.5 kg (28 lbs)
35BL-1	180°	24, 25 5-100	26	12.5 kg (28 lbs)
*Weight with 400' magazine, no lens, no film				

Dimensions of 35BL-4s and 35BL4			
	Length	**Width**	**Height**
35BL-4s with 400' (120m) mag	17.3" (440mm)	12" (305mm)	9.1" (230mm)
35BL-4 with 1000' (300m) mag	21.5" (546mm)	12" (305mm)	12.5" (317mm)
Dimensions of 35BL-1, 2 and 3: same length and height. Width is 11" (280mm)			

Lens: 54mm diameter PL mount. Newer cameras switch from Normal to Super 35.

Early 35BL cameras had Arri bayonet mount. Some cameras were converted to BNC mount.

35BL-2 and BL-1 cameras require lens blimps for silent operation.

Shutter: Rotating mirror shutter. See table.

Viewfinder: Reflex Viewfinder. 35BL-4s and BL-4 viewfinders are a stop brighter than earlier 35BL cameras and feature a larger exit pupil. The finder rotates 90° above and 90° below level with the image upright. Super Wide Angle eyepiece with manual leaf closure and 6.5X magnification standard on 35BL-4s and BL-4 cameras. Adjustable eyecup allows the operator to select the optimum eye-to-exit pupil distance. Finder extenders available for the 35BL-4s and 35BL-4 include a 12.5" standard with switchable contrast viewing filter, and variable magnification up to 2X. For the 35BL-3, 35BL-2 and 35BL-1: 9" standard and 9" anamorphic finder extenders.

Video: Video elbow with Arri and aftermarket video taps from CEI, Jurgens, Denz, Philips, Sony and many others.

Viewing Screens: pullout with Hirschmann forceps to clean and interchange. ArriGlow illuminated frame lines.

Mags: 400' (122m) and 1,000' (300m) coaxial. The 35BL can be handheld with either magazine. Mechanical footage counters are integral.

Accessories: Sound Barney and heated barney.

Connections: Electronic Accessories: Multicamera interlock is achieved with the EXS-2 50/60Hz External Sync Unit. SMPTE time code available for later models.

Motors, Power: 12V DC. Power input through a 4-pin XLR connector on camera. Pin 1 is (-); Pin 4 is +12V. Although most of the industry settled on 4 pin connectors on both ends, some cables have 5-pin XLR male connectors on the battery end.

Arri Accessories

Arri accessories common to most cameras with flat bases—(many 2C cameras still have with handgrip motors, not flat bottoms):

Rods: There are two diameters of lens support/accessory rods in use: 15mm and 19mm. The 19mm rods are centered below the lens; 15mm rods are off-center.

Environmental Protection Equipment: Aftermarket rain covers, splash housings, rain deflectors and underwater housings available.

Camera Support Equipment: Arri Head; Arri Head 2 (newer, lighter, smaller). Arrimotion (small and lightweight moco).

Lens Controls: Arri FF2 or FF3 follow focus. Preston Microforce or Arri LCS/wireless lens control. Lens Control: Arri FF3 follow focus. Preston Microforce zoom control. Iris gears available for remote iris.

Arri Matte Boxes

MB-16 (4 x 4 Studio): two 4" x 4" filters and one 4½" round filter (maximum of four 4" x 4" and one 4½" round). Swing-away mechanism for fast lens changes. Can be equipped with top and side eyebrows.

MB-17B (4 x 4 LW): A lightweight matte box holding two 4" x 4" filters and one 4½" round filter. Swing-away mechanism; can easily be adapted to 15mm or 19mm support rods via the BA bracket adapters. It can also be used on the SR lightweight rods. It can be equipped with a top eyebrow.

MB-16A (4 x 5.6 Studio): A studio matte box holding two 4" x 5.650" filters and one 4½" round filter (maximum of four 4" x 5.6" and one 4½" round). Swing-away mechanism. Can be equipped with top and side eyebrows.

MB-18 (4 x 5.6 Studio): A studio matte box holding three 4" x 5.650" filters and one 138mm filter (maximum of four 4" x 5.650" and one 138mm). Swing-away mechanism for fast lens changes. Can be equipped with top and side eyebrows. Covers Super 16mm.

MB-19 (4 x 5.6 LW): A lightweight matte box holding two 4" x 5.650" filters and one 138mm or 4½" round filter (maximum of three 4" x 5.650" and one 138mm or 4½" round). Swing away mechanism for fast lens changes and can easily be adapted to 15mm or 19mm support rods via the BA bracket adapters. Can also be used on SR lightweight rods. Can be equipped with top and side eyebrows. Covers Super 16mm.

MB-15 (5 x 6 Studio): A studio matte box holding two 5" x 6" filters and one 6", 138mm or 4½" round filter. A rotating stage can be attached, adding two 4" x 4" filters. Swing-away mechanism for fast lens changes. Can be equipped with top and side eyebrows. Covers fixed lenses 14mm and up, as well as most zooms. Geared filter frame.

MB-14 (6.6x6.6 Studio): A studio matte box holding four 6.6" x 6.6" filters and one 6", 138mm or 4½" round filter (maximum of six 6.6" x 6.6" and one 6", 138mm or 4½" round). The four 6.6" x 6.6" filter trays are grouped in two stages with two filter trays each. The two stages can be rotated

Arri Accessories		
Accessory	**19mm Rods**	**15mm Rods**
Camera Baseplate	BP-8	BP-9
Lens Support	LS-7, LS-9	LS-8, LS-10
FF-4 Follow Focus		
Mattebox		

Baseplates for a new generation of Arriflex cameras

Camera	**19mm Rods**	**15mm Rods**
235, 435	BP-8	BP-9
535, 535B	BP-5	BP-3
16 SR3	BP-6	BP-7

New Baseplates for new accessories on old cameras
If you want to use new style matteboxes, lens supports, and accessories with older cameras.

Camera	**19mm Rods**	**15mm Rods**
35 BL1, 2, 3, 4, 4s	BP-5	BP-3
35-3	BP-5	BP-3
16SR1, 16SR2	BP-6	BP-7

Old Baseplates for old accessories on old cameras
If you want to use older style accessories with older cameras.

Camera	**Baseplate**
35bl1, 2, 3, 4, 4s	BP-3
35-3	BP-3
16SR1, 16SR2	SR1

independently of each other, and each stage contains one filter tray with a geared moving mechanism allowing for very precise setting of grad filters. Swing-away mechanism. Can be equipped with top and side eyebrows.

6.6x6.6 Production Matte Box: Covers lenses 12mm and up, as well as most zooms. Interchangeable two, four or six filter stages, rotatable 360°, swing-away for changing lenses. Geared filter frames.

MB-14W: same as MB-14, but with a wider front piece for 9.8mm lenses or longer.

MB-14C: same as MB-14, but with a shorter front piece for close-up lenses.

LMB-3 (4x4 clip-on): A very lightweight matte box that clips to the front of 87mm or 80mm lenses, holding two 4"x4" filters. When using prime lenses with a 80mm front diameter (most Arri/Zeiss prime lenses), a Series 9 filter can be added with an adapter ring. Shade part can be easily removed from the filter stages if only the filter stages are needed. Can be used for 16mm prime lenses 8mm–180mm and 35mm prime lenses 16mm–180mm. It also attaches to the 16mm Vario-Sonar 10–100mm or 11–110mm zoom lens.

Arri Fuses (electronic/motor)	
Camera	**Fuse**
35-2B/C	4 A 5 x 20mm motor circuit
35-3C	¾ A pico / 10 A pico
35-3 1st, 2nd gen.	¾ A pico / 15 A pico
35-3 3rd gen.	¾ A pico / 15 A pico
35-3 BNC Mount	¾ A pico / 15 A pico
235, 435, ES, Adv	Polyfuse
35BL-1, 2	¾ radial micro / 15 A pico
35 BL-3, 4, 4s	1 A pico / 15 A pico 3 A pico accresories (4s only) ½ A pico Arriglow (4, 4s only)
35 BL BNC Mount	¾ A pico / 15 A pico
535 A, 535B	2.5 pico / 15 A pico
Arricam ST, LT	Polyfuse
765	2 A blade type – electronics 15 A blade type – movement 20 A blade type – shutter 2 A blade type – accessories

Part numbers for Arri Fuses					
Pico		**Pico**		**Micro Fuse**	
¼ A	05.07953.0	3 A	05.07956.0	¾ A	05.07962.0
½ A	05.07954.0	5 A	05.07957.0		
¾ A	05.07955.0	7 A	05.07985.0	**5 x 20mm**	
1 A	ZELE-MISC-14	10 A	05.07958.0	4 A	05.07984.0
2.5 A	ZELE-MISC-34	15 A	05.07959.0		

LMB-5 (4x5.650 clip-on): A matte box that clips onto the front of the lens, holding two 4"x5.6" filters. Can be attached to lens front using clamp adapters of the following diameters: 80mm, 87mm, 95mm and 114mm. Can be equipped with a top eyebrow.

LMB-4 (6.6x6.6 clip-on): A matte box that clips onto the front of the lens, holding two 6.6"x6.6" filters. Can be used on 156mm front diameter lenses (like the Zeiss T2.1/10mm) or, with an adapter, on 144mm front diameter lenses (like the Zeiss T2.1/12mm).

Additional Accessories: Bridge plate support system for CG balance and mount for matte box, follow focus, servo zoom drive, and heavy lenses; handheld rig for shoulder operation of the camera.

Many good aftermarket matteboxes and accessories from Chrosziel, Cinetech and many others.

Arriflex Cameras: Flange Focal Distance Chart		
Camera Lens	Mount to Filmgate (mm)	Lens Mount to Groundglass (mm)
35-2B/C	51.970 to 51.980	52.000
35.3C	51.970 to 51.980	52.000
35-3 1st, 2nd gen.	51.990 to 52.000	52.000
35-3 3rd gen.	51.980 to 51.990	52.000
35-3 BNC Mount	61.450 to 61.460	61.470
235	51.98 to 0.01	52.000
435, ES, Adv., Extm.	51.970 to 51.980	52.000
35 BL-1, 2	51.970 to 51.980	52.000
35 BL3, 4, 4s	51.970 to 51.980	52.000
35BL BNC-Mount	61.450 to 61.460	61.470
535A, 535B	51.970 to 51.980	52.000
Arricam ST, LT	51.970 to 51.980	52.000
765	73.500 to 73.500	73.500

Bell & Howell 35mm Eyemo Model 71

Notes, Models: "Beats the Other Fellow to the Pictures" (from original 1926 ad)

71 M–Compact 3 lens turret

71 Q–wide " Spider" three-lens turret.

71 K–single Eyemo mount.

Weight: 11 lbs/4.9 kg, size: 4" x 6" x 8"

Eyemo K

Movement: No registration pins. Pull-down claw on soundtrack side only. Cam-operated single claw. Spring-loaded edge guide and pressure plate.

FPS: 8, 12, 16, 24, 32, 48 fps. Governor controlled

Aperture: Full, Academy centered or full centered. Filter slot behind lens

Displays: Read out/indicators dial on side for 100' body. Veeder root counter, for Q with magazines.

Eyemo Q

Lens: Eyemo Bell & Howell Mount, many conversions to Nikon, PL, Panavision and Canon.

Shutter: 160°. Replacement shutters of different degrees available.

Viewfinder: Nonreflex viewfinder: external with parallax correction and matching objective lenses. Reflex shift over plate for Q model only with full frame viewing and focusing. Taking lens rotate 180° to reflex eye piece.

Loads: 100' (30.5m) daylight spools.

Motors, Power: Spring wind-up, 55' (16.8M) per wind. 6V DC, 12V DC, 24V DC, 110V AC.

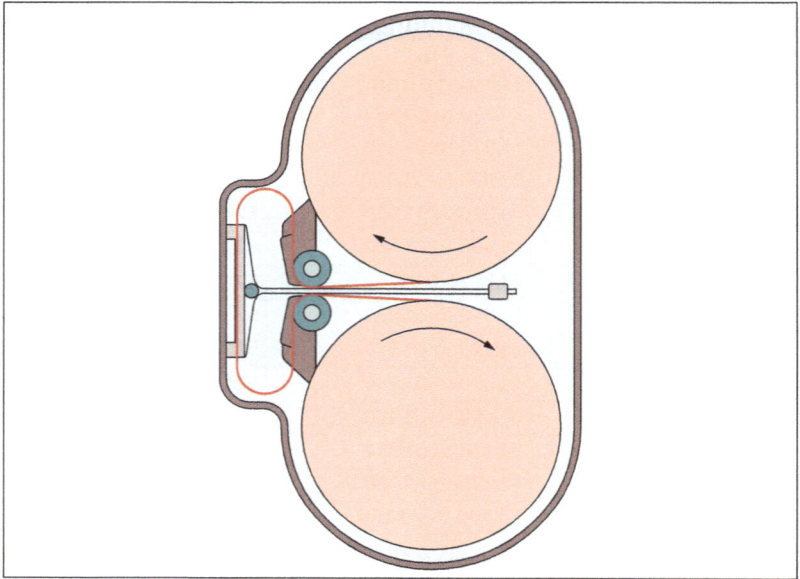

Bell & Howell 35mm Eyemo Threading Diagram
Figure 10. Film takes up emulsion side in. (Daylight load only.)

Mags: 200' (61m) 400' (122m) Some models don't accept magazines.
Misc: Reprinted Instructions Manuals at www.photobooks online.com/
books/manual23.html

Bell & Howell 35mm Steve's Cine Service Conversion

Movement: No registration pins. Pull-down claw on soundtrack side only.
FPS: 4–50 fps.
Aperture: Full: optically centered or full centered
Displays: LED footage and fps.
Lens: Nikon, PL, Panavison and Canon mounts. Since this is often used as
a "crash" camera, be sure your lenses are expendable. That's why Nikon
or Canon still lenses are often used. Some of Steve's conversions have a
neutral mount, with adapters for various mounts.
Shutter: 160°. Replacement shutters of different degrees available.
Viewfinder: Reflex Viewfinder: cube beamsplitter reflex system
(-½ stop loss due to cube beamsplitter and 160° shutter). Viewing
optics use Arriflex eyepieces. Other models have parallax finders (not
reflex).
Video: Black-and-white CCD.
Viewing Screen: Arri III type. All Academy and Super 35 formats.
Loads: Uses 100' (30.5m) daylight spools in camera body.

Accessories: Remote start cables, Crash housing, underwater housings and Clairmont Camera fire housings.

Motors, Power: 12V DC only

Eclair CM-3 16/35mm

Notes: Darling camera of the new wave.

Movement: Easily converts from 35mm to 16mm with two sets of ratchet-type pull-down claws: one on each side for 35mm and a single, smaller claw for 16mm. Adjusting the claw stroke adapts camera to either normal 4-perf pull-down or 2-perf pull-down for Techniscope, or single-perf pull-down for 16mm operation. Pull-down claws mounted on sliding cam-driven plate, which is reached through opening in aperture plate. No disassembly or special tools required. Registration and steadiness achieved by double rear pressure plate and very long side rails. Top plate keeps film flat in focal plane, bottom plate holds film at edges only to keep it properly aligned for pulldown claws.

FPS: 50 fps maximum.

Aperture: Optically centered and Academy centered on some models. Aperture plate made of one piece of steel, hand-polished and undercut to prevent scratching. Aperture plate is part of camera body proper, pressure plates are built into magazine. Raised area in center of aperture portion of pressure plate eliminates breathing. Sliding mattes for film aperture and viewfinder for 16mm. Techniscope or other widescreen ratios. Gel filter behind the lens.

Displays: Built-in tachometer.

Lens: Three-lens divergent cam-lock turret with Camerette CA-1 lens mounts. CA-1 lens mount is large-diameter brass bayonet type. Divergent turret permits mounting 5.7mm focal length and longest telephoto lenses without optical or physical interference.

Shutter: 200° variable front-surfaced mirror reflex shutter; may be varied to 35° by turning knob on left side of camera body.

Viewfinder: Reflex, 360° rotating eyepiece for right or left eye. Adjustable mattes for various aspect ratios.

Viewing Screen: Fixed. Various markings available.

Mags: Quick change (snap-on) 200' (61m) and 400' (122m) displacement type mags. Fixed loop (which may be set from outside at any time). Automatic footage counter. Removal of magazine allows inspection and cleaning of aperture plate and film channel. For Techniscope operation, T-Type magazine operates at either 45' per minute or 90' per minute by merely changing gears. Plastic film cores.

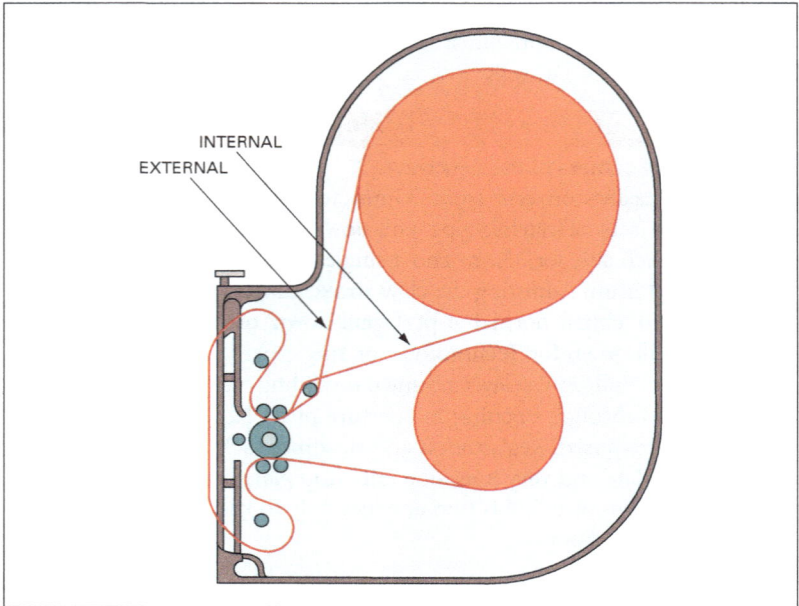

Eclair CM3 400' Magazine
Figure 11. Film takes up emulsion side out.

Accessories: Dovetail adapter to mount to tripod has twin matte box rods. Mattebox with two 3"x3" filter stages, one rotatable and removable, for use with extra-wide-angle lenses.

Sound Blimp has one door to allow sliding camera out on rails for instant magazine change and automatically connects follow focus, lens diaphragm and external eyepiece. Camera may be used with all anamorphic and zoom lenses, in or out of blimp. Full instrumentation capabilities available with single-frame pulse and intervalometer operation.

Aquaflex underwater housing for 35mm Techniscope and 16mm.

Lightweight magnesium tripod. Entire tripod bowl and movements can be lifted from legs and clamped to table edges, doors, ladders, etc.

Motors, Power: Motors mounted on side of camera can be changed in a few seconds.

Basic motor: 6-8V DC rheostat-controlled variable-speed type (also available for 24V power).

Other motors: 6, 12 and 24V DC transistor-controlled regulated motors with variable-speed or constant-speed operation with 50 or 60Hz sync pulse outputs, crystal plus variable also. Stops in viewing position. 115V 60Hz and 220V three-phase, 60Hz AC motors for synchronous sound shooting.

Hand-crank drive also available for 1, 8 or 16 pictures per turn.

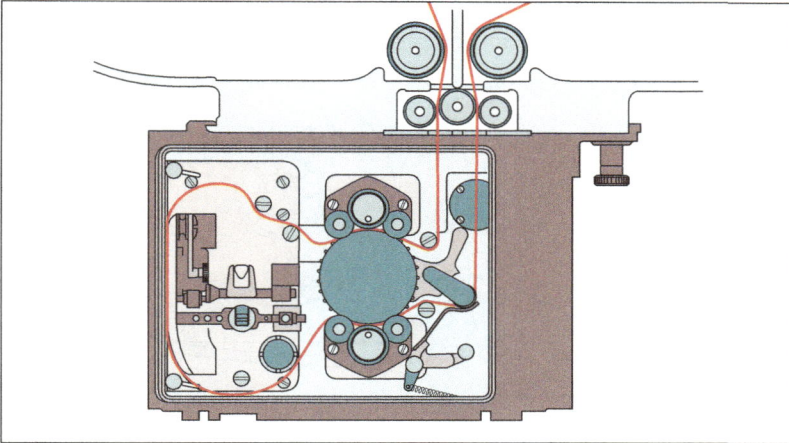

Fries 435 Threading Diagram
Figure 12. Film takes up emulsion side out.

Fries 435

Weight: 26 lbs./11.8 kg body only.
Movement: Mitchell movement
FPS: 2–150 fps. in one-frame increments, crystal controlled.
Aperture: .980" x .735" (24.89mm x 18.67mm), removable aperture plate: Displays: Panel
Lens: BNCR, Panavision, Arri PL mounts
Shutter: Spinning mirror reflex with 170° shutter.
Viewfinder: A light valve allows the operator to direct all the light to the viewfinder, the video-assist, or combo which splits between the two.
Mags: 400' (122m) and 1,000' (300m) displacement
Motors, Power: 30V DC. Equipped with take-up and supply torque motors.

Moviecam Compact

Weight: 13 lbs 10 oz/6.3kg.
Movement: Dual pin registration and double pull-down pins. The movement slides back for easy threading. Loop adjustment.
FPS: 12–32 fps forward or reverse. 2–50 fps forward with moviespeed control. Frame rate speed pre-set buttons.
Aperture: .980" x .735" (24.89mm x 18.67mm). Aperture plates available in all 35mm aspect ratios and easily interchanged. Mattes and masks only at Clairmont by special order.

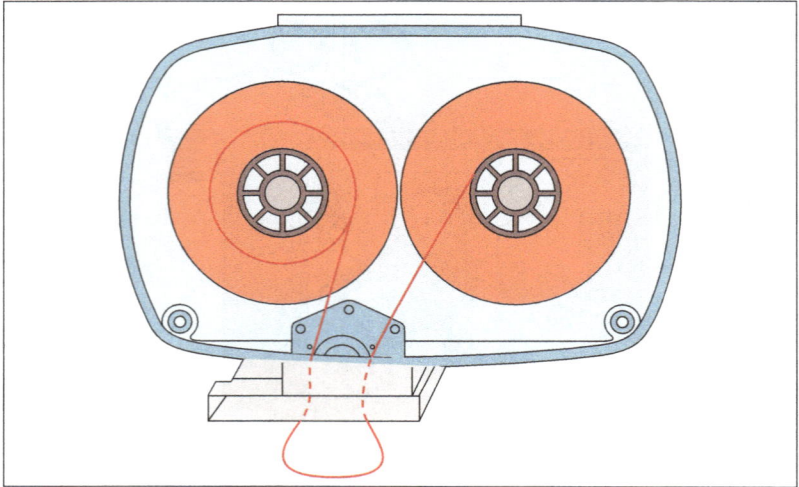

Moviecam Compact Magazine Diagram
Figure 13a. Moviecam standard type magazine. Film takes up emulsion side in.

dB: Under 20dBA.

Displays: Footage and frame rate. Digital counters for frame rate. Flashing control display which indicates incorrect operation or buckle trips. Digital display for forward and reverse. Shutter angles are displayed only on the shutter.

Lens: BNCR and PL mounts. Regular and Super 35mm. Iris gears are available and necessary for speed/iris ramps. Electronic dust check (gate check) button.

Shutter: 180° variable to 45°. Calibrated in segments with positive locks at 45°, 90°, 120°, 144° and 172.8°. Mirror stops automatically in viewing position. 22.5° available on newer cameras.

Viewfinder: Reflex 6.1X magnification viewfinder. Three-position filter wheel (clear, blocked and ND.6). Reflex viewfinder is rotatable 360° while maintaining an erect image. 12" viewfinder extension with built-in 2.4X magnification zoom. 9.22mm eyepiece exit pupil has heated rear element to prevent condensation. The eyepiece diopter is adjustable. Anamorphic viewing system available.

Video: Several flicker-reduced CCD video pick-ups may be attached. 100 percent color or black-and-white, 80/20 optical black-and-white video, 80/20 optical/color video. On board 1.5" monitor and 6.5" color LCD monitors available. All video-assist cameras have built-in iris controls.

Viewing Screen: Interchangeable, available in all aspect ratios. Movielite projects the aspect ratio of the ground glass in selectable combinations

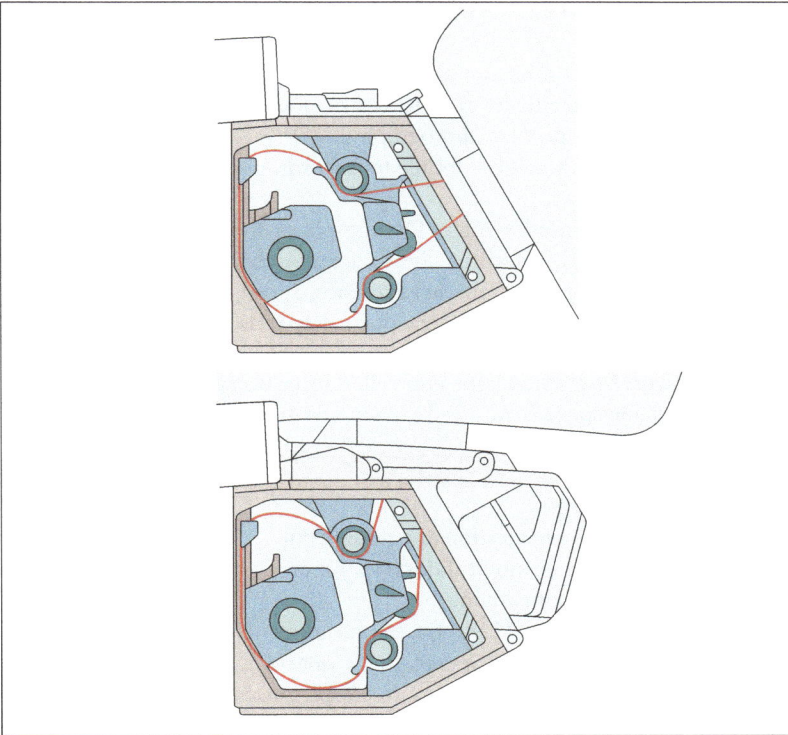

Moviecam Compact Threading Diagrams
Figure 13b & 13c. Top:Slant loading. Bottom: Top Loading. Film takes up emulsion side in.

of all standard formats. Custom Movielite module for Super 35mm and HDTV formats.

Mags: Top- or rear-mounted 500' (152m) and 1,000' (300m). Lightweight composite 400'(122m) and 1,000'(300m) mags. Lightweight 400' (122m) Steadicam mags. All mags have built-in heaters and torque motors. No gear or belt connection to the camera. Each mag has its own mechanical and electronic footage counter with digital display of raw stock with memory. Displacement type mag loading. 2" plastic film cores.

Accessories: Uses Moviecam and Arri baseplates, rods and matte boxes. Arriflex, Chrosziel or Willie Tec follow focus.

Electronic Accessories: Moviespeed attachment plugs into camera right side, and allows speeds to be changed during the shot at programmed rates from 1–50 fps forward and 12–32 fps reverse over user-defined time intervals (set with push-button switches). Fully automatic exposure corrections are made with the iris control servo motor coupled to the lens iris ring.

Running speed can be preset in three-digit accuracy for filming computer screens.

Connections: Synchronization attachment slaves the camera motor to an external pulse for flicker-free generator-powered HMI shooting, filming monitors, or process photography.

Time code plug-in TC-Module for recording AatonCode on specially equipped cameras.

Illuminated on/off switch. TV line phase shifter for synchronizing film with any TV monitor. Sync in and sync out. Cinematography Electronics makes the Compact Precision Speed Plus for the Moviecam Compact. Allows Arri accessory ports. Expands frame rate range from 2–50.999 fps. Also single frame feature.

Motors, Power: Microprocessor-controlled (quartz crystal accuracy) motor with variable speed from 12–32 fps in one-frame increments. 24V DC

Moviecam SL

Weight: 8.25 lbs/3.7kg.

Movement: Dual pin registration and double pull-down pins. The movement slides back for easy threading. Loop adjustment.

FPS: Variable speed from 12–40 fps in one-frame increments. All speeds operate with quartz crystal accuracy. Setting camera to 43 fps causes camera to run 23 fps. Setting camera to run at 49 fps causes camera to run at 29 fps.

Aperture: Full aperture .980" x .735" (24.89mm x 18.67mm).

Aperture Plates available in all 35mm aspect ratios and easily interchangeable. PL lens mount can be oriented for Academy center or full aperture center. Mattes and masks available by special order at Clairmont Cameras.

Displays: Illuminated on/off switch. Frame speed preset buttons. Digital counters for frame rate. Sync in and sync out. Dust check knob. Footage counters on magazines. Shutter angles indicated on shutter.

Lens: PL mount. Regular and Super 35mm.

Shutter: 180°, variable to 22.5°. Calibrated in segments with positive locks at 45°, 90°, 120°, 144° and 172.8°. Mirror stops automatically in viewing position.

Viewfinder: Reflex Viewfinder, 6.1X magnification. 3-position filter wheel (clear, blocked and ND.6). Reflex viewfinder rotates 360° while maintaining an upright image. A 12" viewfinder extension with built-in 2.4X magnification zoom available only at Clairmont. 9.22mm exit pupil has heated rear element to prevent condensation. Eyepiece diopter is adjustable. Anamorphic viewing system also available only at Clairmont.

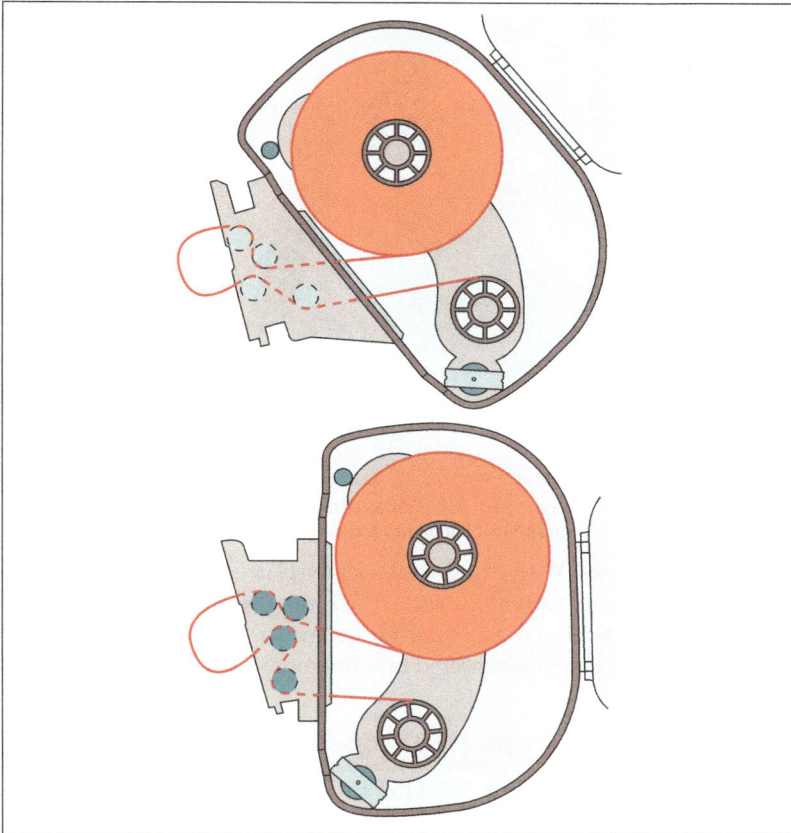

Moviecam SL Magazine Diagrams
Figure 14a & 14b. Active displacement magazines in shoulder-hold and
Steadicam configurations. Film takes up emulsion side in.

Video: Flicker-free CCD video pick-ups. 100 percent color or black-and-white, 80/20 optical black-and-white video. CEI color video.

Viewing Screen: Interchangeable ground glasses in all aspect ratios.

Mags: 400' (122m) lightweight. Rear mounted. All magazines have built-in heaters and torque motors. Electronic footage counter. 400' (122m) lightweight Steadimag with vertical displacement to maintain center of gravity. Moviecam SL is designed to accept magazines from the Moviecam Compact with a special adapter. Specialized magazines for Steadicam.

Magazine Loading: Displacement type. 2" plastic film cores.

Accessories: Uses Moviecam Compact and Arri bridge plates and follow focus units.

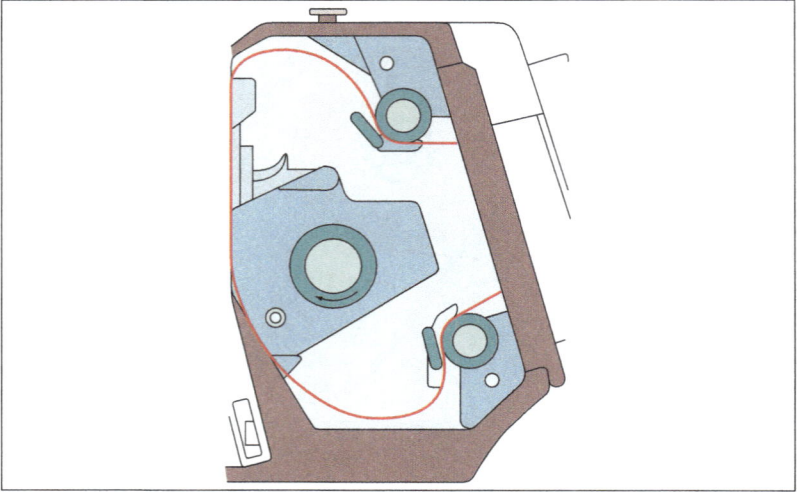

Moviecam SL Threading Diagram
Figure 14c. Film takes up emulsion side in.

Optical Accessories: With of a special adapter plate, all viewfinder systems of the Moviecam Compact may be used with the Moviecam SL, including video systems and the Movielite system.

Motors, Power: Camera is powered by a microprocessor-controlled motor. 24V DC.

Moviecam Super America MK 2

Weight: 29 lbs./13.2 kg with 500' (152 m) of film and 50mm lens.

Movement: Same as Moviecam SL.

FPS: Variable speed from 12–32 fps in one-frame increments. All speeds operate with quartz crystal accuracy.

Aperture: .980"x.735" (24.89mm x 18.67mm). Aperture plate adjustable for full aperture or Academy centered. Easily interchangeable. Mattes and masks available at Clairmont by special order.

dB: 20dB(A).

Displays: Footage and frame rate digital display forward and reverse. Illuminated on/off switch. Frame speed preset buttons. Digital counters for frame rate. Flashing control display indicates incorrect operation or buckle trips. Digital display for forward and reverse. Shutter angle is displayed directly on the shutter via engraved marks. TV line phase shifter for synchronizing film with any TV monitor. Sync in and sync out. Dust check button.

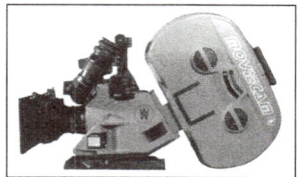

Lens: BNCR and PL mounts.

Shutter: 180°, variable to 45°. Calibrated in segments with positive locks at 45°, 90°, 120°, 144° and 172.8 °. Mirror stops automatically in viewing position.

Viewfinder: Reflex viewfinder (same as SL.)

Video: CCD black-and-white or color video pick-ups, flicker reduced at 24/25 fps, which can easily be plugged into the camera. 1.5" black-and-white onboard monitor or 6.50" CCD color onboard monitor. Iris control for the video system.

Viewing Screen: Interchangeable ground glasses available in all aspect ratios.

Mags: Displacement, rear mounted 500' (152m) and 1,000' (300m) feet. Can be top mounted by using an adapter. All magazines have built-in heaters and torque motors for FWD and REV operation. Each magazine has its own mechanical and electronic footage counter with digital display of raw stock with memory. Additional manual take-up controls. 2" plastic cores.

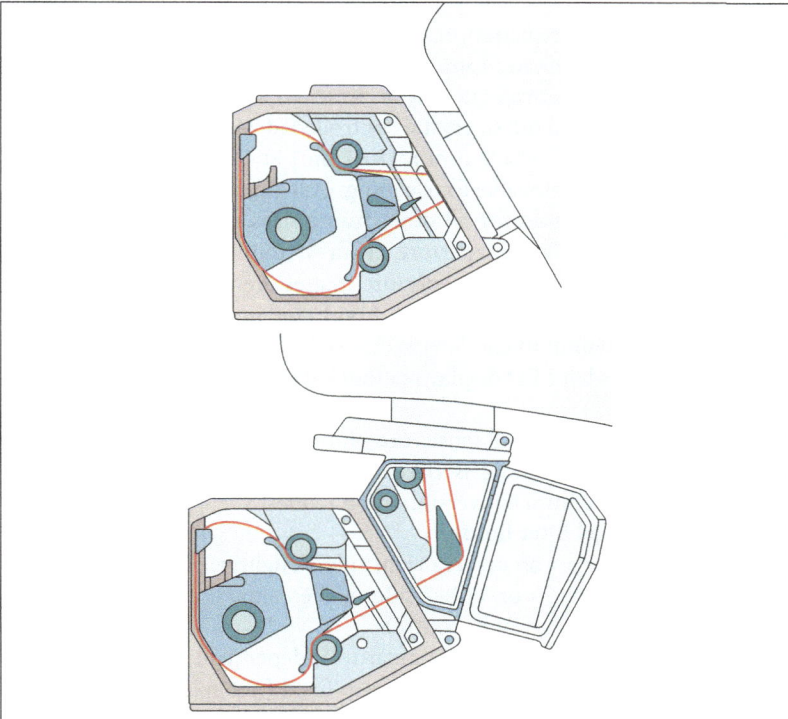

Moviecam Super America MK2 Threading Diagram
Figure 15a & 15b. Top: Slant loading loop adjustment. Bottom: Top loading.
Film takes up emulsion side in.

Accessories: Uses Arriflex bridge plates and follow focus units. Right- and left-hand grips. Carry handles.

Electronic Accessories: Moviespeed and Synchronization attachments — see Movicam Compact.

Connections: Computer diagnosis digitally displays by number any malfunctioning circuit boards. Plug-in boards easily interchangeable in the field. Digiclapper: Built-in automatic slate optically prints dialed scene and take number onto the film.

Power: 24V DC.

Panavision GII Golden Panaflex (PFX-GII)

Notes: Very similar to the Platinum Panaflex. Incorporates most of the features and operates with most of the accessories listed for that camera.

Weight: 24.4 lbs/11.08 kg (body with short eyepiece).

Movement: Dual pin registration, double pulldown claws. Pitch and stroke controls for optimizing camera quietness. 4-perf movement standard, 3-perf available. Movement may be removed for servicing.

FPS: 4–34 fps (forward only), crystal controlled at 24, 25, 29.97, and 30 fps.

Aperture: .980" x .735" (24.89mm x 18.67mm) Style C (SMPTE 59-1998). Aperture Plate removable for cleaning. Full-frame aperture is standard, aperture mattes used for all other frame sizes. A special perforation-locating pin above the aperture ensures trouble-free and rapid film threading. Interchangeable aperture mattes are available for academy, anamorphic, Super 35mm, 1.85:1, 1.66:1, and any other.

dB: Under 24dB with film and lens, measured 3' from the image plane.

Displays: Camera-left LED display readout with footage, film speed and low battery.

Lens: Panavision mount. All lenses are pinned to ensure proper rotational orientation. (Note: This is particularly important with anamorphic lenses.) Super 35mm conversion upon request.

Behind-the-lens gel filter holder.

Iris-rod support on camera right side. A lightweight modular follow focus control works on either side of the camera; optional electronic remote focus and aperture controls.

Shutter: Reflex rotating mirror standard—independent of the focal-pane shutter. Interchangeable, semisilvered, fixed (not spinning) reflex mirror (pellicle) for flicker-free viewing upon request. Focal-plane shutter, infinitely variable and adjustable in-shot. Maximum opening 200°, minimum 50°, with adjustable maximum and minimum opening stops.

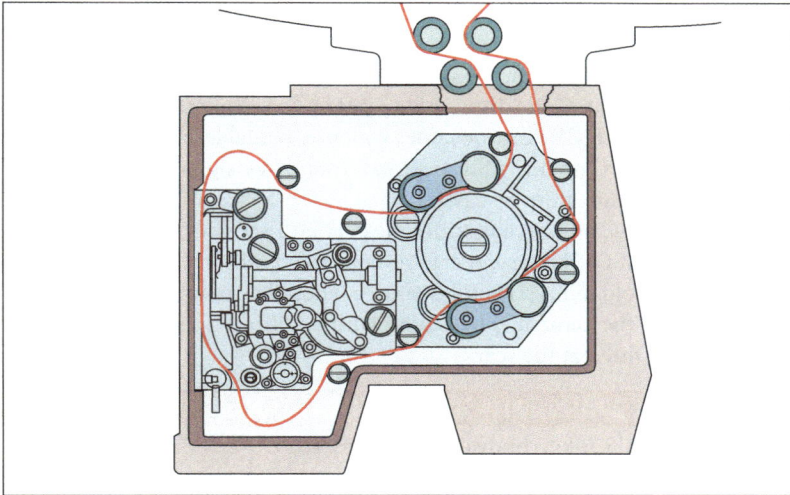

Panavision GII Golden Panaflex Threading Diagram
Figure 16. Film takes up emulsion side out.

Adjustable for synchronization with monitors, etc. Manual and electronic remote-control units.

Viewfinder: High-magnification, orientable viewfinder tube gives a constantly upright image through 360°. Short, intermediate and long viewfinder tubes available. Optical magnifier for critical focusing, deanamorphoser, contrast viewing filter and lightproof shutter. Ocular adjustment with marker bezel to note individual settings. A built-in "Panaclear" eyepiece heater ensures mist-free viewing. Entire optical viewfinder system may be removed and replaced with a video viewfinder display for lightweight camera configuration (e.g., for Steadicam, crane, and remote camera usage). An eyepiece diopter to suit the operator's eyesight can be provided on request.

Video: CCD video systems available in black-and-white or color.

Viewing Screen: Interchangeable ground glasses with any marking or combination of markings. "Panaglow" illuminated reticle system with brightness control is standard. Ground glasses with finer or coarser texture available on request. Provision for a cut frame to be placed in the viewfinder system for optical image matching. Frame cutters available to suit negative or positive perforations.

Mags: Top or rear mounted displacement magazines. 250' (76.2m), 500' (152m), 1,000' (300m), and 2,000' (610m) magazines all available. All can be used on the top of the camera or at the rear (for good balance when handholding). 2,000' (610mm) magazines can be used in the top position only. 3" plastic core required. All others 2".

Electronic Accessories: Special sync boxes available to synchronize the camera with computers, video signals and process projectors in shutter phase synchronization.

Connections: AatonCode time code system (on request) encodes every frame with a SMPTE time code, which is readable by both computer and human. Camera will accept external drive signals via the 10-pin accessory connector.

Motors, Power: Camera, magazines, heaters and accessories all operate off a single 24V DC battery. A crystal-controlled motor drives the system.

Misc: Hand-Holdability: Handles and a shoulder rest provided. When handheld, the camera is best used with a 500' (152m) or 250' (76.2m) magazine fitted at the rear.

Panavision Millenium XL (PFXMXL), XL2

Weight: 11.8 lbs/5.36kg. (body only) 23.6 lbs/10.76 kg (Steadicam configuration: body, 400' (122m) mag w/film, Steadicam plates, 4x5 matte box, lightweight zoom lens).

27.8 lbs/12.6 kg (handheld configuration, all of above plus handheld viewfinder, shoulder pad and right handgrip).

Movement: Dual pin registration, double pull-down claws. Pitch and stroke controls for optimizing camera quietness. 4-perf movement standard, 3-perf available. Movement may be removed for servicing. Special coatings allow for less frequent lubrication.

FPS: *XL:* 3–40 fps. Forward only Crystal speeds selected in $\frac{1}{1000}$th of a frame increments

XL2: 3–50 fps. Forward only. Crystal speeds selected in $\frac{1}{1000}$th of a frame increments.

Aperture: .980" x .735" (24.89mm x 18.67mm) Style C (SMPTE 59-1998).

Aperture Plate removable for cleaning. Full-frame aperture standard, aperture mattes used for all other frame sizes. A special perforation-locating pin above the aperture ensures trouble-free and rapid film threading.

dB: Under 23dB(A) with film and lens, measured 3' from the image plane.

Displays: Pivoting and removable dual-sided LED digital display showing speed, film footage, shutter angle. Rear control panel for speed and shutter setting with full display and connector for included remote speed/shutter controller.

Lens: Panavision titanium positive clamp lens mount. Super 35mm conversion upon request. Camera right iris-rod support supplied.

Behind-the-lens gel filter holder.

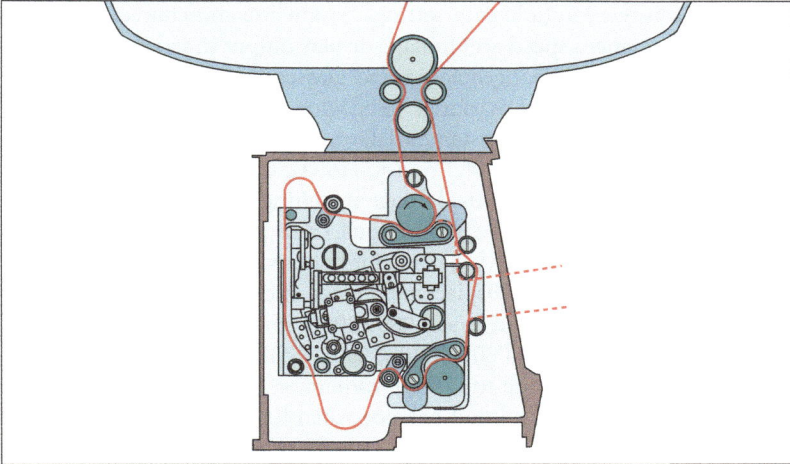

Panavision Millenium XL Threading Diagram
Figure 17. Film takes up emulsion side out.

Shutter: Reflex spinning mirror. Focal plane shutter, infinitely variable and adjustable in-shot, 11.2°–180°; with adjustable maximum and minimum opening stops. Digital display confirms adjustments in $\frac{1}{10}$th-degree increments. System is adjustable for synchronization with monitors, etc. Manual and electronic remote control units.

Viewfinder: Reflex viewfinder detaches for quick conversion to handheld, Steadicam or studio mode. A 5" LCD video monitor can replace the optical viewfinder, often used for handheld. Left- or right-eyed handheld eyepiece. Utilizes Millennium studio viewfinder system, including the telescoping extension eyepiece. Panaglow.

Viewfinder tube is orientable and gives a constantly upright image through 360°. Short and modular-length viewfinder tubes are available. Modular tube can telescope over 3" for optimum viewing position. System incorporates an optical magnifier for critical focusing, a de-anamorphoser, a contrast viewing filter and a lightproof shutter. Wide-range ocular adjustment with marker bezel to note individual settings. A built-in "Panaclear" eyepiece heater ensures mist-free viewing. Entire optical viewfinder system may be easily removed without tools for video viewfinder display for lightweight camera configuration (e.g., for Panaglide, Steadicam, Louma or remote camera usage). An eyepiece diopter to suit the operator's eyesight can be provided on request.

Video: Integrated Color Video Assist, flicker-free at all camera speeds. Internal iris for exposure control. Selectable neutral density filter. Freeze and compare picture modes. Auto color balance or two preset color

temperatures. Multiple gain settings. Frameline and character generator. Film camera speed and footage display output in video display.

Viewing Screen: Interchangeable ground glasses available with any marking or combination of markings. "Panaglow" illuminated reticle system
with brightness control is standard. Ground glasses with finer or coarser
texture available on request. Provision for a cut frame to be placed in the
viewfinder system for optical image matching. Frame cutters available
to suit negative or positive perforations. Clear format screen can replace
ground glass in first viewing plane for better video image.

Mags: Top or rear mounted displacement magazines. Brushless motor driven
200' (76.2m), 400' (122m) and 1,000' (300m) magazines. Traditional 250'
(83m), 500' (152m), 1,000' (300m), 2,000' (610m) magazines available.
All can be used on the top of the camera,or at the rear for minimum
camera height and for good balance when handholding (2,000' magazines can be used in the top position only). 2" plastic cores required, 3"
for 2,000' (610m).

Accessories: Internal servo motor controls electronics for focus, T-stop and
zoom. Wired or wireless remote control. Iris rod bracket with 24V DC
power connectors. Separate remote control for timed speed shutter
compensated shots. Digital Link Smart Shutter controller for speed-iris
and/or shutter ramps, also depth of field shift. Sync box to synchronize
the camera with computers, video signals and projectors for shutter
phase synchronization.

Environmental Protection Equipment: Same as Panavision GII.

Camera Support Equipment: Same as Panavision GII.

Hand-Holdability: Handles and a shoulder rest provided for handholding
the camera. In this configuration, camera is best used with a 200', 250',
400' or 500' magazine fitted at the rear.

Motors, Power: Camera, magazines, heaters and accessories all operate off
a single 24V battery. Separate (dual) brushless drive motors for shutter
and movement, easily retimed for effects. Single variable shutter motor
for ramp functions.

Panavision Millenium (PFX-M)

Weight: 17.5 lbs/7.95 kg. (body only).
29.12 lbs/13.23 kg (Steadicam configuration:
body, 400' (122m) mag w/film, Steadicam
plates, 4"x5.650" clip on matte box, lightweight
zoom lens).
34.2 lbs/15.5 kg (handheld configuration, all of
above plus: focus tube, short eyepiece).

Movement: Same as Milleninium XL.

FPS: 3–50 fps (forward and reverse), crystal controlled at all speeds in $\frac{1}{1000}$th of a second increments.

Aperture: .980" x .735" (24.89mm x 18.67mm) Style C (SMPTE 59-1998). Aperture Plate removable for cleaning. Full-frame aperture is standard; aperture mattes used for all other frame sizes. A special perforation-locating pin above the aperture ensures trouble-free and rapid film threading.

dB: Under 19dB(A) with film and lens, measured 3' from the image plane.

Displays: Pivoting and removable dual-sided LED digital display showing speed, film footage, shutter angle. Additional status indicator and speed/footage display on operator side. Rear control panel for speed and shutter setting with full display and connector for included remote speed/shutter controller.

Lens: Panavision positive clamp lens mount. Super 35mm conversion upon request. Iris-rod support supplied. Lens Controls same as Millenium XL. Behind-the-lens gel filter holder.

Shutter: Same as Millennium XL.

Viewfinder: Same as Millennium XL.

Video: Color video, flicker-free at all camera speeds. Internal iris for exposure control. Clear format replaces the traditional ground glass. Approximately 2000ASA. Freeze and compare picture modes. Electronic de-anamorphoser. RGB output for on-set compositing. Auto color balance or two preset color temperatures. Multiple gain settings.

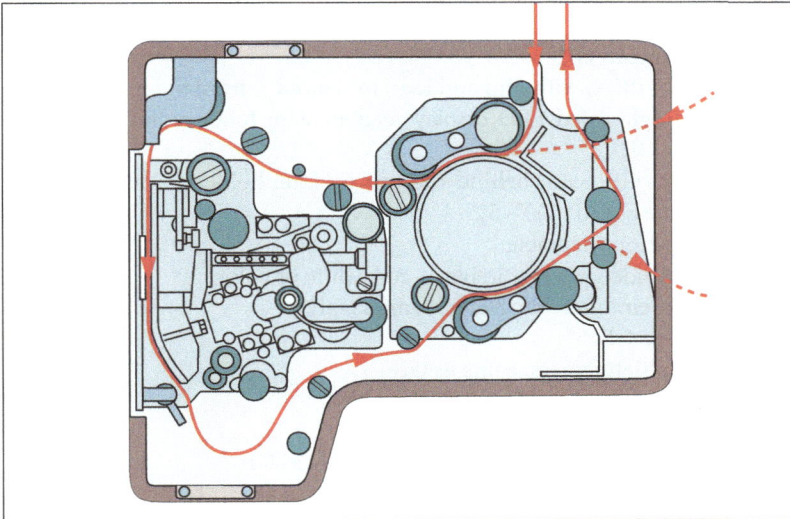

Panavision Millenium Threading Diagram
Figure 18. Film takes up emulsion side out.

Frameline and character generator. Film camera speed and footage display. Outputs to video display. Two composite video outputs, one RGB output.

Viewing Screen: Same as Millennium XL.

Mags: Same as Millennium XL.

Accessories: Same as Millennium XL. Matte Boxes same as GII.

Electronic Accessories: Special sync boxes available to synchronize the camera with computers, video signals and process projectors in shutter phase synchronization.

Additional Accessories: A shutter/speed compensation box comes standard.

Environmental Protection Equipment: Same as GII.

Camera Support Equipment: Same as GII.

Hand-Holdability: Handles and a shoulder-rest are provided for hand-holding the camera. In this configuration camera is best used with a 250' (76.2m), 400',(122m) or 500' (152m) magazine fitted at the rear.

Power: Brushless crystal motor drive. 24V DC.

Panavision Panaflex-X (PFX-X)

Notes: Similar to the GII Golden Panaflex but has a fixed viewfinder system and is not hand-holdable.

Weight: 20.5 lbs/9.31 kg (body only).

Movement: same as GII

FPS: Same as GII: 4–34 fps (forward only), xtal 24, 25, and 29.97.

Aperture: same as GII

dB: Under 24dB(A) with film and lens, measured 3' from the image plane.

Displays: Single-sided LED display readout with footage and film speed. Same as GII

Lens: Same as GII. Same behind-the-lens gel filter holder.

Shutter: Same as GII. 200°–50°

Viewfinder: Nonorientable.

Video: CCD video systems in black-and-white or color.

Viewing Screen: Interchangeable, same as GII

Mags: Same as GII

Accessories: Matte boxes: Same as GII.

Electronic Accessories: Same as GII.

Optical Accessories: Same as GII.

Environmental Protection Equipment: Same as GII.

Camera Support Equipment: Same as GII.

Motors, Power: same as GII (24V DC) and Millenium.

Misc: Camera cannot be handheld.

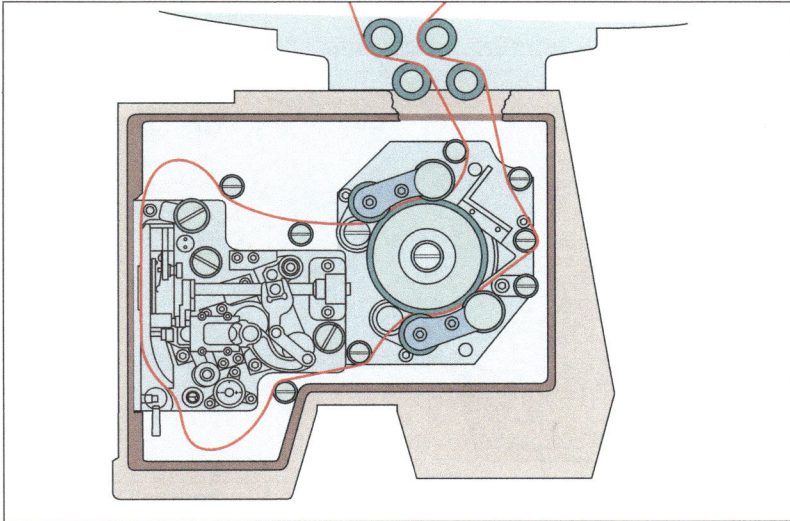

Panavision Panaflex-X Threading Diagram
Figure 19. Film takes up emulsion side out.

Panavision Panaflex Panastar II High-Speed

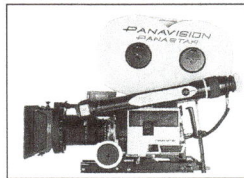

Weight: 24.4 lbs/11.08 kg (body with short eye-piece).

Movement: Dual pin registration. Four pulldown claws. Entire movement may be removed for servicing.

FPS: Camera runs at any speed from 4–120 fps, crystal-controlled at all speeds, and may be adjusted in 1 fps increments. Fwd and rev.

Aperture: .980" x .735" (24.89mm x 18.67mm) Style C (SMPTE 59-1998). Aperture Plate same as Platinum Panaflex.

Displays: Dual-sided LCD display readout with footage, film speed, shutter angle, and time code bits. LED indicators for low battery/film jam/film out/MVMT SW/Mag/RVS.

Lens: Lens mount and lens control information the same as Panavision GII. Behind the lens filter holder.

Shutter: Focal plane shutter with infinitely variable opening and adjustable in-shot. Maximum opening 180°, minimum 45°, with adjustable maximum and minimum opening stops. Digital display allows adjustments in $1/10$th-degree increments. Adjustable for synchronization with monitors, etc. Manual and electronic remote-control units available.

Viewfinder: Reflex. Same as Platinum Panaflex.

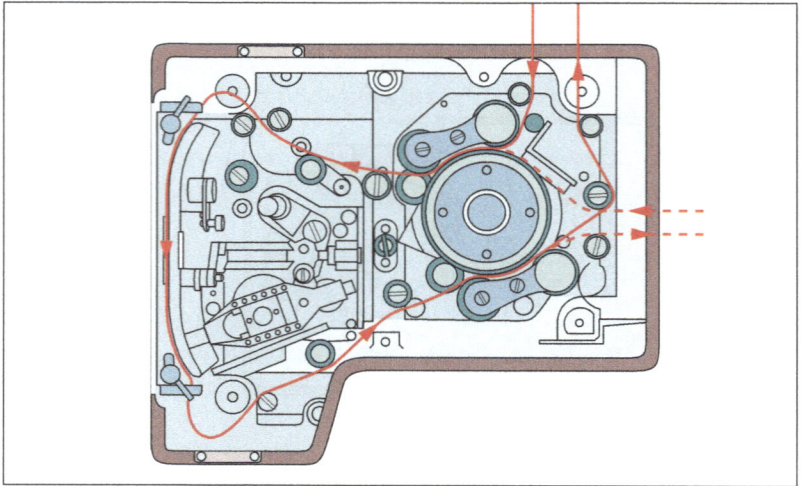

Panavision Panaflex Panastar II High-Speed Threading Diagram
Figure 20a. Film takes up emulsion side out.

Video: Same as Platinum Panaflex.

Viewing Screen: Same as Platinum Panaflex.

Mags: 250'(76.2m) (Note: 250' mag up to 34fps only), 500' (152m) and 1,000' (300m) magazines. Either can be used on the top of the camera or at the rear. 1,000'(300m) reverse-running magazines—film takes up emulsion side *in*.

Film Cores: 2" plastic core required. Note Panastar reverse running-type magazine threading.

Accessories Matte Boxes: Same as Platinum Panaflex.

Optical Accessories: Same as Platinum Panaflex.

Camera Support Equipment: Same as Platinum Panaflex. Handles and a shoulder rest provided.

Connections: The camera will accept external drive signals via the 10-pin accessory connector.

Motors, Power: 24V DC. Batteries same as Platinum Panaflex

Panavision Platinum Panaflex 35mm (PFX-P)

Weight: 24 lbs/10.9 kg (body with short eyepiece).

Movement: Dual pin registration; Double pull-down claws. Pitch and stroke controls for optimizing camera quietness. 4-perf movement standard, 3-perf available. Movement may be removed for servicing.

FPS: 4–36 fps (forward and reverse), crystal-controlled at all speeds and

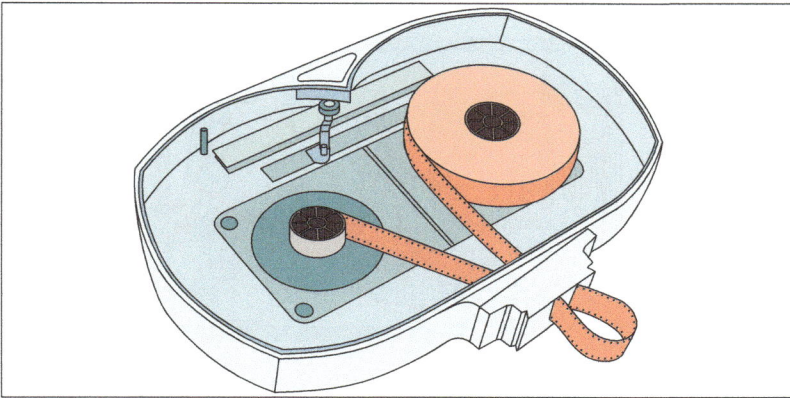

Panastar reverse running type magazine threading
Figure 20b. Film takes up emulsion side in.

adjusted in ¹/₁₀th fps increments.

Aperture: .980" x .735" (24.89mm x 18.67mm) Style C (SMPTE 59-1998).

Aperture Plate: Removable for cleaning. Full-frame aperture is standard, aperture mattes are used for all other frame sizes. A special perforation-locating pin above the aperture ensures trouble-free and rapid film threading.

dB: Under 22dB with film and lens, measured 3' from the image plane.

Displays: Dual-sided LCD display readout with footage, film speed, shutter angle, and time code bits. LED indicators for low battery / low film / film jam/ illegal speed.

Lens: same as Panavision GII. Behind-the-lens gel filter holder.

Shutter: Reflex mirror. Focal plane shutter, infinitely variable and adjustable in-shot. Maximum opening 200°, minimum 50°, with adjustable maximum and minimum opening stops. Digital display allows adjustments in 1/10th-degree increments. Adjustable for synchronization with monitors. Manual and electronic remote-control units.

Viewfinder: Reflex Viewfinder. Same as GII.

Video: Same as GII.

Viewing Screen: Same as GII.

Mags: Same as GII.

Accessories: Matte Boxes same as GII.

Electronic Accessories: Same as GII.

Optical Accessories: Same as GII.

Environmental Protection Equipment: Same as GII.

Camera Support Equipment: Same as GII. Handles and shoulder rest provided for handheld use.

Connections: The camera will accept external drive signals via the 10-pin

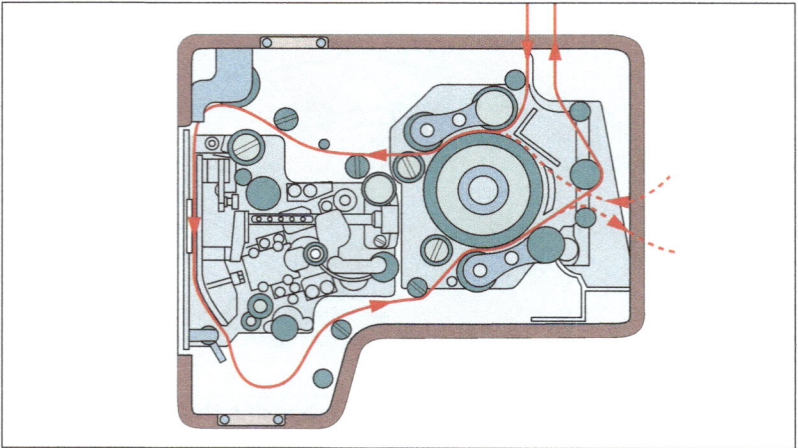

Panavision Platinum Panaflex Threading Diagram
Figure 21a. Film takes up emulsion side out.

accessory connector. AatonCode can be provided on request.

Motors, Power: 24V DC. A crystal-controlled brushless motor drives the system. Batteries: Same as Millennium.

Panavision 35mm Camera Models, Panavision Notes and Accessories

Most cameras in the Panavision system share the following accessories and attributes.

Movement: Dual Pilot pins register in the same perforation holes (immediately below the bottom frameline) as optical printers. This ensures process-plate image steadiness. Entire movement may be removed for servicing.

Lenses: All lenses are pinned to ensure proper rotational orientation. (Note: This is particularly important with anamorphic lenses.)

Panavision supplies a wide range of spherical, anamorphic and specialty lenses, all checked and calibrated by MTF. Primo lenses are all color matched and range from a distortion-free 10mm to 150mm. Primo zoom lenses are equal to Primo lenses in image look and optical performance. All Primo lenses have widely spaced lens focus calibrations and have been especially designed for low veiling glare. Physically long lenses are supplied with adequate-length iris rods for matte box and filter support, ultra-wide-angle lenses are supplied with a suitable sunshade and matte box.

Zoom lenses are supplied with a motor-driven zoom control unit as standard. Iris gears are incorporated into most prime and zoom lenses.

Physically long lenses are supplied with adequate-length iris rods for matte box and filter support, ultra-wide-angle lenses are supplied with a suitable sunshade and matte box.

Lens Control: A lightweight modular follow focus control which can be used from either side of the camera is standard; optional electronic remote focus and aperture controls also available. Zoom lenses supplied with a motordriven zoom control unit as standard. Iris gears incorporated into most prime and zoom lenses.

An eyepiece leveler is supplied with every Panahead to keep the eyepiece position constant while tilting the camera.

Optical Accessories: Front-of-lens optical accessories include an exceptionally wide range of color-control filters, diffusion filters, fog filters, low-contrast filters, black, white and colored nets, full-cover and split diopters, low/high angle inclining prisms.

Matte Boxes: Standard matte box incorporates a sunshade and two 4"x5.650" filters which can be individually slid up and down.

Optional matte box incorporates a sunshade, and two 4"x5.650" filters which can be individually slid up and down.

Special matte boxes incorporating more filter stages, with provision for sliding (motorized if required), rotating and/or tilting and for taking 6.6" square filters optional. Panavision can also supply special sliding diffusers, diopters and image-control filters, to use in matte boxes.

Image Contrast Control: "Panaflasher" light overlay unit is an optional accessory.

Environmental Protection Equipment: All Panaflex cameras and magazines have built-in heaters. Heated covers available to give additional protection to lenses, especially zoom lenses, to keep their operation smooth in intensely cold conditions. Other covers available to pro-

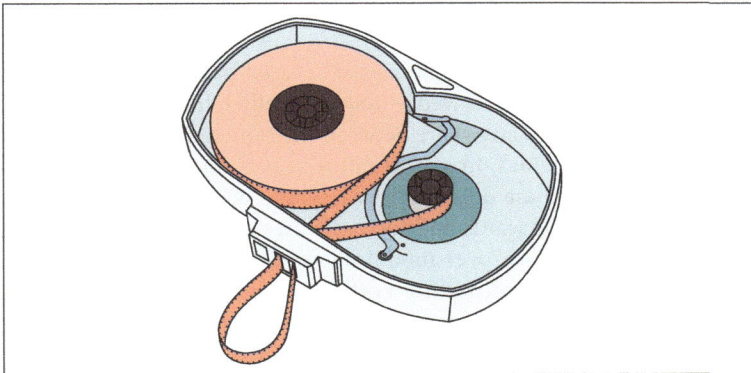

Panavision Film Magazine
Figure 21b. Film takes up emulsion side out.

Panavision 35mm Camera Models				
Camera	Shutter Angles	Frame Rate	dB	Weight
GII Gold	50°-200°	4-34 fps (fwd only) crystal controlled at 24, 25, 29.97	Under 24dB	24.4 lbs/ 11.08 kg (body w/short eyepiece)
Millenium XL	11.2°-180°	3-40 fps (fwd only) crystal controlled at sync speeds	Under 24dB(A)	11.8 lbs/ 5.36 kg (body only)
XL2	Same as XL	3-50 fps (fwd only) crystal controlled at sync speeds	Same as XL	Same as XL
Millennium	11.2°-180°	3-50 fps (fwd & reverse) crystal controlled at sync speeds	Under 19dB(A)	17.5 lbs/ 7.95 kg (body only)
Panaflex-X	50°-200°	4-34 fps (fwd only) crystal controlled at 24, 25, 29.97	Under 24dB(A)	20.5 lbs/ 9.31 kg (body only)
Panastar II	45°-180°	4-120 fps (fwd & reverse) in 1 fps increments		12.5 kg (28 lbs)
Platinum	50°-200°	4-36 fps (fwd & reverse) crystal controlled at sync speeds	Under 22dB(A)	24 lbs/ 10.9 kg (body w/short eyepiece)

tect camera, magazines and lenses from heat, dust, rain and water. Spinning-glass rain deflectors available for use in storm conditions. Autobase available to secure the camera in conditions of vibration, high "g-forces" and other stressful and dangerous conditions. Water box available to protect the camera in shallow water conditions, a hazard box to protect the camera from explosions, collisions and other dangerous situations.

Camera Support Equipment: "Panahead" geared head incorporates a 60° tilt range with a built-in wedge system to allow the operator to select where that range is, anywhere between the camera pointing directly up or directly down, and three gear ratios in both the pan and tilt movements. A sliding base unit enables camera to be attached and detached and to be slid backwards and forwards on the head for optimum balance. "Panatate" turn-over mount allows 360° camera rotation about the lens axis while permitting nodal pan and tilt movements. Nodal adapter available to mount a Panaflex on a Panahead. The normal battery complement is two cased units with built-in chargers. Belt batteries and a newly designed onboard battery for handholding optional.

Photo-Sonics 35mm 4CR

Notes: Reflex rotary prism camera 125–2,500 fps. This is a rotary prism camera and is not pin-registered.

Film Specifications: 35mm B&H perforation .1866" pitch. 1,000' (300m) loads preferable.

Weight: 125 lbs./56.81 kg. with loaded 1,000' (300m) mag, without lens.

Movement: Rotary prism. Continuous film transport. Rotary imaging prism.

FPS: High-speed system: 500–2500 fps in 500-frame intervals. Low-speed system: 250–1,250 fps in 250-frame increments. Special low-speed motor, 125–625 fps available on request.

Aperture: Full-frame 35mm.

Displays: Mechanical footage indicator. Camera ready and power indicators.

Lens: Pentax 6x7 lens mount. 17mm through 165mm Pentax lenses, in addition to zooms and Probe II lenses.

Shutter: Rotary disc, 4C has 72-degree fixed shutter. 36°, 18° or 9° available upon request.

Viewfinder: The 4C utilizes a Jurgens orientable reflex viewfinder system with a behind-the-lens beamsplitter to achieve flickerless reflex viewing. Extension eyepiece with leveling rod.

Video: CEI Color V or III available in NTSC version only.

Viewing Screen: Standard ground glass formats available. Specify when ordering camera package to ensure availability.

Mags: 1000' (300m). Double chamber. 35mm B&H perforation .1866" pitch. Film must be rewound onto dynamically balanced aluminum cores. Twelve cores with each 4CR rental package.

Accessories: Follow Focus: Arri follow focus.

Matte Boxes: 6.6.x6.6 Arri matte box. Heavy-duty tilt plate, high and low

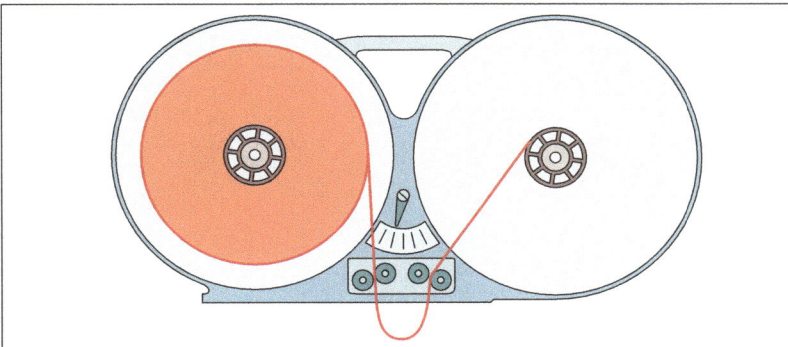

Photo-Sonics 35mm 35-4B/4C magazine
Figure 22a. Film takes up emulsion side in.

hat, flicker meter, 90° angle plate. Raincovers are included with camera package.

Motors, Power: High-speed 208V AC, three phase, 60Hz, Y-connected synchronous speed motor. Surge at maximum frame rate 60 amps (each phase); running 30 amps (each phase). Low-speed 115V AC, single phase, 60Hz, synchronous speed motor. Surge at maximum frame rate: 40 amps; running 20 amps. Power: 208V AC, three phase, Y-connected.

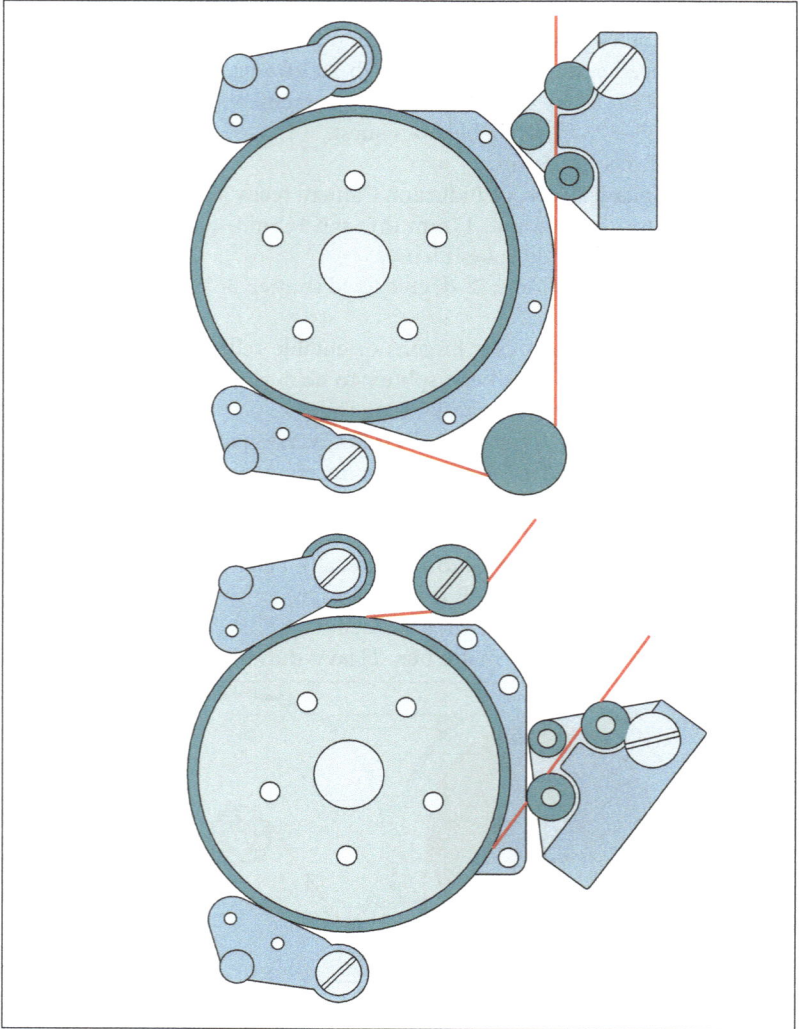

Photo-Sonics 35mm 4CR Threading Diagrams
Figure 22b & 22c. Top: 35 4B. Bottom: 35 4C

Misc: Standard ⅜-16 thread fits most large tripods and heads and may require extension plates on some remote heads.

Photo-Sonics 35mm 4ER

Notes: The 4ER pin registered camera produces solid registration at frame rates from 6–360 fps. Camera is compatible with Unilux strobes (mid-shutter pulse).

Film Specifications: Standard 35mm B&H perforation with .1866" (4.74mm) pitch. 1,000' (300m) loads preferable.

Weight: 125 lbs./56.81 kg with loaded 1,000' (300m) magazine, without lens.

Movement: Intermittent, pin registered. Intermittent with four registration pins, twelve pull-down arms and a vacuum pressure plate to hold the film absolutely stationary and registered during exposure.

FPS: 6–360 fps.

Aperture: Full-frame 35mm. Removable aperture plate.

Displays: Mechanical footage indicator.

Lens: BNCR or Panavision. (Academy centered.)

Shutter: 5° to 120°, adjustable with mechanical indicator.

Viewfinder: The 4ER utilizes a Jurgens/Arriflex reflex, orientable viewfinder system with a behind-the-lens beamsplitter to achieve flickerless reflex viewing. Optional external boresight tool available.

Video: CEI Color V or III availabe in NTSC version only.

Viewing Screen: Most standard ground glasses are available. Specify when ordering camera package to ensure availability.

Mags: 1,000' (300m). Double chamber. Standard plastic 35mm 2" film cores. 35mm B&H perforation .1866" pitch.

Accessories: Environmental Protection Equipment: Same as 4C.

Camera Support Equipment: Same as 4C. Arri follow focus unit with right-hand knob. Zoom Control and Iris Gears available on request.

Electronic Accessories: Optional remote cables, 75' (23m) and 150' (45.7m); remote speed indicator.

Additional Accessories: Extension eyepiece with leveling rod, heavy duty tilt plate, high and low hat, flicker meter, 90-degree angle plate, Panavision lens mount and "L" bracket support adapter with ⅝" support rods, extension eyepiece, follow focus.

Optical Accessories: Various Zeiss T1.3and Nikkor primes, in addition to macro and zoom and Probe II lenses.

Motors, Power: 208V AC, single phase (200V to 250V AC is acceptable). 35 amps surge at 360 fps and 20 amps running. Cannot use batteries. Requires AC power 208V AC single phase.

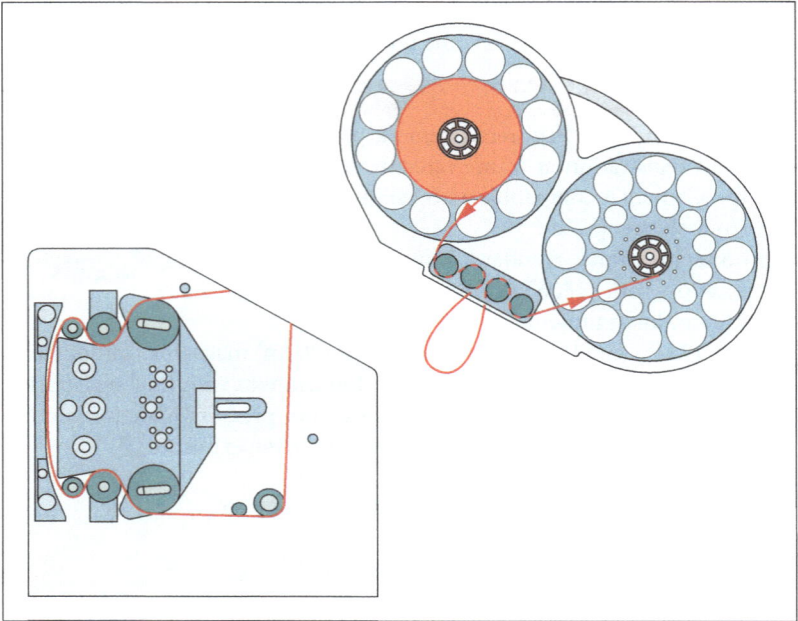

Photo-Sonics 35mm 4E and 4ER Diagrams
Figure 23a & 23b. Film takes up emulsion side out.

Photo-Sonics 35mm 4ML (Reflex and Nonreflex)

Notes: The 4ML reflex is a compact, rugged, pin registered, high-speed camera capable of crystal-controlled filming speeds from 10-200 fps. The 4ML reflex can be configured at only 9" total height with prime lenses and a 400' (122m) magazine. Only 5½" with a 200' (61m) magazine. Compatible with Unilux strobe lighting (midshutter pulse).

Standard B&H perforation .1866" (4.74mm) pitch.

Weight: 28lbs./12.72kg with loaded 400' (122m) mag, without lens.

Movement: Intermittent with two registrations pins and four pulldown arms.

FPS: 10–200 fps.

Aperture: .745" x .995" (18.92mm x 25.27mm). Academy centered.

Displays: Digital readout plate w/accessory port.

Lens: Lens Mount: BNCR, Panavision, Nikon, PL (Warning: Depth restriction with certain lenses—restricted to certain zooms and longer primes.) Various Nikkor lenses (extension tube set for close-focus available), Probe II lens

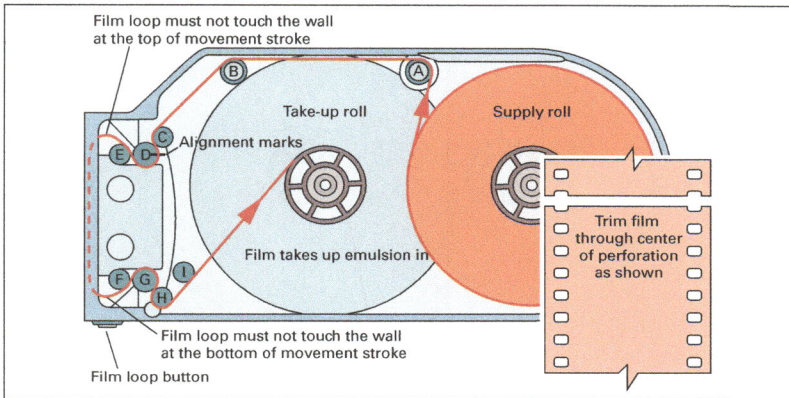

Photo-Sonics 35mm 4ML Magazine Diagram
Figure 24. Film takes up emulsion side in.

Shutter: 144° maximum, adjustable to 72°, 36°, 18°, and 9°.

Viewfinder: A behind-the-lens beamsplitter block provides flickerless reflex viewing. Extension eyepiece. External Viewfinder: Nonreflex model utilizes a boresight tool.

Video: CEI Color V or III available in NTSC version only.

Viewing Screen: TV/Academy/1:1.85 combo standard. Specify ahead for different ground glass.

Mags: 200' (61m) and 400' (122m) displacement, snap-on magazines for quick reloading. Single chamber with daylight cover. 2" film cores.

Accessories: Clamp-on 4x4 two-stage Arri Studio matte box.

Follow Focus: Arri follow focus unit with right-hand knob.

Electronic Accessories: Digital readout plate with accessory port, crystal-controlled filming speeds from 10–200 fps, Unilux strobe lighting (mid-shutter pulse).

Additional Accessories: Compatible with Panavision and Arri lens accessories.

Environmental Protection Equipment: Splash housings depth-rated 12' (3.6m)–15' (4.6m), rain covers.

Power: 28V DC. 12 amps surge, 7 amps running.

Ultracam

Weight: 31 lbs./14.06 kg with 400' (122m) of film and 50mm lens.

Movement: Single claw, dual registration pin. Automatic film location by spring-loaded pin. Pitch adjustment compensated for 3X more change in stroke length at end of stroke

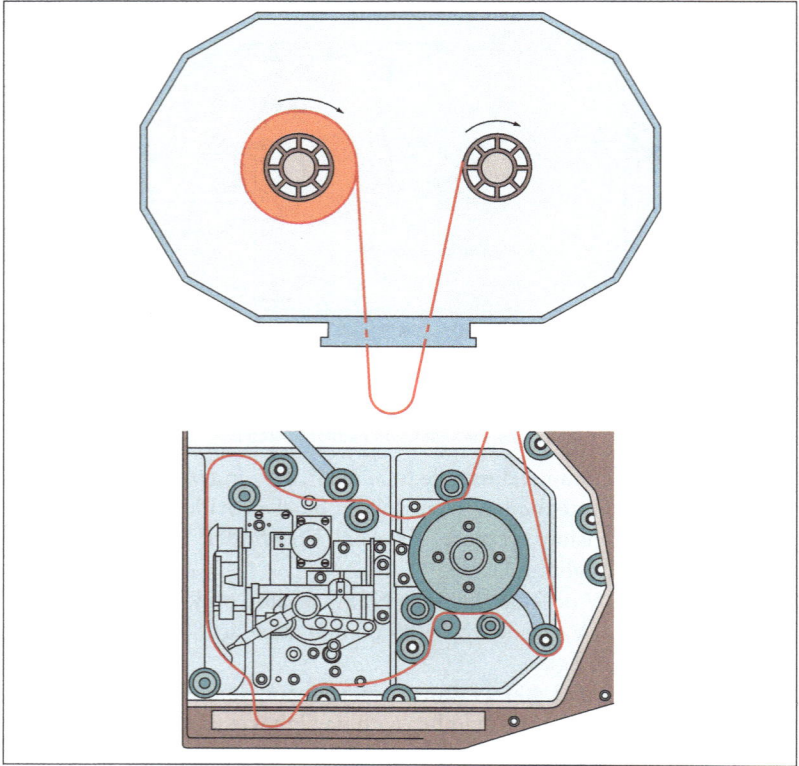

Ultracam Magazine and Threading Diagrams
Figure 25a & 25b. Film takes up emulsion side in.

than at start. Entire movement can be removed for cleaning; coupling is keyed for correct alignment on replacement.

FPS: 8, 12, 16, 18, 20, 24, 25, 30 and 32 fps and by a 10V P-P external pulse of 60X frame rate.

Aperture: Full aperture .985" x .736" (25.02mm x 18.69mm). Aperture plate removes easily for cleaning and lubrication.

dB: Sound level 20 +1dB at 3' with film and 50mm lens.

Displays: Built-in follow focus. LED counter feet/meters may be preset to any reading; battery-operated memory.

Lens: Lens Mount: SBNCR.

Shutter: Focal plane 175° on same shaft with mirror. Rotating, two-blade, half-speed mirror. 41°30' to permit short back-focus lenses.

Viewfinder: Reflex finder, eyepiece rotates 360° using prism to provide upright image. Exit pupil 10mm. 6X to 9X true zoom magnification. Anamorphic correction available. Internal diopter accommodation.

Right- or left-eye operation. Video assist on bayonet mount.

Viewing Screen: Interchangeable.

Mags: 500' (152m) and 1,000' (300m) displacement. Built-in torque motor and electric brake. Either size mounts on camera top or rear.

Accessories: Quick-release balance plate. Swing-away matte box; rotating feature accepts various size filters with two stationary stages and two rotating stages.

Motors, Power: Internal 28V DC optically encoded. Crystal sync +15 ppm over 0° to 130° F. range 50/60Hz and frame rate output pulse.

16MM

Aaton A Minima (Super 16 only)

Weight: 5 lbs./2kg with onboard battery and film.

Movement: single coplanar claw movement and lateral pressure plate ensure vertical and lateral steadiness to ¹⁄₂₀₀₀th of image dimensions. Hair-free gate.

FPS: 1–32 fps crystal speed control, on internal lithium batteries. Runs 50 fps with external NiMH or NiCd battery.

Aperture: 1.66 (7.44mm x 12.4mm).

Aperture Plate: Super 16 only. Super 16-centered lens port and viewfinder.

dB: 29dB ±½dB.

Displays: Illuminated readout displays speed, footage (in feet and meters), ASA, time code, video sync speed, intervalometer setting program.

Lens: Nikon and PL, mount

Shutter: 172.8° spinning reflex mirror shutter.

Viewfinder: DistantEye viewfinder. Removing eye from eyecup doesn't fog the running film.

Video: Black-and-white LCD video-assist.

Viewing Screen: Fiber optic 9X magnification (fixed). Aspect ratio markings: 1.66:1 Super16/1.78:1 16x9 (HDTV) 14x9/1.85:1 and 4:3/1.33:1 (Standard 16 frame indicator). Standard 16 (1.33:1) extraction possible at telecine or printing, centered on Super or Standard frame.

Mags: 200' (61m) coaxial quick-change magazines, "A" wound rolls in Aaton's "flexible" daylight spools. Requires Kodak A-Minima spools. Magazine can be loaded in subdued light without edge fogging using custom Kodak film loads. Requires Kodak A-Minima spools. Cannot use standard metallic 200' (61m) spools or 400' (122m) rolls.

Accessories: Time recording by XTRprod-compatible AatonCode-II matrices, accurate to ¼ of a frame. The camera can be used as a master clock to other Aaton/ASCII devices. Uses 15mm minirods. Chrosziel sunshades and matte boxes.

Sound Blimp: Leather sound barney.

Connections: Lemo6 (accessories), Lemo6 (in base to accept powerbase), Lemo5 (time code). Powerbase provides film/video sync, two Lemo6 connectors, one Lemo2 and one XLR 4.

Motors, Power: Batteries, onboard lithium battery. Four disposable 3V cells (CR17345). Also accepts 10-14V NiMH or NiCd batteries, or any 12V power source with cable.

Tri-phase brushless motor. 400mA with film, 550mA with film and video assist. Built-in intervalometer.

Misc: Built-In incident light meter: via rear dome (not TTL) T-stop and speed differential T-stop. Works with DV-size tripods, Steadicam mini.

Aaton XTRprod

Weight: 13 lbs./6kg with 400' (122m) load, 18 lbs/8.5 kg with 800' (244m) load, and 12V onboard battery.

Movement: Coplanar single claw movement with lateral pressure plate that ensures vertical and lateral steadiness to ½₀₀₀th of image dimensions. Hair-free gate.

FPS: 18 sync speeds including 23.98, 24, 29.97, 30, 48 and 75 fps and crystal-controlled adjustable speeds from 3–75 fps in 0.001 increments via a minijog. Internal phase shift control for TV bar elimination.

Aperture: 1.66. Optical center is switchable for Super 16 and standard 16mm operation.

dB: 20dB -1/+2.

Displays: Illuminated LCD display, speed selection, elapsed footage, remaining footage, ISO selection, battery voltage timer and date. Pre-end and end of film warning, mag ID, full time code readout. Memo-mag allows magnetic recognition by the camera body of seven different magazines. Counter provides LCD display of remaining footage for short-end load or multi-emulsion shoot.

Lens: Interchangeable hard fronts: Arri PL as standard, Aaton, Panavision. Quick centering of lens axis for 16mm to Super 16 conversion formats. Field-convertible quick centering of lens axis, viewfinder and CCD target between formats.

Shutter: Reflex mirror shutter is user adjustable: 180°, 172.8°, 150° for 25 fps under 60Hz lighting, 144°, 135°, 90°, 60°, 45°, 30°, 15°.

Viewfinder: Reflex from shutter. Fiber-optic imaging finder field is 120 percent of standard 16mm frame. Swiveling auto-erect image eyepiece with 10X magnification. 20cm or 40cm extensions and left-eye extender available.

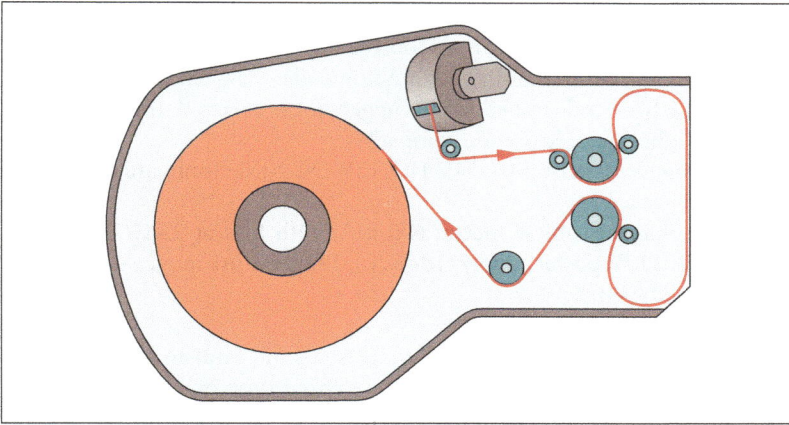

Aaton XTRprod Magazine Diagram
Figure 26. Film takes up emulsion side in.

Field interchangeable standard 16mm/Super16 ground glass with Aatonite markings available. Built-in light meter display in viewfinder, also indicates low battery, out of sync and pre-end and end of film warnings.

Video: Integrated high-definition CCD color video assist. NTSC flicker-free at all camera speeds. Black-and-white video tap available. Film camera time code, footage, camera run status are inserted in both windows and VITC lines. Built-in frameline generator.

Viewing Screen: Quick-release, interchangeable fiber-optic screen available in 1.37, 1.66, 1.78 (16:9) and 1.85 aspect ratios and combinations thereof. Aatonite illuminated markings.

Mags: 400' (122m) and 800' (244m) Coaxial instant preloaded magazine, magnetic drive, feed chamber loaded in dark and loop threaded in daylight. 14- to 15-perf loop length. Twistless film threading and hair-free gate eliminates pressure marks and emulsion pile-up. No time code-related parts to clean. Reads in feet and meters. Magnetically driven take-up with electronic and mechanical counters. Memo-mag indices for magazine ID recognition. Standard 2" plastic core for 400' (122m) mag, 3" plastic core required for 800' (244m) mag.

Accessories: Chrosziel follow focus and matteboxes. Leather sound barney. 15mm screw-in front rods. 15mm and 19mm bridgeplate compatible. Lightweight wide-format, swing-away matte box: two 4" x 5.6" and one 138mm rotating stages. Also accommodates Panavision mattes. Lightweight follow-focus system.

HydroFlex deepwater housing, ScubaCam splashbag.

Eshot intervalometer, CE F/V synchronizer and speed control, and Preston speed aperture computer.

Connections: Electronic Accessories: Inputs; Amph9 (video sync), Lemo6 (power zoom), Lemo8 (phase controllers), Lemo5 (SMPTE and ASCII time code). Time recording with AatonCode: Man-readable figures and SMPTE time code imbedded in rugged dot matrixes ½-frame accuracy over eight hours. Key-code compatible.

Motors, Power: Batteries: 10–14V DC. 12V DC NiMH onboard or external source via cable.

Tri-phase brushless motor. 600 mA, with film at 25°C/77°F under standard 12V power supply (10–12V). Temperature range: -20°C / +4°F to +40°C / +10°F.

Models: XTRplus (BiPhase)

24, 25, 30 fps plus 6–54 fps in 12 steps, no built-in TV bar elimi-nator on XTRplus. No backlight or elapsed time on XTRplus display. Memo-mag allows magnetic recognition by camera of three different magazines. Bottom of camera to lens optical axis distance is 109.2mm to make XTRplus compatible with 35mm camera accessories.

Shutter: True 180-degree front surface mirror essential for 60Hz HMI and video-monitor roll-bar elimination. Stops in viewing position. May be inched for aperture inspection.

LTR Model

Superceded by the XTRs, LTRs are differentiated by the magazine me-chanical drive, no LCD counter and no CCD video-assist compatibility.

Ikonoskop A-Cam SP-16

Notes: Possibly the smallest, lightest MOS Super 16 camera, for the price of a DV camera: About the size of the old GSAP, much lighter, and uses readily available 100' daylight spools.

Weight: 3.3 lbs/1.5kg with lens, internal battery and film.

Movement: Single transport claw

FPS: 6, 10, 12.5, 18, 20, 24, 25, 30, 36, 37, 37.5; timelapse from 1 fps to 1 frame in 24 hours.

Aperture: Super 16

Aperture Plate: Super 16 only. Super 16-centered lens port and viewfinder.

Displays: Backlit LCD main readout with three control buttons shows bat-tery status, film exposed, frame rate and time-lapse mode.

Lens: C mount. Comes with Kinoptik 9mm f/1.5.

Shutter: 160°

Viewfinder: Nonreflex, magnetically-attached, parallel-mounted ocular.

Loads: 100' (30.5 m) daylight spools.

Accessories: ¼" x 20 and ⅜" x 16 tripod mounting threads.

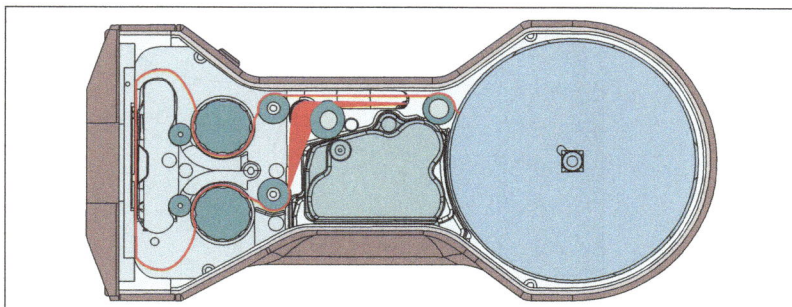

Ikonoskop A-Cam SP-16 Magazine Diagram
Figure 27. Film takes up emulsion side in.

Connections: Main power switch. Start/stop button. Connector for charger and external 12V DC power (runs on 10.8-15 V DC). Requires external power for speeds of 30 and 37.5 fps. Remote on/off connector.

Power: Batteries: Camera comes with single-use lithium battery pack. 1400 mAh, 70 g. Runs 25 rolls at 25 fps at 20°C. A charger or an external power supply must *never* be connected to the camera when using a single-use lithium battery pack.

Optional internal rechargeable Li-Ion battery, 480mAh, 46g, Runs 25 rolls at 25 fps at 20°C. Battery is located under the battery compartment cover on the left side of the camera.

Arriflex 16 BL

Weight: 16.3 lbs./7.39 kg, camera, 400' (122m) magazine and lens

Movement: Pin registered.

FPS: 5–50 fps, forward or reverse, when used with appropriate motor and speed controls.

Aperture: .405" x.295" (10.3mm x 7.5mm). Standard 16mm.

dB: 30dB.

Displays: Tachometer and footage counter.

Lens: Lens Mount: Steel Arri Bayonet mount (lens housings required to maintain minimal camera operating sound levels). All Arriflex Standard or bayonet-mount lenses that cover the 16mm format can be used with lens housings. Standard zoom and telephoto lenses should be used with the bridgeplate support system. Lenses: Fixed focal length Standard and Zeiss Superspeed lenses. Zeiss, Angenieux and Cooke zoom lenses. Some wide-angle lenses may hit shutter.

Shutter: Rotating mirror-shutter system with fixed 180-degree opening ($\frac{1}{48}$th of a second at 24 fps).

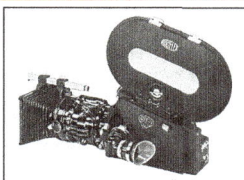

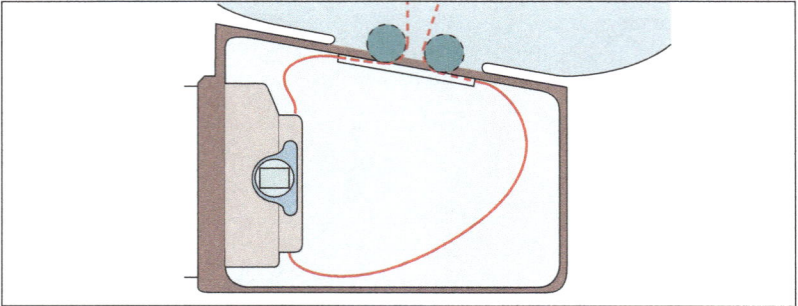

Arriflex 16BL Single System Threading Diagram
Figure 28a. Film takes up emulsion side in.

Viewfinder: Reflex Viewfinder: High-aperture/parallax-free viewing, 10X magnification at the eyepiece. Offset finder accessory available for handheld camera applications for additional operator comfort. Finder extender also available. APEC (Arri Precision Exposure Control): Exposure control system meters behind the lens and displays continuous exposure information (match-needle mode) in the viewfinder.

Video: May be attached to eyepeiece.

Viewing Screen: Noninterchangeable ground glass. Requires trained tech to change, using special tools.

Mags: 200' (61m), 400' (122m) forward and reverse, and 1200' (366m) forward-only magazines. Magazine loading: displacement.

Film Cores: 2" plastic cores. Film core adapter removable to adapt 100' (30.5m) daylight spools.

Accessories: Universal lens housing for use with fixed focal-length lenses when minimal camera operating sound level is required (accepts 3"x3" or a 94mm diameter filter).

Electronic Accessories: Variable speed controls. Jensen, CPT, Tobin.

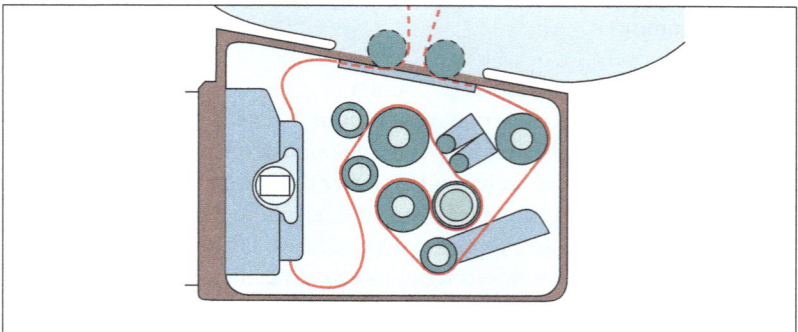

Arriflex 16BL Double System Threading Diagram
Figure 28b. Film takes up emulsion side in.

Additional Accessories: Plug-in single-system sound module and single-system record amplifier. Handholdable.

Optical Accessories: Periscope finder orients image.

Batteries: 12V DC. Accepts blocks and belts.

Camera Support Equipment: Offset finder, assorted lens blimps, speed control, bellows matte box, sound module.

Matte Boxes: Bellows type available for all 16BL lens housings.

Motors, Power: Two motor drive systems available. The 12V DC quartz-controlled motor provides cordless sync-control and automatically stops shutter in viewing position. Speed range is 6, 12, 24 (quartz-controlled) and 48 fps. The Universal motor is transistorized and governor-controlled. A variable speed control accessory will drive the universal motor from 10 fps to 40 fps.

Arriflex 16S; 16M

Models: About 20,000 S (for Standard) cameras made, and 1,500 M (for Magazine) cameras. 16S/B; 16S/B-GS; 16M/B. Main difference— you can use 100' daylight spools in the Arri S body without magazines; Arri M only uses magazines.

Arriflex M

Arriflex 16S/B: accepts 100' (30.5m) daylight spools in body as well as top-mounting torque-motor driven 200' (61m) and 400' (122m) magazines.

Arriflex 16 S/B-GS: (Generator-Start) Pilotone sync generator with built-in start-mark light.

Arriflex S

Arriflex 16M/B: No internal daylight film spool load capacity, takes gear-driven mags—200' (61m), 400' (122m) and 1,200' (366m) coaxial. Accepts all of the accessories in the 16S system except the magazines and power cables.

Weight: 5.8 lbs./2.63 kg

Movement: Pin registered. 16S, 16M and 16BL movements are identical.

FPS: Variable speed range to 75 fps with appropriate motor, forward or reverse.

Aperture: .405" x .295" (10.3mm x 7.5mm). Standard 16mm.

Displays: Tachometer, footage and frame counter.

Lens: divergent three-lens mount turret with two standard and one steel bayonet-lock. Any Arriflex Standard or bayonet mount lens that covers the full 16mm format may be used. Zoom and telephoto lenses require use of the bridgeplate support system.

Shutter: Rotating 180° mirror-shutter.

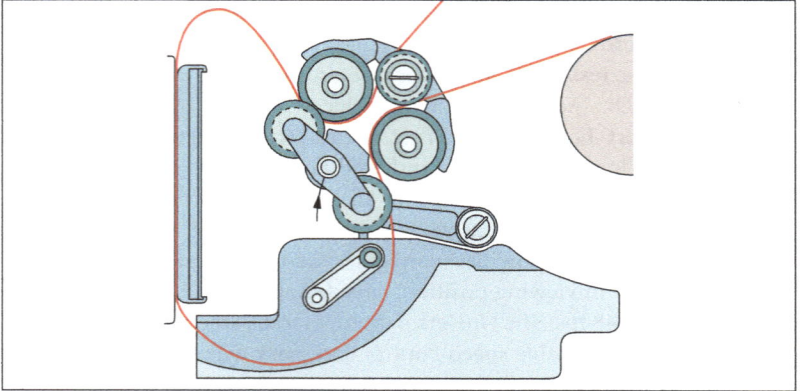

Arriflex 16 S/B Series Threading Diagram
Figure 29a. Film takes up emulsion side in.

Viewfinder: Reflex, parallax-free viewing, 10X image magnification at the eyepiece. An interchangeable ground glass or fiber-optic screen, and an optional APEC exposure control indicator are located within the viewfinder system. APEC: Exposure control system meters behind the lens and displays continuous exposure information (match-needle mode in viewfinder, 16S only).

Viewing Screen: Interchangeable.

Mags: 16S: Accepts 100' (30.5m) daylight spools in body or in mags (core adapter releases from spindle). 200' (61m) and 400' (122m) torque motor-driven magazines. The torque motor drive is essential with 16S magazines and is interchangeable with all 16S magazines of the same film capacity. Lever for forward or reverse.

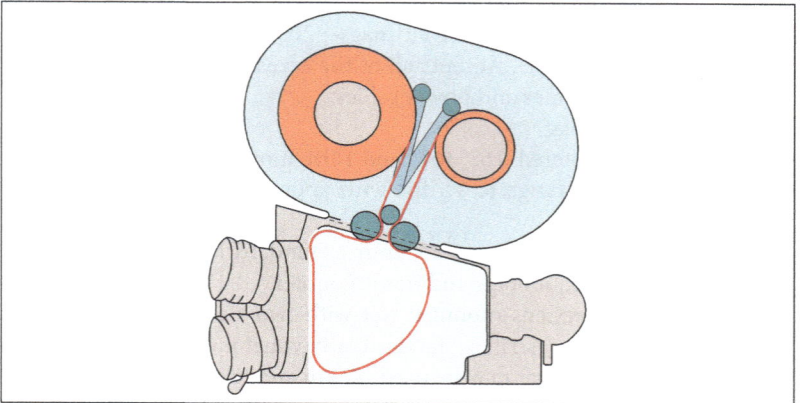

Arriflex 16M Magazine and Threading Diagram
Figure 29b. Film takes up emulsion side in.

16M: 200' (61m), 400' (122m) and 1,200' (366m). Magazines are gear-driven and do not use torque motor drives. The 1,200' (366m) magazine operates in forward only.

Accessories: Bridgeplate support system, adapter for microscope stand and microscope optical link. Fiber-optic screen, periscope viewfinder, finder extender. Norris intervalometer. Sound barney and blimp housings. Standard matte box (16 S/M) with adjustable bellows, a rotary and stationary filter stage. Accepts 2"x2" glass or gelatin filters, and 60mmx100mm glass filters. Universal matte box (16 S/M) with adjustable bellows, a rotary and stationary filter stage. Accepts 3"x3", 3"x4", and 4"x4" glass filters. A 94mm round Pola screen can also be used. Lightweight sunshade and filter holder (Rubber) for 16 S/M accepts 3"x3" filters. Bridge plate support system. Adapter for microscope stand and microscope connector.

Motors, Power: Quartz-regulated, governor-controlled, synchronous and variable-speed motors.

12V DC quartz-motor for 24/25 fps 50/60Hz, variable speeds 5–75 fps, and single-frame forward and reverse capability and Pilotone output.

8V and 12V DC governor motor for 24 fps forward operation only.

8V or 12V DC variable motor for 5–40 fps forward or reverse operation.

110V AC/60Hz synchronous motor and inline power supply for 12V DC, 24 fps operation.

Arriflex 16SR-1, 16SR2

Notes: Over 6,000 still in use. Many conversions and aftermarket adaptations.

Weight: 11–12 lbs./5–5.5 kg, body and magazine, without film and lens.

Movement: Single pull-down claw; single registration pin, with fixed-gap film channel.

FPS: 16SR-1 and 16SR-2 from 5-75 fps with external variable speed control. 16HSR-1 and -2 High-Speed from 10–150 fps with external variable speed control.

Switches located in the camera base of early versions lock in crystal speeds of 24 and 25 fps, 50 and 60Hz and, in later SR cameras, 30 fps. All 16SRs can be modified with a 30 fps kit.

Aperture: Aperture plate is fixed. Standard cameras can be modified to Super 16. Aperture of regular 16SR camera is .295" x .405" (7.5mm x 10.3mm); aperture of Super16 camera is .295" x .484" (7.5mm x 12.3mm).

Super16 conversion cannot be done in the field—requires repositioning of the optical center axis of lens mount, viewfinder, tripod thread and accessory holder by 1mm to the left. Height of Super 16 aperture

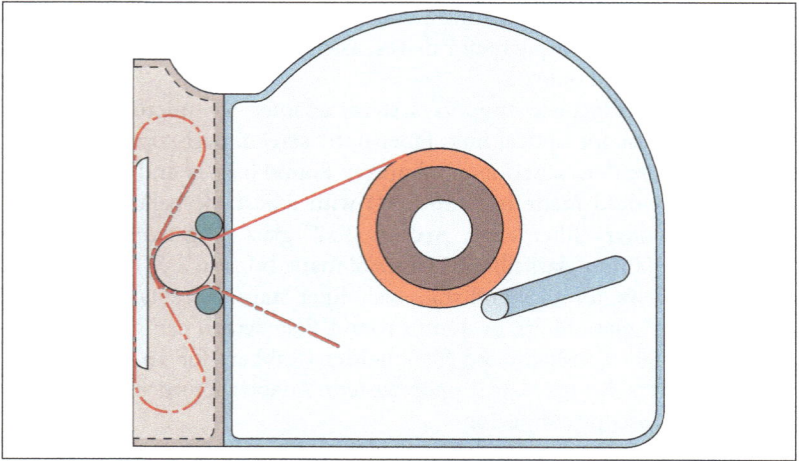

Arriflex 16 SR 1, 2 and 3 Magazine Diagram
Figure 30. Film takes up emulsion side in.

is identical to Standard 16, but the aperture is 2mm wider, pushing into the left perf area on the negative—which is why you use single-perforation film stock.

dB: 22dB–28dB (±2dB)

Displays: Footage remaining on back of magazine, and footage shot on take-up side of magazine (dial settable).

Lens: Bayonet on earlier models and PL on later models and conversions.

Lens Control: Arri Follow Focus 2 or FF3. Preston Microforce or Arri LCS/wireless zoom control.

Shutter: Rotating mirror-shutter.

Viewfinder: Reflex, swing-over viewfinder with parallax-free viewing and 10X magnification at the eyepiece. Swings 190° to either side of the camera for left- and right-side operation. The finder also rotates 360° parallel to camera on either side and swings out 25°. Red out-of-sync LED, and APEC exposure indicator. APEC through-the-lens system provides continuous exposure information (match-needle mode) on four-stop indicator displayed in viewfinder. For film speeds ASA 16–1000. Optional servo-operated automatic exposure control system (with manual override) for complete automatic exposure control with auto-iris lenses available. Super 16 SRs have same exposure meter system in regular 16SRs, but automatic exposure control feature cannot be installed.

Video: OEM removable video "T-bar" viewfinder assembly. optional and necessary for video assist.Aftermarket video assists from Denz, P&S, CEI, others.

	Arriflex 16SR-1, 16SR-2				
Camera	Xtal fps; Variable	dB	Width Body+Mag	Shutter	Mags
16SR-1	24/25; 5-75	28	12 lbs/5.5 kg	180°	Black
16SR-1 Highspeed	24/25; 10-150	N/A	12 lbs/5.5 kg	180° (optional 144°)	Gray & Black
16SR-2	24/25, 24/30; 5-75	22	11 lbs/5 kg	180° (optional 144°)	Black Black
16SR-2 Highspeed	24/25, 24/30; 10-150	28	11 lbs/5 kg	180° (optional 144°)	Gray & Black
16SR-1 S 16	24/25, 24/30; 5-75	22	11 lbs/5 kg	172.8° (optional 144°)	Black
16HSR-2 S16	24/25, 24/30	28	11 lbs/5 kg	172.8° (optional 144°)	Gray & Black

Notes: Over 6,000 still in use. Many conversions and after-market adaptations.

Viewing Screen: Interchangeable fiber-optic viewing screen.

Mags: Rear-mounted coaxial snap-on 400' (122m) mags. Black mags are for the regular speed cameras (up to 75 fps). Gray and black (marked *highspeed*) are for the high speed cameras (up to 150 fps.) You should not interchange them.

Loop formed during loading for quick magazine change. White loop index line on bottom of mag.

2" plastic and collapsible cores, removable to accept 100' (30.5m) and 200' (61m) daylight loads. NASA used 400' (122m) daylight spools by milling off ⅛" of spool's edge.

Accessories: External speed control for operation of standard 16SRs up to 75 fps or 16HSR High-Speed up to 150 fps. 16SR-2 Super 16 cameras time code compatible. Cinematography Electronics 16SR Frameline Glow and Speed Control and intervalometer. Norris intervalometer.

Bridgeplate, lightweight support rods, left and right grips for hand-held operation, finder extender, lightweight follow focus, shoulder set.

Connections: Variable speed control, precision speed controls, external monitor synchronizer, multicamera interlock achieved with FSZ-II sync-control accessory. Modular plug-in electronics boards contain circuitry controlling all electronic functions, including a built-in start-marking system, out-of-sync light, Pilotone output and prewiring for SMPTE 80-bit time code.

Motors, Power: 12V DC . Four-pin connector. Pin 1 is (-); pin 4 is +12V. 12V onboard batteries with onboard battery adapter. Many aftermarket onboard batteries, including adapters for power-tool batteries. Accepts blocks and belts with power cable.

Arriflex 16SR3, 16HSR3, 16SR Adv., 16HSR3 Adv.

Models: 16SR3 (5–75 fps)

16HSR3 High-Speed (5–150 fps)

16SR3 Advanced and HSR-3 Advanced (updated electronics, brighter finder, no APEC exposure meter)

All models thread the same as 16SR-1 and 16SR-2.

Weight: 13.5 lbs/6.1kg. (body + mag). 15.4 lbs/7kg. (body + loaded 400' mag + onboard battery)

Movement: Single pull-down claw; single registration pin, with fixed-gap film channel. 16SR-3 Advanced: Film guide has sapphire rollers on one side, for reduced film dust and improved image steadiness.

FPS: 5–75 fps standard; 5-150 fps high speed. Onboard programmable speeds of 24, 25, 29.97 and 30 fps, and variable crystal speeds from 5–75 fps in the Standard camera, or 5-150 fps in the high-speed 16SR-3, variable in 0.001 increments at crystal accuracy. Speeds continuously variable when the remote unit (RU-1), remote control unit (RCU-1), or wireless remote control unit (WRC-1) is used. Speeds can be programmed from the 16SR-3's onboard LCD with the RU-1 or with the camera control unit (CCU), Arri's standard off-camera programming unit.

Aperture: .405" x .295" (10.3mm x 7.5mm). Easily converts from normal 16mm to Super 16. 16SR-3 Super 16 aperture can be masked for standard 16mm frame. No additional aperture is needed. Universal film gate needs only slight adjustment on Advanced models.

dB: Standard 20dB(A) + 2dB(A).

Displays: LCD Display—set/display frame rates, set/display film counter, display mirror shutter opening (during electronic inching mode), set/display time code and user bits, display TC sensitivity readout, battery voltage and low-battery warning, film end and asynchronous camera speed.

Lens: Standard Arri PL mount will take most 16mm and 35mm format PL mount lenses. Adapters available for 41mm diameter bayonet and standard mount lenses.

Shutter: rotating mirror shutter; manually adjustable when camera is switched. Shutter openings of 90°, 135°, 144°, 172.8°, 180°. Shutter opening indicated on LCD display during electronic inching mode. SR-3 Advanced: Variable (manually) rotating mirror shutter with shutter openings of 45°, 90°, 135°, 144°, 172.8°, 180°.

Arriflex Cameras: Flange Focal Distance Chart		
Camera Lens	**Mount to Filmgate (mm)**	**Lens Mount to Groundglass (mm)**
16S	51.970 to 51.980	52.000
16BL	51.970 to 51.980	52.000
16BLEQ	51.970 to 51.980	52.000
16M	51.970 to 51.980	52.000
16SR-1, 2, 3 Adv.	51.990 to 52.000	52.000
16SR-1, 2, 3 Adv., HS	51.960 to 51.970	52.000

Arri Fuses (electronics/motor)	
Camera	**Fuse**
16S	None
16BL	1 A pico – slanting system
	15 pico – protect wiring harness soldered inline below drive motor
16BLEQ	½ A & spare / 15 A & spare
	Access via coin slot
16M	None
16SR-1, 2, 3 Adv.	¾ A pico / 10 A pico
16SR-1, 2, 3 Adv., HS	¾ A pico / 10 A pico

Viewfinder: Reflex Viewfinder: Reflex viewfinder swings 190° to camera left or camera right, with fully upright image in any position. Finder rotates 360° parallel to the body and can be swung away by 25°. Viewfinder provides automatic upright images at all times. Image can also be manually oriented.

With CCD video assist and flicker-reduction electronics attached, viewfinder swings in a 120° arc. Finder equipped with Arriglow continuously adjustable illuminated framelines for standard 16mm and Super 16. Finder also has warning indications for asynchronous camera speed, film end and low battery.

Finder center can be adjusted to either normal 16mm or Super 16. Switchable magnification built into viewfinder extension. With integrated video system attached, viewfinder can pivot from left to right camera side.

SR3 Advanced: Leaving out the exposure meter and utilizing a specifically designed mirror for the Arriglow results in gain in viewfinder brightness of ¾ of an f-stop.

Video: Takes Arri ½" black-and-white or color CCD video assist, and Arri AFP-2 flicker reduction electronics for bright, flicker-reduced images. Adjustable for standard 16mm and Super 16, with full image of either format on monitor. Changing ratio for color or black-and-white is easy and requires no adjustment. LCD display.

SR-3 Advanced: Video-assist system, IVS-Integrated Video System (can be used on 16SR-3). High-speed, high-resolution and flicker-free from 5 frames on. The IVS has two components: a video electronic module and a CCD module available in PAL and NTSC. Equipped with interchangeable optics with Super and normal 16mm formats. Effective ASA is 4000. Format markings can be electronically inserted into video image for low lighting conditions. Area outside format marking can be darkened electronically to better emphasize viewing area. Time code and camera status indicators such as "standby/run" can be directly inserted into video image.

Viewing Screen: Interchangeable fiber optic viewing screens. ArriGlow.

Mags: Rear mounted coaxial snap-on 400' (122m) and 800' (244m) mags. Loop formed during loading for quick magazine change. 2" plastic and collapsible cores, removable to accept 100' (30.5m) and 200' (61m) daylight loads. Standard 80-bit SMPTE time code module built in. Existing 16SR-2 magazines can be used. 16SR-3 magazines without time code available. Black 16SR mags work on regular speed 16SR-3 cameras. Gray and black 16HSR (marked *highspeed*) work on 16HSR-3 high-speed cameras.

Do not use regular mags on high-speed cameras; do not use high-speed mags on regular cameras.

Accessories: camera handgrip, finder extender, heated eyecup, lightweight support rods, lightweight follow focus, shoulder set, low-mode support, handgrips, matte boxes.

The 16SR-3 uses Arri 19mm rod camera support system. Bridgeplates and lens supports. 15mm rod adapters. Handheld accessories. A wide variety of Arriflex 35mm accessories can be used with the 16SR3.

Matte Boxes: 4x4 production matte box ideal for 16SR-3. Its swing-away design covers lenses 16mm and up, has interchangeable two- and four-frame geared filter stages, is fully rotatable and accepts most support system accessories. Support system includes a full range of matte boxes in 6.6x6.6, 5x5, and a variety of 4x4. See pages 525–528 for a complete list.

Connections: Many 435 and 535 accessories can be used: external synchronizing unit (ESU), remote unit (RU-1), remote switch (RS); RCU, ICU, CCU and laptop computer controller to control or set most functions (speed, footage counters, shutter angles, etc.) 24V-to-12V power converter, multi-accessory connector. Integral 80-bit SMPTE time code. Recording module built into 16SR-3 magazines. Fully complies with SMPTE RP 114 standard.

Motors, Power: 24V DC. Onboard batteries. Accepts blocks and belts. Built-in crystal-controlled 24V DC motor.

Bolex H-16mm

Movement: Single-claw pull-down. No registration pin. Gate has automatic threading device that loops film and inserts it into gate and around sprockets. Rear pressure plate can be removed for cleaning gate. Automatic loop former prevents loss of loop.

FPS: single frame, 8–64 fps

Aperture: Standard. Super 16 on certain models. Fixed aperture plate.

Displays: Footage and frame counters add and subtract. Audible scene-length signal clicks every 28 frames. Single-frame exposure button for instantaneous or time exposures.

Lens: H-16 Rex 5 has three-lens turret for C-mount lenses, other models have large Bolex bayonet mount suitable for heavy zoom and telephoto lenses. Adapter for C-mount lenses and accessories available. Full line of Switar, Vario Switar and Angenieux zoom and standard lenses, matte box, extension tubes. Aspheron wide-angle adapters.

Shutter: Bolex spring-driven cameras (H-16 Rex 5 and H-16 SBM) have 135° variable shutter (some earlier models do not have this feature), which can be opened or closed while camera is running. It can be locked at ¼, ½ and can be opened and closed automatically with Rexofader accessory. Bolex electrically driven cameras (H-16 EBM and H-16 EL) have fixed 170-degree shutter. Shutter speeds electronically controlled 10–50 fps.

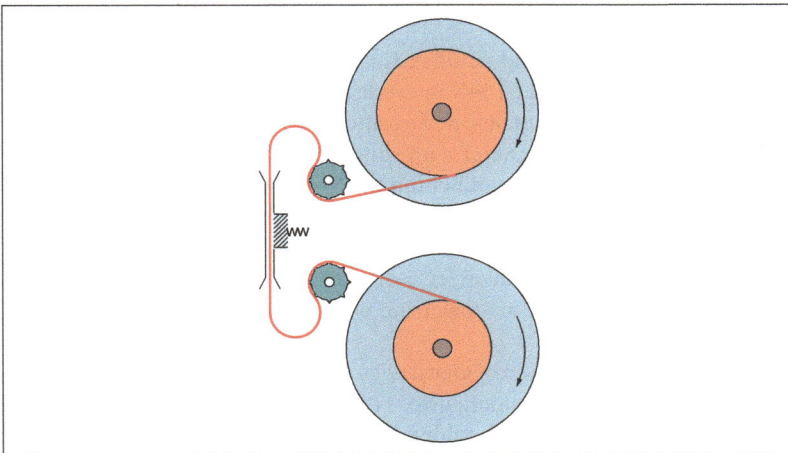

Bolex 16mm Threading Diagram
Figure 31. Film takes up emulsion side in (Daylight spool load only)

Bolex H-16 Models	
Year	**Model**
1933	H-16
1956	H-16 reflex H-16 R
1959	H-16 rex-1 (var. shutter 145°)
1963	H-16 rex-2 (var. shutter 130°)
1963	H-16 rex-3 built-in flat base
1964	H-16 m-3 built-in flat base
1965	H-16 s
1965	H-16 rex-4 1:1 ratio shift
1965	H-16 m-4 1:1 ratio shift
1967	H-16 rex-5 400' magazine saddle, clapper
1967	H-16 m-5 400' magazine saddle
1971	H-16 rex-5 new vf, magnification 13X
1971	H-16 sbm bayonet mount, 400' magazine saddle
1971	H-16 sb bayonet mount, 100' capacity
1971	H-16 ebm built-in electric motor
1975	H-16 el built-in electric motor, exp. meter
1978	H-16 el/tv (series ii) tv mask, x-sync
1978	H-16 sbm/tv tv mask in vf, 13X magnification
1980	H-16 el/tv (series iii) 1600 ASA exp meter
2000	Super 16 conversions

Viewfinder: Flickerless and parallax-free reflex viewfinder via prism reflex finder. Image magnified 14X in eye-level finder and may be continuously viewed in filming or stopped position. H-l6 EL has built-in, through-the-lens silicon light meter with shockproof LED indicators in the VF. All cameras have filter slot behind the lens.

External Viewfinder: External sidefinder on some models.

Film, Mags: All cameras accept 100' (30.5m) daylight loading spools, which can be ejected with built-in lever device.

Optional 400' (122m) magazine with self-contained take-up motor available.

Accessories: Automatic Rexofader device for H-16 REX and SBM available for 40-frame fades. Camera grip, extension tubes for macrocinematography. Cable releases, shoulder brace. *Note:* Many other accessories, such as animation motors, microscope attachments and time-lapse units, are available from other firms. Norris makes intervalometer for

REX 4 and 5, EBM, SBM. Sound blimp. Underwater housing for EL and EB.

Motors, Power: Spring-driven cameras will expose 16½' of film on one winding. Variable-speed motor and electronically stabilized motor suitable for sync pulse, and crystal sync available for spring-driven cameras. H-16 EBM and H-16 EL have 10–50 fps electronically regulated motors built in. H-l6 EL has single frame and electric rewind, instant start and stop. All models accept 400' (122m) magazine with take-up motor. Spring motor may be disengaged. Full 100' (30.5m) film rewind.

Panaflex 16mm – "Elaine"

Notes: Named after a lady who works at Panavision (still does).

Weight: 16.6 lbs/7.54 kg (body with short eyepiece)

Movement: Dual pilot pin registration. Entire movement may be removed for servicing.

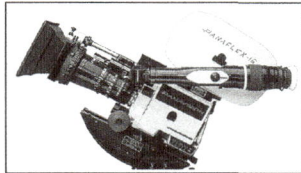

FPS: 4–50 fps, crystal-controlled at all speeds; may be adjusted in ¹⁄₁₀-fps increments.

Aperture: .486" x .295" (12.34mm x 7.49mm) SMPTE 201M—1996. Aperture Plate removable for checking and cleaning. Super l6 aperture plate is standard.

dB: Less than 20dB with film and lens, measured 3' from the image plane.

Displays: Camera speed and footage, LED indicators for low battery/low film/film jam/illegal speed.

Lens: Panavision 16 positive clamp lens mount with index pin. Super 16 lens mount is standard, regular 16 upon request.

Lenses: Panavision/Zeiss Superspeeds and other 16mm image format lenses. 6mm to 135mm (see separate lens list). Wide range of Panavision-engineered zoom lenses by other manufacturers also available. All lenses have widely spaced lens focus calibrations and T-stop marks. Most prime and zoom lenses will cover Super 16.

Lens Control: Lightweight modular follow-focus control that can be used from either side of the camera is standard; optional electronic remote focus and aperture controls also available. Zoom lenses supplied with a motor-driven zoom control unit as standard. Iris gears are incorporated into most prime and zoom lenses.

Shutter: Focal plane shutter with infinitely variable opening, adjustable in shot. Maximum opening 200°, minimum 50°, with adjustable maximum and minimum opening stops; adjustable for critical synchroniza-

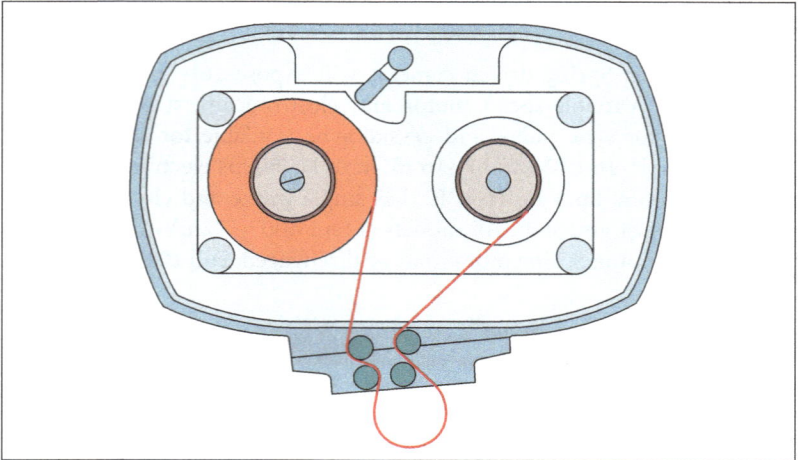

Panavision 16mm Film Magazine
Figure 32a. Film takes up emulsion side out.

tion with computers, TV monitors and HMI lighting at unusual frame rates. Manual and electronic remote control units available.

Viewfinder: Reflex viewfinder, reflex rotating mirror is standard and independent of camera shutter. Viewfinder tube is orientable and gives a constantly upright image through 360°. Short viewfinder provided for handheld operation. Viewfinders may be swung out to suit left- or right-eye viewing. System incorporates optical magnifier for critical

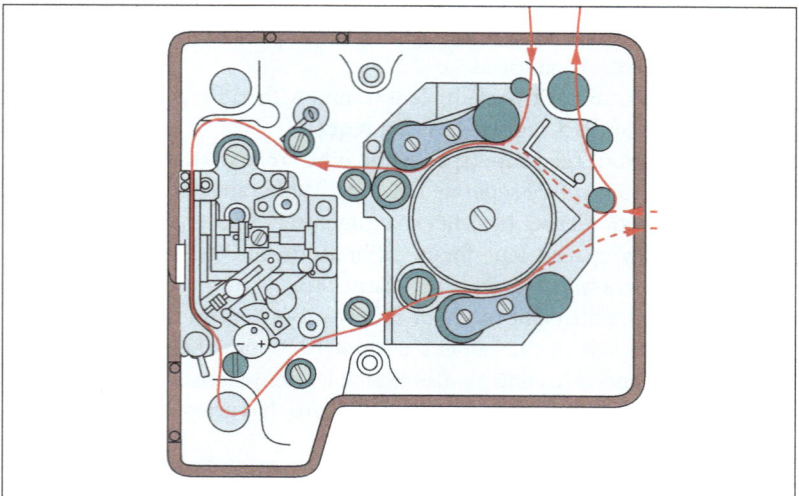

Panaflex 16mm Camera System (The Elaine) Threading Diagram
Figure 32b. Film takes up emulsion side out.

focusing and picture composition, contrast viewing filter and lightproof shutter. Wide-range ocular adjustment with marker bezel to note individual settings. Built-in "Panaclear" eyepiece heater ensures mist-free viewing. Eyepiece leveler supplied to keep eyepiece position constant while tilting the camera up or down. Eyepiece diopter to suit operator's eyesight can be provided on request.

Video: Flicker-free at 24 fps and 30 fps. Auto color balance, normal and boost gain, ND filter, wide sensitivity range.

Viewing Screen: "Panaglow" illuminated reticle system with brightness control is standard.

Mags: 400' (122m) and 1,200' (366m) film magazines available. The 400' (122m) can be rear mounted for good balance when handholding. Magazine loading: displacement, top or rear mount. 2" plastic core required for 400' (122m), 3" for 1,200' (366m) magazine.

Accessories: Heated covers available to give additional protection to lenses, especially zoom lenses, for smooth operation in intensely cold conditions. Other covers available to protect the camera, magazines and lenses from heat, dust, rain and water. Spinning-glass rain deflectors available for use in storm conditions. Autobase available to secure camera in conditions of vibration, high g-forces and other stressful and dangerous forces. Water box available to protect camera in shallow water conditions, and hazard box can be used to protect camera from explosions, collisions and other dangerous situations.

Camera Support Equipment: Standard Panahead. Sliding base unit enables camera to be quickly attached and detached and to be slid backwards and forwards on the head for optimum balance. "Panatate" turnover mount allows 360° camera rotation about the lens axis while permitting nodal pan-and-tilt movements.

Handheld handles and shoulder rest for handholding the camera. In this configuration, camera is best used with 400' (122m) magazine fitted on the rear.

Standard matte box incorporating a sunshade, provision for two 4"x5.650" filters. Special matte boxes incorporating more filter stages, with provision for sliding (motorized if required), rotating and tilting to take 6.6" square filters optional.

Connections: Sync box to synchronize the camera with computers, video signals and projectors for shutter phase synchronization. Camera will accept external drive signals via the 10-pin accessory connector.

Motors, Power: 24V DC. Crystal-controlled brushed motor drives system. Camera, magazines, heaters and accessories operate off a single 24V battery. Belt batteries for handholding optional.

Misc: All Panaflex-16 cameras and magazines have built-in heaters.

SUPER 8MM

Beaulieu 4008

FPS: 2–70 fps (speed select for either 18, 24 or 25 fps). Mechanical single frame.

Aperture: .166"x .224" (4.22mm x 5.69mm).

Displays: Footage.

Lens: C mount with power lens contacts. Power Zoom Lenses available are Schneider 6–66mm or 16–70mm and Angenieux 8–64mm or 6–8mm. Macrocinematography mode

Focusing ring. Built-in electric zoom control. On-lens variable speed. Iris gears on lens governed by camera meter.

Built-in 85 filter, through-the-lens internal meter ISO 12–400 ASA.

Shutter: Guillotine ⅟₉₀th second at 24 fps and ⅟₆₀th at 24 fps variable with frame rate closed lock position.

Viewfinder: Reflex viewfinder.

Viewing Screen: Focusing-screen. Retractable.

Mags: 50' (15m) silent Super 8 or Pro8mm cartridges.

Accessories: Remote cable release.

Power: Onboard 250Ma. 7.2V/3.6V combined.

Beaulieu 6008 Pro

Weight: 2 lbs. 3 oz./1kg. body only.

FPS: 4, 9, 18, 24/25, 36 and 80 fps. Electronic single frame and three time-lapse speeds. Optional crystal control at 24 or 25 fps.

Aperture: .166" x .224" (4.22mm x 5.69mm).

Displays: Some with footage, others with frames.

Lens: Schneider 6-70mm f/1.4 zoom or Beaulieu 7mm-56mm f/1.4 power zoom lens.

Center-weighted TTL metering. ISO 12-400.

Zoom Control: Electric or manual. Iris Gears: Electric.

Shutter: Guillotine, two-position; ⅟₉₀th at 24 and ⅟₆₀th at 24 variable with frame rate speed in closed position.

Viewfinder: Reflex viewfinder

Viewing Screen: Matte focusing screen.

Mags: 50' (15m) sound or silent Super 8 and Pro8mm cartridges, 200' (61m) sound. (Sound ctg. no longer available.)

Accessories: Electromagnetic trigger, remote control, external power supply.

Power: 7.2V AA battery pack.

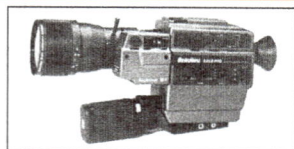

Beaulieu 7008 Pro

Weight: 2.82 lbs/1.28kg, body only.

Movement: Forward and limited reverse.

FPS: 4, 9, 18, 24/25 (optional 24 or 25 fps crystal), 36, 80 fps. Single-frame capabilities and three time-lapse filming speeds.

Aperture: .166" x .224" (4.22mm x 5.69mm).

Displays: Digital readouts for frames and centimeters.

Lens: C mount and Beaulieu power mounts. Automatic control sets lens to minimum depth of field. Zoom Control: Electric or manual.

Shutter: Guillotine, two-position; ⅟₉₀th at 24 and ⅟₆₀th at 24 variable with frame rate speed in closed position.

Viewfinder: Reflex viewfinder

Viewing Screen: Fine-grain focusing screen.

Mags: 50' (15m) sound or silent Super 8 and Pro8mm cartridges. 200' (61m) sound ctg. (sound ctg. no longer available).

Accessories: Center-weighted TTL metering. ISO 12-400. Output sockets, flash synchronization, electromagnetic trigger, remote control. Remote cable release. Fader (in and out.)

Power: Six 1.2VC-Cell NiCd battery packs. Power cable adapter. Quick charger.

Canon 814 XL-S, 1014 XL-S

FPS: 9, 18, 24 and 36 fps.

Aperture: .228" x .165" (5.8mm x 4.2mm).

Displays: Battery check, film end, film transport, sound recording levels, correct exposure, manual aperture indicator, footage indicator.

Lens: 814XL-S has 7–56mm (8:1) f/1.4 with built-in wide angle and tele-photo macro mechanisms. 1014XL-S has 6.5–65mm (10:1) f/1.4 with wide angle and telephoto macro mechanisms. Zoom control: two-speed electric or manual. 85 filter switch, filter rings, 4.3mm wide-angle attachment for 1014XL-S and 4.5mm wide-angle attachment for the 814XL-S, 1.4x 67 teleconverter, close-up lens attachment,

Shutter: Semi-disc rotating, automatic or manual 150° and 250°.

Viewfinder: Single-lens reflex viewfinder with split image rangefinder.

Mags: 50' (15m) sound or silent Super 8 and Pro8mm cartridges.

Accessories: Film Mode Dial allows lap-dissolves (1014XL-S only), fade-in/fade-out, timed interval filming, single-frame filming, light meter, microphones, earphones, intervalometer, self-timer, remote control, flash socket. Chest Pod II, extension cord.

Power: Six AA-size 1.5V alkaline manganese, carbon zinc, or NiCd. 9V power pack available.

Nautica

Notes: Underwater camera, no housing required. Watertight to 30' (9.1m).
FPS: Single frame and 18 fps.
Displays: Depth indicator, footage counter.
Lens: Fixed 9–30mm Panorama-Viennon f/1.9 zoom. Exposure is auto-matic. Aspheric wide-angle attachment needed for underwater. Focus is automatic. Zoom lever.
Mags: 50' (15m) sound or silent Super 8 and Pro8mm cartridges.
Accessories: Cable release.
Power: Two AA batteries.

Nikon R8, R10

FPS: 18, 24, 54 fps. Single frame.
Displays: F-numbers, exposure warning, film end, shutter opening, footage, battery.
Lens: Fixed Cine-Nikkor zoom lens. 7–70mm (10:1) f/1.4 macro. 67mm front attachment size. Two-speed power zoom with manual override.
Shutter: Variable shutter from 160° to 0°.
Viewfinder: Reflex viewfinder, SLR with split-image rangefinder.
Mags: 50' (15m) sound or silent Super 8 and Pro8mm cartridges.
Accessories: Exposure meter, 100 frame rewind, automatic fade-in/fade-out with manual override, double exposure, reverse filming, remote con-trol, flash sync.
Power: Six AA 1.5V.

Pro8mm Pro II

FPS: 23.97, 24, 25, 29.97 and 30 fps crystal controlled. 4, 9, 18, 24, 36 and 80 fps non-crystal. New crystal also features built-in phase control so TV monitors can be shot without video bar. Single frame function with variable shutter rate for animation ef-fects. Intervalometer for timed exposures.
Aperture: .166" x .224" (4.22mm x 5.69mm). Optional mask for 1.85 Acad-emy.
Displays: Visual display in viewfinder indicating an absolute crystal lock. Liquid crystal display frame and centimeter counters keep track of exact footage transported in forward and reverse. Two-stage LED informs user when camera service is required.
Lens: C mount and custom Beaulieu power mount. Lenses: Angenieux 6-90mm T1.6. Schneider 6-70mm. 3mm superwide prime. Superwide

elements can be removed from lens to obtain 6mm focal length. Nikon compatible 60–300mm telephoto. Anamorphic Lens System. Aspect ratio is 2.35:1 (1.75X squeeze) and lens is mounted with custom brackets. Same lens can also be used with any standard projector to permit widescreen projection. C-mount adapters allow various non-C-mount lenses to be used.

Lens Control Unit for variable power zoom and aperture control. These features include manual override.

Viewfinder: Reflex viewfinder

Viewing Screen: Focusing screen.

Mags: 50' (15m) sound or silent Super 8 and Pro8mm cartridges. 200' (61m) sound ctg. (Sound ctg. no longer available.)

Accessories: Additional Accessories: Motor-driven rewind is included to perform dissolves and double exposures. Hard-shell sound blimp made from industrial-grade aluminum and sound-absorbing foam (-22dB effective). Rental only.

Motors, Power: 12V DC input. Regulated and fused for 12V DC battery belt. Microprocessor crystal-controlled 1.5 amp motor.

65MM

Arriflex 765

Movement: Microprocessor control technology to link two quartz-controlled DC motors in a direct drive configuration to control shutter and film transport. No belts or mechanical couplings used in drive system. Dual registration pins, triple-pin pull-down claws and user-adjustable pitch control to optical printer standards.

FPS: Quartz-accurate sync at 15/24/25/29.97/30/60/75 fps onboard; 2–100 fps with the CCU; 24 fps reverse; and 1 fps with the 765's remote control unit. Run-up time is less than 1 second at 24 fps.

Aperture: 2.17" x 1.004" (55mm x 25.5mm).

dB: 25dB at 24 fps; 28.5dB(A) at 30 fps.

Displays: LCD tachometer and footage displays: digital camera left/right; audible and visible out-of-sync; low battery; feet/meters footage display.

Lens: 64mm diameter Maxi-PL lens mount; flange focal distance of 63.5mm; designed for Arri Maxi-PL prime and RTH Cooke zoom, wide-angle and telephoto lenses. Lenses: Arri/Zeiss 65mm format lenses include 30mm, 40mm, 50mm, 60mm, 80mm, 100mm, 110mm, 120mm, 150mm, 250mm, 350mm, 2x Mutar Extender, and a 38–210mm zoom.

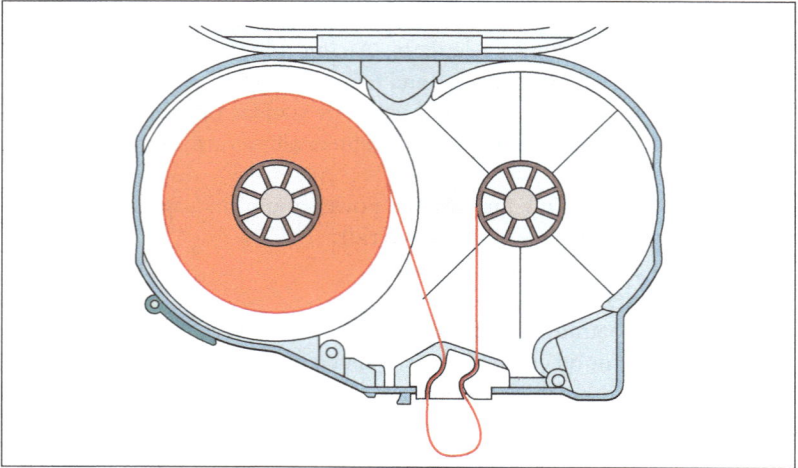

Arriflex 765 Magazine
Figure 33a. Film takes up emulsion side in.

Shutter: Rotating, microprocessor-controlled silicon mirror shutter, mechanically variable from 15° to 165°, including 144°, 172.8°, and 180°.

Viewfinder: Reflex viewfinder has built-in optical turret that permits on-the-fly selection of either 80:20 or 100:0 video/viewing ratios, and has switchable ND.6 contrast viewing glass, ArriGlow illuminated frame lines, and finder extender with built-in 2X image magnification. Short

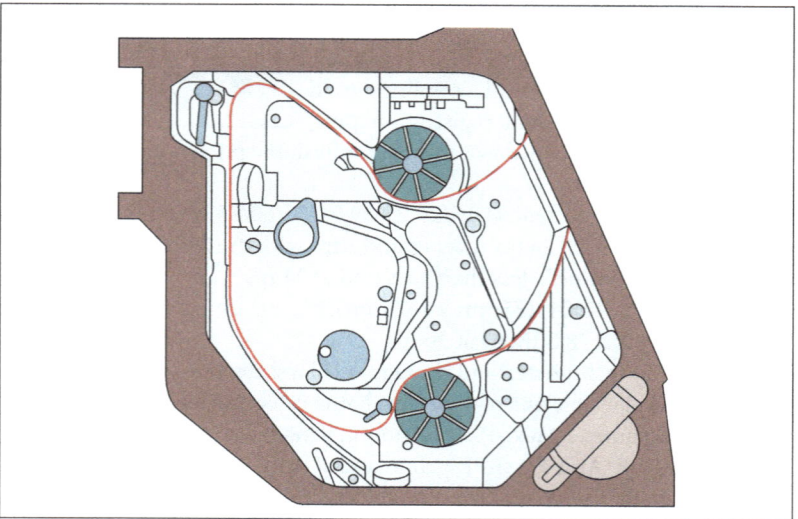

Arriflex 765 Threading Diagram
Figure 33b. Film takes up emulsion side in.

finder (for portable operation) and video finder are also available. Wide-angle eyepiece with manual iris closure, 8X magnification, and +2 diopter adjustment standard. In-finder displays: out-of-sync and film-end.

Video: Video Optics Module: Color and black-and-white CCD video tap cameras with flicker reduction and iris control.

Viewing Screen: Interchangeable with full range of aspect ratios.

Mags: 400' (122m) and 1,000' (300m) displacement with microprocessor-controlled torque motors. Microprocessor samples and adjusts feed/take-up tension and all other functions continuously. Automatic connection and data transfer to camera via multiplug pin plug. Mechanical and digital LCD counters.

Accessories: 6.6"x6.6" swing-away production matte box covers all 65mm format lenses. Has two fully rotatable two-filter stages. Geared filter frames. Bridgeplate support system for balance and mount for matte box, follow focus, servo zoom drive and heavy lenses. Finder extender and leveling rod.

Camera Control Unit (CCU) remotely turns 765 on and off, and activates speed change from up to 100' (30.5m) away.

Variable Speed and Sync Unit: VSSU module allows remote speed changes between 6 and 100 fps noncrystal; provides synchronization with external PAL or NTSC video signal (50/60Hz) via up to 100' BNC cable.

Barney and heated barney.

Motors, Power: Power input via a three-pin connector:
pin 1 is (-), pin 2 is + 24V.

Fries Model 865 65mm/8-perf.

Notes: A large-format 65mm 8-perf camera for special venue productions.

Weight: Camera body 45 lbs/20.45kg, 1000' (300m) mag 13.5 lbs/6.13kg.

Movement: Dual registration pins and six pull-down claws. A cam and eccentric mounted on a single shaft actuate pull down and operate register pins.

Film specifications: 65mm KS-1866.

FPS: 2–72 fps forward or 2–30 fps reverse. All speeds crystal controlled.

Aperture: Photographed aperture is 2.072" x 1.450" (52.63mm x 36.83mm). Removable aperture and pressure plates for ease of cleaning. Aperture plate: optically centered.

Displays: Footage counters.

Lens: Universal bayonet type with large port diameter. Special mounts available. Complete series of Hasselblad lenses available.

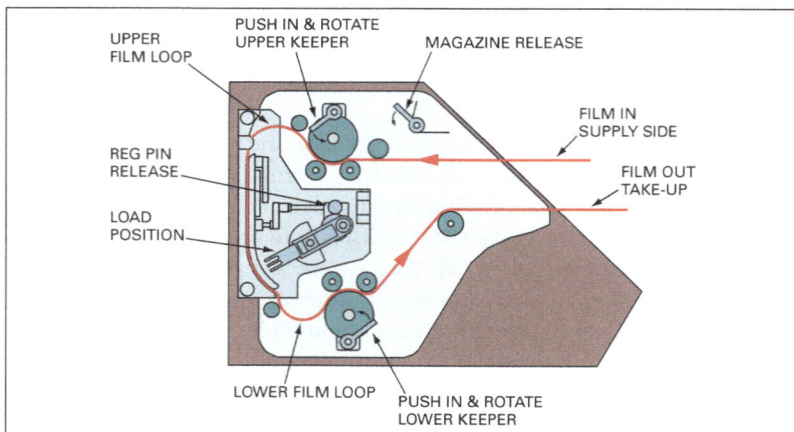

Fries 865 65mm/8-perf. Threading Diagram
Figure 34. Film takes up emulsion side out.

Shutter: 170-degree fixed opening blanking shutter.

Viewfinder: Reflex viewfinder, rotating mirror reflex image. Viewfinder is orientable through a full 360° and self-corrected through approximately 180°. Lightvalve allows operator to direct to viewing system, to video assist, or to combo, which splits light between both viewing and video assist.

Video: Video tap with ½" CCD chip camera, color or black-and-white.

Mags: Displacement magazines with torque motor take-up and hold-back. Standard 65mm 3" plastic cores.

Accessories: Remote on/off. Standard Arri matte box.

Motors, Power: 30V DC. Internal 30V DC crystal-controlled motor.

Mitchell FC, BFC (65mm)

Notes, Models: Scaled up design of 35mm rackover Mitchell NC and BNC. B models are blimped.

Movement: Dual register pins, four-prong pulldown; adjustable stroke. Timing marks on shutter and movement facilitate removal and reassembly.

FPS: Single frame to 32 fps.

Aperture: Removable aperture plate with built-in matte slot. Slot for dual gel filters.

Displays: Mechanical. Footage and frames.

Shutter: Focal plane 175° maximum, variable to 0° in 10-degree increments. Phase and opening indicator on back of camera. Some models have automatic 4' fade in or out.

Viewfinder: Non-reflex models-external large screen erecting finder with parallax correction coupled by camera-to-lens focus knob

Viewing Screen: Interchangeable.

Mags: 400' (122m), 1,000' (300m), 1,200' (366m) double compartment sound insulated. Plastic film cores (that come with film) on feed side, collapsible and removable on take-up side.

    See Mitchell 35mm for threading diagram

Accessories: Film matte punch

Motors, Power: Detachable motors. Synchronous motors are sound insulated. Crystal sync 30V DC with 50/60Hz signal, mirror-positioning circuit and audible offspeed indicator. Power requirements vary with motor.

MSM Model 8870 65mm/8-perf.

Movement: MSM Monoblock high-speed, dual register pins, claw engages six perfs. Shrinkage adjustment changes stroke and entry position. Indexable loop-setting sprockets have independent locking keeper rollers. Vacuum backplate ensures filmplane accuracy, removes without tools for cleaning. Removable for cleaning and lubrication.

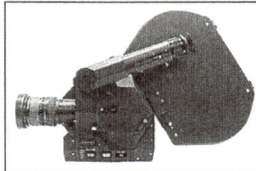

FPS: From time-lapse to 60 fps forward, also to 30 fps reverse. Crystal sync from 5–60 fps in .001 increments.

Aperture: 2.072" x 1.485" (52.63mm x 37.72mm). Aperture plate removable for cleaning and lubrication.

Displays: Status LEDs for power, heat, low battery, mag ready, buckle and speed sync. Two illuminated LCD footage counters. Digital battery volt/amp meter. Circuit breakers for camera, mag, heat and accessories. Control port allows operation from handheld remote or interface with computers and external accessories.

Lens: MSM 75mm diameter x 80mm flange depth. BNC-style lens mount is vertically adjustable 7mm for flat or dome screen composition. Mount accepts modified Zeiss (Hasselblad), Pentax, Mamiya and other large-format lenses.

Shutter: Focal plane shutter, manually variable from 172.8° to 55° with stops at 144° and 108°.

Viewfinder: Reflex viewfinder, spinning mirror reflex. Finder rotates 360° with upright image, which can be manually rotated for unusual setups. Finder shows 105 percent of frame, magnifier allows critical focusing at center of interest. Single lever controls internal filter and douser. Heated eyepiece has large exit pupil and long eye relief. High resolution black-and-white or optional color CCD video tap is built into camera door with swing-away 50/50 beamsplitter. Viewfinder removes completely for aerial or underwater housing use.

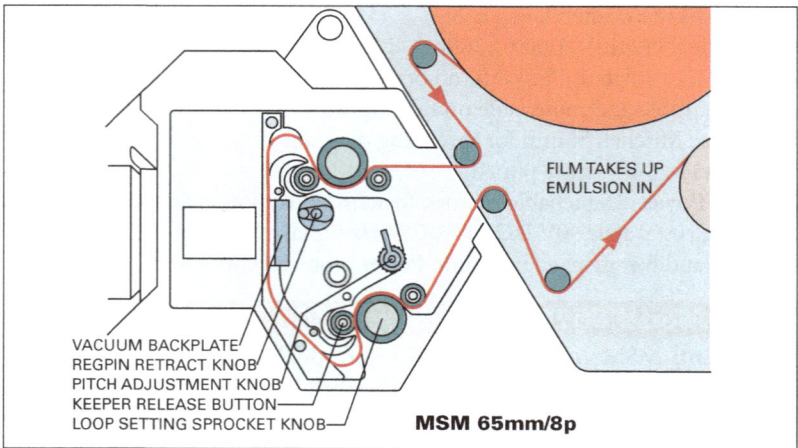

MSM 8870 65mm/8 perf. Threading Diagram
Figure 35.

Viewing Screen: Interchangeable ground glasses with register pins for film clips.

Mags: 1,000' (300m) displacement magazines use MSM TiltLock mount. Magazines lock to camera with pair of 8mm hardened pins and can tilt away from operator to allow easier camera threading. Optional minimum profile 1,000' (300m) coaxial magazines use same mount without tilt feature. Both magazines operate bidirectionally at all camera speeds. Positive camlock secures mag in running position and switches power to motor and heater contacts in mag foot. Expanding core hubs have integral DC servo motors controlled by film tension in both directions, with soft startup to eliminate slack. Tightwind rollers guide film winding for smooth solid rolls at any camera angle. Noncontact light traps feature infrared end-of-film sensors.

Accessories: 15mm matte rods are on Arri BL centers for accessory compatibility and use standard Arri accessories.

Motors, Power: Integrated.

Panavision System-65 65mm

Movement: Four pull-down claws. Pitch adjustment to optimize camera quietness. Entire movement may be removed for servicing. Dual pilot pin registration ensures FPS: 4-30 fps.

Aperture: .906" x 2.072" (23.01mm x 52.63mm).

Aperture plate removable for checking and cleaning. Full-frame aperture is standard, aperture mattes used for all

other frame sizes. A special perforation-locating pin above aperture ensures trouble-free and rapid film threading.

Interchangeable aperture mattes available. Anamorphic, Super 35, 1.85:1, l.66:l and any other as required. Special hard mattes available on request.

Behind-the-lens gel filter holder.

dB: 24 Db(A)

Lens: Panavision positive clamp lens mount for maintaining critical flange focal depth setting. All lenses pinned to ensure proper rotational orientation. (*Note:* This is particularly important with anamorphic lenses.) Iris-rod support supplied. Lenses: Exceptionally wide range of spherical, anamorphic, speciality, and primo lenses available.

Shutter: Focal plane shutter with infinitely variable opening and adjustable in shot. Maximum opening: 180°; minimum: 40° with adjustable maximum and minimum opening stops. Digital display allows adjustments

Panavision 65mm AC/SPC Magazine and Threading Diagram
Figure 36. Film takes up emulsion side out.

in $\frac{1}{10}°$ increments. Micrometer adjustment allows critical synchronization with computers, TV monitors and HMI lighting at unusual frame rates. Manual and electronic remote-control units available.

Viewfinder: Reflex viewfinder, reflex rotating mirror standard and independent of light shutter system. Interchangeable semisilvered fixed reflex mirror for flicker-free viewing optional.

Viewfinder tube is orientable and gives a constantly upright image through 360°. Short, intermediate and long viewfinder tubes available. System incorporates an optical magnifier for critical focusing and picture composition, a de-anamorphoser, a contrast viewing filter and a lightproof shutter. Wide-range ocular adjustment with marker bezel to note individual settings. Built-in "Panaclear" eyepiece heater ensures mist-free viewing. Adjustable eyepiece leveling link-arm. Entire optical viewfinder system may be removed and replaced with video viewfinder display for lightweight camera configuration. An eyepiece diopter to suit operator's eyesight can be provided.

Video: State-of-the-art CCD video systems available in black-and-white or color.

Viewing Screen: Interchangeable ground glasses available with any marking or combination of markings. "Panaglow" illuminated reticle system with brightness control standard. Ground glasses with finer or coarser texture available. Provision for a cut frame to be placed in viewfinder system for optical image matching. Frame cutters available to suit negative or positive perforations.

Mags: 500' (152m) and 1000' (300m) magazines available. Both can be used on top of the camera for minimum camera length, or at rear for minimum camera height.

Accessories: Almost all Panaflex 35mm front-of-lens optical accessories and filters can be used on System-65 cameras.

All System-65 cameras and magazines have built-in heaters for operation in any temperature. Heated covers available to give additional protection to lenses, especially zoom lenses. Other covers available to protect camera, magazines and lenses. Spinning-glass rain deflectors available. Autobase available to secure the camera in conditions of vibration, high g-forces and other stressful and dangerous conditions. Water box available to protect camera in shallow water conditions, a hazard box to protect camera from explosions, collisions and other dangerous situations.

Camera Support Equipment: "Super Panahead" geared head incorporates a 60° tilt range with a built-in wedge system to allow operator to select where that range is, anywhere between the camera pointing directly up or directly down, and three gear ratios in both the pan and tilt movements. A sliding base unit enables camera to be quickly attached and detached and to be slid backwards and forwards on the head for optimum balance. "Panapod" tripods with carbon fiber legs are available in a range of sizes.

Power: Camera, magazines, heaters and accessories operate off a single 24V DC battery.

Panavision System 65mm Hand-Holdable

Weight: 35 lbs/15.88kg with 500' (152m) magazine and film

Movement: Dual pilot pin registration ensures process-plate image steadiness. Pilot pins register in same perforation holes (immediately below the bottom frame line) as optical printers. Four pull-down claws. Entire movement may be removed for servicing.

FPS: Camera runs at any speed from 4–72 fps. Motor is crystal-controlled at all speeds and may be adjusted in 1-fps increments.

Aperture: .906" x 2.072" (23.01mm x 52.63mm). Aperture Plate optically centered. Removable for checking and cleaning.

Displays: Single-sided display fps/footage/ low battery.

Lens: Panavision positive clamp lens mount for maintaining critical flange focal depth setting. All lenses pinned to ensure proper rotational orientation. Lenses are interchangeable with the System-65 Studio Camera.

Shutter: 172.8° fixed-opening focal plane shutter.

Viewfinder: Reflex viewfinder. Two models available; one has rotating mirror, the other a semisilvered, fixed reflex mirror for flicker-free viewing and is especially suitable for Panaglide, Steadicam, Louma and remote camera operation.

Viewfinder tube is orientatable and gives a constantly upright image through 180°. Short and long viewfinder tubes available for handheld and tripod usage. System incorporates optical magnifier for critical focusing and picture composition, contrast viewing filter and lightproof shutter. Wide-range ocular adjustment with marker bezel to note individual settings. A built-in "Panaclear" eyepiece heater ensures mist-free viewing. Adjustable leveler link arm supplied with every Panahead to keep eyepiece position constant while tilting camera up or down. An eyepiece diopter to suit operator's eyesight can be provided on request.

Video: State-of-the-art CCD video systems available in black-and-white or color. Flicker-free images possible with the pellicle reflex system.

Viewing Screen: Interchangeable ground glasses available with any marking or combination of markings. "Panaglow" illuminated reticle system

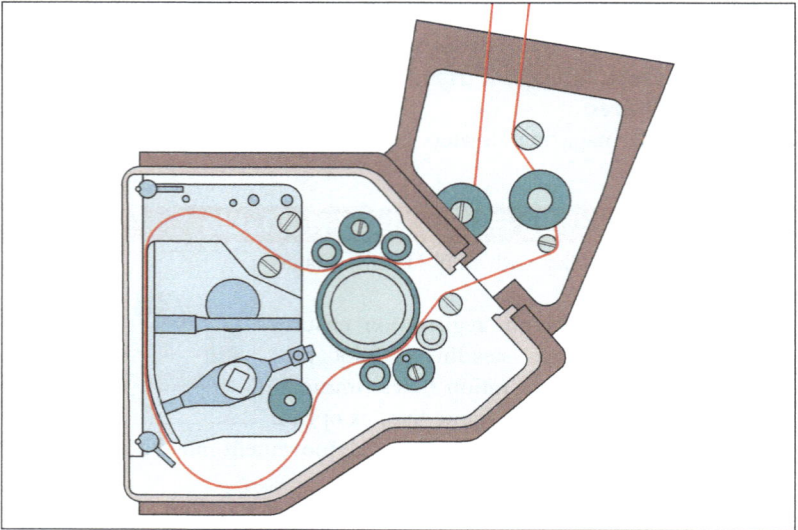

Panavision 65mm HH Threading Diagram
Figure 37. Note: The extension unit is used only for top-magazine configurations.
Film takes up emulsion side out.

with brightness control standard. Ground glasses with finer or coarser texture available.

Mags: 250' (76m), 500' (152m), and 1000' (300m) magazines are available. 1000' (300m) reverse-running magazines available on request.

Same as Panavision PSR 200°.

Accessories: Interchangeable with System-65 Studio camera. Focus control can be used from either side of the camera. Zoom lenses are supplied with an electronic zoom control unit as standard.

Standard matte box incorporating a sunshade, provision for two 4"x5.650" filters which can be individually slid up and down. Special matte boxes incorporating more filter stages with provision for sliding (motorized if required), rotating and/or tilting and for taking 6.6" square filters optional. Panavision can also supply special sliding diffusers, diopters and image-control filters, etc., to use in matte boxes.

Lightweight System-65 hand-holdable cameras are ideal for use with Panaglide and Steadicam floating camera rigs and on remotely controlled camera cranes. They can also be used with "Panatate" 360° turnover rig.

Connections: Special sync boxes available to synchronize the camera with a main power supply, computers, video signals and process projectors in shutter phase synchronization. Internal heaters.

Motors, Power: 24V DC. Camera, heaters and accessories operate off a single 24V Ni-Cad battery. Belt batteries available for handholding.

VISTAVISION 35MM

MSM Model 8812 35mm/8-perf. VistaVision

Movement: MSM Monoblock high-speed, triple-register pins, claw engages four perfs. Shrinkage adjustment changes stroke and entry position. Indexable loop-setting sprockets have independent locking keeper rollers. Movement removes easily for cleaning and lubrication. Vacuum backplate ensures film plane accuracy, removes without tools for cleaning.

FPS: Frame rates from time-lapse to 72 fps forward, to 30 fps reverse. Crystal sync from 5–72 fps in .001 increments.

Aperture: 1.485" x .992" (37.72mm x 25.2mm). Aperture removes easily for cleaning and lubrication.

Displays: Status LEDs for power, heat, low battery, mag ready, buckle and speed sync. Two illuminated LCD footage counters. Digital battery volt/amp meter. Circuit breakers for camera, mag, heat and accessories. Control port allows operation from handheld remote or interface with computers and external accessories.

Lens: BNC lens mount. 15mm matte rods are on Arri BL centers for accessory compatibility.

Shutter: Focal plane shutter, manually variable from 172.8° to 55° with stops at 144° and 108°.

Viewfinder: Reflex viewfinder, spinning mirror reflex. Inter-changeable ground glasses with register pins for film clips. Finder rotates 360° with

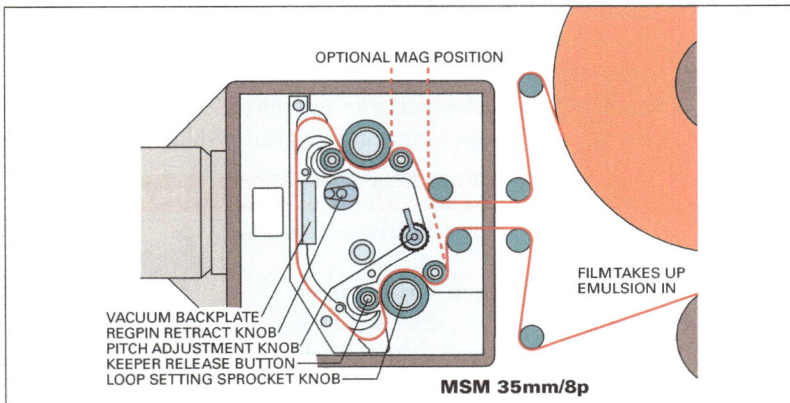

MSM 8812 Threading Diagram
Figure 38.

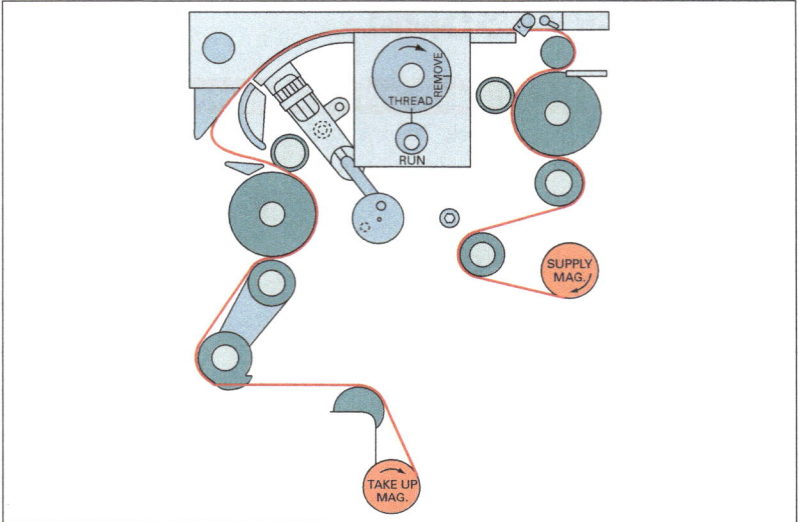

Wilcam W-7 Threading Diagram
Figure 39. Film takes up emulsion side in.

upright image, image can be manually rotated for unusual setups. Finder shows 105 percent of frame, magnifier allows critical focusing at center of interest. Single lever controls internal filter and douser. Heated eyepiece has large exit pupil and long eye relief. High-resolution black-and-white CCD videotap built into camera door with swing-away 50/50 beamsplitter. Viewfinder removes completely for aerial or underwater housing use.

Mags: 400' (122m) and 1,000' (300m) displacement magazines operate bidirectionally at all camera speeds. Positive camlock secures the mag in running position and switches power to motor and heater contacts in mag foot. Expanding core hubs have integral DC servo motors controlled by film tension in both directions, with soft startup to eliminate slack. Tightwind rollers guide film winding for smooth solid rolls at any camera angle. Noncontact light traps feature infrared end-of-film sensors.

Wilcam W-7 VistaVision High Speed (pic, one diagram)

Notes: VistaVision 35mm/8-perf. Designed for operation at 200 fps.

Weight: 110 lbs/50kg with 50mm lens and film.

Movement: Three dual-register pins. Two claw pins. Transport claws never enter registration pin perforations.

FPS: 200 fps.

Aperture: VistaVision. Aperture plate optically centered full.

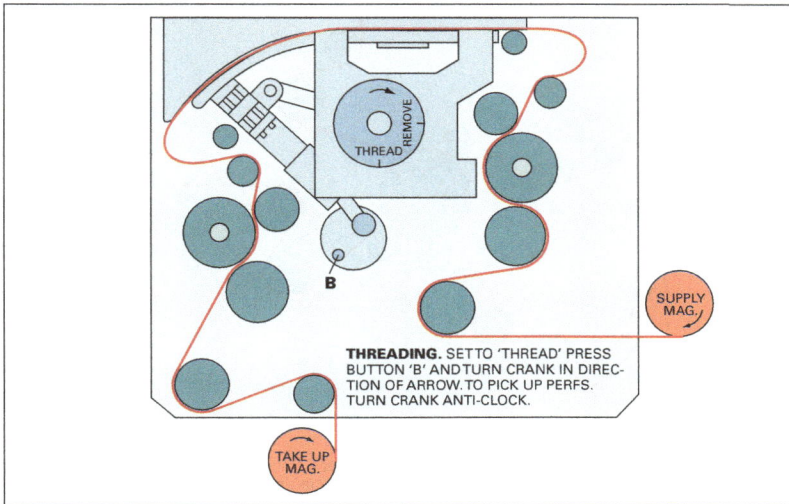

Wilcam 2-9 Threading Diagram
Figure 40. Film takes up emulsion side in.

Lens: BNCR. Lenses: 14mm f/2.8 Canon, 19mm f/2.8 Leitz, 25mm T2.8 Zeiss, 28mm T1.8 Zeiss, 35mm T1.4 Zeiss, 50mm T1.4 Zeiss, 85mm T1.4 Zeiss, 135mm T1.8 Zeiss, 35-140mm f/1.4 Vivitar zoom. Also 200mm, 400mm and 600mm.

Shutter: Beryllium mirror with tungsten counterweights.

Viewfinder: Reflex viewfinder, Rotating mirror. Uses servo motors for constant upright image while eyepiece is rotated.

Mags: 1,000' (300m). Coaxial. 2" plastic cores. Magazine drive gear-driven through torque motors permanently mounted on camera body.

Accessories: Wilcam 4" x 5.65", also standard Arriflex 6.6" x 6.6" matte boxes

Power: 48V DC required.

Wilcam W-9 VistaVision Lightweight

Notes: VistaVision 35mm/8 perf. Designed for general-purpose use. Maximum speed 100 fps.

Weight: 37 lbs/16.81 kg with 50mm lens and film.

Movement: Three dual-register pins. Two claw pins. Transport claws never enter registration pin perforations

FPS: 100 fps.

Aperture: VistaVision.

Lens: BNCR Lenses: 14mm f/2.8 Canon, 19mm f/2.8 Leitz, 25mm T2.8 Zeiss, 28mm T1.8 Zeiss, 35mm T1.4 Zeiss, 50mm T1.4 Zeiss, 85mm

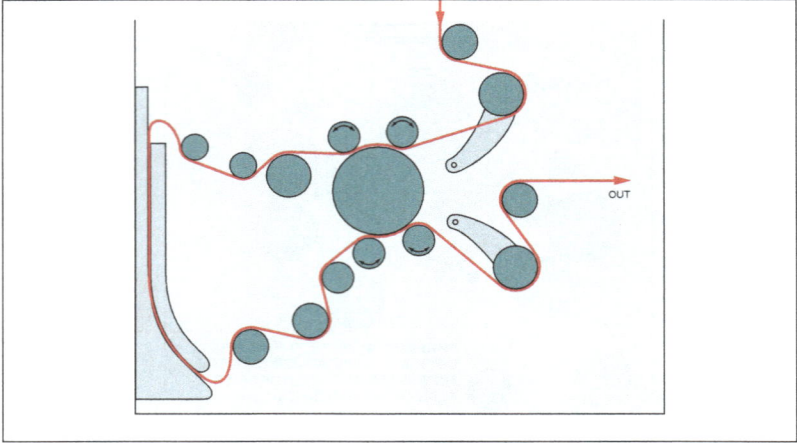

Wilcam W-11 Threading Diagram
Figure 41. Film takes up emulsion side out.

T1.4 Zeiss, 135mm T1.8 Zeiss, 35-140mm f/1.4 Vivitar zoom. Also 200mm, 400mm and 600mm.

Shutter: 180-degree Beryllium mirror with tungsten counterweights.

Viewfinder: Reflex viewfinder, Rotating mirror. Uses servo motors for constant upright image while eyepiece is rotated.

Mags: 1,000' (300m). Coaxial. 2" plastic cores. Magazine drive torque motors mounted on each magazine.

Accessories: Wilcam 4"x5.65", also standard Arriflex 6.6"x6.6" matte boxes

Wilcam W-11 VistaVision Sound Camera

Notes: VistaVision 35mm 8-perf. Designed for soundstage shooting.

Weight: 60lbs/27.27kg with 50mm lens and 1,000' (300m) of film.

Movement: Three dual-register pins. Two pairs in conventional location, one pair .050-wide perforations trailing. Two claw pins. Transport claws never enter registration pin perforations.

FPS: Crystal sync at 24, 25 and 30 fps.

Aperture: VistaVision. Aperture plate optically centered and full centered.

dB: Noise level in operating condition with a prime lens is 25dB(A) at 3' in front of camera.

Lens: BNCR lenses: 14mm f/2.8 Canon, 19mm f/2.8, Leitz, 25mm T2.8 Zeiss, 28mm T1.8 Zeiss, 35mm T1.4 Zeiss, 50mm T1.4 Zeiss, 85mm T1.4 Zeiss, 135mm T1.8 Zeiss, 35-140mm f/1.4 Vivitar zoom. Also 200mm, 400mm and 600mm.

Lens Control: Follow focus on left side of camera. Detachable.

Shutter: Half-speed, 144°. Beryllium mirror driven by second motor, phase-locked to camera motor.

Viewfinder: Reflex viewfinder, automatic image erection with manual override for odd angle viewing. 10X magnifier for critical focusing.

Video: Built-in Sony CCD video camera.

Viewing Screen: Ground glass with locating pins for film clip.

Mags: 1,000' (300m). Coaxial. 2" plastic cores. Supply on right side of camera, take-up on rear. Magazine Drive: Hysteresis clutch with sensing arms in camera body for correct film tension.

Accessories: Wilcam 4"x5.65", also standard Arriflex 6.6"x6.6" matte boxes

Motors, Power: 36V. Current: 3 Amperes.

IMAX

IMAX 3-D

Notes: Dual-strip camera comprised of two separate movements and film-handling systems all contained in single camera body. To properly record 3-D images, lenses are separated by the same interocular as the average human eye interocular of 2.85". Behind each of the taking lenses are beamsplitter mirrors that reflect right eye image up to right eye movement, and left eye image is reflected down to left eye movement. The beamsplitter mirrors also allow some light to pass through to provide for through-the-lens viewing.

Weight: 215 lbs/97.52 kg (camera, lens and 1,000' (300m) magazine); 329 lbs/149.23 kg (camera, lens and 2,500' (762m) magazine)

Movement: Two separate movements, with pull-down driven by counterbalanced crankshaft; has six claw pins and six register pins. Uses a vacuum backplate in the aperture to hold film flat for steadier images and more uniform focus.

FPS: Variable crystal speed from 1–36 fps. Camera speed can be synchronized to external reference signal. Draws 9 amps at 36V DC running at 24 fps.

Aperture: Shoots two images simultaneously on separate film strips where each negative is 15 perf x 65mm—film travels horizontally.

Lens: Custom-design IMAX lens carriage that holds pair of lenses mounted in single-lens block.

Lens Control: Remote focus and iris controller, wireless remote focus and iris controller, clip-on 3.3"x6.6" filters.

Lenses: Lens pairs mounted in single-lens block with optics supplied by Zeiss, except where noted. Include integrated iris drive and convergence motors where applicable. Fixed interocular at 2.85": 30mm T3.1

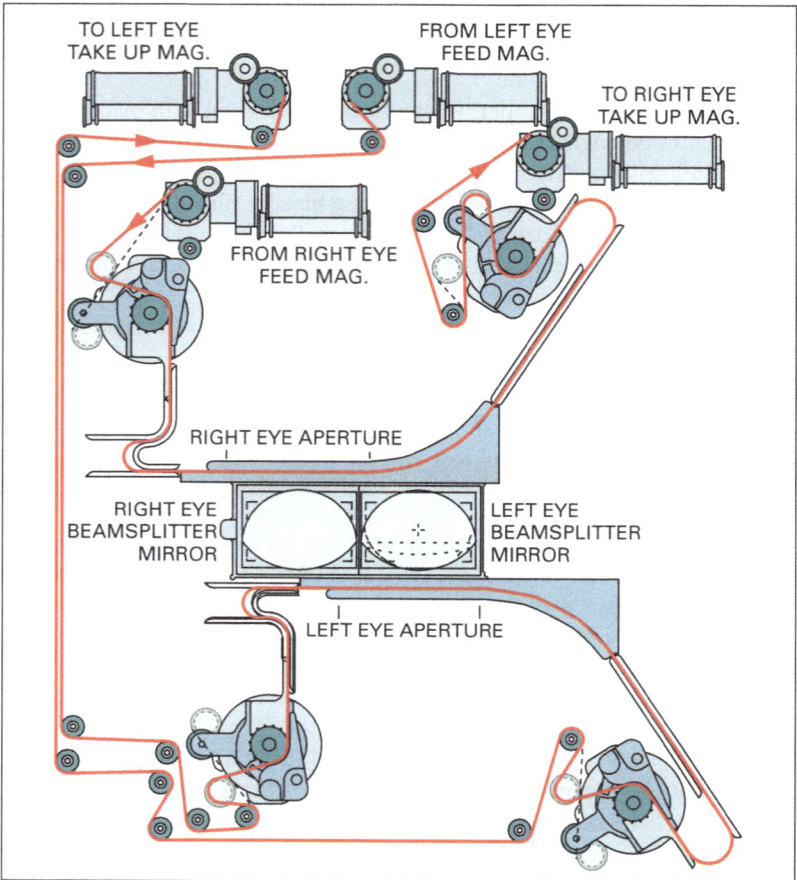

Imax 3-D Threading Diagram
Figure 42. Film takes up emulsion side out.

(Hughes Leitz), 40mm T4.3, 60mm T3.8, 80mm T3.1. Adjustable convergence: 50mm f/4, 60mm T3.8, 80mm T3.1, 105mm f/4 macro (Rodenstock), 250mm f/5.6.

Shutter: Focal plane shutter, manually variable from 172.8° to 55° with stops at 144° and 108°.

Viewfinder: Beamsplitter reflex viewfinding (70/30 split) with Imax 3-D and Imax 3-D dome reticle markings on ground glass. Viewfinder is orientable and has 10X magnifier.

Mags: Normally equipped with (four) 1,000' (300m) single-chamber magazines (3 minutes at 24 fps). Or (four) 2,500' (762m) magazines (7.5 minutes at 24 fps).

Accessories: 3-D underwater housing (depth rated to 120' (36.6m)), weather barney, matte box (with one 14" x 14" filter stage), sunshade (with mattes), 3-D microscope, viewfinder monitors, environmental box, motorized remote head, Vinten fluid head, Cartoni fluid head, parallax-corrected video assist (mounted above taking lenses).

IW5, IW5A

Notes: IW5 and IW5A are general-purpose mirrored-shutter reflex cameras. The quietest of all IMAX cameras, although not suitable for sync sound without a blimp. Very durable and robust cameras, ideal for rough environments.

IW5A is a slightly later version of IW5. IW5A uses many aluminum, parts in place of magnesium making for a more robust camera body but at the expense of a little more weight (10 lbs difference). IW5A uses an upgraded set of electronics, but the camera operational features remain the same.

Weight: IW5 88 lbs/39.91 kg (camera plus lens and 1,000' (300m) magazine with film). IW5A, 98 lbs/ 44.45 kg (camera plus lens and 1,000' (300m) magazine with film). IW5A, 155 lbs/ 70.3 kg (camera plus lens and 2,500' (762m) magazine with film).

Movement: Pull-down is a combination cam and pin-driven system. Has four register pins and four claws with adjustable pitch control. Movement is removable for easy cleaning and lubrication. Uses vacuum backplate in aperture to hold film flat for steadier images and more uniform focus.

FPS: Variable frame rate from 1–36 fps, crystal speed at 24 and 25 fps. Camera speed can be synchronized to an external reference signal. Current draw is 9 amps at 30V DC running at 24 fps.

Aperture: Negative is 15 perf x 65mm, film travels horizontally.

Lens: Custom-design IMAX bayonet lens mount.

BNC lens mount. 15mm matte rods on Arri BL centers for accessory compatibility.

Lenses: Custom-packaged for the IW5/IW5A camera with optics supplied by Zeiss (except where noted): Wide-angle 30mm f/3.5 (fisheye), 40mm f/4; medium 50mm f/2.8, 60mm f/3.5, 80mm f/2.8; long 110mm f/2, 120mm f/4, 150mm f/2.8, 250mm f/4, 350mm f/5.6, 500mm f/8, 800mm f/4 (Pentax), 1000mm f/8 catadioptic (Pentax); zoom 75–150mm f/4.5 (Schneider), 300–1200mm f/11 (Canon/Century).

Shutter: Focal plane shutter with fixed 155° opening. Wings can be added to close down to 10° opening for intervalometer shooting.

Viewfinder: Spinning mirror reflex viewfinding with IMAX and IMAX Dome reticle markings on ground glass. Finder rotates 360° with manual upright image correction. Footage and camera speed displayed in viewfinder.

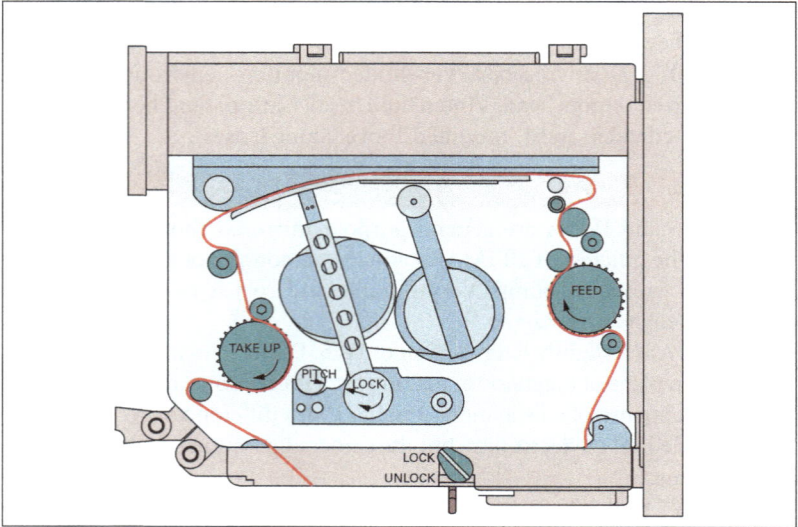

IW5 Threading Diagram
Figure 43. Film takes up emulsion side out.

Video: Video tap is modular in design, using color CCD camera.

Mags: Normally equipped with (two) 1000' (300m) dual coaxially stacked magazines (3 minutes at 24 fps). IW5A also uses 2500' (762m) magazine (7.5 minutes at 24 fps).

Accessories: Norris intervalometer, spinning disc, video assist, video lid and extension eyepiece.

Follow focus with Arri whip extension. Pentax director's finder (shoots still photos using camera lenses listed below), Preston FIZ controller and Microforce zoom controller, Preston Radio transmitter, 2X Pentax extender (for 800mm and 1000mm Pentax lenses only), extension tubes (10mm, 20mm and 40mm lengths), diopter lenses 0.5, 1 and 2.

Arri 6.6"x6.6" three stage mattebox. Sound Blimp. HydroFlex underwater housing (depth rating 150' (45.7m)), rain barney and heater barney.

MKII L/W and H/S

Notes: MKII-L/W and MKII-H/S are based on same MKII camera design and are identical in appearance and features, with one optimized for weight and the other for higher speeds.

MKII-L/W and MKII-H/S are beamsplitter reflex cameras intended for special applications where a light or high-speed camera is required in very rough or remote environments. MKII-H/S contains beryllium movement parts, and camera body was allowed to remain slightly heavier than MKII-L/W for improved image resolution when running at higher speeds.

Weight: MKII-L/W 59 lbs/26.8 kg (camera plus lens and 1,000' (300m) magazine with film), 46 lbs/20.9 kg. (camera plus lens and 500' (152m) magazine with film). MKII-H/S 68 lbs/30.84 kg (camera plus lens and 1,000' (300m) magazine with film), 55 lbs/24.95 kg (camera plus lens and 500' (152m) magazine with film).

Movement: Pull-down is a cam-driven claw arm. Four register pins and four claw pins. Uses vacuum backplate in aperture to hold film flat for steadier images and more uniform focus.

FPS: MKII-L/W has variable frame rate from 1–36 fps, crystal speed at 24 and 25 fps. MKII-H/S has variable frame rate from 1–4 fps, crystal speed at 24 and 25 fps. Camera speed can be synchronized to external reference signal. Both cameras draw 9 amps at 30V DC running at 24 fps.

Aperture: Negative is 15 perf x 65mm, film travels horizontally.

Lens: Custom-design IMAX bayonet lens mount.

Lenses: Custom-packaged for MKII-L/W and MKII-H/S with optics supplied by Zeiss (except where noted). Uses same lenses as IW5 and IW5A.

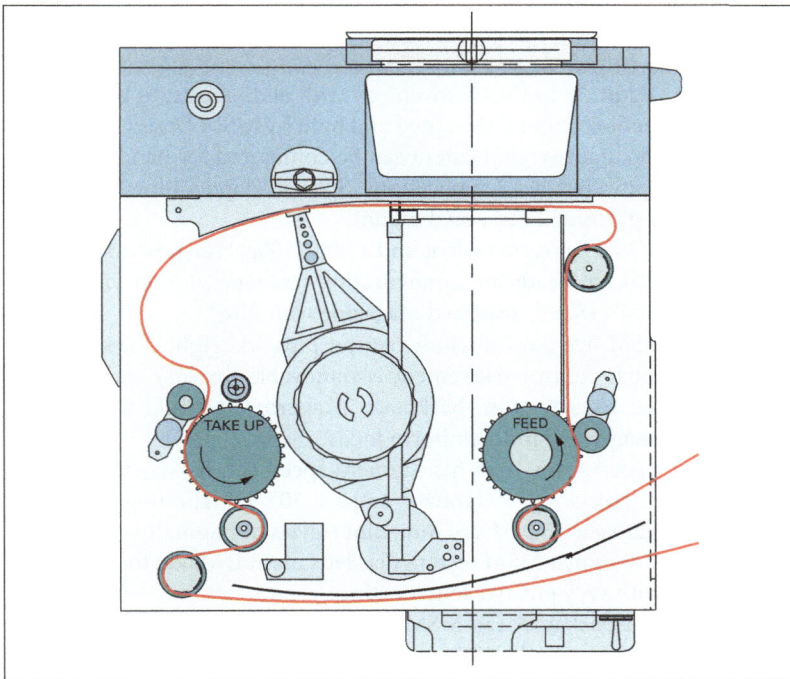

MKII L/W and H/S Threading Diagram
Figure 44. Film takes up emulsion side out.

Shutter: Flat-blade shutter with fixed 155° opening interchangeable with shutters with smaller openings for intervalometer use or shooting with HMIs.

Viewfinder: Beamsplitter reflex viewfinding (50/50 split) with IMAX and IMAX Dome reticle markings on ground glass. Finder is fixed straight to back of camera with 8X magnifier.

Video: No video tap due to beamsplitter light levels, but has video lid for 100-percent video in remote environments.

Mags: Normally equipped with 1,000' (300m) Mitchell dual-chamber magazine (3 minutes at 24 fps) or Mitchell 500' (152m)magazine (1.5 minutes at 24 fps).

Accessories: Norris intervalometer, spinning disc and video assist.

Pentax director's finder (shoots still photos using camera lenses listed below), Preston FIZ controller and Microforce zoom controller, Preston Radio transmitter, 2X Pentax extender (for 800mm and 1000mm Pentax lenses only), extension tubes (10mm, 20mm and 40mm lengths), diopter lenses 0.5, 1 and 2.

Arri 6.6"x6.6" three-stage matte box. Sound Blimp. MKII underwater housing (depth rating 120' (36.6m)), rain barney and heater barney.

MSM 9801

Notes: Latest addition to IMAX inventory with all the features of a normal 435 production camera. Designed and built by MSM Design of Hayden Lake, Idaho, lightweight camera can be configured for handheld, Steadicam or powered-head applications. Special adapter allows it to fly in Spacecam gyrostabilized aerial mount.

Weight: 56 lbs/25.4 kg (camera, lens and 1,000' (300m) magazine with film). 38 lbs/17.24 kg Steadicam configuration (camera without viewfinder, lens and 500' (152m) displaced magazine with film).

Movement: MSM five-bar link, four register pins and eight claws with adjustable pitch control. Movement is removable for easy cleaning and lubrication. Uses vacuum backplate in aperture to hold film flat for steadier images and more uniform focus.

FPS: Crystal speed from 1–36 fps. Camera speed can be synchronized to external reference signal. Draws 6 amps at 30V DC running 24 fps.

Aperture: Negative is 15 perf x 65mm, film travels horizontally.

Lens: Custom-designed MSM rectangular lens mount. Makes for quick lens changes with very positive lens locating.

Lenses: Custom-packaged for MSM 9801 with optics supplied by Zeiss (except where noted): Wide-angle 30mm f/3.5 (fisheye), 40mm f/4; medium 50mm f/2.8, 60mm f/3.5, 80mm f/2.8; long 110mm f/2, 120mm f/4, 150mm f/2.8, 250mm f/4, 350mm f/4, 500mm f/8, 800mm

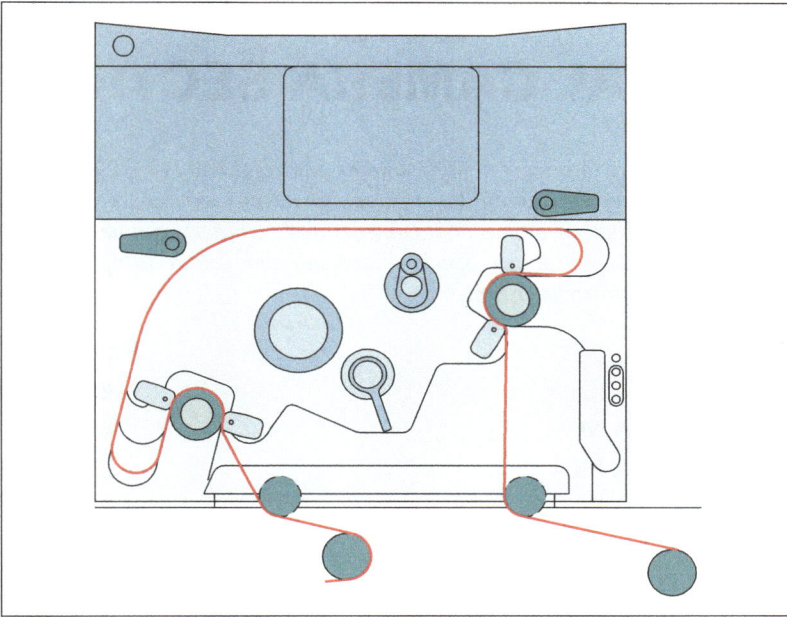

MSM 9801 Threading Diagram
Figure 45. On 1000' magazine film takes up emulsion side in.
500' magazine takes up emulsion side out.

f/6.7 (Pentax); zoom 75–150mm f/4.5 (Schneider), 300–1200mm f/11 (Canon/Century); macro 120mm slant focus (Nikon).

Shutter: Focal plane shutter with fixed 180-degree opening.

Viewfinder: Spinning mirror reflex viewfinding. IMAX and IMA
    Dome reticle markings on ground glass with register pins for film clips. Finder rotates 360° with constant upright image.

Video: Integrated color CCD video tap. Viewfinder is detachable to reduce weight for aerial shooting or Steadicam applications.

Mags: Normally equipped with 1,000' (300m) dual-chamber, coaxially stacked magazine (3 minutes at 24 fps). Also uses 500' (152m) displacement magazine (1.5 minutes at 24 fps) with automatic compensation for center of gravity shift of film roll.

Accessories: Norris intervalometer, Hi-G plate, Spacecam adapter.
    Built-in follow focus. Preston FIZ controller (focus, iris, zoom), Preston radio transmitter, 1.4X Pentax extender (for 800mm Pentax only).
    Arri 6.6"x6.6" three-stage matte box. Sound blimp. MKII underwater housing (depth rating 120' (36.6m)), rain barney and heater barney. HydroFlex shallow water housing (depth rated to 15' (4.6m)), weather barney.

2012
DIGITAL CAMERA SECTION

Note: *There are too many digital cameras and recorders being used today, with the technology in constant flux, to create an all-inclusive list; these entries represent a selection of professional cameras and recorders commonly being used for cinema applications. Specifications can change due to updating of firmware and software over time.*

CAMERAS

ARRI ALEXA

Overview: A Super 35 single-sensor digital camera with an electronic shutter and viewfinder. Integrated shoulder arch and receptacles for 15mm lightweight rods. Internal HD recording to memory cards using Apple ProRes 422/4444 codec family (Avid DNxHD codecs possible with license key). Onboard HD/certified data recorder devices can be attached. Data mode output delivers uncompressed 12-bit 2.88K ARRIRAW data in 16:9 aspect ratio. HD mode output delivers standard 10-bit (or 12-bit for ProRes4444) 1080P HD images in 16:9 aspect ratio.

Weight: Body only: 6.3 kg (13.8 lb) / body + EVF w/mounting bracket and handle: 7.7 kg (16.9 lb).

Body dimensions (LxWxH): 33.92 x 15.3 x 15.8cm (12.95" x 6.02" x 6.22").

Sensor: S35mm CMOS with Bayer CFA; Dual Gain Architecture (DGA). 3392 x 2200 pixels: 3168 x 1782 active photosites used for Surround View/recorded area is 2880 x 1620 pixels.

Active sensor dimensions: Surround View for EVF is 26.14 x 14.70mm (1.029" x 0.579"). Recorded area is 23.76 x 13.37mm (.935" x .526")/image circle is 27.26mm (1.073").

Quantization: Dual 14-bit A/D data combined into 16-bits.

Lens mount: ARRI Exchangeable Mount (ELM); ships with PL mount.

Sound level: Less than 20dB(A) at 24 fps w/lens attached and fan set to "regular".

Sensitivity: At 24 fps/180° shutter, suggested rating of ISO 800.

Frame rates: ProRes 422 HQ: 0.75-60 fps (0.75–120 fps w/high-speed license key/64 GB SxS card required for frame rates over 60 fps). ProRes 4444: 0.75–40 fps (0.75–60 fps on 64 GB cards). HD-SDI: 0.75–60 fps. ARRIRAW: 0.75–60 fps. All speeds can be set with 0.001 fps precision.

Electronic shutter: 5° to 358° with 1/10th degree precision.

White balance: Separate red/blue and green/magenta balance available through Auto White Balance or manual setting. Red/blue: 2000–11000°K, adjustable in 100°K steps, with presets of 3200°K (tungsten), 4300°K (fluorescent), 5600°K (daylight), 7000°K (cool daylight). Green/magenta: -8 to +8 CC, 1CC = 035 Kodak CC values or ⅛ Rosco values.

On-set monitoring: 1080P 4:2:2 YUV HD monitor output (single-link 422 1.5G HD-SDI) with frame rates of 23.976, 24, 25, 29.97, or 30 fps. Signal format can be changed in camera menu. Monitor signal can use either Rec.709, P3 or Log-C gamma independent of gamma selected for recording.

Recording device: Integrated SxS memory card recorder for compressed

HD or external recorder for uncompressed HD or 2.88K ARRIRAW (proprietary) data. Two SxS card slots.

Recording format: Using SxS recorder: Apple ProRes codecs (10-bit: 422 Proxy, 422 LT, 422, 422 HQ; 12-bit: 4444). DNxHD 145 (8-bit 4:2:2) and DNxHD 220x (10-bit 4:2:2) codecs are available with license key. DNxHD 4:4:4 available by end of 2012. Uncompressed 10-bit 1080P 4:4:4 RGB or 4:2:2 YCbCr or 12-bit 2.88K ARRIRAW data can be sent to external recorder. Can record Rec.709, P3 or Log-C gamma.

Recording time: On 32 GB SxS card, using ProRes 422 at 30 fps, 25 mins.; using ProRes 4444 at 30 fps, 11 mins.

Menu display/controls: Main control is a 3" LCD screen on the camera right side w/buttons and jogwheel to make selections. Three assignable buttons plus three function buttons on left (operator) side. More controls on EVF for viewfinder adjustments and other image parameters.

Indicators: Warnings appear on main display, EVF, and monitor-out.

Operating temperature: -20°C to +45C (-4°F to +113°F) at 95% max. humidity.

Video connectors: HD-SDI/1.5G/3G/T-Link out (BNC x2), monitor out (BNC).

Power connectors: 24V DC in (2-pin Fischer), 12V DC out (2-pin LEMO), RS 24V DC out (3-pin Fischer x2).

Other connectors: Ethernet (10-pin LEMO), audio in (5-pin XLR), TC (5-pin LEMO), EVF (16-pin custom LEMO), RET/Sync-In (BNC), EXT (16-pin LEMO), stereo headphone (3.5mm minijack).

Power: 24V DC (10.5V to 34V).

Power consumption: 85W for camera + EVF w/o accessories.

Accessories: Accepts the whole range of ARRI matte boxes, 15mm or 19mm rod systems, follow focus and ARRI electronic accessories, including remote control unit (RCU-1), lens control system (LCS), lens data system (LDS), wireless remote system (WRS), remote control on/off switch (RS-4).

Misc: Extra attachment points for rigging. SD card slot for importing ARRI Look Files, camera set-up files, frame line files, feature license keys and custom lens tables for Lens Data Archive (LDA). Stores capture stills from rec. out image path. Also used for software updates.

ARRI ALEXA M

Overview: Based on the ALEXA Plus 4:3, but with the camera head containing the sensor and lens mount is separate from the body

containing the image processing and recording. Ideal for dual-camera 3-D rigs and other situations where a small and lightweight camera body is needed (Steadicams, aerial and underwater photography, etc.) See ALEXA and ALEXA Plus 4:3 specs for anything not listed below.

Weight: Camera head: 2.9 kg (6.4 lb)/body: 5.5 kg (12.1 lb).

Body dimensions (LxWxH): Camera head: 21.1cm x 12.9cm x 14.9cm (8.31" x 5.08" x 5.87")/body: 32.3cm x 15.3cm x 15.8cm (12.72" x 6.02" x 6.22").

Additional connectors: SMPTE 304M hybrid fiber optical link (LEMO / one each on camera head and body). Camera head also has its own 24V DC in (2-pin Fischer) and 24V DC remote start/accessory power out (3-pin Fischer x2).

Power: Minimum 15V DC input to body is required to power camera head through SMPTE hybrid fiber cable up to 50m, w/o accessories. Camera head has one 10.5V to 34V DC power input used to power the head independently from the camera body.

Power consumption: 40W for camera head; 85W for body.

ARRI ALEXA Plus

Overview: Shares most of the same technical data as the ALEXA, but with built-in support for the ARRI wireless remote system,cmotion cvolution lens control system, and ARRI LDS (lens data system) including lens data mount and lens data archive for lenses without built-in LDS. Also has one additional monitor out, one additional RS (remote start), two LCS (lens control system), one LDD (lens data display) and three lens motor connectors, built-in motion sensors and Quick Switch BNC connectors. Assistive displays on EVF-1 and monitor out: electronic level (horizontal gauge). Automated sync of lens settings for 3-D applications in master/slave mode. SD card for importing custom lens tables for the lens data archive. ALEXA Plus 4:3 model allows a taller 4:3 area of the sensor to be used, which is ideal for anamorphic photography. Anamorphic desqueeze w/licence key. Only specs which differ from the standard ALEXA are listed:

Weight: Body only: 7.0 kg (15.4 lb)/body + EVF w/mounting bracket and handle: 8.4 kg (18.5 lb).

Body dimensions (LxWxH): 33.2cm x 17.5cm x 15.8cm (12.95" x 6.89" x 6.22").

Sensor: S35mm CMOS with Bayer CFA; dual gain architecture (DGA). 3392 x 2200 pixels. 4:3 model: 3168 x 2160 active photosites for Surround View/recorded area is 2880 x 2160 pixels. 16:9 model: 3168 x 1940 for Surround View/recorded area is 2880 x 1620 pixels.

Active sensor dimensions: 4:3 model: Surround View for EVF is 26.14mm x 17.82mm (1.029" x .702")/recorded area is 23.76mm x 17.82mm (.935" x .702")/image circle is 29.70mm (1.169"). 16:9 model: Surround View for EVF is 26.14mm x 16.00mm (1.029" x 0.630"). Recorded area is 23.76mm x 13.37mm (.935" x .526")/image circle is 27.26mm (1.073").

Video connectors: HD-SDI/1.5G/3G/T-Link out (BNC x2), monitor out (BNC x2).

Power connectors: 24V DC in (2-pin Fischer), 12V DC out (2-pin LEMO), RS 24V DC out (3-pin Fischer x3).

Other connectors: Ethernet (10-pin LEMO), audio in (5-pin XLR), time code (5-pin LEMO), EVF (16-pin custom LEMO), RET/Sync-In (BNC), EXT (16-pin LEMO), stereo headphone (3.5mm TRS), lens control system (5-pin Fischer x2), lens data display (5-pin Fischer), iris (12-pin Fischer), zoom (12-pin Fischer), focus (12-pin Fischer).

Power: 24V DC (10.5V to 34V).

Power consumption: 85W for camera + EVF w/o accessories.

ARRI ALEXA Studio

Overview: A Super 35 single-sensor digital camera with a rotating mirror shutter and an optical viewfinder. Also has internal ND filters and built-in support for ARRI wireless remote system (WRS),cmotion evolution lens control system, and ARRI lens data system  (LDS). Integrated shoulder arch and receptacles for 15mm lightweight rods. Internal 16:9 HD recording to memory cards using Apple ProRes 422/4444 codec family (Avid DNxHD codecs possible with license key). Onboard HD/certified data recorder devices can be attached. Data mode output delivers uncompressed 12-bit 2.88K ARRIRAW data using 4:3 or 16:9 area of the sensor. HD mode output delivers standard 10-bit (or 12-bit for ProRes4444) 1080P HD images in 16:9 aspect ratio. 4:3 sensor mode is ideal for 2X anamorphic photography; the optical viewfinder can be modified for unsqueezing anamorphic images.

Weight: Body only: 8 kg (17.6 lb)/body + optical viewfinder and handle: 10.2 kg (22.5 lb).

Body dimensions (LxWxH): 40.2cm x 26.8cm x 24.1cm (15.85" x 10.55" x 9.49").

Sensor: S35mm CMOS with Bayer CFA; Dual Gain Architecture (DGA). 3392 x 2200 pixels: 3168 x 2160 active photosites for EVF Surround View. Recorded area in 4:3 mode is 2880 x 2160 pixels; in 16:9 mode, 2880 x 1620 pixels (downsampled to 1920 x 1080 for HD recording).

Active sensor dimensions: Surround View for OVF is 26.14 x 19mm

(1.029" x .748")/Surround View for EVF is 26.14mm x 17.82mm (1.029" x .702"). Recorded area in 4:3 mode is 23.76mm x 17.82mm (.935" x .702"); in 16:9 mode, 23.76mm x 13.37mm (0.935" x 0.526"). Image circle in 4:3 mode is 29.70mm (1.169"); in 16:9 mode, 27.26mm/1.073".

Quantization: Dual 14-bit A/D data combined into 16-bits.

Lens mount: ARRI Exchangeable Mount (ELM); ships with PL mount with dual Lens Data System (LDS) contacts.

Sound level: Less than 20dB(A) at 24 fps w/mirror shutter on, lens attached, and fan set to "regular".

Sensitivity: At 24 fps/180° shutter, suggested rating of ISO 800.

Frame rates: 4:3 raw, mirror shutter on or off: 0.75–48 fps. 16:9 raw, mirror shutter off: 0.75–120 fps. 16:9 raw, mirror shutter on: 0.75–60 fps. ProRes 422: 0.75–60 fps. ProRes 4444: 0.75–40 fps. HD-SDI: 0.75–60 fps (4:2:2 dual-link 1.5G or single-link 3G). 4:4:4 RGB: 0.75–60 fps (dual-link 3G). All speeds can be set with 0.001 fps precision.

Shutter: Mirror shutter: 11.2° to 180°/electronic shutter: 5° to 358°. Shutter angle setting precision: 1/10th degree. At some frame rates, mirror shutter needs to be less than 180°.

White balance: Separate red/blue and green/magenta balance available through auto white balance or manual setting. Red/blue: 2000-11000°K, adjustable in 100°K steps, with presets of 3200°K (tungsten), 4300°K (fluorescent), 5600°K (daylight), 7000°K (cool daylight). Green/magenta: -8 to +8 CC, 1CC = 035 Kodak CC values or 1/8 Rosco values.

On-set monitoring: 1080P 4:2:2 YUV HD monitor output (single-link 422 1.5G HD-SDI) with frame rates of 23.976, 24, 25, 29.97, or 30 fps. Signal format can be changed in camera menu. Monitor signal can use either Rec.709, P3 or Log-C gamma independent of gamma selected for recording.

Recording device: Attached SxS memory card recorder for compressed HD (16 x 9) or external recorder for uncompressed HD or 2.88K raw data (4 x 3 or 16 x 9). SxS recorder has two card slots.

Recording formats: Using SxS recorder: Apple ProRes codecs (10-bit: 422 Proxy, 422 LT, 422, 422 HQ, 12-bit: 4444). DNxHD 145 (8-bit 4:2:2) and DNxHD 220x (10-bit 4:2:2) codecs are available with license key. DNxHD 4:4:4 available by end of 2012. Uncompressed 10-bit 1080P 4:4:4 RGB or 4:2:2 YCbCr (16:9) or 12-bit 2.88K ARRIRAW data (4:3 or 16:9) can be sent to external recorder. Can record Rec.709, P3 or Log-C gamma.

Recording time: On 32 GB SxS card, using ProRes 422 at 30 fps, 25 mins.; using ProRes 4444 at 30 fps, 11 mins. For data recorder time limits, see manufacturer specs.

Menu display/controls: Main control is a 3" LCD screen on the camera right side w/buttons and jogwheel to make selections. Three assignable buttons plus three function buttons on left (operator) side.

Indicators: Warnings appear on main display, EVF, and monitor-out.

Operating temperature: -10°C to +45°C (+14°F to +113°F) at 95% max. humidity.

Video/data connectors: HD-SDI / 1.5G/3G / T-Link out (BNC x2), monitor out (BNC x2).

Power connectors: 24V DC in (2-pin Fischer), 12V DC out (2-pin LEMO), RS 24V DC out (3-pin Fischer x3).

Other connectors: Ethernet (10-pin LEMO), audio in (5-pin XLR), time code (5-pin LEMO), EVF (16-pin custom LEMO), RET/Sync-In (BNC), EXT (16-pin LEMO), headphone jack (3.5mm TRS), lens control system (5-pin Fischer x2), lens data display (5-pin Fischer), iris (12-pin Fischer), zoom (12-pin Fischer), focus (12-pin Fischer).

Power: 24V DC (10.5V to 34V).

Power consumption: 90W for camera + OVF w/o accessories. When running over 30 fps with mirror shutter on, supply voltage of 18V or more is recommended.

Accessories: Accepts the whole range of ARRI matte boxes, 15mm or 19mm rod systems, follow focus and ARRI electronic accessories, including remote control unit (RCU-1), lens control system (LCS), lens data system (LDS), wireless remote system (WRS), remote control on/off switch (RS-4).

Misc: Extra attachment points for rigging. SD card slot for importing ARRI Look Files, camera set-up files, frame line files, feature license keys and custom lens tables for lens data archive (LDA). Stores capture stills from rec out image path. Also used for software updates.

ARRI D-21

Overview: A Super 35 single-sensor digital camera with an optical viewfinder/spinning mirror shutter. No internal recorder; however, an HD or data recorder can be attached to the camera. Using a 4:3 sensor, data mode output delivers uncompressed 12-bit ARRI-RAW data in 4:3 or 16:9 aspect ratio. HD mode output delivers standard 10-bit 1080P HD images in 16:9 aspect ratio.

Mscope anamorphic mode outputs a 4:3 1920 x 1440 RGB image (with a 2X optical squeeze) split into two 1920x720 frames (within a 1920x1080 HD signal each); this can be recombined in post. Single-link HD-SDI preview out displays a desqueezed 2.66:1 letterboxed HD signal. Image can be resized and cropped in post to standard 2.40 : 1 aspect ratio.

Weight: Body only: 9.3 kg (20.5 lb)/body + viewfinder: 11.6 kg (25.5 lb).

Body dimensions (LxWxH): With viewfinder + handle: 39cm x 27cm x 30cm (15.35" x 10.83" x 11.81"); w/o handle, height is 23cm (9.06").

Sensor: S35mm CMOS with Bayer CFA. 2880 x 2160 active photosites. Recorded area in 4:3 data mode is 2880 x 2160 pixels; in 16:9 data mode, 2880 x 1620. In HD mode: 2880 x 1620 pixels are downsampled to 1920 x 1080 pixels.

Active sensor dimensions: Data mode: 23.76mm x 17.82mm (0.935" x 0.702"). HD mode: 23.76mm x 13.36mm (.935" x .526").

Quantization: 12-bit A/D.

Lens mount: PL with dual lens data system (LDS) contacts.

Sound level: Less than 20dB(A) at 24 fps.

Sensitivity: At 24 fps/180° shutter, suggested base sensitivity of ISO 200.

Frame rates: 16:9 data mode: 1–30 fps. 4:3 data mode: 1–25 fps. HD mode: 1–60 fps. Does not run in reverse. All speeds can be set with 0.001 fps precision.

Mechanical shutter: Spinning reflex mirror shutter, electronically adjustable in 0.1° steps from 11.2° to 180° using electronic accessories such as RCU or WRC. Adjustable through camera menu at: 11.2°, 22.5°, 30°, 45°, 60°, 75°, 90°, 105°, 120°, 135°, 144°, 172.8°, and 180°.

Optical viewfinder: Two models: spherical or one switchable between spherical and anamorphic. Both have following features: adjustable in two axes with automatic or manual image compensation, laterally extendable for left-eye operation, illuminated framelines (ARRIGLOW, adjustable in brightness). Optional medium or long finder extender. Long extender includes magnifier. Optional heated eyecup or auto-closing heated eyecup.

Viewing screen: Interchangeable, uses digital ground glasses for 23.76mm (0.9354") image width.

On-set monitoring: 1080P 4:2:2 YUV HD output (single-link HD-SDI) and SD (PAL or NTSC) output (downscaled from captured image) or optional optical video tap, showing view of ground glass including area surrounding captured area, using integrated video system (IVS) optional.

Recording device: External HD or data recorder connected to single or dual-link HD-SDI.

Recording format: HD mode: up to 30 fps for 1080PsF 10-bit 4:2:2 YCbCr (single-link HD-SDI) or 1080PsF 10-bit 4:4:4 RGB (dual-link HD-SDI) and up to 60 fps for 1080PsF 10-bit 4:2:2 YCbCr (dual-link HD-SDI). Data mode: 2880 x 2160 uncompressed 12-bit raw data at 24 and 25 fps or 2880 x 1620 uncompressed 12-bit raw data at 30 fps using proprietary transmission protocol mapped into RGBA HD-SDI stream according to SMPTE 372M. Can output images using Rec.709, Extended Range Rec.709, and Log-C gamma.

Menu display/controls: To set basic camera parameters, use display on left side, similar to 435 display. Individual buttons for: *run, phase* (electronic inching), *norm, ps/ccu,* display *lock.* Use *mode, sel* and *set* buttons for setting: fps, beeper volume, beeper at start and/or stop, enable/disable mirror shutter, mirror shutter angle, frame counter reset. To set digital imaging parameters, use menus available on SD video monitoring output.

Indicators: Async operation and digital systems diagnostics, temperature, and power supply.

Operating temperature: 0°C to 40°C (+32°F to +104°F) at 95% max. humidity.

Video/data connectors: Dual-link HD-SDI out (BNC x2), composite video out (BNC x2), Y/C (S-Video/4-pin mini-DIN).

Power connectors: 24V DC in (BAT, 2-pin Fischer), 12V DC accessory out (11-pin Fischer), RS 24V DC out (3-pin Fischer).

Other connectors: HD clock pulse out/v-sync (BNC x2), lens control system (5-pin Fischer x2), lens data display (5-pin Fischer), camera control unit (RS232), ACC, iris (12-pin Fischer), zoom (12-pin Fischer), focus (12-pin Fischer), URM-3 radio receiver port.

Power: 24V DC (20.5V to 36V).

Power consumption: Camera w/o accessories: 1.9A (standby w/mirror shutter not rotating)/at 24 fps w/mirror shutter rotating: 21A.

Accessories: Accepts the whole range of ARRI matte boxes, 15mm or 19mm rod systems, follow focus and ARRI electronic accessories, including remote control unit (RCU-1), lens control system (LCS), lens data system (LDS), wireless remote system (WRS), remote control on/off switch (RS-4), integrated video system (IVS), external synchronization unit (ESU-1). Note that the FEM-2 or UMC-3 is needed for operation of WRC-1. Specifically for D-20: low mode support set for Steadicam operation or underslung use and top-mounting of accessories without bridge plate. Flash Mag Mounting Bracket (FMB-1), Sony Fibre Interface (SFI-1).

Misc: Extra attachment points for rigging.

Canon C300

Overview: A small Super 35 single-sensor digital camera. C300PL model comes with PL lens mount. Records to Compact Flash (CF) cards.

Weight: Body only: 1.4 kg (3.2 lb)/body w/grip unit and belt, monitor unit, BP-955 battery and two CF cards: 2.52 kg (5.6 lb).

Body dimensions (LxWxH): Minimal configuration C300: 17.1cm x 13.3cm x 17.9cm (6.73" x 5.2" x 7.05") / C300PL: 17.7cm x 13.1cm x 17.9cm (6.97" x 5.2" x 7.05").

Sensor: S35mm CMOS with Bayer CFA, 3840 x 2160 active photosites.

Active sensor dimensions: 24.4mm x 13.5mm (.961" x .532").

Quantization: 14-bit A/D.

Lens mount: Canon EF or PL.

Behind-the-lens ND filters: Off, ND.60, ND1.2, ND2.4.

Sensitivity: Recommended ISO 640 (0dB). Can be set in 1-stop increments: ISO 320, ISO 400 to ISO 12800, then 20000; ⅓-stop increments: ISO 320 to ISO 20000. Gain in 3dB increments: -6dB to 30dB; 0.5dB increments: 0dB to 24dB. 54dB S/N ratio (at ISO 850 using Canon Log gamma.)

Frame rates: 23.98, 24, 25, 29.97, 50, 59.94. 1080P max. rate is 29.97. 1080i max rate is 59.94. 720P max rate is 59.94.

Electronic shutter: Selectable as speed (⅓-stop increments, ¼-stop increments) or shutter angle (11.5° to 360°). Clear Scan, slow, off.

White balance: Custom white balance (A and B), color temperature setting (2,000°K to 15,000°K); two presets (daylight 5400°K and tungsten 3200°K) that can be adjusted.

Viewfinder: Attached 4" LCD and ½" EVF.

On-set monitoring: HDMI out or HD-SDI out.

Recording device: Internal recorder using removable Compact Flash (CF) memory cards (two slots). Can send uncompressed 8-bit 4:2:2 HD signal via HD-SDI to external recorder.

Recording format: MPEG-2 Long GOP codec stored as MXF files. 8-bit 4:2:2 at 50 Mbps: 1920 x 1080 (23.98P, 24P, 25P, 29.97P, 50i, 59.94i)/1280 x 720 (23.98P, 24P, 25P, 29.97P, 50P, 59.94P). 8-bit 4:2:0 at 35 Mbps: 1920 x 1080 (23.98P, 25P, 29.97P, 50i, 59.94i)/1280 x 720 (23.98P, 25P, 29.97P, 50P, 59.94P). 8-bit 4:2:0 at 25 Mbps: 1440 x 1080 (23.98P, 25P, 29.97P, 50i, 59.94i). Can record customizable Rec.709 or Canon Log gamma. 2-channel linear PCM audio (16-bit / 48 kHz). Metadata. Also captures still images as JPEGs.

Recording time: 16 GB card: 40 min. (50 Mbps)/55 min. (35 Mbps)/80 min. (25 Mbps).

Menu display/controls: Menu button and joystick/set button at rear and side, plus operation controls on side; info displayed on LCD/EVF.

Operating temperature: 0°C to +40°C (+32°F to +104°F).

Video connectors: HDMI out, single-link HD-SDI out (BNC),

Audio connectors: Ch1/Ch2 audio in (3-pin XLR x2), mic in (3.5mm minijack), stereo headphone (3.5mm minijack).

Power connectors: Powered through battery pack or with adaptor to DC in.

Other connectors: Wireless file transmitter (WFT) terminal, EXT (x2), remote (2.5mm minijack), sync out (BNC), genlock in (BNC), time code I/O (BNC), grip connection terminal.

Power: 7.4V DC (battery pack), 8.4V DC (dc in).

Power consumption: LCD + EVF at 24 fps: approx. 11.7W. EVF only: approx. 10.7W. 20.9W max rated power consumption.

Panasonic AJ-HDC27H VariCam

Overview: A ⅔" three-sensor 720P camcorder that allows shooting at variable frame rates, recording always at 60P to an internal DVCPRO HD VTR. Frame rates may be changed during recording.

Weight: Body only: approx. 4.5 kg (9.9 lb)/typical configuration w/ ENG lens: 7.0 kg (15.4 lb).

Body dimensions (LxWxH): 13.2cm x 20.4cm x 31.3cm (5.25" x 8" x 12.31").

Sensor: Three ⅔" CCD (IT type), 1280 x 720 active photosites per sensor.

Active sensor dimensions: 9.58mm x 5.39mm (.3772" x .2122").

Quantization: 14-bit A/D (model HDC27F is 10-bit).

Lens mount: ⅔" bayonet type (B4).

Sensitivity: f/12.0 at 2000 lux.

Frame rates: 4–60P (in single increments), interval recording.

Electronic shutter: ¹⁄₆₀, ¹⁄₁₀₀, ¹⁄₁₂₀, ¹⁄₂₅₀, ¹⁄₅₀₀, ¹⁄₁₀₀₀, ¹⁄₂₀₀₀. 45°, 90°, 120°, 144°, 172.8°, 180°/0.8–97.2% variable.

Built-in filters: Dual-stage: A: Cross, B: 3200°K (clear), C: 4300°K, D: 6300°K, 1: clear, 2: ¼ND, 3: ¹⁄₁₆ND, 4: ¹⁄₆₄ND.

Electronic viewfinder: Standard 2" black-and-white 720P CRT viewfinder (AJ-HVF27); color viewfinders available from third-party vendors.

On-set monitoring: 720P HD output (single-link HD-SDI).

Recording device: Internal DVCPRO HD VTR or external HD recording system.

Recording format: 720P (59.94 or 60Hz) 10-bit 4:2:2 YCbCr (single-link HD-SDI). DVCPRO HD recording reduces this to compressed 8-bit 4:2:2 960 x 720 pixel signal at 100 Mbps.

Menu display/controls: Thru viewfinder or external monitor. Side LCD panel displays TC, audio levels, battery level, tape length, etc. Also switches for: recording start/stop, two user assignable switches, power on/off, gain (L,M,H), save/standby, bars/camera, WB preset/A/B, audio levels, setting TC, switching shutter speed, white/black balance

Indicators: Tally, error.

Operating temperature: 0°C to +40°C (+32°F to +104°F).

Operating humidity: Less than 85%.

Tape: ¼" DVCPRO HD "L size" cassette. Recommended: Panasonic AJ-HP46LP.

Recoding time: Max. 46 min. with AJ-HP46LP.

Fast-forward/rewind time: Approx. 3 min. with AJ-HP46LP.

Video connectors: Single-link HD-SDI out (BNC x2), tri-level sync (BNC), time code in (BNC), time code out (BNC).

Audio connectors: Audio in (Ch1/Ch2, female 3-pin XLR), audio out (male 5-pin XLR), mic in (phantom +48V female 3-pin XLR), stereo head-phone (3.5mm minijack).

Power connectors: 12V DC in (male 4-pin XLR), 12V DC out (female 4-pin, 11 to 17V DC, max 100mA).

Other connectors: Lens (12-pin), remote (8-pin), ECU (6-pin), EVF (20-pin).

Power: 12V DC (11V to 17V).

Power consumption: 33W (w/o VF, save rec mode) / 39W (typical set-up and conditions).

Panasonic AJ-HPX3700 VariCam

Overview: A ⅔" three-sensor 1080P camcorder that records onto P2 cards using AVC-Intra 100 (10-bit 4:2:2 full raster sampling), AVC-Intra 50 and DVCPRO HD codecs. Dual-link HD-SDI output allows external recorder to capture 10-bit 4:4:4 Log. Scan reverse (image flip) function can be used to correct image inversion from certain lens adaptors. Seven gamma modes including film-rec. Gamma corrected for monitor and viewfinder display can be selected separately from recorded gamma.

Weight: Body only: approx. 4.5 kg (9.9 lb)/typical configuration w/ENG lens: 7.0 kg (15.4 lb).

Body dimensions (LxWxH): 13.2cm x 20.4cm x 31.3cm (5.25" x 8" x 12.31").

Sensor: Three ⅔" CCD (IT type), 1920 x 1080 active photosites per sensor.

Active sensor dimensions: 9.58mm x 5.39mm (.3772" x .2122").

Quantization: 14-bit A/D.

Lens mount: ⅔" bayonet type (B4).

Sensitivity: f/10.0 at 2000 lux.

Frame rates: 1–30P (in single increments), interval recording.

Electronic shutter: ¹⁄₆₀, ¹⁄₁₀₀, ¹⁄₁₂₀, ¹⁄₂₅₀, ¹⁄₅₀₀, ¹⁄₁₀₀₀, ¹⁄₂₀₀₀. Shutter angles can be selected. Synchro scan function.

Built-in filters: Dual-stage: A: Cross, B: 3200K (clear), C: 4300K, D: 6300K, 1: clear, 2: ¼ND, 3: ¹⁄₁₆ND, 4: ¹⁄₆₄ND.

Electronic viewfinder: Standard 2" black-and-white 720P CRT viewfinder (AJ-HVF27); color viewfinders available from third-party vendors.

On-set monitoring: 1080P HD output (single-link HD-SDI).

Recording device: Internal AVC-Intra 100/50 and DVCPRO HD to P2 cards

(16 GB, 32 GB, 64 GB). SD/SDHC memory card slot allows metadata files to be recorded; also allows scene files and firmware updates to be loaded.

Recording format: 1080P (59.94 or 60Hz) 10-bit 4:2:2 (single-link HD-SDI) or 4:4:4 (dual-link HD-SDI). DVCPRO HD recording reduces this to compressed 8-bit 4:2:2 1440 x 1080 pixel signal at 100 Mbps.

Menu display/controls: Thru viewfinder or external monitor. Side LCD panel displays TC, audio levels, battery level, tape length, etc. Also switches for: recording start/stop, two user assignable switches, power on/off, gain (L,M,H), save/standby, bars/camera, WB preset/A/B, audio levels, setting TC, switching shutter speed, white/black balance.

Indicators: Tally, error.

Operating temperature: 0°C to + 40°C (+32°F to +104°F).

Operating humidity: Less than 85%.

Recoding time: Five P2 card slots, 64 GB per card, allows 800 minutes of 24P/1080 content.

Video connectors: Single-link HD-SDI out (BNC x2), tri-level sync (BNC), time code in (BNC), time code out (BNC).

Audio connectors: Audio in (Ch1/Ch2, female 3-pin XLR), audio out (male 5-pin XLR), mic in (phantom +48V female 3-pin XLR), stereo headphone (3.5mm minijack).

Power connectors: 12V DC in (male 4-pin XLR), 12V DC out (female 4-pin, 11 to 17V DC, max 100mA).

Other connectors: Lens (12-pin), remote (8-pin), ECU (6-pin), EVF (20-pin).

Power: 12V DC (11V to 17V).

Power consumption: 33W (w/o VF, SAVE REC MODE) / 39W (typical set-up and conditions).

Panavision Genesis

Overview: A Super 35 single-sensor digital camera. Sensor delivers full 1920 x 1080 pixel resolution for each color channel. Multiple progressive-scan frame rates possible as well as 1080/50i and 1080/60i. Electronic viewfinder only. Sony SRW-1 VTR, Panavision SSR, or Sony SR-R1 can be positioned either in top or rear position, like a Panaflex magazine. Camera can also be used without the SRW-1, connected to a separate recorder via single or dual-link HD-SDI cables.

Weight: Body + top handle: 6.83 kg (15.5 lb), viewfinder + bracket: 1.75 kg (3.85 lb), VTR: 5.72 kg (12.6 lb).

Body dimensions (LxWxH): 22.1cm x 22.86cm x 20.32cm (8.7" x 9" x 8").

Sensor: S35mm CCD with RGB-striped CFA, 5760 x 2160 active photosites.

Active sensor dimensions: 23.622mm x 13.2842mm (.930" x .523").

Quantization: 14-bit A/D.

Lens mount: PV.

Sound level: Camera only (tethered VTR): 22.5dB(A). Camera with VTR rear-mounted: 26dB(A). Camera with VTR top-mounted: 26dB(A). Camera w/SSR rear-mounted: 25 db(A). Camera with SSR top-mounted: 25.5 db(A). (All values 3 feet from film plane).

Sensitivity: At 24 fps with a ¼₈-sec. shutter speed, suggested rating of ISO 400.

Frame rates: Fixed speeds are 23.98P, 24P, 25P, 29.97P, 30P, 59.94P, 60P, and 59.94i and 60i. Variable rate can be set between 1–30 fps (4:4:4) or 1–50 fps (4:2:2).

Electronic shutter: Adjustable from 3.8° to 360°.

Electronic viewfinder: Sony HD color viewfinder with diopter. Option for two viewfinders at once. Programmable frame lines and transparent mask.

On-set monitoring: 1080P HD output (single-link HD-SDI).

Recording device: Attached Sony SRW-1 HDCAM SR VTR or Panavision SSR-1 flash memory device, or cabled to external HD recorder, via single or dual-link HD-SDI. Video is fed automatically to SRW-1 or SSR through top or rear connector. See separate Sony SRW-1and Panavision SSR entries for details.

Recording format: Up to 30 fps for 1080P 10-bit 4:4:4 RGB (SMPTE 372M dual-link HD-SDI) or 1080P 10-bit 4:2:2 YCbCr (SMPTE 292M single-link HD-SDI); up to 50 fps for 1080P 10-bit 4:2:2 YCbCr (dual-link HD-SDI). Output uses "Panalog" transfer curve to create Log signal. SQ mode is 440 Mbps, for recording 4:2:2 (2.7:1 compression)/4:4:4 (4:1 compression); HQ mode is 880 Mbps (double-speed) for recording 4:4:4 with only 2:1 compression.

Menu display/controls: Viewfinder or side LCD panel. Programmable LCD menu gives fast access to frequently used camera settings. Also: recording start/stop, three assignable switches, on/off.

Indicators: Tally/error.

Operating temperature: -20°C to +40°C (-4°F to +104°F).

Operating humidity: Less than 85%.

Tape: ½" HDCAM SR cassette. Recommended: Sony BCT-40SR.

Tape speed: Approx. 77.4mm/s (at 24P).

Recording time: SQ mode: 50 min. (at 24P). HQ mode: 25 min. (at 24P).

Fast-forward/rewind time: Approx. 5 min.

Video connectors: Single-link HD-SDI (BNC), dual-link HD-SDI w/optional GADC adaptor (BNC x2), gen lock (BNC), reference out (BNC).

Power connectors: 24V/12V DC in (8-pin LEMO), 12V DC out (3-pin LEMO), 24V DC out (2-pin LEMO).

Other connectors: Sony RS232 (multipin x1), metadata, analog and digital zoom motor, 24V iris rod bracket, focus and T-stop motors.

NOTE: SRW-1 only has Ch1/Ch2 audio input, time code in/out, and an earphone jack. All other inputs and outputs are on the SRPC-1. For this reason, when separating the SRW-1 unit from the Panavision Genesis, you need to attach an interface box to the camera and use the SRPC-1 with the SRW-1. Then you can connect the camera to the separate recorder through HD-SDI cables for picture.

Accessories: Accepts the entire range of Panaflex accessories including matte boxes, follow focus, etc. Panavision base plate.

Power: 12V DC (camera) and 24V DC (accessories).

Power consumption: 30 fps or less: 5A, 30 to 50 fps: 7.5A, Sony EVF: 0.5A, VTR: 5A, Astro onboard monitor: 1.1A.

RED EPIC

Overview: A Super 35 single-sensor digital camera. Electronic shutter and viewfinder. Records 16-bit raw data up to 5.1K using REDCODE RAW wavelet compression. HDRx™ feature can extend dynamic range. Lower resolution modes involve cropping the sensor to smaller dimensions, allowing frame rates above 120 fps. Can also be used as a 14MP still camera.

Optional Pro I/O Module is available for increased video and audio connections (see below).

Weight: Body only: 2.27 kg (5 lb).

Body dimensions (LxWxH): 14.8cm x 9.8cm x 14.67cm (5.83" x 3.86" x 5.78").

Sensor: S35mm CMOS with Bayer CFA, 5120 x 2700 active photosites.

Active sensor dimensions: 27.7mm x 14.6mm (1.09" x .575").

Quantization: 16-bit A/D.

Lens mount: PL. Other mounts available incl. Canon EF and Nikkor.

Sensitivity: Suggested rating of ISO 800. 66 db S/N ratio.

Frame rates: Project rates: 23.98, 24, 25, 29.97, 47.96, 48, 50, 59.94 fps / varispeed rates: 1–120 fps (5K, 4.5K), 1–150 fps (4K), 1–200 fps (3K), 1–300 fps (2K).

Electronic shutter: Variable speed shutter with pre-programmed presets at $\frac{1}{24}$ to $\frac{1}{2000}$ seconds.

Viewfinder: Attachable BOMB EVF (OLED), 5" REDtouch-LCD (5" or 9"), or RED-LCD (7").

On-set monitoring: Preview HD-SDI or HDMI output in 1080P or 720P 10-bit 4:2:2 up to 60Hz.

Recording device: Mounted RED-MAG SSD module (64, 128, 256, 512 GB media).

Recording format: Using selectable levels (18:1 to 3:1) of REDCODE RAW compression: 5K raw (full frame, 2:1, 2.40 : 1, and 1.20 for 2X anamorphic photography), 4.5K raw (2.40 : 1), 4K raw (16:9, HD, 2:1, and 1.20), 3K and 2K raw (16:9, HD, 2:1, and 1.20). 1.20 mode unsqueezes 2X anamorphic image for letterboxed 2.40 display on monitors and in viewfinder. Clean HD-SDI signal (10-bit 4:2:2 720P or 1080P) can be sent to external recorders. Two channels audio (24-bit, 48 kHz). Optional four-channel analog audio and AES/EBU digital audio input via Pro I/O module.

Menu display/controls: Menu accessible through attachable BOMB EVF (when used with side handle), REDtouch-LCD, or detachable wireless REDMOTE controller.

Operating temperature: 0°C to +40°C (+32°F to +104°F).

Video connectors: EVF-LCD, HD-SDI (BNC), HDMI, Video Sync (4-pin LEMO).

Audio connectors: Audio in (3.5mm minijack x2/+48V phantom power), stereo headphones (3.5mm minijack).

Power connectors: 12V DC in (6-pin LEMO).

Other connectors: RS232 control (4-pin LEMO), Ethernet GIG-E (9-pin LEMO).

Power: 12V DC (11.5V to 17V).

Power consumption: 60W.

Misc: Remote control through wireless device (REDMOTE), Ethernet, RS232, or GPI trigger using video sync connector or via optional Pro I/O module. User assignable buttons.

Pro I/O Module

Attaches to the rear of the camera for increased I/O connections.

Weight: 1.09 kg (2.4 lb).

Dimensions (LxWxH): 9.76cm x 9.8cm x 10.9cm (3.84" x 3.86" x 4.29").

Video connectors: EVF/LCD, genlock (BNC), program HD-SDI (BNC), preview HD-SDI (BNC).

Audio connectors: Audio in (3-pin XLR x2 / +48V phantom power), audio out (5-pin XLR), AES input (7-pin LEMO) allows two to four channels of 24-bit 48 KHz digital audio ingest.

Power connectors: 12V DC out (4-pin LEMO) supplies unregulated 11.5V to 17V battery pass-through power. GPIO trigger/tally function (4-pin LEMO) also supplies unregulated 11.5V to 17V battery pass-through power.

Other connectors: RS232 control (10-pin LEMO), time code (5-pin LEMO).

Operating temperature: 0°C to +40°C (+32°F to +104°F).

Power consumption: 25W (excluding power draw of attached devices).

RED ONE

Overview: A Super 35 single-sensor digital camera. Electronic viewfinder with SurroundView™ feature, which shows a 10% area outside the picture composition. Delivers 12-bit raw data (4.5K and below) using REDCODE RAW wavelet compression. Later units will have the larger 5K Mysterium-X sensor, which is 30 x 15mm, and can use its higher ISO rating, but are restricted to recording the same 4.5K area of the original Mysterium sensor.

Weight: Body only: approx. 4.54 kg (10 lb).

Sensor: S35mm CMOS with Bayer CFA, 4520 x 2540 active photosites. Max. recorded area is 4480 x 2304 pixels, the rest is used for overscan area for monitoring.

Active sensor dimensions: 24.4mm x 13.7mm (.961" x .539"). Max. recorded area is 24.2mm x 12.5mm.

Quantization: 12-bit A/D.

Lens mount: PL. Other mounts available.

Sensitivity: Suggested rating of ISO 800 w/Mysterium-X sensor (ISO 320 with original Mysterium sensor). 66 db S/N ratio.

Frame rates: Project rates: 23.98, 24, 25, 29.97 fps (4.5K, 4K); also 50, 59.94 fps (3K, 2K). Varispeed rates: 1–30 fps (4.5K, 4K); 1–60 fps (3K); 1–120 fps (2K).

Electronic shutter: Variable speed shutter with pre-programmed presets at $\frac{1}{24}$ to $\frac{1}{2000}$ seconds.

Viewfinder: Color LCD RED-EVF (1280 x 848 pixels, progressive-scan, w/SurroundView, framelines, exposure meter).

On-set monitoring: Preview HD-SDI or HDMI output in 720P 10-bit 4:2:2 at 50/60 Hz, to RED-EVF, RED-LCD, or other monitors.

Recording device: Attached RED-FLASH (16 GB CF card) or RED SSD (64, 128, 256 GB) module.

Recording format: 12-bit REDCODE RAW files (using compression in selectable levels).

Menu display/controls: Embedded interactive menu visible through EVF and onboard LCD, plus rear black-and-white LCD display panel w/ joystick control. Display info includes media capacity remaining, battery capacity remaining, selected ASA, shutter speed, frame rate, color temp, clip name, time code, exposure histogram, Focus Assist, waveform, audio levels.

Indicators: Tally.

Operating temperature: 0°C to +40°C (+32°F to +104°F).

Video connectors: RED-EVF, RED-LCD (custom 16-pin data + power), remote (USB-2), digital magazine (custom 16-pin LEMO w/ e-SATA + power), time code (5-pin LEMO), genlock (DIN 1.0/2.3).

Audio connectors: Audio in (3-pin mini-XLR x4), audio out (5-pin mini-XLR), stereo headphones (3.5mm minijack).

Power connectors: 12V DC in (6-pin LEMO), aux. power out/GPI/O (4-pin LEMO).

Other connectors: AUX 232, lens remote, USB-2 Peripheral, SDIO.

Power: 12V DC (11.5V to 17V).

Power consumption: Approx. 65W (depending on configuration and mode).

Misc: Metadata, 4-channel audio (24-bit / 48kHz), FCP and QuickTime Player compatibility, RED-ALERT and REDCINE processing, DPX/TIFF export and alternate codec transcoding applications.

RED Scarlet-X

Overview: A Super 35 single-sensor digital camera. Electronic shutter and viewfinder. Delivers 16-bit raw data up to 5.1K using REDCODE RAW wavelet compression. HDRx™ feature can extend dynamic range. Lower resolution modes involve cropping the sensor to smaller dimensions, allowing frame rates up to 120 fps. Can also be used as a 14MP still camera.

Optional Pro I/O Module is available for increased video and audio connections (see Red EPIC entry for details).

Weight: Body only: 2.27 kg (5 lb).

Body dimensions (LxWxH): 14.8cm x 9.8cm x 14.67cm (5.83" x 3.86" x 5.78").

Sensor: S35mm CMOS with Bayer CFA, 5120 x 2700 active photosites.

Active sensor dimensions: 27.7mm x 14.6mm (1.09" x .575").

Quantization: 16-bit A/D.

Lens mount: Nikkor or Canon EF. PL mount optional.

Sensitivity: Suggested rating of ISO 800. 66 db S/N ratio.

Frame rates: Project rates: 23.98, 24, 25, 29.97, 47.96, 48, 50, 59.94 fps/varispeed rates: 1–12 fps (5K full-frame), 1–30 fps (4K HD), 1–48 fps (3K HD), 1-60 fps (1080P), 1-120 fps (1K).

Electronic shutter: Variable speed shutter with pre-programmed presets at $1/24$ to $1/2000$ seconds.

Viewfinder: Attachable BOMB EVF (OLED), REDtouch-LCD (5" or 9"), or RED-LCD (7").

On-set monitoring: Preview HD-SDI or HDMI output in 1080P or 720P 10-bit 4:2:2 up to 60 Hz.

Recording device: Mounted RED-MAG SSD module (64, 128, 256, 512 GB media).

Recording format: Using selectable levels (18:1 to 3:1) of REDCODE RAW compression: 5K raw (full frame), 4K raw (HD), 3K (HD), 1080P, 1K. Clean HD-SDI signal (10-bit 4:2:2 720P or 1080P) can be sent to external recorders. Two channels audio (24-bit, 48 kHz). Optional four-channel analog audio and AES/EBU digital audio input via the Pro I/O module.

Menu display/controls: Menu accessible through attachable BOMB EVF (when used with side handle), REDtouch-LCD, or detachable wireless REDMOTE device.

Operating temperature: 0°C to +40°C (+32°F to +104°F).

Video connectors: EVF-LCD, HD-SDI (BNC), HDMI, Video Sync (4-pin LEMO).

Audio connectors: Audio in (3.5mm minijack x2 / +48V phantom power), stereo headphones (3.5mm minijack).

Power connectors: 12V DC in (6-pin LEMO).

Other connectors: RS232 control (4-pin LEMO), Ethernet GIG-E (9-pin LEMO).

Power: 12V DC (11.5V to 17V).

Power consumption: 60W.

Misc: remote control through wireless device (REDMOTE), Ethernet, RS232, or GPI trigger using video sync connector or via optional Pro I/O module. User assignable buttons.

Silicon Imaging SI-2K

Overview: A ⅔" single-sensor digital camera. The SI-2K is composed of two components, the removable sensor head (also called the SI-2K MINI) which is then connected via network interface to an embedded Intel Core 2 Duo cPCI boardset running a customized version of Windows XP designed specifically for running the camera control software. Because the control software runs on a PC OS platform, it can also be installed on a generic PC such as a laptop, and the MINI head tethered up to 100 meters away via gigabit Ethernet. Raw sensor data from the camera head can be transmitted at up to 100 Mbps over the network interface. An optical viewfinder version of the SI-2K MINI head is also available, and can be swapped out with the non-optical viewfinder SI-2K MINI sensor block in the SI-2K.

Weight: Sensor head (SI-2K MINI) only: approx. .454 kg (1 lb); camera + sensor head: 4.99 kg (11 lb).

Dimensions (LxWxH): 26.6cm x 14.9cm x 16.5cm (10.47" x 5.87" x 6.5").

Sensor: ⅔" CMOS sensor with Bayer CFA, 2048 x 1152 active photosites.

Active sensor dimensions: 10.2mm x 5.76mm (.402" x .227").

Quantization: 12-bit A/D.

Lens mount: Universal lens mount system with adapters for PL, B4, c-mount, and F-mount.

Sound level: High fan mode: 35 db(A)/low fan mode: 21 db(A).

Sensitivity: At 24 fps with $\frac{1}{48}$-sec. shutter speed, suggested rating of ISO 250.

Frame rates: Possible frame rates vary at each resolution. At 2K and 1080P: 23.98P, 24P, 25P, 29.97P, 30P. Higher rates up to 85 and 150 fps possible through windowing of the sensor either at 1280 x 720 or 960 x 540 pixels. 720/60P provided for 60 fps smooth-motion broadcast work.

Electronic shutter: Selectable shutter angles/shutter speeds of $\frac{1}{48}$, $\frac{1}{50}$, $\frac{1}{60}$, $\frac{1}{72}$, $\frac{1}{100}$, $\frac{1}{120}$, $\frac{1}{250}$, $\frac{1}{500}$, $\frac{1}{1000}$. Additional long exposure shutter modes available up to 5 seconds (suggested limit—longer times available but create too much dark current noise).

On-set monitoring: 720P output (HDMI or VGA) at 1280 x 720 pixels via GPU video card output.

Recording device: Onto either 2.5" hard drives or flash discs compatible with SATA specification. Also any USB compatible device able to sustain 20 Mbps.

Recording format: 2048 x 1152 compressed (CineForm) 10-bit raw data or uncompressed 12-bit raw data. 720P via HDMI or VGA for monitoring purposes only.

Menu display/controls: Touchscreen interface with control over all camera functions such as shutter, gain, frame rates, resolution, as well as integrated IRIDAS 3D LUT color correction system, and frame-store system.

Accessories: P+S Technik supplied MINI-rig system for camera-head only operation, record trigger controls, optical viewfinder option, OLED electronic viewfinder via VGA interface, and shoulder-mount system.

Video connectors: Gigabit Ethernet (x2), USB 2.0 (x2), VGA, HDMI, genlock input, camera control input, record trigger input.

Power connectors: 12V DC power out (x2), lens power out (12-pin Hirose).

Power: 12V DC (12V to 17V); Anton Bauer mount included.

Power consumption: 5A average power consumption; 8A peak consumption (during record).

Sony F23 CineAlta

Overview: A 1080/60P 4:4:4 camera with three Power HAD EX $\frac{2}{3}$" (RGB) CCDs. With a wide color gamut prism block and digital signal processing up to 36 bits, color space is not limited to broadcast ITU-709 standards (television color palette). Electronic viewfinder only. The F23 records to an attached

SRW-1 tape recorder or SR-R1 memory recorder; the camera signal can also be sent to an external recorder. With attached SRW-1 or SR-R1, the F23 can record 1–60 fps for overcranking, undercranking, speed ramp effects, time lapse and interval recording. Results can be reviewed immediately on the set without any additional gear. Camera operates in either cine mode using S-Log gamma setting allowing 700% dynamic range or in custom mode with full engineering control available including hypergamma. Reinforced steel B4 lens mount.

Weight: Approx. 5.0 kg (11 lb); with attached SRW-1 approx. 9.5 kg (21 lb).

Body dimensions (LxWxH): body only: 21.6cm x 19.9cm x 20.4cm (8⅝" x 7⅞" x 8⅛"); w/top-mounted SRW-1 VTR (LxH): 29.4cm x 41.2cm (11⅝" x 16¼"); w/rear-mounted SRW-1 VTR (LxH): 38.8cm x 30.7cm (15⅜" x 12⅛").

Sensor: Three ⅔" CCD (Hyper HAD EX), 1920 x 1080 active photosites per sensor.

Active sensor dimensions: 9.58mm x 5.39mm (.3772" x .2122").

Quantization: 14-bit A/D.

Lens mount: ⅔" bayonet type (B4).

Built-in filters: Dual-stage: A: 3200°K (clear), B: 4300°K, C: 5600°K, D: 6300°K, E: ½ND ND1: CLEAR, ND2: ¼ND, ND3: ¹⁄₁₆ND, ND4: ¹⁄₆₄ND, ND5: CAP.

Sound level: Camera only (tethered VTR): 22.5dB(A). Camera with VTR rear-mounted: 26dB(A). Camera with VTR top-mounted: 26dB(A). Camera w/SSR rear-mounted: 25 db(A). Camera with SSR top-mounted: 25.5 db(A). (All values 3 feet from film plane).

Sensitivity: f/10.0 at 2000 lux, 89.9% reflective. At 24 fps with a ¹⁄₄₈-sec. shutter speed, the exposure index is approx. equivalent to ISO 400.

Frame rates: Fixed speeds are 23.98P, 24P, 25P, 29.97P, 30P, 59.94P, 60P, and 59.94i and 60i. Variable rates: 1–60 fps (4:4:4 or 4:2:2)/interval recording, time lapse and speed ramps possible.

Electronic shutter: Variable mode shutter angles from 4.2° to 360° are achievable. Settings are either OFF, or VARIABLE (4.2°–360°) or STEP (eight user-defined settings chosen from 4.2°–360°).

Electronic viewfinder: Sony HDVF-C30W LCD color viewfinder (w/ 3.5" LCD screen).

On-set monitoring: 1080P/1080i (single or dual link HD-SDI) / SD (NTSC/PAL).

Recording device: Attached Sony SRW-1 HDCAM SR VTR or SR-R1 memory recorder, or cabled to an external recorder via single or dual-link HD-SDI. Video is fed automatically to SRW-1 / SR-R1 through top or rear connector. See separate Sony SRW-1 and SR-R1 entries for additional details.

Recording format: 1080P or 1080i, 10-bit 4:4:4 (RGB) or 4:2:2 (YCbCr) using HDCAM-SR compression. SR-Lite (220 Mbps) and SR-SQ (440 Mbps) are supported as standard; SR-HQ (880 Mbps) is supported on SRW-1. SR-HQ and uncompressed recording are supported on SR-R1 as an option with the SRK-R311. S-Log, Hypergamma, and Rec.709 gamma options.

Menu display/controls: LCD viewfinder, monitor out or side blue EL display panel. Programmable LCD and EL panel menu gives fast access to frequently used camera settings. Also: recording start/stop, three assignable switches, on/off. Separate assistant panel (wired remote control device) with blue EL display also available.

Indicators: Tally/error/assignable.

Operating temperature: 0°C to +40°C (+32°F to +104°F).

Operating humidity: Less than 85%.

Video connectors: Genlock in (BNC), test out/VBS/HD Y (BNC), monitor out/single-link HD-SDI out (BNC x2), dual-link HD-SDI out or two HD-SDI 4:2:2 via Interface Box (BNC x2).

Audio connectors: audio in (3-pin XLR x2).

Power connectors: 12V/24V DC in (8-pin male LEMO), DC in (4-pin male XLR, camera only via interface module), 12V DC out (11-pin Fischer, max 4A), 24V DC out (3-pin Fischer, max 5.5A).

Other connectors: Lens (12-pin Hirose), RMB/MSU remote (8-pin Hirose), viewfinder (20-pin Sony x2), external I/O (5-pin female LEMO), network (RJ-45, 10Base-T/100Base-TX).

NOTE: SRW-1 only has Ch1/Ch2 audio input, time code in/out, and an earphone jack. All other inputs and outputs are on the SRPC-1. For this reason, when separating the SRW-1 unit from the Sony F23 camera, you need to attach an interface box to the camera and use the SRPC-1 with the SRW-1. Then you can connect the camera to the separate recorder through HD-SDI cables for picture.

Power: 12V DC (10.5V to 17V) / 24V DC (pass-thru for accessory out only). 150W power supply recommended.

Power consumption: 56W (w/o lens, viewfinder, at 24P).

Sony F35 CineAlta

Overview: A Super 35 single-sensor (RGB-striped CCD) digital camera. Sensor delivers full 1920 x 1080 pixel resolution for each color channel. The F35 records to an attached SRW-1 tape recorder or SR-R1 memory recorder; camera signal can also be sent to an external recorder. With attached SRW-1 or SR-R1, the F35 can record 1 - 60 fps for overcranking,

undercranking, speed ramp effects, time lapse and interval recording. Results can be reviewed immediately on the set without any additional gear. Camera operates in either Cine Mode using S-Log Gamma setting allowing 800% dynamic range or in Custom Mode with full engineering control available including Hypergamma. Electronic viewfinder only.

Weight: Body + top handle: 6.83 kg (15.5 lb), viewfinder 850g (1.13 lb), VTR: 5.72 kg (12.6 lb).

Body dimensions (LxWxH): Body only: 21.6cm x 19.9cm x 20.4cm (8⅝" x 7⅞" x 8⅛"); w/top-mounted SRW-1 VTR (LxH): 29.4cm x 41.2cm (11⅝" x 16¼"); w/rear-mounted SRW-1 VTR (LxH): 38.8cm x 30.7cm (15⅜" x 12⅛").

Sensor: S35mm CCD with RGB-striped filter, 5760 x 2160 active photosites.

Active sensor dimensions: 23.622mm x 13.2842mm (.930" x .523").

Quantization: 14-bit A/D.

Lens mount: PL or PV.

Sound level: Camera only (tethered VTR): 22.5dB(A)/camera with VTR rear-mounted: 26dB(A)/camera with VTR top-mounted: 26dB(A)/camera w/SSR rear-mounted: 25 db(A)/camera with SSR top-mounted: 25.5 db(A). (All values 3 feet from film plane).

Sensitivity: At 24 fps with a ¹⁄₄₈-sec. shutter speed, suggested rating of 400 ASA.

Frame rates: Fixed speeds are 23.98P, 24P, 25P, 29.97P, 30P, 59.94P, 60P, and 59.94i and 60i. Variable rate can be set between 1–60 fps (4:4:4 or 4:2:2).

Electronic shutter: Adjustable from 3.8° to 360°.

Electronic viewfinder: Sony HD color viewfinder with diopter. Option for two viewfinders at once. Programmable frame lines and transparent mask.

On-set monitoring: 1080P HD output (single-link HD-SDI).

Recording device: Attached Sony SRW-1 HDCAM SR VTR or SR-R1 memory recorder, or cabled to external recorder, via single or dual-link HD-SDI. Video is fed automatically to SRW-1/SR-R1 through top or rear connector. See separate Sony SRW-1 and SR-R1 entries for additional details.

Recording format: 1080P 10-bit or 12 bit 4:4:4 RGB or 1080P 10-bit 4:2:2 YCbCr using HDCAM-SR compression. SR-Lite (220 Mbps) and SR-SQ (440 Mbps) are supported as standard; SR-HQ (880 Mbps) is supported on SRW-1. SR-HQ and uncompressed recording are supported on SR-R1 as an option with the SRK-R311. S-Log, Hypergamma, and Rec.709 gamma options.

Menu display/controls: viewfinder or side LCD panel. Programmable LCD menu gives fast access to frequently used camera settings. Also: recording start/stop, three assignable switches, on/off.

Indicators: Tally, error, assignable.

Operating temperature: -20°C to +40°C (-4°F to +104°F).

Operating humidity: Less than 85%.

Video connectors: Single-link HD-SDI (BNC), genlock in (BNC), reference out (BNC), sync out (BNC).

Power connectors: 24V/12V DC in (11-pin Fisher), 12V DC out (3-pin Fisher), 24V DC out.

Other connectors: Sony RS232 (multipin), metadata, record trigger on 3-pin Fisher.

NOTE: SRW-1 only has Ch1/Ch2 audio input, time code in/out, and an earphone jack. All other inputs and outputs are on the SRPC-1. For this reason, when separating the SRW-1 unit from the F35, you need to attach an interface box to the camera and use the SRPC-1 with the SRW-1.

Accessories: Accepts the entire range of ARRI or Panaflex accessories including matte boxes, follow focus, etc.

Power: 12V DC (10.5V to 17V); 24V DC (pass thru for accessory out only). 150W power supply recommended.

Power consumption: 30 fps or less: 5A, 30 to 50 fps: 7.5A, Sony viewfinder: 0.5A, VTR: 5A.

Sony F65 CineAlta

Overview: A Super 35 single-sensor CMOS digital camera. 8K (20MP) sensor with 17:9 aspect ratio delivers full 4K resolution. Electronic viewfinder. F65 has a mechanical rotating shutter to eliminate rolling shutter effect. Uses a dockable memory recorder (SR-R4) for 16-bit raw data.

Weight: Body only: 5 kg (11 lb)/body + top handle, viewfinder bracket, viewfinder: 7.3 kg (16 lb)/body + top handle, viewfinder bracket, viewfinder, SR-R4 Memory Recorder: 9.3 kg (20.5 lb).

Body dimensions (LxWxH): 25.4cm x 22.9cm x 20.3cm (10" x 9" x 8").

Sensor: S35mm CMOS w/ Q67-style CFA (Bayer pattern rotated 45 degrees), 8192 x 2160 active photosites.

Active sensor dimensions: 24.7mm x 13.1mm (.972" x .516").

Quantization: 16-bit A/D.

Lens mount: PL or PV.

Behind-the-lens ND filters: ND.9, 1.2, 1.5, 1.8 (3, 4, 5, 6 stops).

Sensitivity: Suggested rating of ISO 800.

Frame rates: 1–120 fps.

Shutter: 4.2° to 360° (electronic shutter)/11.2° to 180° (mechanical rotary shutter).

Electronic viewfinder: Color LCD viewfinder (HDVF-C30W) with diopter; other viewfinders available.

On-set monitoring: 1080P HD output (single-link HD-SDI).

Recording device: Dockable Sony SR-S4 recorder using SRMemory cards.

Recording format: 16-bit linear raw or MPEG-4 SStP files (HDCAM-SR native.) RAW options: F65RAW-SQ, F65RAW-Lite, and F65RAW-HFR. The F65RAW-SQ mode uses a mild compression for highest possible image quality is the priority. The F65RAW-Lite mode uses a higher compression which extends the recording time by reducing the image file size. F65RAW-HFR mode allows the F65, with the SR-R4, to record over 24 minutes of 120P content on a single SR-1TS55 (1 TB) card. HD SStP options: RGB HD files (1920 x 1080) recorded as 10-bit 4:4:4 or 12-bit 4:4:4 and 10-bit 4:2:2 MPEG-4 SStP files.

Recording time: Raw mode to SR-R4 using 1TB card: 60 min. (at 24P).

Menu display/controls: Viewfinder or side LCD panel. Four assignable buttons. Wired or wireless to iPad or Android tablets.

Indicators: Recording (hideable), diagnosis, docking.

Operating temperature: 0°C to +40°C (+32°F to +104°F).

Video connectors: HD-SDI out (BNC x2), HD-Y out (BNC), genlock in (BNC).

Power connectors: 12V/24V DC in (8-pin male LEMO) / 12V DC out (11-pin), 24V DC out (3-pin).

Other connectors: Viewfinder (20-pin), lens (12-pin), remote (8-pin) external input/output (5-pin female LEMO), Ethernet (RJ-45 type), 10BASE-T, 100BASE-TX lens mount hot shoe (4-pin x2), conforming to ARRI LDS (Lens Data System) and Cooke /i.

Power: 12 DC (10.5V to 17V) for camera, 24V DC (20V to 30V) for accessories.

Power consumption: Approx. 65W at 24 fps (mechanical rotary shutter operating, without lens, viewfinder); 102W w/ SR-R4 onboard.

Sony HDC-F950 CineAlta

Overview: A 1080/60P 4:4:4 camera with three ⅔" (RGB) CCDs. Requires external HD recorder. Electronic viewfinder only. The HDC-F950 provides full-bandwidth digital 4:4:4 RGB signal processing and output capability. 4:4:4 HD can be sent via dual-link HD-SDI to recorder,  or via single optical fiber cable to HDCU-F950 Camera Control Unit or to SRPC-1 processor unit (w/ HKSR-101 option installed) for SRW-1 HDCAM SR recorder. The HDC-F950 has the ability to do time exposures (slow shutter). The HKC-T950 HD CCD block adaptor is a small unit containing just the lens mount and imaging block, separated from the DSP inside the main camera body by up to 10 meters, or 50 meters with an optional cable. This has been adapted for 3-D systems (using two "T-blocks" side by side), plus unique shooting situations that require a small camera unit.

Weight: Body only: approx. 5.1 kg (11.24 lb).

Body dimensions (LxWxH): 36.0cm x 13.3cm x 27.6cm (14.17" x 5.24" x 10.87").

Sensor: Three ⅔" CCD (FIT type), 1920 x 1080 active photosites per sensor.

Active sensor dimensions: 9.58mm x 5.39mm (.3772" x .2122").

Quantization: 14-bit A/D.

Lens mount: ⅔" bayonet type (B4).

Sensitivity: f/10.0 at 2000 lux, 89.9% reflective. At 24 fps, $\frac{1}{48}$-second shutter speed, the exposure index is approx. equivalent to ISO 320.

Frame/field rates: 23.98P, 24P, 25P, 29.97P, 30P, 50i, 59.94i, 60i

Electronic shutter: (24P mode): off, $\frac{1}{32}$, $\frac{1}{48}$, $\frac{1}{60}$, $\frac{1}{96}$, $\frac{1}{125}$, $\frac{1}{250}$, $\frac{1}{500}$, $\frac{1}{1000}$. ECS (ClearScan) 24–2200Hz (minimum setting depends on frame rate selected).

Built-in filters: dual-stage: A: Cross (or 5600°K on later versions), B: 3200°K, C: 4300°K, D: 6300°K, 1: clear, 2: ¼ND, 3: $\frac{1}{16}$ND, 4: $\frac{1}{64}$ND.

Electronic viewfinder: 2" black-and-white CRT viewfinder (HDVF-20A) or color LCD viewfinder (HDVF-C30W); other viewfinders available.

On-set monitoring: 1080P/1080i HD (single-link HD-SDI).

Recording device: Any external HD recorder.

Recording format: 1080P or 1080i 10-bit 4:2:2 YCbCr (thru single-link HD-SDI) or 10-bit 4:4:4 RGB (thru dual-link HD-SDI or optical fiber cable).

Menu display/controls: Viewfinder (for access to menu using thumbwheel) or side LCD panel (for TC, audio, etc.) Also switches for: record start/stop, two assignable switches, power on/off. white balance, etc.

Indicators: Tally/error.

Operating temperature: -20°C to +45°C (-4°F to +113°F).

Operating humidity: 25% to 80% relative humidity.

Video connectors: Dual-link HD-SDI out (BNC x2), single-link HD-SDI out (BNC), test out (BNC), genlock in (BNC), optical fiber out.

Audio connectors: Ch1/Ch2 audio in (3-pin female XLR x2), mic in (3-pin female XLR), stereo headphone (3.5mm minijack).

Power connectors: 12V DC in (4-pin male XLR, 11 to 17V DC), 12V DC out (4-pin male, 10.5 to 17V).

Other connectors: Lens (12-pin), remote (8-pin), EVF (20-pin), external I/O (20-pin).

Power: 12V DC (11V to 17V).

Power consumption: 33W.

Sony HDW-F900 CineAlta

Overview: A ⅔" 3-CCD camcorder capable of capturing images at 23.98/24/25/29.97/30P (progressive-scan) or 50/59.94/60i (interlace-scan) at 1920 x 1080 pixel resolution, recording to an internal HDCAM VTR.

Weight: Body w/ ENG lens, tape, and battery: approx. 8 kg (17 lb).

Body dimensions (LxWxH): With handle: 34.0cm x 14.0cm x 26.5cm (13.39" x 5.51" x 10.43").

Sensor: Three ⅔" CCD (FIT type), 1920 x 1080 active photosites per sensor.

Active sensor dimensions: 9.58mm x 5.39mm (.3772" x .2122").

Quantization: 10-bit A/D.

Lens mount: ⅔" bayonet type (B4).

Sensitivity: f/10.0 at 2000 lux, 89.9% reflective. At 24 fps, ¹⁄₄₈-second shutter speed, the exposure index is approx. equivalent to ISO 320.

Frame/field rates: 23.98P, 24P, 25P, 29.97P, 30P, 50i, 59.94i, 60i.

Electronic shutter: (24P mode): ¹⁄₃₂, ¹⁄₄₈, ¹⁄₆₀, ¹⁄₉₆, ¹⁄₁₂₅, ¹⁄₂₅₀, ¹⁄₅₀₀, ¹⁄₁₀₀₀. ECS (ClearScan) 24 to 7000 Hz (minimum setting depends on frame rate selected).

Built-in filters: Dual-stage: A: Cross (or 5600°K on later versions), B: 3200°K, C: 4300°K, D: 6300°K, 1: clear, 2: ¼ND, 3: ¹⁄₁₆ND, 4: ¹⁄₆₄ND.

Electronic viewfinder: 2" black-and-white CRT viewfinder (HDVF-20A) or color LCD viewfinder (HDVF-C30W); other viewfinders available.

On-set monitoring: 1080P/1080i HD (three analog HD connectors); single-link HD-SDI output possible w/ HDCA-901 adaptor.

Recording device: Internal HDCAM VTR or external HD recorder.

Recording format: 1080P/1080i 10-bit 4:2:2 YCbCr (thru single-link HD-SDI). HDCAM recording reduces this to compressed 8-bit 3:1:1 1440 x 1080 pixel signal.

Menu display/controls: Viewfinder (for access to menu using thumbwheel) or side LCD panel (for TC, audio, etc.) Also switches for: record start/stop, two assignable switches, power on/off. white balance, etc.

Indicators: Tally/error.

Operating temperature: 0°C to +40°C (+32°F to +104°F).

Operating humidity: 25% to 80% relative humidity.

Tape: ½" HDCAM cassette. Recommended: Sony BCT-40HD/22HD.

Tape speed: Approx. 77.4mm/s (24P mode).

Recording time: Max. 50 min. with BCT-40HD (24P mode).

Fast-forward/Rewind time: Approx. 6 min. with BCT-40HD.

Video connectors: Analog YPbPr video output (BNC x3), genlock video in (BNC), time code in (BNC), time code out (BNC).

Audio connectors: Ch1/Ch2 audio in (3-pin female XLR x2), mic in (3-pin female XLR), audio out (5-pin male XLR), stereo headphone (3.5mm minijack).

Power connectors: 12V DC in (4-pin male XLR, 11 to 17V DC), 12V DC out (4-pin male XLR, 11 to 17V DC).

Other connectors: Lens (12-pin), remote (8-pin), ECU (6-pin), EVF (20-pin).

Power: 12V DC (11V to 17V).

Power consumption: 42W (with 12V power supply, REC mode, with HDVF-20A).

Misc.: Sony HDCA-901 is a commonly used adaptor that allows HD-SDI output (BNC x2), as well as audio recording to Ch3/Ch4 (female 3-pin XLR x2), audio monitor output (4-pin male XLR) and stereo headphone (3.5mm minijack). Panavision and Clairmont Cameras made various revisions to the F900; as a result, the menu access button on the front was moved onto a separate control unit. Panavised F900 has a dedicated Panavision lens mount to accept Panavision Digital Lens.

Sony HDW-F900R CineAlta

Overview: A major revision of the Sony F900 with many physical improvements, not just an updated version. The F900R records images in accordance with the CIF (Common Image Format) standard, which specifies a sampling structure of 1920 x 1080 pixels, rather than re-ducing 1920 to 1440 horizontal pixels as the HDCAM recorder does in the earlier F900. There is also a picture cache board, a 2:3 pull-down option for monitoring 24P as 60i to reduce flicker, a downconverter for SD monitoring purposes, a slow-shutter board, and two HD-SDI outputs. 12-bit A/D conversion rather than 10-bit. The body is 20% shorter and 2.6 kg lighter than the previous model. The size is also smaller because the commonly-used HDCA-901 adaptor is no longer needed to get HD-SDI outputs. The B4 lens mount has been reinforced. Enhanced image controls such as HyperGamma provided. Stop motion and time-lapse photography now possible with HKDW-703 picture cache board. Image inversion possible with HKDW-905R board.

Only the specifications that differ from the F900 are listed below.

Weight: Body w/ ENG lens, tape, and battery: approx. 5.4 kg (11.91 lb).

Body dimensions (LxWxH): Without handle: 30.8cm x 12.7cm x 20.6cm (12.13" x 5" x 8.11"); w/ handle, height is 26.9cm (10.59").

Quantization: 14-bit A/D.

Frame/field rates: Same as F900, plus interval recording w/ HKDW-703 board.

Electronic shutter: Same as F900, plus slow-shutter w/ HKDW-905R board.

Electronic viewfinder: 2" black-and-white CRT viewfinder (HDVF-20A) or color LCD viewfinder (HDVF-C30W); other viewfinders available.

On-set monitoring: 1080P/1080i HD (single-link HD-SDI), SD (NTSC/PAL).

Operating humidity: 25% to 85% relative humidity.

Video connectors: Single-link HD-SDI out (BNC x2), test/SD out (BNC), genlock video in (BNC), time code in (BNC), time code out (BNC).

Power consumption: 38W (with 12V power supply, REC mode, with HDVF-20A).

Sony PMW-F3 CineAlta

Overview: A small, affordable Super 35 single-sensor digital camera with electronic shutter, viewfinder, and 3.5" LCD. Records 1920 x 1080 HD to internal SxS cards using 8-bit 4:2:0 XDCAM codec. Can send out 10-bit 4:2:2/4:4:4 HD in S-Log gamma to external recorders. 3D-LINK option for controlling two bodies in a stereoscopic rig with a single remote controller. Interval recording function. PMW-F3K model comes with a T/2.0 35mm, 50mm, and 85mm lens.

Weight: 2.4 kg (5.29 lb).

Body dimension (LxWxH): 21.0cm x 15.1cm x 18.9cm (8.27" x 5.94" x 7.44").

Sensor: S35mm CMOS (Exmor) with Bayer CFA. 2468 x 1398 active photosites.

Active sensor dimensions: 23.6mm x 13.3mm (.929" x .524"). 27.1mm diagonal.

Quantization: 14-bit A/D.

Lens mount: PL (with supplied lens mount adapter).

Built-in filters: Off: Clear, 1: $\frac{1}{8}$ND, 2: $\frac{1}{64}$ND.

Sensitivity: Recommended ISO 400 (video gamma mode) or ISO 800 (S-Log gamma mode). 63dB (Y) signal-to-noise ratio.

Gain: -3, 0, 3, 6, 9, 12, 18dB, AGC.

White balance: Preset, Memory A, Memory B/ATW.

Frame rates: 720P: 1–60 fps selectable (17–60 fps when HD-SDI Dual Link is active); 1080P: 1–30 fps selectable (17–30 fps when HD-SDI Dual Link is active).

Electronic shutter: $\frac{1}{32}$–$\frac{1}{2000}$ sec./slow shutter: 2, 3, 4, 5, 6, 7, 8 frame accumulation.

Electronic viewfinder: 0.45-inch, 16 x 9, 852 x 480 pixels.

Onboard LCD: 3.5-inch, 16 x 9, hybrid (semi-transmissive) type, 640 x 480 pixels.

On-set monitoring: HD-SDI out or HDMI out to monitor.

Recording device: Internal SxS Express Card34 recorder, 2-slots. 16GB, 32GB, 64GB cards.

Recording format: 8-bit 4:2:0 XDCAM codec using internal recorder. HD HQ mode (35 Mbps): 1920 x 1080/59.94i, 50i, 29.97P, 25P, 23.98P; 1440 x 1080/59.94P, 50P, 29.97P, 25P, 23.98P; 1280 x 720/59.94P, 50P, 29.97P, 25P, 23.98P. HD SP mode (25 Mbps): 1440 x 1080/59.94i, 50i (23.98P is recorded as 59.94i w/2-3 pull-down). SD mode (DVCAM): 720 x 480/59.94i, 29.97P or 720 x 576/50i, 25P. 10-bit 4:2:2 or 4:4:4 out to external recorder using HD-SDI single or dual-link. Gamma modes: Standard (x6), Cine (x4), S-Log (with RGB and S-LOG option).

Recording time: In HQ mode, 16GB card: approx. 50 min./32GB card: approx. 100 min./64GB card: approx. 200 min.

Menu display/controls: External switches on camera body plus through LCD and EVF. Also can use IR Remote Commander.

Indicators: Tally/battery/error.

Operating temperature: 0°C to +40°C (+32°F to +104°F).

Video connectors: SDI out (BNC), HD-SDI dual-link out (BNC x2), HD-Y or composite video out (BNC), HDMI out (Type A).

Audio connectors: Ch.1/Ch.1 audio in (3-pin XLR x2), Ch.1/Ch.2 audio out (RCA phono jacks x2), stereo headphone (3.5mm minijack).

Power connectors: DC in (4-pin XLR).

Other connectors: Genlock in (BNC), time code in (BNC), time code out (BNC), i.Link HDV/DV (4-pin), remote (8-pin), USB (Mini-B/USB2.0), option (USB Type A), spare (10-pin round).

Power requirements: 12V DC (10.5V to 17.0V).

Power consumption: Approx. 18W (HD-SDI dual-link off, EVF on, LCD monitor off); max. 24W (HD-SDI dual-link on, EVF On, LCD monitor on).

Accessories: PL lens mount adapter, stereo mic, windscreen, IR remote, shoulder strap, CD-ROM (XDCAM browser, SxS device driver software, PDF version operation manual), operational manual, warranty card, PL lens kit (PMW-F3K only).

Vision Research Phantom Flex

Overview: A Super 35 single-sensor digital camera. The camera has a limited internal memory buffer and an attachable flash memory Cine-Mag. Electronic viewfinder only. The camera captures and outputs uncompressed 12-bit raw 2.5K data at frame rates in excess of 2500 fps. The full sensor is slightly larger than that of Super 35 (25.6mm instead

of Super 35's 24mm width) which means that some lenses may vignette when using the full sensor. The sensor can be cropped in any resolution or frame shape desired.

Weight: Basic camera w/o CineMag or viewfinder: 5.33 kg (11.75 lb).

Body dimensions (LxWxH): 29.21cm x 12.70cm x 13.97cm (11.5" x 5.0" x 5.5").

Sensor: S35mm CMOS with Bayer CFA, 2560 x 1600 active photosites.

Active sensor dimensions: 25.6 x 16mm (1" x .63").

Quantization: 12-bit A/D.

Lens Mount: PL standard, also PV, Nikon F, Canon EOS (powered).

Sound level: Less than 20dB at all speeds.

Sensitivity: At 24 fps/180° shutter, suggested rating of ISO 1200 for minimal noise level.

Frame rates: Dependent on chosen vertical resolution. At the full height of 1600, maximum speed is 1455 fps. At 1080 height, 2570 fps. At 720 height, 5350 fps. An HQ mode eliminates the need for Black Referencing but cuts available frame rates approximately in half. The camera can shoot at any frame rate from 1 fps to the maximum available speed in single digit intervals. Does not run in reverse.

Electronic shutter: Adjustable from 2 microseconds (0.017° at 24 fps) to 360°.

Electronic viewfinder: HD color viewfinder with diopter and flip-out panel.

On-set monitoring: Dual HD-SDI outputs can either be two separate 4:2:2 feeds (one with optional menu display) or a single dual-link 4:4:4 feed for recording alternative.

Recording device: High-speed internal RAM memory buffer (8 GB, 16 GB, 32 GB) and CineMag (128 GB, 256 GB, 512 GB); also 4:2:2 / 4:4:4 HD can be sent to external recorder.

Recording format: Uncompressed 12-bit raw data at various resolutions (2560 x 1600 pixels is max.). Raw data can be translated into other file formats or read directly in post. Two BNC video connectors can be set to output all the common HD-SDI 4:2:2 formats or dual-link 4:4:4 formats. At 1080P resolution, the 512 GB CineMag can hold 132 minutes of material when played back at 24 fps.

Menu display/controls: Basic parameters controlled via a rotary dial and three buttons on operator side. Simple menu in viewfinder and/or video output for video monitoring settings (gain, color, gamma, matrix), black balance, resolution, frame rate, shutter angle and trigger setting. All other controls via a computer interface (Gigabit Ethernet connection) or by accessory RCU or PCU controllers.

Video connectors: HD-SDI out (BNC x2).

Power connectors: 24V DC in (3-pin Fischer x2), 12V DC accessory power out (4-pin Fischer x2).

Other connectors: Viewfinder out (Fischer-7, w/12V accessory out), record trigger (BNC), time code in (BNC), time code out (BNC), frame sync (BNC), genlock (BNC), remote port (5-pin Fischer).

Power: 24V DC (operates up to 36V DC).

Power consumption: 4A draw in capture mode, 2.5A in standby or playback modes, viewfinder 0.5A, CineMag 0.8A, accessory outputs rated up to 1.5A at 12V DC.

Accessories: Compatible with ARRI 15mm or 19mm sliding baseplates, as well as ARRI lightweight 15mm front rods (60mm center-to-center) for handheld use. Compatible with all matteboxes, follow focuses, zoom controls, etc. designed for these systems.

Vision Research Phantom HD Gold

Overview: A Super 35 single-sensor digital camera. The camera has a limited internal memory buffer and an attachable flash memory CineMag. Electronic viewfinder only. The camera captures and outputs uncompressed 14-bit 2K raw data at frame rates in excess of 1000 fps. The full sensor is a large square that slightly exceeds the size of Super 35 (25.6mm instead of Super-35's 24mm width) which means that some lenses may vignette when using the full sensor. When windowed to 1920 x 1080 pixels, the image width is the same 24mm width as Super 35. The square sensor can be cropped in any resolution desired, allowing a 2.40 frame or even the use of standard 2X anamorphic optics.

Weight: Basic camera w/o CineMag or viewfinder: 5.44 kg (12 lb).

Body dimensions (LxWxH): 29.21cm x 13.97cm x 19.05cm (11.5" x 5.5" x 7.5").

Sensor: S35mm CMOS with Bayer CFA, 2048 x 2048 active photosites.

Active sensor dimension: 25.6mm x 25.6mm (1" x 1").

Quantization: 14-bit A/D.

Lens mount: PL standard, PV, Nikon F, Hasselblad large format and Mamiya medium format mounts also available.

Sound level: Less than 20dB at all speeds.

Sensitivity: At 24 fps/180° shutter, suggested rating of ISO 600 for minimal noise level.

Frame rates: Dependent on chosen vertical resolution. At the full height of 2048, maximum speed is 560 fps. At 1080 height, 1052 fps. At 720 height, 1576 fps. At the anamorphic image area height of 1488, 760 fps. The camera can shoot at any frame rate from 1 fps to the maximum available speed in single digit intervals. Does not run in reverse.

Electronic shutter: Adjustable from 2 microseconds (0.017° at 24 fps) to 360°.

Electronic viewfinder: HD color viewfinder with diopter and flip-out panel.

On-set monitoring: HD-SDI output is typically looped through onboard HD monitor to other HD set monitors and downconverters.

Recording device: High-speed internal RAM memory buffer (8 GB, 16 GB, 32 GB) and CineMag (128 GB, 256 GB, 512 GB); also 4:2:2 HD can be sent to external recorder.

Recording format: Uncompressed 14-bit raw data (8-bit, 10-bit, and 12-bit are also selectable) at various resolutions; 2048 x 2048 is max. resolution. Data can be translated into other file formats or read directly in post. HD-SDI can send 4:2:2 HD formats to external recorder. At 1080P resolution, the 512 GB CineMag can hold 132 minutes of material when played back at 24 fps.

Menu display/controls: Basic parameters controlled via a rotary dial and two buttons on operator side. Simple menu in viewfinder and/or video output for video monitoring settings (gain, color, gamma, matrix), black balance, resolution, frame rate shutter, angle and trigger setting. All other controls via a computer interface (Gigabit Ethernet connection) or by accessory RCU or PCU controllers.

Video connectors: HD-SDI out (BNC).

Power connectors: 24V DC in (3-pin Fischer).

Other connectors: Viewfinder out (7-pin Fischer, w/12V accessory out), capture port [8-pin Fischer. with breakout cable to BNCs for record trigger, time code in, time code out, frame sync (sychronization in/out port) and strobe (for syncing a strobe light)], remote port (5-pin Fischer).

Power: 24V DC (operates up to 36V DC).

Power consumption: 4A draw in Capture mode, 2.5A in standby or playback modes, viewfinder 0.5A, CineMag 0.8A, accessory output rated up to 1.5A at 12V DC.

Accessories: Compatible with ARRI 15mm or 19mm sliding baseplates, as well as ARRI lightweight 15mm front rods (60mm center-to-center) for handheld use. Compatible with all matte boxes, follow focuses, zoom controls, etc. designed for these systems. Accessory breakout box available for additional 12V and 24V power outputs and 12V onboard battery power for camera. Shares all accessories designed for the Phantom 65.

Vision Research Phantom Miro M320S

Overview: A compact, lightweight 35mm single-sensor digital camera. The camera has an internal memory buffer and an interchangeable flash memory CineFlash module mounted in the camera. Electronic viewfinder only. The camera captures and  outputs uncompressed 12-bit raw 2K data at frame rates in excess of 1450 fps. The full sensor is slightly smaller than that of Super 35 (19.6mm instead of Super 35's 24mm width) which means that lenses will appear more telephoto than on a Super 35 camera. The sensor can be cropped in any resolution or frame shape desired.

Weight: Basic camera without CineFlash or viewfinder: 1.36 kg (3.0 lb).

Body dimensions (LxWxH): 19.05cm x 10.16cm x 8.89cm (7.5" x 4.0" x 3.5").

Sensor: 35mm CMOS with Bayer CFA, 1920 x 1200 active photosites.

Active sensor dimensions: 19.6mm x 12mm (.772" x .472").

Quantization: 12-bit A/D.

Lens mount: PL standard, also PV, Nikon F, Canon EOS (powered.)

Sound level: Less than 20dB all speeds.

Sensitivity: At 24fps/180° shutter, suggested rating of ISO 1200 for minimal noise level.

Frame rates: Dependent on chosen vertical resolution. At the full height of 1200, maximum speed is 1380 fps. At 1080 height, 1540 fps. At 720 height, 32800 fps. The camera can shoot at any frame rate from 24 fps to the maximum available speed in single digit intervals. Does not run in reverse.

Electronic shutter: Adjustable from 2 microseconds (0.017° at 24 fps) to 360°.

Electronic viewfinder: HD color viewfinder with diopter and flip-out panel.

On-set monitoring: Full HD-SDI 4:2:2 output in all standard formats.

Recording device: High-speed internal RAM memory buffer (3 GB, 6 GB, 12 GB) and CineFlash (60 GB, 120 GB, 240 GB); also 4:2:2 HD can be sent to external recorder.

Recording format: Uncompressed 12-bit raw data at various resolutions (1920 x 1200 is max). This can be translated into other file formats or read directly in post. HD-SDI out can send all common HD 4:2:2 formats to external recorder. At 1080P resolution, the 240G CineFlash can hold 66 minutes of material when played back at 24 fps.

Menu display/controls: To save in size and weight, only a record trigger and a reset button are located on the front of the camera; all other controls via a computer interface via Gigabit Ethernet connection or by accessory RCU or PCU controllers.

Video connectors: HD-SDI (BNC).

Power connectors: DC in (Sony BP-U battery mount).

Other connectors: Ethernet (8-pin Fischer), capture (12-pin Fischer with breakout to BNCs for record trigger, time code in, time code out, strobe sync), Power/RS-232 (remote control, 6-pin Fischer), frame sync (BNC).

Power: 12V to 28V DC (accepts Sony BP-U series onboard battery).

Power consumption: 65W.

Accessories: compatible with ARRI 15mm or 19mm sliding baseplates, as well as ARRI lightweight 15mm front rods (60mm center to center) for handheld use. Compatible with all matte boxes, follow focuses, zoom controls, etc. designed for these systems.

Vision Research Phantom 65 Gold

Overview: A 65mm single-sensor digital camera. The camera has a limited internal memory buffer and an attachable flash memory Cine-Mag. Electronic viewfinder only. The camera captures and outputs uncompressed 14-bit 4K raw data at frame rates in excess of 140 fps.

Weight: basic camera w/o CineMag or viewfinder: 5.44 kg (12 lb).

Body dimensions (LxWxH): 30.8cm x 13.9cm x 19.4cm (12.3" x 5.47" x 7.62").

Sensor: 65mm CMOS with Bayer CFA, 4096 x 2440 active photosites.

Active sensor dimensions: 51.2mm x 30.5mm (2.02" x 1.2").

Quantization: 14-bit A/D.

Lens mount: Arriflex Super-PL (aka Mega-PL) standard, Panavision Super-PV, Hasselblad large format and Mamiya medium format mounts also available. Standard PL, PV and Nikon F mounts can also be used but lenses designed for these mounts may not cover the sensor's image area.

Sound level: Less than 20dB at all speeds.

Sensitivity: At 24 fps/180° shutter, suggested rating of ISO 600 for minimal noise level.

Frame rates: 1fps to 145 fps in single digit intervals. Windowed for 1.85 aspect, 162 fps. Windowed for 2.40 aspect ratio, 220 fps. Does not run in reverse.

Electronic shutter: Adjustable from 2 microseconds (0.017° @ 24 fps) to 360°.

Electronic viewfinder: HD color viewfinder with diopter and flip-out panel.

On-set monitoring: HD-SDI output is typically looped through onboard HD monitor to other HD set monitors and downconverters.

Recording device: High-speed internal RAM memory buffer (8 GB, 16 GB, 32 GB) and CineMag (128 GB, 256 GB, 512 GB); also 4:2:2 HD can be sent to external recorder.

Recording format: Uncompressed 14-bit raw data at various resolutions (4096 x 2440 is max.). This can be translated into other file formats or read directly in post. HD-SDI out can all common HD 4:2:2 formats to external recorder. At full sensor resolution, the 512 GB CineMag can hold more than 32 minutes of material when played back at 24 fps.

Menu display/controls: Basic parameters controlled via a rotary dial and two buttons on operator side. Simple menu in viewfinder and/or video output for video monitoring settings (gain, color, gamma, matrix), black balance, resolution, frame rate shutter angle and trigger setting. All other controls via a computer interface via Gigabit Ethernet connection or RCU or PCU controllers.

Video connectors: HD-SDI (BNC).

Power connectors: 24V DC in (3-pin Fischer).

Other connectors: Viewfinder out (7-pin Fischer w/12V accessory out), capture port [8-pin Fischer. with breakout cable to BNCs for record trigger, time code in, time code out, frame sync (sychronization in/out port) and strobe (for syncing a strobe light)], remote port (5-pin Fischer).

Power: 24V DC (operates up to 36V DC).

Power consumption: 4A draw in capture mode, 2.5A in standby or playback modes, viewfinder 0.5A, CineMag 0.8A, accessory output rated up to 1.5A at 12V DC.

Accessories: Compatible with ARRI 15mm or 19mm sliding baseplates, as well as ARRI lightweight 15mm frontrods (60mm center-to-center) for handheld use. Compatible with all matteboxes, followfocuses, zoom controls, etc. designed for these systems. Accessory breakout box available for additional 12V and 24V power outputs and 12V onboard battery power for camera. Shares all accessories designed for the Phantom HD.

ONBOARD RECORDERS

Cinedeck EX

Overview: This onboard recorder is compatible with HDMI/HD-SDI/LAN cameras and records to a wide choice of codecs in .MOV, MXF, MP4 and other wrappers via HDMI and single/dual-link 3G/HD-SDI. It also records to popular camera and playback formats including AVC-Intra, XDCAM HD, and H.264. It has a 7" high-res preview/focus/playback monitor with touchscreen user interface. Brighter screen option (Hi-Brite) for improved visibility in daylight shooting. Can mount an onboard battery.

Weight: 1.8 kg (4 lb).

Dimensions (LxWxH): 20.3cm x 8.9cm x 12.7cm (8" x 3.5" x 5").

Menu display/controls: Touchscreen interface on 7" screen. Real-tme composite and per-channel waveform and histogram, onscreen reticle overlays. Remote operation via Ethernet or WiFi.

Recording media: 2.5" SSD.

Recording format: Uncompressed 10-bit HD, uncompressed 8-bit or 10-bit 4:2:2 HD, all Apple Pro-Res codecs including 4444, all Avid DNxHD codecs (MFX or .MOV), Avid Meridien JFIF, CineForm, AVC-Intra, XDCAM HD, XDCAM EX, H.264 or DPX/C. Supports 1080i (50, 60i), 1080P or PsF (23.98, 24, 25, 29.97, 30), 1080 P or PsF (50, 59.94, 60

CineForm only), 720P (50, 59.94, 60), PAL/NTSC, SI-2K uncompressed 12-bit raw 2K (w/ SI-2K option).

Connectors: DC in (2-pin), 12V DC accessories out (4-pin), RS232/422 COM port, HDMI in, HDMI out, VGA out, analog audio in (XLR), analog audio in (3-pin), tethered remote record (4-pin), time code sync port (5-pin), HD-SDI in (BNC x2), HD-SDI out (BNC x2), stereo headphone, USB (x2), ESATA, LAN Port, digital/analog audio, component and composite video.

Power: 12-28V DC.

Power consumption: 50–60W (Hi-Brite model draws 60-70W).

Codex ARRIRAW

Overview: A solid-state flash memory recorder designed to be mounted onto the camera. Can record two channels of ARRIRAW (ideal for 3-D work) up to 30 fps, or single channel of ARRIRAW up to 60 fps, plus audio and metadata, to removable datapacks. LUT's can be loaded for monitor-out preview.

Weight: 2.5 kg (5.7 lb).

Dimensions (LxWxH): 19.87cm x 10.95cm x 11.5cm (7.8" x 4.3" x 4.5").

Menu display/controls: Touch-based control surface unit; interface can be run locally or remotely on a computer. GPI trigger.

Recording media: Solid-state datapacks (256 GB, 480 GB, 512 GB) plus HS (high-speed) and LW (lightweight) datapacks.

Recording format: 12-bit ARRIRAW/0–60 fps Variframe. 16/24-bit audio at 48 kHz, AES or HD-SDI embedded.

Operating temperature: 5°C to +40°C (+23°F to +104°F).

Connectors: HD-SDI or T-Link/1.5G or 3G (BNC x4); in 1.5G mode, can record up to two cameras single or dual-link (ARRIRAW or HD); in 3G mode, can record up tp two cameras single-link and one camera dual-link (ARRIRAW or HD), 4:2:2 out (BNC x2), 4:4:4 out (BNC), genlock (BNC), LTC time code (5-pin LEMO), GPI record trigger (7-pin LEMO), RS422 interface (6-pin LEMO), network interface (Gigabit Ethernet), two channels analog audio I/O (Mini XLR x2), stereo headphone (3.5mm jack), DC power in (5-pin LEMO).

Power: 12–34V DC.

Power consumption: Approx. 30W (w/ standard datapack at 30 fps); peaks around 40W (when recording ARRIRAW 4:3 at 48 fps w/ high-speed datapack). 18W in standby.

Codex Onboard M

Overview: A solid-state flash memory recorder designed to be mounted onto the camera. Can record ARRIRAW, uncompressed or wavelet encoded HD, plus audio and metadata, to removable datapacks. A Codex media station can offload material faster than real-time. LUT's can be loaded for monitor-out preview.

Weight: 2.5 kg (5.7 lb).

Dimensions (LxWxH): 19.87cm x 10.95cm x 11.5cm (7.8" x 4.3" x 4.5").

Menu display/controls: Touch-based control surface unit that can be mounted or used handheld; interface can be run locally or remotely on a computer. GPI trigger.

Recording media: Solid-state datapacks (256 GB, 480 GB, 512 GB) plus HS (high-speed) and LW (lightweight) datapacks.

Recording format: 8-bit or 10-bit 1080PsF or 4:4:4 RGB or 4:2:2 YCbCr (23.98, 24, 25, 29.97, 30 fps)/8-bit or 10-bit 1080PsF 4:2:2 YCbCr using dual-link HD-SDI (47.96, 48, 50, 59.94, 60 fps)/8-bit or 10-bit 720P 4:4:4 RGB or 4:2:2 YCbCr (59.94, 60 fps)/12-bit ARRIRAW/0–60 fps Variframe. Uncompressed, or can use wavelet compression. 16/24-bit audio at 48 kHz, AES or HD-SDI embedded.

Operating temperature: 5°C to +40°C (+23°F to +104°F).

Connectors: HD-SDI or T-Link/1.5G or 3G (BNC x4); in 1.5G mode, can record up to two cameras single or dual-link (ARRIRAW or HD); in 3G mode, can record up tp two cameras single-link and one camera dual-link (ARRIRAW or HD), 4:2:2 out (BNC x2), 4:4:4 out (BNC), genlock (BNC), LTC time code (5-pin LEMO), GPI record trigger (7-pin LEMO), RS422 interface (6-pin LEMO), network interface (Gigabit Ethernet), two channels analog audio I/O (Mini XLR x2), stereo head-phone (3.5mm jack), DC power in (5-pin LEMO).

Power: 12–34V DC.

Power consumption: Approx. 30W (w/standard datapack at 30 fps); peaks around 40W (when recording ARRIRAW 4:3 at 48 fps w/high-speed datapack). 18W in standby.

Codex Onboard S

Overview: A solid-state flash memory recorder designed for use with compact HD cameras (such as the Canon C300, Sony F3). Can record uncompressed or wavelet encoded HD, plus audio and metadata, to removable capture drive. A Codex media station or Codex Vault can offload material faster than real time. Audio is recorded through em-bedded video stream. LUT's can be loaded for monitor-out preview.

Weight: 1.2 kg (2.7 lb).

Dimensions (LxWxH): 18.75cm x 8.29cm x 13.9cm (7.38" x 3.26" x 5.47").

Menu display/controls: Touch-based control surface; interface can be run locally or remotely on a computer. GPI trigger.

Recording media: Solid-state 240-480 GB capture drive.

Recording format: 8-bit or 10-bit 1080PsF 4:4:4 RGB or 4:2:2 YCbCr (23.98, 24, 25, 29.97, 30 fps)/8-bit or 10-bit 1080PsF 4:2:2 YCbCr using dual-link HD-SDI (47.96, 48, 50, 59.94, 60 fps)/8-bit or 10-bit 720P 4:4:4 RGB or 4:2:2 YCbCr (59.94, 60 fps)/0–60 fps Variframe. Uncompressed, or can use wavelet compression. 16/24-bit audio at 48 kHz, HD-SDI embedded.

Operating temperature: 5°C to +40°C (+23°F to +104°F).

Connectors: HD-SDI for dual-link 4:4:4 or two single-link 4:2:2 in (BNC 2x), 3G-SDI in (BNC x2), 4:4:4 out (BNC), 4:2:2 out (BNC x2), LTC time code (5-pin LEMO), GPI record trigger (7-pin LEMO), RS422 interface (6-pin LEMO), network interface (Gigabit Ethernet), stereo headphone (3.5mm jack), DC power in (5-pin LEMO).

Power: 12–34V DC.

Power consumption: Approx. 30W at 30 fps. 18W in standby.

Convergent Design Gemini

Overview: A small solid-state recorder with a built-in 5" LCD monitor using removable SSD media. There are two models, the Gemini 4:4:4 and the Gemini RAW; both can record uncompressed ARRIRAW data (16:9 and 4:3) with full metadata, but the Gemini Raw has greater processing power, more inputs and outputs, can record up to four cameras simultaneously (in certain modes), and can record 4K raw data from the Canon C500. Both models also record to compressed formats such as Avid DNxHD. Real-time decompression and de-Bayering for playback, with or without a LUT. Stereo 3-D support. Gemini RAW also capable of 4K monitoring using 4-SDI from de-Bayered 4K raw input, as well as multistream (x4) playback and live switcher.

Weight: .612 kg (1.35 lb).

Dimensions (LxWxH): 13.8cm x 3.7cm x 12.0cm (5.4" x 1.45" x 4.7").

Menu display/controls: Touch-sensitive LCD w/intuitive menu system.

Recording media: 1.8" SSD (two slots). 256 GB or 512 GB. Automatic spanning from one SSD to the next and Dual master recording option.

Recording format: Gemini 4:4:4: 10-bit 4:4:4 (uncompressed DPX) or 4:2:2 (compressed Avid DNxHD) 1080P (up to 60 fps)/12-bit ARRIRAW 16:9 (up to 60 fps) and 4:3 (up to 48 fps)/ARRIRAW and Stereo 3D are extra options. Gemini RAW: adds QuadHD/4K Canon raw (up to 60 fps)/ HD/2K raw (from Weisscam, P+S Technik, IndieCam, IO Industries, Lux Media Plan cameras, up to 60 fps)/can record raw data to CinemaDNG files / Avid DNxHD supported for 1080P YCbCr up to 120 fps (60 fps support for 1080P 4:4:4 RGB planned). Parallel recording up to two (Gemini 4:4:4) or four (Gemini RAW) 1080/30P streams (DNxHD-220) or four 30P HD/raw streams provided cameras are genlocked.

Operating temperature: -10°C to +40°C (+14°F to +104°F).

Connectors: Gemini RAW: six programmable HD/3G-SDI ports (BNC x6), configurable as: (4-in/2-out) or (2-in/4-out). Gemini 4:4:4: HD/3G-SDI single or dual-link in (BNC x2), HD-SDI out (BNC x2), HDMI out. Both devices: DC power in (4-pin Hirose), audio in (3.5mm jack), audio out/stereo headphone (3.5mm jack).

Power: Gemini RAW: 6-25V DC / Gemini 4:4:4: 6-19V DC.

Power consumption: 8-15W.

Panavision SSR-1

Overview: A small, dockable, solid-state flash memory recorder. It is about half the weight and size of the SRW-1 VTR (2.7 kg vs. 5.72 kg) on the Panavison Genesis, making it well-suited for Steadicam and handheld work, or tight shooting spaces.

Weight: 2.7 kg (6 lb).

Dimensions (LxWxH): 24.0cm x 13.5cm x 12.0cm (9.5" x 5.3" x 4.7").

Menu display/controls: 3.5" color LCD display w/thumbwheel for access. SSR-1 controls: standard VTR controls, cue clips, jog frame, display rotate, brightness, keyboard lock. Dedicated record buttons for quick start. Functions controlled by Genesis camera: record on/off, record review, frame rate selection, format (4:2:2 or 4:4:4) selection, tally light control, PB/EE control.

Recording media: No separate media.

Recording format: Fully uncompressed 10-bit 4:4:4 RGB or 4:2:2 YCbCr, or dual 4:2:2, plus 16 audio channels from HD-SDI, 2 from analog inputs. Also 4:4:4:4 RGB + Alpha Channel when SSRD docking station is used with SSR-1.

Recording time: 21 min. of uncompressed 10-bit 4:4:4 at 24P; 17 min. at 30P/43 min. of uncompressed 10-bit 4:2:2 at 24P; 34 min. at 30P.

Indicators: Tally/error.

Operating temperature: -20°C to +40°C (-4°F to +104°F).

Operating humidity: 5–95%.

Connectors: Docking (multipin), dual-link HD-SDI in (BNC x2), dual-link HD-SDI out (BNC x2), single-link HD-SDI (BNC), NTSC/PAL composite video (BNC), genlock in (BNC), time code in (BNC), network interface (100BaseT Ethernet), audio in (line level x2), accessory (8-pin LEMO software definable functions: 2 GPI in, 2 GPO out), 12V DC in (male 4-pin XLR).

SSRD docking station: Provides HD-SDI out w/embedded audio from SSR-1. SSR-1 can record when mounted to SSRD. Docking station acts as VTR when connected via 9-pin remote connector. It has a 12V DC in and dual-link HD-SDI in and out.

Power: 12V DC (11V to 17V).

Power consumption: Low power standby: 0.5A, record: 3.3A.

Sony SR-R1

Overview: The SR-R1 is mountable memory recorder for any camera with HD-SDI interface. Dual-link HD-SDI/3G-SDI is supported. Dual-stream capability for 3-D recording. Uses MPEG4 SStP format (HDCAM SR native); SR-Lite and SR-SQ are standard; optional SR-HQ and uncompressed HD are supported. Removable SSD memory media. 16 channels of 24-bit audio. Operating with the Sony PMW-F3 camera, the SR-R1 is able to make frame accurate recordings on both the camera's internal SxS card and the SRMemory media. Also can be mounted directly to the Sony F23 and F35 with a third-party adapter.

Weight: Without SRMemory card + control panel: 1.9 kg (4.2 lb).

Dimenions (LxWxH): 19.0cm x 14.1cm x 9.7cm (7.4" x 5.6" x 3.82").

Menu display/controls: Detachable control panel (SRK-CP1). RS422 remote control.

Recording media: SRMemory SSD (256 GB, 512 GB, 1 TB).

Recording format: 10-bit 4:4:4 RGB and 4:2:2 YCbCr using MPEG4 SStP compression/SR-Lite (220 Mbps), SR-SQ (440 Mbps). 1–30 fps (4:4:4) or 1-60 fps (4:2:2). Up to 16 channels of 24-bit audio recording. Dual-stream 3D 4:2:2 HD mode (with SRK-R301 option, dual 3G-SDI for RGB 3D). SR-HQ (880 Mbps) and uncompressed 10-bit or 12-bit HD supported as option with SRK-R311 (as DPX files).

Recording time: Example: 311 min. of 1080/23.98PsF SR-SQ onto a 1 TB SRMemory card.

Indicators: Tally/error, power, lid lock.

Operating temperature: 0°C to +40°C (+32°F to +104°F).

Operating humidity: 10% to 95%.

Connectors: HD-SDI in (BNC x2), HD-SDI out (BNC x2), time code in (BNC), time code out (BNC), aux in, SDI embedded digital audio (BNC), Ch 1/2 audio in (3-pin XLR x2), stereo headphone (3.5mm jack), control panel, remote control (14-pin female), DC in (4-pin XLR).

Power: 11-17V DC.

Power consumption: 4:2:2 SR-Lite at 23.98PsF: 30W.

Sony SR-R4

Overview: The SR-R4 is the companion dockable recorder for the Sony F65. It records uncompressed 16-bit raw (linear) data at a data rate up to 5.5 Gbps, as well as 2K raw high-speed footage. HD recording in the MPEG-4 SStP format (HDCAM-SR native). Removable SSD memory media. Docks directly to the F65 camera; no external cable required. 16 channels of 24-bit audio.

Weight: Without SRMemory card + control panel: 1.8 kg (3.97 lb).

Dimenions (LxWxH): 19.0cm x 14.1cm x 8.9cm (7.4" x 5.6" x 3.5").

Menu display/controls: Through camera or with detachable control panel (SRK-CP1).

Recording media: SRMemory SSD (256 GB, 512 GB, 1 TB).

Recording format: Uncompressed 16-bit F65RAW, HD MPEG-4 SStP. Variable-frame rate image capturing from 1 fps to 60 fps (4K); 1 fps to 120 fps (2K). Up to 16 channels of 24-bit audio recording.

Recording time: 60 min. of raw recording onto a 1 TB SRMemory card at 24 fps.

Indicators: Tally/error, power, lid lock.

Operating temperature: 0°C to +40°C (+32°F to +104°F).

Operating humidity: 10% to 95%.

Connectors: Camera connector (multipin D-sub optical), time code in (BNC), time code out (BNC), Ch 1/2 audio in (3-pin XLR x2), stereo headphone (3.5mm jack), control panel.

Power: 11-17V DC.

Power consumption: 37W/total F65 + SR-R4 onboard: 102W.

Sony SRW-1

Overview: This is actually a two-part unit, the tape recorder (SRW-1) and the processor (SRPC-1). In a Panavision Genesis or Sony F23, F35, many of the SRPC-1 processor functions are built into the camera, allowing the VTR portion, the SRW-1, to be attached to either top or back of camera like a film magazine, or detached but cable-connected. The SRW-1/SRPC-1 offers 1080-line HD recordings with minimal compression at multiple frame rates onto HDCAM SR videotape. The SRW-1/SRPC-1 connects to HD cameras via HD-SDI (single-link or dual-link) or optional optical fiber cable to create a convenient, portable full-bandwidth 4:4:4 RGB image capturing system. The SRPC-1 processing functions include 2:3 pull-down insertion for 525-line downconversion, and RGB (4:4:4) to YCbCr (4:2:2) color space conversion. The system has three recording modes: SQ (Standard Quality) at 440 Mbps, HQ (High Quality) at 880 Mbps with a 2:1 compression ratio for RGB 4:4:4, and 3D mode where two separate 4:2:2 HD-SDI inputs can be recorded simultaneously to the same tape. The deck can also record 720P. The control panel is detachable for remote use using a cable. With the HKSR-102 option installed, recording 4:4:4 1080P HD at frame rates from 1-30P is possible and 4:2:2 at frame rates, 1-60P. With both the HKSR 102 and HKSR 103 option installed 4:4:4 at frame rates from 1-60P is possible.

Weight: SRPC-1 + SRW-1: 8.5 kg (18.74 lb). SRW-1 only: 5.72 kg (12.6 lb).

Dimensions (LxWxH): When viewed with the SRW-1 on top of the SRPC-1: 27.9cm x 13.9cm x 39.9cm (10.98" x 5.47" x 15.71"). The SRW-1 portion is about half that height.

Menu display/controls: VTR LCD menu panel (SRWC) plugs into VTR CTRL PANEL via multipin cable. Panel latches on to VTR top. Menu system enables many settings, including time code hour and audio levels. Control panel is detachable for remote use with a cable.

Recording media: ½" HDCAM SR videotape cassette. Recommended: Sony BCT-40SR.

Recording format: SQ mode: compressed 10-bit 4:4:4 RGB or 4:2:2 YCbCr at 440 Mbps. HQ mode: mildly-compressed 10-bit 4:4:4 or uncompressed 4:2:2 at 880 Mbps. 3-D mode: dual 4:2:2 at 440 Mbps per signal. 12 channels of 24-bit audio at 48 kHz.

Tape speed: Approx. 77.4mm/s (24P mode).

Fast-forward/rewind time: Approx. 5 min. with BCT-40SR.

Recording time: SQ mode: max. 50 min. with BCT-40SR (at 24P). HQ mode: 25 min. (at 24P).

Operating temperature: 0°C to +40°C (32°F to +104°F).

Operating humidity: 25–80%.

Video/data connectors: Dual-link HD-SDI in (BNC x2), dual-link HD-SDI out (BNC x2), HD reference video in (BNC x1), SD reference video in (BNC x1), SDI video out (BNC x1), single-link HD-SDI out (BNC x1), time code in (BNC x1).With optional HKSR-1, fiber cable for 4:4:4 RGB HD-SDI in for SRPC-1.

Audio connectors: Digital audio in (BNC x2), analog audio in (female 3-pin XLR x4), digital audio out (ch1/ch2, D-sub multi connector), earphones (stereo minijack).

Other connectors: Remote input (D-sub 9-pin female, Sony 9-pin remote interface).

NOTE: SRW-1 only has Ch1/Ch2 audio input, time code in/out, and an earphone jack. All other inputs and outputs are on the SRPC-1. For this reason, when separating the SRW-1 unit from a Panavision Genesis or Sony F23 camera, you need to attach an interface box to the camera and use the SRPC-1 with the SRW-1. Then you can connect the camera to the separate recorder through HD-SDI cables for picture.

Power connectors: 12V DC in (male 4-pin XLR x1).

Power: 12V DC (11V to 17V).

Power consumption: SRW-1: 60W. SRPC-1: 35W.

S.Two OB-1

Overview: A solid-state flash memory recorder designed to be mounted onto the camera. Can record ARRIRAW (4:3 or 16:9) or uncompressed

HD, plus audio and metadata, to removable FlashMag. FlashMag can be downloaded using FlashDock or FlashPort, a high-speed playback, transfer, and archive device that can be used on location. Viewing LUTs can be loaded for preview output.

Weight: With FlashMag, under 3 kg (6.6 lb).

Dimensions (LxWxH): 20.3cm x 10.8cm x 12.7cm (8" x 4.25" x 5").

Menu display/controls: Menu keypad w/LCD screen info. GPI trigger.

Recording media: 500 GB FlashMag (holds 42 min. of uncompressed data).

Recording format: 4:4:4 RGB 1080PsF (23.98, 24, 25, 29.97, 30, 48, 50, 59.94, 60PsF); 2x 4:4:4 RGB 1080PsF for 3D (23.98, 24, 25, 29.97, 30PsF); 4:2:2 YCbCr 1080PsF (23.98, 24, 25, 29.97, 30, 48, 50, 59.94, 60PsF); 2x 4:2:2 YCbCr 1080PsF for 3D (23.98, 24, 25, 29.97, 30PsF); 4:2:2 720P (50, 59.94, 60 fps); 4:4:4 RGB 1080P (23.98, 24, 25, 29.97, 30P); 4:2:2 YCbCr 1080P (23.98, 24, 25, 29.97, 30, 48, 50, 59.94, 60P); 2x 4:2:2 YCbCr 1080P for 3D (23.98, 24, 25, 29.97, 30P); 12-bit ARRIRAW (4:3 or 16:9) as DPX or .ARI files (23.98, 24, 25, 29.97, 30 fps), 12-bit ARRIRAW anamorphic as DPX or .ARI files, with desqueeze output to monitors.

Operating temperature: -5°C to +55°C (+23°F to +131°F).

Connectors: HD-SDI dual-link in (BNC x2), 4:2:2 HD-SDI in (BNC x2), HD-SDI dual-link out (BNC x2), 4:2:2 HD-SDI out (BNC x2), network interface (Gigabit Ethernet), USB 2.0, RS422/Remote Port/GPI trigger (12-pin Hirose), LTC I/O (5-pin LEMO), two-channel audio in (5-pin Mini XLR), DC power in (3-pin Fischer).

Power: 12/24V DC (10V to 36V).

Power consumption: under 20W at 12/24V DC.

Vision Research Phantom CineMag-II

Overview: A compact, rugged, high-speed, uncompressed, camera-mountable solid state recorder. Ideal for all shooting applications involving the Phantom cameras. Available in 128 GB, 256 GB and 512 GB versions. In order to increase capacity, increase download speeds, and use of footage shot at different bit-depths, all raw images are log-encoded 10-bit. When the clips are downloaded from the CineMag to a computer, they are relinearized and once again stored as 14-bit (or whatever they started as). The lighter and thinner CineMag-II superceded the original CineMag in 2010, but they are cross-compatible.

Weight: 0.9 kg (2 lb).

Dimensions (LxWxH): 19.2cm x 12.6cm x 4.0cm (5.5" x 4.9" x 1.5").

Menu display/controls: Controlled by camera and/or Phantom application, onboard display includes memory remaining, write activity, write protect, magazine enabled, and power LED's.

Recording format: Uncompressed raw data (8–14 bit accepting), saved internally as 10-bit log raw but converts back to original linear upon export.

Recording times: examples given, frame rate and overall resolution can vary.

256G CineMag: 2048 x 1080 at 24fps: 66 min.; 2048 x 1080 at 450fps (max. write speed at given resolution): 3 min. 32 sec.; 4096 x 2440 at 24fps: 15 min. 15 sec.; 4096 x 2440 at 90fps (max. write speed at given resolution): 4 min.

512G CineMag: 2048 x 1080 at 24fps: 132 min.; 2048 x 1080 at 450fps (max. write speed at given resolution): 7 min. 4 sec.; 4096 x 2440 at 24fps: 30 min. 30 sec.; 4096 x 2440 at 90fps (max. write speed at given resolution): 8 min.

Operating temperature: 0°C to +40°C (+32°F to +104°F).

Operating humidity: 80%, noncondensing at +5°C (+41°F).

Connector: proprietary 96-pin pogo-pin data bus.

Power consumption: 1.5A.

Jon Fauer, ASC is an award-winning director of photography and director who often writes and lectures about cameras, equipment, techniques, technology, film history and the future of film. He is the author of eight best-selling books on cinematography and digital imaging. These publications are available at www.theasc.com.

M. David Mullen, ASC is a member of the Academy of Motion Picture Arts and Sciences. He has photographed more than thirty independent feature films and two television series. He has received two IFP Independent Spirit Award nominations for Best Cinematography, the first for Twin Falls Idaho *(2000) and the second for* Northfork *(2004).*

Table Reference

Cine Lens List

The Cine Lens List includes most of the current lenses available for rental or purchase. Many of these lenses are no longer made, but are available used or remounted. Many "House" brands exist that are reworked versions of still camera lenses and older cine lenses. For complete data, see your local rental house or lens manufacturer.

ANGENIEUX

35mm Prime Lenses
14.5mm f/3.5	1'
18.5mm f/2.2	
24mm f/2.2	
28mm f/1.8	
32mm f/1.8	
40mm f/1.8	
50mm f/.95	
75mm f/1.8	
100mm f/2	

35mm Zoom Lenses
17–102mm T2.9 HR	2'6"
20–120mm T2.9	3'
25–250mm T3.5 HR	5'7"
25–250mm T3.7 HP	5'7"
25–250mm T4.2	5'6"
25–625mm T8	4'4"
35–140mm f/3.5	

16mm Prime Lenses
5.9mm T1.9	
Fixed @ 4'–inf.	
10mm f/1.8	f.f.
14.5mm T3.9	f.f.
15mm f/1.3	10"
25mm f/.95	18"
25mm f/1.4	20"
25mm f/1.8	20"
28mm f/1.2	20"
50mm f/1.5	2'
75mm f/2.5	3'
100mm f/2.5	3'
150mm f/2.7	5'

16mm Zoom Lenses
9.5–57mm T1.9	2'
9.5–95mm T2.8	2'6"
10–150mm T2.3	5'
12–120mm T2.5	5'
12–240mm T4.2	5'
12.5–75mm T2.5	4'
16–44mm T1.3	5'
17–68mm f/2.2	4'
17.5–70mm T2.5	4'

Super 16 Zoom Lenses
7–81mm T2.4 HR	2'
11–66mm T2.6	2'
11.5–138mm T2.3 HR	5'
15–300mm T5	5'

Optimo 35mm Zoom Lenses
15–40mm T2.6	2'
28–76mm T2.6	2'
45–120mm T2.8	3' 1"
17–80mm T2.2	2'
19.5–94mm	2' 0.5"
24–290mm &2.8	4'
28–340mm T3.2	4' 0.5"

Optimo DP Digital Zoom Lenses (D)
16–42mm T2.8	2'
30–80mm T2.8	2'

ARRIFLEX
VARIABLE PRIMES
(See Zeiss 35mm Zoom
Arri Variable Primes)

BAUSCH & LOMB
35mm Prime Lenses
Super Baltar Series Lenses
20mm T2.3	1'6"
25mm T2.3	1'6"
35mm T2.3	1'6"
50mm T2.3	1'6"
75mm T2.3	1'10"
100mm T2.3	4'
150mm T3	6'

Baltar Series Lenses
25mm T2.5	2'
30mm T2.5	2'
35mm T2.5	2'
40mm T2.5	2'
50mm T2.5	2'
75mm T2.5	3'
100mm T2.5	4'
152mm T2.8	9'
225mm T4	

16mm Prime Lenses
Baltars Series Lenses
15mm T2.5	2'
17.5mm T2.5	2'
20mm T2.5	2'
25mm T2.5	2'
30mm T2.5	2'
35mm T2.5	2'
40mm T2.5	2'
50mm T2.5	2'
75mm T2.5	3'
100mm T2.5	4'
152mm T2.8	9'

B&L CINEMASCOPE
35mm Anamorphic Prime Lenses
40mm f/2.3
50mm f/2.3
75mm f/2.8
100mm f/2.8
150mm f/3.5

BERTHIOT
16mm Prime Lenses
Cinor Series Lenses
10mm f/1.9
25mm f/1.4
75mm f/2.5
100mm f/3.5
145mm f/4.5

Lytar Series Lenses
25mm f/1.8

16mm Zoom Lenses
Pan Cinor Lenses
17.5–85mm T2.6	
17.5–85mm f/3.8	
25–100mm f/3.4	7'
28–154mm T4.7	

Monital Series Lenses
12–120mm T3.8

CANON
(Also see Century Precision & OpTex)
16mm Zoom Lenses
7–63mm T2.6	2'
8–64mm T2.4	2'

Super 16 Zoom Lenses
11.5–138mm T2.4	3'6"
11–165mm T2.5	3'6"

EF Cinema Prime Lenses (D)
( )* = distance from front of lens
24mm T1.5	(1')*
50mm T1.3	(1'6")*
85mm T1.3	(3'2")*

EF Cinema Zoom Lenses (D)
( )* = distance from front of lens
14.5–60mm T2.6	(2'4")*
15.5–47mm T2.8	(1'8")*
30–105mm T2.8	(2')*
30–300mm T2.9-37	(5')*

CENTURY PRECISION

35mm Prime Lenses
6mm T2.8	
(Century/Nikkor Fisheye)	1'
7.5mm T5 (Century)	3'
8mm T2.8	
(Century/Nikkor Fisheye)	1'1"
9.8mm T2.3	
(Century/Kinoptic)	8.5"
14mm T2.8 (Canon)	10"

Cooke/Century Speed Panchro (Close Focus) Lenses
18mm T2.2	5.5"
25mm T2.2	5.5"
32mm T2.3	6.5"
40mm T2.3	7"
50mm T2.3	8"
75mm T2.3	1'3"
100mm T2.8	1'5"

Cooke/Century Speed Panchro Lenses
18mm T2.2	1'
25mm T2.2	1'
32mm T2.3	1'
40mm T2.3	1'
50mm T2.3	1'6"
75mm T2.3	2'
100mm T2.8	3'
152mm T3.2 (Macro 1:2)	2'3"

Century/Canon Telephoto Lenses
200mm T2	10'
200mm T2 Mark II	8'
300mm T2.8	9'9"
300mm T3 Mark II	15'
400mm T2.8	15'
400mm T3 Mark II	15'
400mm T4.5	13'
500mm T4.5	15'3"
600mm T4.5	27'
800mm T5.6	45'

Century/Canon Telephoto Lenses (EOS & FD)
200mm f/2 (EOS MK II)	
300mm f/3 (EOS MK II)	
300mm f/2.8 (FD MK I)	
400mm f/3 (EOS MK II)	
400mm f/2.8 (FD MK I)	

Century/Nikkor Telephoto Lenses
200mm T2	9'
200mm T4 (Micro-Nikkor 1:2)	
300mm T2.4	13'
300mm T2.8	13'
400mm T2.8	13'2"
500mm T4	15'6"
600mm T4	25'
800mm T5.6	27'
1000mm T6.1	25'

35mm Zoom Lenses
17–35mm T3	
(Century/Canon-Compact)	1'4"
23–460mm T8	
(Century/Angenieux)	5'
28–70mm T3	
(Century/Minolta-Compact)	3'
50–300mm f/4.5 (Canon)	
50–300mm f/4.5 (Nikon)	
150–60mm T6.7	10'
150–600mm T6.7	
(Century/Canon)	9'9"

16mm Prime Lenses
1.9mm T2.8 (extreme fisheye)	f.f.
3.5mm T2 (fisheye)	2'
5.9mm f/1.8	f.f.
10mm f/1.8	

Super 16 Prime Lenses
6mm Series 2000 T1.9	
(4.5 w/Wide Angle Adapter)	1'

Super 16 Zoom Lenses
11.5–215mm T2.6 –T3.5	
(Century/Fujinon)	4'

Special Purpose Lenses
Century/Canon Tilt Focus Lenses
24mm T4	1'
45mm T2.8	1'4"
90mm T2.8	1'8"

Clairmont/Century Swing/Shift Lens System
14mm T2.8 (Canon)	0
18mm T3.8 (Nikkor)	0
20mm T3.2 (Nikkor)	0
24mm T3.8 (Olympus)	0
28mm T3.8 (Pentax)	0
35mm T3.2 (Canon)	
approx. 6" (½")	
45mm T2.8 (Canon)	
55mm T2.8 (Mamiya)	
75mm T2.8 (Pentax)	
90mm T2.8 (Canon)	
105mm T2.4 (Nikkor)	2'6"
135mm T4 (Pentax)	
150mm T2.8 (Zeiss)	5'
150mm T3.5 (Pentax)	

Swing/Shift Macro Lenses
120mm T4	
(Zeiss/Clairmont 1:1)	1'8"
135mm T5.6	
(Zeiss/Clairmont 1:1)	1'8"

Optical Accessories
Double Asphere Wide-Angle Adapter
35mm Format
(Converts: 16mm=12mm, 18mm=16)
16mm Format
(Converts: 8=6mm, 9.5=7mm, 12=9mm, 10–100mm=7mm, 11–110=7.3)
Super 16 Format (6mm=4.5)

Optical Extenders:
1.4X (PL to PL) (1½-stop loss)
2X (PL to PL) (2-stop loss)

Fish Eye Adapter:
35mm Format
(Zeiss lens examples:
16mmCF=10.5mm,
18mm=11.5mm)
16mm Format
(Zeiss lens examples:
8mm=5mm, 9.5mm=6mm,
12=7mm,
10–100 zoom=5.5mm,
11–110 zoom=5.7)
$^2/_3$" Video-to-Super 16
Mount Transformer

Low Angle Prism
(½-stop loss)

Periscope T3.8
(1-stop loss)

Series 2000 Mark II Periscope T4
(w/ a fixed T2.8 lens setting)

CINEMA PRODUCTS

35mm Prime Lenses
K-35 High Speed Aspheric (CP/Canon) Lenses
18mm T1.4
24mm T1.4
35mm T1.4
55mm T1.4
85mm T1.4

16mm Prime Lenses
Ultra T (CP/Canon) Lenses
9.5mm T1.2
12.5mm T1.2
16mm T1.2
25mm T1.2

CINE MAGIC

35mm Special Purpose Lenses
Cinewand Probe Lens System T5.6
10mm
12mm
16mm
24mm
32mm
40mm
60mm

Revolution Dual-swivel Snorkel/Probe T7.5 Lens System
Mini-PL mount Lenses:
(Standard PL-mount adapter
also available)
9.5mm
12mm
16mm
20mm
24mm
32mm
40mm
60mm

CLAIRMONT

35mm Prime Lenses

14mm T2.8	
(Clairmont/Canon)	10"
20mm T2.8	
(Clairmont/Canon)	10"
1000mm T4.5	70'

35mm Zoom Lenses

140–420mm T2.7	
(Clairmont/Isco)	
150–600mm T8	10'
(Clairmont/Canon)	

35mm Anamorphic Prime Lenses
Clairmont Anamorphic Prime Lenses

22mm T2.4	
32mm T2.3	2'6"
40mm T2.3	3'
50mm T2.3	3'
75mm T2.8	3'
100mm T3.4	5'

Anamorphic Telephoto Lenses

360mm T4.5 (Zeiss)	5'
400mm T4 (Nikkor)	9'
400mm T6	
(Nikkor Macro 1:2)	1'7"
600mm T4 (Nikkor)	13'
600mm T4.5 (Canon)	9'9"
800mm T5.6 (Nikkor)	13'2"
800mm T5.6 (Canon)	12'3"
1000mm T6.3 (Nikkor)	15'6"
1000mm T8 (Canon)	15'3"
1200mm T6.3 (Nikkor)	25'
1200mm T6.3 (Canon)	25'
1600mm T9 (Nikkor)	25'
1600mm T9 (Canon)	45'
2000mm T8	
(Clairmont/Canon)	70'

35mm Anamorphic Zoom Lenses

28-140 T4.5 (Cooke)	2'4"
34-204 T4.5 (Angenieux)	2'6"
36-200 T4.5 (Cooke)	2'4"
40-200 T4.5 (Cooke)	2'4"
50–500mm T5.6	
(Cooke MK II)	5'6"
50–500mm T5.6	
(Cooke MK III)	5'6"
50–500mm T5.6	
(Angenieux HR)	5'7"
300–1200mm T11	
(Clairmont)	10'

Special Purpose Lenses
Blurtar Lenses

(single element vignette-focus lenses)

28mm T2.3	
40mm T2.6	
50mm T3	
75mm T3.8	

Clairmont/Century Swing/Shift Lens System

14mm T2.8 (Canon)		0
18mm T3.8 (Nikkor)		0
20mm T3.2 (Nikkor)		0
24mm T3.8 (Olympus)		0
28mm T3.8 (Pentax)		0
35mm T3.2		
(Canon)	approx. 6" (½")	
50mm T4		
(Zeiss)	approx. 1' (4")	
60mm T3.5		
(Zeiss)	approx. 1' (4")	
80mm T2.8		
(Zeiss)	approx. 1'4" (9")	
105mm T2.4 (Nikkor)		2'6"
110mm T2.4		
(Zeiss)	approx. 3'	
150mm T2.8 (Zeiss)		5'

Swing/Shift Macro Lenses

120mm T4	
(Zeiss/Clairmont 1:1)	1'8"
135mm T5.6	
(Zeiss/Clairmont 1:1)	1'8"

InfinFX K2 T22 Long Distance Macro Lens System

#1 Objective Lens	
(1.3X Magnification)	1'5"
#2 Objective Lens	
(1.6X Magnification)	1'4"
#3 Objective Lens	
(2.1X Magnification)	1'
#4 Objective Lens	
(3.9X Magnification)	6"
#5 Objective Lens	
(5.3X Magnification)	4"
#6 Objective Lens	
(10X Magnification)	1.9"

Microscope T51-T60 (PL mount) Lens System

4X Objective Lens
10X Objective Lens
40X Objective Lens

Pinhole Lens f48-f143 (50mm equivalent)

Nikkor Fisheye Lens

6mm T2.8	9'

V3 Moving Optical Element Prime Lenses

The MOE system is based on a moving optical element lens that captures different points of view relative to the plane of focus. These slight shifts cause the viewer to interpret multiple depth layers by displacing objects from one another in the frame.

24mm T2.3	2'
35mm T1.6	2'3"
50mm T1.4	2'3"
85mm T2.1	2'6"
135mm T2.8	4'3"

Optical Accessories

Baby Periscope T5.6
Image Shaker
Revolution Lens System
Rifle Scope
Spy EFX (Night vision front attachment)
Squishy Lens

COOKE

5/i Prime Lenses

18mm T1.4	1'2"
25mm T1.4	1'2"
32mm T1.4	1'2"
40mm T1.4	1'4"
50mm T1.4	1'8"
65mm T1.4	2'
75mm T1.4	2'3"
100mm T1.4	2'6"
135mm T1.4	2'7"

35mm Prime Lenses

S4 & S4/i (information) Lenses
(S4/i lenses are compatible with Arri's LDS system)

14mm T2	9"
16mm T2	9"
18mm T2	9"
21mm T2	9"
25mm T2	9"
27mm T2	10"
32mm T2	1'
35mm T2	1'2"
40mm T2	1'4"
50mm T2	1'8"
65mm T2	2'3"
75mm T2	2'6"
100mm T2	3'
135mm T2	5' (2'6" at T4)

S2 & S3 Speed Panchro Lenses

18mm T2.2	1'
25mm T2.2	1'
32mm T2.3	1'
40mm T2.3	1'
50mm T2.3	1'6"
75mm T2.3	2'
100mm T2.8 (Deep Field)	3'
152mm T3.2 (Macro 1:2)	2'3"

S3 Speed Panchros (Close Focus) Lenses

18mm T2.2	5.5"
25mm T2.2	5.5"
32mm T2.3	6.5"
40mm T2.3	7"
50mm T2.3	8"
75mm T2.3	1'3"
100mm T2.8	1'5"

Double Speed Panchro

28mm T2.5	2'

Panchro/i "Mini S4"
Prime Lenses

18mm T2.8	10"
25mm T2.8	10"
32mm T2.8	12"
50mm T2.8	1'8"
75mm T2.8	2'6"
100mm T2.8	3'
135mm T2.8	3'3"

SK4 Wide Angle 16mm/S16
Prime Lenses

6mm T2	8"
9.5mm T2	8"
12mm T2	8"

35mm Zoom Lenses

14–70mm T3.1	
(Wide Angle Varotal)	2'4"
18–100mm T3 (Varotal)	2'4"
20–60mm T3.1 (Varopanchro)	2'4"
20–100mm T3.1 (Varotal)	2'4"
25–250mm f/2.8	
(MK I Super Cine Varotal)	5'6"
25–250mm T3.9	
(MK II Cine Varotal)	5'6"
25–250mm T3.7	
(MK III Cinetal)	5'6"

35mm Zoom Lens

S4/i 15–40mm T2 (CXX)	1'6"

16mm Zoom Lenses

9–50mm T2.5 (Varokinetal)	1'6"

Super 16 Zoom Lenses

10–30mm T1.6 (Veropanchro)	
10.4–52mm T2.8 (Varokinetal)	1'6"

EASTMAN KODAK

16mm Prime Lenses
Cine-Ektar Series Lenses

15mm f/2.5	6"
20mm f/3.5	
25mm f/1.4	
25mm f/1.9	
50mm f/1.9	
63mm f/2	2'

Anastigmat Series Lenses

50mm f/1.6	2'
63mm f/2.7	1'6"
102mm f/2.7	4'6"
153mm f/4	

ELGEET

35mm Prime Lenses
Cine-Navitar Series Lenses

13mm f/1.5	1'
25.4mm f/2.0	1'
50mm f/2.0	2'
75mm f/1.9	3'
150mm f/3.8	6'

Cine-Tel Series

75mm f/2.9	3'
100mm f/2.7	2'6"

ELITE

35mm Prime Lenses

9.6mm T2.1	10"
10mm T2.4	
(Lightweight)	10"
12mm T1.9	10"
14mm T1.9	10"
16mm T1.6	10"
18mm T1.3	10"
20mm T1.3	10"
22mm T1.3	10"
24mm T1.3	10"
28mm T1.3	10"
35mm T1.3	1'8"
40mm T1.3	1'8"
50mm T1.3	2'4"
60mm T1.3	2'4"
75mm T1.3	3'4"
100mm T1.6	3'4"
135mm T1.9	5'
180mm T2.8	6'6"
200mm T2.8	6'6"

35mm Zoom Lenses

25–80mm T3.2 (Lightweight)	3'
120–520mm T3	11'

35mm Anamorphic
Prime Lenses

21mm T2.8	2'6"
24.5mm T2.1	3'
32mm T2.1	3'
40mm T2.1	3'
50mm T2.1	3'
75mm T2.1	3'
100mm T2.1	3'
135mm T2.5	5'
180mm T2.8	5'
250mm T3	5'

35mm Anamorphic
Zoom Lenses

40–160mm T4	3'
(Lightweight)	
240–1040mm T4	11'

16mm Prime Lenses

4mm T2.2	f.f.

Super 16 Prime Lenses

4.5mm T2.2 (Fisheye)	4"
6.6mm T1.3	8"
7mm T1.3	8"
8mm T1.3	10"
9.5mm T1.3	10"
12mm T1.3	10"
16mm T1.3	10"
20mm T1.3	10'
25mm T1.3	10"
35mm T1.3	10"
50mm T1.3	1'8"

Super 16 Zoom Lenses

10-100 T2.5	1'6"

Special Purpose Lenses

200mm T1.3	
(Reverse Perspective)	
focuses 4' to 6' only	

EYEMO

35mm Prime Lenses
Canon Lenses

14mm T2.8	10"
17mm T4	10"
20mm T2.8	10"
24mm T2.8	1'3"
35mm T2.8	1'

Nikkor Lenses

8mm T2.8 (Fisheye)	1'1"
15mm T3.5	1'
18mm T2.8	10"
20mm T2.8	10"
24mm T2	1'
28mm T1.4	1'3"
28mm T2	
35mm T1.4	1'
35mm T2	
50mm T1.4	2'
55mm T2.8	
105mm T2.8	

FUJINON

Premier Zoom Lenses

14.5–45mm T2.0	2'3"
18–85mm T2.0	2"7"
24–180mm T2.6	4"1"
75–400mm T2.8-3.8	6'6"
19–90mm Cabrio T2.9	2'9.5"

Arri Alura Lightweight
Zoom Lenses (D)

15.5–45mm T2.8	2'
30–80mm T2.8	2'

Arri Alura Studio Zoom Lenses

18–80mm T2.6	2'4"
45–250mm t2.6	3'11"

HAWK

(See Vantage Film Lenses)

INNOVISION

16mm & 35mm
Special Purpose Lenses
Probe II+ - T6.3 (35mmFormat),
T4 (16mm/Video Formats)

9mm (35mm format),
5mm (16mm format)
12mm (35mm format),
7mm (16mm format)
16mm (35mm format),
9.5mm (16mm format)
20mm (35mm format),
12.5mm (16mm format)
32mm (35mm format),
18mm (16mm format)
40mm (35mm format),
24mm (16mm format)

Probe II - T5.6 (35mm Format),
T2.8 (16mm/Video Formats)

9mm (35mm format),
5mm (16mm format)
12mm (35mm format),
7mm (16mm format)
16mm (35mm format),

9.5mm (16mm format)
20mm (35mm format),
12.5mm (16mm format)
32mm (35mm format),
18mm (16mm format)
40mm (35mm format),
24mm (16mm format)

**High Resolution Probe II &
Probe II+ Prime Lenses**
12mm
20mm
28mm
40mm
55mm

**Probe I - T16 (35mm Format),
T8 (16mm/Video Formats)***
* (1-Stop loss w/90° Attachment)
10mm (35mm format),
5mm (16mm format)
14mm (35mm format),
6.5mm (16mm format)
16mm (35mm format),
9mm (16mm format)
24mm (35mm format),
12.5mm (16mm format)
32mm (35mm format),
18mm (16mm format)
50mm (35mm format),
28mm (16mm format)
75mm (35mm format),
40mm (16mm format)
100mm (35mm format),
60mm (16mm format)

6000 Series
35mm Format: 30mm T45
16mm Format: 20mm T30

KENWORTHY/ NETTMAN SNORKEL

The lens on the camera will be 4.1 times
net focal length of the combined optical
system with the periscope included. For
35mm, Kenworthy/Nettman can supply a
T/3 18mm, combined focal length, (Pentax
75mm, PL or BNC mount) or a T/4.5 Zoom
19.5–39mm, combined focal length, (Pentax 80–160mm, PL or BNC mount). The
customer may supply Zeiss in 85–180mm
range. For Arri 16mm SR the client supplies these primes: 35mm, 40mm, 50mm,
60mm. Divide by 4.1 for combined focal
length. For Panavision use these Panaflex
Spherical Primes: SP type 75mm, 100,
& 150mm, which net at 18mm, 24.4mm
and 36.6mm. When ordering SP 75mm,
specify late model design with serial # approx. SP75-94. Earlier designs may cause
vignetting. Panavision zooms are too
large. Use the modified Pentax 80–160mm
with the Panavision mount. For Panavision
Anamorphic there are no zooms available.
Use primes T/3.5 Series C Panatar 150mm
which will look like an anamorphic 37mm.
Longer focal length Panatar primes may
work. Anamorphic alternative: Super 35
with spherical lenses using Arriflex or
Panavision cameras.

KERN-PAILLARD
**16mm Prime Lenses
Switar Series Lenses**
10mm f/1.6	8"
16mm f/1.8	8"
25mm f/1.4	1'6"
50mm f/1.4	3'
75mm f/1.9	5'

Pizar Series Lenses
26mm f/1.9	1'6"
50mm f/1.8	

Yvar/Macro-Yvar Series Lenses
16mm f/2.8	1'
75mm f/2.8	5'
100mm f/3.3	8'
150mm f/4	13'

Macro-Switar Series Lenses
50mm f/1.4

16mm Zoom Lenses
16–86mm f/2.5

KILFITT
**35mm Prime Lenses
Tele-Kilar Series Lenses**
150mm f/3.5	5'
300mm f/4	5'6"
300mm f/5.6	10'

Fern-Kilar Serise Lenses
400mm f/4
600mm f/5.6

Macro-Kilar Series Lenses
40mm f/2.8	4"
(Macro 1:1)	
90mm f/2.8	6"
(Macro 1:1)	

KINOPTICS
35mm Prime Lenses
9.8mm f/1.8 (Tegea)	8.5"
18mm f/1.8 (Apochromat)	
28mm f/2 (Apochromat)	9"
32mm f/1.9	
32mm f/2.8	
35mm f/2 (Apochromat)	
40mm f/2 (Apochromat)	
50mm f/2 (Apochromat)	
75mm f/2 (Apochromat)	
100mm f/2 (Apochromat)	3'
150mm f/2.5 (Apochromat)	
210mm f/2.8 (Special-Cine)	
300mm f/3.5 (Special-Cine)	
500mm f/5.6 (Aplanat)	
1000mm f/8 (Kinoptar)	

16mm & Super 16 Prime Lenses
1.9mm f/1.9 (Super Tegea)
5.7mm f/1.8 (Tegea)
9mm f/1.5 (Apochromat)
12.5mm f/2.5 (Apochromat)
18mm f/1.8 (Apochromat)
25mm f/2 (Apochromat)
28mm f/2 (Apochromat)
32mm f/1.9
32mm f/2.8

35mm f/1.3 (Fulgior Apochromat)
35mm f/2 (Apochromat)
40mm f/2 (Apochromat)
50mm f/2 (Apochromat)
75mm f/2 (Apochromat)
100mm f/2 (Apochromat)
150mm f/2.5 (Apochromat)
210mm f/2.8 (Special-Cine)
300mm f/3.5 (Special-Cine)
500mm f/5.6 (Aplanat)
1000mm f/8 (Kinoptar)

**16mm, Super 16 & 35mm
Macro Lenses**
50mm T2.5	
(Macro-Apochromat 1:1)	8"
75mm T2.5	
(Macro-Apochromat 1:1)	2'6"
100mm T2.5	
(Macro-Apochromat 1:1)	4'
150mm T3	
(Macro-Apochromat 1:1)	2'

KINETAL
16mm Prime Lenses
9mm T2
12.5mm T2
17.5mm T2
25mm T2
37.5mm T2
50mm T2
75mm T2
100mm T2.8
150mm T4

KISH OPTICS
Optical Accessories
Rear Anamorphic Attachment (PL)
Mesmerizer
Mini-Mesmerizer
(35mm format: 50mm widest angle,
16mm format: 25mm)

Rear Zoom-Mesmerizer
(PL or Panavision Mount)
(1 √3-stop loss)

Kaleida-Lens
(PL or Panavision Mount)
T2.8 Maximum aperture.

KOWA
**35mm Prime Lenses
Prominar Series Lenses**
15mm T4	1'
18mm T2.6	1'
25mm T2.3	1'6"
32mm T2.3	1'6"
40mm T2.3	2'6"
50mm T2.3	2'6"
75mm T2.3	2'8"
100mm T2.6	5'

LEICA

Summilux-C Prime Lenses

16mm T1.4	1'2"
18mm T1.4	1'2"
21mm T1.4	1'2"
25mm T1.4	1'
35mm T1.4	1'
40mm T1.4	1'4"
50mm T1.4	1'8"
65mm T1.4	1'5"
75mm T1.4	2'3"
100mm T1.4	2'11"

LOMO

35mm Anamorphic Prime Lenses

22mm T3.6	3'
30mm T3.2	3'
35mm T2.4	3'
50mm T2.4	3'
75mm T2.4	3'
100mm T3.2	5'
150mm T4.5	7'
300mm T5.6	11'
500mm T8	11'

65mm Prime Lenses

28mm T3.8	
40mm T3.4	
56mm T2.9	
75mm T2.9	
100mm T2.9	
150mm T3	

OPPENHEIMER-NIKKOR

35mm Prime Lenses

8mm T3.2

OPTAR

35mm Prime Lenses
Zome Series Lenses

25–80mm T3.3	3'

OPTEX

35mm Prime Lenses

10mm f/2.8 (OpTex/Canon)	
10.5mm T2.1	6"
(OpTex/Zeiss)	
14mm f/2.8 (OpTex/Canon)	
20mm f/2.8 (OpTex/Canon)	

Optex/Nikkor (Close Focus) Lenses

15mm T3.5	7"
20mm T2.8	6"
24mm T2.8	6"
28mm T2.8	6.5"
35mm T2.8	8"

Telephoto Lenses

100mm T2 (Optex/Canon)	3'6"
135mm T2 (Optex/Canon)	5'
150mm T3 (OpTex)	
180mm f/2 (OpTex/Nikon)	
200mm f/2.8 (OpTex/Canon)	
200mm f/1.8 (OpTex/Canon)	9'

200mm f/2 (OpTex/Nikon)	
200mm f/4 (OpTex/Pentax-Macro)	
300mm f/2 (OpTex/Canon)	
300mm f/2.8 (OpTex/Canon)	
300mm T2.1 (Nikon)	
300mm f/3.2 (OpTex/Canon Mk-IIIB)	
400mm f/2.8 (OpTex/Canon)	
800mm f/5.6 (OpTex/Canon)	
1000mm f/11 (OpTex/Nikon)	

Macro Lenses

50mm f/3.5 (OpTex/Canon)	
60mm f/2.8 (OpTex/Leica)	10.63"
100mm T5.6	
(Auto Compensating Iris)	1'2"
(OpTex)	
200mm f/4 (OpTex/Pentax)	

35mm Zoom Lenses

150–600mm f5.6 (OpTex/Canon)	10'

Macro Zoom Lenses

7.8–164mm T2-T2.8

16mm & Super 16 Prime Lenses

4mm T1.9 (OpTex)	
fixed focus @ 4'–inf.	
5.5mm T1.9 (OpTex)	8"
8mm T1.9 (OpTex)	1'3"
150mm T3	

16mm Zoom Lenses

5–30mm f3.5 (OpTex/Canon)	

Super 16 Zoom Lenses

6–60mm T2.4 (OpTex/Canon)	
7–63mm T2.4 (OpTex/Canon)	2'
10.3–216mm T3.3	
(OpTex/Canon)	4'
10.5–158mm T2.4	
10.5–210mm T2.4-T4	4'
10.8–60mm T3 (OpTex/RTH Cooke)	
12–120mm T2.4 (OpTex/Zeiss)	5'
14.5–480mm T3-T5	
(OpTex/Canon)	9'

Special Purpose Lenses

Excellence Periscope/
Probe System T2.8 (Super 16),
T5.6 (35mm),

T8 Anamorphic

60° (14mm–Super 16,
28mm–35mm,
56mm–Anamorphic)

79° (10mm–Super 16,
20mm–35mm,
40mm–Anamorphic)

100° (7mm–Super 16,
14mm–35mm,
28mm–Anamorphic)

120° (5mm–Super 16,
10mm–35mm,
20mm–Anamorphic)

Optical Accessories

2X Extenders: For 16mm, S16 and
35mm Format Lenses.

1.4X Extender

OTTO NEMENZ

35mm Prime Lenses
Eyemo Lenses

14mm T2.8 (Canon)	10"
15mm T3.5 (Nikkor)	1'
17mm T4 (Canon)	10"
18mm T2.8 (Nikkor)	10"
20mm T2.8 (Canon)	10"
20mm T2.8 (Nikkor)	10"
24mm T2.8 (Canon)	1'3"
24mm T2 (Nikkor)	1'
28mm T1.4 (Nikkor)	1'3"
35mm T1.4 (Nikkor)	1'
35mm T2.8 (Canon)	1'
50mm T1.4 (Nikkor)	2'

P+S TECHNIK

35mm Special Purpose Lenses

T-Rex Superscope System T7.1
(PL, BNC, Panavision mounts)

PANAVISION LENSES

35mm Prime Lenses
Primo Series Lenses

10mm T1.9	2'
14.5mm T1.9	2'
17.5mm T1.9	2'
21mm T1.9	2'
27mm T1.9	2'
35mm T1.9	2'
40mm T1.9	2'
50mm T1.9	2'
75mm T1.9	3'
100mm T1.9	3'
150mm T1.9	5'9"
210mm T2.8	5'10"
(150mm w/ 1.4X Primo Extender)	

Primo Classic Series (Close Focus) Lenses

21mm T1.9 (1:5)	9.5"
24mm T1.7 (1:4)	
w/ soft effect	10"
27mm T1.9 (1:2.5)	9.5"
30mm T1.7 (1:3.5)	
w/ soft effect	10"
35mm T1.9 (1:3)	11"
50mm T1.9 (1:1.25)	11"
65mm T1.7 (1:1.8)	
w/soft effect	13.5"
85mm T1.7 (1:3)	
w/ soft effect	16.5"
100mm T1.9 (1:2)	16"
125mm T1.8 (1:2.5)	
w/ soft effect	25.5"

Primo Close Focus Lenses

11.5mm T1.9	
(14.5mm w/ low distortion Wide Angle Adapter)	
14.5mm T1.9 (1:6.5)	8.25"
17.5mm T1.9 (1:4.5)	7.5"
21mm T1.9 (1:5)	9.5"
27mm T1.9 (1:3)	9.5"
35mm T1.9 (1:3)	11"

Ultra Speed "Z" Series Lenses

14mm T1.9	2'
24mm T1.3	2'
29mm T1.3	2'
35mm T1.4	2'
50mm T1.4	2'
85mm T1.4	2'
100mm T2	3'
135mm T2	5'
180mm T2.8	5'
252mm T4	5'1"
(180mm w/1.4X Primo Extender)	

Super Speed "Z" Series Lenses

14mm T1.9	2'
24mm T1.9	2'
29mm T1.9	2'
35mm T1.9	2'
50mm T1.9	2'
85mm T1.9	2'6"
100mm T2	3'
135mm T2	5'
180mm T2	5'
252mm T2.8	5'1"
(180mm w/ 1.4X Primo Extender)	

Ultra Speed Lenses

14mm T1.9	2'
17mm T1.9	2'
20mm T1.9	2'6"
24mm T1.3	2'
29mm T1.3	2'3"
35mm T1.3	2'
40mm T1.3	2'
50mm T1	2'
75mm T1.6	2'
100mm T1.6	4'
125mm T1.6	3'6"
150mm T1.5	5'

Super Speed Lenses

24mm T2	2'
28mm T2	2'
35mm T1.6	2'
50mm T1.4	2'–2'3"
55mm T1.1	2'6"

Normal Speed Lenses

8mm T2.8 (Nikon Fisheye)	1'
8mm T2.8 (Distortion Lens)	14"
9.8mm T2.8	2'
16mm T2.8	1'9"
20mm T3 or T4	2'6"
24mm T2.8	2'3"
28mm T2.8	2'
32mm T2.8	2'
35mm T2	1'9"–2'
40mm T2	2'
50mm T2	2'3"–2'6"
75mm T2	2'6"–2'9"
100mm T2.4	3'6"
150mm T2.8	5'

Telephoto Lenses (Panavised)

200mm T2 (Canon)	8'
200mm T2 (Nikon)	9'
200mm T2 (Ultra Speed)	6'
280mm T2.8 (Canon)	8'1"
(Canon 200mm w/1.4X Primo Extender)	
280mm T2.8 (Nikon)	9'1"
(Nikon 200mm w/1.4X Primo Extender)	
300mm T2.8 (Ultra Speed)	15'
300mm T2.8 (Canon)	10'
300mm T2 (Nikon)	11'
420mm T2.8 (Nikon)	11'
(Nikon 300mm w/1.4X Primo Extender)	
400mm T4 (Panavision)	15'
400mm T2.8 (Nikon)	15'
400mm T2.8 (Canon)	15'
560mm T4 (Canon)	15'
(Canon 400mm w/1.4X Primo Extender)	
500mm T4 (Panavision)	23'
600mm T4 (Nikon)	25'
600mm T4.5 (Canon)	27'
840mm T6.3 (Canon)	27'
(Canon 600mm w/1.4X Primo Extender)	
800mm T5.6 (Canon)	45'
1120mm T8 (Canon)	45'
(Canon 800mm w/1.4X Primo Extender)	
1000mm T6 (Nikon)	25'

35mm Zoom Lenses

14.5–50mm T2.2 (Primo Macro)	2'6"
17.5–75mm T2.3 (Primo 4:1)	2'9"
24–275mm T2.8 (Primo11:1)	4'
135–420mm T2.8 (Primo 3:1)	8'6"
27–68mm T2.8 Lightweight I	3'
17.5–34mm T2.8 Lightweight II	1'6"
85–200mm T4 Lightweight III	4'
17–102mm T2.9 (Angenieux/Panavision)	2'6"
20–120mm T3 (Angenieux/Panavision)	3'6"
20–60mm T3 (Cooke/Panavision)	2'6"
20–100mm T3.1 (Cooke/Panavision)	2'6"
25–250mm T4 Super Panazoom (Cooke)	5'6"
150–600mm T6.3 (Canon/Panavision)	10'

Compact Zoom Lenses

19–90mm T2.8	2'3"
15–40mm T2.75	2'
27–75mm T2.75	2'6"
60–125mm T2.75	3'6"

Macro and Specialty Lenses
Macro Lenses

50mm T1 (1:2)	9"
90mm T2 (1:0.7)	14.75"
100mm T2 (1:2.5)	18"
180mm T4 (1:0.35)	15.5"
(90mm w/ 2X Primo Extender)	
100mm T2 (1:2.5)	18"
140mm T2.8 (1:1.8)	19"
(100mm w/ 1.4X Primo Extender)	
200mm T4 (1:2)	27"
280mm T5.6 (1:1.4)	28"
(200mm w/ 1.4X Primo Extender)	

Close Focus/Macro Lenses

17mm T1.9	10"
20mm T4	8"
24mm T2.8	8"
28mm T2.8	8"
35mm T2	8"
40mm T2.8 (1:2)	
60mm T2.8 (1:2)	
90mm T2.8 (1:2)	
100mm T2.8 (1:2)	

Frazier T7.1 Lens System

14mm (gives 9.9mm)
17mm (gives 12mm)
20mm (gives 14mm)
24mm (gives 17mm)
28mm (gives 20mm)
35mm (gives 25mm)
45mm (gives 32mm)
50mm (gives 35mm)
85mm (gives 60mm)
105mm (gives 75mm)
135mm (gives 95mm)
15mm (Sigma Fisheye)

Portrait Lenses

14mm T1.9	2'
16mm T2.8	1'9"
20mm T3	2'
24mm T2.8	2'3"
28mm T1.9	2'
35mm T1.4 (Zeiss)	2'
35mm T1.6	2'
35mm T2	2'
50mm T1.4	2'3"
50mm T2	2'6"
75mm T2	2'6"

Flare Lenses

14mm T1.9	2'
17mm T1.9	2'
20mm T3	2'6"
24mm T2.8	2'3"
28mm T1.9	2'
32mm T2.8	2'
35mm T2	1'6"
40mm T2	2'
50mm T2.3	2'3"
75mm T2	2'
100mm T1.6	4'
125mm T1.6	3'6"

Slant Focus Lenses (Bellowless)
24mm T3.5 (Close Focus)	12"
34mm T4.9 (Close Focus)	13"
(24mm w/ 1.4X Primo Extender)	
45mm T2.8 (Close Focus)	16"
63mm T4 (Close Focus)	17"
(45mm w/ 1.4X Primo Extender)	

Panavision/Century Swing Shift Lenses (F/D)
14mm T2.8
18mm T2.8
24mm T4
28mm T3.5
35mm T2.8
45mm T2.8
55mm T2.8
75mm T2.8
90mm T2.8
105mm T2.4
135mm T4.5
150mm T3.5

35mm Special Purpose Lenses
6mm T2.9 (Fisheye)	1'6"
6mm T3.5 (Nikon Fisheye)	10'6"

35mm Anamorphic Prime Lenses
Primo Series Anamorphic
35mm T2	3'6"
40mm T2	3'6"
50mm T2	3'6"
75mm T2	4'6"
100mm T2	4'6"

Primo Close Focus Series Anamorphic Lenses
35mm T2	2'9"
40mm T2	2'9"
50mm T2	2'9"
75mm T2	2'6"
100mm T2	2'6"

"G" Series Anamorphic Lenses
25mm T2.6	2'6"
30mm T2.6	2'6"
35mm T2.6	3'
40mm T2.6	3'
50mm T2.6	3'
60mm T2.6	3'
75mm T2.6	3'
100mm T3	3'

"E" Series Anamorphic Lenses
28mm T2.3	5'
35mm T2	5'
40mm T2	5'
50mm T2	5'
75mm T2	5'
85mm T2	5'
100mm T2.3	5'
135mm T2.8	3'9"
180mm T2.8	4'6"
252mm T4	4'7"
(180mm w/ 1.4X Primo Extender)	

"C" Series Anamorphic Lenses
30mm T3	4'
35mm T2.3	2'9"
40mm T2.8	2'6"

50mm T2.3	2'6"
60mm T2.8	3'6"
75mm T2.5	4'6"
100mm T2.8	4'6"
150mm T3.5	5'
180mm T2.8	7'
252mm T4	7'1"
(180mm w/ 1.4X Primo Extender)	

"C" Series Anamorphic Flare Lenses
40mm T2.8	2'6"
50mm T2.3	2'6"
75mm T2.8	3'6"
100mm T3.5	4'

Super High-Speed Anamorphic Lenses
24mm T1.6	6'
35mm T1.4	4'6"
50mm T1.1	4'
50mm T1.4	4'
55mm T1.4	4'
75mm T1.8	4'6"
100mm T1.8	4'6"

35mm Anamorphic Telephoto Lenses
360mm T4	5'6"
400mm T3.5 (Nikon)	9'
400mm T3 (Canon)	8'
600mm T4 (Nikon)	13'
600mm T4.5 (Canon)	27'
800mm T5.6 (Canon)	15'
1000mm T5.6	22'
1200mm T8 (Canon)	27'
2000mm T9	30'

35mm Anamorphic Zoom Lenses
38–85mm T2.8	2'
48–550mm T4.5 (Primo 11:1)	4'1"
270–840mm T4.5 (Primo 3:1)	8'7"
40–200mm T4.5	
(Super Panazoom/Cooke)	2'6"
50–500mm T5.6	
(Super Panazoom/Cooke)	5'6"

Special Purpose 35mm Anamorphic Lenses
25mm T2.5	
(Wide Angle Distortion)	5'
55mm T2.5 (Close Focus)	10"
90mm T4.3	
(Slant Focus w/ Close Focus)	17"
100mm T2.8	
(Insert or Process)	4'6"
150mm T3.2	
(Macro Panatar 1:1.5)	17"
200mm T3.2	
(Macro Panatar 1:2)	18"
250mm T3.2	
(Macro Panatar 1:2)	29"

65mm Panavision Prime Lenses
21mm T3	1'6"
24mm T3.5	1'6"
28mm T3	3'
35mm T2.8	1'6"
35mm T2.8	1'9"

40mm T2.8	1'6"
50mm T2	2'
50mm T2	2'6"
55mm T2.8	3'6"
75mm T2	2'3"
75mm T2.3	2'9"
100mm T2	2'
100mm T2.5	3'6"
150mm T2	4'
180mm T2	5'6"
200mm T2	8'
300mm T2.8 (Zeiss)	8'
300mm T2.8 (Canon)	10'
400mm T2.8 (Canon)	12'
800mm T5.6 (Canon)	40'

Primo Series Lenses
75mm T1.9	3'
100mm T1.9	3'
150mm T1.9	5'9"

65mm Zoom Lens
60–360mm T6.3	8'

65mm Special Purpose Lenses
19mm T4.5 (Fisheye)	1'6"
24mm T3.5 (Fisheye)	1'
55mm T4 (Macro)	11"

Optical Accessories
Optex Periscope
(Panavision Mount)
Century Precision Periscope
(Panavision Mount)
2X Extender
1.4X Extender

RED DIGITAL CINEMA
Prime Lenses (D)
18mm T1.8	1'
25mm T1.8	1'
35mm T1.8	1'
50mm T1.8	1'
85mm T1.8	2'
100mm T1.8	2'6"
300mm T2.9	8'

Zoom Lenses (D)
( )* = distance from front of lens
17–50mm T2.9	(4")*
18–85mm T2.9	(2'4")*

RANK-TAYLOR-HOBSON
35mm Prime Lenses
Speed Panchro Series Lenses
18mm f/1.7
25mm f/1.8
32mm f/2
40mm f/2
50mm f/2
75mm f/2
100mm f/2
16mm Prime Lenses
Kinetal Series Lenses
9mm f/1.9
12.5mm f/1.8
17.5mm f/1.8

25mm f/1.8
37.5mm f/1.8
50mm f/1.4   3'
75mm f/2.6
100mm f/2.6
150mm f/3.8

REVOLUTION
(See Cine Magic)

ROESSEL-CPT
CPT Superscope Prime Lenses
10mm T5.7
15mm T5.7
25mm T5.7
40mm T5.7
60mm T5.7

Special Purpose Lenses
Supersnorkel T8
T-Rex T7.1

SCHNEIDER
35mm Prime Lenses
Cinegon Series Lenses
18mm f/2

Cine-Xenar II Series Lenses (D)
25mm T2.2   11"
35mm T2.1   13"
50mm T2   14"
75mm T2   18"
95mm T2   26"

Cine-Xenar III Series Lenses (D)
18mm T2.2   11"
25mm T2.2   11"
35mm T2.1   11"
50mm T2   14"
75mm T2   18"
95mm T2   26"

Cine-Xenon Series Lenses
24mm T1.4   1'1"
28mm T2.2   1'8"
35mm T2.2   2'
40mm T2.2   2'6"
50mm T2.2   3'6"
75mm T2.2   5'
100mm T2.2   5'
300mm T2.2

35mm Zoom Lenses
Televariogon Series Lenses
80–240mm f/4

16mm Prime Lenses
Cinegon Series Lenses
10mm f/1.8   8"
11.5f/1.8
16mm T2   10"
18mm T2
25mm T1.4   1'1"
28mm f/1.8

Cine-Xenon Series Lenses
16mm f/2
25mm T2   1'1"
28mm T2.2   1'8"
35mm T2.2   2'
40mm T2.2   2'6"

50mm T2.2   3'6"
75mm T2.2   5'
100mm T2.2   5'
300mm T2.2

Tele-Xenar Series Lenses
100mm f2.8

16mm Zoom Lenses
10–100mm T2.2
16–60mm T2.2
16–80mm

TECHNOVISION
35mm Prime Lenses
9mm T2.8   10"
9.5 mm T2.8
12 mm T2.1 (Technovision-Zeiss)
12mm T2.1   8"
15 mm T3.5 (Technovision-Leitz)
18mm T1.6
18 mm T1.4 (Technovision-Zeiss)
24mm T1.4 (Technovision)
50mm T1.6 (Technovision-Leitz)
80mm T1.4 (Technovision-Leitz)

High Speed Lenses
18mm T1.4
25mm T1.4
35mm T1.4
50mm T1.4
85mm T1.4

Technovision-Leitz Lenses
15mm T2.3
19mm T2.3
24mm T2.3
35mm T2.3
50mm T2.3
60mm T2.3
80mm T2.3
100mm T2.3
135mm T2.3
180mm T2.3

Macro Lenses
50mm T1.6
60mm T1.4
80mm T1.4
85mm T1.4
100mm T1.4
135mm T1.4
180mm T1.4
40mm T1.8 (Technovision)
50mm T1.4 (Technovision)
60mm T2.3 (Technovision-Leitz)
80mm T2.3 (Technovision-Leitz)
85mm T1.4 (Technovision)
100mm T2.3 (Technovision-Leitz)
135mm T2.3 (Technovision-Leitz)
180mm T2.3 (Technovision-Leitz)

TECHNOVISION/ COOKE
(Close Focus) Lenses
18mm T2.3
25mm T2.3
32mm T2.3
40mm T2.3

50mm T2.2   3'6"
75mm T2.2   5'
100mm T2.2   5'
300mm T2.2

50mm T2.3
75mm T2.3
100mm T2.3

35mm Zoom Lenses
Technovision/Cooke Lenses
14–42mm T3.1
18.5–55.5mm T2.3   2'4"
15–75mm T3.1
18–90mm T2.3   2'7"
25–250mm T2.3

35mm Anamorphic
Prime Lenses
High-Speed
Anamorphic Lenses
20mm TI.4   3'6"
35mm TI.4   3'
40mm TI.4   3'
50mm TI.4   3'
85mm TI.6   3'

Anamorphic Prime Lenses
25mm T2   3'6"
32mm T2.1   4'
40mm T2.1   3'6"
50mm T2.1   3'
85mm T2.1   4'
100mm T2   3'6"
135mm T2.3   4'
270mm T3.5   5'

Anamorphic Prime Lenses
32mm T2.8   3'5"
40mm T2.5   3'
50mm T2.5   3'
75mm T2.8   3'
100mm T2.8   3'
150mm T3.5   3'
152mm T3   3'5"
200mm T4   2'

Anamorphic Prime Lenses
40mm T2.3   3'
50mm T2.3   3'
75mm T2.5   3'
100mm T2.8   3'

Compact Anamorphic Lenses
40mm T2.3   3'
50mm T2.3   3'
75mm T2.8   3'
100mm T3.4   5'
150mm T3.5   3'

Telephoto Anamorphic Lenses
200mm T3.5 (Techno/Nikon)
200mm T3.2 (Techno/Nikon)
400mm T3.6 (Techno/Nikon)   9'
500mm T3 (Techno/Olympus)
600mm T4.5 (Techno/Canon)   10'
800mm T4.5 (Techno/Canon)   15'
1000mm T6.3 (Techno/Canon)   20'
1200mm T6.3 (Techno/Canon)   27'
1600mm T11 (Techno/Canon)   45'
2000mm T11 (Techno/Pentax)   30'

Macro Anamorphic Lenses
50mm TI.4
200mm T4

35mm Anamorphic Zoom Lenses

28–84mm T4.5 (Techno/Cooke)	
28–140mm T4.5 (Techno/Cooke)	2'4"
30–150mm T4.5 (Techno/Cooke)	
40–120mm T4.5 (Techno/Cooke)	2'4"
40–200mm T4.5 (Techno/Cooke)	2'6"
50–500mm T4 (Techno/Cooke)	5'6"
50–500mm T5.6 (Techno/Cooke)	5'6"
300–1200mm T8 (Techno/Canon)	10'

TODD-AO

35mm Anamorphic Prime Lenses

28mm T3.9	5'
35mm T1.4	2'6"
55mm T1.4	1'6"
75mm T2.5	3'
100mm T3.4	3'
200mm T4 (Macro 1:1)	1'6"

65mm Prime Lenses

28mm f/3.2
40mm f/2.8
50mm f/2
60mm f/2
75mm f/2.8
100mm f/2.8
150mm f/2.8

65mm Zoom Lenses

60–150mm f/2.8
100–300mm f/4

VAN-DIEMEN

35mm Prime Lenses
Leica Motion Picture Lenses

15mm T3.7 (Super Elmarit)
19mm T3 (Elmarit)
35mm T3 (Elmarit)
50mm T2.1 (Summicron)

Leica Compact Macro Prime Lenses

24mm T3 (Elmarit)
28mm T3 (Elmarit)
35mm T1.5 (Summilux)
50mm T1.5 (Summilux)
60mm T3 (Elmarit)
75mm T1.5 (Summilux)
80mm T1.5 (Summilux)

Leica Variable Pitch Full Macro Lenses

60mm T3 (Elmarit)
80mm T1.5 (Summilux)
90mm T3 (Elmarit)
90mm T2.1 (Summicron)
100mm T3 (Elmarit)
135mm T3 (Elmarit)
180mm T3 (Elmarit)

Leica APO Telephoto Modular Lenses (Head Units & Focus Modules)

Head A= 280mm T3
Head A + Focus Module
  Factor 1 = 280mm T3
Head A + Focus Module
  Factor 1.4 = 400mm T4.2
Head A + Focus Module
  Factor 2 = 560mm T5.8
Head B= 400mm T3
Head B + Focus Module
  Factor 1 = 400mm T3
Head B + Focus Module
  Factor 1.4 = 560mm T4.2
Head B + Focus Module
  Factor 2 = 800mm T5.8

VANTAGE FILM LENSES

35mm Prime Lenses
VantageOne Lenses

17.5mm T1	1'
21mm T1	1'
25mm T1	1'
32mm T1	1'
40mm T1	1'2"
50mm T1	1'2"
65mm T1	1'2"
90mm T1	1'8"
120mm T1	2'6"

35mm Zoom Lenses

10–24mm T2.5	
150–450mm T2.8 (Hawk)	9'9"
17–35mm T2.8 (Vantage Lightweight)	11"
Super Wide Zoom (Hawk) 100–300mm T2.2	
Telephoto Zoom (Hawk) 150–450 T2.8	9'9"
17–35mm T2.8 (Vantage Lightweight)	11"

35mm Macro Lenses
Vantage Macro Lenses (Leica)

19mm T2.8
21mm T2.8
24mm T2.8
28mm T2.8
35mm T2.8
60mm T2.8
90mm T2.8
135mm T2.8
180mm T2.8

35mm Anamorphic Prime Lenses
Hawk V-Series Lenses

25mm T2.2 (2'9" w/matched Diopter #1, 2'1" w/Diopter #2)	3'6"
30mm T2.2	2'9"
35mm T2.2	2'6"
40mm T2.2	2'6"
50mm T2.2 (close focus)	2'
60mm T2.2 (close focus)	2'
75mm T2.2 (close focus)	2'

100mm T2.2	3'6"
135mm T3	3'6"
120mm T3	1'6"
180mm T3	6'6"
250mm T3	6'6"

Hawk V-Plus Lenses (2X squeeze)

35mm T2.2	2'6"
40mm T2.2	2'6"
50mm T2.2	2'
65mm T3 (super close focus)	1'2"
75mm T2.2	2'
85mm T2.2	2'
100mm T2.2	3'3"
120mm T3.5 (super close focus)	1'5"
135mm T3	3'3"
150mm T3	3'3"

Hawk V-Lite Lenses (2X squeeze)

28mm T2.2	2'7"
35mm T2.2	3'3"
45mm T2.2	3'3"
55mm T2.2	3'3"
65mm T2.2	3'3"
80mm T2.2	3'3"
110mm T3	3'3"
140mm T3.5	3'3"

Hawk V-Lite Lenses (1.3X squeeze)

20mm T2.2	2'
24mm T2.2	2'
28mm T2.2	2'7"
35mm T2.2	3'3"
45mm T2.2	3'3"
55mm T2.2	3'3"
65mm T2.2	3'3"
80mm T2.2	3'3"
110mm T3	3'3"
140mm T3.5	3'3"

Hawk V-Lite Vintage '74 Lenses (2X squeeze)

28mm T2.3	2'7"
35mm T2.3	3'3"
45mm T2.3	3'3"
55mm T2.3	3'3"
65mm T2.3	3'3"
80mm T2.3	3'3"
110mm T3.1	3'3"
140mm T3.7	3'3"

Hawk C-Series Lenses (2X squeeze)

40mm T2.2	3'6"
50mm T2.2	3'6"
60mm T2.2	3'6"
75mm T2.2	3'6"
100mm T3	3'6"

35mm Anamorphic Zoom Lenses
Hawk V-Series Lenses

46–230mm T4	1'6"
300–900mm T4	9'9"

Hawk V-Plus Lenses
(2X squeeze)
45–90mm T2.8	2'6"
80–180mm T2.8	3'3"

Hawk V-Plus Zoom Lenses
(1.3X squeeze)
30–60mm T2.8	2'
45–90mm T2.8	2'6"
80–180mm T2.8	3'3"

Hawk C-Series Lenses
55–165mm T4	3'6"

16mm Anamorphic Prime Lenses
Hawk V-Lite 16 Lenses
(2X squeeze)
14mm T1.5	2'7"
18mm T1.5	3'3"
24mm T1.5	3'3"
28mm T1.5	3'3"
35mm T1.5	3'3"

Hawk V-Lite 16 Lenses
(1.3X squeeze)
14mm T1.5	2'7"
18mm T1.5	3'3"
24mm T1.5	3'3"
28mm T1.5	3'3"
35mm T1.5	3'3"

Optical Accessories
Hawk Anamorphic
Rear Attachment (1-stop loss)
Hawk V 350mm 1.4X Extender
(extends a 250mm to 350mm)
Vantage 6mm Fisheye Attachment
for Nikon 8mm
Vantage 0.7X Reducer
(1-stop gain)

WILCAM/ VISTAVISION LENSES
35mm Prime Lenses
19mm T2.8 (BNC)	9"
24mm T1.4 (BNC)	9"
28mm T1.4 (BNC)	10"
35mm T1.4 (BNC)	12"
50mm T1.4 (BNC)	18"
85mm T1.4 (BNC)	2'
100mm T2 (Macro Schneider)	
135mm T1.8 (BNC)	3'

Zeiss BNC Wilcam Lenses
25mm T2.8	1'
35mm T1.4	1'
50mm T1.4	1'3"
85mm T1.4	1'

35mm Zoom Lenses
35–140mm T3.5 (BNC)	5'5"
50–300mm T4.5 (BNC)	8'

WOLLENSAK
35mm Prime Lenses
Fastair Pro Raptar Series Lenses
13mm f/2.3	1'2"
17mm f/2.3	1'4"
25mm f/2.3	1'1"

50mm f/2.3	2'3"
76mm f/2.5	2'4"
101mm f/2.5	3'9"
152mm f/3.8	6'9"

Fastax Raptar Series Lenses
25mm f/2.5	1'6"
35mm f/2.5	2'4"
50mm f/2.5	2'
75mm f/2.5	8'
101mm f/3.5	20'
152mm f/4.5	25'
254mm f/4.5	
305mm f/4.5	
356mm f/4.5	
380mm f/4.5	
406mm f/5.6	
457mm f/5.6	

Velostigmat Series Lenses
35mm f/2	2'6"
50mm f/3.5	1'6"
105mm f/3.5	8'

Mirrotel Series Lenses
508mm f/5.6	
610mm f/5.6	
1016mm f/8	
2032mm f/14	

16mm Prime Lenses
Cine Raptar Series Lenses
12.7mm f/1.5	1'6"
13mm f/1.2	1'
17mm f/2	
f.f. (15–inf. @ f/2.7)	
17mm f/2.5	10"
17mm f/2.7	10"
25mm f/1.5	2'
25mm f/1.9	2'
40mm f/1.5	2'
50mm f/1.5	2'
50mm f/1.9	1'6"
50mm f/3.5	2'6"
75mm f/2.5	3'
75mm f/2.8	3'
75mm f/4	3'
100mm f/4.5	4'6"
150mm f/4.5	9'

ZEISS
35mm Prime Lenses
Ultra Prime & Ultra Prime LDS (Lens Data System) Lenses
8mm (R) T2.8	1'
10mm T2.1 (Distagon)	1'3"
12mm T1.9 (Distagon)	1'
14mm T1.9 (Distagon)	9"
16mm T1.9 (Distagon)	9"
20mm T1.9 (Distagon)	1'
24mm T1.9 (Distagon)	1'
28mm T1.9 (Distagon)	1'3"
32mm T1.9 (Distagon)	1'3"
40mm T1.9 (Distagon)	1'6"
50mm T1.9 (Planar)	2'
65mm T1.9 (Planar)	2'3"
85mm T1.9 (Planar)	3'

100mm T1.9 (Sonnar)	3'3"
135mm T1.9 (Sonnar)	5'
180mm T1.9 (Sonnar)	8'6"

Super Speed Prime Lenses
18mm T1.3 (Distagon)	10"
25mm T1.3 (Distagon)	10"
35mm T1.3 (Distagon)	14"
50mm T1.3 (Planar)	2'4"
65mm T1.3 (Planar)	2'4"
85mm T1.3 (Planar)	3'

Standard Prime Lenses
10mm T2.1 (Distagon)	14"
12mm T2.1 (Distagon)	10"
14mm T2 (Distagon)	9"
16mm T2.1 (Distagon)	10"
20mm T2.1 (Distagon)	8"
24mm T2.1 (Distagon)	1'2"
28mm T2.1 (Distagon)	11"
32mm T2.1 (Planar)	2'
40mm T2.1 (Planar)	1'4"
50mm T2.1 (Planar)	1'5"
60mm T3	
(Planar/Macro 1:2)	11" (4")
85mm T2.1 (Planar)	3'
100mm T2.1 (Planar)	3'4"
135mm T2.1 (Planar)	5'
180mm T3 (Sonnar)	5'
300mm T4 (Sonnar)	10'

Master Prime Lenses
12mm T1.3	1'4"
14mm T1.3	1'2"
16mm T1.3	1'2"
18mm T1.3	1'2"
21mm T1.3	1'2"
25mm T1.3	1'2"
27mm T1.3	1'2"
32mm T1.3	1'2"
35mm T1.3	1'2"
40mm T1.3	1'4"
50mm T1.3	1'8"
65mm T1.3	2'1"
75mm T1.3	2'7"
100mm T1.3	3'4"
135mm T1.3	3'3"
150mm T1.3	

Close Focus Standard Prime Lenses
16mm T2.1 (Distagon)	6"
18mm T1.3 (Super Speeds)	9"
24mm T2.1 (Distagon)	6"
25mm T1.3 (Super Speeds)	9"
32mm T2.1 (Planar)	9"

Arri Macro Prime Lenses
( )* = distance from front of lens
16mm T2.1 (1:4)	5.5" (1.5")*
24mm T2.1 (1:4)	6.5" (2.5")*
32mm T2.1 (1:4)	7.5" (3.5")*
40mm T2.1 (1:4)	9" (5")*
50mm T3 (1:1)	7.5" (2")*
100mm T3 (1:1)	1' 2" (6")*
200mm T4.3 (1:2)	1'11"

Master Macro			40mm T1.9	2'6"		**Compact Prime CP.2**		
100mm T2		1'1.75"	50mm T1.9	2'6"		**Super Speed Lenses**		
(@ inf: T4.3 @CF)			60mm T1.9	3'		35mm T1.5		1'
(from film/sensor plane)			75mm T1.9	3'		50mm T1.5		1'6"
Telephoto Lenses			100mm T1.9	4'		85mm T1.5		3'3"
300mm T3		11'6"	135mm T1.9	5'		**Digiprime Lenses (⅔" sensor)**		
						3.9mm T1.9		1'8"
35mm Zoom Lenses			**16mm/Ultra 16 Prime Lenses**			5mm T1.9		1'8"
Arri Variable Prime Lenses			(formerly Super 16 Ultra)			7mm T1.6		1'8"
(Vario-Sonnar)			18mm T1.3	1'		10mm T1.6		1'8"
16–30mm T2.2 VP1		2'	25mm T1.3	1'		14mm T1.6		1'8"
29–60mm T2.2 VP2		2'9"	35mm T1.3	1'2"		20mm T1.6		1'8"
55–105mm T2.2 VP3		2'9"	50mm T1.3	1'4"		28mm T1.6		1'8"
Master Zoom Lens						40mm T1.6		1'8"
16.5–110mm T2.6		2'4"	**Digital Prime Lenses**			52mm T1.6		1'8"
			Compact Prime CP.2 Lenses			70mm T1.6		1'1"
35mm Anamorphic			15mm T2.9	1'		135mm T1.9		2'11"
Prime Lenses			18mm T2.1	10"		**Digital Zoom Lenses**		
Arriscope Prime			21mm T2.1	7"		**Compact Zoom CZ.2**		
Anamorphic Lenses			25mm T2.1	10"		28–80mm T2.9		2'8"
40mm T2.3		3'3"	28mm T2.1	10"		70–200mm T2.9		5'
50mm T2.3		3'3"	35mm T2.1	1'		**Lightweight Zoom LWZ.2**		
75mm T2.3		3'9"	50mm T2.1	1'6"		15.5–45mm T2.6		1'6"
100mm T3.5		4'	85mm T2.1	3'3"		**DigiZoom Lenses (⅔" sensor)**		
135mm T3		4'6"	100mm T2.1	2'6"		6–24mm T1.9		1' 10"
Master Anamorphic			135mm T2.1	3'3"		17–112mm T1.9		2'5.5"
Prime Lenses			50mm T2.1 (macro)	10"				
35mm T1.9		2'6"	(from image plane)					

SPECIAL PURPOSE LENSES

Swing Shift Lens

The Clairmont Swing Shift Lens System consists of a multi axis moveable lens board receiver attached to a Arriflex style PL lens mount by a rubber bellows. Specially modified lenses are attached to the receiver board by two captive screws. The assembly is able to move the entire lens in the following directions: tilt up and down, swing side to side, shift position and focus right to left, or up and down. Tilting/swinging the lens plane alters the focus; tilting/swinging the film plane alters the shape. By combining the various parameters of movement, different and unusual effects can be accomplished such as increased or decreased depth of field, selective planes of focus, repositioning of image without changing placement of the camera, correction or addition of image distortion. The focal lengths available are, 20mm, 24mm, 28mm, 35mm, 50mm, 60mm, and 80mm.

Panavision 24mm T3.5 or 45mm T2.8 Slant Focus Lens

The plane of focus of this lens can be tilted in any direction (including vertical and diagonal) as well as horizontal by adjusting the rear lens rotating mount.

If the lens focus is set on an object near the center of the field of view, the plane of focus can be tilted so that objects (left side of frame and/or right side of frame) located along this tilted plane of focus will also be sharp.

If there is not an object near the center of the field of view, measure the distance to the near and far object and set the focus at an average between the two distances. The plane of focus can now be tilted so that the two objects will be brought into focus. In all situations, an object near the center of the field of view should still be in focus after tilting the lens.

Due to the tilting nature of this lens, it cannot be used with a Panaflex follow focus. For the initial focus and any change in focus, eye focusing is necessary. This lens accepts a 1.4X Primo extender with negligible change in performance and no change in operation. The focal length becomes 63mm with a maximum aperture of T4.0. If filters are used with this lens they should (when ever possible) be glass filters in front of the lens. If needed, the lens does accept a 40.5mm rear filter.

CONTINENTAL CAMERA SYSTEMS REMOTELY-CONTROLLED

"Pitching Lens" f/3.9 Optical Relay

Concept: A system to remotely control a prime lens that is mounted at the end of an optical relay tube. In normal configuration the 18" tube extends downward from the camera. The prime lens is mounted at right angles to the tube and can tilt 15° up to 90° down. The entire system rotates 380°. This allows lenses such as Nikkor or Arriflex to get into very small areas. Use of an anamorphic element between the end of relay tube and camera allows a spherical lens to produce an anamorphic image on film. Because focus is controlled in the relay tube, it is possible to continuously follow focus from ½ inch to infinity thus greatly extending the normal focus range of most prime lenses. The system may also be mounted vertically (as in a submarine) or extended straight out in a horizontal position.

Clear length of relay: 18" Maximum diameter: 3"

Control of Lens: Control console with built-in video monitor. Pressure sensitive joystick for pan and tilt operation. System power requirements 110V, 220V or 24V DC.

Cameras: Arriflex IIC, Norelco PCP90 (video), Mitchell R35, Lightweight Technicolor VistaVision equipped with Nikon mount.

Focus: Remotely controlled from hand-held unit. Focus speed is proportional to focus command.

Taking Formats: 16mm, 35mm anamorphic, VistaVision.

Optics: Nikon mount through adapter rings can use a wide assortment of Nikkor and Arriflex lenses from 7.2 mm to 100mm. Speed of system is f/3.9 to f/32. Prime lens is set wide open and aperture controlled in the relay system.

Suspension: Standard dolly with small jib arm and C.C.S. balanced cross arm at camera end of jib. Large telescopic billboard cranes and Chapman "Titan" cranes can be used.

Kenworthy Snorkel Camera Systems

A remote image taking system with operator and camera components removed from shooting area. The camera looks into a periscope-like optical relay tube that extends downward below the camera and ends with a small front-surfaced mirror. Since the mass of the camera with operator is removed from the shooting area ,considerations of scene staging are concerned only with the small end (1¼"x 1¼" at the mirror) of the tube. The tilting mirror is remotely controlled, as are other functions such as pan, focus, roll, zoom and iris. The mirror system permits more intimate shooting (due to its small size) than do add-on right-angled lens periscopes. It also permits tilting up in constricted situations because the mirror, rather than the tube/camera combination, does the tilting. The system allows viewpoints in tight quarters reachable from overhead, or from very low viewpoints or in miniature sets. Pans and tilts are on system nodal point. An added waterproof tube permits underwater or transition shots.

There are two systems available:

The Kenworthy Nettman Snorkel features fast optics and lightweight, interchangeable formats, and carries a shorter tube for use on light weight dollies. The cameras are butterfly VistaVision, 65mm, and 16mm film and ⅔" video cameras. Camera lenses are used.

Type B Kenworthy Snorkel is designed for shooting actors with dialogue at moderate lighting levels. It carries a longer tube (48" or 66") which permits more overhead clearance for deeper penetration into four-walled sets or water tanks. This system uses 35mm only: Arriflex, Mitchell Mark II, Panaflex or other similar cameras. The Panacam is used for video. System lenses are used on the Type B; 28 mm & 50mm T8 for film 13mm T5.6 for video. Both systems can use anamorphic lenses. Type B requires a camera crane.

With both systems a console is used with a video monitor and pan, tilt and lens controls.

Dynalens

An optical stabilizing device mounted on the camera optical axis for compensating for image motion due to vibration of the camera.

A pair of gyro sensors detect rapid motion and drive two gimbal-mounted glass plates, between which is a liquid filled cell. One plate moves around a vertical axis and the other around a horizontal axis in a manner which deviates the light path opposite to the vibratory movement, causing the image to stay still relative to the image receptor (film or video).

A low-frequency-response, manually operated potentiometer on the control module adjusts the frequency sensitivity of the unit so controlled panning or tilting may be done.

The Dynalens is available in 2.3" diameter for 16mm film or small video cameras and 3.8" and 8" for larger format cameras. The maximum useful angular deviation is +6°.

EXTREME CLOSE-UP CINEMATOGRAPHY

There are two basic methods for focusing a lens on very close objects: 1) by adding extension tubes or extension bellows and 2) by employing plus diopter supplementary lenses in front of the normal lens.

Extension Tubes or Bellows

Generally speaking, extension tubes or bellows produce the best overall results since the lens itself is not altered- it is simply placed further away from the film plane so that it can produce a sharp image of an object at very close distances.

Extension tubes should not be employed with wide-angle or zoom lenses. They work best with normal or semi-telephoto lenses. For practical purposes the diaphragm of a normal focal length lens may be considered the point at which the light rays cross (the rear nodal point). For simplicity the close-up tables on page 810–818 show measurements from the diaphragm (not necessarily the diaphragm actuating the ring.) to the object being filmed and from the diaphragm to the film plane.

Conventional lenses of moderate focal length usually will develop a better quality image if reversed in their mounts when the distance from the lens to the film plane is greater than the distance from the lens to the object. Specially designed close working lenses should be used if a great deal of ultraclose filming is required.

Since depth of field is shallow at close distances, even when the lens is stopped down, try to keep the object or the area being filmed in as compact as a space, from front to back, as possible. Camera, lens tube, or bellows, and object must be held as rigid and vibrationless as possible during filming.

When a lens is focused closer than ten times its focal length its effective aperture, rather than its marked aperture, must be taken into consideration. Long extension tubes decrease lens speed considerably since the farther the lens is moved from the film plane the more its speed is proportionately reduced.

Image to Object manifestation, or reduction, ratios are based on the size of the actual film frame compared to the size of the object being photographed. Close-up tables can thus be used with either 16mm or 35mm cameras because comparisons are "area for area" since similar focal length lenses with similar extension will deliver the same ratio- with a smaller portion of the object being filmed on 16mm than on 35mm. The first number of the ratio is the film image- the second is the object. Thus 1:1 means that the size of the image on the film equals the size of the object being filmed. (Note: Any lens at twice its normal focal length will be an equal distance from the object being photographed, and shoot its actual size. Thus a 2-inch lens at 4 inches from the film will also be 4 inches from the object and record an object area the same size as the film area. A 3-inch lens will perform the same way at 6 inches from the film and the object. A 4-inch lens at 8 inches, etc.)

1 to 1 is a good starting point to compute ratios, exposures, etc. With a 16mm camera an object area the size of the full frame (.404" x .295") can thus be filmed with any lens at twice its focal length. The same holds true for a 35mm camera except that a larger object area (.866" x .630" say 1 to 5 (film area is ⅕ the size of object area), would require much less extension. Greater magnification, say 5 to 1 (film area is five times the size of the object area) would require much longer extension.

Depth of field is identical at the same magnification (not lens extension!) and same f-stop for any focal length lens. Nothing is gained as far as depth of field is concerned by using a shorter focal length lens for the same size image. Since the f-stop is the only factor to consider any convenient focal length lens may be used.

The simplest method for finding the exposure factor is to add "1" to the scale of reproduction and multiply the result by itself. Thus for a scale of 1:2 (film area is ½ the size of object area), ½ + 1 or 1.5 x 1.5 equals 2.25. Similarly, for same-size reproduction or 1:1, 1 + 1 equals 2. 2 x 2 equals 4 (or 2 stops increase). 3:1 would be 3 + 1 equals 4. 4 x 4 equals 16 (or 4 stops increase).

Exposure for extreme close-ups can best be determined by an incident light meter. The effective aperture should be used for determining the light.

Diopter Lenses

Extreme close-ups may be filmed by employing positive supplementary lenses, generally of a weak meniscus form, called diopter lenses, in front of the normal lens.

The power of these positive supplementary lenses is commonly expressed in diopters. The power in diopters is the reciprocal of the focal length in meters. The plus sign indicates a positive, or converging lens. Thus, a +3 diopter lens has a focal length of ⅓ meter, or 39.3 inches divided by 3 or approximately 13 inches. A +2 diopter lens would have a focal length of approximately 20 inches. A +1 would be one meter or roughly 40 inches. In other words, the positive diopter lens alone will form an image of a distant object when held at its respective focal length. When two such lenses are used together, their combined power is practically equal to the sum of both powers. A +2 and a +3, for instance, would equal a +5 and possess a focal length of approximately 8 inches (39.3 divided by 5 equals approximately 8).

When two diopter lenses are combined, the highest power should be closest to the prime lens. Plus diopters should be placed in front of the prime lens with their convex (outward curve) side toward the subject. If an arrow is engraved on the rim of the diopter lens mount, it should point toward the subject.

High power plus diopter lenses, such as +8 or +10, are not practical to manufacture for large diameter prime lenses because their optical performance would be inferior. Best screen quality results with lower power diopters. It is better to use a longer focal length lens and a less powerful plus diopter lens, then to employ a high power diopter on a short focal length lens.

A plus diopter lens placed in front of a conventional lens set at infinity all form a sharp image at its particular focal length. Thus a cine lens may be focused for extreme close-ups, without the necessity of racking it out with the extension tubes or bellows, simply by placing a plus diopter lens, of the required focal length, in front of it. The distance at which a diopter lens can be focused is decreased, however, by racking the normal lens out to its nearest focusing distance. Cine lens may be focused much closer, therefore, with the same power diopter lens, by simply utilizing closer focus settings on the lens.

Diopter lenses may be focused at the same distance with any focal length lens, since their power remains the same. The magnification will vary, however, depending on the focal length of the actual camera lens employed.

The longer the focal length of the prime lens, the smaller the area covered by the same power diopter lens. The shorter the focal length of the prime lens, the closer the camera will have to be positioned to the subject and the more powerful the diopter lens required- to cover the same area as a longer focal length lens. There are several advantages in employing longer focal length lenses; a less powerful plus diopter lens is required and results are better; more space is available between camera and subject for lighting; the same area may be panned with a shorter arc so the subject is not distorted.

Diopter lenses alter the basic lens design and therefore require stopping the lens down for reasonable sharpness. Since illuminating a small area generally presents no problem (except heat) it is a simple matter to close down to f/8 or f/11. Diopter lenses on the order of +½, +1, +2 or +3 will give satisfactorily sharp results with normal focal length or semi-telephoto lenses.

Plus diopter lenses shorten the focal length of the prime lens. (See: Plus Diopter Lenses Focal Length Conversion Table page 747.) A 100mm prime lens with a +3 diopter lens, for instance, becomes 76.91mm in focal length. The indicated f-number, therefore, should be divided by
approximately 1.4 to get its true value. In practice, however, the use of close-up diopter lenses does not require any change in exposure setting; because the change in effective f-number exactly compensates for the exposure change caused by increased image size.

OPTICAL LENS EXTENDER EXPOSURE FACTORS

1.4X = Factor of 2 — 1 Stop increase

1.6X = Factor of 2.5 — 1 1/3 Stop Increase

2X = Factor of 4 — 2 Stop Increase

Magnification squared = Factor

Example: 1.4 x 1.4 = 1.96 closest factor 2

Non-Optical Extension Tube or Bellows Exposure Factors

Distance of lens from film plane squared,
divided by the focal length squared = factor.

Example:

50mm lens + 50mm extension =
factor of 4 — 2 stop increase.

$$\frac{(50 + 50)^2}{50^2} = \frac{10,000}{2500} = 4$$

Comparison of lens "depths" for collimatation of lens (not for setting flange depth of camera)

Arri (2.04")	52.00mm	Nikon (1.831")	46.5mm	Lecia R (1.85")	47.00mm
Panavision (2.2500")	57.15mm	Canon (1.659")	42.14mm	Leica M (1.10")	27.95mm
BNCR (2.42")	61.47mm				

This chart is for reference only; note there are different standards
for collimation or setup, often set by rental house.

Split-Field Diopter Lenses

Split-field diopter lenses are partial lenses, cut so that they cover only a portion of the prime lens. They are generally cut in half, although they may be positioned in front of the prime lens so that more or less than half is covered. They may be compared with bi-focals for human vision, in which the eye may focus near and far. They have an advantage over bifocals, however, in that they may be focused sharply on both near and far subjects simultaneously.

The depth of field of the prime lens is not extended. The split-field diopter lens simply permits focusing on a very close subject on one side of the frame, while a distant subject is photographed normally through the uncovered portion of the prime lens. Generally, the area in between will not be in focus. There are instances, such as using a zoom lens with a small aperture at the wide-angle position, when sharpness may extend all the way from the ultra-close-up to the distant subject. The split-diopter equipped lens possesses two distinct depths of field: one for the close subject (which may be very shallow or possess no depth whatsoever) and another for the distant subject (which will be the normal depth of field for the particular focal length lens and f-stop in use). It is important, therefore, to exclude subject matter from the middle distance because it will create a situation where the foreground is sharp, the middle distance out of focus and the distant subject sharp.

Split-field diopter lenses require ground glass focusing to precisely line-up both foreground and background subjects and visually check focus on each. This is particularly important with zoom lenses, which may require camera movement during the zoom.

Very unusual effects are possible, which would otherwise require two separate shots, which would be later combined in an optical printer via a matting process. Making such split shots in the camera permits viewing the scene as it will appear, rather than waiting for both shots to be optically printed onto one film.

The proper power split-field diopter lens is positioned in front of the taking lens on the same side as the near object- so that it is sharply focused on one side of the frame. The uncovered portion of the conventional or zoom lens is focused in the usual manner on the distant subject. (*Note:* Use the Plus Diopter Lenses Focus Conversion Table on page 818 to find near and far focusing distances with various power diopter lenses.)

The edge of the split-diopter lens should be positioned, if possible, so that it lines up with a straight edge in the background- such as the corner of a room, the edge of a column or a bookcase. Eliminating the edge may prove difficult under certain conditions, particularly with a zoom lens because the edge will shift across the frame slightly when the lens is zoomed. It is wise to leave space between the foreground and background subjects so that they do not overlap and each is removed from the lens edge. This will minimize "blending". The split-diopter need not be lined up vertically- it may be used horizontally or at any angle to cover a foreground subject on top, bottom, either side or at an angle across the frame.

The split may sometimes be "covered" by filming both foreground and background against a distant neutral background for a "limbo" effect. The can of wax, for instance, may be placed on a table so that it appears against the same distant neutral background as the housewife.

Lighting may be employed to lighten or darken the background area where the split occurs, to make it less noticeable. Lighting should generally be balanced so that both near and far subjects may be varied, of course, for pictorial effects. Either foreground or background may be filmed in silhouette, or kept in darkness so that one or the other may be fully illuminated during the scene. Since the diopter lens requires no increase in exposure, balancing the lights is a simple matter.

Formulas

By R. Evans Wetmore. P. E.
ASC Associate Member

1 LENS FORMULAS

The formulas given in this section are sufficiently accurate to solve most practical problems encountered in cinematography. Many of the equations, however, are approximations or simplifications of very complex optical relationships. Therefore, shooting tests should always be considered when using these formulas, especially in critical situations.

1.1 Hyperfocal distance

The hyperfocal distance (H) is the focus distance setting of a lens where all objects from half the focus distance setting through infinity are in acceptable focus. Acceptable focus is characterized by a parameter called the circle of confusion (Cc). The lens aperture setting and the circle of confusion affect the hyperfocal distance. The formula for hyperfocal distance is:

$$H = \frac{F^2}{fC_c} \tag{1}$$

where F = focal length of lens
f = f-stop of lens
C_c = circle of confusion

All values in this and the following equations must be in the same units, e.g., millimeters, inches, etc. For instance, when using a circle of confusion value measured in inches, the lens focal length must be in inches, and the resulting answer will be in inches. (Note: f-stop has no dimensions and so is not affected by the type of units used.)

As mentioned above, the circle of confusion characterizes the degree of acceptable focus. The smaller the circle of confusion is the higher the resulting image sharpness. For practical purposes the following values have been used in computing depth of field and hyperfocal distances in this manual:

35mm photography = 0.001 inch ($\frac{1}{1000}$ inch) or 0.025mm

16mm photography = 0.005 inch ($\frac{5}{10,000}$ inch) or 0.013mm

1.2 Depth of field

For a discussion on the concept of depth of field, please see the introduction to the depth of field tables. It should be understood that the detemination of depth of field involves a subjective judgement that requires taking into account the conditions under which the final projected image will be viewed.

The following two formulas are for calculating the depth of field. To use these equations one must first calculate the hyperfocal distance from Equation 1.

$$D_n = \frac{HS}{H + (S - F)} \tag{2}$$

$$D_f = \frac{HS}{H - (S - F)} \tag{3}$$

where D_n = Camera to Near Limit
D_f = Camera to Far Limit
H = Hyperfocal Distance
S = Distance from Camera to Subject
F = Focal Length of Lens

The total depth of field is equal to $D_f - D_n$.

The following shows how the above equations can be used to make hyperfocal and depth of field calculations:

Example: A 35mm camera lens of 50mm focal length is focused at 20 feet and is set to f/2.8. Over what range of distances will objects be in acceptable focus?

First convert all the units to the same system. In this example inches will be used. Therefore, the 50mm focal length will be converted to 2 inches. (This is an approximation as 50mm is exactly 1.969 inches, but 2 inches is close enough for normal work.) Also the 20 feet converts to 240 inches (20 × 12). The circle of confusion is 0.001 inches for 35mm photography.

Using Equation 1 and filling in the converted values yields:

$$H = \frac{2^2}{2.8 \times 0.001} = \frac{4}{0.0028} = 1429 \text{ inches} = 119 \text{ feet}$$

Using the hyperfocal distance just calculated and equations 2 and 3, we can now calculate the near and far distances that will be in acceptable focus.

Courtesy of Panavision's Tak Miyagishima.

TAK'S TIPS

CC (in inches)	Decimal of CC	Constant
Multiplication Constants for Calculating Hyperfocal Distance for Circle of Confusions in Feet		
$1/500$	0.002	0.06458
$1/707$	0.0014	0.09226
$1/1000$	0.001	0.12917
$1/1414$	0.0007	0.18452
$1/1666$	0.0006	0.21528
$1/2500$	0.0005	0.32292

Example: For CC = .0005
F = 35mm f /4

$$H = \frac{.32292 \times 35^2}{4} = 98.89'$$

$$D_n = \frac{1429 \times 240}{1429 + (240\text{-}2)} = 205.7 \text{ inches} = 17.1 \text{ feet}$$

$$D_f = \frac{1429 \times 240}{1429 - (240\text{-}2)} = 288 \text{ inches} = 24 \text{ feet}$$

Therefore, when a 50mm lens at f/2.8 is focused at 20 feet, everything from 17.1 feet to 24.0 feet will be in acceptable focus. The total depth of field for this example is:

$$D_{total} = D_f - D_n = 24.0 - 17.1 = 6.9 \text{ feet}$$

If a more approximate answer is all that is needed, equations 2 and 3 may be simplified to

$$D_n = \frac{HS}{H + S} \tag{4}$$

$$D_f = \frac{HS}{H - S} \tag{5}$$

Using these equations, D_n and D_f are:

$$D_n = \frac{119 \times 20}{119 + 20} \approx 17 \text{ feet}$$

$$D_f = \frac{119 \times 240}{119 - (20)} \approx 24 \text{ feet}$$

Therefore, $D_{total} = 24\text{-}17 = 7$ feet

1.2.1 Finding lens settings when D_n and D_f are known

When the near and far focus requirements are known, equations 4, 5 and 1 can be rearranged as follows:

$$L_s = \frac{2D_nD_f}{D_n + D_f} \tag{6}$$

$$H = \frac{2D_nD_f}{D_n - D_f} \tag{7}$$

$$f = \frac{F^2}{HC_c} \tag{8}$$

where D_n = Camera to Near Limit
D_f = Camera to Far Limit
H = Hyperfocal Distance
L_s = Lens Focus Distance Setting
F = Focal Length of Lens
f = f-stop Setting of Lens
C_c = Circle of confusion

Example: A scene is being photographed on 35mm using a 75mm lens. Everything in the scene from 15 to 27 feet must be in acceptable focus. How must the lens f-stop and focus be set?

First convert all distances and focal lengths to inches. Focal length is 2.953 inches (75 ÷ 25.40). D_n is 180 inches (15 × 12), and D_f is 324 inches (27 × 12).

$$L_s = \text{focus distance setting} = \frac{2 \times 180 \times 324}{180 + 324} = 231 \text{ inches} = 19.3 \text{ feet}$$

$$H = \text{hyperfocal distance} = \frac{2 \times 180 \times 324}{324 - 180} = 810 \text{ inches} = 67.5 \text{ feet}$$

$$\text{f-stop} = \frac{2.953^2}{0.001 \times 810} = \text{f}/10.77 = \text{f}/11$$

Therefore, focus the lens to 19.3 feet, and set the f-stop to f/11.

1.3 Depth of focus

Depth of focus should not be confused with depth of field as they are very different and do not refer to the same thing.

Depth of focus is the range of distance between the lens and the film plane

Courtesy of Panavision's Tak Miyagishima.

TAK'S TIPS

SIMPLIFIED DEPTH OF FIELD

$$\frac{1}{D_n} = \frac{1}{S} + \frac{1}{H}$$

$$\frac{1}{D_f} = \frac{1}{S} - \frac{1}{H}$$

D_n = Camera to Near Limit
D_f = Camera to Far Limit
H = Hyperfocal Distance
S = Distance from Camera to Subject

where acceptable focus is maintained. This range is quite small and is measured usually in very small units such as thousandths of an inch.

For an image to be in sharp focus, the distance from the lens to the film must be held to very tight tolerances, hence the design of motion-picture cameras which holds the film very securely during exposure. Any buckling of the film or anything that shifts the film's postition in the aperture can cause a deterioration of focus.

The following equation provides a good approximation of the depth of focus of a lens:

$$\text{Depth of Focus} \approx \frac{Ff}{1000} \tag{9}$$

where F = focal length of lens (in mm)
f = f-stop of lens

Example: A 50mm f/2.8 lens has the following depth of focus:

$$\frac{50 \times 2.8}{1000} = 0.14 \text{ mm} = 0.0055 \text{ inch}$$

As this is the total depth of focus, the film must stay within plus or minus half that value which is about ±0.00275 inch or ±0.07mm. This dimension is equal to the approximate value of a single strand of human hair. This is a very small value indeed which further amplifies the statement above about the need for precision in the gate and aperture area of the camera.

1.4 Lens viewing angles

The angle, either horizonal or vertical, that a lens images onto the film frame may be calculated using the following equation:

$$\Theta = 2atan \left(\frac{ARs}{2F}\right) \quad (10)$$

where F = focal length of lens
        A = camera aperture height or width
        R_s = squeeze ratio (use 1.0 for spherical lenses
             and Scope vertical and use 2.0 for
             Scope horizontal)
        Θ = viewing angle

The inverse tangent (written as atan, arctan, or tan-1) can be found with many pocket calculators. Alternately Table 1 relates atan to Θ
Example: What are horizontal and vertical viewing angles for a 75mm Scope lens?

A typical Scope camera aperture is 0.868" wide by 0.735" high. Converting 75mm to inches yields 2.953 inches (75÷25.4 = 2.953)

$$Horizontal\ Angle = 2\ atan\ \frac{0.868 \times 2.0}{2 \times 2.953} = 32.8°$$

$$2\ atan\ \frac{1.736}{5.906} = .2939$$

$$atan\ of\ .2939 = 16.4°$$
$$2\ atan = 32.8°$$

$$Vertical\ Angle = 2atan\ \frac{0.735 \times 1.0}{2 \times 2.953} = 14.2°$$

$$2\ atan\ \frac{0.735}{5.906} = .1244$$

$$atan\ of\ .1244 = 7.1°$$
$$2\ atan = 14.2°$$

1.5 Lens, subject, distance, and image size relationships

Using the simple drawing on the previous page, the relationships between camera distance, object size, image size, and lens focal length for spherical lenses may easily be calculated in the following equation:

TABLE 1: *ATAN* TABLE

Inverse Tangent Function							
Angle	atan	Angle	atan	Angle	atan	Angle	atan
1°	.018	12°	.213	23°	.424	34°	.675
2°	.035	13°	.231	24°	.445	35°	.700
3°	.052	14°	.249	25°	.466	36°	.727
4°	.070	15°	.268	26°	.488	37°	.754
5°	.088	16°	.287	27°	.510	38°	.781
6°	.105	17°	.306	28°	.532	39°	.810
7°	.123	18°	.325	29°	.554	40°	.839
8°	.141	19°	.344	30°	.577	41°	.869
9°	.158	20°	.364	31°	.601	42°	.900
10°	.176	21°	.384	32°	.625	43°	.933
11°	.194	22°	.404	33°	.649	44°	.966
						45°	1.000

$$\frac{O}{A} = \frac{D}{F} \tag{11}$$

where F = focal length of lens
D = distance to object being photographed
O = size of object being photographed
A = aperture size
Θ = viewing angle

Equation 11 may be rewritten in any of the following ways depending on the problem being solved:

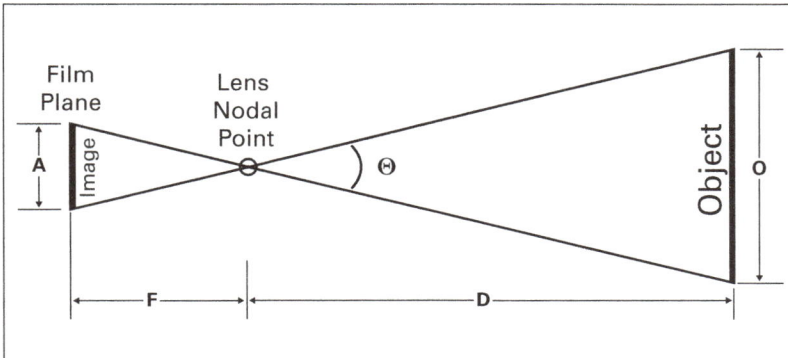

$$D = \frac{OF}{A} \tag{12}$$

$$O = \frac{AD}{F} \tag{13}$$

$$F = \frac{AD}{O} \tag{14}$$

$$A = \frac{OF}{D} \tag{15}$$

1.6 Lens apertures –T- versus f-stops

The f number of a lens is its focal length divided by the diameter of its lens pupil. Stated mathematically

$$f = \frac{F}{D_a} \tag{16}$$

where F = focal length of lens
D_a = diameter of aperture
f = f-stop value of lens

The T-stop of a lens controls the transmission of light through a lens. The same logarithmic progression of numbers is used for T-stops as for f-stops. If a lens lost no light passing through it, the f- and T-stops would be equal, but as no lens passes light through it without loss, the f- and T-stops for lenses are not the same. (See ANSI PH22.90 for more information.)

The rule is: Use f-stops for computing depth of field, and use T-stops for setting exposure.

When setting the f/T-stop on a lens, first always open the lens to its widest aperture, and then set the desired f/T-stop value. This practice removes the effects of backlash in the lens mechanism and insures repeatable results.

1.7 Lens displacement for focusing

When a lens is focused at infinity, the distance from the film plane to the lens nodal point is nominally equal to the focal length of the lens. For instance, a 50mm lens, when focused at infinity, has 50mm between the film plane and the nodal point of the lens. However, when a lens is focused closer than infinity, the lens must be moved away from the film plane to maintain focus. The following equation computes the amount of displacement from the infinity position needed to focus on an object not at infinity.

$$d = \frac{F^2}{a - F} \tag{17}$$

where F = focal length of lens
          a = distance to object being photographed
          d = lens displacement from infinity position

Example: The displacement from the infinity position of a 50mm (2 inch) lens focused at 10 feet is as follows:

Converting all distances to inches and applying Equation 17 yields

$$d = \frac{2^2}{120\text{-}2} = \frac{4}{118} = 0.031 \text{ inches}$$

2 SHOOTING PRACTICES

2.1 Running times, feet, and frames
The Table 2 shows the linear sound speed of common theatrical film gages and the number of frames per foot.

2.1.1 Footage-versus-time relationship

$$T_F = St \tag{18}$$

where T_F = total footage
          S = speed of film (in ft/min)
          t = time (in minutes)

Example: How many feet of 35 mm film run through a sound camera in 4 and a half minutes?

$$T_F = 90 \times 4.5 = 405 \text{ feet}$$

TABLE 2: SPEED & FRAME INFORMATION FOR COMMON FILM GAGES

Film Gage (in mm)	Linear Speed (ft/min)	Frames per Foot
16	36	40
35	90	16
65/70	112.5	12.8

2.1.2 Footage in feet and frames

$$F_T = \frac{tF_s}{F_F} \qquad (19)$$

where F_T = total footage
     F_s = frames per second
     t = time (in seconds)
     F_F = frames per foot

Example: How much film goes through a 16mm sound camera in 8 seconds?

$$F_T = \frac{8 \times 24}{40} = 4.8 \text{ feet}$$

To convert the decimal to frames, multiply the decimal part by number of frames per foot:

$$.8 \times 40 = 32$$

Therefore, the answer is 4 feet 32 frames.

2.2 Computing exposure times
The following equations relate frame rate, shutter angle, and exposure time:

$$T_e = \frac{1}{\dfrac{S\,360}{\alpha}} \qquad (20) \qquad \text{and} \qquad \alpha = 360ST_e \qquad (21)$$

where α = shutter angle (in degrees)
      S = frames per second
      T_e = exposure time (in second)

Example: What is the exposure time when shooting at 24 frames per second with a 180° shutter?

$$T_e = \frac{1}{\dfrac{24 \times 360}{180}} = \frac{1}{48} \text{ second}$$

2.3 Frame rates for miniatures
To make the action in minatures look convincing, it is often necessary to shoot at frame rates faster than 24 fps. The exact frame rate for a

HIGH SPEED FOLUMAS

Times Normal Speed = frame rate ÷ normal frame rate (24 or 30 fps)
Example: 360 ÷ 24 = 15 times normal speed

Frames Exposed = frame rate x event duration
Example: 360 x .5 second = 180 frames exposed

Screen Time = frame rate x event duration ÷ normal frame rate (24 or 30 fps)
Example: 360 x .5 ÷ 24 = 7.5 seconds screen time

Frame Rate Required = screen time ÷ event duration x transfer rate
Example: 7.5 seconds ÷ .5 x 24 = 360 fps required

Running Time = frames per foot x footage ÷ frame rate
Example: 16 x 1000' ÷ 360 = 44.4 seconds running time

Screen Time for Moving Objects = field of view ÷ 20' per second x 360 fps ÷24 = 1.5 seconds screen time
Example: 2' field of view ÷ 20' per second x 360 fps ÷ 24 = 1.5 seconds screen time

Notes:
Field of view and object velocity must be in same type measurement (inches, feet)
Falling objects will increase in velocity (use velocity charts to determine event time)

given miniature shot must be determined by shooting test footage. Even skilled minature cinematographers will shoot tests to confirm proper effect on film.

Shooting frame rate depends on, among other things, subject matter, direction of movement in relation to the camera position, and minature scale. Generally, however, the smaller the minature, the faster the required frame rate. Also as magnification decreases, the necessary frame rate drops.

The following may be used as a guide and a starting point:

$$R_f = 24 \sqrt{\frac{1}{S}} \tag{22}$$

where R_f = frame rate
S = scale of miniature

Example: What frame rate should be used to shoot a 1:4 (quarter scale) miniature?

$$R_f = 24 \sqrt{\frac{1}{0.25}} = 24 \sqrt{4} = 24 \times 2 = 48 \text{ fps}$$

2.4 Image blur

When shooting high speed photography, the question often comes up: what frame rate is needed to reduce the image blur to an acceptable amount. This question is especially important to cinematographers shooting fast moving subject such as missile tests, horse races, airplanes, etc.

The following equations may be used to calculate the blur of an image caused by the movment of an object during exposure:

$$m = \frac{F}{D} \tag{23}$$

$$d = vtm \tag{24}$$

$$d = \frac{d}{tm} \tag{25}$$

where D = object to lens distance
          F = taking focal length
         m = magnification
         d = image movement during exposure
         v = object speed
         t = exposure

Example: What is the image blur of a thin vertical line painted on the side of a racing car moving at 153 miles per hour when shot from 33.3 feet away with a 2 inch lens at 48 fps with a shuter angle of 180°?

First, all of the units have to be brought to common units; in this case inches and seconds are a good choice. Therefore, D is 400 inches (12×33.3) and v is 2693 in/sec ($153 \times 5280 \times 12 \div 3600$)

$$m = \frac{F}{D} = \frac{2}{400} = \frac{1}{200}$$

$$d = 2693 \times \frac{1}{96} \times \frac{1}{200} = 0.14 \text{ inch}$$

3 LIGHT AND EXPOSURE

3.1 Units for measuring light

The terms used to measure light can often be confusing. The three main measures of light are intensity, illumination, and brightness. Each refers to a very different characteristic.

3.2 Intensity (I)

The unit of intensity is the candle or candela. The name, not surprisingly, comes from the fact that a standard wax candle was used for many years as the standard source of light. The luminous inensity from one candle was, therefore, one candle power.

Another unit which is also encountered in discussions about luminous intensity is the lumen. One candle power emits one lumen in a standard three dimensional cone called a steradian.

3.3 Illumination (E)

The unit of illumination is the foot candle which is one lumen falling onto one square foot. (In the SI system, the unit is the lux which is 1 lumen/m2.) In simple terms the foot candle measures the amount of light falling on a surface, hence the term illumination.

3.4 Brightness (B)

When light falls upon a surface some of that light is reflected. The unit of brightness is the foot-lambert which is $1/\pi$ candles being relfected from a one square foot area. The reflected light give the surface a "bright" appearance, hence the term brightness.

3.5 Exposure using incident light

The following equation may be used to find the required number of foot candles required for a given film speed, f-stop, and exposure time:

$$E = \frac{25 f^2}{St} \tag{26}$$

where E = Illumination in foot candles
           f = T-stop of taking lens (use f-stop if lens
              does not have T-stop markings)
           t = exposure time (in seconds)
           S = film speed (in ASA)

Example: How many foot candles are required to expose an ASA 100 film for $\frac{1}{50}$ second at f/2.0?

$$E = \frac{25 \times 2.0^2}{100 \times \frac{1}{50}} = \frac{100}{2} = 50 \, foot \, candles$$

Equation 26 may be simplified for shooting at 24 fps with a shutter angle of 172.8° which gives an effective exposure of $\frac{1}{50}$ second.

$$E = \frac{1250 f^2}{S} \tag{27}$$

Example: How many foot candles are required to expose an ASA 200 film shooting at 24 fps at f/4.0?

$$E = \frac{1250 \times 4.0^2}{200} = \frac{20000}{200} = 100 \; foot\; candles$$

3.6 Exposure using extention tubes or bellows

When using a bellows or extension tube to move the lens further than normal from the film plane, use the following formula to calculate the required increase in exposure:

$$\Delta = \frac{(d + F)^2}{F^2} \tag{28}$$

where Δ = Exposure Multiplier
              d = length of extension tube or bellows
              F = lens focal length

Example: A 3 inch lens is moved 150mm further from the film plane by a bellows. The exposure time before the lens was moved was ¹⁄₄₈ of a second. What is the new exposure time?

First the units must be made the same. A 3 inch lens has a focal length of 76.2mm (3 × 25.4). Then using the above equation

$$\Delta = \frac{(150 + 76.2)^2}{76.2^2} = 8.812$$

Then multiply the old exposure time of ¹⁄₄₈ by Δ to get the new exposure time of

$$\tfrac{1}{48} \times 8.812 = 0.184$$

0.184 seconds is approximately ⅕ second which is the new, corrected exposure time. Alternately, if depth of field is not an issue, the exposure could also be corrected by a three stop increase in aperture. (Remember that each stop doubles the exposure, so for a roughly nine-fold increase, 3+ stops are needed.) Also, the esposure could be corrected by increasing the illumination approximately ninefold.

It should also be noted that vignetting may occur when using extention tubes or bellows. It is good practice, therefore, to check the corners of the image for proper exposure prior to production shooting when using extension tubes or bellows.

3.7 Shooting close-ups with diopters

Often in shooting extreme close-ups supplemental lens called "diopters"[1] are affixed to the front of a prime lens. These "diopters" allow very close focusing.

Diopters for all practical purposes do not affect many of the characteristics of the prime lens. For instance, the f-stop of lens is not affected by a positive diopter.[2] Also the depth of field calculations are unaffected. Principally, the diopter allows for much closer than normal focusing by the prime lens.

When using diopters it is a good idea to stop the prime lens down to at least f/8 as diopters do add lens abberations which degrade the image quality. By stopping down, these degradations may be minimized.

---

1. A diopter is actually a unit that measures the focal length of a lens. A diopter is 1/focal length where the focal length is expressed in meters. For example, a lens with a focal length of 500 mm(0.5 meters) has a strength of 2 diopters (1/0.5 = 2.0).

---

2. Negative diopters are rarely, if ever, used in motion picture work.

Conversion of Feet Per Seconds to Miles Per Hours

Feet Per Second	to	Miles Per Hour*	Feet Per Second	to	Miles Per Hour*
1¼		1	44		30
3		2	51		35
7		5	59		40
9		6	66		45
10½		7	73		50
12		8	80		55
13		9	88		60
14½		10	110		75
15		11	147		100
17½		12	183		125
22		15	220		150
29		20	257		200
37		25			* rounded off

1.4667 x MPH = feet per second
88 x MPH = Feet per minute

1 Nautical mile = 6080 feet
1 Land or Statute mile = 5280 feet
1 Kilometer = 3280 feet

Distance and Velocity of Free Falling Body

Distance	Velocity	Time
0	0	0
16	32	1
64	64	2
144	96	3
256	128	4
400	160 (max)	5
Feet	Feet Per Seconds	Seconds

Conversion Tables

Feet to Meters		Meters to Feet			Inches to Millimeters	
ft	**m**	**m**	**ft**	**in**	**in**	**mm**
3 =	.91	1 =	3	3	1/16 =	1.6
4 =	1.22	1¼ =	4	1	1/8 =	3.2
5 =	1.52	1½ =	4	11	3/16 =	4.8
6 =	1.83	2 =	6	7	¼ =	6.4
7 =	2.13	2⅙ =	8	2	5/16 =	7.9
8 =	2.44	3 =	9	10	3/8 =	9.5
9 =	2.74	4 =	13	1	7/16 =	11.1
10 =	3.05	5 =	16	5	½ =	12.7
12 =	3.66	6 =	19	8	9/16 =	14.3
15 =	4.57	7 =	23		5/8 =	15.9
20 =	6.10	8 =	26	3	11/16 =	17.5
25 =	7.62	9 =	29	6	¾ =	19.1
30 =	9.14	10 =	32	10	13/16 =	20.7
40 =	12.19	15 =	49	3	7/8 =	22.2
50 =	15.24	20 =	65	7	15/16 =	23.8
75 =	22.86	30 =	98	5	1 =	25.4
100 =	30.48	50 =	164		2 =	50.8
150 =	45.72	55 =	180		3 =	76.2
200 =	60.96	60 =	196	9	4 =	101.6
300 =	91.44	70 =	229	7	5 =	127.0
400 =	121.92	80 =	262	6	6 =	152.4
500 =	152.40	90 =	295	3	7 =	177.8
1000 =	304.80	100 =	328		8 =	203.2
					9 =	228.6
					10 =	254.0

Millimeters to Inches		Inches to Centimeters		Centimeters to Inches	
mm	**in**	**in**	**cm**	**cm**	**in**
1 =	.04	1 =	2.54	1 =	00.4
2 =	.08	2 =	5.08	2 =	00.8
3 =	.12	3 =	7.62	3 =	01.2
4 =	.16	4 =	10.16	4 =	01.6
5 =	.20	5 =	12.70	5 =	02.0
6 =	.24	6 =	15.24	6 =	02.4
7 =	.28	7 =	17.78	7 =	02.8
8 =	.32	8 =	20.32	8 =	03.1
9 =	.36	9 =	22.86	9 =	03.5
10 =	.39	10 =	25.40	10 =	03.9
12 =	.47	11 =	27.94	11 =	04.3
14 =	.55	12 =	30.48	12 =	04.7
16 =	.63	13 =	33.02	13 =	05.1
18 =	.71	14 =	35.56	14 =	05.5
20 =	.79	15 =	38.10	15 =	05.9
22 =	.87	16 =	40.64	16 =	06.3
24 =	.94	17 =	43.18	17 =	06.7
25 =	.98	18 =	45.72	18 =	07.1
25.4 =	1.00	19 =	48.26	19 =	07.5
26 =	1.02	20 =	50.80	20 =	07.9
27 =	1.06	21 =	53.34	21 =	08.3
28 =	1.1	22 =	55.88	22 =	08.7
29 =	1.14	23 =	58.42	23 =	09.0
30 =	1.18	24 =	60.96	24 =	09.4
35 =	1.37	25 =	63.50	25 =	09.8
40 =	1.57	30 =	76.20	25.4 =	10.0

LENS FOCAL LENGTH
Converted from Millimeters into Inches

mm	in	mm	in	mm	in
12½ =	½	140 =	5³/₅	290 =	11³/₅
15 =	³/₅	150 =	6	295 =	11⁴/₅
20 =	⁴/₅	155 =	6¹/₅	300 =	12
25 =	1	160 =	6²/₅	305 =	12¹/₅
28 =	1¹/₈	165 =	6³/₅	310 =	12²/₅
30 =	1¹/₅	170 =	6⁴/₅	315 =	12³/₅
32 =	1¹/₄	175 =	7	320 =	12⁴/₅
35 =	1²/₅	180 =	7¹/₅	325 =	13
38 =	1½	185 =	7²/₅	330 =	13¹/₅
40 =	1⁵/₈	190 =	7³/₅	335 =	13²/₅
45 =	1⁴/₅	195 =	7⁴/₅	340 =	13³/₅
50 =	2	200 =	8	350 =	14
55 =	2¹/₅	205 =	8¹/₅	355 =	14¹/₅
60 =	2²/₅	210 =	8²/₅	360 =	14²/₅
65 =	2³/₅	215 =	8³/₅	365 =	14³/₅
70 =	2⁴/₅	220 =	8⁴/₅	370 =	14⁴/₅
75 =	3	225 =	9	375 =	15
80 =	3¹/₅	230 =	9¹/₅	385 =	15²/₅
85 =	3²/₅	235 =	9²/₅	400 =	16
90 =	3³/₅	240 =	9³/₅	415 =	16³/₅
95 =	3⁴/₅	245 =	9⁴/₅	425 =	17
100 =	4	250 =	10	435 =	17²/₅
105 =	4¹/₅	255 =	10¹/₅	450 =	18
110 =	4²/₅	260 =	10²/₅	465 =	18³/₅
115 =	4³/₅	265 =	10³/₅	475 =	19
120 =	4⁴/₅	270 =	10⁴/₅	485 =	19²/₅
125 =	5	275 =	11	495 =	19⁴/₅
130 =	5¹/₅	280 =	11¹/₅	500 =	20
135 =	5²/₅	285 =	11²/₅		

The table is rounded off for practical purposes. Actually 25.4mm equals 1 inch.

Decimal Equivalents of Fractions and Equivalents of Fractions of an Inch in mm.

1/8	1/10	1/32	1/64	1/128	mm	Decim. of an Inch	1/8	1/10	1/32	1/64	1/128	mm	Decim. of an Inch
				1	.198	.0078125					65	12.898	.5078125
			1	2	.397	.0156250			33		66	13.097	.515625
				3	.595	.0234375					67	13.295	.5234375
		1	2	4	.794	.031250			17	34	68	13.494	.531250
				5	.992	.0390625					69	13.692	.5390625
			3	6	1.191	.046875				35	70	13.891	.546875
				7	1.389	.0546875					71	14.089	.5546875
	1	2	4	8	1.588	.062500		9	18	36	72	14.288	.562500
				9	1.786	.0703125					73	14.486	.5703125
			5	10	1.984	.078125				37	74	14.684	.578125
				11	2.183	.0859375					75	14.883	.5859375
		3	6	12	2.381	.093750			19	38	76	15.081	.593750
				13	2.580	.1015625					77	15.280	.6015625
			7	14	2.778	.109375				39	78	15.478	.609375
				15	2.977	.1171875					79	15.677	.6171875
1	2	4	8	16	3.175	.125000	5	10	20	40	80	15.875	.625000
				17	3.373	.1328125					81	16.073	.6328125
			9	18	3.572	.140625				41	82	16.272	.640625
				19	3.770	.1484375					83	16.470	.6484375
		5	10	20	3.969	.156250			21	42	84	16.669	.656250
				21	4.167	.1640625					85	16.867	.6640625
			11	22	4.366	.171875				43	86	17.066	.671875
				23	4.564	.1796875					87	17.264	.6796875
	3	6	12	24	4.763	.187500		11	22	44	88	17.463	.687500
				25	4.961	.1953125					89	17.661	.6953125
			13	26	5.159	.203125				45	90	17.859	.703125
				27	5.358	.2109375					91	18.058	.7109375
		7	14	28	5.556	.218750			23	46	92	18.256	.718750
				29	5.755	.2265625					93	18.455	.7265625
			15	30	5.953	.234375				47	94	18.653	.734375
				31	6.152	.2421875					95	18.852	.7421875
2	4	8	16	32	6.350	.250000	6	12	24	48	96	19.050	.750000
				33	6.548	.2578125					97	19.248	.7578125
			17	34	6.747	.265625				49	98	19.447	.765625
				35	6.945	.2734375					99	19.645	.7734375
		9	18	36	7.144	.281250			25	50	100	19.844	.781250
				37	7.342	.2890625					101	20.042	.7890625
			19	38	7.541	.296875				51	102	20.241	.796875
				39	7.739	.3046875					103	20.439	.8046875
	5	10	20	40	7.938	.312500		13	26	52	104	20.638	.812500
				41	8.136	.3203125					105	20.836	.8203125
			21	42	8.334	.328125				53	106	21.034	.828125
				43	8.533	.3359375					107	21.233	.8359375
		11	22	44	8.731	.343750			27	54	108	21.431	.843750
				45	8.930	.3515625					109	21.630	.8515625
			23	46	9.128	.359375				55	110	21.828	.859375
				47	9.327	.3671875					111	22.027	.8671875
3	6	12	24	48	9.525	.375000	7	14	28	56	112	22.225	.875000
				49	9.723	.3828125					113	22.423	.8828125
			25	50	9.922	.390625				57	114	22.622	.890625
				51	10.120	.3984375					115	22.820	.8984375
		13	26	52	10.319	.406250			29	58	116	23.019	.906250
				53	10.517	.4140625					117	23.217	.9140625
			27	54	10.716	.421875				59	118	23.416	.921875
				55	10.914	.4296875					119	23.614	.9296875
	7	14	28	56	11.113	.437500		15	30	60	120	23.813	.937500
				57	11.311	.4453125					121	24.011	.9453125
			29	58	11.509	.453125				61	122	24.209	.953125
				59	11.708	.4609375					123	24.408	.9609375
		15	30	60	11.906	.46875			31	62	124	24.606	.96875
				61	12.105	.4765625					125	24.805	.9765625
			31	62	12.303	.484375				63	126	25.003	.984375
				63	12.502	.4921875					127	25.202	.9921875
4	8	16	32	64	12.700	.500000	8	16	32	64	128	25.400	1.0000000

OHM's Law Formulas
(D.C. or 100% P_f A.C. Circuits)

	To find:		
W = (Watts)	E x I	I^2R	$\dfrac{E^2}{R}$
E = (Volts)	I x R	$\sqrt{W \times R}$	$\dfrac{W}{I}$
I = (Amperes)	$\dfrac{E}{R}$	$\sqrt{\dfrac{W}{R}}$	$\dfrac{W}{E}$
R = (Ohms)	$\dfrac{E}{I}$	$\dfrac{E^2}{W}$	$\dfrac{W}{I^2}$

1ø A.C. Power: W = I x E x P_f
3ø A.C. Power: W = 1.73 x I x E x P_f

Watts = Power   E = Electromotive Force

Ohms = Resistance P_f = Power Factor

Amperes = Current

1 Kilo-Watt = 1,000 Watts
1 Kilo-Watt = 1.344 Input H.P.
1 Horse Power = 746 Watts
1 Ampere = 1,000 Milli-Amperes
1 Meg Ohm = 1,000,000 Ohms

Ohm's Law

The formulas for D.C. and A.C. differ when inductance (L.) and capacity (C.) are involved in A.C. circuits. When L and/or C are used in A.C. circuits, these reactances (X) cause leading or lagging currents vs. voltage. The subsequent apparent and true powers differ by the ratio known as the Power Factor (Pf). More complex formulas, or lab measurements are used to determine the Power Factor involved. Usually Ohms Law can be applied to line loss with reasonable accuracy in A.C. motor circuits, by using the equipment name-plate data. It is highly recommended to use larger instead of smaller conductors when in doubt of the actual load conditions.

VOLTAGE DROP OF COPPERWIRE
(D.C. or 100% Power Factor A.C. Circuits)

Single Phase (1ø)

$$\text{Voltage Drop} = \frac{\text{Amperes x Feet x 21.6}}{\text{Circular Mills}}$$

Three Phase (3ø)

$$\text{Voltage Drop} = \frac{\text{Amperes x Feet x 18.7}}{\text{Circular Mills}}$$

Amperes = Amperes of Load Current (Amps)
Feet = Length of Conductors One Way
Circular Mills = Cross Sectional Area of Conductor
          in Circular Mills (C.M.)

Example:
        100 feet #14 Ga. Cable
        1000 Watt (1 K.W.) Lamp
        117 Volt Source
        (1000W @ 117V = 8.5 Amps)

$$\frac{\text{8.5A x 100 Feet x 21.6}}{\text{4107 (C.M.)}} = 4.5 \text{ Volts Drop (V.D.)}$$

Voltage Available at Load = 117 - 4.5 = 112.5 Volts

Note: Increasing conductor length increases the voltage drop. The V.D. is subtracted from the source voltage and the difference is the voltage available at the load. This indicates that undersize, or overly long conductors result in too low a voltage at the load. Low voltage reduces light output and lowers color temperature of lamps. It also decreases the efficiency of motors, with subsequent increased heat losses. Generally a 5% V.D. can be tolerated (or, 5.85V on a 117 volt line). Voltage regulation varies from power houses, and a range of 105V to 135V is not uncommon over a few hours of time. The 117 volt mean should be used in calculations, and care exercised to measure the source and load voltage when more precise control is desired.

To find amps (load) divide watts by volts.
Example: 1000 watts ÷ by 120 volts = 8.3 amps.

How to Use the Following Tables

1) Know the total amount power at your supply point.
2) Be sure your supply has ample fusing.
3) Compute the amperage load (Table 1) for the maximum units of lighting equipment you expect to use and be sure it does not exceed your total supply. The quantity of and variety of lights should be sufficient to provide flexibility in all photographic situations and since all will not be used at one time, only the maximum number of lights to be used at one time will form the basis for computing amperage load.
4) Relate your available power to the current carrying capacities in Table 2 and decide on adequate cables.
5) See Table 3 for Cable Voltage Drop at different distances.

TABLE 1

INCANDESCENT LAMPS

Globe Wattage	Globe Amperage
200	1.7
500	4.2
650	5.4
750	6.3
1,000	8.3
1,500	12.5
2,000	16.7
5,000	41.6
10,000	83.3
20,000/208	86.0A @ 208V
20,000/220	99.2 @ 240V

HMI

Globe Wattage	Globe Amperage
200	5
575	7
1,200	15
2,500	25
4,000	38
6,000	65
12,000	70A @ 240V
18,000	75A @ 240V
	105A @ 208V

Courtesy of Mole-Richardson.

TABLE 1 — CONTINUED

ARC LAMPS AT 115–120 VOLTS

Type Number	Amperage
40	40
90	120
170	150
450, 4591, 4581	225
4601, 4611, 4691	225

TABLE 2

COPPER CABLE TYPE SC ENTERTAINMENT 90°C

Type SC Entertainment 90°C

AWG Size of Conductors	Ampacity* **	
	Numbers of Conductors	
	1	2†
8	80	74
6	105	99
4	140	130
2	190	174
2/0	300	-
4/0	405	-

* Based on 2002 NEC.
** Additional capacity can be obtained by paralleling cables.
† Number of conductors carrying current in a single jacket.

TABLE 3

CABLE VOLTAGE DROP

Cable Size	Amp @120V	100 ft	200 ft	300 ft	400 ft	500 ft	600 ft
4Ø	300A	116.6	112.8	109.5	105.6	102	98.4
2Ø	225A	115.9	111.9	107.7	102.8	99.6	–
#2	140A	114.7	109.3	104.8	98.3	–	–
#4	105A	113.6	107.1	100.7	–	–	–
#6	80A	112.2	106	96.5	–	–	–
#8	60A	110.6	101.1	–	–	–	–

Distribution Systems

For A.C. determine whether you have a Single (1∅) Phase 4-Wire or Three (3∅) Phase 5-Wire System and use Figures 1 and 2 as a guide in laying out your distribution system.

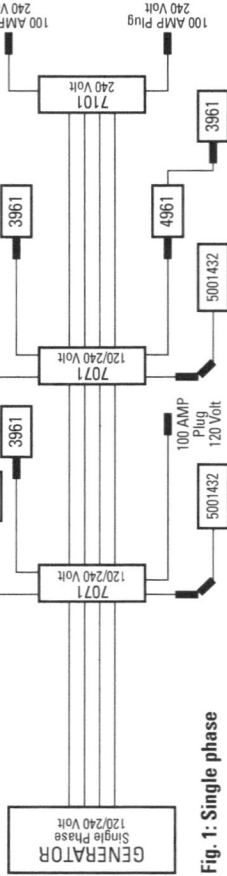

Fig. 1: Single phase

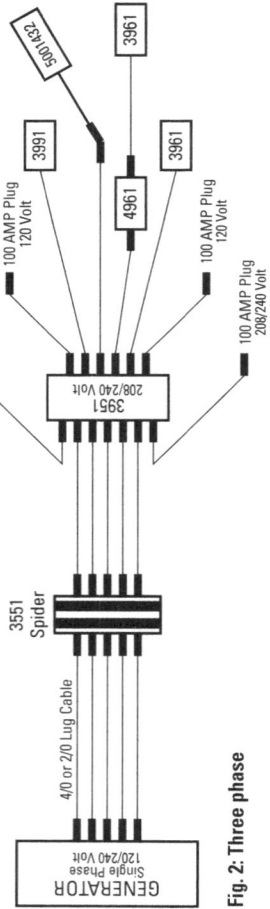

Fig. 2: Three phase

Distribution Systems — Continued

For D.C. determine whether you have a Two or Three-Wire System and use either Figure 3 or 4 as a guide in laying out your distribution system.

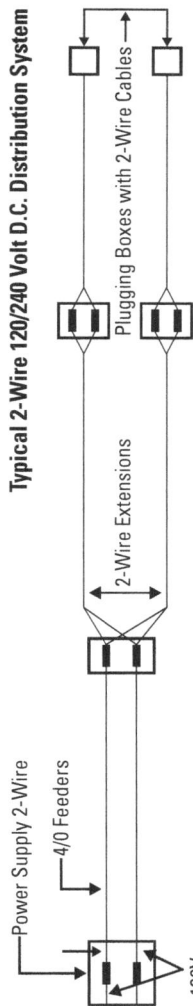

Typical 2-Wire 120/240 Volt D.C. Distribution System

Plugging Boxes with 2-Wire Cables

2-Wire Extensions

Power Supply 2-Wire

4/0 Feeders

120V

Fig. 3: Two-wire system

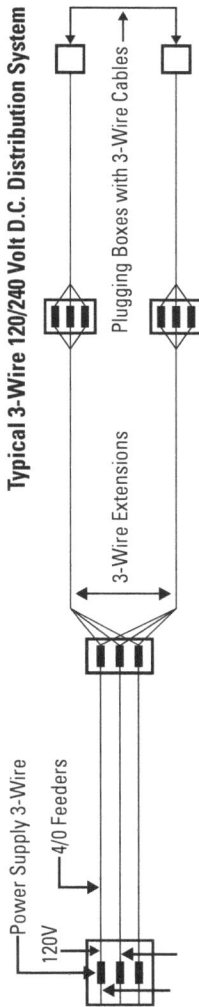

Typical 3-Wire 120/240 Volt D.C. Distribution System

Plugging Boxes with 3-Wire Cables

3-Wire Extensions

Power Supply 3-Wire

4/0 Feeders

120V

Fig. 4: Three-wire system

Courtesy of Mole-Richardson.

Measurement Conversion Factors

Use multiplying factor to convert from one system to the other.
Example: 6 feet x .3048 = 1.8288 meters.

English to Metric Factors		Metric to English Factors	
Yards to meters (m)	.914	Meters to yards (yd)	1.09
Feet to meters (m)	.3048	Meters to feet (ft)	3.28
		Centimeters to feet (ft)	.03281
		Centimeters to inches (in)	.3937
Inches to millimeters (mm)	25.4	Millimeters to inches (in)	.0394
Miles to kilometers (km)	1.61	Kilometers to miles (mi)	.621
Pounds to kilograms (kg)	.454	Kilograms to pounds (lb)	2.21
Ounces to grams (g)	28.4	Grams to ounces (oz)	.0353
Gallons to liters (l)	3.79	Liters to gallons (gal)	.264
Quarts to liters (l)	.946	Liters to quarts (qt)	1.06
Fluid ounces to milliliters (ml)	29.6	Milliliters to fluid ounces (fl oz)	.0338

1 inch = 25.4mm = 2.54cm =.0254m
1 foot = 304.8mm = 30.48cm = .3048m
1yard = .9144m

Depth of Field Tables Introduction

These comprehensive "All Formats Depth of Field Tables" will provide you with depth of field information for virtually all of the currently used 16, 35, and 65mm lenses. You will also find tables for Super 8mm and additional 16mm tables beginning on page 800.

Please see the chapter on lenses for a more thorough discussion of this subject.

These tables are computed mathematically, and should be used as a guide only. Depth of field is a useful concept within limits. Technically speaking, an object is only in focus at one precise point in space. Depth of field determines the range in front of and behind a designated focusing distance, where an object still appears to be acceptably in focus. A low resolving film stock or lens may appear to have greater depth of field, because the "in focus" image is already so soft, it is more difficult to determine when it goes further out of focus. Conversely, a very sharp, high contrast lens may appear to have shallow depth of field, because the "in focus" image has such clarity, it is much easier to notice when it slips out of a range of acceptable focus.

These tables can be nothing other than generic in their information. They will give you a very close approximation of any given focal length's depth of field characteristics. Truly precise Depth of Field calculations cannot be performed without knowing the size of a specific lens' entrance pupil.

That being said, these charts should be very helpful, unless you are trying to measure down to an accuracy of less than a couple of inches. If you are demanding that level of precision, then you must shoot a test of the lens in question, because no calculation can provide the empirical data a visual evaluation can.

These tables are calculated based on a circle of confusion of 0.001" ($\frac{1}{1000}$"). To calculate a depth of field based upon a more critical circle of confusion of half that size (0.0005" or $\frac{5}{10,000}$"), find your chosen f-stop at the distance desired, then read the depth of field data two columns to the left. The 0.0005" circle of confusion can be used for lenses of greater sharpness or contrast, or for a more traditional method of determining 16mm depth of field.

One more note: you will see some lenses at certain distances that indicate a depth of field of effectively nothing (e.g.: 10' 0" to 10' 0"). This means the depth of field is less than an inch, and we recommend that a test is shot to determine such a critical depth of field. Charts should never be relied upon when exploring such narrow fields of focus.

For further discussion on this subject *see pages 136 and 140.*

These tables were compiled with the invaluable help of Evans Wetmore, P.E. Evans is Vice-President of Advanced Engineering in the News Technology Group, of Fox NewsCorp. A fellow of SMPTE; his feature film credits include the special effects engineering for Star Trek, the Motion Picture, Blade Runner, *and* Brainstorm.

5.9mm — ALL FORMATS DEPTH OF FIELD TABLE

CIRCLE OF CONFUSION=0.0010 inches

FOCUS (feet)	f/1.4 NEAR	f/1.4 FAR	f/2 NEAR	f/2 FAR	f/2.8 NEAR	f/2.8 FAR	f/4 NEAR	f/4 FAR	f/5.6 NEAR	f/5.6 FAR	f/8 NEAR	f/8 FAR	f/11 NEAR	f/11 FAR	f/16 NEAR	f/16 FAR	f/22 NEAR	f/22 FAR
Hyper. Dist.	3' 3"		2' 3"		1' 7"		1' 1"		0' 10"		0' 7"		0' 5"		0' 3"		0' 2"	
2	1' 3"	5' 3"	1' 1"	INF	0' 11"	INF	0' 9"	INF	0' 7"	INF	0' 5"	INF	0' 4"	INF	0' 3"	INF	0' 2"	INF
2½	1' 5"	11' 0"	1' 2"	INF	1' 0"	INF	0' 9"	INF	0' 7"	INF	0' 6"	INF	0' 4"	INF	0' 3"	INF	0' 2"	INF
3	1' 7"	INF	1' 3"	INF	1' 1"	INF	0' 10"	INF	0' 8"	INF	0' 6"	INF	0' 4"	INF	0' 3"	INF	0' 2"	INF
3½	1' 8"	INF	1' 4"	INF	1' 1"	INF	0' 10"	INF	0' 8"	INF	0' 6"	INF	0' 4"	INF	0' 3"	INF	0' 2"	INF
4	1' 9"	INF	1' 5"	INF	1' 2"	INF	0' 11"	INF	0' 8"	INF	0' 6"	INF	0' 4"	INF	0' 3"	INF	0' 2"	INF
4½	1' 11"	INF	1' 6"	INF	1' 2"	INF	0' 11"	INF	0' 8"	INF	0' 6"	INF	0' 5"	INF	0' 3"	INF	0' 2"	INF
5	2' 0"	INF	1' 7"	INF	1' 3"	INF	0' 11"	INF	0' 8"	INF	0' 6"	INF	0' 5"	INF	0' 3"	INF	0' 2"	INF
5½	2' 0"	INF	1' 7"	INF	1' 3"	INF	0' 11"	INF	0' 8"	INF	0' 6"	INF	0' 5"	INF	0' 3"	INF	0' 2"	INF
6	2' 1"	INF	1' 8"	INF	1' 3"	INF	0' 11"	INF	0' 9"	INF	0' 6"	INF	0' 5"	INF	0' 3"	INF	0' 2"	INF

6½	2' 2" INF	1' 8" INF	1' 3" INF	1' 0" INF	0' 9" INF	0' 6" INF	0' 5" INF	0' 3" INF	0' 2" INF
7	2' 2" INF	1' 8" INF	1' 4" INF	1' 0" INF	0' 9" INF	0' 6" INF	0' 5" INF	0' 3" INF	0' 2" INF
8	2' 4" INF	1' 9" INF	1' 4" INF	1' 0" INF	0' 9" INF	0' 6" INF	0' 5" INF	0' 3" INF	0' 2" INF
9	2' 4" INF	1' 10" INF	1' 4" INF	1' 0" INF	0' 9" INF	0' 6" INF	0' 5" INF	0' 3" INF	0' 2" INF
10	2' 5" INF	1' 10" INF	1' 5" INF	1' 0" INF	0' 9" INF	0' 6" INF	0' 5" INF	0' 3" INF	0' 2" INF
12	2' 6" INF	1' 11" INF	1' 5" INF	1' 0" INF	0' 9" INF	0' 6" INF	0' 5" INF	0' 3" INF	0' 2" INF
14	2' 7" INF	1' 11" INF	1' 5" INF	1' 1" INF	0' 9" INF	0' 6" INF	0' 5" INF	0' 3" INF	0' 2" IN
16	2' 8" INF	2' 0" INF	1' 6" INF	1' 1" INF	0' 9" INF	0' 7" INF	0' 5" INF	0' 3" INF	0' 2" INF
18	2' 9" INF	2' 0" INF	1' 6" INF	1' 1" INF	0' 9" INF	0' 7" INF	0' 5" INF	0' 3" INF	0' 2" INF
20	2' 9" INF	2' 0" INF	1' 6" INF	1' 1" INF	0' 9" INF	0' 7" INF	0' 5" INF	0' 3" INF	0' 2" INF
25	2' 10" INF	2' 1" INF	1' 6" INF	1' 1" INF	0' 9" INF	0' 7" INF	0' 5" INF	0' 3" INF	0' 2" INF
50	3' 0" INF	2' 2" INF	1' 7" INF	1' 1" INF	0' 9" INF	0' 7" INF	0' 5" INF	0' 3" INF	0' 2" INF

For circle of confusion = .0005 use depth data two columns left of chosen F-Stop.

8mm — ALL FORMATS DEPTH OF FIELD TABLE

CIRCLE OF CONFUSION=0.0010 inches

FOCUS (feet)		f/1.4	f/2	f/2.8	f/4	f/5.6	f/8	f/11	f/16	f/22
Hyper. Dist.		5'11"	4'2"	2'11"	2'1"	1'6"	1'0"	0'9"	0'6"	0'5"
2	NEAR	1'6"	1'4"	1'2"	1'0"	0'10"	0'8"	0'7"	0'5"	0'4"
	FAR	3'0"	3'10"	6'0"	INF	INF	INF	INF	INF	INF
2½	NEAR	1'9"	1'7"	1'4"	1'2"	0'11"	0'9"	0'7"	0'5"	0'4"
	FAR	4'4"	6'3"	15'5"	INF	INF	INF	INF	INF	INF
3	NEAR	2'0"	1'9"	1'6"	1'3"	1'0"	0'9"	0'7"	0'5"	0'4"
	FAR	6'1"	10'8"	INF	INF	INF	INF	INF	INF	INF
3½	NEAR	2'2"	1'11"	1'7"	1'4"	1'1"	0'10"	0'7"	0'5"	0'4"
	FAR	8'6"	21'11"	INF	INF	INF	INF	INF	INF	INF
4	NEAR	2'5"	2'0"	1'8"	1'4"	1'1"	0'10"	0'8"	0'6"	0'4"
	FAR	12'3"	INF	INF	INF	INF	INF	INF	INF	INF
4½	NEAR	2'7"	2'2"	1'9"	1'5"	1'1"	0'10"	0'8"	0'6"	0'4"
	FAR	18'7"	INF	INF	INF	INF	INF	INF	INF	INF
5	NEAR	2'9"	2'3"	1'10"	1'6"	1'2"	0'10"	0'8"	0'6"	0'4"
	FAR	31'9"	INF	INF	INF	INF	INF	INF	INF	INF
5½	NEAR	2'10"	2'4"	1'11"	1'6"	1'2"	0'10"	0'8"	0'6"	0'4"
	FAR	INF	INF	INF	INF	INF	INF	INF	INF	INF
6	NEAR	3'0"	2'5"	2'0"	1'7"	1'2"	0'11"	0'8"	0'6"	0'4"
	FAR	INF	INF	INF	INF	INF	INF	INF	INF	INF

F-Stop									
6½	3'1" INF	2'6" INF	2'0" INF	1'7" INF	1'2" INF	0'11" INF	0'8" INF	0'6" INF	0'4" INF
7	3'3" INF	2'7" INF	2'1" INF	1'7" INF	1'3" INF	0'11" INF	0'8" INF	0'6" INF	0'4" INF
7½	3'5" INF	2'9" INF	2'2" INF	1'8" INF	1'3" INF	0'11" INF	0'8" INF	0'6" INF	0'4" INF
9	3'7" INF	2'10" INF	2'3" INF	1'8" INF	1'3" INF	0'11" INF	0'8" INF	0'6" INF	0'4" INF
10	3'9" INF	2'11" INF	2'3" INF	1'9" INF	1'3" INF	0'11" INF	0'8" INF	0'6" INF	0'4" INF
12	4'0" INF	3'1" INF	2'4" INF	1'9" INF	1'4" INF	0'11" INF	0'8" INF	0'6" INF	0'4" INF
14	4'2" INF	3'2" INF	2'5" INF	1'10" INF	1'4" INF	1'0" INF	0'9" INF	0'6" INF	0'4" INF
16	4'4" INF	3'3" INF	2'6" INF	1'10" INF	1'4" INF	1'0" INF	0'9" INF	0'6" INF	0'4" INF
18	4'5" INF	3'4" INF	2'6" INF	1'10" INF	1'4" INF	1'0" INF	0'9" INF	0'6" INF	0'4" INF
20	4'7" INF	3'5" INF	2'7" INF	1'11" INF	1'5" INF	1'0" INF	0'9" INF	0'6" INF	0'4" INF
25	4'9" INF	3'7" INF	2'8" INF	1'11" INF	1'5" INF	1'0" INF	0'9" INF	0'6" INF	0'4" INF
50	5'3" INF	3'10" INF	2'9" INF	2'0" INF	1'5" INF	1'0" INF	0'9" INF	0'6" INF	0'4" INF

For circle of confusion = .0005 use depth data two columns left of chosen F-Stop.

9.8mm — ALL FORMATS DEPTH OF FIELD TABLE

CIRCLE OF CONFUSION=0.0010 inches

FOCUS (feet)	f/1.4 NEAR	f/1.4 FAR	f/2 NEAR	f/2 FAR	f/2.8 NEAR	f/2.8 FAR	f/4 NEAR	f/4 FAR	f/5.6 NEAR	f/5.6 FAR	f/8 NEAR	f/8 FAR	f/11 NEAR	f/11 FAR	f/16 NEAR	f/16 FAR	f/22 NEAR	f/22 FAR
Hyper. Dist.	8' 10"		6' 2"		4' 5"		3' 1"		2' 3"		1' 7"		1' 2"		0' 9"		0' 7"	
2	1' 8"	2' 7"	1' 6"	2' 11"	1' 5"	3' 7"	1' 3"	5' 6"	1' 1"	INF	0' 11"	INF	0' 9"	INF	0' 7"	INF	0' 5"	INF
2½	1' 11"	3' 6"	1' 9"	4' 2"	1' 7"	5' 8"	1' 5"	12' 3"	1' 2"	INF	1' 0"	INF	0' 9"	INF	0' 7"	INF	0' 6"	INF
3	2' 3"	4' 6"	2' 0"	5' 9"	1' 10"	9' 1"	1' 6"	INF	1' 3"	INF	1' 0"	INF	0' 10"	INF	0' 7"	INF	0' 6"	INF
3½	2' 6"	5' 9"	2' 3"	7' 11"	2' 0"	16' 1"	1' 8"	INF	1' 4"	INF	1' 1"	INF	0' 10"	INF	0' 8"	INF	0' 6"	INF
4	2' 9"	7' 3"	2' 5"	11' 1"	2' 1"	INF	1' 9"	INF	1' 5"	INF	1' 1"	INF	0' 11"	INF	0' 8"	INF	0' 6"	INF
4½	3' 0"	9' 1"	2' 7"	16' 1"	2' 3"	INF	1' 10"	INF	1' 6"	INF	1' 2"	INF	0' 11"	INF	0' 8"	INF	0' 6"	INF
5	3' 2"	11' 5"	2' 9"	25' 1"	2' 4"	INF	1' 11"	INF	1' 7"	INF	1' 2"	INF	0' 11"	INF	0' 8"	INF	0' 6"	INF
5½	3' 5"	14' 4"	2' 11"	INF	2' 6"	INF	2' 0"	INF	1' 7"	INF	1' 3"	INF	0' 11"	INF	0' 8"	INF	0' 6"	INF
6	3' 7"	18' 5"	3' 1"	INF	2' 7"	INF	2' 1"	INF	1' 7"	INF	1' 3"	INF	0' 11"	INF	0' 8"	INF	0' 6"	INF

f									
6½	0' 6" INF	0' 8" INF	1' 0" INF	1' 3" INF	1' 8" INF	2' 1" INF	2' 8" INF	3' 2" INF	3' 9" 4' 1"
7	0' 6" INF	0' 8" INF	1' 0" INF	1' 3" INF	1' 8" INF	2' 2" INF	2' 9" INF	3' 4" INF	3' 11" 2' 9"
8	0' 6" INF	0' 9" INF	1' 0" INF	1' 4" INF	1' 9" INF	2' 3" INF	2' 10" INF	3' 6" INF	4' 3" INF
9	0' 6" INF	0' 9" INF	1' 0" INF	1' 4" INF	1' 9" INF	2' 4" INF	3' 0" INF	3' 8" INF	4' 6" INF
10	0' 6" INF	0' 9" INF	1' 0" INF	1' 4" INF	1' 10" INF	2' 4" INF	3' 1" INF	3' 10" INF	4' 8" INF
12	0' 6" INF	0' 9" INF	1' 0" INF	1' 5" INF	1' 10" INF	2' 6" INF	3' 3" INF	4' 1" INF	5' 1" INF
14	0' 7" INF	0' 9" INF	1' 1" INF	1' 5" INF	1' 11" INF	2' 7" INF	3' 4" INF	4' 4" INF	5' 5" INF
16	0' 7" INF	0' 9" INF	1' 1" INF	1' 5" INF	1' 11" INF	2' 7" INF	3' 6" INF	4' 6" INF	5' 9" INF
18	0' 7" INF	0' 9" INF	1' 1" INF	1' 5" INF	2' 0" INF	2' 8" INF	3' 7" INF	4' 7" INF	5' 11" INF
20	0' 7" INF	0' 9" INF	1' 1" INF	1' 6" INF	2' 0" INF	2' 8" INF	3' 8" INF	4' 9" INF	6' 2" INF
25	0' 7" INF	0' 9" INF	1' 1" INF	1' 6" INF	2' 0" INF	2' 9" INF	3' 9" INF	5' 0" INF	6' 7" INF
50	0' 7" INF	0' 9" INF	1' 1" INF	1' 6" INF	2' 1" INF	2' 11" INF	4' 1" INF	5' 6" INF	7' 6" INF

For circle of confusion = .0005 use depth data two columns left of chosen F-Stop.

10mm — ALL FORMATS DEPTH OF FIELD TABLE

CIRCLE OF CONFUSION=0.0010 inches

Hyper. Dist.	f/1.4 9'3"		f/2 6'6"		f/2.8 4'7"		f/4 3'3"		f/5.6 2'4"		f/8 1'7"		f/11 1'2"		f/16 0'10"		f/22 0'7"	
FOCUS (feet)	NEAR	FAR	NEAR	FAR	NEAR	FAR	NEAR	FAR	NEAR	FAR	NEAR	FAR	NEAR	FAR	NEAR	FAR	NEAR	FAR
2	1'8"	2'7"	1'6"	2'11"	1'5"	3'6"	1'3"	5'1"	1'1"	13'7"	0'11"	INF	0'9"	INF	0'7"	INF	0'6"	INF
2½	2'0"	3'5"	1'10"	4'1"	1'8"	5'4"	1'5"	10'7"	1'2"	INF	1'0"	INF	0'10"	INF	0'7"	INF	0'6"	INF
3	2'3"	4'5"	2'1"	5'7"	1'10"	8'5"	1'7"	INF	1'4"	INF	1'1"	INF	0'10"	INF	0'8"	INF	0'6"	INF
3½	2'7"	5'7"	2'3"	7'7"	2'0"	14'1"	1'8"	INF	1'5"	INF	1'1"	INF	0'11"	INF	0'8"	INF	0'6"	INF
4	2'10"	7'0"	2'6"	10'4"	2'2"	28'7"	1'10"	INF	1'6"	INF	1'2"	INF	0'11"	INF	0'8"	INF	0'6"	INF
4½	3'0"	8'9"	2'8"	14'7"	2'3"	INF	1'11"	INF	1'6"	INF	1'2"	INF	0'11"	INF	0'8"	INF	0'6"	INF
5	3'3"	10'10"	2'10"	21'8"	2'5"	INF	2'0"	INF	1'7"	INF	1'3"	INF	0'11"	INF	0'8"	INF	0'6"	INF
5½	3'5"	13'6"	3'0"	35'10"	2'6"	INF	2'1"	INF	1'8"	INF	1'3"	INF	1'0"	INF	0'8"	INF	0'6"	INF
6	3'8"	17'0"	3'1"	INF	2'7"	INF	2'1"	INF	1'8"	INF	1'3"	INF	1'0"	INF	0'9"	INF	0'6"	INF

F-Stop									
6½	0'6" INF	0'9" INF	1'0" INF	1'4" INF	1'9" INF	2'2" INF	2'8" INF	3'3" INF	3'10" / 21'9"
7	0'7" INF	0'9" INF	1'0" INF	1'4" INF	1'9" INF	2'3" INF	2'9" INF	3'4" INF	4'0" / 28'7"
8	0'7" INF	0'9" INF	1'0" INF	1'4" INF	1'10" INF	2'4" INF	2'11" INF	3'7" INF	4'4" / 58'7"
9	0'7" INF	0'9" INF	1'1" INF	1'4" INF	1'10" INF	2'5" INF	3'1" INF	3'9" INF	4'7" INF
10	0'7" INF	0'9" INF	1'1" INF	1'5" INF	1'11" INF	2'5" INF	3'2" INF	3'11" INF	4'10" INF
12	0'7" INF	0'9" INF	1'1" INF	1'5" INF	1'11" INF	2'7" INF	3'4" INF	4'2" INF	5'3" INF
14	0'7" INF	0'9" INF	1'1" INF	1'6" INF	2'0" INF	2'8" INF	3'6" INF	4'5" INF	5'7" INF
16	0'7" INF	0'9" INF	1'1" INF	1'6" INF	2'0" INF	2'8" INF	3'7" INF	4'7" INF	5'10" INF
18	0'7" INF	0'9" INF	1'1" INF	1'6" INF	2'1" INF	2'9" INF	3'8" INF	4'9" INF	6'1" INF
20	0'7" INF	0'9" INF	1'1" INF	1'6" INF	2'1" INF	2'9" INF	3'9" INF	4'11" INF	6'4" INF
25	0'7" INF	0'9" INF	1'1" INF	1'6" INF	2'1" INF	2'10" INF	3'11" INF	5'2" INF	6'9" INF
50	0'7" INF	0'10" INF	1'2" INF	1'7" INF	2'2" INF	3'0" INF	4'3" INF	5'9" INF	7'10" INF

For circle of confusion = .0005 use depth data two columns left of chosen F-Stop.

12mm — ALL FORMATS DEPTH OF FIELD TABLE

CIRCLE OF CONFUSION=0.0010 inches

FOCUS (feet)		f/1.4	f/2	f/2.8	f/4	f/5.6	f/8	f/11	f/16	f/22
Hyper. Dist.		13' 3"	9' 4"	6' 8"	4' 8"	3' 4"	2' 4"	1' 8"	1' 2"	0' 10"
2	NEAR	1' 9"	1' 8"	1' 7"	1' 5"	1' 3"	1' 1"	0' 11"	0' 9"	0' 7"
	FAR	2' 4"	2' 6"	2' 10"	3' 5"	4' 11"	12' 9"	INF	INF	INF
2½	NEAR	2' 1"	2' 0"	1' 10"	1' 8"	1' 5"	1' 3"	1' 0"	0' 10"	0' 8"
	FAR	3' 1"	3' 5"	4' 0"	5' 4"	9' 8"	INF	INF	INF	INF
3	NEAR	2' 5"	2' 3"	2' 1"	1' 10"	1' 7"	1' 4"	1' 1"	0' 10"	0' 8"
	FAR	3' 10"	4' 5"	5' 5"	8' 3"	INF	INF	INF	INF	INF
3½	NEAR	2' 9"	2' 7"	2' 4"	2' 0"	1' 9"	1' 5"	1' 2"	0' 11"	0' 8"
	FAR	4' 9"	5' 7"	7' 4"	13' 8"	INF	INF	INF	INF	INF
4	NEAR	3' 1"	2' 10"	2' 6"	2' 2"	1' 10"	1' 6"	1' 2"	0' 11"	0' 8"
	FAR	5' 8"	7' 0"	9' 11"	27' 0"	INF	INF	INF	INF	INF
4½	NEAR	3' 4"	3' 0"	2' 8"	2' 4"	1' 11"	1' 7"	1' 3"	0' 11"	0' 9"
	FAR	6' 9"	8' 8"	13' 8"	INF	INF	INF	INF	INF	INF
5	NEAR	3' 8"	3' 3"	2' 10"	2' 5"	2' 0"	1' 7"	1' 3"	0' 11"	0' 9"
	FAR	8' 0"	10' 9"	19' 9"	INF	INF	INF	INF	INF	INF
5½	NEAR	3' 11"	3' 6"	3' 0"	2' 6"	2' 1"	1' 8"	1' 4"	1' 0"	0' 9"
	FAR	9' 4"	13' 4"	30' 11"	INF	INF	INF	INF	INF	INF
6	NEAR	4' 2"	3' 8"	3' 2"	2' 8"	2' 2"	1' 8"	1' 4"	1' 0"	0' 9"
	FAR	10' 11"	16' 9"	INF	INF	INF	INF	INF	INF	INF

F-Stop									
6½	4' 4" 12' 8"	3' 10" 21' 3"	3' 4" INF	2' 9" INF	2' 2" INF	1' 9" INF	1' 4" INF	1' 0" INF	0' 9" INF
7	4' 7" 14' 8"	4' 0" 27' 10"	3' 5" INF	2' 10" INF	2' 3" INF	1' 9" INF	1' 4" INF	1' 0" INF	0' 9" INF
8	5' 0" 20' 0"	4' 4" 55' 7"	3' 8" INF	2' 11" INF	2' 4" INF	1' 10" INF	1' 5" INF	1' 0" INF	0' 9" INF
9	5' 4" 27' 8"	4' 7" INF	3' 10" INF	3' 1" INF	2' 5" INF	1' 10" INF	1' 5" INF	1' 0" INF	0' 9" INF
10	5' 9" 39' 11"	4' 10" INF	4' 0" INF	3' 2" INF	2' 6" INF	1' 11" INF	1' 5" INF	1' 1" INF	0' 9" INF
12	6' 4" INF	5' 3" INF	4' 3" INF	3' 4" INF	2' 7" INF	1' 11" INF	1' 6" INF	1' 1" INF	0' 10" INF
14	6' 10" INF	5' 7" INF	4' 6" INF	3' 6" INF	2' 8" INF	2' 0" INF	1' 6" INF	1' 1" INF	0' 10" INF
16	7' 3" INF	5' 11" INF	4' 8" INF	3' 7" INF	2' 9" INF	2' 0" INF	1' 6" INF	1' 1" INF	0' 10" INF
18	7' 8" INF	6' 2" INF	4' 10" INF	3' 8" INF	2' 10" INF	2' 1" INF	1' 7" INF	1' 1" INF	0' 10" INF
20	8' 0" INF	6' 4" INF	5' 0" INF	3' 9" INF	2' 10" INF	2' 1" INF	1' 7" INF	1' 1" INF	0' 10" INF
25	8' 8" INF	6' 9" INF	5' 3" INF	3' 11" INF	2' 11" INF	2' 2" INF	1' 7" INF	1' 1" INF	0' 10" INF
50	10' 6" INF	7' 10" INF	5' 10" INF	4' 3" INF	3' 1" INF	2' 3" INF	1' 8" INF	1' 2" INF	0' 10" INF

For circle of confusion = .0005 use depth data two columns left of chosen F-Stop.

14mm — ALL FORMATS DEPTH OF FIELD TABLE

CIRCLE OF CONFUSION=0.0010 inches

FOCUS (feet)	f/1.4 NEAR	f/1.4 FAR	f/2 NEAR	f/2 FAR	f/2.8 NEAR	f/2.8 FAR	f/4 NEAR	f/4 FAR	f/5.6 NEAR	f/5.6 FAR	f/8 NEAR	f/8 FAR	f/11 NEAR	f/11 FAR	f/16 NEAR	f/16 FAR	f/22 NEAR	f/22 FAR
Hyper. Dist.	18' 1"		12' 8"		9' 1"		6' 4"		4' 6"		3' 2"		2' 4"		1' 7"		1' 2"	
2	1' 10"	2' 3"	1' 9"	2' 4"	1' 8"	2' 7"	1' 6"	2' 11"	1' 5"	3' 6"	1' 3"	5' 3"	1' 1"	13' 3"	0' 11"	INF	0' 9"	INF
2½	2' 2"	2' 11"	2' 1"	3' 1"	2' 0"	3' 5"	1' 10"	4' 1"	1' 7"	5' 6"	1' 5"	11' 2"	1' 3"	INF	1' 0"	INF	0' 10"	INF
3	2' 7"	3' 7"	2' 5"	3' 11"	2' 3"	4' 5"	2' 1"	5' 8"	1' 10"	8' 8"	1' 7"	INF	1' 4"	INF	1' 1"	INF	0' 10"	INF
3½	2' 11"	4' 4"	2' 9"	4' 10"	2' 6"	5' 8"	2' 3"	7' 8"	2' 0"	14' 10"	1' 8"	INF	1' 5"	INF	1' 1"	INF	0' 10"	INF
4	3' 3"	5' 1"	3' 1"	5' 10"	2' 9"	7' 1"	2' 6"	10' 8"	2' 2"	INF	1' 9"	INF	1' 6"	INF	1' 2"	INF	0' 11"	INF
4½	3' 7"	6' 0"	3' 4"	6' 11"	3' 0"	8' 10"	2' 8"	15' 2"	2' 3"	INF	1' 10"	INF	1' 6"	INF	1' 2"	INF	0' 11"	INF
5	3' 11"	6' 11"	3' 7"	8' 3"	3' 3"	11' 1"	2' 10"	23' 0"	2' 5"	INF	1' 11"	INF	1' 7"	INF	1' 3"	INF	0' 11"	INF
5½	4' 3"	7' 11"	3' 10"	9' 8"	3' 5"	13' 10"	2' 11"	39' 9"	2' 6"	INF	2' 0"	INF	1' 8"	INF	1' 3"	INF	0' 11"	INF
6	4' 6"	8' 11"	4' 1"	11' 4"	3' 7"	17' 7"	3' 1"	INF	2' 7"	INF	2' 1"	INF	1' 8"	INF	1' 3"	INF	1' 0"	INF

f-stop									
6½	1'0" INF	1'3" INF	1'9" INF	2'2" INF	2'8" INF	3'3" INF	3'10" / 22'9"	4'4" / 13'3"	4'9" / 10'1"
7	1'0" INF	1'4" INF	1'9" INF	2'2" INF	2'9" INF	3'4" INF	3'11" / 30'4"	4'6" / 15'6"	5'1" / 11'4"
8	1'0" INF	1'4" INF	1'10" INF	2'3" INF	2'11" INF	3'7" INF	4'3" INF	4'11" / 21'6"	5'7" / 14'3"
9	1'0" INF	1'4" INF	1'10" INF	2'4" INF	3'0" INF	3'9" INF	4'6" INF	5'3" / 30'9"	6'0" / 17'10"
10	1'0" INF	1'4" INF	1'11" INF	2'5" INF	3'1" INF	3'11" INF	4'9" INF	5'7" / 46'10"	6'5" / 22'3"
12	1'0" INF	1'5" INF	1'11" INF	2'6" INF	3'4" INF	4'2" INF	5'2" INF	6'2" INF	7'3" / 35'5"
14	1'1" INF	1'5" INF	2'0" INF	2'7" INF	3'5" INF	4'4" INF	5'6" INF	6'8" INF	7'11" / 61'4"
16	1'1" INF	1'5" INF	2'0" INF	2'8" INF	3'6" INF	4'7" INF	5'9" INF	7'1" INF	8'6" INF
18	1'1" INF	1'6" INF	2'1" INF	2'8" INF	3'7" INF	4'8" INF	6'0" INF	7'5" INF	9'0" INF
20	1'1" INF	1'6" INF	2'1" INF	2'9" INF	3'8" INF	4'10" INF	6'3" INF	7'9" INF	9'6" INF
25	1'1" INF	1'6" INF	2'1" INF	2'10" INF	3'10" INF	5'1" INF	6'8" INF	8'5" INF	10'6" INF
50	1'2" INF	1'6" INF	2'2" INF	3'0" INF	4'2" INF	5'7" INF	7'8" INF	10'1" INF	13'3" INF

For circle of confusion = .0005 use depth data two columns left of chosen F-Stop.

16mm — ALL FORMATS DEPTH OF FIELD TABLE

CIRCLE OF CONFUSION=0.0010 inches

FOCUS (feet)	Hyper. Dist.	f/1.4 23'7" NEAR / FAR	f/2 16'6" NEAR / FAR	f/2.8 11'10" NEAR / FAR	f/4 8'3" NEAR / FAR	f/5.6 5'11" NEAR / FAR	f/8 4'2" NEAR / FAR	f/11 3'0" NEAR / FAR	f/16 2'1" NEAR / FAR	f/22 1'6" NEAR / FAR
2		1'10" / 2'2"	1'9" / 2'3"	1'9" / 2'5"	1'7" / 2'7"	1'6" / 3'0"	1'4" / 3'9"	1'3" / 5'8"	1'0" / INF	0'10" / INF
2½		2'3" / 2'9"	2'2" / 2'11"	2'1" / 3'2"	1'11" / 3'7"	1'9" / 4'3"	1'7" / 6'2"	1'5" / 13'5"	1'2" / INF	0'11" / INF
3		2'8" / 3'5"	2'7" / 3'8"	2'5" / 4'0"	2'3" / 4'8"	2'0" / 6'0"	1'9" / 10'5"	1'6" / INF	1'3" / INF	1'0" / INF
3½		3'1" / 4'1"	2'11" / 4'5"	2'9" / 4'11"	2'6" / 6'0"	2'3" / 8'5"	1'11" / 21'1"	1'8" / INF	1'4" / INF	1'1" / INF
4		3'5" / 4'10"	3'3" / 5'3"	3'0" / 6'0"	2'8" / 7'8"	2'5" / 12'1"	2'1" / INF	1'9" / INF	1'4" / INF	1'1" / INF
4½		3'9" / 5'7"	3'7" / 6'2"	3'3" / 7'3"	2'11" / 9'9"	2'7" / 18'3"	2'2" / INF	1'10" / INF	1'5" / INF	1'2" / INF
5		4'2" / 6'4"	3'10" / 7'2"	3'6" / 8'7"	3'2" / 12'5"	2'9" / 30'10"	2'3" / INF	1'11" / INF	1'6" / INF	1'2" / INF
5½		4'6" / 7'2"	4'2" / 8'2"	3'9" / 10'3"	3'4" / 16'2"	2'10" / INF	2'4" / INF	1'11" / INF	1'6" / INF	1'2" / INF
6		4'10" / 8'0"	4'5" / 9'4"	4'0" / 12'1"	3'6" / 21'5"	3'0" / INF	2'6" / INF	2'0" / INF	1'7" / INF	1'3" / INF

F-Stop									
6½	5' 1" / 8' 11"	4' 8" / 10' 8"	4' 2" / 14' 4"	3' 8" / 29' 6"	3' 1" / INF	2' 6" / INF	2' 1" / INF	1' 7" / INF	1' 3" / INF
7	5' 5" / 9' 11"	4' 11" / 12' 1"	4' 5" / 17' 0"	3' 10" / 43' 10"	3' 3" / INF	2' 7" / INF	2' 1" / INF	1' 7" / INF	1' 3" / INF
8	6' 0" / 12' 1"	5' 5" / 15' 5"	4' 9" / 24' 6"	4' 1" / INF	3' 5" / INF	2' 9" / INF	2' 2" / INF	1' 8" / INF	1' 3" / INF
9	6' 6" / 14' 6"	5' 10" / 19' 7"	5' 1" / 37' 2"	4' 4" / INF	3' 7" / INF	2' 10" / INF	2' 3" / INF	1' 8" / INF	1' 4" / INF
10	7' 0" / 17' 3"	6' 3" / 25' 1"	5' 5" / 63' 5"	4' 6" / INF	3' 9" / INF	2' 11" / INF	2' 4" / INF	1' 9" / INF	1' 4" / INF
12	8' 0" / 24' 3"	7' 0" / 43' 3"	6' 0" / INF	4' 11" / INF	4' 0" / INF	3' 1" / INF	2' 5" / INF	1' 9" / INF	1' 4" / INF
14	8' 10" / 34' 2"	7' 7" / 89' 6"	6' 5" / INF	5' 3" / INF	4' 2" / INF	3' 2" / INF	2' 6" / INF	1' 10" / INF	1' 4" / INF
16	9' 7" / 49' 3"	8' 2" / INF	6' 10" / INF	5' 6" / INF	4' 4" / INF	3' 4" / INF	2' 6" / INF	1' 10" / INF	1' 5" / INF
18	10' 3" / 75' 0"	8' 8" / INF	7' 2" / INF	5' 8" / INF	4' 5" / INF	3' 4" / INF	2' 7" / INF	1' 11" / INF	1' 5" / INF
20	10' 10" / 128' 8"	9' 1" / INF	7' 5" / INF	5' 10" / INF	4' 7" / INF	3' 5" / INF	2' 7" / INF	1' 11" / INF	1' 5" / INF
25	12' 2" / INF	10' 0" / INF	8' 0" / INF	6' 3" / INF	4' 9" / INF	3' 7" / INF	2' 8" / INF	2' 0" / INF	1' 5" / INF
50	16 1" / INF	12' 5" / INF	9' 7" / INF	7' 1" / INF	5' 3" / INF	3' 10" / INF	2' 10" / INF	2' 0" / INF	1' 6" / INF

For circle of confusion = .0005 use depth data two columns left of chosen F-Stop.

18mm — ALL FORMATS DEPTH OF FIELD TABLE

CIRCLE OF CONFUSION = 0.0010 inches

Hyper. Dist.	f/1.4 29'11"		f/2 20'11"		f/2.8 14'11"		f/4 10'6"		f/5.6 7'6"		f/8 5'3"		f/11 3'10"		f/16 2'7"		f/22 1'11"	
FOCUS (feet)	NEAR	FAR	NEAR	FAR	NEAR	FAR	NEAR	FAR	NEAR	FAR	NEAR	FAR	NEAR	FAR	NEAR	FAR	NEAR	FAR
2	1'11"	2'2"	1'10"	2'2"	1'9"	2'4"	1'8"	2'5"	1'7"	2'8"	1'6"	3'2"	1'4"	4'1"	1'2"	7'9"	1'0"	INF
2½	2'4"	2'9"	2'3"	2'10"	2'2"	3'0"	2'0"	3'3"	1'11"	3'9"	1'8"	4'8"	1'6"	7'0"	1'4"	INF	1'1"	INF
3	2'9"	3'4"	2'8"	3'6"	2'6"	3'9"	2'4"	4'2"	2'2"	4'11"	1'11"	6'10"	1'8"	13'3"	1'5"	INF	1'2"	INF
3½	3'2"	3'11"	3'0"	4'2"	2'10"	4'7"	2'8"	5'3"	2'5"	6'6"	2'1"	10'3"	1'10"	INF	1'6"	INF	1'3"	INF
4	3'6"	4'7"	3'4"	4'11"	3'2"	5'5"	2'11"	6'5"	2'7"	8'6"	2'3"	16'3"	2'0"	INF	1'7"	INF	1'4"	INF
4½	3'11"	5'3"	3'9"	5'9"	3'6"	6'5"	3'2"	7'10"	2'10"	11'1"	2'5"	29'9"	2'1"	INF	1'8"	INF	1'4"	INF
5	4'3"	6'0"	4'1"	6'7"	3'9"	7'6"	3'5"	9'6"	3'0"	14'9"	2'7"	INF	2'2"	INF	1'9"	INF	1'5"	INF
5½	4'8"	6'9"	4'4"	7'5"	4'0"	8'8"	3'7"	11'6"	3'2"	20'3"	2'8"	INF	2'3"	INF	1'9"	INF	1'5"	INF
6	5'0"	7'6"	4'8"	8'5"	4'4"	9'11"	3'10"	13'11"	3'4"	29'3"	2'10"	INF	2'4"	INF	1'10"	INF	1'5"	INF

F-Stop									
6½	5' 4" / 8' 3"	5' 0" / 9' 5"	4' 7" / 11' 5"	4' 0" / 16' 11"	3' 6" / INF	2' 11" / INF	2' 5" / INF	1' 11" / INF	1' 6" / INF
7	5' 8" / 9' 1"	5' 3" / 10' 6"	4' 9" / 13' 1"	4' 2" / 20' 10"	3' 8" / INF	3' 0" / INF	2' 6" / INF	1' 11" / INF	1' 6" / INF
8	6' 4" / 10' 11"	5' 10" / 12' 11"	5' 3" / 17' 1"	4' 7" / 33' 2"	3' 11" / INF	3' 2" / INF	2' 7" / INF	2' 0" / INF	1' 7" / INF
9	6' 11" / 12' 10"	6' 4" / 15' 9"	5' 8" / 22' 5"	4' 10" / 61' 11"	4' 1" / INF	3' 4" / INF	2' 8" / INF	2' 0" / INF	1' 7" / INF
10	7' 6" / 15' 0"	6' 9" / 19' 1"	6' 0" / 29' 10"	5' 2" / INF	4' 3" / INF	3' 5" / INF	2' 9" / INF	2' 1" / INF	1' 7" / INF
12	8' 7" / 20' 0"	7' 8" / 27' 11"	6' 8" / 59' 8"	5' 7" / INF	4' 7" / INF	3' 8" / INF	2' 11" / INF	2' 2" / INF	1' 8" / INF
14	9' 7" / 26' 3"	8' 5" / 41' 11"	7' 3" / INF	6' 0" / INF	4' 11" / INF	3' 10" / INF	3' 0" / INF	2' 3" / INF	1' 8" / INF
16	10' 5" / 34' 3"	9' 1" / 67' 2"	7' 9" / INF	6' 4" / INF	5' 1" / INF	3' 11" / INF	3' 1" / INF	2' 3" / INF	1' 8" / INF
18	11' 3" / 45' 0"	9' 8" / 126' 3"	8' 2" / INF	6' 8" / INF	5' 4" / INF	4' 1" / INF	3' 2" / INF	2' 3" / INF	1' 9" / INF
20	12' 0" / 60' 1"	10' 3" / INF	8' 7" / INF	6' 11" / INF	5' 5" / INF	4' 2" / INF	3' 2" / INF	2' 4" / INF	1' 9" / INF
25	13' 8" / 150' 11"	11' 5" / INF	9' 4" / INF	7' 5" / INF	5' 9" / INF	4' 4" / INF	3' 4" / INF	2' 4" / INF	1' 9" / INF
50	18' 9" / INF	14' 9" / INF	11' 6" / INF	8' 8" / INF	6' 6" / INF	4' 9" / INF	3' 6" / INF	2' 6" / INF	1' 10" / INF

For circle of confusion = .0005 use depth data two columns left of chosen F-Stop.

20mm — ALL FORMATS DEPTH OF FIELD TABLE

CIRCLE OF CONFUSION=0.0010 inches

FOCUS (feet)	f/1.4 36'11" NEAR / FAR	f/2 25'10" NEAR / FAR	f/2.8 18'5" NEAR / FAR	f/4 12'11" NEAR / FAR	f/5.6 9'3" NEAR / FAR	f/8 6'6" NEAR / FAR	f/11 4'8" NEAR / FAR	f/16 3'3" NEAR / FAR	f/22 2'4" NEAR / FAR
2	1'11" / 2'1"	1'10" / 2'2"	1'10" / 2'3"	1'9" / 2'4"	1'8" / 2'6"	1'6" / 2'10"	1'5" / 3'5"	1'3" / 5'0"	1'1" / 11'4"
2½	2'4" / 2'8"	2'3" / 2'9"	2'3" / 2'11"	2'1" / 3'1"	2'0" / 3'5"	1'10" / 4'0"	1'8" / 5'2"	1'5" / 10'2"	1'3" / INF
3	2'9" / 3'3"	2'8" / 3'5"	2'7" / 3'7"	2'5" / 3'11"	2'3" / 4'5"	2'1" / 5'6"	1'10" / 8'0"	1'7" / INF	1'4" / INF
3½	3'2" / 3'10"	3'1" / 4'0"	2'11" / 4'4"	2'9" / 4'9"	2'7" / 5'7"	2'3" / 7'6"	2'0" / 13'0"	1'8" / INF	1'5" / INF
4	3'7" / 4'6"	3'6" / 4'9"	3'4" / 5'1"	3'1" / 5'9"	2'10" / 7'0"	2'6" / 10'3"	2'2" / 24'8"	1'10" / INF	1'6" / INF
4½	4'0" / 5'1"	3'10" / 5'5"	3'8" / 5'11"	3'4" / 6'10"	3'0" / 8'8"	2'8" / 14'4"	2'4" / INF	1'11" / INF	1'7" / INF
5	4'5" / 5'9"	4'2" / 6'2"	3'11" / 6'10"	3'7" / 8'1"	3'3" / 10'9"	2'10" / 21'2"	2'5" / INF	2'0" / INF	1'7" / INF
5½	4'10" / 6'5"	4'7" / 7'0"	4'3" / 7'10"	3'10" / 9'6"	3'6" / 13'5"	3'0" / 34'8"	2'7" / INF	2'1" / INF	1'8" / INF
6	5'2" / 7'2"	4'11" / 7'9"	4'6" / 8'10"	4'1" / 11'1"	3'8" / 16'10"	3'2" / INF	2'8" / INF	2'1" / INF	1'8" / INF

Hyper. Dist.

F-Stop									
6½	1' 9" INF	2' 2" INF	2' 9" INF	3' 3" INF	3' 10" 21' 6"	4' 4" 12' 1"	4' 10" 10' 0"	5' 2" 8' 8"	5' 6" 7' 10"
7	1' 9" INF	2' 3" INF	2' 10" INF	3' 5" INF	4' 0" 28' 2"	4' 7" 15' 1"	5' 1" 11' 3"	5' 6" 9' 7"	5' 11" 8' 7"
8	1' 10" INF	2' 4" INF	3' 0" INF	3' 7" INF	4' 4" 57' 2"	4' 11" 20' 9"	5' 7" 14' 0"	6' 1" 11' 7"	6' 7" 10' 2"
9	1' 10" INF	2' 5" INF	3' 1" INF	3' 9" INF	4' 7" INF	5' 4" 29' 2"	6' 1" 17' 5"	6' 8" 13' 9"	7' 3" 11' 10"
10	1' 11" INF	2' 5" INF	3' 3" INF	3' 11" INF	4' 10" INF	5' 8" 43' 4"	6' 6" 21' 8"	7' 3" 16' 3"	7' 11" 13' 8"
12	2' 0" INF	2' 7" INF	3' 5" INF	4' 3" INF	5' 3" INF	6' 3" INF	7' 3" 34' 0"	8' 2" 22' 4"	9' 1" 17' 9"
14	2' 0" INF	2' 8" INF	3' 6" INF	4' 5" INF	5' 7" INF	6' 9" INF	8' 0" 57' 2"	9' 1" 30' 5"	10' 2" 22' 6"
16	2' 1" INF	2' 8" INF	3' 8" INF	4' 7" INF	6' 1" INF	7' 2" INF	8' 7" 117' 3"	9' 11" 41' 9"	11' 2" 28' 2"
18	2' 1" INF	2' 9" INF	3' 9" INF	4' 9" INF	6' 4" INF	7' 6" INF	9' 2" INF	10' 7" 58' 10"	12' 1" 35' 0"
20	2' 1" INF	2' 9" INF	3' 10" INF	4' 11" INF	6' 9" INF	7' 10" INF	9' 7" INF	11' 3" 87' 7"	13' 0" 43' 6"
25	2' 2" INF	2' 10" INF	4' 0" INF	5' 2" INF	7' 10" INF	8' 6" INF	10' 8" INF	12' 9" INF	14' 11" 77' 1"
50	2' 3" INF	3' 0" INF	4' 4" INF	5' 9" INF		10' 3" INF	13' 6" INF	17' 1" INF	21' 3" INF

For circle of confusion = .0005 use depth data two columns left of chosen F-Stop.

24mm — ALL FORMATS DEPTH OF FIELD TABLE

CIRCLE OF CONFUSION=0.0010 inches

FOCUS (feet)	f/1.4		f/2		f/2.8		f/4		f/5.6		f/8		f/11		f/16		f/22	
Hyper. Dist.	53' 2"		37' 2"		26' 7"		18' 7"		13' 3"		9' 4"		6' 9"		4' 8"		3' 5"	
	NEAR	FAR	NEAR	FAR	NEAR	FAR	NEAR	FAR	NEAR	FAR	NEAR	FAR	NEAR	FAR	NEAR	FAR	NEAR	FAR
2	1' 11"	2' 1"	1' 11"	2' 1"	1' 10"	2' 2"	1' 10"	2' 3"	1' 9"	2' 4"	1' 8"	2' 6"	1' 7"	2' 10"	1' 5"	3' 5"	1' 3"	4' 8"
2½	2' 5"	2' 7"	2' 4"	2' 8"	2' 3"	2' 9"	2' 3"	2' 10"	2' 1"	3' 1"	2' 0"	3' 5"	1' 10"	3' 11"	1' 8"	5' 3"	1' 5"	8' 10"
3	2' 10"	3' 2"	2' 9"	3' 3"	2' 8"	3' 4"	2' 7"	3' 7"	2' 6"	3' 10"	2' 3"	4' 4"	2' 1"	5' 3"	1' 10"	8' 1"	1' 7"	INF
3½	3' 3"	3' 9"	3' 2"	3' 10"	3' 1"	4' 0"	2' 11"	4' 3"	2' 9"	4' 9"	2' 7"	5' 6"	2' 4"	7' 1"	2' 0"	13' 3"	1' 9"	INF
4	3' 9"	4' 4"	3' 7"	4' 6"	3' 6"	4' 8"	3' 4"	5' 1"	3' 1"	5' 8"	2' 10"	6' 11"	2' 6"	9' 6"	2' 2"	25' 6"	1' 10"	INF
4½	4' 2"	4' 11"	4' 0"	5' 1"	3' 10"	5' 5"	3' 8"	5' 11"	3' 5"	6' 9"	3' 1"	8' 7"	2' 9"	13' 0"	2' 4"	INF	1' 11"	INF
5	4' 7"	5' 6"	4' 5"	5' 9"	4' 3"	6' 2"	3' 11"	6' 10"	3' 8"	7' 11"	3' 3"	10' 7"	2' 11"	18' 4"	2' 5"	INF	2' 0"	INF
5½	5' 0"	6' 1"	4' 10"	6' 5"	4' 7"	6' 11"	4' 3"	7' 9"	3' 11"	9' 3"	3' 6"	13' 2"	3' 1"	27' 9"	2' 6"	INF	2' 1"	INF
6	5' 5"	6' 9"	5' 2"	7' 2"	4' 11"	7' 9"	4' 7"	8' 10"	4' 2"	10' 10"	3' 8"	16' 6"	3' 2"	INF	2' 8"	INF	2' 2"	INF

f-stop									
6½	5' 10" / 7' 5"	5' 7" / 7' 10"	5' 3" / 8' 7"	4' 10" / 9' 11"	4' 5" / 12' 7"	3' 10" / 21' 0"	3' 4" / INF	2' 9" / INF	2' 3" / INF
7	6' 2" / 8' 1"	5' 11" / 8' 7"	5' 7" / 9' 6"	5' 1" / 11' 2"	4' 7" / 14' 7"	4' 0" / 27' 4"	3' 6" / INF	2' 10" / INF	2' 4" / INF
8	7' 0" / 9' 5"	6' 7" / 10' 2"	6' 2" / 11' 5"	5' 7" / 13' 11"	5' 0" / 19' 10"	4' 4" / 54' 0"	3' 8" / INF	3' 0" / INF	2' 5" / INF
9	7' 8" / 10' 10"	7' 3" / 11' 10"	6' 9" / 13' 7"	6' 1" / 17' 4"	5' 5" / 27' 5"	4' 7" / INF	3' 11" / INF	3' 1" / INF	2' 6" / INF
10	8' 5" / 12' 4"	7' 11" / 13' 8"	7' 3" / 16' 0"	6' 6" / 21' 5"	5' 9" / 39' 6"	4' 10" / INF	4' 1" / INF	3' 2" / INF	2' 7" / INF
12	9' 10" / 15' 6"	9' 1" / 17' 8"	8' 3" / 21' 9"	7' 4" / 33' 5"	6' 4" / INF	5' 3" / INF	4' 4" / INF	3' 4" / INF	2' 8" / INF
14	11' 1" / 19' 0"	10' 2" / 22' 4"	9' 2" / 29' 5"	8' 0" / 55' 8"	6' 10" / INF	5' 7" / INF	4' 7" / INF	3' 6" / INF	2' 9" / INF
16	12' 4" / 22' 10"	11' 2" / 28' 0"	10' 0" / 39' 11"	8' 7" / 111' 1"	7' 3" / INF	5' 11" / INF	4' 9" / INF	3' 7" / INF	2' 10" / INF
18	13' 6" / 27' 2"	12' 2" / 34' 9"	10' 9" / 55' 4"	9' 2" / INF	7' 8" / INF	6' 2" / INF	4' 11" / INF	3' 8" / INF	2' 10" / INF
20	14' 7" / 32' 0"	13' 0" / 43' 1"	11' 5" / 79' 11"	9' 8" / INF	8' 0" / INF	6' 4" / INF	5' 1" / INF	3' 9" / INF	2' 11" / INF
25	17' 0" / 47' 1"	15' 0" / 75' 9"	12' 11" / INF	10' 8" / INF	8' 8" / INF	6' 10" / INF	5' 4" / INF	3' 11" / INF	3' 0" / INF
50	25' 9" / INF	21' 4" / INF	17' 4" / INF	13' 7" / INF	10' 6" / INF	7' 10" / INF	6' 0" / INF	4' 3" / INF	3' 2" / INF

For circle of confusion = .0005 use depth data two columns left of chosen F-Stop.

25mm — ALL FORMATS DEPTH OF FIELD TABLE

CIRCLE OF CONFUSION=0.0010 inches

FOCUS (feet)		f/1.4	f/2	f/2.8	f/4	f/5.6	f/8	f/11	f/16	f/22
Hyper. Dist.		57' 8"	40' 4"	28' 10"	20' 2"	14' 5"	10' 1"	7' 4"	5' 1"	3' 8"
2	NEAR	1' 11"	1' 11"	1' 11"	1' 10"	1' 9"	1' 8"	1' 7"	1' 5"	1' 4"
	FAR	2' 1"	2' 1"	2' 2"	2' 3"	2' 4"	2' 6"	2' 8"	3' 3"	4' 2"
2½	NEAR	2' 5"	2' 4"	2' 4"	2' 3"	2' 2"	2' 0"	1' 11"	1' 8"	1' 6"
	FAR	2' 7"	2' 8"	2' 9"	2' 10"	3' 0"	3' 3"	3' 9"	4' 10"	7' 4"
3	NEAR	2' 10"	2' 10"	2' 9"	2' 7"	2' 6"	2' 4"	2' 2"	1' 11"	1' 8"
	FAR	3' 2"	3' 3"	3' 4"	3' 6"	3' 9"	4' 3"	5' 0"	7' 1"	14' 8"
3½	NEAR	3' 4"	3' 3"	3' 2"	3' 0"	2' 10"	2' 7"	2' 5"	2' 1"	1' 10"
	FAR	3' 9"	3' 10"	4' 0"	4' 3"	4' 7"	5' 4"	6' 7"	10' 10"	INF
4	NEAR	3' 9"	3' 8"	3' 6"	3' 4"	3' 2"	2' 11"	2' 7"	2' 3"	1' 11"
	FAR	4' 3"	4' 5"	4' 8"	5' 0"	5' 6"	6' 6"	8' 7"	17' 11"	INF
4½	NEAR	4' 2"	4' 1"	3' 11"	3' 8"	3' 5"	3' 2"	2' 10"	2' 5"	2' 1"
	FAR	4' 10"	5' 1"	5' 4"	5' 9"	6' 6"	8' 0"	11' 4"	INF	INF
5	NEAR	4' 7"	4' 5"	4' 3"	4' 0"	3' 9"	3' 4"	3' 0"	2' 6"	2' 2"
	FAR	5' 6"	5' 8"	6' 0"	6' 7"	7' 7"	9' 9"	15' 2"	INF	INF
5½	NEAR	5' 0"	4' 10"	4' 8"	4' 4"	4' 0"	3' 7"	3' 2"	2' 8"	2' 3"
	FAR	6' 1"	6' 4"	6' 9"	7' 6"	8' 10"	11' 11"	21' 0"	INF	INF
6	NEAR	5' 5"	5' 3"	5' 0"	4' 8"	4' 3"	3' 9"	3' 4"	2' 9"	2' 4"
	FAR	6' 8"	7' 0"	7' 7"	8' 6"	10' 2"	14' 6"	31' 0"	INF	INF

f								
6½	5' 10" 7' 4"	5' 7" 7' 9"	5' 4" 8' 4"	4' 11" 9' 6"	4' 6" 11' 9"	4' 0" 17' 10"	3' 6" INF	2' 10" INF	2' 4" INF
7	6' 3" 7' 11"	6' 0" 8' 5"	5' 8" 9' 3"	5' 3" 10' 8"	4' 9" 13' 6"	4' 2" 22' 3"	3' 7" INF	2' 11" INF	2' 5" INF
8	7' 0" 9' 3"	6' 8" 9' 11"	6' 3" 11' 0"	5' 9" 13' 2"	5' 2" 17' 9"	4' 6" 37' 2"	3' 10" INF	3' 1" INF	2' 6" INF
9	7' 10" 10' 8"	7' 4" 11' 7"	6' 10" 13' 0"	6' 3" 16' 2"	5' 7" 23' 7"	4' 9" INF	4' 1" INF	3' 3" INF	2' 7" INF
10	8' 6" 12' 1"	8' 0" 13' 3"	7' 5" 15' 3"	6' 8" 19' 8"	5' 11" 32' 1"	5' 1" INF	4' 3" INF	3' 4" INF	2' 8" INF
12	9' 11" 15' 2"	9' 3" 17' 0"	8' 6" 20' 5"	7' 7" 29' 4"	6' 7" 69' 3"	5' 6" INF	4' 7" INF	3' 7" INF	2' 10" INF
14	11' 3" 18' 5"	10' 5" 21' 4"	9' 5" 27' 1"	8' 3" 45' 1"	7' 1" INF	5' 11" INF	4' 10" INF	3' 9" INF	2' 11" INF
16	12' 6" 22' 1"	11' 6" 26' 5"	10' 4" 35' 9"	8' 11" 75' 9"	7' 7" INF	6' 2" INF	5' 1" INF	3' 10" INF	3' 0" INF
18	13' 9" 26' 1"	12' 6" 32' 4"	11' 1" 47' 7"	9' 6" INF	8' 0" INF	6' 6" INF	5' 3" INF	3' 11" INF	3' 1" INF
20	14' 10" 30' 7"	13' 5" 39' 6"	11' 10" 64' 8"	10' 1" INF	8' 5" INF	6' 9" INF	5' 5" INF	4' 1" INF	3' 1" INF
25	17' 5" 44' 0"	15' 5" 65' 4"	13' 5" 184' 2"	11' 2" INF	9' 2" INF	7' 2" INF	5' 8" INF	4' 3" INF	3' 3" INF
50	26' 10" 372' 3"	22' 4" INF/	18' 4" INF	14' 5" INF	11' 2" INF	8' 5" INF	6' 5" INF	4' 7" INF	3' 5" INF

For circle of confusion = .0005 use depth data two columns left of chosen F-Stop.

28mm — ALL FORMATS DEPTH OF FIELD TABLE

CIRCLE OF CONFUSION=0.0010 inches

FOCUS (feet)	f/1.4 — 72' 4" NEAR / FAR	f/2 — 50' 8" NEAR / FAR	f/2.8 — 36' 2" NEAR / FAR	f/4 — 25' 4" NEAR / FAR	f/5.6 — 18' 1" NEAR / FAR	f/8 — 12' 8" NEAR / FAR	f/11 — 9' 2" NEAR / FAR	f/16 — 6' 4" NEAR / FAR	f/22 — 4' 7" NEAR / FAR
2	1' 11" / 2' 1"	1' 11" / 2' 1"	1' 11" / 2' 1"	1' 10" / 2' 2"	1' 10" / 2' 3"	1' 9" / 2' 4"	1' 8" / 2' 6"	1' 6" / 2' 10"	1' 5" / 3' 5"
2½	2' 5" / 2' 7"	2' 5" / 2' 7"	2' 4" / 2' 8"	2' 3" / 2' 9"	2' 2" / 2' 11"	2' 1" / 3' 1"	2' 0" / 3' 5"	1' 10" / 4' 0"	1' 8" / 5' 3"
3	2' 11" / 3' 2"	2' 10" / 3' 2"	2' 9" / 3' 3"	2' 8" / 3' 5"	2' 7" / 3' 7"	2' 5" / 3' 11"	2' 3" / 4' 5"	2' 1" / 5' 7"	1' 10" / 8' 2"
3½	3' 4" / 3' 8"	3' 3" / 3' 9"	3' 2" / 3' 10"	3' 1" / 4' 1"	2' 11" / 4' 4"	2' 9" / 4' 9"	2' 7" / 5' 7"	2' 3" / 7' 7"	2' 0" / 13' 6"
4	3' 10" / 4' 3"	3' 9" / 4' 4"	3' 7" / 4' 6"	3' 6" / 4' 9"	3' 3" / 5' 1"	3' 1" / 5' 9"	2' 10" / 6' 11"	2' 6" / 10' 5"	2' 2" / 26' 6"
4½	4' 3" / 4' 10"	4' 2" / 4' 11"	4' 0" / 5' 1"	3' 10" / 5' 5"	3' 7" / 5' 11"	3' 4" / 6' 11"	3' 1" / 8' 8"	2' 8" / 14' 10"	2' 4" / INF
5	4' 8" / 5' 4"	4' 7" / 5' 6"	4' 5" / 5' 9"	4' 2" / 6' 2"	3' 11" / 6' 10"	3' 7" / 8' 2"	3' 3" / 10' 9"	2' 10" / 22' 3"	2' 5" / INF
5	5' 1" / 5' 11"	5' 0" / 6' 2"	4' 9" / 6' 6"	4' 6" / 7' 0"	4' 3" / 7' 10"	3' 10" / 9' 7"	3' 6" / 13' 4"	3' 0" / 37' 10"	2' 6" / INF
6	5' 7" / 6' 6"	5' 4" / 6' 10"	5' 2" / 7' 2"	4' 10" / 7' 10"	4' 6" / 8' 11"	4' 1" / 11' 3"	3' 8" / 16' 9"	3' 1" / INF	2' 8" / INF

F-Stop									
6½	6' 0" / 7' 2"	5' 9" / 7' 5"	5' 6" / 7' 11"	5' 2" / 8' 8"	4' 10" / 10' 1"	4' 4" / 13' 2"	3' 10" / 21' 5"	3' 3" / INF	2' 9" / INF
7	6' 5" / 7' 9"	6' 2" / 8' 1"	5' 11" / 8' 8"	5' 6" / 9' 8"	5' 1" / 11' 4"	4' 6" / 15' 5"	4' 0" / 28' 1"	3' 4" / INF	2' 10" / INF
8	7' 3" / 9' 0"	6' 11" / 9' 6"	6' 7" / 10' 3"	6' 1" / 11' 8"	5' 7" / 14' 3"	4' 11" / 21' 4"	4' 4" / 56' 9"	3' 7" / INF	2' 11" / INF
9	8' 0" / 10' 3"	7' 8" / 10' 11"	7' 3" / 11' 11"	6' 8" / 13' 11"	6' 0" / 17' 9"	5' 3" / 30' 5"	4' 7" / INF	3' 9" / INF	3' 1" / INF
10	8' 10" / 11' 7"	8' 4" / 12' 5"	7' 10" / 13' 9"	7' 2" / 16' 5"	6' 6" / 22' 1"	5' 7" / 46' 0"	4' 10" / INF	3' 11" / INF	3' 2" / INF
12	10' 4" / 14' 4"	9' 9" / 15' 8"	9' 0" / 17' 11"	8' 2" / 22' 8"	7' 3" / 35' 2"	6' 2" / INF	5' 3" / INF	4' 2" / INF	3' 4" / INF
14	11' 9" / 17' 4"	11' 0" / 19' 4"	10' 1" / 22' 9"	9' 0" / 31' 1"	7' 11" / 60' 8"	6' 8" / INF	5' 7" / INF	4' 5" / INF	3' 6" / INF
16	13' 1" / 20' 6"	12' 2" / 23' 4"	11' 1" / 28' 7"	9' 10" / 43' 1"	8' 6" / INF	7' 1" / INF	5' 10" / INF	4' 7" / INF	3' 7" / INF
18	14' 5" / 23' 11"	13' 4" / 27' 10"	12' 0" / 35' 8"	10' 7" / 61' 6"	9' 1" / INF	7' 5" / INF	6' 1" / INF	4' 8" / INF	3' 8" / INF
20	15' 8" / 27' 7"	14' 4" / 33' 0"	12' 11" / 44' 6"	11' 2" / 93' 7"	9' 6" / INF	7' 9" / INF	6' 4" / INF	4' 10" / INF	3' 9" / INF
25	18' 7" / 38' 2"	16' 9" / 49' 2"	14' 10" / 80' 4"	12' 7" / INF	10' 6" / INF	8' 5" / INF	6' 9" / INF	5' 1" / INF	3' 11" / INF
50	29' 7" / 161' 3"	25' 2" / INF	21' 0" / INF	16' 10" / INF	13' 4" / INF	10' 1" / INF	7' 9" / INF	5' 8" / INF	4' 3" / INF

For circle of confusion = .0005 use depth data two columns left of chosen F-Stop.

32mm — ALL FORMATS DEPTH OF FIELD TABLE

CIRCLE OF CONFUSION=0.0010 inches

FOCUS (feet)	f/1.4 (94' 6") NEAR	FAR	f/2 (66' 2") NEAR	FAR	f/2.8 (47' 3") NEAR	FAR	f/4 (33' 1") NEAR	FAR	f/5.6 (23' 7") NEAR	FAR	f/8 (16' 6") NEAR	FAR	f/11 (12' 0") NEAR	FAR	f/16 (8' 3") NEAR	FAR	f/22 (6' 0") NEAR	FAR
2	2' 0"	2' 0"	1' 11"	2' 1"	1' 11"	2' 1"	1' 11"	2' 1"	1' 10"	2' 2"	1' 10"	2' 3"	1' 9"	2' 4"	1' 8"	2' 7"	1' 6"	2' 11"
2½	2' 5"	2' 7"	2' 5"	2' 7"	2' 5"	2' 8"	2' 4"	2' 8"	2' 3"	2' 9"	2' 2"	2' 11"	2' 1"	3' 1"	1' 11"	3' 6"	1' 9"	4' 2"
3	2' 11"	3' 1"	2' 10"	3' 2"	2' 10"	3' 2"	2' 9"	3' 3"	2' 8"	3' 5"	2' 7"	3' 8"	2' 5"	3' 11"	2' 3"	4' 7"	2' 0"	5' 9"
3½	3' 5"	3' 8"	3' 4"	3' 8"	3' 3"	3' 9"	3' 2"	3' 11"	3' 1"	4' 1"	2' 11"	4' 5"	2' 9"	4' 11"	2' 6"	5' 11"	2' 3"	8' 0"
4	3' 10"	4' 2"	3' 9"	4' 3"	3' 8"	4' 4"	3' 7"	4' 6"	3' 5"	4' 9"	3' 3"	5' 3"	3' 0"	5' 11"	2' 9"	7' 7"	2' 5"	11' 4"
4½	4' 4"	4' 9"	4' 3"	4' 10"	4' 1"	5' 0"	4' 0"	5' 2"	3' 10"	5' 6"	3' 7"	6' 2"	3' 4"	7' 1"	2' 11"	9' 7"	2' 7"	16' 9"
5	4' 9"	5' 3"	4' 8"	5' 5"	4' 6"	5' 7"	4' 4"	5' 10"	4' 2"	6' 4"	3' 10"	7' 1"	3' 7"	8' 5"	3' 2"	12' 3"	2' 9"	26' 11"
5½	5' 2"	5' 10"	5' 1"	6' 0"	4' 11"	6' 3"	4' 9"	6' 7"	4' 6"	7' 2"	4' 2"	8' 2"	3' 10"	10' 0"	3' 4"	15' 10"	2' 11"	INF
6	5' 8"	6' 5"	5' 6"	6' 7"	5' 4"	6' 10"	5' 1"	7' 4"	4' 10"	8' 0"	4' 5"	9' 4"	4' 0"	11' 9"	3' 6"	20' 11"	3' 0"	INF

F-Stop									
6½	3' 2" / INF	3' 8" / 28' 9"	4' 3" / 13' 11"	4' 8" / 10' 7"	5' 1" / 8' 11"	5' 5" / 8' 1"	5' 9" / 7' 6"	5' 11" / 7' 2"	6' 1" / 7' 0"
7	3' 3" / INF	3' 10" / 42' 2"	4' 5" / 16' 5"	4' 11" / 12' 0"	5' 5" / 9' 11"	5' 10" / 8' 10"	6' 1" / 8' 2"	6' 4" / 7' 10"	6' 6" / 7' 7"
8	3' 6" / INF	4' 1" / INF	4' 10" / 23' 4"	5' 5" / 15' 4"	6' 0" / 12' 0"	6' 5" / 10' 6"	6' 10" / 9' 7"	7' 2" / 9' 1"	7' 5" / 8' 9"
9	3' 8" / INF	4' 4" / INF	5' 2" / 34' 7"	5' 10" / 19' 6"	6' 6" / 14' 5"	7' 1" / 12' 4"	7' 7" / 11' 1"	7' 11" / 10' 5"	8' 3" / 9' 11"
10	3' 9" / INF	4' 7" / INF	5' 6" / 56' 6"	6' 3" / 24' 11"	7' 1" / 17' 3"	7' 8" / 14' 3"	8' 3" / 12' 8"	8' 8" / 11' 9"	9' 1" / 11' 2"
12	4' 0" / INF	4' 11" / INF	6' 0" / INF	7' 0" / 42' 9"	8' 0" / 24' 2"	8' 10" / 18' 9"	9' 7" / 16' 0"	10' 2" / 14' 8"	10' 8" / 13' 9"
14	4' 3" / INF	5' 3" / INF	6' 6" / INF	7' 7" / 87' 9"	8' 10" / 34' 0"	9' 10" / 24' 2"	10' 10" / 19' 10"	11' 7" / 17' 9"	12' 2" / 16' 5"
16	4' 5" / INF	5' 6" / INF	6' 11" / INF	8' 2" / INF	9' 7" / 48' 11"	10' 10" / 30' 10"	12' 0" / 24' 1"	12' 11" / 21' 1"	13' 8" / 19' 3"
18	4' 6" / INF	5' 8" / INF	7' 3" / INF	8' 8" / INF	10' 3" / 74' 3"	11' 8" / 39' 3"	13' 1" / 29' 0"	14' 2" / 24' 8"	15' 2" / 22' 2"
20	4' 8" / INF	5' 10" / INF	7' 6" / INF	9' 1" / INF	10' 10" / 126' 10"	12' 6" / 50' 3"	14' 1" / 34' 7"	15' 4" / 28' 7"	16' 6" / 25' 4"
25	4' 10" / INF	6' 3" / INF	8' 2" / INF	10' 0" / INF	12' 2" / INF	14' 3" / 101' 2"	16' 4" / 52' 10"	18' 2" / 40' 1"	19' 9" / 33' 11"
50	5' 5" / INF	7' 1" / INF	9' 9" / INF	12' 5" / INF	16' 1" / INF	19' 11" / INF	24' 4" / INF	28' 6" / 203' 8"	32' 9" / 106' 0"

For circle of confusion = .0005 use depth data two columns left of chosen F-Stop.

35mm — ALL FORMATS DEPTH OF FIELD TABLE

CIRCLE OF CONFUSION = 0.0010 inches

FOCUS (feet)	f/1.4 113'0" NEAR	f/1.4 FAR	f/2 79'1" NEAR	f/2 FAR	f/2.8 56'6" NEAR	f/2.8 FAR	f/4 39'7" NEAR	f/4 FAR	f/5.6 28'3" NEAR	f/5.6 FAR	f/8 19'9" NEAR	f/8 FAR	f/11 14'5" NEAR	f/11 FAR	f/16 9'11" NEAR	f/16 FAR	f/22 7'2" NEAR	f/22 FAR
2	2'0"	2'0"	1'11"	2'1"	1'11"	2'1"	1'11"	2'1"	1'10"	2'2"	1'10"	2'3"	1'9"	2'4"	1'8"	2'6"	1'7"	2'9"
2½	2'5"	2'7"	2'5"	2'7"	2'5"	2'7"	2'4"	2'8"	2'4"	2'9"	2'3"	2'10"	2'2"	3'0"	2'0"	3'4"	1'11"	3'9"
3	2'11"	3'1"	2'11"	3'1"	2'10"	3'2"	2'10"	3'3"	2'9"	3'4"	2'7"	3'6"	2'6"	3'9"	2'4"	4'3"	2'2"	5'0"
3½	3'5"	3'7"	3'4"	3'8"	3'4"	3'9"	3'3"	3'10"	3'2"	4'0"	3'0"	4'3"	2'10"	4'7"	2'7"	5'4"	2'5"	6'7"
4	3'10"	4'2"	3'10"	4'2"	3'9"	4'4"	3'8"	4'5"	3'6"	4'8"	3'4"	5'0"	3'2"	5'6"	2'10"	6'7"	2'7"	8'8"
4½	4'4"	4'8"	4'3"	4'9"	4'2"	4'11"	4'1"	5'1"	3'11"	5'4"	3'8"	5'9"	3'5"	6'6"	3'1"	8'1"	2'10"	11'6"
5	4'10"	5'3"	4'9"	5'4"	4'7"	5'6"	4'5"	5'8"	4'3"	6'1"	4'0"	6'8"	3'9"	7'7"	3'4"	9'11"	3'0"	15'7"
5½	5'3"	5'9"	5'2"	5'11"	5'0"	6'1"	4'10"	6'4"	4'7"	6'10"	4'4"	7'7"	4'0"	8'9"	3'7"	12'1"	3'2"	21'11"
6	5'8"	6'4"	5'7"	6'6"	5'5"	6'8"	5'3"	7'1"	5'0"	7'7"	4'7"	8'6"	4'3"	10'2"	3'9"	14'10"	3'4"	33'0"

f-stop									
6½	6'2" / 6'11"	6'0" / 7'1"	5'10" / 7'4"	5'7" / 7'9"	5'4" / 8'5"	4'11" / 9'7"	4'6" / 11'8"	3'11" / 18'4"	3'5" / INF
7	6'7" / 7'5"	6'5" / 7'8"	6'3" / 8'0"	6'0" / 8'6"	5'8" / 9'3"	5'2" / 10'9"	4'9" / 13'5"	4'2" / 23'1"	3'7" / INF
8	7'6" / 8'7"	7'3" / 8'11"	7'0" / 9'4"	6'8" / 10'0"	6'3" / 11'1"	5'9" / 13'4"	5'2" / 17'8"	4'5" / 39'6"	3'10" / INF
9	8'4" / 9'9"	8'1" / 10'2"	7'9" / 10'8"	7'4" / 11'7"	6'10" / 13'2"	6'3" / 16'4"	5'7" / 23'6"	4'9" / INF	4'0" / INF
10	9'2" / 11'0"	8'11" / 11'5"	8'6" / 12'1"	8'0" / 13'4"	7'5" / 15'5"	6'8" / 20'0"	5'11" / 32'0"	5'0" / INF	4'3" / INF
12	10'10" / 13'5"	10'5" / 14'1"	9'11" / 15'2"	9'3" / 17'2"	8'5" / 20'9"	7'6" / 30'1"	6'7" / 69'1"	5'5" / INF	4'6" / INF
14	12'6" / 16'0"	11'11" / 17'0"	11'3" / 18'7"	10'4" / 21'7"	9'5" / 27'6"	8'3" / 47'0"	7'1" / INF	5'10" / INF	4'9" / INF
16	14'0" / 18'7"	13'4" / 20'0"	12'6" / 22'3"	11'5" / 26'9"	10'3" / 36'7"	8'10" / 81'3"	7'7" / INF	6'2" / INF	5'0" / INF
18	15'6" / 21'5"	14'8" / 23'3"	13'8" / 26'4"	12'5" / 32'10"	11'0" / 49'1"	9'5" / INF	8'0" / INF	6'5" / INF	5'2" / INF
20	17'0" / 24'3"	16'0" / 26'9"	14'10" / 30'10"	13'4" / 40'3"	11'9" / 67'6"	10'0" / INF	8'5" / INF	6'8" / INF	5'4" / INF
25	20'6" / 32'1"	19'0" / 36'6"	17'4" / 44'8"	15'4" / 67'5"	13'4" / INF	11'1" / INF	9'2" / INF	7'1" / INF	5'7" / INF
50	34'8" / 89'6"	30'8" / 135'4"	26'7" / INF	22'1" / INF	18'1" / INF	14'2" / INF	11'2" / INF	8'3" / INF	6'4" / INF

For circle of confusion = .0005 use depth data two columns left of chosen F-Stop.

37.5mm — ALL FORMATS DEPTH OF FIELD TABLE

CIRCLE OF CONFUSION=0.0010 inches

FOCUS (feet)	f/1.4 129' 9" NEAR/FAR	f/2 90' 10" NEAR/FAR	f/2.8 64' 10" NEAR/FAR	f/4 45' 5" NEAR/FAR	f/5.6 32' 5" NEAR/FAR	f/8 22' 8" NEAR/FAR	f/11 16' 6" NEAR/FAR	f/16 11' 4" NEAR/FAR	f/22 8' 3" NEAR/FAR
2	2' 0" / 2' 0"	2' 0" / 2' 1"	1' 11" / 2' 1"	1' 11" / 2' 1"	1' 11" / 2' 1"	1' 10" / 2' 2"	1' 10" / 2' 3"	1' 9" / 2' 5"	1' 8" / 2' 7"
2½	2' 5" / 2' 7"	2' 5" / 2' 7"	2' 5" / 2' 7"	2' 5" / 2' 8"	2' 4" / 2' 8"	2' 3" / 2' 10"	2' 2" / 2' 11"	2' 1" / 3' 2"	1' 11" / 3' 6"
3	2' 11" / 3' 1"	2' 11" / 3' 1"	2' 10" / 3' 2"	2' 10" / 3' 2"	2' 9" / 3' 4"	2' 8" / 3' 5"	2' 7" / 3' 8"	2' 5" / 4' 0"	2' 3" / 4' 7"
3½	3' 5" / 3' 7"	3' 4" / 3' 8"	3' 4" / 3' 8"	3' 3" / 3' 9"	3' 2" / 3' 11"	3' 1" / 4' 1"	2' 11" / 4' 5"	2' 8" / 5' 0"	2' 6" / 5' 11"
4	3' 11" / 4' 1"	3' 10" / 4' 2"	3' 9" / 4' 3"	3' 8" / 4' 4"	3' 7" / 4' 7"	3' 5" / 4' 10"	3' 3" / 5' 3"	3' 0" / 6' 1"	2' 9" / 7' 6"
4½	4' 4" / 4' 8"	4' 4" / 4' 9"	4' 3" / 4' 10"	4' 1" / 5' 0"	4' 0" / 5' 2"	3' 9" / 5' 7"	3' 7" / 6' 1"	3' 3" / 7' 4"	2' 11" / 9' 7"
5	4' 10" / 5' 2"	4' 9" / 5' 3"	4' 8" / 5' 5"	4' 6" / 5' 7"	4' 4" / 5' 11"	4' 1" / 6' 4"	3' 10" / 7' 1"	3' 6" / 8' 9"	3' 2" / 12' 3"
5½	5' 3" / 5' 9"	5' 2" / 5' 10"	5' 1" / 6' 0"	4' 11" / 6' 3"	4' 9" / 6' 7"	4' 5" / 7' 2"	4' 2" / 8' 2"	3' 9" / 10' 5"	3' 4" / 15' 9"
6	5' 9" / 6' 3"	5' 8" / 6' 5"	5' 6" / 6' 7"	5' 4" / 6' 11"	5' 1" / 7' 4"	4' 9" / 8' 1"	4' 5" / 9' 4"	3' 11" / 12' 5"	3' 6" / 20' 10"

Hyper. Dist. row (per f-stop): f/1.4 = 129' 9", f/2 = 90' 10", f/2.8 = 64' 10", f/4 = 45' 5", f/5.6 = 32' 5", f/8 = 22' 8", f/11 = 16' 6", f/16 = 11' 4", f/22 = 8' 3"

f-stop									
6½	6' 2" / 6' 10"	6' 1" / 7' 0"	5' 11" / 7' 3"	5' 8" / 7' 7"	5' 5" / 8' 1"	5' 1" / 9' 0"	4' 8" / 10' 7"	4' 2" / 14' 10"	3' 8" / 28' 7"
7	6' 8" / 7' 5"	6' 6" / 7' 7"	6' 4" / 7' 10"	6' 1" / 8' 3"	5' 9" / 8' 11"	5' 4" / 10' 0"	4' 11" / 12' 0"	4' 4" / 17' 9"	3' 10" / 41' 11"
8	7' 7" / 8' 6"	7' 4" / 8' 9"	7' 2" / 9' 1"	6' 10" / 9' 8"	6' 5" / 10' 7"	5' 11" / 12' 3"	5' 5" / 15' 4"	4' 9" / 26' 2"	4' 1" / INF
9	8' 5" / 9' 8"	8' 2" / 10' 0"	7' 11" / 10' 5"	7' 6" / 11' 2"	7' 1" / 12' 5"	6' 6" / 14' 9"	5' 10" / 19' 6"	5' 1" / 41' 3"	4' 4" / INF
10	9' 4" / 10' 10"	9' 0" / 11' 3"	8' 8" / 11' 10"	8' 3" / 12' 9"	7' 8" / 14' 5"	7' 0" / 17' 8"	6' 3" / 24' 11"	5' 4" / INF	4' 7" / INF
12	11' 0" / 13' 3"	10' 7" / 13' 10"	10' 2" / 14' 8"	9' 6" / 16' 3"	8' 9" / 18' 11"	7' 11" / 25' 2"	7' 0" / 42' 9"	5' 10" / INF	4' 11" / INF
14	12' 8" / 15' 8"	12' 2" / 16' 6"	11' 6" / 17' 10"	10' 9" / 20' 2"	9' 10" / 24' 6"	8' 8" / 36' 0"	7' 7" / 87' 8"	6' 4" / INF	5' 3" / INF
16	14' 3" / 18' 3"	13' 7" / 19' 5"	12' 10" / 21' 2"	11' 10" / 24' 7"	10' 9" / 31' 4"	9' 5" / 53' 2"	8' 2" / INF	6' 8" / INF	5' 6" / INF
18	15' 10" / 20' 11"	15' 0" / 22' 5"	14' 1" / 24' 10"	12' 11" / 29' 8"	11' 7" / 40' 1"	10' 1" / 84' 8"	8' 8" / INF	7' 0" / INF	5' 8" / INF
20	17' 4" / 23' 7"	16' 5" / 25' 7"	15' 4" / 28' 10"	13' 11" / 35' 7"	12' 5" / 51' 8"	10' 8" / INF	9' 1" / INF	7' 3" / INF	5' 10" / INF
25	21' 0" / 30' 11"	19' 7" / 34' 5"	18' 1" / 40' 7"	16' 2" / 55' 3"	14' 2" / 107' 3"	11' 11" / INF	10' 0" / INF	7' 10" / INF	6' 3" / INF
50	36' 1" / 81' 3"	32' 3" / 110' 11"	28' 3" / 216' 4"	23' 10" / INF	19' 8" / INF	15' 8" / INF	12' 5" / INF	9' 3" / INF	7' 1" / INF

For circle of confusion = .0005 use depth data two columns left of chosen F-Stop.

40mm — ALL FORMATS DEPTH OF FIELD TABLE

CIRCLE OF CONFUSION=0.0010 inches

FOCUS (feet)	f/1.4 147'7" NEAR / FAR	f/2 103'4" NEAR / FAR	f/2.8 73'10" NEAR / FAR	f/4 51'8" NEAR / FAR	f/5.6 36'11" NEAR / FAR	f/8 25'10" NEAR / FAR	f/11 18'9" NEAR / FAR	f/16 12'11" NEAR / FAR	f/22 9'5" NEAR / FAR
2	2'0" / 2'0"	2'0" / 2'0"	1'11" / 2'1"	1'11" / 2'1"	1'11" / 2'1"	1'10" / 2'2"	1'10" / 2'3"	1'9" / 2'4"	1'8" / 2'6"
2½	2'6" / 2'6"	2'5" / 2'7"	2'5" / 2'7"	2'5" / 2'7"	2'4" / 2'8"	2'3" / 2'9"	2'3" / 2'10"	2'1" / 3'1"	2'0" / 3'4"
3	2'11" / 3'1"	2'11" / 3'1"	2'11" / 3'1"	2'10" / 3'2"	2'9" / 3'3"	2'8" / 3'4"	2'7" / 3'6"	2'5" / 3'10"	2'4" / 4'4"
3½	3'5" / 3'7"	3'5" / 3'7"	3'4" / 3'8"	3'3" / 3'9"	3'2" / 3'10"	3'1" / 4'0"	3'0" / 4'3"	2'9" / 4'9"	2'7" / 5'5"
4	3'11" / 4'1"	3'10" / 4'2"	3'10" / 4'3"	3'9" / 4'4"	3'7" / 4'6"	3'6" / 4'8"	3'4" / 5'0"	3'1" / 5'9"	2'10" / 6'10"
4½	4'4" / 4'8"	4'4" / 4'8"	4'3" / 4'9"	4'2" / 4'11"	4'0" / 5'1"	3'10" / 5'5"	3'8" / 5'10"	3'4" / 6'10"	3'1" / 8'5"
5	4'10" / 5'2"	4'9" / 5'3"	4'8" / 5'4"	4'7" / 5'6"	4'5" / 5'9"	4'2" / 6'2"	4'0" / 6'9"	3'8" / 8'0"	3'4" / 10'5"
5½	5'4" / 5'8"	5'3" / 5'10"	5'2" / 5'11"	5'0" / 6'2"	4'10" / 6'5"	4'7" / 6'11"	4'3" / 7'8"	3'11" / 9'5"	3'6" / 12'10"
6	5'9" / 6'3"	5'8" / 6'4"	5'7" / 6'6"	5'5" / 6'9"	5'2" / 7'2"	4'11" / 7'9"	4'7" / 8'9"	4'2" / 11'0"	3'8" / 16'0"

F-Stop									
6½	3' 10" / 20' 2"	4' 4" / 12' 10"	4' 10" / 9' 10"	5' 3" / 8' 8"	5' 7" / 7' 10"	5' 9" / 7' 5"	6' 0" / 7' 1"	6' 1" / 6' 11"	6' 3" / 6' 10"
7	4' 1" / 26' 0"	4' 7" / 14' 11"	5' 2" / 11' 0"	5' 6" / 9' 6"	5' 11" / 8' 7"	6' 2" / 8' 1"	6' 5" / 7' 9"	6' 7" / 7' 6"	6' 8" / 7' 4"
8	4' 4" / 49' 3"	5' 0" / 20' 6"	5' 8" / 13' 9"	6' 2" / 11' 6"	6' 7" / 10' 2"	6' 11" / 9' 5"	7' 3" / 8' 11"	7' 5" / 8' 8"	7' 7" / 8' 5"
9	4' 8" / INF	5' 4" / 28' 9"	6' 1" / 17' 1"	6' 8" / 13' 8"	7' 3" / 11' 10"	7' 8" / 10' 10"	8' 0" / 10' 3"	8' 3" / 9' 10"	8' 6" / 9' 7"
10	4' 11" / INF	5' 8" / 42' 5"	6' 7" / 21' 1"	7' 3" / 16' 2"	7' 11" / 13' 8"	8' 5" / 12' 4"	8' 10" / 11' 7"	9' 2" / 11' 1"	9' 4" / 10' 9"
12	5' 4" / INF	6' 3" / INF	7' 4" / 32' 7"	8' 3" / 22' 2"	9' 1" / 17' 8"	9' 9" / 15' 7"	10' 4" / 14' 4"	10' 9" / 13' 7"	11' 1" / 13' 1"
14	5' 8" / INF	6' 9" / INF	8' 1" / 53' 6"	9' 1" / 30' 3"	10' 2" / 22' 5"	11' 0" / 19' 2"	11' 9" / 17' 3"	12' 4" / 16' 2"	12' 10" / 15' 5"
16	5' 11" / INF	7' 2" / INF	8' 8" / 103' 0"	9' 11" / 41' 6"	11' 2" / 28' 1"	12' 3" / 23' 1"	13' 2" / 20' 5"	13' 10" / 18' 11"	14' 5" / 17' 11"
18	6' 2" / INF	7' 7" / INF	9' 3" / INF	10' 8" / 58' 5"	12' 2" / 34' 11"	13' 4" / 27' 6"	14' 6" / 23' 9"	15' 4" / 21' 9"	16' 1" / 20' 6"
20	6' 5" / INF	7' 11" / INF	9' 9" / INF	11' 4" / 86' 7"	13' 0" / 43' 4"	14' 5" / 32' 6"	15' 9" / 27' 4"	16' 9" / 24' 9"	17' 8" / 23' 1"
25	6' 10" / INF	8' 7" / INF	10' 9" / INF	12' 9" / INF	14' 11" / 76' 8"	16' 11" / 48' 2"	18' 8" / 37' 8"	20' 2" / 32' 11"	21' 5" / 30' 1"
50	7' 11" / INF	10' 3" / INF	13' 8" / INF	17' 1" / INF	21' 3" / INF	25' 5" / INF	29' 10" / 154' 2"	33' 9" / 96' 8"	37' 4" / 75' 6"

For circle of confusion = .0005 use depth data two columns left of chosen F-Stop.

50mm — ALL FORMATS DEPTH OF FIELD TABLE

CIRCLE OF CONFUSION=0.0010 inches

FOCUS (feet)	f/1.4 NEAR	f/1.4 FAR	f/2 NEAR	f/2 FAR	f/2.8 NEAR	f/2.8 FAR	f/4 NEAR	f/4 FAR	f/5.6 NEAR	f/5.6 FAR	f/8 NEAR	f/8 FAR	f/11 NEAR	f/11 FAR	f/16 NEAR	f/16 FAR	f/22 NEAR	f/22 FAR
Hyper. Dist.	230' 8"		161' 6"		115' 4"		80' 9"		57' 8"		40' 4"		29' 4"		20' 2"		14' 8"	
2	2' 0"	2' 0"	2' 0"	2' 0"	2' 0"	2' 0"	1' 11"	2' 1"	1' 11"	2' 1"	1' 11"	2' 1"	1' 11"	2' 2"	1' 10"	2' 2"	1' 9"	2' 3"
2½	2' 6"	2' 6"	2' 6"	2' 6"	2' 5"	2' 7"	2' 5"	2' 7"	2' 5"	2' 7"	2' 4"	2' 8"	2' 4"	2' 9"	2' 3"	2' 10"	2' 2"	3' 0"
3	3' 0"	3' 0"	2' 11"	3' 1"	2' 11"	3' 1"	2' 11"	3' 1"	2' 10"	3' 2"	2' 10"	3' 3"	2' 9"	3' 4"	2' 8"	3' 6"	2' 6"	3' 9"
3½	3' 5"	3' 7"	3' 5"	3' 7"	3' 5"	3' 7"	3' 4"	3' 8"	3' 4"	3' 9"	3' 3"	3' 10"	3' 2"	3' 11"	3' 0"	4' 2"	2' 10"	4' 6"
4	3' 11"	4' 1"	3' 11"	4' 1"	3' 10"	4' 2"	3' 10"	4' 2"	3' 9"	4' 3"	3' 8"	4' 5"	3' 6"	4' 7"	3' 4"	4' 11"	3' 2"	5' 5"
4½	4' 5"	4' 7"	4' 5"	4' 7"	4' 4"	4' 8"	4' 3"	4' 9"	4' 2"	4' 10"	4' 1"	5' 0"	3' 11"	5' 3"	3' 8"	5' 9"	3' 6"	6' 5"
5	4' 11"	5' 1"	4' 10"	5' 2"	4' 10"	5' 3"	4' 9"	5' 4"	4' 7"	5' 5"	4' 6"	5' 8"	4' 4"	6' 0"	4' 0"	6' 7"	3' 9"	7' 5"
5½	5' 5"	5' 8"	5' 4"	5' 8"	5' 3"	5' 9"	5' 2"	5' 11"	5' 0"	6' 1"	4' 10"	6' 4"	4' 8"	6' 9"	4' 4"	7' 6"	4' 0"	8' 8"
6	5' 10"	6' 2"	5' 9"	6' 3"	5' 9"	6' 4"	5' 7"	6' 6"	5' 5"	6' 8"	5' 3"	7' 0"	5' 0"	7' 6"	4' 8"	8' 5"	4' 4"	10' 0"

F-Stop									
6½	6' 4" / 6' 8"	6' 3" / 6' 9"	6' 2" / 6' 11"	6' 0" / 7' 1"	5' 10" / 7' 4"	5' 7" / 7' 9"	5' 4" / 8' 3"	4' 11" / 9' 6"	4' 6" / 11' 5"
7	6' 10" / 7' 3"	6' 9" / 7' 4"	6' 7" / 7' 5"	6' 5" / 7' 8"	6' 3" / 7' 11"	6' 0" / 8' 5"	5' 8" / 9' 1"	5' 3" / 10' 7"	4' 9" / 13' 1"
8	7' 9" / 8' 3"	7' 8" / 8' 5"	7' 6" / 8' 7"	7' 4" / 8' 10"	7' 1" / 9' 3"	6' 8" / 9' 11"	6' 4" / 10' 11"	5' 9" / 13' 1"	5' 3" / 17' 2"
9	8' 8" / 9' 4"	8' 6" / 9' 6"	8' 4" / 9' 9"	8' 1" / 10' 1"	7' 10" / 10' 8"	7' 5" / 11' 6"	6' 11" / 12' 11"	6' 3" / 16' 0"	5' 7" / 22' 7"
10	9' 7" / 10' 5"	9' 5" / 10' 8"	9' 3" / 10' 11"	8' 11" / 11' 5"	8' 7" / 12' 1"	8' 0" / 13' 3"	7' 6" / 15' 0"	6' 9" / 19' 6"	6' 0" / 30' 4"
12	11' 5" / 12' 8"	11' 2" / 12' 11"	10' 11" / 13' 4"	10' 6" / 14' 1"	9' 11" / 15' 1"	9' 3" / 17' 0"	8' 7" / 20' 1"	7' 7" / 29' 0"	6' 8" / 62' 0"
14	13' 2" / 14' 11"	12' 11" / 15' 4"	12' 6" / 15' 11"	11' 11" / 16' 11"	11' 3" / 18' 5"	10' 5" / 21' 4"	9' 6" / 26' 6"	8' 4" / 44' 6"	7' 2" / INF
16	15' 0" / 17' 2"	14' 7" / 17' 9"	14' 1" / 18' 7"	13' 5" / 19' 11"	12' 7" / 22' 1"	11' 6" / 26' 4"	10' 5" / 34' 9"	9' 0" / 74' 4"	7' 8" / INF
18	16' 8" / 19' 6"	16' 3" / 20' 3"	15' 7" / 21' 4"	14' 9" / 23' 1"	13' 9" / 26' 1"	12' 6" / 32' 3"	11' 2" / 45' 10"	9' 7" / INF	8' 2" / INF
20	18' 5" / 21' 11"	17' 10" / 22' 10"	17' 1" / 24' 2"	16' 1" / 26' 6"	14' 11" / 30' 6"	13' 5" / 39' 4"	11' 11" / 61' 8"	10' 1" / INF	8' 6" / INF
25	22' 7" / 28' 0"	21' 8" / 29' 7"	20' 7" / 31' 10"	19' 1" / 36' 1"	17' 6" / 43' 11"	15' 6" / 65' 0"	13' 7" / 162' 4"	11' 2" / INF	9' 3" / INF
50	41' 1" / 63' 9"	38' 2" / 72' 4"	34' 11" / 88' 1"	30' 11" / 130' 8"	26' 10" / 368' 4"	22' 4" / INF	18' 6" / INF	14' 5" / INF	11' 5" / INF

For circle of confusion = .0005 use depth data two columns left of chosen F-Stop.

75mm — ALL FORMATS DEPTH OF FIELD TABLE

CIRCLE OF CONFUSION=0.0010 inches

FOCUS (feet)	f/1.4		f/2		f/2.8		f/4		f/5.6		f/8		f/11		f/16		f/22	
Hyper. Dist.	519' 0"		363' 3"		259' 6"		181' 8"		129' 9"		90' 10"		66' 1"		45' 5"		33' 0"	
	NEAR	FAR	NEAR	FAR	NEAR	FAR	NEAR	FAR	NEAR	FAR	NEAR	FAR	NEAR	FAR	NEAR	FAR	NEAR	FAR
2	2' 0"	2' 0"	2' 0"	2' 0"	2' 0"	2' 0"	2' 0"	2' 0"	2' 0"	2' 0"	2' 0"	2' 0"	1' 11"	2' 1"	1' 11"	2' 1"	1' 11"	2' 1"
2½	2' 6"	2' 6"	2' 6"	2' 6"	2' 6"	2' 6"	2' 6"	2' 6"	2' 5"	2' 7"	2' 5"	2' 7"	2' 5"	2' 7"	2' 5"	2' 8"	2' 4"	2' 8"
3	3' 0"	3' 0"	3' 0"	3' 0"	3' 0"	3' 0"	2' 11"	3' 1"	2' 11"	3' 1"	2' 11"	3' 1"	2' 11"	3' 2"	2' 10"	3' 2"	2' 9"	3' 3"
3½	3' 6"	3' 6"	3' 6"	3' 6"	3' 5"	3' 7"	3' 5"	3' 7"	3' 5"	3' 7"	3' 5"	3' 8"	3' 4"	3' 8"	3' 3"	3' 9"	3' 2"	3' 11"
4	4' 0"	4' 0"	4' 0"	4' 1"	3' 11"	4' 1"	3' 11"	4' 1"	3' 11"	4' 1"	3' 10"	4' 2"	3' 9"	4' 3"	3' 8"	4' 4"	3' 7"	4' 6"
4½	4' 6"	4' 6"	4' 5"	4' 7"	4' 5"	4' 7"	4' 5"	4' 7"	4' 4"	4' 8"	4' 4"	4' 9"	4' 3"	4' 10"	4' 1"	5' 0"	4' 0"	5' 2"
5	4' 11"	5' 1"	4' 11"	5' 1"	4' 11"	5' 1"	4' 10"	5' 2"	4' 10"	5' 2"	4' 9"	5' 3"	4' 8"	5' 5"	4' 6"	5' 7"	4' 4"	5' 10"
5½	5' 5"	5' 7"	5' 5"	5' 7"	5' 5"	5' 7"	5' 4"	5' 8"	5' 3"	5' 9"	5' 2"	5' 10"	5' 1"	6' 0"	4' 11"	6' 3"	4' 9"	6' 6"
6	5' 11"	6' 1"	5' 11"	6' 1"	5' 10"	6' 2"	5' 10"	6' 2"	5' 9"	6' 3"	5' 8"	6' 5"	5' 6"	6' 7"	5' 4"	6' 10"	5' 1"	7' 3"

f	1	2	3	4	5	6	7	8	9
6½	5' 6" / 8' 0"	5' 9" / 7' 6"	5' 11" / 7' 2"	6' 1" / 7' 0"	6' 2" / 6' 10"	6' 3" / 6' 9"	6' 4" / 6' 8"	6' 5" / 6' 7"	6' 5" / 6' 7"
7	5' 10" / 8' 10"	6' 1" / 8' 3"	6' 4" / 7' 10"	6' 6" / 7' 7"	6' 8" / 7' 5"	6' 9" / 7' 3"	6' 10" / 7' 2"	6' 10" / 7' 2"	6' 11" / 7' 1"
8	6' 6" / 10' 5"	6' 10" / 9' 8"	7' 2" / 9' 1"	7' 4" / 8' 9"	7' 7" / 8' 6"	7' 8" / 8' 4"	7' 9" / 8' 3"	7' 10" / 8' 2"	7' 11" / 8' 1"
9	7' 1" / 12' 3"	7' 7" / 11' 2"	7' 11" / 10' 5"	8' 3" / 10' 0"	8' 5" / 9' 8"	8' 7" / 9' 5"	8' 8" / 9' 4"	8' 9" / 9' 3"	8' 10" / 9' 2"
10	7' 9" / 14' 2"	8' 3" / 12' 9"	8' 9" / 11' 9"	9' 0" / 11' 2"	9' 4" / 10' 10"	9' 6" / 10' 7"	9' 8" / 10' 5"	9' 9" / 10' 3"	9' 10" / 10' 2"
12	8' 10" / 18' 8"	9' 6" / 16' 2"	10' 2" / 14' 7"	10' 7" / 13' 9"	11' 0" / 13' 2"	11' 3" / 12' 10"	11' 6" / 12' 7"	11' 7" / 12' 5"	11' 9" / 12' 3"
14	9' 11" / 24' 0"	10' 9" / 20' 1"	11' 7" / 17' 8"	12' 2" / 16' 6"	12' 8" / 15' 8"	13' 0" / 15' 2"	13' 4" / 14' 9"	13' 6" / 14' 7"	13' 8" / 14' 5"
16	10' 10" / 30' 7"	11' 11" / 24' 6"	12' 11" / 21' 0"	13' 8" / 19' 4"	14' 3" / 18' 3"	14' 9" / 17' 6"	15' 1" / 17' 0"	15' 4" / 16' 9"	15' 6" / 16' 6"
18	11' 8" / 38' 11"	12' 11" / 29' 7"	14' 2" / 24' 7"	15' 1" / 22' 4"	15' 10" / 20' 10"	16' 5" / 19' 11"	16' 10" / 19' 4"	17' 2" / 18' 11"	17' 5" / 18' 8"
20	12' 6" / 49' 9"	13' 11" / 35' 5"	15' 5" / 28' 6"	16' 5" / 25' 7"	17' 4" / 23' 7"	18' 0" / 22' 5"	18' 7" / 21' 8"	19' 0" / 21' 2"	19' 3" / 20' 9"
25	14' 3" / 99' 10"	16' 2" / 55' 0"	18' 2" / 40' 0"	19' 8" / 34' 4"	21' 0" / 30' 11"	22' 0" / 28' 11"	22' 10" / 27' 8"	23' 5" / 26' 10"	23' 10" / 26' 3"
50	19' 11" / INF	23' 10" / INF	28' 6" / 202' 8"	32' 4" / 110' 7"	36' 2" / 81' 1"	39' 3" / 68' 10"	41' 11" / 61' 10"	44' 0" / 57' 11"	45' 8" / 55' 4"

For circle of confusion = .0005 use depth data two columns left of chosen F-Stop.

85mm — ALL FORMATS DEPTH OF FIELD TABLE

CIRCLE OF CONFUSION=0.0010 inches

FOCUS (feet)	f/1.4 666' 7" NEAR	FAR	f/2 466' 7" NEAR	FAR	f/2.8 333' 4" NEAR	FAR	f/4 233' 4" NEAR	FAR	f/5.6 166' 8" NEAR	FAR	f/8 116' 8" NEAR	FAR	f/11 84' 10" NEAR	FAR	f/16 58' 4" NEAR	FAR	f/22 42' 5" NEAR	FAR
2	2' 0"	2' 0"	2' 0"	2' 0"	2' 0"	2' 0"	2' 0"	2' 0"	2' 0"	2' 0"	2' 0"	2' 0"	2' 0"	2' 0"	1' 11"	2' 1"	1' 11"	2' 1"
2½	2' 6"	2' 6"	2' 6"	2' 6"	2' 6"	2' 6"	2' 6"	2' 6"	2' 6"	2' 6"	2' 5"	2' 7"	2' 5"	2' 7"	2' 5"	2' 7"	2' 5"	2' 8"
3	3' 0"	3' 0"	3' 0"	3' 0"	3' 0"	3' 0"	3' 0"	3' 0"	2' 11"	3' 1"	2' 11"	3' 1"	2' 11"	3' 1"	2' 10"	3' 2"	2' 10"	3' 2"
3½	3' 6"	3' 6"	3' 6"	3' 6"	3' 6"	3' 6"	3' 5"	3' 7"	3' 5"	3' 7"	3' 5"	3' 7"	3' 4"	3' 8"	3' 4"	3' 8"	3' 3"	3' 9"
4	4' 0"	4' 0"	4' 0"	4' 0"	3' 11"	4' 1"	3' 11"	4' 1"	3' 11"	4' 1"	3' 11"	4' 2"	3' 10"	4' 2"	3' 9"	4' 3"	3' 8"	4' 5"
4½	4' 6"	4' 6"	4' 6"	4' 6"	4' 5"	4' 7"	4' 5"	4' 7"	4' 5"	4' 7"	4' 4"	4' 8"	4' 3"	4' 9"	4' 2"	4' 10"	4' 1"	5' 0"
5	5' 0"	5' 0"	4' 11"	5' 1"	4' 11"	5' 1"	4' 11"	5' 1"	4' 10"	5' 2"	4' 10"	5' 3"	4' 9"	5' 4"	4' 8"	5' 5"	4' 6"	5' 8"
5½	5' 5"	5' 7"	5' 5"	5' 7"	5' 5"	5' 7"	5' 5"	5' 8"	5' 4"	5' 8"	5' 3"	5' 9"	5' 2"	5' 10"	5' 1"	6' 0"	4' 11"	6' 3"
6	5' 11"	6' 1"	5' 11"	6' 1"	5' 11"	6' 1"	5' 10"	6' 2"	5' 10"	6' 3"	5' 9"	6' 4"	5' 7"	6' 5"	5' 6"	6' 8"	5' 3"	6' 11"

f-stop									
6½	6'5" / 6'7"	6'5" / 6'7"	6'5" / 6'7"	6'4" / 6'8"	6'3" / 6'9"	6'2" / 6'10"	6'1" / 7'0"	5'10" / 7'3"	5'8" / 7'7"
7	6'11" / 7'1"	6'11" / 7'1"	6'10" / 7'2"	6'10" / 7'2"	6'9" / 7'4"	6'7" / 7'5"	6'6" / 7'7"	6'3" / 7'11"	6'1" / 8'4"
8	7'11" / 8'1"	7'10" / 8'2"	7'10" / 8'2"	7'9" / 8'3"	7'8" / 8'5"	7'6" / 8'7"	7'4" / 8'10"	7'1" / 9'3"	6'9" / 9'9"
9	8'11" / 9'1"	8'10" / 9'2"	8'9" / 9'3"	8'8" / 9'4"	8'7" / 9'6"	8'4" / 9'9"	8'2" / 10'0"	7'10" / 10'7"	7'6" / 11'4"
10	9'10" / 10'2"	9'10" / 10'3"	9'9" / 10'4"	9'7" / 10'5"	9'5" / 10'7"	9'3" / 10'11"	9'0" / 11'4"	8'7" / 12'0"	8'2" / 13'0"
12	11'10" / 12'3"	11'8" / 12'4"	11'7" / 12'5"	11'5" / 12'8"	11'3" / 12'11"	10'11" / 13'4"	10'7" / 13'11"	10'0" / 15'0"	9'5" / 16'7"
14	13'9" / 14'4"	13'7" / 14'5"	13'5" / 14'7"	13'3" / 14'10"	12'11" / 15'3"	12'6" / 15'10"	12'1" / 16'8"	11'4" / 18'4"	10'7" / 20'8"
16	15'8" / 16'5"	15'6" / 16'7"	15'3" / 16'10"	15'0" / 17'2"	14'7" / 17'8"	14'1" / 18'6"	13'6" / 19'8"	12'7" / 21'11"	11'8" / 25'5"
18	17'6" / 18'6"	17'4" / 18'9"	17'1" / 19'0"	16'9" / 19'6"	16'3" / 20'2"	15'8" / 21'3"	14'11" / 22'9"	13'10" / 25'10"	12'8" / 30'11"
20	19'5" / 20'7"	19'2" / 20'11"	18'11" / 21'3"	18'5" / 21'10"	17'11" / 22'8"	17'1" / 24'1"	16'3" / 26'1"	14'11" / 30'3"	13'8" / 37'5"
25	24'1" / 26'0"	23'9" / 26'5"	23'3" / 27'0"	22'7" / 28'0"	21'9" / 29'4"	20'8" / 31'9"	19'4" / 35'3"	17'7" / 43'5"	15'10" / 59'11"
50	46'6" / 54'0"	45'2" / 56'0"	43'6" / 58'9"	41'3" / 63'6"	38'6" / 71'3"	35'1" / 87'2"	31'6" / 120'9"	27'0" / 338'11"	23'0" / INF

For circle of confusion = .0005 use depth data two columns left of chosen F-Stop.

100mm — ALL FORMATS DEPTH OF FIELD TABLE

CIRCLE OF CONFUSION=0.0010 inches

Hyper. Dist.	f/1.4 INF		f/2 645' 10"		f/2.8 461' 4"		f/4 322' 11"		f/5.6 230' 8"		f/8 161' 6"		f/11 117' 5"		f/16 80' 9"		f/22 58' 9"	
FOCUS (feet)	NEAR	FAR	NEAR	FAR	NEAR	FAR	NEAR	FAR	NEAR	FAR	NEAR	FAR	NEAR	FAR	NEAR	FAR	NEAR	FAR
2	2' 0"	2' 0"	2' 0"	2' 0"	2' 0"	2' 0"	2' 0"	2' 0"	2' 0"	2' 0"	2' 0"	2' 0"	2' 0"	2' 0"	2' 0"	2' 1"	1' 11"	2' 1"
2½	2' 6"	2' 6"	2' 6"	2' 6"	2' 6"	2' 6"	2' 6"	2' 6"	2' 6"	2' 6"	2' 6"	2' 6"	2' 5"	2' 7"	2' 5"	2' 7"	2' 5"	2' 7"
3	3' 0"	3' 0"	3' 0"	3' 0"	3' 0"	3' 0"	3' 0"	3' 0"	3' 0"	3' 0"	2' 11"	3' 1"	2' 11"	3' 1"	2' 11"	3' 1"	2' 10"	3' 2"
3½	3' 6"	3' 6"	3' 6"	3' 6"	3' 6"	3' 6"	3' 6"	3' 6"	3' 5"	3' 7"	3' 5"	3' 7"	3' 5"	3' 7"	3' 4"	3' 8"	3' 4"	3' 8"
4	4' 0"	4' 0"	4' 0"	4' 0"	4' 0"	4' 0"	3' 11"	4' 1"	3' 11"	4' 1"	3' 11"	4' 1"	3' 11"	4' 2"	3' 10"	4' 2"	3' 9"	4' 3"
4½	4' 6"	4' 6"	4' 6"	4' 6"	4' 6"	4' 6"	4' 5"	4' 7"	4' 5"	4' 7"	4' 5"	4' 7"	4' 4"	4' 8"	4' 3"	4' 9"	4' 2"	4' 10"
5	5' 0"	5' 0"	5' 0"	5' 0"	4' 11"	5' 1"	4' 11"	5' 1"	4' 11"	5' 1"	4' 10"	5' 2"	4' 10"	5' 2"	4' 9"	5' 4"	4' 8"	5' 5"
5½	5' 6"	5' 6"	5' 5"	5' 7"	5' 5"	5' 7"	5' 5"	5' 7"	5' 5"	5' 8"	5' 4"	5' 8"	5' 3"	5' 9"	5' 2"	5' 11"	5' 1"	6' 0"
6	6' 0"	6' 0"	5' 11"	6' 1"	5' 11"	6' 1"	5' 11"	6' 1"	5' 10"	6' 2"	5' 10"	6' 3"	5' 9"	6' 4"	5' 7"	6' 5"	5' 6"	6' 8"

6½	6' 5" / 6' 7"	6' 5" / 6' 7"	6' 5" / 6' 7"	6' 5" / 6' 8"	6' 4" / 6' 8"	6' 3" / 6' 9"	6' 2" / 6' 10"	6' 0" / 7' 0"	5' 11" / 7' 3"
7	6' 11" / 7' 1"	6' 11" / 7' 1"	6' 11" / 7' 1"	6' 10" / 7' 2"	6' 10" / 7' 3"	6' 9" / 7' 4"	6' 7" / 7' 5"	6' 6" / 7' 8"	6' 3" / 7' 11"
8	7' 11" / 8' 1"	7' 11" / 8' 1"	7' 10" / 8' 2"	7' 10" / 8' 2"	7' 9" / 8' 3"	7' 8" / 8' 5"	7' 6" / 8' 7"	7' 4" / 8' 10"	7' 1" / 9' 2"
9	8' 11" / 9' 1"	8' 11" / 9' 1"	8' 10" / 9' 2"	8' 9" / 9' 3"	8' 8" / 9' 4"	8' 6" / 9' 6"	8' 5" / 9' 9"	8' 2" / 10' 1"	7' 10" / 10' 7"
10	9' 11" / 10' 1"	9' 10" / 10' 2"	9' 10" / 10' 3"	9' 9" / 10' 4"	9' 7" / 10' 5"	9' 5" / 10' 8"	9' 3" / 10' 11"	8' 11" / 11' 4"	8' 7" / 12' 0"
12	11' 10" / 12' 2"	11' 9" / 12' 3"	11' 8" / 12' 4"	11' 7" / 12' 5"	11' 5" / 12' 8"	11' 2" / 12' 11"	10' 11" / 13' 4"	10' 6" / 14' 0"	10' 0" / 15' 0"
14	13' 10" / 14' 3"	13' 9" / 14' 4"	13' 7" / 14' 5"	13' 5" / 14' 7"	13' 3" / 14' 11"	12' 11" / 15' 4"	12' 6" / 15' 10"	12' 0" / 16' 10"	11' 4" / 18' 3"
16	15' 9" / 16' 3"	15' 7" / 16' 5"	15' 6" / 16' 7"	15' 3" / 16' 10"	15' 0" / 17' 2"	14' 7" / 17' 9"	14' 1" / 18' 6"	13' 5" / 19' 10"	12' 8" / 21' 10"
18	17' 8" / 18' 4"	17' 6" / 18' 6"	17' 4" / 18' 9"	17' 1" / 19' 1"	16' 9" / 19' 6"	16' 3" / 20' 3"	15' 8" / 21' 2"	14' 9" / 23' 1"	13' 10" / 25' 9"
20	19' 7" / 20' 5"	19' 5" / 20' 8"	19' 2" / 20' 11"	18' 10" / 21' 4"	18' 5" / 21' 10"	17' 10" / 22' 9"	17' 2" / 24' 0"	16' 1" / 26' 5"	15' 0" / 30' 1"
25	24' 4" / 25' 8"	24' 1" / 26' 0"	23' 9" / 26' 5"	23' 3" / 27' 1"	22' 7" / 28' 0"	21' 8" / 29' 6"	20' 8" / 31' 8"	19' 2" / 36' 0"	17' 7" / 43' 1"
50	47' 5" / 52' 10"	46' 5" / 54' 2"	45' 2" / 56' 0"	43' 4" / 59' 1"	41' 2" / 63' 9"	38' 3" / 72' 3"	35' 2" / 86' 8"	30' 11" / 130' 0"	27' 1" / 324' 9"

For circle of confusion = .0005 use depth data two columns left of chosen F-Stop.

105mm — ALL FORMATS DEPTH OF FIELD TABLE

CIRCLE OF CONFUSION=0.0010 inches

FOCUS (feet)	f/1.4 NEAR/FAR	f/2 NEAR/FAR	f/2.8 NEAR/FAR	f/4 NEAR/FAR	f/5.6 NEAR/FAR	f/8 NEAR/FAR	f/11 NEAR/FAR	f/16 NEAR/FAR	f/22 NEAR/FAR
Hyper. Dist.	INF	712' 0"	508' 7"	356' 0"	254' 4"	178' 0"	129' 6"	89' 0"	64' 9"
5	5' 0" / 5' 0"	5' 0" / 5' 0"	4' 11" / 5' 1"	4' 11" / 5' 1"	4' 11" / 5' 1"	4' 10" / 5' 2"	4' 10" / 5' 2"	4' 9" / 5' 3"	4' 8" / 5' 5"
5½	5' 6" / 5' 6"	5' 6" / 5' 6"	5' 5" / 5' 7"	5' 5" / 5' 7"	5' 5" / 5' 7"	5' 4" / 5' 8"	5' 3" / 5' 9"	5' 2" / 5' 10"	5' 1" / 6' 0"
6	6' 0" / 6' 0"	5' 11" / 6' 1"	5' 11" / 6' 1"	5' 11" / 6' 1"	5' 10" / 6' 2"	5' 10" / 6' 2"	5' 9" / 6' 3"	5' 8" / 6' 5"	5' 6" / 6' 7"
6½	6' 6" / 6' 6"	6' 5" / 6' 7"	6' 5" / 6' 7"	6' 5" / 6' 7"	6' 4" / 6' 8"	6' 3" / 6' 9"	6' 2" / 6' 10"	6' 1" / 7' 0"	5' 11" / 7' 2"
7	6' 11" / 7' 1"	6' 11" / 7' 1"	6' 11" / 7' 1"	6' 10" / 7' 2"	6' 10" / 7' 2"	6' 9" / 7' 3"	6' 8" / 7' 5"	6' 6" / 7' 7"	6' 4" / 7' 10"
8	7' 11" / 8' 1"	7' 11" / 8' 1"	7' 11" / 8' 1"	7' 10" / 8' 2"	7' 9" / 8' 3"	7' 8" / 8' 4"	7' 7" / 8' 6"	7' 4" / 8' 9"	7' 2" / 9' 1"
9	8' 11" / 9' 1"	8' 11" / 9' 1"	8' 10" / 9' 2"	8' 9" / 9' 3"	8' 8" / 9' 4"	8' 7" / 9' 6"	8' 5" / 9' 8"	8' 2" / 10' 0"	7' 11" / 10' 5"
10	9' 11" / 10' 1"	9' 10" / 10' 2"	9' 10" / 10' 2"	9' 9" / 10' 3"	9' 8" / 10' 5"	9' 6" / 10' 7"	9' 4" / 10' 10"	9' 0" / 11' 3"	8' 8" / 11' 9"
12	11' 10" / 12' 2"	11' 10" / 12' 2"	11' 9" / 12' 3"	11' 7" / 12' 5"	11' 6" / 12' 7"	11' 3" / 12' 10"	11' 0" / 13' 2"	10' 7" / 13' 10"	10' 2" / 14' 8"

14	13'10" / 14'2"	13'9" / 14'3"	13'8" / 14'5"	13'6" / 14'7"	13'3" / 14'10"	13'0" / 15'2"	12'8" / 15'8"	12'2" / 16'6"	11'7" / 17'9"
16	15'9" / 16'3"	15'8" / 16'4"	15'6" / 16'6"	15'4" / 16'9"	15'1" / 17'1"	14'8" / 17'7"	14'3" / 18'2"	13'7" / 19'5"	12'11" / 21'1"
18	17'8" / 18'4"	17'7" / 18'5"	17'5" / 18'8"	17'2" / 18'11"	16'10" / 19'4"	16'5" / 20'0"	15'10" / 20'10"	15'0" / 22'5"	14'2" / 24'9"
20	19'7" / 20'5"	19'6" / 20'7"	19'3" / 20'10"	18'11" / 21'2"	18'7" / 21'8"	18'0" / 22'6"	17'4" / 23'7"	16'5" / 25'8"	15'4" / 28'9"
25	24'5" / 25'7"	24'2" / 25'11"	23'10" / 26'3"	23'5" / 26'10"	22'9" / 27'8"	22'0" / 29'0"	21'0" / 30'11"	19'7" / 34'7"	18'1" / 40'5"
50	47'8" / 52'7"	46'9" / 53'9"	45'7" / 55'5"	43'11" / 58'1"	41'10" / 62'2"	39'1" / 69'4"	36'2" / 81'1"	32'1" / 113'1"	28'4" / 214'8"
75	69'10" / 80'11"	67'11" / 83'9"	65'5" / 87'11"	62'0" / 94'11"	58'0" / 106'2"	52'10" / 129'2"	47'7" / 177'2"	40'9" / 465'3"	34'10" / INF
100	91'1" / 110'10"	87'9" / 116'3"	83'7" / 124'4"	78'2" / 138'10"	71'10" / 164'5"	64'1" / 227'2"	56'6" / 434'4"	47'2" / INF	39'5" / INF
125	111'4" / 142'5"	106'5" / 151'6"	100'5" / 165'7"	92'7" / 192'4"	83'11" / 245'2"	73'6" / 417'1"	63'8" / INF	52'1" / INF	42'9" / INF
150	130'9" / 175'11"	123'11" / 189'11"	115'11" / 212'6"	105'7" / 258'9"	94'5" / 364'6"	81'6" / 941'9"	69'7" / INF	55'11" / INF	45'3" / INF
175	149'4" / 211'3"	140'6" / 231'11"	130'3" / 266'6"	117'5" / 343'6"	103'9" / 558'9"	88'4" / INF	74'6" / INF	59'1" / INF	47'4" / INF
200	167'2" / 248'10"	156'2" / 277'11"	143'7" / 329'3"	128'2" / 455'5"	112'0" / 930'9"	94'3" / INF	78'8" / INF	61'8" / INF	49'0" / INF

For circle of confusion = .0005 use depth data two columns left of chosen F-Stop.

135mm — ALL FORMATS DEPTH OF FIELD TABLE

CIRCLE OF CONFUSION=0.0010 inches

FOCUS (FEET)	f/1.4 NEAR/FAR	f/2 NEAR/FAR	f/2.8 NEAR/FAR	f/4 NEAR/FAR	f/5.6 NEAR/FAR	f/8 NEAR/FAR	f/11 NEAR/FAR	f/16 NEAR/FAR	f/22 NEAR/FAR
Hyper. Dist.	INF	INF	INF	588' 6"	420' 4"	294' 3"	214' 0"	147' 2"	107' 0"
5	5' 0" / 5' 0"	5' 0" / 5' 0"	5' 0" / 5' 0"	5' 0" / 5' 0"	4' 11" / 5' 1"	4' 11" / 5' 1"	4' 11" / 5' 1"	4' 10" / 5' 2"	4' 10" / 5' 3"
5½	5' 6" / 5' 6"	5' 6" / 5' 6"	5' 6" / 5' 6"	5' 5" / 5' 7"	5' 5" / 5' 7"	5' 5" / 5' 7"	5' 4" / 5' 8"	5' 4" / 5' 8"	5' 3" / 5' 9"
6	6' 0" / 6' 0"	6' 0" / 6' 0"	6' 0" / 6' 0"	5' 11" / 6' 1"	5' 11" / 6' 1"	5' 11" / 6' 1"	5' 10" / 6' 2"	5' 9" / 6' 3"	5' 8" / 6' 4"
6½	6' 6" / 6' 6"	6' 6" / 6' 6"	6' 5" / 6' 7"	6' 5" / 6' 7"	6' 5" / 6' 7"	6' 4" / 6' 8"	6' 4" / 6' 8"	6' 3" / 6' 9"	6' 2" / 6' 11"
7	7' 0" / 7' 0"	7' 0" / 7' 0"	6' 11" / 7' 1"	6' 11" / 7' 1"	6' 11" / 7' 1"	6' 10" / 7' 2"	6' 10" / 7' 3"	6' 8" / 7' 4"	6' 7" / 7' 5"
8	8' 0" / 8' 0"	7' 11" / 8' 1"	7' 11" / 8' 1"	7' 11" / 8' 1"	7' 10" / 8' 2"	7' 10" / 8' 3"	7' 9" / 8' 4"	7' 7" / 8' 5"	7' 6" / 8' 7"
9	8' 11" / 9' 1"	8' 11" / 9' 1"	8' 11" / 9' 1"	8' 10" / 9' 2"	8' 10" / 9' 2"	8' 9" / 9' 3"	8' 8" / 9' 4"	8' 6" / 9' 7"	8' 4" / 9' 9"
10	9' 11" / 10' 1"	9' 11" / 10' 1"	9' 11" / 10' 1"	9' 10" / 10' 2"	9' 9" / 10' 3"	9' 8" / 10' 4"	9' 7" / 10' 6"	9' 5" / 10' 8"	9' 2" / 11' 0"
12	11' 11" / 12' 1"	11' 11" / 12' 1"	11' 10" / 12' 2"	11' 9" / 12' 3"	11' 8" / 12' 4"	11' 7" / 12' 6"	11' 5" / 12' 8"	11' 2" / 13' 0"	10' 10" / 13' 5"

14	13' 11" / 14' 1"	13' 10" / 14' 2"	13' 9" / 14' 3"	13' 8" / 14' 4"	13' 7" / 14' 6"	13' 5" / 14' 8"	13' 2" / 14' 11"	12' 10" / 15' 5"	12' 5" / 16' 0"
16	15' 10" / 16' 2"	15' 9" / 16' 3"	15' 9" / 16' 4"	15' 7" / 16' 5"	15' 5" / 16' 7"	15' 2" / 16' 11"	14' 11" / 17' 3"	14' 6" / 17' 11"	14' 0" / 18' 9"
18	17' 10" / 18' 2"	17' 9" / 18' 3"	17' 8" / 18' 5"	17' 6" / 18' 7"	17' 3" / 18' 9"	17' 0" / 19' 2"	16' 8" / 19' 7"	16' 1" / 20' 5"	15' 6" / 21' 6"
20	19' 9" / 20' 3"	19' 8" / 20' 4"	19' 7" / 20' 6"	19' 4" / 20' 8"	19' 1" / 21' 0"	18' 9" / 21' 5"	18' 4" / 22' 0"	17' 8" / 23' 1"	16' 11" / 24' 6"
25	24' 8" / 25' 4"	24' 6" / 25' 6"	24' 3" / 25' 9"	24' 0" / 26' 1"	23' 7" / 26' 7"	23' 1" / 27' 3"	22' 5" / 28' 3"	21' 5" / 30' 0"	20' 4" / 32' 5"
50	48' 7" / 51' 6"	48' 0" / 52' 2"	47' 3" / 53' 2"	46' 1" / 54' 7"	44' 9" / 56' 8"	42' 10" / 60' 2"	40' 7" / 65' 1"	37' 5" / 75' 5"	34' 2" / 93' 2"
75	71' 10" / 78' 6"	70' 6" / 80' 1"	68' 11" / 82' 4"	66' 7" / 85' 11"	63' 8" / 91' 2"	59' 10" / 100' 5"	55' 7" / 115' 1"	49' 9" / 152' 1"	44' 2" / 247' 4"
100	94' 5" / 106' 4"	92' 2" / 109' 3"	89' 5" / 113' 5"	85' 6" / 120' 4"	80' 10" / 131' 0"	74' 9" / 151' 2"	68' 3" / 187' 0"	59' 8" / 309' 3"	51' 10" / INF
125	116' 5" / 135' 0"	113' 0" / 139' 10"	108' 10" / 146' 9"	103' 2" / 158' 7"	96' 5" / 177' 8"	87' 10" / 216' 9"	79' 0" / 299' 1"	67' 8" / 814' 9"	57' 9" / INF
150	137' 9" / 164' 8"	133' 1" / 171' 10"	127' 4" / 182' 5"	119' 7" / 201' 1"	110' 8" / 232' 10"	99' 5" / 305' 0"	88' 4" / 498' 1"	74' 5" / INF	62' 7" / INF
175	158' 6" / 195' 3"	152' 5" / 205' 6"	144' 11" / 220' 10"	135' 0" / 248' 10"	123' 8" / 299' 3"	109' 10" / 430' 2"	96' 5" / 949' 4"	80' 0" / INF	66' 6" / INF
200	178' 9" / 226' 11"	171' 0" / 240' 10"	161' 8" / 262' 3"	149' 4" / 302' 7"	135' 7" / 380' 9"	119' 2" / 621' 5"	103' 6" / INF	84' 11" / INF	69' 10" / INF

For circle of confusion = .0005 use depth data two columns left of chosen F-Stop.

150mm — ALL FORMATS DEPTH OF FIELD TABLE

CIRCLE OF CONFUSION=0.0010 inches

FOCUS (feet)	f/1.4 INF		f/2 INF		f/2.8 726'7"		f/4 519'0"		f/5.6 363'3"		f/8 264'2"		f/11 181'8"		f/16 132'1"		f/22 90'10"	
Hyper. Dist.	NEAR	FAR	NEAR	FAR	NEAR	FAR	NEAR	FAR	NEAR	FAR	NEAR	FAR	NEAR	FAR	NEAR	FAR	NEAR	FAR
5	5' 0"	5' 0"	5' 0"	5' 0"	5' 0"	5' 0"	4' 11"	5' 1"	4' 11"	5' 1"	4' 11"	5' 1"	4' 11"	5' 2"	4' 10"	5' 2"	4' 9"	5' 3"
5½	5' 6"	5' 6"	5' 6"	5' 6"	5' 6"	5' 6"	5' 5"	5' 7"	5' 5"	5' 7"	5' 5"	5' 7"	5' 4"	5' 8"	5' 4"	5' 9"	5' 3"	5' 10"
6	6' 0"	6' 0"	6' 0"	6' 0"	5' 11"	6' 1"	5' 11"	6' 1"	5' 11"	6' 1"	5' 11"	6' 2"	5' 10"	6' 2"	5' 9"	6' 3"	5' 8"	6' 5"
6½	6' 6"	6' 6"	6' 6"	6' 6"	6' 5"	6' 7"	6' 5"	6' 7"	6' 5"	6' 7"	6' 4"	6' 8"	6' 4"	6' 9"	6' 3"	6' 10"	6' 1"	7' 0"
7	7' 0"	7' 0"	6' 11"	7' 1"	6' 11"	7' 1"	6' 11"	7' 1"	6' 11"	7' 2"	6' 10"	7' 2"	6' 9"	7' 3"	6' 8"	7' 4"	6' 6"	7' 6"
8	8' 0"	8' 0"	7' 11"	8' 1"	7' 11"	8' 1"	7' 11"	8' 1"	7' 10"	8' 2"	7' 9"	8' 3"	7' 8"	8' 4"	7' 7"	8' 6"	7' 5"	8' 9"
9	8' 11"	9' 1"	8' 11"	9' 1"	8' 11"	9' 1"	8' 10"	9' 2"	8' 10"	9' 3"	8' 9"	9' 4"	8' 7"	9' 5"	8' 5"	9' 7"	8' 3"	9' 11"
10	9' 11"	10' 1"	9' 11"	10' 1"	9' 10"	10' 2"	9' 10"	10' 2"	9' 9"	10' 3"	9' 8"	10' 4"	9' 6"	10' 7"	9' 4"	10' 9"	9' 1"	11' 2"
12	11' 11"	12' 1"	11' 10"	12' 2"	11' 10"	12' 2"	11' 9"	12' 3"	11' 8"	12' 5"	11' 6"	12' 7"	11' 3"	12' 10"	11' 0"	13' 2"	10' 8"	13' 9"

14	13' 10" 14' 2"	13' 10" 14' 2"	13' 9" 14' 3"	13' 8" 14' 4"	13' 6" 14' 6"	13' 4" 14' 9"	13' 0" 15' 1"	12' 8" 15' 7"	12' 2" 16' 5"
16	15' 10" 16' 2"	15' 9" 16' 3"	15' 8" 16' 4"	15' 6" 16' 6"	15' 4" 16' 9"	15' 1" 17' 0"	14' 9" 17' 6"	14' 4" 18' 2"	13' 8" 19' 4"
18	17' 9" 18' 3"	17' 8" 18' 4"	17' 7" 18' 5"	17' 5" 18' 8"	17' 2" 18' 11"	16' 11" 19' 3"	16' 5" 19' 11"	15' 11" 20' 9"	15' 1" 22' 4"
20	19' 9" 20' 3"	19' 8" 20' 5"	19' 6" 20' 7"	19' 3" 20' 9"	19' 0" 21' 2"	18' 7" 21' 7"	18' 1" 22' 5"	17' 5" 23' 6"	16' 6" 25' 6"
25	24' 7" 25' 5"	24' 5" 25' 7"	24' 2" 25' 10"	23' 10" 26' 3"	23' 5" 26' 10"	22' 11" 27' 7"	22' 0" 28' 11"	21' 1" 30' 8"	19' 8" 34' 3"
50	48' 4" 51' 9"	47' 9" 52' 6"	46' 10" 53' 8"	45' 8" 55' 3"	44' 0" 57' 11"	42' 1" 61' 6"	39' 3" 68' 9"	36' 4" 80' 0"	32' 4" 109' 11"
75	71' 4" 79' 1"	70' 0" 80' 10"	68' 0" 83' 7"	65' 7" 87' 7"	62' 3" 94' 4"	58' 6" 104' 5"	53' 2" 127' 2"	47' 11" 172' 0"	41' 2" 417' 7"
100	93' 7" 107' 4"	91' 3" 110' 7"	87' 11" 115' 10"	83' 11" 123' 9"	78' 6" 137' 9"	72' 8" 160' 5"	64' 7" 221' 2"	57' 0" 405' 3"	47' 9" INF
125	115' 2" 136' 9"	111' 7" 142' 0"	106' 9" 150' 10"	100' 10" 164' 5"	93' 1" 190' 2"	85' 0" 236' 5"	74' 2" 397' 5"	64' 4" INF	52' 9" INF
150	136' 0" 167' 2"	131' 1" 175' 3"	124' 5" 188' 10"	116' 5" 210' 8"	106' 3" 254' 11"	95' 10" 345' 6"	82' 3" 847' 11"	70' 4" INF	56' 8" INF
175	156' 3" 198' 11"	149' 10" 210' 4"	141' 1" 230' 4"	131' 0" 263' 8"	118' 3" 336' 9"	105' 5" 515' 6"	89' 3" INF	75' 5" INF	59' 11" INF
200	175' 10" 231' 10"	167' 9" 247' 7"	156' 11" 275' 8"	144' 6" 324' 11"	129' 1" 443' 8"	113' 11" 816' 9"	95' 4" INF	79' 8" INF	62' 7" INF

For circle of confusion = .0005 use depth data two columns left of chosen F-Stop.

200mm — ALL FORMATS DEPTH OF FIELD TABLE

CIRCLE OF CONFUSION=0.0010 inches

FOCUS (feet)	f/1.4 INF NEAR/FAR	f/2 INF NEAR/FAR	f/2.8 INF NEAR/FAR	f/4 INF NEAR/FAR	f/5.6 645' 10" NEAR/FAR	f/8 469' 8" NEAR/FAR	f/11 322' 11" NEAR/FAR	f/16 234' 10" NEAR/FAR	f/22 161' 6" NEAR/FAR
5	5'0" / 5'0"	5'0" / 5'0"	5'0" / 5'0"	5'0" / 5'0"	5'0" / 5'0"	4'11" / 5'1"	4'11" / 5'1"	4'11" / 5'1"	4'10" / 5'2"
5½	5'6" / 5'6"	5'6" / 5'6"	5'6" / 5'6"	5'6" / 5'6"	5'6" / 5'6"	5'5" / 5'7"	5'5" / 5'7"	5'5" / 5'7"	5'4" / 5'8"
6	6'0" / 6'0"	6'0" / 6'0"	6'0" / 6'0"	6'0" / 6'0"	5'11" / 6'1"	5'11" / 6'1"	5'11" / 6'1"	5'10" / 6'2"	5'10" / 6'2"
6½	6'6" / 6'6"	6'6" / 6'6"	6'6" / 6'6"	6'6" / 6'6"	6'5" / 6'7"	6'5" / 6'7"	6'5" / 6'7"	6'4" / 6'8"	6'3" / 6'9"
7	7'0" / 7'0"	7'0" / 7'0"	7'0" / 7'0"	6'11" / 7'1"	6'11" / 7'1"	6'11" / 7'1"	6'10" / 7'2"	6'10" / 7'2"	6'9" / 7'3"
8	8'0" / 8'0"	8'0" / 8'0"	7'11" / 8'1"	7'11" / 8'1"	7'11" / 8'1"	7'11" / 8'2"	7'10" / 8'2"	7'9" / 8'3"	7'8" / 8'5"
9	9'0" / 9'0"	9'0" / 9'0"	8'11" / 9'1"	8'11" / 9'1"	8'11" / 9'1"	8'10" / 9'2"	8'9" / 9'3"	8'8" / 9'4"	8'7" / 9'6"
10	10'0" / 10'0"	9'11" / 10'1"	9'11" / 10'1"	9'11" / 10'1"	9'10" / 10'2"	9'10" / 10'2"	9'9" / 10'4"	9'7" / 10'5"	9'5" / 10'7"
12	11'11" / 12'1"	11'11" / 12'1"	11'11" / 12'1"	11'10" / 12'2"	11'10" / 12'3"	11'9" / 12'4"	11'7" / 12'5"	11'5" / 12'7"	11'3" / 12'11"

14	13' 11" / 14' 1"	13' 11" / 14' 1"	13' 10" / 14' 2"	13' 10" / 14' 2"	13' 9" / 14' 4"	13' 7" / 14' 5"	13' 5" / 14' 7"	13' 3" / 14' 10"	12' 11" / 15' 3"
16	15' 11" / 16' 1"	15' 10" / 16' 2"	15' 10" / 16' 2"	15' 9" / 16' 3"	15' 8" / 16' 5"	15' 6" / 16' 6"	15' 3" / 16' 10"	15' 0" / 17' 1"	14' 7" / 17' 8"
18	17' 11" / 18' 1"	17' 10" / 18' 2"	17' 9" / 18' 3"	17' 8" / 18' 4"	17' 6" / 18' 6"	17' 4" / 18' 8"	17' 1" / 19' 0"	16' 9" / 19' 5"	16' 3" / 20' 2"
20	19' 10" / 20' 2"	19' 10" / 20' 3"	19' 8" / 20' 4"	19' 7" / 20' 5"	19' 5" / 20' 7"	19' 3" / 20' 10"	18' 10" / 21' 3"	18' 6" / 21' 10"	17' 10" / 22' 9"
25	24' 9" / 25' 3"	24' 8" / 25' 4"	24' 6" / 25' 6"	24' 4" / 25' 8"	24' 1" / 26' 0"	23' 9" / 26' 4"	23' 3" / 27' 0"	22' 8" / 27' 11"	21' 9" / 29' 5"
50	49' 1" / 51' 0"	48' 8" / 51' 4"	48' 2" / 52' 0"	47' 6" / 52' 10"	46' 5" / 54' 2"	45' 3" / 55' 10"	43' 4" / 59' 0"	41' 4" / 63' 4"	38' 4" / 72' 0"
75	72' 11" / 77' 3"	72' 1" / 78' 2"	70' 11" / 79' 7"	69' 5" / 81' 7"	67' 3" / 84' 9"	64' 9" / 89' 1"	61' 0" / 97' 5"	57' 0" / 109' 9"	51' 4" / 139' 0"
100	96' 4" / 104' 0"	94' 11" / 105' 8"	92' 10" / 108' 4"	90' 3" / 112' 1"	86' 8" / 118' 2"	82' 7" / 126' 10"	76' 6" / 144' 5"	70' 3" / 173' 4"	61' 11" / 259' 11"
125	119' 3" / 131' 4"	117' 1" / 134' 0"	114' 0" / 138' 4"	110' 2" / 144' 6"	104' 10" / 154' 10"	98' 10" / 170' 0"	90' 3" / 203' 3"	81' 9" / 265' 8"	70' 7" / 543' 9"
150	141' 10" / 159' 2"	138' 9" / 163' 3"	134' 5" / 169' 7"	129' 1" / 179' 0"	121' 10" / 195' 1"	113' 10" / 219' 11"	102' 7" / 279' 1"	91' 8" / 412' 0"	77' 11" / INF
175	163' 11" / 187' 8"	159' 11" / 193' 3"	154' 2" / 202' 4"	147' 2" / 215' 9"	137' 10" / 239' 9"	127' 8" / 278' 4"	113' 8" / 380' 4"	100' 5" / 679' 3"	84' 2" / INF
200	185' 8" / 216' 9"	180' 6" / 224' 3"	173' 3" / 236' 6"	164' 6" / 255' 1"	152' 10" / 289' 4"	140' 5" / 347' 6"	123' 8" / 522' 8"	108' 2" / 1322' 11"	89' 6" / INF

For circle of confusion = .0005 use depth data two columns left of chosen F-Stop.

300mm — ALL FORMATS DEPTH OF FIELD TABLE

CIRCLE OF CONFUSION=0.0010 inches

Cell values shown as NEAR / FAR.

FOCUS (feet)	f/2	f/2.8	f/4	f/5.6	f/8	f/11	f/16	f/22	f/32
Hyper. Dist.	INF	INF	INF	INF	INF	INF	INF	INF	363' 3"
10	10'0" / 10'0"	10'0" / 10'0"	10'0" / 10'0"	9'11" / 10'1"	9'11" / 10'1"	9'11" / 10'1"	9'11" / 10'2"	9'10" / 10'2"	9'9" / 10'3"
12	12'0" / 12'0"	12'0" / 12'0"	11'11" / 12'1"	11'11" / 12'1"	11'11" / 12'1"	11'11" / 12'2"	11'10" / 12'2"	11'9" / 12'3"	11'8" / 12'5"
14	14'0" / 14'0"	13'11" / 14'1"	13'11" / 14'1"	13'11" / 14'1"	13'11" / 14'2"	13'10" / 14'2"	13'9" / 14'3"	13'8" / 14'4"	13'6" / 14'6"
16	16'0" / 16'0"	15'11" / 16'1"	15'11" / 16'1"	15'11" / 16'1"	15'10" / 16'2"	15'9" / 16'3"	15'8" / 16'4"	15'7" / 16'6"	15'4" / 16'8"
18	17'11" / 18'1"	17'11" / 18'1"	17'11" / 18'1"	17'10" / 18'2"	17'9" / 18'3"	17'9" / 18'4"	17'7" / 18'5"	17'5" / 18'7"	17'2" / 18'11"
20	19'11" / 20'1"	19'11" / 20'1"	19'10" / 20'2"	19'10" / 20'2"	19'9" / 20'3"	19'8" / 20'4"	19'6" / 20'6"	19'4" / 20'9"	19'0" / 21'1"
25	24'11" / 25'1"	24'10" / 25'2"	24'10" / 25'2"	24'9" / 25'4"	24'7" / 25'5"	24'5" / 25'7"	24'2" / 25'10"	23'11" / 26'2"	23'5" / 26'9"
50	49'7" / 50'5"	49'5" / 50'7"	49'2" / 50'10"	48'10" / 51'3"	48'4" / 51'9"	47'9" / 52'5"	46'10" / 53'7"	45'9" / 55'1"	44'1" / 57'10"

	1	2	3	4	5	6	7	8	9
75	74' 1" / 76' 0"	73' 8" / 76' 4"	73' 2" / 77' 0"	72' 5" / 77' 9"	71' 4" / 79' 0"	70' 1" / 80' 8"	68' 1" / 83' 6"	65' 9" / 87' 3"	62' 4" / 94' 2"
100	98' 4" / 101' 9"	97' 8" / 102' 5"	96' 8" / 103' 6"	95' 5" / 105' 0"	93' 7" / 107' 4"	91' 5" / 110' 4"	88' 0" / 115' 9"	84' 3" / 123' 1"	78' 7" / 137' 6"
125	122' 5" / 127' 9"	121' 4" / 128' 10"	119' 11" / 130' 7"	117' 11" / 132' 11"	115' 2" / 136' 8"	111' 10" / 141' 7"	106' 9" / 150' 9"	101' 3" / 163' 4"	93' 2" / 189' 9"
150	146' 3" / 153' 11"	144' 10" / 155' 7"	142' 8" / 158' 1"	139' 11" / 161' 7"	136' 1" / 167' 2"	131' 6" / 174' 7"	124' 6" / 188' 8"	117' 0" / 208' 11"	106' 4" / 254' 4"
175	169' 11" / 180' 5"	168' 0" / 182' 8"	165' 1" / 186' 2"	161' 6" / 191' 0"	156' 3" / 198' 10"	150' 3" / 209' 6"	141' 2" / 230' 1"	131' 8" / 260' 11"	118' 4" / 335' 11"
200	193' 5" / 207' 1"	190' 10" / 210' 1"	187' 2" / 214' 8"	182' 6" / 221' 2"	175' 11" / 231' 9"	168' 4" / 246' 5"	157' 0" / 275' 5"	145' 3" / 320' 10"	129' 3" / 442' 4"
250	239' 9" / 261' 2"	235' 10" / 265' 11"	230' 3" / 273' 5"	223' 3" / 284' 1"	213' 5" / 301' 8"	202' 4" / 327' 1"	186' 2" / 380' 4"	169' 11" / 472' 10"	148' 4" / 794' 10"
300	285' 4" / 316' 3"	279' 10" / 323' 3"	272' 0" / 334' 5"	262' 3" / 350' 6"	248' 10" / 377' 9"	233' 10" / 418' 4"	212' 6" / 509' 10"	191' 7" / 691' 1"	164' 7" / 1695' 10"
350	330' 2" / 372' 4"	322' 10" / 382' 1"	312' 6" / 397' 9"	299' 7" / 420' 9"	282' 3" / 460' 8"	263' 1" / 522' 7"	236' 5" / 673' 7"' 1"	210' 9" / 030' 11"	178' 6" / INF
400	374' 4" / 429' 6"	364' 11" / 442' 6"	351' 9" / 463' 8"	335' 6" / 495' 2"	313' 10" / 551' 5"	290' 4" / 642' 8"	258' 2" / 887' 3"' 1"	227' 11" / 633' 6"	190' 7" / INF

For circle of confusion = .0005 use depth data two columns left of chosen F-Stop.

400mm — ALL FORMATS DEPTH OF FIELD TABLE

CIRCLE OF CONFUSION=0.0010 inches

FOCUS (feet)	Hyper. Dist. f/2 INF NEAR/FAR	f/2.8 INF NEAR/FAR	f/4 INF NEAR/FAR	f/5.6 INF NEAR/FAR	f/8 INF NEAR/FAR	f/11 INF NEAR/FAR	f/16 INF NEAR/FAR	f/22 INF NEAR/FAR	f/32 INF NEAR/FAR
10	10' 0" / 10' 0"	10' 0" / 10' 0"	10' 0" / 10' 0"	10' 0" / 10' 0"	10' 0" / 10' 0"	9' 11" / 10' 1"	9' 11" / 10' 1"	9' 11" / 10' 1"	9' 10" / 10' 2"
12	12' 0" / 12' 0"	12' 0" / 12' 0"	12' 0" / 12' 0"	12' 0" / 12' 0"	11' 11" / 12' 1"	11' 11" / 12' 1"	11' 11" / 12' 1"	11' 10" / 12' 2"	11' 10" / 12' 2"
14	14' 0" / 14' 0"	14' 0" / 14' 0"	14' 0" / 14' 0"	13' 11" / 14' 1"	13' 11" / 14' 1"	13' 11" / 14' 1"	13' 10" / 14' 2"	13' 10" / 14' 2"	13' 9" / 14' 3"
16	16' 0" / 16' 0"	16' 0" / 16' 0"	15' 11" / 16' 1"	15' 11" / 16' 1"	15' 11" / 16' 1"	15' 11" / 16' 2"	15' 10" / 16' 2"	15' 9" / 16' 3"	15' 8" / 16' 4"
18	18' 0" / 18' 0"	18' 0" / 18' 0"	17' 11" / 18' 1"	17' 11" / 18' 1"	17' 11" / 18' 1"	17' 10" / 18' 2"	17' 9" / 18' 3"	17' 8" / 18' 4"	17' 7" / 18' 6"
20	20' 0" / 20' 0"	19' 11" / 20' 1"	19' 11" / 20' 1"	19' 11" / 20' 1"	19' 10" / 20' 2"	19' 10" / 20' 2"	19' 9" / 20' 4"	19' 7" / 20' 5"	19' 5" / 20' 7"
25	24' 11" / 25' 1"	24' 11" / 25' 1"	24' 11" / 25' 1"	24' 10" / 25' 2"	24' 9" / 25' 3"	24' 8" / 25' 4"	24' 7" / 25' 6"	24' 5" / 25' 8"	24' 1" / 25' 11"
50	49' 9" / 50' 3"	49' 8" / 50' 4"	49' 6" / 50' 6"	49' 4" / 50' 8"	49' 1" / 51' 0"	48' 9" / 51' 4"	48' 2" / 52' 0"	47' 6" / 52' 9"	46' 6" / 54' 1"

75	74' 6" 75' 6"	74' 3" 75' 9"	73' 11" 76' 1"	73' 6" 76' 6"	72' 11" 77' 2"	72' 2" 78' 1"	70' 11" 79' 6"	69' 7" 81' 5"	67' 4" 84' 8"
100	99' 1" 101' 0"	98' 8" 101' 4"	98' 2" 101' 11"	97' 5" 102' 9"	96' 4" 104' 0"	95' 0" 105' 7"	92' 11" 108' 3"	90' 6" 111' 9"	86' 9" 118' 0"
125	123' 6" 126' 6"	122' 11" 127' 2"	122' 1" 128' 1"	120' 11" 129' 4"	119' 3" 131' 3"	117' 3" 133' 10"	114' 1" 138' 3"	110' 5" 143' 11"	104' 11" 154' 7"
150	147' 10" 152' 2"	147' 0" 153' 1"	145' 10" 154' 5"	144' 2" 156' 4"	141' 10" 159' 2"	139' 0" 162' 11"	134' 6" 169' 6"	129' 6" 178' 2"	121' 11" 194' 10"
175	172' 1" 178' 0"	171' 0" 179' 3"	169' 4" 181' 1"	167' 2" 183' 8"	164' 0" 187' 7"	160' 2" 192' 10"	154' 3" 202' 2"	147' 8" 214' 8"	137' 11" 239' 5"
200	196' 3" 203' 11"	194' 9" 205' 6"	192' 7" 208' 0"	189' 9" 211' 5"	185' 9" 216' 8"	180' 10" 223' 8"	173' 4" 236' 4"	165' 1" 253' 8"	152' 11" 288' 10"
250	244' 1" 256' 2"	241' 10" 258' 9"	238' 6" 262' 8"	234' 3" 268' 1"	228' 1" 276' 8"	220' 9" 288' 2"	209' 8" 309' 7"	197' 8" 340' 0"	180' 6" 406' 7"
300	291' 7" 308' 11"	288' 4" 312' 8"	283' 7" 318' 5"	277' 6" 326' 5"	268' 11" 339' 3"	258' 10" 356' 9"	243' 8" 390' 3"	227' 8" 439' 10"	205' 2" 558' 1"
350	338' 7" 362' 3"	334' 3" 367' 4"	327' 10" 375' 4"	319' 9" 386' 6"	308' 5" 404' 7"	295' 3" 429' 9"	275' 7" 479' 5"	255' 3" 556' 7"	227' 3" 760' 8"
400	385' 2" 416' 1"	379' 6" 422' 10"	371' 4" 433' 5"	361' 0" 448' 5"	346' 6" 473' 0"	330' 0" 507' 9"	305' 8" 578' 7"	280' 10" 694' 11"	247' 4" 1045' 3"

For circle of confusion = .0005 use depth data two columns left of chosen F-Stop.

SETUPS (Approximate Distance) — 8mm FIELD OF VIEW

	Full Aperture	Academy 1.33:1	Academy 1.66:1	Academy 1.85:1	Anamorphic 2.40:1	Super 35 1.85:1	Super 35 2.40:1	VistaVision	VistaVision 1.85:1	VistaVision 2.40:1	65mm
Ext Close Up	0' 4"	0' 4"	0' 5"	0' 6"	NA	0' 6"	0' 7"	0' 3"	0' 4"	0' 5"	NA
Close Up	0' 6"	0' 7"	0' 8"	0' 9"	NA	0' 9"	0' 11"	0' 4"	0' 5"	0' 7"	NA
Medium Shot	0' 11"	1' 1"	1' 4"	1' 5"	NA	1' 4"	1' 9"	0' 8"	0' 10"	1' 1"	NA
Full Figure	2' 7"	3' 0"	3' 7"	4' 0"	NA	3' 8"	4' 10"	1' 11"	2' 4"	3' 1"	NA
Angle of View	V 98.8° H 114.5°	V 87.4° H 105.3°	V 76.5° H 105.3°	V 70.6° H 105.3°	NA	V 78.1° H 112.6°	V 64.0° H 112.6°	V 115.1° H 134.0°	V 113.8° H 134.0°	V 89.2° H 134.0°	
2	4' 8" / 6' 3"	4' 0" / 5' 6"	3' 4" / 5' 6"	3' 0" / 5' 6"	NA / NA	3' 3" / 6' 0"	2' 6" / 6' 0"	6' 3" / 9' 5"	5' 1" / 9' 5"	3' 11" / 9' 5"	NA / NA
2½	5' 10" / 7' 9"	5' 0" / 6' 10"	4' 2" / 6' 10"	3' 9" / 6' 10"	NA / NA	4' 1" / 7' 6"	3' 2" / 7' 6"	7' 9" / 11' 9"	6' 4" / 11' 9"	4' 11" / 11' 9"	NA / NA
3	7' 0" / 9' 4"	6' 0" / 8' 3"	5' 0" / 8' 3"	4' 5" / 8' 3"	NA / NA	4' 10" / 9' 0"	3' 9" / 9' 0"	9' 4" / 14' 2"	7' 8" / 14' 2"	5' 11" / 14' 2"	NA / NA
3½	8' 2" / 10' 11"	7' 0" / 9' 7"	5' 10" / 9' 7"	5' 2" / 9' 7"	NA / NA	5' 8" / 10' 6"	4' 5" / 10' 6"	10' 11" / 16' 6"	8' 11" / 16' 6"	6' 11" / 16' 6"	NA / NA
4	9' 4" / 12' 6"	8' 0" / 11' 0"	6' 8" / 11' 0"	5' 11" / 11' 0"	NA / NA	6' 6" / 12' 0"	5' 0" / 12' 0"	12' 6" / 18' 10"	10' 2" / 18' 10"	7' 11" / 18' 10"	NA / NA
4½	10' 6" / 14' 0"	9' 0" / 12' 4"	7' 5" / 12' 4"	6' 8" / 12' 4"	NA / NA	7' 4" / 13' 6"	5' 8" / 13' 6"	14' 0" / 21' 3"	11' 6" / 21' 3"	8' 10" / 21' 3"	NA / NA
5	11' 8" / 15' 7"	10' 0" / 13' 9"	8' 3" / 13' 9"	7' 5" / 13' 9"	NA / NA	8' 1" / 15' 0"	6' 3" / 15' 0"	15' 7" / 23' 7"	12' 9" / 23' 7"	9' 10" / 23' 7"	NA / NA
5½	12' 10" / 17' 2"	11' 0" / 15' 1"	9' 1" / 15' 1"	8' 2" / 15' 1"	NA / NA	8' 11" / 16' 6"	6' 11" / 16' 6"	17' 2" / 25' 11"	14' 0" / 25' 11"	10' 10" / 25' 11"	NA / NA

6	14' 0" / 18' 8"	12' 0" / 16' 6"	9' 11" / 16' 6"	8' 11" / 16' 6"	NA / NA	9' 9" / 18' 0"	7' 6" / 18' 0"	18' 8" / 28' 3"	15' 4" / 28' 3"	11' 10" / 28' 3"	NA / NA	
6½	15' 2" / 20' 3"	13' 0" / 17' 10"	10' 9" / 17' 10"	9' 8" / 17' 10"	NA / NA	10' 7" / 19' 6"	8' 2" / 19' 6"	20' 3" / 30' 8"	16' 7" / 30' 8"	12' 10" / 30' 8"	NA / NA	
7	16' 4" / 21' 10"	14' 0" / 19' 3"	11' 7" / 19' 3"	10' 5" / 19' 3"	NA / NA	11' 4" / 21' 0"	8' 9" / 21' 0"	21' 10" / 33' 0"	17' 10" / 33' 0"	13' 10" / 33' 0"	NA / NA	
8	18' 8" / 24' 11"	16' 0" / 22' 0"	13' 3" / 22' 0"	11' 11" / 22' 0"	NA / NA	13' 0" / 24' 0"	10' 0" / 24' 0"	24' 11" / 37' 9"	20' 5" / 37' 9"	15' 9" / 37' 9"	NA / NA	
9	21' 0" / 28' 0"	18' 0" / 24' 9"	14' 11" / 24' 9"	13' 4" / 24' 9"	NA / NA	14' 7" / 27' 0"	11' 3" / 27' 0"	28' 0" / 42' 5"	22' 11" / 42' 5"	17' 9" / 42' 5"	NA / NA	
10	23' 4" / 31' 2"	20' 0" / 27' 6"	16' 7" / 27' 6"	14' 10" / 27' 6"	NA / NA	16' 3" / 30' 0"	12' 6" / 30' 0"	31' 2" / 47' 2"	25' 6" / 47' 2"	19' 9" / 47' 2"	NA / NA	
12	28' 0" / 37' 5"	24' 0" / 33' 0"	19' 11" / 33' 0"	17' 10" / 33' 0"	NA / NA	19' 6" / 36' 0"	15' 0" / 36' 0"	37' 5" / 56' 7"	30' 7" / 56' 7"	23' 8" / 56' 7"	NA / NA	
14	32' 8" / 43' 7"	28' 1" / 38' 6"	23' 2" / 38' 6"	20' 10" / 38' 6"	NA / NA	22' 9" / 42' 0"	17' 6" / 42' 0"	43' 7" / 66' 0"	35' 8" / 66' 0"	27' 7" / 66' 0"	NA / NA	
16	37' 4" / 49' 10"	32' 1" / 44' 0"	26' 6" / 44' 0"	23' 9" / 44' 0"	NA / NA	26' 0" / 48' 0"	20' 0" / 48' 0"	49' 10" / 75' 5"	40' 10" / 75' 5"	31' 7" / 75' 5"	NA / NA	
18	42' 0" / 56' 1"	36' 1" / 49' 6"	29' 10" / 49' 6"	26' 9" / 49' 6"	NA / NA	29' 2" / 54' 0"	22' 6" / 54' 0"	56' 1" / 84' 10"	45' 11" / 84' 10"	35' 6" / 84' 10"	NA / NA	
20	46' 8" / 62' 4"	40' 1" / 55' 0"	33' 2" / 55' 0"	29' 9" / 55' 0"	NA / NA	32' 5" / 60' 0"	25' 0" / 60' 0"	62' 4" / 94' 4"	51' 0" / 94' 4"	39' 5" / 94' 4"	NA / NA	
25	58' 4" / 77' 10"	50' 1" / 68' 9"	41' 5" / 68' 9"	37' 2" / 68' 9"	NA / NA	40' 7" / 75' 0"	31' 3" / 75' 0"	77' 10" / 117' 10"	63' 9" / 117' 10"	49' 4" / 117' 10"	NA / NA	
50	116' 8" / 155' 9"	100' 2" / 137' 6"	82' 10" / 137' 6"	74' 4" / 137' 6"	NA / NA	81' 1" / 150' 0"	62' 7" / 150' 0"	155' 9" / 235' 9"	127' 6" / 235' 9"	98' 7" / 235' 9"	NA / NA	

SETUPS (Approximate Distance) — 9.8mm FIELD OF VIEW

	Full Aperture	Academy 1.33:1	Academy 1.66:1	Academy 1.85:1	Anamorphic 2.40:1	Super 35 1.85:1	Super 35 2.40:1	VistaVision	VistaVision 1.85:1	VistaVision 2.40:1	65mm
Ext Close Up	0' 5"	0' 6"	0' 7"	0' 7"	NA	0' 7"	0' 9"	NA	NA	NA	NA
Close Up	0' 7"	0' 9"	0' 10"	1' 0"	NA	0' 11"	1' 2"	NA	NA	NA	NA
Medium Shot	1' 2"	1' 4"	1' 7"	1' 9"	NA	1' 8"	2' 1"	NA	NA	NA	NA
Full Figure	3' 2"	3' 8"	4' 5"	4' 11"	NA	4' 6"	5' 11"	NA	NA	NA	NA
Angle of View	V 87.2° H 103.6°	V 75.9° H 93.8°	V 65.6° H 93.8°	V 60.1° H 93.8°		V 67.0° H 101.5°	V 54.1° H 101.5°				
2	3' 10" / 5' 1"	3' 3" / 4' 6"	2' 8" / 4' 6"	2' 5" / 4' 6"	NA / NA	2' 8" / 4' 11"	2' 1" / 4' 11"	NA / NA	NA / NA	NA / NA	NA / NA
2½	4' 9" / 6' 4"	4' 1" / 5' 7"	3' 5" / 5' 7"	3' 0" / 5' 7"	NA / NA	3' 4" / 6' 1"	2' 7" / 6' 1"	NA / NA	NA / NA	NA / NA	NA / NA
3	5' 9" / 7' 8"	4' 11" / 6' 9"	4' 1" / 6' 9"	3' 8" / 6' 9"	NA / NA	4' 0" / 7' 4"	3' 1" / 7' 4"	NA / NA	NA / NA	NA / NA	NA / NA
3½	6' 8" / 8' 11"	5' 9" / 7' 10"	4' 9" / 7' 10"	4' 3" / 7' 10"	NA / NA	4' 8" / 8' 7"	3' 7" / 8' 7"	NA / NA	NA / NA	NA / NA	NA / NA
4	7' 7" / 10' 2"	6' 7" / 9' 0"	5' 5" / 9' 0"	4' 10" / 9' 0"	NA / NA	5' 4" / 9' 10"	4' 1" / 9' 10"	NA / NA	NA / NA	NA / NA	NA / NA
4½	8' 7" / 11' 5"	7' 4" / 10' 1"	6' 1" / 10' 1"	5' 6" / 10' 1"	NA / NA	6' 0" / 11' 0"	4' 7" / 11' 0"	NA / NA	NA / NA	NA / NA	NA / NA
5	9' 6" / 12' 9"	8' 2" / 11' 3"	6' 9" / 11' 3"	6' 1" / 11' 3"	NA / NA	6' 7" / 12' 3"	5' 1" / 12' 3"	NA / NA	NA / NA	NA / NA	NA / NA
5½	10' 6" / 14' 0"	9' 0" / 12' 4"	7' 5" / 12' 4"	6' 8" / 12' 4"	NA / NA	7' 3" / 13' 6"	5' 7" / 13' 6"	NA / NA	NA / NA	NA / NA	NA / NA

6	11' 5" / 15' 3"	9' 10" / 13' 6"	8' 1" / 13' 6"	7' 3" / 13' 6"	NA NA	7' 11" / 14' 8"	6' 2" / 14' 8"	NA NA	NA NA	NA NA	NA NA
6½	12' 5" / 16' 6"	10' 8" / 14' 7"	8' 10" / 14' 7"	7' 11" / 14' 7"	NA NA	8' 7" / 15' 11"	6' 8" / 15' 11"	NA NA	NA NA	NA NA	NA NA
7	13' 4" / 17' 10"	11' 5" / 15' 9"	9' 6" / 15' 9"	8' 6" / 15' 9"	NA NA	9' 3" / 17' 2"	7' 2" / 17' 2"	NA NA	NA NA	NA NA	NA NA
8	15' 3" / 20' 4"	13' 1" / 17' 11"	10' 10" / 17' 11"	9' 8" / 17' 11"	NA NA	10' 7" / 19' 7"	8' 2" / 19' 7"	NA NA	NA NA	NA NA	NA NA
9	17' 2" / 22' 11"	14' 9" / 20' 2"	12' 2" / 20' 2"	10' 11" / 20' 2"	NA NA	11' 11" / 22' 1"	9' 2" / 22' 1"	NA NA	NA NA	NA NA	NA NA
10	19' 1" / 25' 5"	16' 4" / 22' 5"	13' 6" / 22' 5"	12' 2" / 22' 5"	NA NA	13' 3" / 24' 6"	10' 3" / 24' 6"	NA NA	NA NA	NA NA	NA NA
12	22' 10" / 30' 6"	19' 8" / 26' 11"	16' 3" / 26' 11"	14' 7" / 26' 11"	NA NA	15' 11" / 29' 5"	12' 3" / 29' 5"	NA NA	NA NA	NA NA	NA NA
14	26' 8" / 35' 7"	22' 11" / 31' 5"	18' 11" / 31' 5"	17' 0" / 31' 5"	NA NA	18' 7" / 34' 3"	14' 4" / 34' 3"	NA NA	NA NA	NA NA	NA NA
16	30' 6" / 40' 8"	26' 2" / 35' 11"	21' 8" / 35' 11"	19' 5" / 35' 11"	NA NA	21' 2" / 39' 2"	16' 4" / 39' 2"	NA NA	NA NA	NA NA	NA NA
18	34' 3" / 45' 9"	29' 5" / 40' 5"	24' 4" / 40' 5"	21' 10" / 40' 5"	NA NA	23' 10" / 44' 1"	18' 5" / 44' 1"	NA NA	NA NA	NA NA	NA NA
20	38' 1" / 50' 10"	32' 9" / 44' 11"	27' 1" / 44' 11"	24' 3" / 44' 11"	NA NA	26' 6" / 49' 0"	20' 5" / 49' 0"	NA NA	NA NA	NA NA	NA NA
25	47' 8" / 63' 7"	40' 11" / 56' 1"	33' 10" / 56' 1"	30' 4" / 56' 1"	NA NA	33' 1" / 61' 3"	25' 6" / 61' 3"	NA NA	NA NA	NA NA	NA NA
50	95' 3" / 127' 2"	81' 9" / 112' 3"	67' 8" / 112' 3"	60' 8" / 112' 3"	NA NA	66' 3" / 122' 6"	51' 1" / 122' 6"	NA NA	NA NA	NA NA	NA NA

SETUPS (Approximate Distance) — 10mm FIELD OF VIEW

	Full Aperture	Academy 1.33:1	Academy 1.66:1	Academy 1.85:1	Anamorphic 2.40:1	Super 35 1.85:1	Super 35 2.40:1	VistaVision	VistaVision 1.85:1	VistaVision 2.40:1	65mm
Ext Close Up	0' 5"	0' 6"	0' 7"	0' 8"	NA	0' 7"	0' 9"	NA	NA	NA	NA
Close Up	0' 7"	0' 9"	0' 11"	1' 0"	NA	0' 11"	1' 2"	NA	NA	NA	NA
Medium Shot	1' 2"	1' 4"	1' 8"	1' 10"	NA	1' 8"	2' 2"	NA	NA	NA	NA
Full Figure	3' 3"	3' 9"	4' 6"	5' 1"	NA	4' 7"	6' 0"	NA	NA	NA	NA
Angle of View	V 86.1° H 102.4°	V 74.8° H 97.7°	V 64.5° H 92.7°	V 59.1° H 92.1°		V 66.0° H 100.4°	V 53.2° H 100.4°				
2	3' 9" / 5' 0"	3' 2" / 4' 5"	2' 8" / 4' 5"	2' 5" / 4' 5"	NA / NA	2' 7" / 4' 10"	2' 0" / 4' 10"	NA / NA	NA / NA	NA / NA	NA / NA
2½	4' 8" / 6' 3"	4' 0" / 5' 6"	3' 4" / 5' 6"	3' 0" / 5' 6"	NA / NA	3' 3" / 6' 0"	2' 6" / 6' 0"	NA / NA	NA / NA	NA / NA	NA / NA
3	5' 7" / 7' 6"	4' 10" / 6' 7"	4' 0" / 6' 7"	3' 7" / 6' 7"	NA / NA	3' 11" / 7' 2"	3' 0" / 7' 2"	NA / NA	NA / NA	NA / NA	NA / NA
3½	6' 6" / 8' 9"	5' 7" / 7' 8"	4' 8" / 7' 8"	4' 2" / 7' 8"	NA / NA	4' 7" / 8' 5"	3' 6" / 8' 5"	NA / NA	NA / NA	NA / NA	NA / NA
4	7' 6" / 10' 0"	6' 5" / 8' 10"	5' 4" / 8' 10"	4' 9" / 8' 10"	NA / NA	5' 2" / 9' 7"	4' 0" / 9' 7"	NA / NA	NA / NA	NA / NA	NA / NA
4½	8' 5" / 11' 3"	7' 3" / 9' 11"	6' 0" / 9' 11"	5' 4" / 9' 11"	NA / NA	5' 10" / 10' 10"	4' 6" / 10' 10"	NA / NA	NA / NA	NA / NA	NA / NA
5	9' 4" / 12' 6"	8' 0" / 11' 0"	6' 8" / 11' 0"	5' 11" / 11' 0"	NA / NA	6' 6" / 12' 0"	5' 0" / 12' 0"	NA / NA	NA / NA	NA / NA	NA / NA
5½	10' 3" / 13' 8"	8' 10" / 12' 1"	7' 4" / 12' 1"	6' 6" / 12' 1"	NA / NA	7' 2" / 13' 2"	5' 6" / 13' 2"	NA / NA	NA / NA	NA / NA	NA / NA

6	NA NA	NA NA	NA NA	NA NA	6' 0" / 14' 5"	7' 9" / 14' 5"	NA NA	7' 2" / 13' 2"	7' 11" / 13' 2"	9' 7" / 13' 2"	11' 2" / 14' 11"
6½	NA NA	NA NA	NA NA	NA NA	6' 6" / 15' 7"	8' 5" / 15' 7"	NA NA	7' 9" / 14' 4"	8' 7" / 14' 4"	10' 5" / 14' 4"	12' 2" / 16' 2"
7	NA NA	NA NA	NA NA	NA NA	7' 0" / 16' 10"	9' 1" / 16' 10"	NA NA	8' 4" / 15' 5"	9' 3" / 15' 5"	11' 3" / 15' 5"	13' 1" / 17' 5"
8	NA NA	NA NA	NA NA	NA NA	8' 0" / 19' 2"	10' 5" / 19' 2"	NA NA	9' 6" / 17' 7"	10' 7" / 17' 7"	12' 10" / 17' 7"	14' 11" / 19' 11"
9	NA NA	NA NA	NA NA	NA NA	9' 0" / 21' 7"	11' 8" / 21' 7"	NA NA	10' 8" / 19' 10"	11' 11" / 19' 10"	14' 5" / 19' 10"	16' 10" / 22' 5"
10	NA NA	NA NA	NA NA	NA NA	10' 0" / 24' 0"	13' 0" / 24' 0"	NA NA	11' 11" / 22' 0"	13' 3" / 22' 0"	16' 0" / 22' 0"	18' 8" / 24' 11"
12	NA NA	NA NA	NA NA	NA NA	12' 0" / 28' 10"	15' 7" / 28' 10"	NA NA	14' 3" / 26' 5"	15' 11" / 26' 5"	19' 3" / 26' 5"	22' 5" / 29' 11"
14	NA NA	NA NA	NA NA	NA NA	14' 0" / 33' 7"	18' 2" / 33' 7"	NA NA	16' 8" / 30' 10"	18' 7" / 30' 10"	22' 5" / 30' 10"	26' 2" / 34' 11"
16	NA NA	NA NA	NA NA	NA NA	16' 0" / 38' 5"	20' 9" / 38' 5"	NA NA	19' 0" / 35' 2"	21' 3" / 35' 2"	25' 8" / 35' 2"	29' 10" / 39' 10"
18	NA NA	NA NA	NA NA	NA NA	18' 0" / 43' 2"	23' 4" / 43' 2"	NA NA	21' 5" / 39' 7"	23' 10" / 39' 7"	28' 10" / 39' 7"	33' 7" / 44' 10"
20	NA NA	NA NA	NA NA	NA NA	20' 0" / 48' 0"	26' 0" / 48' 0"	NA NA	23' 9" / 44' 0"	26' 6" / 44' 0"	32' 1" / 44' 0"	37' 4" / 49' 10"
25	NA NA	NA NA	NA NA	NA NA	25' 0" / 60' 0"	32' 5" / 60' 0"	NA NA	29' 9" / 55' 0"	33' 2" / 55' 0"	40' 1" / 55' 0"	46' 8" / 62' 4"
50	NA NA	NA NA	NA NA	NA NA	50' 0" / 120' 0"	64' 11" / 120' 0"	NA NA	59' 5" / 110' 0"	66' 4" / 110' 0"	80' 2" / 110' 0"	93' 4" / 124' 7"

SETUPS (Approximate Distance) — 12mm FIELD OF VIEW

	Full Aperture	Academy 1.33:1	Academy 1.66:1	Academy 1.85:1	Anamorphic 2.40:1	Super 35 1.85:1	Super 35 2.40:1	VistaVision	VistaVision 1.85:1	VistaVision 2.40:1	65mm
Ext Close Up	0' 6"	0' 7"	0' 8"	0' 9"	NA	0' 8"	0' 11"	NA	NA	NA	NA
Close Up	0' 9"	0' 10"	1' 1"	1' 2"	NA	1' 1"	1' 5"	NA	NA	NA	NA
Medium Shot	1' 5"	1' 7"	2' 0"	2' 2"	NA	2' 0"	2' 7"	NA	NA	NA	NA
Full Figure	3' 10"	4' 6"	5' 5"	6' 1"	NA	5' 7"	7' 2"	NA	NA	NA	NA
Angle of View	V 75.8° H 92.1°	V 65.0° H 82.2°	V 55.5° H 82.2°	V 50.5° H 82.2°		V 56.8° H 90.0°	V 45.3° H 90.0°				
2	3' 1" 4' 2"	2' 8" 3' 8"	2' 3" 3' 8"	2' 0" 3' 8"	NA NA	2' 2" 4' 0"	1' 8" 4' 0"	NA NA	NA NA	NA NA	NA NA
2½	3' 11" 5' 2"	3' 4" 4' 7"	2' 9" 4' 7"	2' 6" 4' 7"	NA NA	2' 8" 5' 0"	2' 1" 5' 0"	NA NA	NA NA	NA NA	NA NA
3	4' 8" 6' 3"	4' 0" 5' 6"	3' 4" 5' 6"	3' 0" 5' 6"	NA NA	3' 3" 6' 0"	2' 6" 6' 0"	NA NA	NA NA	NA NA	NA NA
3½	5' 5" 7' 3"	4' 8" 6' 5"	3' 10" 6' 5"	3' 6" 6' 5"	NA NA	3' 9" 7' 0"	2' 11" 7' 0"	NA NA	NA NA	NA NA	NA NA
4	6' 3" 8' 4"	5' 4" 7' 4"	4' 5" 7' 4"	4' 0" 7' 4"	NA NA	4' 4" 8' 0"	3' 4" 8' 0"	NA NA	NA NA	NA NA	NA NA
4½	7' 0" 9' 4"	6' 0" 8' 3"	5' 0" 8' 3"	4' 5" 8' 3"	NA NA	4' 10" 9' 0"	3' 9" 9' 0"	NA NA	NA NA	NA NA	NA NA
5	7' 9" 10' 5"	6' 8" 9' 2"	5' 6" 9' 2"	4' 11" 9' 2"	NA NA	5' 5" 10' 0"	4' 2" 10' 0"	NA NA	NA NA	NA NA	NA NA
5½	8' 7" 11' 5"	7' 4" 10' 1"	6' 1" 10' 1"	5' 5" 10' 1"	NA NA	5' 11" 11' 0"	4' 7" 11' 0"	NA NA	NA NA	NA NA	NA NA

6	9' 4" 12' 6"	8' 0" 11' 0"	6' 8" 11' 0"	5' 11" 11' 0"	NA NA	6' 6" 12' 0"	5' 0" 12' 0"	NA NA	NA NA	NA NA	NA NA
6½	10' 1" 13' 6"	8' 8" 11' 11"	7' 2" 11' 11"	6' 5" 11' 11"	NA NA	7' 0" 13' 0"	5' 5" 13' 0"	NA NA	NA NA	NA NA	NA NA
7	10' 11" 14' 6"	9' 4" 12' 10"	7' 9" 12' 10"	6' 11" 12' 10"	NA NA	7' 7" 14' 0"	5' 10" 14' 0"	NA NA	NA NA	NA NA	NA NA
8	12' 5" 16' 7"	10' 8" 14' 8"	8' 10" 14' 8"	7' 11" 14' 8"	NA NA	8' 8" 16' 0"	6' 8" 16' 0"	NA NA	NA NA	NA NA	NA NA
9	14' 0" 18' 8"	12' 0" 16' 6"	9' 11" 16' 6"	8' 11" 16' 6"	NA NA	9' 9" 18' 0"	7' 6" 18' 0"	NA NA	NA NA	NA NA	NA NA
10	15' 7" 20' 9"	13' 4" 18' 4"	11' 1" 18' 4"	9' 11" 18' 4"	NA NA	10' 10" 20' 0"	8' 4" 20' 0"	NA NA	NA NA	NA NA	NA NA
12	18' 8" 24' 11"	16' 0" 22' 0"	13' 3" 22' 0"	11' 11" 22' 0"	NA NA	13' 0" 24' 0"	10' 0" 24' 0"	NA NA	NA NA	NA NA	NA NA
14	21' 9" 29' 1"	18' 8" 25' 8"	15' 6" 25' 8"	13' 10" 25' 8"	NA NA	15' 2" 28' 0"	11' 8" 28' 0"	NA NA	NA NA	NA NA	NA NA
16	24' 11" 33' 3"	21' 4" 29' 4"	17' 8" 29' 4"	15' 10" 29' 4"	NA NA	17' 4" 32' 0"	13' 4" 32' 0"	NA NA	NA NA	NA NA	NA NA
18	28' 0" 37' 5"	24' 0" 33' 0"	19' 11" 33' 0"	17' 10" 33' 0"	NA NA	19' 6" 36' 0"	15' 0" 36' 0"	NA NA	NA NA	NA NA	NA NA
20	31' 1" 41' 6"	26' 9" 36' 8"	22' 1" 36' 8"	19' 10" 36' 8"	NA NA	21' 8" 40' 0"	16' 8" 40' 0"	NA NA	NA NA	NA NA	NA NA
25	38' 11" 51' 11"	33' 5" 45' 10"	27' 7" 45' 10"	24' 9" 45' 10"	NA NA	27' 0" 50' 0"	20' 10" 50' 0"	NA NA	NA NA	NA NA	NA NA
50	77' 9" 103' 10"	66' 9" 91' 8"	55' 3" 91' 8"	49' 6" 91' 8"	NA NA	54' 1" 100' 0"	41' 8" 100' 0"	NA NA	NA NA	NA NA	NA NA

SETUPS (Approximate Distance) — 14mm FIELD OF VIEW

	Full Aperture	Academy 1.33:1	Academy 1.66:1	Academy 1.85:1	Anamorphic 2.40:1	Super 35 1.85:1	Super 35 2.40:1	VistaVision	VistaVision 1.85:1	VistaVision 2.40:1	65mm
Ext Close Up	0' 7"	0' 8"	0' 10"	0' 11"	NA	0' 10"	1' 1"	0' 5"	0' 6"	0' 8"	NA
Close Up	0' 10"	1' 0"	1' 3"	1' 4"	NA	1' 3"	1' 8"	0' 8"	0' 10"	1' 0"	NA
Medium Shot	1' 7"	1' 11"	2' 3"	2' 7"	NA	2' 4"	3' 0"	1' 3"	1' 6"	1' 1"	NA
Full Figure	4' 6"	5' 3"	6' 4"	7' 1"	NA	6' 6"	8' 5"	3' 4"	4' 1"	5' 4"	NA
Angle of View	V 67.4° H 83.3°	V 57.3° H 73.6°	V 48.5° H 73.6°	V 44.1° H 73.6°		V 49.7° H 81.2°	V 39.3° H 81.2°	V 83.9° H 106.8°	V 72.1° H 106.8°	V 58.8° H 106.8°	
2	2' 8" / 3' 7"	2' 3" / 3' 2"	1' 11" / 3' 2"	1' 8" / 3' 2"	NA / NA	1' 10" / 3' 5"	1' 5" / 3' 5"	3' 7" / 5' 5"	2' 11" / 5' 5"	2' 3" / 5' 5"	NA / NA
2½	3' 4" / 4' 5"	2' 10" / 3' 11"	2' 4" / 3' 11"	2' 1" / 3' 11"	NA / NA	2' 4" / 4' 3"	1' 9" / 4' 3"	4' 5" / 6' 9"	3' 8" / 6' 9"	2' 10" / 6' 9"	NA / NA
3	4' 0" / 5' 4"	3' 5" / 4' 9"	2' 10" / 4' 9"	2' 7" / 4' 9"	NA / NA	2' 9" / 5' 2"	2' 2" / 5' 2"	5' 4" / 8' 1"	4' 4" / 8' 1"	3' 5" / 8' 1"	NA / NA
3½	4' 8" / 6' 3"	4' 0" / 5' 6"	3' 4" / 5' 6"	3' 0" / 5' 6"	NA / NA	3' 3" / 6' 0"	2' 6" / 6' 0"	6' 3" / 9' 5"	5' 1" / 9' 5"	3' 11" / 9' 5"	NA / NA
4	5' 4" / 7' 1"	4' 7" / 6' 3"	3' 9" / 6' 3"	3' 5" / 6' 3"	NA / NA	3' 9" / 6' 10"	2' 10" / 6' 10"	7' 1" / 10' 9"	5' 10" / 10' 9"	4' 6" / 10' 9"	NA / NA
4½	6' 0" / 8' 0"	5' 2" / 7' 1"	4' 3" / 7' 1"	3' 10" / 7' 1"	NA / NA	4' 2" / 7' 9"	3' 3" / 7' 9"	8' 0" / 12' 1"	6' 7" / 12' 1"	5' 1" / 12' 1"	NA / NA
5	6' 8" / 8' 11"	5' 9" / 7' 10"	4' 9" / 7' 10"	4' 3" / 7' 10"	NA / NA	4' 8" / 8' 7"	3' 7" / 8' 7"	8' 11" / 13' 6"	7' 3" / 13' 6"	5' 8" / 8' 7"	NA / NA
5½	7' 4" / 9' 9"	6' 4" / 8' 8"	5' 3" / 8' 8"	4' 8" / 8' 8"	NA / NA	5' 1" / 9' 5"	3' 11" / 9' 5"	9' 9" / 14' 10"	8' 0" / 14' 10"	6' 2" / 14' 10"	NA / NA

6	NA NA	8' 0" / 10' 8"	6' 10" / 9' 5"	5' 8" / 9' 5"	5' 1" / 9' 5"	NA NA	5' 7" / 10' 3"	4' 3" / 10' 3"	10' 8" / 16' 2"	8' 9" / 16' 2"	6' 9" / 16' 2"
6½	NA NA	8' 8" / 11' 7"	7' 5" / 10' 3"	6' 2" / 10' 3"	5' 6" / 10' 3"	NA NA	6' 0" / 11' 2"	4' 8" / 11' 2"	11' 7" / 17' 6"	9' 6" / 17' 6"	7' 4" / 17' 6"
7	NA NA	9' 4" / 12' 6"	8' 0" / 11' 0"	6' 8" / 11' 0"	5' 11" / 11' 0"	NA NA	6' 6" / 12' 0"	5' 0" / 12' 0"	12' 6" / 18' 10"	10' 2" / 18' 10"	7' 11" / 18' 10"
8	NA NA	10' 8" / 14' 3"	9' 2" / 12' 7"	7' 7" / 12' 7"	6' 10" / 12' 7"	NA NA	7' 5" / 13' 9"	5' 9" / 13' 9"	14' 3" / 21' 7"	11' 8" / 21' 7"	9' 0" / 21' 7"
9	NA NA	12' 0" / 16' 0"	10' 4" / 14' 2"	8' 6" / 14' 2"	7' 8" / 14' 2"	NA NA	8' 4" / 15' 5"	6' 5" / 15' 5"	16' 0" / 24' 3"	13' 1" / 24' 3"	10' 2" / 24' 3"
10	NA NA	13' 4" / 17' 10"	11' 5" / 15' 9"	9' 6" / 15' 9"	8' 6" / 15' 9"	NA NA	9' 3" / 17' 2"	7' 2" / 17' 2"	17' 10" / 26' 11"	14' 7" / 26' 11"	11' 3" / 26' 11"
12	NA NA	16' 0" / 21' 4"	13' 9" / 18' 10"	11' 4" / 18' 10"	10' 2" / 18' 10"	NA NA	11' 2" / 20' 7"	8' 7" / 20' 7"	21' 4" / 32' 4"	17' 6" / 32' 4"	13' 6" / 32' 4"
14	NA NA	18' 8" / 24' 11"	16' 0" / 22' 0"	13' 3" / 22' 0"	11' 11" / 22' 0"	NA NA	13' 0" / 24' 0"	10' 0" / 24' 0"	24' 11" / 37' 9"	20' 5" / 37' 9"	15' 9" / 37' 9"
16	NA NA	21' 4" / 28' 6"	18' 4" / 25' 2"	15' 2" / 25' 2"	13' 7" / 25' 2"	NA NA	14' 10" / 27' 5"	11' 5" / 27' 5"	28' 6" / 43' 1"	23' 4" / 43' 1"	18' 0" / 43' 1"
18	NA NA	24' 0" / 32' 0"	20' 7" / 28' 3"	17' 1" / 28' 3"	15' 3" / 28' 3"	NA NA	16' 8" / 30' 10"	12' 10" / 30' 10"	32' 0" / 48' 6"	26' 3" / 48' 6"	20' 3" / 48' 6"
20	NA NA	26' 8" / 35' 7"	22' 11" / 31' 5"	18' 11" / 31' 5"	17' 0" / 31' 5"	NA NA	18' 7" / 34' 3"	14' 4" / 34' 3"	35' 7" / 53' 11"	29' 2" / 53' 11"	22' 6" / 53' 11"
25	NA NA	33' 4" / 44' 6"	28' 7" / 39' 3"	23' 8" / 39' 3"	21' 3" / 39' 3"	NA NA	23' 2" / 42' 10"	17' 10" / 42' 10"	44' 6" / 67' 4"	36' 5" / 67' 4"	28' 2" / 67' 4"
50	NA NA	66' 8" / 89' 0"	57' 3" / 78' 7"	47' 4" / 78' 7"	42' 5" / 78' 7"	NA NA	46' 4" / 85' 9"	35' 9" / 85' 9"	89' 0" / 134' 9"	72' 10" / 134' 9"	56' 4" / 134' 9"

SETUPS (Approximate Distance) — 16mm FIELD OF VIEW

	Full Aperture	Academy 1.33:1	Academy 1.66:1	Academy 1.85:1	Anamorphic 2.40:1	Super 35 1.85:1	Super 35 2.40:1	VistaVision	VistaVision 1.85:1	VistaVision 2.40:1	65mm
Ext Close Up	0' 8"	0' 9"	0' 11"	1' 0"	NA	0' 11"	1' 2"	NA	NA	NA	NA
Close Up	1' 0"	1' 2"	1' 5"	1' 7"	NA	1' 5"	1' 10"	NA	NA	NA	NA
Medium Shot	1' 10"	2' 2"	2' 7"	2' 11"	NA	2' 8"	3' 6"	NA	NA	NA	NA
Full Figure	5' 2"	6' 0"	7' 3"	8' 1"	NA	7' 5"	9' 7"	NA	NA	NA	NA
Angle of View	V 60.5° H 75.8°	V 51.1° H 66.4°	V 43.1° H 66.4°	V 39.0° H 66.4°		V 44.2° H 73.7°	V 34.7° H 73.7°				
2	2' 4" / 3' 1"	2' 0" / 2' 9"	1' 8" / 2' 9"	1' 6" / 2' 9"	NA / NA	1' 7" / 3' 0"	1' 3" / 3' 0"	NA / NA	NA / NA	NA / NA	NA / NA
2½	2' 11" / 3' 11"	2' 6" / 3' 5"	2' 1" / 3' 5"	1' 10" / 3' 5"	NA / NA	2' 0" / 3' 9"	1' 7" / 3' 9"	NA / NA	NA / NA	NA / NA	NA / NA
3	3' 6" / 4' 8"	3' 0" / 4' 1"	2' 6" / 4' 1"	2' 3" / 4' 1"	NA / NA	2' 5" / 4' 6"	1' 11" / 4' 6"	NA / NA	NA / NA	NA / NA	NA / NA
3½	4' 1" / 5' 5"	3' 6" / 4' 10"	2' 11" / 4' 10"	2' 7" / 4' 10"	NA / NA	2' 10" / 5' 3"	2' 2" / 5' 3"	NA / NA	NA / NA	NA / NA	NA / NA
4	4' 8" / 6' 3"	4' 0" / 5' 6"	3' 4" / 5' 6"	3' 0" / 5' 6"	NA / NA	3' 3" / 6' 0"	2' 6" / 6' 0"	NA / NA	NA / NA	NA / NA	NA / NA
4½	5' 3" / 7' 0"	4' 6" / 6' 2"	3' 9" / 6' 2"	3' 4" / 6' 2"	NA / NA	3' 8" / 6' 9"	2' 10" / 6' 9"	NA / NA	NA / NA	NA / NA	NA / NA
5	5' 10" / 7' 9"	5' 0" / 6' 10"	4' 2" / 6' 10"	3' 9" / 6' 10"	NA / NA	4' 1" / 7' 6"	3' 2" / 7' 6"	NA / NA	NA / NA	NA / NA	NA / NA
5½	6' 5" / 8' 7"	5' 6" / 7' 7"	4' 7" / 7' 7"	4' 1" / 7' 7"	NA / NA	4' 6" / 8' 3"	3' 5" / 8' 3"	NA / NA	NA / NA	NA / NA	NA / NA

	C1	C2	C3	C4	C5	C6	C7	C8	C9	C10	C11
6	NA / NA	NA / NA	NA / NA	NA / NA	3' 9" / 9' 0"	4' 10" / 9' 0"	NA / NA	4' 5" / 8' 3"	5' 0" / 8' 3"	6' 0" / 8' 3"	7' 0" / 9' 4"
6½	NA / NA	NA / NA	NA / NA	NA / NA	4' 1" / 9' 9"	5' 3" / 9' 9"	NA / NA	4' 10" / 8' 11"	5' 5" / 8' 11"	6' 6" / 8' 11"	7' 7" / 10' 1"
7	NA / NA	NA / NA	NA / NA	NA / NA	4' 5" / 10' 6"	5' 8" / 10' 6"	NA / NA	5' 2" / 9' 7"	5' 10" / 9' 7"	7' 0" / 9' 7"	8' 2" / 10' 11"
8	NA / NA	NA / NA	NA / NA	NA / NA	5' 0" / 12' 0"	6' 6" / 12' 0"	NA / NA	5' 11" / 11' 0"	6' 8" / 11' 0"	8' 0" / 11' 0"	9' 4" / 12' 6"
9	NA / NA	NA / NA	NA / NA	NA / NA	5' 8" / 13' 6"	7' 4" / 13' 6"	NA / NA	6' 8" / 12' 4"	7' 5" / 12' 4"	9' 0" / 12' 4"	10' 6" / 14' 0"
10	NA / NA	NA / NA	NA / NA	NA / NA	6' 3" / 15' 0"	8' 1" / 15' 0"	NA / NA	7' 5" / 13' 9"	8' 3" / 13' 9"	10' 0" / 13' 9"	11' 8" / 15' 7"
12	NA / NA	NA / NA	NA / NA	NA / NA	7' 6" / 18' 0"	9' 9" / 18' 0"	NA / NA	8' 11" / 16' 6"	9' 11" / 16' 6"	12' 0" / 16' 6"	14' 0" / 18' 8"
14	NA / NA	NA / NA	NA / NA	NA / NA	8' 9" / 21' 0"	11' 4" / 21' 0"	NA / NA	10' 5" / 19' 3"	11' 7" / 19' 3"	14' 0" / 19' 3"	16' 4" / 21' 10"
16	NA / NA	NA / NA	NA / NA	NA / NA	10' 0" / 24' 0"	13' 0" / 24' 0"	NA / NA	11' 11" / 22' 0"	13' 3" / 22' 0"	16' 0" / 22' 0"	18' 8" / 24' 11"
18	NA / NA	NA / NA	NA / NA	NA / NA	11' 3" / 27' 0"	14' 7" / 27' 0"	NA / NA	13' 4" / 24' 9"	14' 11" / 24' 9"	18' 0" / 24' 9"	21' 0" / 28' 0"
20	NA / NA	NA / NA	NA / NA	NA / NA	12' 6" / 30' 0"	16' 3" / 30' 0"	NA / NA	14' 10" / 27' 6"	16' 7" / 27' 6"	20' 0" / 27' 6"	23' 4" / 31' 2"
25	NA / NA	NA / NA	NA / NA	NA / NA	15' 8" / 37' 6"	20' 3" / 37' 6"	NA / NA	18' 7" / 34' 4"	20' 9" / 34' 4"	25' 1" / 34' 4"	29' 2" / 38' 11"
50	NA / NA	NA / NA	NA / NA	NA / NA	31' 3" / 75' 0"	40' 7" / 75' 0"	NA / NA	37' 2" / 68' 9"	41' 5" / 68' 9"	50' 1" / 68' 9"	58' 4" / 77' 10"

SETUPS (Approximate Distance) — 18mm FIELD OF VIEW

	Full Aperture	Academy 1.33:1	Academy 1.66:1	Academy 1.85:1	Anamorphic 2.40:1	Super 35 1.85:1	Super 35 2.40:1	VistaVision	VistaVision 1.85:1	VistaVision 2.40:1	65mm
Ext Close Up	0'9"	0'10"	1'0"	1'2"	0'9"	1'0"	1'4"	0'7"	0'8"	0'10"	NA
Close Up	1'1"	1'4"	1'7"	1'9"	1'2"	1'7"	2'1"	0'10"	1'0"	1'4"	NA
Medium Shot	2'1"	2'5"	2'11"	3'3"	2'1"	3'0"	3'11"	1'7"	1'11"	2'6"	NA
Full Figure	5'9"	6'9"	8'2"	9'1"	5'10"	8'4"	10'10"	4'4"	5'4"	6'10"	NA
Angle of View	V 54.8° H 69.3°	V 46.0° H 60.4°	V 38.6° H 60.4°	V 34.9° H 60.4°	V 52.6° H 99.6°	V 39.7° H 67.4°	V 31.1° H 67.4°	V 69.9° H 92.7°	V 59.1° H 92.7°	V 47.3° H 92.7°	
2	2'1" / 2'9"	1'9" / 2'5"	1'6" / 2'5"	1'4" / 2'5"	2'1" / 4'11"	1'5" / 2'8"	1'1" / 2'8"	2'9" / 4'2"	2'3" / 4'2"	1'9" / 4'2"	NA / NA
2½	2'7" / 3'6"	2'3" / 3'1"	1'10" / 3'1"	1'8" / 3'1"	2'7" / 6'1"	1'10" / 3'4"	1'5" / 3'4"	3'6" / 5'3"	2'10" / 5'3"	2'2" / 5'3"	NA / NA
3	3'1" / 4'2"	2'8" / 3'8"	2'3" / 3'8"	2'0" / 3'8"	3'1" / 7'4"	2'2" / 4'0"	1'8" / 4'0"	4'2" / 6'3"	3'5" / 6'3"	2'8" / 6'3"	NA / NA
3½	3'8" / 4'10"	3'1" / 4'3"	2'7" / 4'3"	2'4" / 4'3"	3'7" / 8'7"	2'6" / 4'8"	1'11" / 4'8"	4'10" / 7'4"	4'0" / 7'4"	3'1" / 7'4"	NA / NA
4	4'2" / 5'6"	3'7" / 4'11"	2'11" / 4'11"	2'8" / 4'11"	4'2" / 9'9"	2'11" / 5'4"	2'3" / 5'4"	5'6" / 8'5"	4'6" / 8'5"	3'6" / 8'5"	NA / NA
4½	4'8" / 6'3"	4'0" / 5'6"	3'4" / 5'6"	3'0" / 5'6"	4'8" / 11'0"	3'3" / 6'0"	2'6" / 6'0"	6'3" / 9'5"	5'1" / 9'5"	3'11" / 9'5"	NA / NA
5	5'2" / 6'11"	4'5" / 6'1"	3'8" / 6'1"	3'4" / 6'1"	5'2" / 12'3"	3'7" / 6'8"	2'9" / 6'8"	6'11" / 10'6"	5'8" / 10'6"	4'5" / 10'6"	NA / NA
5½	5'8" / 7'7"	4'11" / 6'9"	4'1" / 6'9"	3'8" / 6'9"	5'8" / 13'5"	4'0" / 7'4"	3'1" / 7'4"	7'7" / 11'6"	6'3" / 11'6"	4'10" / 11'6"	NA / NA

6	6' 3" 8' 4"	5' 4" 7' 4"	4' 5" 7' 4"	4' 0" 7' 4"	6' 2" 14' 8"	4' 4" 8' 0"	3' 4" 8' 0"	8' 4" 12' 7"	6' 10" 12' 7"	5' 3" 12' 7"	NA NA
6½	6' 9" 9' 0"	5' 9" 7' 11"	4' 9" 7' 11"	4' 4" 7' 11"	6' 9" 15' 11"	4' 8" 8' 8"	3' 7" 8' 8"	9' 0" 13' 7"	7' 4" 13' 7"	5' 8" 13' 7"	NA NA
7	7' 3" 9' 8"	6' 3" 8' 7"	5' 2" 8' 7"	4' 7" 8' 7"	7' 3" 17' 1"	5' 1" 9' 4"	3' 11" 9' 4"	9' 8" 14' 8"	7' 11" 14' 8"	6' 2" 14' 8"	NA NA
8	8' 4" 11' 1"	7' 1" 9' 9"	5' 11" 9' 9"	5' 3" 9' 9"	8' 3" 19' 7"	5' 9" 10' 8"	4' 5" 10' 8"	11' 1" 16' 9"	9' 1" 16' 9"	7' 0" 16' 9"	NA NA
9	9' 4" 12' 6"	8' 0" 11' 0"	6' 8" 11' 0"	5' 11" 11' 0"	9' 4" 22' 0"	6' 6" 12' 0"	5' 0" 12' 0"	12' 6" 18' 10"	10' 2" 18' 10"	7' 11" 18' 10"	NA NA
10	10' 4" 13' 10"	8' 11" 12' 3"	7' 4" 12' 3"	6' 7" 12' 3"	10' 4" 24' 5"	7' 3" 13' 4"	5' 7" 13' 4"	13' 10" 20' 11"	11' 4" 20' 11"	8' 9" 20' 11"	NA NA
12	12' 5" 16' 7"	10' 8" 14' 8"	8' 10" 14' 8"	7' 11" 14' 8"	12' 5" 29' 4"	8' 8" 16' 0"	6' 8" 16' 0"	16' 7" 25' 2"	13' 7" 25' 2"	10' 6" 25' 2"	NA NA
14	14' 6" 19' 5"	12' 6" 17' 1"	10' 4" 17' 1"	9' 3" 17' 1"	14' 6" 34' 3"	10' 1" 18' 8"	7' 9" 18' 8"	19' 5" 29' 4"	15' 10" 29' 4"	12' 3" 29' 4"	NA NA
16	16' 7" 22' 2"	14' 3" 19' 7"	11' 9" 19' 7"	10' 7" 19' 7"	16' 6" 39' 1"	11' 6" 21' 4"	8' 11" 21' 4"	22' 2" 33' 6"	18' 2" 33' 6"	14' 0" 33' 6"	NA NA
18	18' 8" 24' 11"	16' 0" 22' 0"	13' 3" 22' 0"	11' 11" 22' 0"	18' 7" 44' 0"	13' 0" 24' 0"	10' 0" 24' 0"	24' 11" 37' 9"	20' 5" 37' 9"	15' 9" 37' 9"	NA NA
20	20' 9" 27' 8"	17' 10" 24' 5"	14' 9" 24' 5"	13' 2" 24' 5"	20' 8" 48' 11"	14' 5" 26' 8"	11' 1" 26' 8"	27' 8" 41' 11"	22' 8" 41' 11"	17' 6" 41' 11"	NA NA
25	25' 11" 34' 7"	22' 3" 30' 7"	18' 5" 30' 7"	16' 6" 30' 7"	25' 10" 61' 1"	18' 0" 33' 4"	13' 11" 33' 4"	34' 7" 52' 5"	28' 4" 52' 5"	21' 11" 52' 5"	NA NA
50	51' 10" 69' 3"	44' 6" 61' 1"	36' 10" 61' 1"	33' 0" 61' 1"	51' 8" 122' 2"	36' 1" 66' 8"	27' 10" 66' 8"	69' 3" 104' 9"	56' 8" 104' 9"	43' 10" 104' 9"	NA NA

SETUPS (Approximate Distance) — 20mm FIELD OF VIEW

	Full Aperture	Academy 1.33:1	Academy 1.66:1	Academy 1.85:1	Anamorphic 2.40:1	Super 35 1.85:1	Super 35 2.40:1	VistaVision	VistaVision 1.85:1	VistaVision 2.40:1	65mm
Ext Close Up	0' 10"	0' 11"	1' 2"	1' 3"	NA	1' 2"	1' 6"	0' 7"	0' 9"	0' 11"	NA
Close Up	1' 3"	1' 5"	1' 9"	2' 0"	NA	1' 10"	2' 4"	0' 11"	1' 2"	1' 6"	NA
Medium Shot	2' 4"	2' 8"	3' 3"	3' 8"	NA	3' 4"	4' 4"	1' 9"	2' 1"	2' 9"	NA
Full Figure	6' 5"	7' 6"	9' 1"	10' 1"	NA	9' 3"	12' 0"	4' 10"	5' 11"	7' 7"	NA
Angle of View	V 50.0° H 63.8°	V 41.8° H 55.3°	V 35.0° H 55.3°	V 31.6° H 55.3°		V 36.0° H 61.9°	V 28.1° H 61.9°	V 64.4° H 86.6°	V 54.0° H 86.6°	V 43.0° H 86.6°	
2	1' 10" / 2' 6"	1' 7" / 2' 2"	1' 4" / 2' 2"	1' 2" / 2' 2"	NA / NA	1' 4" / 2' 5"	1' 0" / 2' 5"	2' 6" / 3' 9"	2' 0" / 3' 9"	1' 7" / 3' 9"	NA / NA
2½	2' 4" / 3' 1"	2' 0" / 2' 9"	1' 8" / 2' 9"	1' 6" / 2' 9"	NA / NA	1' 7" / 3' 0"	1' 3" / 3' 0"	3' 1" / 4' 9"	2' 7" / 4' 9"	2' 0" / 4' 9"	NA / NA
3	2' 10" / 3' 9"	2' 5" / 3' 4"	2' 0" / 3' 4"	1' 9" / 3' 4"	NA / NA	1' 11" / 3' 7"	1' 6" / 3' 7"	3' 9" / 5' 8"	3' 1" / 5' 8"	2' 4" / 5' 8"	NA / NA
3½	3' 3" / 4' 4"	2' 10" / 3' 10"	2' 4" / 3' 10"	2' 1" / 3' 10"	NA / NA	2' 3" / 4' 2"	1' 9" / 4' 2"	4' 4" / 6' 7"	3' 7" / 6' 7"	2' 9" / 6' 7"	NA / NA
4	3' 9" / 5' 0"	3' 2" / 4' 5"	2' 8" / 4' 5"	2' 5" / 4' 5"	NA / NA	2' 7" / 4' 10"	2' 0" / 4' 10"	5' 0" / 7' 7"	4' 1" / 7' 7"	3' 2" / 7' 7"	NA / NA
4½	4' 2" / 5' 7"	3' 7" / 4' 11"	3' 0" / 4' 11"	2' 8" / 4' 11"	NA / NA	2' 11" / 5' 5"	2' 3" / 5' 5"	5' 7" / 8' 6"	4' 7" / 8' 6"	3' 7" / 8' 6"	NA / NA
5	4' 8" / 6' 3"	4' 0" / 5' 6"	3' 4" / 5' 6"	3' 0" / 5' 6"	NA / NA	3' 3" / 6' 0"	2' 6" / 6' 0"	6' 3" / 9' 5"	5' 1" / 9' 5"	3' 11 / 9' 5"	NA / NA
5½	5' 2" / 6' 10"	4' 5" / 6' 1"	3' 8" / 6' 1"	3' 3" / 6' 1"	NA / NA	3' 7" / 6' 7"	2' 9" / 6' 7"	6' 10" / 10' 4"	5' 7" / 10' 4"	4' 4" / 10' 4"	NA / NA

NA NA	4'9" 11'4"	6'1" 11'4"	7'6" 11'4"	3'0" 7'2"	3'11" 7'2"	NA NA	3'7" 6'7"	4'0" 6'7"	4'10" 6'7"	5'7" 7'6"	**6**
NA NA	5'2" 12'3"	6'8" 12'3"	8'1" 12'3"	3'3" 7'10"	4'3" 7'10"	NA NA	3'10" 7'2"	4'4" 7'2"	5'3" 7'2"	6'1" 8'1"	**6½**
NA NA	5'6" 13'2"	7'2" 13'2"	8'9" 13'2"	3'6" 8'5"	4'7" 8'5"	NA NA	4'2" 7'8"	4'8" 7'8"	5'7" 7'8"	6'6" 8'9"	**7**
NA NA	6'4" 15'1"	8'2" 15'1"	10'0" 15'1"	4'0" 9'7"	5'2" 9'7"	NA NA	4'9" 8'10"	5'4" 8'10"	6'5" 8'10"	7'6" 10'0"	**8**
NA NA	7'1" 17'0"	9'2" 17'0"	11'3" 17'0"	4'6" 10'10"	5'10" 10'10"	NA NA	5'4" 9'11"	6'0" 9'11"	7'3" 9'11"	8'5" 11'3"	**9**
NA NA	7'11" 18'10"	10'2" 18'10"	12'6" 18'10"	5'0" 12'0"	6'6" 12'0"	NA NA	5'11" 11'0"	6'8" 11'0"	8'0" 11'0"	9'4" 12'6"	**10**
NA NA	9'6" 22'8"	12'3" 22'8"	14'11" 22'8"	6'0" 14'5"	7'9" 14'5"	NA NA	7'2" 13'2"	7'11" 13'2"	9'7" 13'2"	11'2" 14'11"	**12**
NA NA	11'0" 26'5"	14'3" 26'5"	17'5" 26'5"	7'0" 16'10"	9'1" 16'10"	NA NA	8'4" 15'5"	9'3" 15'5"	11'3" 15'5"	13'1" 17'5"	**14**
NA NA	12'7" 30'2"	16'4" 30'2"	19'11" 30'2"	8'0" 19'2"	10'5" 19'2"	NA NA	9'6" 17'7"	10'7" 17'7"	12'10" 17'7"	14'11" 19'11"	**16**
NA NA	14'2" 33'11"	18'4" 33'11"	22'5" 33'11"	9'0" 21'7"	11'8" 21'7"	NA NA	10'8" 19'10"	11'11" 19'10"	14'5" 19'10"	16'10" 22'5"	**18**
NA NA	15'9" 37'9"	20'5" 37'9"	24'11" 37'9"	10'0" 24'0"	13'0" 24'0"	NA NA	11'11" 22'0"	13'3" 22'0"	16'0" 22'0"	18'8" 24'11"	**20**
NA NA	19'9" 47'2"	25'6" 47'2"	31'2" 47'2"	12'6" 30'0"	16'3" 30'0"	NA NA	14'10" 27'6"	16'7" 27'6"	20'0" 27'6"	23'4" 31'2"	**25**
NA NA	39'5" 94'4"	51'0" 94'4"	62'4" 94'4"	25'0" 60'0"	32'5" 60'0"	NA NA	29'9" 55'0"	33'2" 55'0"	40'1" 55'0"	46'8" 62'4"	**50**

SETUPS (Approximate Distance) — 24mm FIELD OF VIEW

	Full Aperture	Academy 1.33:1	Academy 1.66:1	Academy 1.85:1	Anamorphic 2.40:1	Super 35 1.85:1	Super 35 2.40:1	VistaVision	VistaVision 1.85:1	VistaVision 2.40:1	65mm
Ext Close Up	1' 0"	1' 1"	1' 4"	1' 6"	1' 0"	1' 5"	1' 10"	0' 9"	0' 11"	1' 2"	0' 9"
Close Up	1' 6"	1' 9"	2' 1"	2' 4"	1' 6"	2' 2"	2' 10"	1' 1"	1' 4"	1' 9"	1' 3"
Medium Shot	2' 9"	3' 3"	3' 11"	4' 4"	2' 10"	4' 0"	5' 2"	2' 1"	2' 7"	3' 4"	2' 3"
Full Figure	7' 9"	9' 0"	10' 10"	12' 1"	7' 9"	11' 1"	14' 5"	5' 9"	7' 1"	9' 2"	6' 3"
Angle of View	V 42.5° H 54.8°	V 35.3° H 47.2°	V 29.5° H 47.2°	V 26.6° H 47.2°	V 40.7° H 83.2°	V 30.3° H 53.1°	V 23.6° H 53.1°	V 55.3° H 76.3°	V 46.0° H 76.3°	V 36.4° H 76.3°	V 49.4° H 90.7°
2	1' 7" / 2' 1"	1' 4" / 1' 10"	1' 1" / 1' 10"	1' 0" / 1' 10"	1' 7" / 3' 8"	1' 1" / 2' 0"	0' 10" / 2' 0"	2' 1" / 3' 2"	1' 8" / 3' 2"	1' 4" / 3' 2"	1' 11" / 4' 5"
2½	1' 11" / 2' 7"	1' 8" / 2' 3"	1' 5" / 2' 3"	1' 3" / 2' 3"	1' 11" / 4' 7"	1' 4" / 2' 6"	1' 1" / 2' 6"	2' 7" / 3' 11"	2' 1" / 3' 11"	1' 8" / 3' 11"	2' 5" / 5' 6"
3	2' 4" / 3' 1"	2' 0" / 2' 9"	1' 8" / 2' 9"	1' 6" / 2' 9"	2' 4" / 5' 6"	1' 7" / 3' 0"	1' 3" / 3' 0"	3' 1" / 4' 9"	2' 7" / 4' 9"	2' 0" / 4' 9"	2' 11" / 6' 7"
3½	2' 9" / 3' 8"	2' 4" / 3' 2"	1' 11" / 3' 2"	1' 9" / 3' 2"	2' 9" / 6' 5"	1' 11" / 3' 6"	1' 6" / 3' 6"	3' 8" / 5' 6"	3' 0" / 5' 6"	2' 4" / 5' 6"	3' 4" / 7' 8"
4	3' 1" / 4' 2"	2' 8" / 3' 8"	2' 3" / 3' 8"	2' 0" / 3' 8"	3' 1" / 7' 4"	2' 2" / 4' 0"	1' 8" / 4' 0"	4' 2" / 6' 3"	3' 5" / 6' 3"	2' 8" / 6' 3"	3' 10" / 8' 9"
4½	3' 6" / 4' 8"	3' 0" / 4' 1"	2' 6" / 4' 1"	2' 3" / 4' 1"	3' 6" / 8' 3"	2' 5" / 4' 6"	1' 11" / 4' 6"	4' 8" / 7' 1"	3' 10" / 7' 1"	2' 11" / 7' 1"	4' 4" / 9' 10"
5	3' 11" / 5' 2"	3' 4" / 4' 7"	2' 9" / 4' 7"	2' 6" / 4' 7"	3' 10" / 9' 2"	2' 8" / 5' 0"	2' 1" / 5' 0"	5' 2" / 7' 10"	4' 3" / 7' 10"	3' 3" / 7' 10"	4' 10" / 11' 0"
5½	4' 3" / 5' 9"	3' 8" / 5' 0"	3' 0" / 5' 0"	2' 9" / 5' 0"	4' 3" / 10' 1"	3' 0" / 5' 6"	2' 4" / 5' 6"	5' 9" / 8' 8"	4' 8" / 8' 8"	3' 7" / 8' 8"	5' 3" / 12' 1"

	A	B	C	D	E	F	G	H	I	J	K
6	4'8" / 6'3"	4'0" / 5'6"	3'4" / 5'6"	3'0" / 5'6"	4'8" / 11'0"	3'3" / 6'0"	2'6" / 6'0"	6'3" / 9'5"	5'1" / 9'5"	3'11" / 9'5"	5'9" / 13'2"
6½	5'1" / 6'9"	4'4" / 5'11"	3'7" / 5'11"	3'3" / 5'11"	5'0" / 11'11"	3'6" / 6'6"	2'9" / 6'6"	6'9" / 10'3"	5'6" / 10'3"	4'3" / 10'3"	6'3" / 14'3"
7	5'5" / 7'3"	4'8" / 6'5"	3'10" / 6'5"	3'6" / 6'5"	5'5" / 12'10"	3'9" / 7'0"	2'11" / 7'0"	7'3" / 11'0"	5'11" / 11'0"	4'7" / 11'0"	6'9" / 15'4"
8	6'3" / 8'4"	5'4" / 7'4"	4'5" / 7'4"	4'0" / 7'4"	6'2" / 14'8"	4'4" / 8'0"	3'4" / 8'0"	8'4" / 12'7"	6'10" / 12'7"	5'3" / 12'7"	7'8" / 17'7"
9	7'0" / 9'4"	6'0" / 8'3"	5'0" / 8'3"	4'5" / 8'3"	7'0" / 16'6"	4'10" / 9'0"	3'9" / 9'0"	9'4" / 14'2"	7'8" / 14'2"	5'11" / 14'2"	8'8" / 19'9"
10	7'9" / 10'5"	6'8" / 9'2"	5'6" / 9'2"	4'11" / 9'2"	7'9" / 18'4"	5'5" / 10'0"	4'2" / 10'0"	10'5" / 15'9"	8'6" / 15'9"	6'7" / 15'9"	9'7" / 21'11"
12	9'4" / 12'6"	8'0" / 11'0"	6'8" / 11'0"	5'11" / 11'0"	9'4" / 22'0"	6'6" / 12'0"	5'0" / 12'0"	12'6" / 18'10"	10'2" / 18'10"	7'11" / 18'10"	11'6" / 26'4"
14	10'11" / 14'6"	9'4" / 12'10"	7'9" / 12'10"	6'11" / 12'10"	10'10" / 25'8"	7'7" / 14'0"	5'10" / 14'0"	14'6" / 22'0"	11'11" / 22'0"	9'2" / 22'0"	13'5" / 30'8"
16	12'5" / 16'7"	10'8" / 14'8"	8'10" / 14'8"	7'11" / 14'8"	12'5" / 29'4"	8'8" / 16'0"	6'8" / 16'0"	16'7" / 25'2"	13'7" / 25'2"	10'6" / 25'2"	15'4" / 35'1"
18	14'0" / 18'8"	12'0" / 16'6"	9'11" / 16'6"	8'11" / 16'6"	13'11" / 33'0"	9'9" / 18'0"	7'6" / 18'0"	18'8" / 28'3"	15'4" / 28'3"	11'10" / 28'3"	17'3" / 39'6"
20	15'7" / 20'9"	13'4" / 18'4"	11'1" / 18'4"	9'11" / 18'4"	15'6" / 36'8"	10'10" / 20'0"	8'4" / 20'0"	20'9" / 31'5"	17'0" / 31'5"	13'2" / 31'5"	19'2" / 43'10"
25	19'5" / 25'11"	16'8" / 22'11"	13'10" / 22'11"	12'5" / 22'11"	19'4" / 45'10"	13'6" / 25'0"	10'5" / 25'0"	25'11" / 39'3"	21'3" / 39'3"	16'5" / 39'3"	24'0" / 54'10"
50	38'11" / 51'11"	33'5" / 45'10"	27'7" / 45'10"	24'9" / 45'10"	38'9" / 91'8"	27'0" / 50'0"	20'10" / 50'0"	51'11" / 78'7"	42'6" / 78'7"	32'10" / 78'7"	47'11" / 109'8"

SETUPS (Approximate Distance) — 25mm FIELD OF VIEW

	Full Aperture	Academy 1.33:1	Academy 1.66:1	Academy 1.85:1	Anamorphic 2.40:1	Super 35 1.85:1	Super 35 2.40:1	VistaVision	VistaVision 1.85:1	VistaVision 2.40:1	65mm
Ext Close Up	1' 0"	1' 2"	1' 5"	1' 7"	1' 0"	1' 5"	1' 10"	0' 9"	0' 11"	1' 2"	0' 10"
Close Up	1' 7"	1' 10"	2' 2"	2' 5"	1' 7"	2' 3"	2' 11"	1' 2"	1' 5"	1' 10"	1' 3"
Medium Shot	2' 11"	3' 5"	4' 1"	4' 7"	2' 11"	4' 2"	5' 5"	2' 2"	2' 8"	3' 5"	2' 4"
Full Figure	8' 0"	9' 4"	11' 4"	12' 7"	8' 1"	11' 7"	15' 0"	6' 0"	7' 4"	9' 6"	6' 6"
Angle of View	V 40.9° H 52.9°	V 34.0° H 45.5°	V 28.3° H 45.5°	V 25.5° H 45.5°	V 39.2° H 80.9°	V 29.1° H 51.3°	V 22.6° H 53.1°	V 53.4° H 74.1°	V 44.4° H 74.1°	V 35.0° H 74.1°	V 49.4° H 92.9°
2	1' 6" / 2' 0"	1' 3" / 1' 9"	1' 1" / 1' 9"	0' 11" / 1' 9"	1' 6" / 3' 6"	1' 0" / 1' 11"	0' 10" / 1' 11"	2' 0" / 3' 0"	1' 8" / 3' 0"	1' 3" / 3' 0"	1' 10" / 4' 3"
2½	1' 10" / 2' 6"	1' 7" / 2' 2"	1' 4" / 2' 2"	1' 2" / 2' 2"	1' 10" / 4' 5"	1' 4" / 2' 5"	1' 0" / 2' 5"	2' 6" / 3' 9"	2' 0" / 3' 9"	1' 7" / 3' 9"	2' 4" / 5' 3"
3	2' 3" / 3' 0"	1' 11" / 2' 8"	1' 7" / 2' 8"	1' 5" / 2' 8"	2' 3" / 5' 3"	1' 7" / 2' 11"	1' 2" / 2' 11"	3' 0" / 4' 6"	2' 5" / 4' 6"	1' 11" / 4' 6"	2' 9" / 6' 4"
3½	2' 7" / 3' 6"	2' 3" / 3' 1"	1' 10" / 3' 1"	1' 8" / 3' 1"	2' 7" / 6' 2"	1' 10" / 3' 4"	1' 5" / 3' 4"	3' 6" / 5' 3"	2' 10" / 5' 3"	2' 2" / 5' 3"	3' 3" / 7' 4"
4	3' 0" / 4' 0"	2' 7" / 3' 6"	2' 1" / 3' 6"	1' 11" / 3' 6"	3' 0" / 7' 0"	2' 1" / 3' 10"	1' 7" / 3' 10"	4' 0" / 6' 0"	3' 3" / 6' 0"	2' 6" / 6' 0"	3' 8" / 8' 5"
4½	3' 4" / 4' 6"	2' 11" / 4' 0"	2' 5" / 4' 0"	2' 2" / 4' 0"	3' 4" / 7' 11"	2' 4" / 4' 4"	1' 10" / 4' 4"	4' 6" / 6' 9"	3' 8" / 6' 9"	2' 10" / 6' 9"	4' 2" / 9' 6"
5	3' 9" / 5' 0"	3' 2" / 4' 5"	2' 8" / 4' 5"	2' 5" / 4' 5"	3' 9" / 8' 10"	2' 7" / 4' 10"	2' 0" / 4' 10"	5' 0" / 7' 7"	4' 1" / 7' 7"	3' 2" / 7' 7"	4' 7" / 10' 6"
5½	4' 1" / 5' 6"	3' 6" / 4' 10"	2' 11" / 4' 10"	2' 7" / 4' 10"	4' 1" / 9' 8"	2' 10" / 5' 3"	2' 2" / 5' 3"	5' 6" / 8' 4"	4' 6" / 8' 4"	3' 6" / 8' 4"	5' 1" / 11' 7"

6	4' 6" 6' 0"	3' 10" 5' 3"	3' 2" 5' 3"	2' 10" 5' 3"	4' 6" 10' 7"	3' 1" 5' 9"	2' 5" 5' 9"	6' 0" 9' 1"	4' 11" 9' 1"	3' 9" 9' 1"	5' 6" 12' 8"
6½	4' 10" 6' 6"	4' 2" 5' 9"	3' 5" 5' 9"	3' 1" 5' 9"	4' 10" 11' 5"	3' 4" 6' 3"	2' 7" 6' 3"	6' 6" 9' 10"	5' 4" 9' 10"	4' 1" 9' 10"	6' 0" 13' 8"
7	5' 3" 7' 0"	4' 6" 6' 2"	3' 9" 6' 2"	3' 4" 6' 2"	5' 2" 12' 4"	3' 8" 6' 9"	2' 10" 6' 9"	7' 0" 10' 7"	5' 9" 10' 7"	4' 5" 10' 7"	6' 5" 14' 9"
8	6' 0" 8' 0"	5' 2" 7' 0"	4' 3" 7' 0"	3' 10" 7' 0"	5' 11" 14' 1"	4' 2" 7' 8"	3' 2" 7' 8"	8' 0" 12' 1"	6' 6" 12' 1"	5' 1" 12' 1"	7' 4" 16' 10"
9	6' 9" 9' 0"	5' 9" 7' 11"	4' 9" 7' 11"	4' 3" 7' 11"	6' 8" 15' 10"	4' 8" 8' 8"	3' 7" 8' 8"	9' 0" 13' 7"	7' 4" 13' 7"	5' 8" 13' 7"	8' 3" 18' 11"
10	7' 6" 10' 0"	6' 5" 8' 10"	5' 4" 8' 10"	4' 9" 8' 10"	7' 5" 17' 7"	5' 2" 9' 7"	4' 0" 9' 7"	10' 0" 15' 1"	8' 2" 15' 1"	6' 4" 15' 1"	9' 2" 21' 1"
12	9' 0" 12' 0"	7' 8" 10' 7"	6' 4" 10' 7"	5' 8" 10' 7"	8' 11" 21' 1"	6' 3" 11' 6"	4' 10" 11' 6"	12' 0" 18' 1"	9' 9" 18' 1"	7' 7" 18' 1"	11' 1" 25' 3"
14	10' 5" 13' 11"	9' 0" 12' 4"	7' 5" 12' 4"	6' 8" 12' 4"	10' 5" 24' 8"	7' 3" 13' 5"	5' 7" 13' 5"	13' 11" 21' 1"	11' 5" 21' 1"	8' 10" 21' 1"	12' 11" 29' 6"
16	11' 11" 15' 11"	10' 3" 14' 1"	8' 6" 14' 1"	7' 7" 14' 1"	11' 11" 28' 2"	8' 4" 15' 4"	6' 5" 15' 4"	15' 11" 24' 2"	13' 1" 24' 2"	10' 1" 24' 2"	14' 9" 33' 8"
18	13' 5" 17' 11"	11' 6" 15' 10"	9' 7" 15' 10"	8' 7" 15' 10"	13' 5" 31' 8"	9' 4" 17' 3"	7' 2" 17' 3"	17' 11" 27' 2"	14' 8" 27' 2"	11' 4" 27' 2"	16' 7" 37' 11"
20	14' 11" 19' 11"	12' 10" 17' 7"	10' 7" 17' 7"	9' 6" 17' 7"	14' 10" 35' 2"	10' 5" 19' 2"	8' 0" 19' 2"	19' 11" 30' 2"	16' 4" 30' 2"	12' 7" 30' 2"	18' 5" 42' 1"
25	18' 8" 24' 11"	16' 0" 22' 0"	13' 3" 22' 0"	11' 11" 22' 0"	18' 7" 44' 0"	13' 0" 24' 0"	10' 0" 24' 0"	24' 11" 37' 9"	20' 5" 37' 9"	15' 9" 37' 9"	23' 0" 52' 8"
50	37' 4" 49' 10"	32' 1" 44' 0"	26' 6" 44' 0"	23' 9" 44' 0"	37' 2" 88' 0"	26' 0" 48' 0"	20' 0" 48' 0"	49' 10" 75' 5"	40' 10" 75' 5"	31' 7" 75' 5"	46' 0" 105' 3"

SETUPS (Approximate Distance) — 28mm FIELD OF VIEW

	Full Aperture	Academy 1.33:1	Academy 1.66:1	Academy 1.85:1	Anamorphic 2.40:1	Super 35 1.85:1	Super 35 2.40:1	VistaVision	VistaVision 1.85:1	VistaVision 2.40:1	65mm
Ext Close Up	1' 1"	1' 4"	1' 7"	1' 9"	1' 2"	1' 7"	2' 1"	0' 10"	1' 0"	1' 4"	0' 11"
Close Up	1' 9"	2' 0"	2' 6"	2' 9"	1' 9"	2' 6"	3' 3"	1' 4"	1' 7"	2' 1"	1' 5"
Medium Shot	3' 3"	3' 9"	4' 7"	5' 1"	3' 3"	4' 8"	6' 1"	2' 5"	3' 0"	3' 10"	2' 8"
Full Figure	9' 0"	10' 6"	12' 8"	14' 2"	9' 0"	12' 11"	16' 9"	6' 9"	8' 3"	10' 8"	7' 4"
Angle of View	V 36.9° H 47.9°	V 30.5° H 41.0°	V 25.4° H 41.0°	V 22.9° H 41.0°	V 35.2° H 74.5°	V 26.1° H 46.4°	V 20.3° H 46.4°	V 48.4° H 67.9°	V 40.0° H 67.9°	V 31.5° H 67.9°	
2	1' 4" / 1' 9"	1' 2" / 1' 7"	0' 11" / 1' 7"	0' 10" / 1' 7"	1' 4" / 3' 2"	0' 11" / 1' 9"	0' 9" / 1' 9"	1' 9" / 2' 8"	1' 5" / 2' 8"	1' 2" / 2' 8"	NA / NA
2½	1' 8" / 2' 3"	1' 5" / 2' 0"	1' 2" / 2' 0"	1' 1" / 2' 0"	1' 8" / 3' 11"	1' 2" / 2' 2"	0' 11" / 2' 2"	2' 3" / 3' 4"	1' 10" / 3' 4"	1' 5" / 3' 4"	NA / NA
3	2' 0" / 2' 8"	1' 9" / 2' 4"	1' 5" / 2' 4"	1' 3" / 2' 4"	2' 0" / 4' 9"	1' 5" / 2' 7"	1' 1" / 2' 7"	2' 8" / 4' 0"	2' 2" / 4' 0"	1' 8" / 4' 0"	NA / NA
3½	2' 4" / 3' 1"	2' 0" / 2' 9"	1' 8" / 2' 9"	1' 6" / 2' 9"	2' 4" / 5' 6"	1' 7" / 3' 0"	1' 3" / 3' 0"	3' 1" / 4' 9"	2' 7" / 4' 9"	2' 0" / 4' 9"	NA / NA
4	2' 8" / 3' 7"	2' 3" / 3' 2"	1' 11" / 3' 2"	1' 8" / 3' 2"	2' 8" / 6' 3"	1' 10" / 3' 5"	1' 5" / 3' 5"	3' 7" / 5' 5"	2' 11" / 5' 5"	2' 3" / 5' 5"	NA / NA
4½	3' 0" / 4' 0"	2' 7" / 3' 6"	2' 2" / 3' 6"	1' 11" / 3' 6"	3' 0" / 7' 1"	2' 1" / 3' 10"	1' 7" / 3' 10"	4' 0" / 6' 1"	3' 3" / 6' 1"	2' 6" / 6' 1"	NA / NA
5	3' 4" / 4' 5"	2' 10" / 3' 11"	2' 4" / 3' 11"	2' 1" / 3' 11"	3' 4" / 7' 10"	2' 4" / 4' 3"	1' 9" / 4' 3"	4' 5" / 6' 9"	3' 8" / 6' 9"	2' 10" / 6' 9"	NA / NA
5½	3' 8" / 4' 11"	3' 2" / 4' 4"	2' 7" / 4' 4"	2' 4" / 4' 4"	3' 8" / 8' 8"	2' 7" / 4' 9"	2' 0" / 4' 9"	4' 11" / 7' 5"	4' 0" / 7' 5"	3' 1" / 7' 5"	NA / NA

	1	2	3	4	5	6	7	8	9	10	11
6	4' 0" / 5' 4"	3' 5" / 4' 9"	2' 10" / 4' 9"	2' 7" / 4' 9"	4' 0" / 9' 5"	2' 9" / 5' 2"	2' 2" / 5' 2"	5' 4" / 8' 1"	4' 4" / 8' 1"	3' 5" / 8' 1"	NA / NA
6½	4' 4" / 5' 9"	3' 9" / 5' 1"	3' 1" / 5' 1"	2' 9" / 5' 1"	4' 4" / 10' 3"	3' 0" / 5' 7"	2' 4" / 5' 7"	5' 9" / 8' 9"	4' 9" / 8' 9"	3' 8" / 8' 9"	NA / NA
7	4' 8" / 6' 3"	4' 0" / 5' 6"	3' 4" / 5' 6"	3' 0" / 5' 6"	4' 8" / 11' 0"	3' 3" / 6' 0"	2' 6" / 6' 0"	6' 3" / 9' 5"	5' 1" / 9' 5"	3' 11" / 9' 5"	NA / NA
8	5' 4" / 7' 1"	4' 7" / 6' 3"	3' 9" / 6' 3"	3' 5" / 6' 3"	5' 4" / 12' 7"	3' 9" / 6' 10"	2' 10" / 6' 10"	7' 1" / 10' 9"	5' 10" / 10' 9"	4' 6" / 10' 9"	NA / NA
9	6' 0" / 8' 0"	5' 2" / 7' 1"	4' 3" / 7' 1"	3' 10" / 7' 1"	6' 0" / 14' 2"	4' 2" / 7' 9"	3' 3" / 7' 9"	8' 0" / 12' 1"	6' 7" / 12' 1"	5' 1" / 12' 1"	NA / NA
10	6' 8" / 8' 11"	5' 9" / 7' 10"	4' 9" / 7' 10"	4' 3" / 7' 10"	6' 8" / 15' 9"	4' 8" / 8' 7"	3' 7" / 8' 7"	8' 11" / 13' 6"	7' 3" / 13' 6"	5' 8" / 13' 6"	NA / NA
12	8' 0" / 10' 8"	6' 10" / 9' 5"	5' 8" / 9' 5"	5' 1" / 9' 5"	8' 0" / 18' 10"	5' 7" / 10' 3"	4' 3" / 10' 3"	10' 8" / 16' 2"	8' 9" / 16' 2"	6' 9" / 16' 2"	NA / NA
14	9' 4" / 12' 6"	8' 0" / 11' 0"	6' 8" / 11' 0"	5' 11" / 11' 0"	9' 4" / 22' 0"	6' 6" / 12' 0"	5' 0" / 12' 0"	12' 6" / 18' 10"	10' 2" / 18' 10"	7' 11" / 18' 10"	NA / NA
16	10' 8" / 14' 3"	9' 2" / 12' 7"	7' 7" / 12' 7"	6' 10" / 12' 7"	10' 7" / 25' 2"	7' 5" / 13' 9"	5' 9" / 13' 9"	14' 3" / 21' 7"	11' 8" / 21' 7"	9' 0" / 21' 7"	NA / NA
18	12' 0" / 16' 0"	10' 4" / 14' 2"	8' 6" / 14' 2"	7' 8" / 14' 2"	11' 11" / 28' 3"	8' 4" / 15' 5"	6' 5" / 15' 5"	16' 0" / 24' 3"	13' 1" / 24' 3"	10' 2" / 24' 3"	NA / NA
20	13' 4" / 17' 10"	11' 5" / 15' 9"	9' 6" / 15' 9"	8' 6" / 15' 9"	13' 3" / 31' 5"	9' 3" / 17' 2"	7' 2" / 17' 2"	17' 10" / 26' 11"	14' 7" / 26' 11"	11' 3" / 26' 11"	NA
25	16' 8" / 22' 3"	14' 4" / 19' 8"	11' 10" / 19' 8"	10' 7" / 19' 8"	16' 7" / 39' 3"	11' 7" / 21' 5"	8' 11" / 21' 5"	22' 3" / 33' 8"	18' 3" / 33' 8"	14' 1" / 33' 8"	NA / NA
50	33' 4" / 44' 6"	28' 7" / 39' 3"	23' 8" / 39' 3"	21' 3" / 39' 3"	33' 2" / 78' 7"	23' 2" / 42' 10"	17' 10" / 42' 10"	44' 6" / 67' 4"	36' 5" / 67' 4"	28' 2" / 67' 4"	NA / NA

SETUPS (Approximate Distance) — 32mm FIELD OF VIEW

	Full Aperture	Academy 1.33:1	Academy 1.66:1	Academy 1.85:1	Anamorphic 2.40:1	Super 35 1.85:1	Super 35 2.40:1	VistaVision	VistaVision 1.85:1	VistaVision 2.40:1	65mm
Ext Close Up	1' 3"	1' 6"	1' 10"	2' 0"	1' 3"	1' 10"	2' 5"	1' 0"	1' 2"	1' 6"	1' 1"
Close Up	2' 0"	2' 4"	2' 10"	3' 2"	2' 0"	2' 11"	3' 9"	1' 6"	1' 10"	2' 4"	1' 7"
Medium Shot	3' 9"	4' 4"	5' 3"	5' 10"	3' 9"	5' 4"	6' 11"	2' 9"	3' 5"	4' 5"	3' 0"
Full Figure	10' 3"	12' 0"	14' 6"	16' 2"	10' 4"	14' 10"	19' 2"	7' 8"	9' 5"	12' 2"	8' 4"
Angle of View	V 32.5° H 42.5°	V 26.9° H 36.3°	V 22.3° H 36.3°	V 20.1° H 36.3°	V 31.1° H 67.3°	V 22.9° H 41.1°	V 17.8° H 41.1°		V 35.4° H 61.0°	V 27.7° H 61.0°	
2	1' 2" / 1' 7"	1' 0" / 1' 4"	0' 10" / 1' 4"	0' 9" / 1' 4"	1' 2" / 2' 9"	0' 10" / 1' 6"	0' 8" / 1' 6"	NA / NA	1' 3" / 2' 4"	1' 0" / 2' 4"	NA / NA
2½	1' 6" / 1' 11"	1' 3" / 1' 9"	1' 0" / 1' 9"	0' 11" / 1' 9"	1' 5" / 3' 5"	1' 0" / 1' 11"	0' 9" / 1' 11"	NA / NA	1' 7" / 2' 11"	1' 3" / 2' 11"	NA / NA
3	1' 9" / 2' 4"	1' 6" / 2' 1"	1' 3" / 2' 1"	1' 1" / 2' 1"	1' 9" / 4' 1"	1' 3" / 2' 3"	0' 11" / 2' 3"	NA / NA	1' 11" / 3' 6"	1' 6" / 3' 6"	NA / NA
3½	2' 1" / 2' 9"	1' 9" / 2' 5"	1' 5" / 2' 5"	1' 4" / 2' 5"	2' 0" / 4' 10"	1' 5" / 2' 8"	1' 1" / 2' 8"	NA / NA	2' 3" / 4' 2"	1' 9" / 4' 2"	NA / NA
4	2' 4" / 3' 1"	2' 0" / 2' 9"	1' 8" / 2' 9"	1' 6" / 2' 9"	2' 4" / 5' 6"	1' 7" / 3' 0"	1' 3" / 3' 0"	NA / NA	2' 7" / 4' 9"	2' 0" / 4' 9"	NA / NA
4½	2' 8" / 3' 6"	2' 3" / 3' 1"	1' 10" / 3' 1"	1' 8" / 3' 1"	2' 7" / 6' 2"	1' 10" / 3' 5"	1' 5" / 3' 5"	NA / NA	2' 10" / 5' 4"	2' 3" / 5' 4"	NA / NA
5	2' 11" / 3' 11"	2' 6" / 3' 5"	2' 1" / 3' 5"	1' 10" / 3' 5"	2' 11" / 6' 10"	2' 0" / 3' 9"	1' 7" / 3' 9"	NA / NA	3' 2" / 5' 11"	2' 6" / 5' 11"	NA / NA
5½	3' 3" / 4' 3"	2' 9" / 3' 9"	2' 3" / 3' 9"	2' 1" / 3' 9"	3' 2" / 7' 7"	2' 3" / 4' 2"	1' 9" / 4' 2"	NA / NA	3' 6" / 6' 6"	2' 9" / 6' 6"	NA / NA

6	3'6" / 4'8"	3'0" / 4'1"	2'6" / 4'1"	2'3" / 4'1"	3'6" / 8'3"	2'5" / 4'6"	1'11" / 4'6"	NA / NA	3'10" / 7'1"	2'11" / 7'1"	NA / NA
6½	3'10" / 5'1"	3'3" / 4'6"	2'8" / 4'6"	2'5" / 4'6"	3'9" / 8'11"	2'8" / 4'11"	2'0" / 4'11"	NA / NA	4'2" / 7'8"	3'2" / 7'8"	NA / NA
7	4'1" / 5'5"	3'6" / 4'10"	2'11" / 4'10"	2'7" / 4'10"	4'1" / 9'7"	2'10" / 5'3"	2'2" / 5'3"	NA / NA	4'6" / 8'3"	3'5" / 8'3"	NA / NA
8	4'8" / 6'3"	4'0" / 5'6"	3'4" / 5'6"	3'0" / 5'6"	4'8" / 11'0"	3'3" / 6'0"	2'6" / 6'0"	NA / NA	5'1" / 9'5"	3'11" / 9'5"	NA / NA
9	5'3" / 7'0"	4'6" / 6'2"	3'9" / 6'2"	3'4" / 6'2"	5'3" / 12'4"	3'8" / 6'9"	2'10" / 6'9"	NA / NA	5'9" / 10'7"	4'5" / 10'7"	NA / NA
10	5'10" / 7'9"	5'0" / 6'10"	4'2" / 6'10"	3'9" / 6'10"	5'10" / 13'9"	4'1" / 7'6"	3'2" / 7'6"	NA / NA	6'4" / 11'9"	4'11" / 11'9"	NA / NA
12	7'0" / 9'4"	6'0" / 8'3"	5'0" / 8'3"	4'5" / 8'3"	7'0" / 16'6"	4'10" / 9'0"	3'9" / 9'0"	NA / NA	7'8" / 14'2"	5'11" / 14'2"	NA / NA
14	8'2" / 10'11"	7'0" / 9'7"	5'10" / 9'7"	5'2" / 9'7"	8'2" / 19'3"	5'8" / 10'6"	4'5" / 10'6"	NA / NA	8'11" / 16'6"	6'11" / 16'6"	NA / NA
16	9'4" / 12'6"	8'0" / 11'0"	6'8" / 11'0"	5'11" / 11'0"	9'4" / 22'0"	6'6" / 12'0"	5'0" / 12'0"	NA / NA	10'2" / 18'10"	7'11" / 18'10"	NA / NA
18	10'6" / 14'0"	9'0" / 12'4"	7'5" / 12'4"	6'8" / 12'4"	10'6" / 24'9"	7'4" / 13'6"	5'8" / 13'6"	NA / NA	11'6" / 21'3"	8'10" / 21'3"	NA / NA
20	11'8" / 15'7"	10'0" / 13'9"	8'3" / 13'9"	7'5" / 13'9"	11'7" / 27'6"	8'1" / 15'0"	6'3" / 15'0"	NA / NA	12'9" / 23'7"	9'10" / 23'7"	NA / NA
25	14'7" / 19'6"	12'6" / 17'2"	10'4" / 17'2"	9'3" / 17'2"	14'6" / 34'4"	10'2" / 18'9"	7'10" / 18'9"	NA / NA	15'11" / 29'6"	12'4" / 29'6"	NA / NA
50	29'2" / 38'11"	25'1" / 34'4"	20'9" / 34'4"	18'7" / 34'4"	29'1" / 68'9"	20'3" / 37'6"	15'8" / 37'6"	NA / NA	31'10" / 58'11"	24'8" / 58'11"	NA / NA

SETUPS (Approximate Distance) — 35mm FIELD OF VIEW

	Full Aperture	Academy 1.33:1	Academy 1.66:1	Academy 1.85:1	Anamorphic 2.40:1	Super 35 1.85:1	Super 35 2.40:1	VistaVision	VistaVision 1.85:1	VistaVision 2.40:1	65mm
Ext Close Up	1' 5"	1' 8"	2' 0"	2' 2"	1' 5"	2' 0"	2' 7"	1' 1"	1' 3"	1' 8"	1' 2"
Close Up	2' 2"	2' 7"	3' 1"	3' 5"	2' 2"	3' 2"	4' 1"	1' 8"	2' 0"	2' 7"	1' 9"
Medium Shot	4' 1"	4' 9"	5' 9"	6' 5"	4' 1"	5' 10"	7' 7"	3' 1"	3' 9"	4' 10"	3' 4"
Full Figure	11' 3"	13' 1"	15' 10"	17' 8"	11' 4"	16' 2"	21' 0"	8' 5"	10' 4"	13' 4"	9' 2"
Angle of View	V 29.9° H 39.2°	V 24.6° H 33.3°	V 20.4° H 33.3°	V 18.4° H 33.3°	V 28.5° H 62.7°	V 21.0° H 37.9°	V 16.3° H 37.9°	V 39.6° H 56.6°	V 32.5° H 56.6°	V 25.4° H 56.6°	V 36.4° H 73.9°
2	1' 1" / 1' 5"	0' 11" / 1' 3"	0' 9" / 1' 3"	0' 8" / 1' 3"	1' 1" / 2' 6"	0' 9" / 1' 4"	0' 7" / 1' 4"	1' 5" / 2' 2"	1' 2" / 2' 2"	0' 11" / 2' 2"	1' 4" / 3' 0"
2½	1' 4" / 1' 9"	1' 2" / 1' 7"	0' 11" / 1' 7"	0' 10" / 1' 7"	1' 4" / 3' 2"	0' 11" / 1' 9"	0' 9" / 1' 9"	1' 9" / 2' 8"	1' 5" / 2' 8"	1' 2" / 2' 8"	1' 8" / 3' 9"
3	1' 7" / 2' 2"	1' 4" / 1' 11"	1' 2" / 1' 11"	1' 0" / 1' 11"	1' 7" / 3' 9"	1' 1" / 2' 1"	0' 10" / 2' 1"	2' 2" / 3' 3"	1' 9" / 3' 3"	1' 4" / 3' 3"	2' 0" / 4' 6"
3½	1' 10" / 2' 6"	1' 7" / 2' 2"	1' 4" / 2' 2"	1' 2" / 2' 2"	1' 10" / 4' 5"	1' 4" / 2' 5"	1' 0" / 2' 5"	2' 6" / 3' 9"	2' 0" / 3' 9"	1' 7" / 3' 9"	2' 4" / 5' 3"
4	2' 2" / 2' 10"	1' 10" / 2' 6"	1' 6" / 2' 6"	1' 4" / 2' 6"	2' 1" / 5' 0"	1' 6" / 2' 9"	1' 2" / 2' 9"	2' 10" / 4' 4"	2' 4" / 4' 4"	1' 10" / 4' 4"	2' 8" / 6' 0"
4½	2' 5" / 3' 2"	2' 1" / 2' 10"	1' 8" / 2' 10"	1' 6" / 2' 10"	2' 5" / 5' 8"	1' 8" / 3' 1"	1' 3" / 3' 1"	3' 2" / 4' 10"	2' 7" / 4' 10"	2' 0" / 4' 10"	3' 0" / 6' 9"
5	2' 8" / 3' 7"	2' 3" / 3' 2"	1' 11" / 3' 2"	1' 8" / 3' 2"	2' 8" / 6' 3"	1' 10" / 3' 5"	1' 5" / 3' 5"	3' 7" / 5' 5"	2' 11" / 5' 5"	2' 3" / 5' 5"	3' 3" / 7' 6"
5½	2' 11" / 3' 11"	2' 6" / 3' 5"	2' 1" / 3' 5"	1' 10" / 3' 5"	2' 11" / 6' 11"	2' 0" / 3' 9"	1' 7" / 3' 9"	3' 11" / 5' 11"	3' 2" / 5' 11"	2' 6" / 5' 11"	3' 7" / 8' 3"

	1	2	3	4	5	6	7	8	9	10	11
6	3' 2" 4' 3"	2' 9" 3' 9"	2' 3" 3' 9"	2' 0" 3' 9"	3' 2" 7' 6"	2' 3" 4' 1"	1' 9" 4' 1"	4' 3" 6' 6"	3' 6" 6' 6"	2' 8" 6' 6"	3' 11" 9' 0"
6½	3' 6" 4' 8"	3' 0" 4' 1"	2' 6" 4' 1"	2' 2" 4' 1"	3' 5" 8' 2"	2' 5" 4' 5"	1' 10" 4' 5"	4' 8" 7' 0"	3' 9" 7' 0"	2' 11" 7' 0"	4' 3" 9' 9"
7	3' 9" 5' 0"	3' 2" 4' 5"	2' 8" 4' 5"	2' 5" 4' 5"	3' 9" 8' 10"	2' 7" 4' 10"	2' 0" 4' 10"	5' 0" 7' 7"	4' 1" 7' 7"	3' 2" 7' 7"	4' 7" 10' 6"
8	4' 3" 5' 8"	3' 8" 5' 0"	3' 0" 5' 0"	2' 9" 5' 0"	4' 3" 10' 1"	3' 0" 5' 6"	2' 3" 5' 6"	5' 8" 8' 7"	4' 8" 8' 7"	3' 7" 8' 7"	5' 3" 12' 0"
9	4' 10" 6' 5"	4' 1" 5' 8"	3' 5" 5' 8"	3' 1" 5' 8"	4' 9" 11' 4"	3' 4" 6' 2"	2' 7" 6' 2"	6' 5" 9' 8"	5' 3" 9' 8"	4' 1" 9' 8"	5' 11" 13' 6"
10	5' 4" 7' 1"	4' 7" 6' 3"	3' 9" 6' 3"	3' 5" 6' 3"	5' 4" 12' 7"	3' 9" 6' 10"	2' 10" 6' 10"	7' 1" 10' 9"	5' 10" 10' 9"	4' 6" 10' 9"	6' 7" 15' 0"
12	6' 5" 8' 7"	5' 6" 7' 6"	4' 7" 7' 6"	4' 1" 7' 6"	6' 4" 15' 1"	4' 5" 8' 3"	3' 5" 8' 3"	8' 7" 12' 11"	7' 0" 12' 11"	5' 5" 12' 11"	7' 11" 18' 1"
14	7' 6" 10' 0"	6' 5" 8' 10"	5' 4" 8' 10"	4' 9" 8' 10"	7' 5" 17' 7"	5' 2" 9' 7"	4' 0" 9' 7"	10' 0" 15' 1"	8' 2" 15' 1"	6' 4" 15' 1"	9' 2" 21' 1"
16	8' 6" 11' 5"	7' 4" 10' 1"	6' 1" 10' 1"	5' 5" 10' 1"	8' 6" 20' 1"	5' 11" 11' 0"	4' 7" 11' 0"	11' 5" 17' 3"	9' 4" 17' 3"	7' 3" 17' 3"	10' 6" 24' 1"
18	9' 7" 12' 10"	8' 3" 11' 4"	6' 10" 11' 4"	6' 1" 11' 4"	9' 7" 22' 7"	6' 8" 12' 4"	5' 2" 12' 4"	12' 10" 19' 5"	10' 6" 19' 5"	8' 1" 19' 5"	11' 10" 27' 1"
20	10' 8" 14' 3"	9' 2" 12' 7"	7' 7" 12' 7"	6' 10" 12' 7"	10' 7" 25' 2"	7' 5" 13' 9"	5' 9" 13' 9"	14' 3" 21' 7"	11' 8" 21' 7"	9' 0" 21' 7"	13' 2" 30' 1"
25	13' 4" 17' 10"	11' 5" 15' 9"	9' 6" 15' 9"	8' 6" 15' 9"	13' 3" 31' 5"	9' 3" 17' 2"	7' 2" 17' 2"	17' 10" 26' 11"	14' 7" 26' 11"	11' 3" 26' 11"	16' 5" 37' 7"
50	26' 8" 35' 7"	22' 11" 31' 5"	18' 11" 31' 5"	17' 0" 31' 5"	26' 7" 62' 10"	18' 7" 34' 3"	14' 4" 34' 3"	35' 7" 53' 11"	29' 2" 53' 11"	22' 6" 53' 11"	32' 10" 75' 2"

SETUPS (Approximate Distance) — **40mm FIELD OF VIEW**

Format	Ext Close Up	Close Up	Medium Shot	Full Figure	Angle of View	2	2½	3	3½	4	4½	5	5½
Full Aperture	1' 7"	2' 6"	4' 8"	12' 10"	V 26.3° H 34.6°	0' 11" / 1' 3"	1' 2" / 1' 7"	1' 5" / 1' 10"	1' 8" / 2' 2"	1' 10" / 2' 6"	2' 1" / 2' 10"	2' 4" / 3' 1"	2' 7" / 3' 5"
Academy 1.33:1	1' 10"	2' 11"	5' 5"	15' 0"	V 21.6° H 29.4°	0' 10" / 1' 1"	1' 0" / 1' 4"	1' 2" / 1' 8"	1' 5" / 1' 11"	1' 7" / 2' 2"	1' 10" / 2' 6"	2' 0" / 2' 9"	2' 2" / 3' 0"
Academy 1.66:1	2' 3"	3' 6"	6' 6"	18' 1"	V 17.9° H 29.4°	0' 8" / 1' 1"	0' 10" / 1' 4"	1' 0" / 1' 8"	1' 2" / 1' 11"	1' 4" / 2' 2"	1' 6" / 2' 6"	1' 8" / 2' 9"	1' 10" / 3' 0"
Academy 1.85:1	2' 6"	3' 11"	7' 3"	20' 2"	V 16.1° H 29.4°	0' 7" / 1' 1"	0' 9" / 1' 4"	0' 11" / 1' 8"	1' 0" / 1' 11"	1' 2" / 2' 2"	1' 4" / 2' 6"	1' 6" / 2' 9"	1' 8" / 3' 0"
Anamorphic 2.40:1	1' 7"	2' 6"	4' 8"	12' 11"	V 25.1° H 56.1°	0' 11" / 2' 2"	1' 2" / 2' 9"	1' 5" / 3' 4"	1' 8" / 3' 10"	1' 10" / 4' 5"	2' 1" / 4' 11"	2' 4" / 5' 6"	2' 7" / 6' 1"
Super 35 1.85:1	2' 4"	3' 7"	6' 8"	18' 6"	V 18.4° H 33.4°	0' 8" / 1' 2"	0' 10" / 1' 6"	1' 0" / 1' 10"	1' 2" / 2' 1"	1' 4" / 2' 5"	1' 6" / 2' 8"	1' 7" / 3' 0"	1' 9" / 3' 4"
Super 35 2.40:1	3' 0"	4' 8"	8' 8"	24' 0"	V 14.3° H 33.4°	0' 6" / 1' 2"	0' 8" / 1' 6"	0' 9" / 1' 10"	0' 11" / 2' 1"	1' 0" / 2' 5"	1' 2" / 2' 8"	1' 3" / 3' 0"	1' 5" / 3' 4"
VistaVision	1' 2"	1' 10"	3' 6"	9' 8"	V 34.9° H 50.5°	1' 3" / 1' 11"	1' 7" / 2' 4"	1' 10" / 2' 10"	2' 2" / 3' 4"	2' 6" / 3' 9"	2' 10" / 4' 3"	3' 1" / 4' 9"	3' 5" / 5' 2"
VistaVision 1.85:1	1' 6"	2' 3"	4' 3"	11' 9"	V 28.6° H 50.5°	1' 0" / 1' 11"	1' 3" / 2' 4"	1' 6" / 2' 10"	1' 9" / 3' 4"	2' 0" / 3' 9"	2' 4" / 4' 3"	2' 7" / 4' 9"	2' 10" / 5' 2"
VistaVision 2.40:1	1' 11"	3' 0"	5' 6"	15' 3"	V 22.3° H 50.5°	0' 9" / 1' 11"	1' 0" / 2' 4"	1' 2" / 2' 10"	1' 5" / 3' 4"	1' 7" / 3' 9"	1' 9" / 4' 3"	2' 0" / 4' 9"	2' 2" / 5' 2"
65mm	1' 4"	2' 0"	3' 9"	10' 5"	V 30.9° H 62.5°	1' 2" / 2' 8"	1' 5" / 3' 3"	1' 9" / 3' 11"	2' 0" / 4' 7"	2' 4" / 5' 3"	2' 7" / 5' 11"	2' 11" / 6' 7"	3' 2" / 7' 3"

	6	6½	7	8	9	10	12	14	16	18	20	25	50
	3'5" / 7'11"	3'9" / 8'7"	4'0" / 9'3"	4'7" / 10'6"	5'2" / 11'10"	5'9" / 13'2"	6'11" / 15'9"	8'1" / 18'5"	9'2" / 21'1"	10'4" / 23'8"	11'6" / 26'4"	14'5" / 32'11"	28'9" / 65'9"
	2'4" / 5'8"	2'7" / 6'2"	2'9" / 6'7"	3'2" / 7'7"	3'7" / 8'6"	3'11" / 9'5"	4'9" / 11'4"	5'6" / 13'2"	6'4" / 15'1"	7'1" / 17'0"	7'11" / 18'10"	9'10" / 23'7"	19'9" / 47'2"
	3'1" / 5'8"	3'4" / 6'2"	3'7" / 6'7"	4'1" / 7'7"	4'7" / 8'6"	5'1" / 9'5"	6'1" / 11'4"	7'2" / 13'2"	8'2" / 15'1"	9'2" / 17'0"	10'2" / 18'10"	12'9" / 23'7"	25'6" / 47'2"
	3'9" / 5'8"	4'1" / 6'2"	4'4" / 6'7"	5'0" / 7'7"	5'7" / 8'6"	6'3" / 9'5"	7'6" / 11'4"	8'9" / 13'2"	10'0" / 15'1"	11'3" / 17'0"	12'6" / 18'10"	15'7" / 23'7"	31'2" / 47'2"
	1'6" / 3'7"	1'8" / 3'11"	1'9" / 4'2"	2'0" / 4'10"	2'3" / 5'5"	2'6" / 6'0"	3'0" / 7'2"	3'6" / 8'5"	4'0" / 9'7"	4'6" / 10'10"	5'0" / 12'0"	6'3" / 15'0"	12'6" / 30'0"
	1'11" / 3'7"	2'1" / 3'11"	2'3" / 4'2"	2'7" / 4'10"	2'11" / 5'5"	3'3" / 6'0"	3'11" / 7'2"	4'7" / 8'5"	5'2" / 9'7"	5'10" / 10'10"	6'6" / 12'0"	8'1" / 15'0"	16'3" / 30'0"
	2'9" / 6'7"	3'0" / 7'2"	3'3" / 7'8"	3'9" / 8'10"	4'2" / 9'11"	4'8" / 11'0"	5'7" / 13'2"	6'6" / 15'5"	7'5" / 17'7"	8'4" / 19'10"	9'4" / 22'0"	11'7" / 27'6"	23'3" / 55'0"
	1'9" / 3'4"	1'11" / 3'7"	2'1" / 3'10"	2'5" / 4'5"	2'8" / 4'11"	3'0" / 5'6"	3'7" / 6'7"	4'2" / 7'8"	4'9" / 8'10"	5'4" / 9'11"	5'11" / 11'0"	7'5" / 13'9"	14'10" / 27'6"
	2'0" / 3'4"	2'2" / 3'7"	2'4" / 3'10"	2'8" / 4'5"	3'0" / 4'11"	3'4" / 5'6"	4'0" / 6'7"	4'8" / 7'8"	5'4" / 8'10"	6'0" / 9'11"	6'8" / 11'0"	8'3" / 13'9"	16'7" / 27'6"
	2'5" / 3'4"	2'7" / 3'7"	2'10" / 3'10"	3'2" / 4'5"	3'7" / 4'11"	4'0" / 5'6"	4'10" / 6'7"	5'7" / 7'8"	6'5" / 8'10"	7'3" / 9'11"	8'0" / 11'0"	10'0" / 13'9"	20'0" / 27'6"
	2'10" / 3'9"	3'0" / 4'1"	3'3" / 4'4"	3'9" / 5'0"	4'2" / 5'7"	4'8" / 6'3"	5'7" / 7'6"	6'6" / 8'9"	7'6" / 10'0"	8'5" / 11'3"	9'4" / 12'6"	11'8" / 15'7"	23'4" / 31'2"

SETUPS (Approximate Distance) — 50mm FIELD OF VIEW

	Full Aperture V 21.1° H 28.0°	Academy 1.33:1 V 17.4° H 23.7°	Academy 1.66:1 V 14.4° H 23.7°	Academy 1.85:1 V 12.9° H 23.7°	Anamorphic 2.40:1 V 20.2° H 46.2°	Super 35 1.85:1 V 14.8° H 27.0°	Super 35 2.40:1 V 11.4° H 27.0°	VistaVision V 28.3° H 41.3°	VistaVision 1.85:1 V 23.1° H 41.3°	VistaVision 2.40:1 V 17.9° H 41.3°	65mm V 24.9° H 51.8°
Ext Close Up	2' 0"	2' 4"	2' 10"	3' 2"	2' 0"	2' 11"	3' 9"	1' 6"	1' 10"	2' 5"	1' 8"
Close Up	3' 1"	3' 8"	4' 5"	4' 11"	3' 2"	4' 6"	5' 10"	2' 4"	2' 10"	3' 8"	2' 6"
Medium Shot	5' 10"	6' 9"	8' 2"	9' 1"	5' 10"	8' 4"	10' 10"	4' 4"	5' 4"	6' 10"	4' 8"
Full Figure	16' 1"	18' 9"	22' 8"	25' 3"	16' 2"	23' 1"	30' 0"	12' 0"	14' 9"	19' 0"	13' 0"
2	0' 9" / 1' 0"	0' 8" / 0' 11"	0' 6" / 0' 11"	0' 6" / 0' 11"	0' 9" / 1' 9"	0' 6" / 1' 0"	0' 5" / 1' 0"	1' 0" / 1' 6"	0' 10" / 1' 6"	0' 8" / 1' 6"	0' 11" / 2' 1"
2½	0' 11" / 1' 3"	0' 10" / 1' 1"	0' 8" / 1' 1"	0' 7" / 1' 1"	0' 11" / 2' 2"	0' 8" / 1' 2"	0' 6" / 1' 2"	1' 3" / 1' 11"	1' 0" / 1' 11"	0' 9" / 1' 11"	1' 2" / 2' 8"
3	1' 1" / 1' 6"	1' 0" / 1' 4"	0' 10" / 1' 4"	0' 9" / 1' 4"	1' 1" / 2' 8"	0' 9" / 1' 5"	0' 7" / 1' 5"	1' 6" / 2' 3"	1' 3" / 2' 3"	0' 11" / 2' 3"	1' 5" / 3' 2"
3½	1' 4" / 1' 9"	1' 1" / 1' 6"	0' 11" / 1' 6"	0' 10" / 1' 6"	1' 4" / 3' 1"	0' 11" / 1' 8"	0' 8" / 1' 8"	1' 9" / 2' 8"	1' 5" / 2' 8"	1' 1" / 2' 8"	1' 7" / 3' 8"
4	1' 6" / 2' 0"	1' 3" / 1' 9"	1' 1" / 1' 9"	0' 11" / 1' 9"	1' 6" / 3' 6"	1' 0" / 1' 11"	0' 10" / 1' 11"	2' 0" / 3' 0"	1' 8" / 3' 0"	1' 3" / 3' 0"	1' 10" / 4' 3"
4½	1' 8" / 2' 3"	1' 5" / 2' 0"	1' 2" / 2' 0"	1' 1" / 2' 0"	1' 8" / 4' 0"	1' 2" / 2' 2"	0' 11" / 2' 2"	2' 3" / 3' 5"	1' 10" / 3' 5"	1' 5" / 3' 5"	2' 1" / 4' 9"
5	1' 10" / 2' 6"	1' 7" / 2' 2"	1' 4" / 2' 2"	1' 2" / 2' 2"	1' 10" / 4' 5"	1' 4" / 2' 5"	1' 0" / 2' 5"	2' 6" / 3' 9"	2' 0" / 3' 9"	1' 7" / 3' 9"	2' 4" / 5' 3"
5½	2' 1" / 2' 9"	1' 9" / 2' 5"	1' 6" / 2' 5"	1' 4" / 2' 5"	2' 1" / 4' 10"	1' 5" / 2' 8"	1' 1" / 2' 8"	2' 9" / 4' 2"	2' 3" / 4' 2"	1' 9" / 4' 2"	2' 6" / 5' 9"

6	2'3" / 3'0"	1'11" / 2'8"	1'7" / 2'8"	1'5" / 2'8"	2'3" / 5'3"	1'7" / 2'11"	1'2" / 2'11"	3'0" / 4'6"	2'5" / 4'6"	1'11" / 4'6"	2'9" / 6'4"
6½	2'5" / 3'3"	2'1" / 2'10"	1'9" / 2'10"	1'7" / 2'10"	2'5" / 5'9"	1'8" / 3'1"	1'4" / 3'1"	3'3" / 4'11"	2'8" / 4'11"	2'1" / 4'11"	3'0" / 6'10"
7	2'7" / 3'6"	2'3" / 3'1"	1'10" / 3'1"	1'8" / 3'1"	2'7" / 6'2"	1'10" / 3'4"	1'5" / 3'4"	3'6" / 5'3"	2'10" / 5'3"	2'2" / 5'3"	3'3" / 7'4"
8	3'0" / 4'0"	2'7" / 3'6"	2'1" / 3'6"	1'11" / 3'6"	3'0" / 7'0"	2'1" / 3'10"	1'7" / 3'10"	4'0" / 6'0"	3'3" / 6'0"	2'6" / 6'0"	3'8" / 8'5"
9	3'4" / 4'6"	2'11" / 4'0"	2'5" / 4'0"	2'2" / 4'0"	3'4" / 7'11"	2'4" / 4'4"	1'10" / 4'4"	4'6" / 6'9"	3'8" / 6'9"	2'10" / 6'9"	4'2" / 9'6"
10	3'9" / 5'0"	3'2" / 4'5"	2'8" / 4'5"	2'5" / 4'5"	3'9" / 8'10"	2'7" / 4'10"	2'0" / 4'10"	5'0" / 7'7"	4'1" / 7'7"	3'2" / 7'7"	4'7" / 10'6"
12	4'6" / 6'0"	3'10" / 5'3"	3'2" / 5'3"	2'10" / 5'3"	4'6" / 10'7"	3'1" / 5'9"	2'5" / 5'9"	6'0" / 9'1"	4'11" / 9'1"	3'9" / 9'1"	5'6" / 12'8"
14	5'3" / 7'0"	4'6" / 6'2"	3'9" / 6'2"	3'4" / 6'2"	5'2" / 12'4"	3'8" / 6'9"	2'10" / 6'9"	7'0" / 10'7"	5'9" / 10'7"	4'5" / 10'7"	6'5" / 14'9"
16	6'0" / 8'0"	5'2" / 7'0"	4'3" / 7'0"	3'10" / 7'0"	5'11" / 14'1"	4'2" / 7'8"	3'2" / 7'8"	8'0" / 12'1"	6'6" / 12'1"	5'1" / 12'1"	7'4" / 16'10"
18	6'9" / 9'0"	5'9" / 7'11"	4'9" / 7'11"	4'3" / 7'11"	6'8" / 15'10"	4'8" / 8'8"	3'7" / 8'8"	9'0" / 13'7"	7'4" / 13'7"	5'8" / 13'7"	8'3" / 18'11"
20	7'6" / 10'0"	6'5" / 8'10"	5'4" / 8'10"	4'9" / 8'10"	7'5" / 17'7"	5'2" / 9'7"	4'0" / 9'7"	10'0" / 15'1"	8'2" / 15'1"	6'4" / 15'1"	9'2" / 21'1"
25	9'4" / 12'6"	8'0" / 11'0"	6'8" / 11'0"	5'11" / 11'0"	9'4" / 22'0"	6'6" / 12'0"	5'0" / 12'0"	12'6" / 18'10"	10'2" / 18'10"	7'11" / 18'10"	11'6" / 26'4"
50	18'8" / 24'11"	16'0" / 22'0"	13'3" / 22'0"	11'11" / 22'0"	18'7" / 44'0"	13'0" / 24'0"	10'0" / 24'0"	24'11" / 37'9"	20'5" / 37'9"	15'9" / 37'9"	23'0" / 52'8"

SETUPS (Approximate Distance) — 75mm FIELD OF VIEW

	Full Aperture	Academy 1.33:1	Academy 1.66:1	Academy 1.85:1	Anamorphic 2.40:1	Super 35 1.85:1	Super 35 2.40:1	VistaVision	VistaVision 1.85:1	VistaVision 2.40:1	65mm
Ext Close Up	3' 0"	3' 6"	4' 3"	4' 9"	3' 0"	4' 4"	5' 7"	2' 3"	2' 9"	3' 7"	2' 5"
Close Up	4' 8"	5' 6"	6' 7"	7' 4"	4' 8"	6' 9"	8' 9"	3' 6"	4' 3"	5' 7"	3' 10"
Medium Shot	8' 8"	10' 2"	12' 3"	13' 8"	8' 9"	12' 6"	16' 3"	6' 6"	8' 0"	10' 4"	7' 1"
Full Figure	24' 1"	28' 1"	33' 11"	37' 10"	24' 2"	34' 8"	45' 0"	18' 1"	22' 1"	28' 6"	19' 7"
Angle of View	V 14.2° H 18.8°	V 11.6° H 15.9°	V 9.6° H 15.9°	V 8.6° H 15.9°	V 13.5° H 31.7°	V 9.9° H 18.2°	V 7.6° H 18.2°	V 19.1° H 28.2°	V 15.5° H 28.2°	V 12.0° H 28.2°	V 16.8° H 35.9°
2	0' 6" / 0' 8"	0' 5" / 0' 7"	0' 4" / 0' 7"	0' 4" / 0' 7"	0' 6" / 1' 2"	0' 4" / 0' 8"	0' 3" / 0' 8"	0' 8" / 1' 0"	0' 7" / 1' 0"	0' 5" / 1' 0"	0' 7" / 1' 5"
2½	0' 7" / 0' 10"	0' 6" / 0' 9"	0' 5" / 0' 9"	0' 5" / 0' 9"	0' 7" / 1' 6"	0' 5" / 0' 10"	0' 4" / 0' 10"	0' 10" / 1' 3"	0' 8" / 1' 3"	0' 6" / 1' 3"	0' 9" / 1' 9"
3	0' 9" / 1' 0"	0' 8" / 0' 11"	0' 6" / 0' 11"	0' 6" / 0' 11"	0' 9" / 1' 9"	0' 6" / 1' 0"	0' 5" / 1' 0"	1' 0" / 1' 6"	0' 10" / 1' 6"	0' 8" / 1' 6"	0' 11" / 2' 1"
3½	0' 10" / 1' 2"	0' 9" / 1' 0"	0' 7" / 1' 0"	0' 7" / 1' 0"	0' 10" / 2' 1"	0' 7" / 1' 1"	0' 6" / 1' 1"	1' 2" / 1' 9"	0' 11" / 1' 9"	0' 9" / 1' 9"	1' 1" / 2' 5"
4	1' 0" / 1' 4"	0' 10" / 1' 2"	0' 8" / 1' 2"	0' 8" / 1' 2"	1' 0" / 2' 4"	0' 8" / 1' 3"	0' 6" / 1' 3"	1' 4" / 2' 0"	1' 1" / 2' 0"	0' 10" / 2' 0"	1' 3" / 2' 10"
4½	1' 1" / 1' 6"	1' 0" / 1' 4"	0' 10" / 1' 4"	0' 9" / 1' 4"	1' 1" / 2' 8"	0' 9" / 1' 5"	0' 7" / 1' 5"	1' 6" / 2' 3"	1' 3" / 2' 3"	0' 11" / 2' 3"	1' 5" / 3' 2"
5	1' 3" / 1' 8"	1' 1" / 1' 6"	0' 11" / 1' 6"	0' 10" / 1' 6"	1' 3" / 2' 11"	0' 10" / 1' 7"	0' 8" / 1' 7"	1' 8" / 2' 6"	1' 4" / 2' 6"	1' 1" / 2' 6"	1' 6" / 3' 6"
5½	1' 4" / 1' 10"	1' 2" / 1' 7"	1' 0" / 1' 7"	0' 10" / 1' 7"	1' 4" / 3' 3"	0' 11" / 1' 9"	0' 9" / 1' 9"	1' 10" / 2' 9"	1' 6" / 2' 9"	1' 2" / 2' 9"	1' 8" / 3' 10"

	A	B	C	D	E	F	G	H	I	J	K
6	1'10" 4'3"	1'3" 3'0"	1'8" 3'0"	2'0" 3'0"	0'10" 1'11"	1'0" 1'11"	1'6" 3'6"	0'11" 1'9"	1'1" 1'9"	1'3" 1'9"	1'6" 2'0"
6½	2'0" 4'7"	1'4" 3'3"	1'9" 3'3"	2'2" 3'3"	0'10" 2'1"	1'1" 2'1"	1'7" 3'10"	1'0" 1'11"	1'2" 1'11"	1'5" 1'11"	1'7" 2'2"
7	2'2" 4'11"	1'6" 3'6"	1'11" 3'6"	2'4" 3'6"	0'11" 2'3"	1'3" 2'3"	1'9" 4'1"	1'1" 2'1"	1'3" 2'1"	1'6" 2'1"	1'9" 2'4"
8	2'5" 5'7"	1'8" 4'0"	2'2" 4'0"	2'8" 4'0"	1'1" 2'7"	1'5" 2'7"	2'0" 4'8"	1'3" 2'4"	1'5" 2'4"	1'9" 2'4"	2'0" 2'8"
9	2'9" 6'4"	1'11" 4'6"	2'5" 4'6"	3'0" 4'6"	1'2" 2'11"	1'7" 2'11"	2'3" 5'3"	1'5" 2'8"	1'7" 2'8"	1'11" 2'8"	2'3" 3'0"
10	3'1" 7'0"	2'1" 5'0"	2'9" 5'0"	3'4" 5'0"	1'4" 3'2"	1'9" 3'2"	2'6" 5'10"	1'7" 2'11"	1'9" 2'11"	2'2" 2'11"	2'6" 3'4"
12	3'8" 8'5"	2'6" 6'0"	3'3" 6'0"	4'0" 6'0"	1'7" 3'10"	2'1" 3'10"	3'0" 7'0"	1'11" 3'6"	2'1" 3'6"	2'7" 3'6"	3'0" 4'0"
14	4'4" 9'10"	2'11" 7'0"	3'10" 7'0"	4'8" 7'0"	1'10" 4'6"	2'5" 4'6"	3'6" 8'3"	2'3" 4'1"	2'6" 4'1"	3'0" 4'1"	3'6" 4'8"
16	4'11" 11'3"	3'4" 8'1"	4'4" 8'1"	5'4" 8'1"	2'2" 5'1"	2'9" 5'1"	4'0" 9'5"	2'6" 4'8"	2'10" 4'8"	3'5" 4'8"	4'0" 5'4"
18	5'6" 12'8"	3'9" 9'1"	4'11" 9'1"	6'0" 9'1"	2'5" 5'9"	3'1" 5'9"	4'6" 10'7"	2'10" 5'3"	3'2" 5'3"	3'10" 5'3"	4'6" 6'0"
20	6'2" 14'0"	4'2" 10'1"	5'5" 10'1"	6'8" 10'1"	2'8" 6'5"	3'6" 6'5"	4'11" 11'9"	3'2" 5'10"	3'6" 5'10"	4'3" 5'10"	5'0" 6'8"
25	7'8" 17'7"	5'3" 12'7"	6'10" 12'7"	8'4" 12'7"	3'4" 8'0"	4'4" 8'0"	6'2" 14'8"	4'0" 7'4"	4'5" 7'4"	5'4" 7'4"	6'3" 8'4"
50	15'4" 35'1"	10'6" 25'2"	13'7" 25'2"	16'7" 25'2"	6'8" 16'0"	8'8" 16'0"	12'5" 29'4"	7'11" 14'8"	8'10" 14'8"	10'8" 14'8"	12'5" 16'7"

SETUPS (Approximate Distance) — 85mm FIELD OF VIEW

	Full Aperture V 12.5° H 16.7°	Academy 1.33:1 V 10.3° H 14.1°	Academy 1.66:1 V 8.5° H 14.1°	Academy 1.85:1 V 7.6° H 14.1°	Anamorphic 2.40:1 V 11.9° H 28.1°	Super 35 1.85:1 V 8.7° H 16.1°	Super 35 2.40:1 V 6.7° H 16.1°	VistaVision V 16.8° H 25.0°	VistaVision 1.85:1 V 13.7° H 25.0°	VistaVision 2.40:1 V 10.6° H 25.0°	65mm
Ext Close Up	3' 5"	4' 0"	4' 10"	5' 4"	3' 5"	4' 11"	6' 4"	2' 7"	3' 2"	4' 0"	2' 9"
Close Up	5' 4"	6' 2"	7' 6"	8' 4"	5' 4"	7' 8"	9' 11"	4' 0"	4' 10"	6' 3"	4' 4"
Medium Shot	9' 10"	11' 6"	13' 11"	15' 6"	9' 11"	14' 2"	18' 5"	7' 5"	9' 0"	11' 8"	8' 0"
Full Figure	27' 4"	31' 10"	38' 6"	42' 11"	27' 5"	39' 4"	51' 0"	20' 6"	25' 0"	32' 4"	22' 2"
2	0' 5" / 0' 7"	0' 5" / 0' 6"	0' 4" / 0' 6"	0' 3" / 0' 6"	0' 5" / 1' 0"	0' 4" / 0' 7"	0' 3" / 0' 7"	0' 7" / 0' 11"	0' 6" / 0' 11"	0' 4" / 0' 11"	NA / NA
2½	0' 7" / 0' 9"	0' 6" / 0' 8"	0' 5" / 0' 8"	0' 4" / 0' 8"	0' 7" / 1' 4"	0' 5" / 0' 8"	0' 4" / 0' 8"	0' 9" / 1' 1"	0' 7" / 1' 1"	0' 6" / 1' 1"	NA / NA
3	0' 8" / 0' 11"	0' 7" / 0' 9"	0' 6" / 0' 9"	0' 5" / 0' 9"	0' 8" / 1' 7"	0' 5" / 0' 10"	0' 4" / 0' 10"	0' 11" / 1' 4"	0' 9" / 1' 4"	0' 7" / 1' 4"	NA / NA
3½	0' 9" / 1' 0"	0' 8" / 0' 11"	0' 7" / 0' 11"	0' 6" / 0' 11"	0' 9" / 1' 10"	0' 6" / 1' 0"	0' 5" / 1' 0"	1' 0" / 1' 7"	0' 10" / 1' 7"	0' 8" / 1' 7"	NA / NA
4	0' 11" / 1' 2"	0' 9" / 1' 0"	0' 7" / 1' 0"	0' 7" / 1' 0"	0' 10" / 2' 1"	0' 7" / 1' 2"	0' 6" / 1' 2"	1' 2" / 1' 9"	1' 0" / 1' 9"	0' 9" / 1' 9"	NA / NA
4½	1' 0" / 1' 4"	0' 10" / 1' 2"	0' 8" / 1' 2"	0' 8" / 1' 2"	1' 0" / 2' 4"	0' 8" / 1' 3"	0' 6" / 1' 3"	1' 4" / 2' 0"	1' 1" / 2' 0"	0' 10" / 2' 0"	NA / NA
5	1' 1" / 1' 6"	0' 11" / 1' 4"	0' 9" / 1' 4"	0' 8" / 1' 4"	1' 1" / 2' 7"	0' 9" / 1' 5"	0' 7" / 1' 5"	1' 6" / 2' 3"	1' 2" / 2' 3"	0' 11" / 2' 3"	NA / NA
5½	1' 2" / 1' 7"	1' 0" / 1' 5"	0' 10" / 1' 5"	0' 9" / 1' 5"	1' 2" / 2' 10"	0' 10" / 1' 7"	0' 8" / 1' 7"	1' 7" / 2' 5"	1' 4" / 2' 5"	1' 0" / 2' 5"	NA / NA

6	1'4" / 1'9"	1'2" / 1'7"	0'11" / 1'7"	0'10" / 1'7"	1'4" / 3'1"	0'11" / 1'8"	0'8" / 1'8"	1'9" / 2'8"	1'5" / 2'8"	1'1" / 2'8"	NA / NA
6½	1'5" / 1'11"	1'3" / 1'8"	1'0" / 1'8"	0'11" / 1'8"	1'5" / 3'4"	1'0" / 1'10"	0'9" / 1'10"	1'11" / 2'11"	1'7" / 2'11"	1'2" / 2'11"	NA / NA
7	1'6" / 2'1"	1'4" / 1'10"	1'1" / 1'10"	1'0" / 1'10"	1'6" / 3'7"	1'1" / 2'0"	0'10" / 2'0"	2'1" / 3'1"	1'8" / 3'1"	1'4" / 3'1"	NA / NA
8	1'9" / 2'4"	1'6" / 2'1"	1'3" / 2'1"	1'1" / 2'1"	1'9" / 4'2"	1'3" / 2'3"	0'11" / 2'3"	2'4" / 3'7"	1'11" / 3'7"	1'6" / 3'7"	NA / NA
9	2'0" / 2'8"	1'8" / 2'4"	1'5" / 2'4"	1'3" / 2'4"	2'0" / 4'8"	1'4" / 2'6"	1'1" / 2'6"	2'8" / 4'0"	2'2" / 4'0"	1'8" / 4'0"	NA / NA
10	2'2" / 2'11"	1'11" / 2'7"	1'7" / 2'7"	1'5" / 2'7"	2'2" / 5'2"	1'6" / 2'10"	1'2" / 2'10"	2'11" / 4'5"	2'5" / 4'5"	1'10" / 4'5"	NA / NA
12	2'8" / 3'6"	2'3" / 3'1"	1'10" / 3'1"	1'8" / 3'1"	2'7" / 6'3"	1'10" / 3'5"	1'5" / 3'5"	3'6" / 5'4"	2'11" / 5'4"	2'3" / 5'4"	NA / NA
14	3'1" / 4'1"	2'8" / 3'7"	2'2" / 3'7"	1'11" / 3'7"	3'1" / 7'3"	2'2" / 3'11"	1'8" / 3'11"	4'1" / 6'3"	3'4" / 6'3"	2'7" / 6'3"	NA / NA
16	3'6" / 4'8"	3'0" / 4'2"	2'6" / 4'2"	2'3" / 4'2"	3'6" / 8'3"	2'5" / 4'6"	1'11" / 4'6"	4'8" / 7'1"	3'10" / 7'1"	3'0" / 7'1"	NA / NA
18	3'11" / 5'3"	3'5" / 4'8"	2'10" / 4'8"	2'6" / 4'8"	3'11" / 9'4"	2'9" / 5'1"	2'1" / 5'1"	5'3" / 8'0"	4'4" / 8'0"	3'4" / 8'0"	NA / NA
20	4'5" / 5'10"	3'9" / 5'2"	3'1" / 5'2"	2'10" / 5'2"	4'4" / 10'4"	3'1" / 5'8"	2'4" / 5'8"	5'10" / 8'11"	4'10" / 8'11"	3'9" / 8'11"	NA / NA
25	5'6" / 7'4"	4'9" / 6'6"	3'11" / 6'6"	3'6" / 6'6"	5'6" / 12'11"	3'10" / 7'1"	2'11" / 7'1"	7'4" / 11'1"	6'0" / 11'1"	4'8" / 11'1"	NA / NA
50	11'0" / 14'8"	9'5" / 12'11"	7'10" / 12'11"	7'0" / 12'11"	10'11" / 25'11"	7'8" / 14'1"	5'11" / 14'1"	14'8" / 22'2"	12'0" / 22'2"	9'3" / 22'2"	NA / NA

SETUPS (Approximate Distance) — 100mm FIELD OF VIEW

	Full Aperture	Academy 1.33:1	Academy 1.66:1	Academy 1.85:1	Anamorphic 2.40:1	Super 35 1.85:1	Super 35 2.40:1	VistaVision	VistaVision 1.85:1	VistaVision 2.40:1	65mm
Ext Close Up	4' 0"	4' 8"	5' 8"	6' 4"	4' 0"	5' 9"	7' 6"	3' 0"	3' 8"	4' 9"	3' 3"
Close Up	6' 3"	7' 3"	8' 10"	9' 10"	6' 3"	9' 0"	11' 8"	4' 8"	5' 9"	7' 5"	5' 1"
Medium Shot	11' 7"	13' 6"	16' 4"	18' 3"	11' 8"	16' 8"	21' 8"	8' 8"	10' 7"	13' 9"	9' 5"
Full Figure	32' 2"	37' 5"	45' 3"	50' 6"	32' 3"	46' 3"	59' 11"	24' 1"	29' 5"	38' 0"	26' 1"
Angle of View	V 10.7° H 14.2°	V 8.7° H 12.0°	V 7.2° H 12.0°	V 6.5° H 12.0°	V 10.2° H 24.1°	V 7.4° H 13.7°	V 5.7° H 13.7°	V 14.3° H 21.4°	V 11.6° H 21.4°	V 9.0° H 21.4°	V 12.6° H 27.3°
2	0' 4" / 0' 6"	0' 4" / 0' 5"	0' 3" / 0' 5"	0' 3" / 0' 5"	0' 4" / 0' 11"	0' 3" / 0' 6"	0' 2" / 0' 6"	0' 6" / 0' 9"	0' 5" / 0' 9"	0' 4" / 0' 9"	0' 6" / 1' 1"
2½	0' 6" / 0' 7"	0' 5" / 0' 7"	0' 4" / 0' 7"	0' 4" / 0' 7"	0' 6" / 1' 1"	0' 4" / 0' 7"	0' 3" / 0' 7"	0' 7" / 0' 11"	0' 6" / 0' 11"	0' 5" / 0' 11"	0' 7" / 1' 4"
3	0' 7" / 0' 9"	0' 6" / 0' 8"	0' 5" / 0' 8"	0' 4" / 0' 8"	0' 7" / 1' 4"	0' 5" / 0' 9"	0' 4" / 0' 9"	0' 9" / 1' 2"	0' 7" / 1' 2"	0' 6" / 1' 2"	0' 8" / 1' 7"
3½	0' 8" / 0' 10"	0' 7" / 0' 9"	0' 6" / 0' 9"	0' 5" / 0' 9"	0' 8" / 1' 6"	0' 5" / 0' 10"	0' 4" / 0' 10"	0' 10" / 1' 4"	0' 9" / 1' 4"	0' 7" / 1' 4"	0' 10" / 1' 10"
4	0' 9" / 1' 0"	0' 8" / 0' 11"	0' 6" / 0' 11"	0' 6" / 0' 11"	0' 9" / 1' 9"	0' 6" / 1' 0"	0' 5" / 1' 0"	1' 0" / 1' 6"	0' 10" / 1' 6"	0' 8" / 1' 6"	0' 11" / 2' 1"
4½	0' 10" / 1' 1"	0' 9" / 1' 0"	0' 7" / 1' 0"	0' 6" / 1' 0"	0' 10" / 2' 0"	0' 7" / 1' 1"	0' 5" / 1' 1"	1' 1" / 1' 8"	0' 11" / 1' 8"	0' 9" / 1' 8"	1' 0" / 2' 4"
5	0' 11" / 1' 3"	0' 10" / 1' 1"	0' 8" / 1' 1"	0' 7" / 1' 1"	0' 11" / 2' 2"	0' 8" / 1' 2"	0' 6" / 1' 2"	1' 3" / 1' 11"	1' 0" / 1' 11"	0' 9" / 1' 11"	1' 2" / 2' 8"
5½	1' 0" / 1' 4"	0' 11" / 1' 3"	0' 9" / 1' 3"	0' 8" / 1' 3"	1' 0" / 2' 5"	0' 9" / 1' 4"	0' 7" / 1' 4"	1' 4" / 2' 1"	1' 1" / 2' 1"	0' 10" / 2' 1"	1' 3" / 2' 11"

	C1	C2	C3	C4	C5	C6	C7	C8	C9	C10	C11
6	1'5" / 3'2"	0'11" / 2'3"	1'3" / 2'3"	1'6" / 2'3"	0'7" / 1'5"	0'9" / 1'5"	1'1" / 2'8"	0'9" / 1'4"	0'10" / 1'4"	1'0" / 1'4"	1'1" / 1'6"
6½	1'6" / 3'5"	1'0" / 2'5"	1'4" / 2'5"	1'7" / 2'5"	0'8" / 1'7"	0'10" / 1'7"	1'3" / 2'10"	0'9" / 1'5"	0'10" / 1'5"	1'1" / 1'5"	1'3" / 1'7"
7	1'7" / 3'8"	1'1" / 2'8"	1'5" / 2'8"	1'9" / 2'8"	0'8" / 1'8"	0'11" / 1'8"	1'4" / 3'1"	0'10" / 1'6"	0'11" / 1'6"	1'1" / 1'6"	1'4" / 1'9"
8	1'10" / 4'3"	1'3" / 3'0"	1'8" / 3'0"	2'0" / 3'0"	0'10" / 1'11"	1'0" / 1'11"	1'6" / 3'6"	0'11" / 1'9"	1'1" / 1'9"	1'3" / 1'9"	1'6" / 2'0"
9	2'1" / 4'9"	1'5" / 3'5"	1'10" / 3'5"	2'3" / 3'5"	0'11" / 2'2"	1'2" / 2'2"	1'8" / 4'0"	1'1" / 2'0"	1'2" / 2'0"	1'5" / 2'0"	1'8" / 2'3"
10	2'4" / 5'3"	1'7" / 3'9"	2'0" / 3'9"	2'6" / 3'9"	1'0" / 2'5"	1'4" / 2'5"	1'10" / 4'5"	1'2" / 2'2"	1'4" / 2'2"	1'7" / 2'2"	1'10" / 2'6"
12	2'9" / 6'4"	1'11" / 4'6"	2'5" / 4'6"	3'0" / 4'6"	1'2" / 2'11"	1'7" / 2'11"	2'3" / 5'3"	1'5" / 2'8"	1'7" / 2'8"	1'11" / 2'8"	2'3" / 3'0"
14	3'3" / 7'4"	2'2" / 5'3"	2'10" / 5'3"	3'6" / 5'3"	1'5" / 3'4"	1'10" / 3'4"	2'7" / 6'2"	1'8" / 3'1"	1'10" / 3'1"	2'3" / 3'1"	2'7" / 3'6"
16	3'8" / 8'5"	2'6" / 6'0"	3'3" / 6'0"	4'0" / 6'0"	1'7" / 3'10"	2'1" / 3'10"	3'0" / 7'0"	1'11" / 3'6"	2'1" / 3'6"	2'7" / 3'6"	3'0" / 4'0"
18	4'2" / 9'6"	2'10" / 6'9"	3'8" / 6'9"	4'6" / 6'9"	1'10" / 4'4"	2'4" / 4'4"	3'4" / 7'11"	2'2" / 4'0"	2'5" / 4'0"	2'11" / 4'0"	3'4" / 4'6"
20	4'7" / 10'6"	3'2" / 7'7"	4'1" / 7'7"	5'0" / 7'7"	2'0" / 4'10"	2'7" / 4'10"	3'9" / 8'10"	2'5" / 4'5"	2'8" / 4'5"	3'2" / 4'5"	3'9" / 5'0"
25	5'9" / 13'2"	3'11" / 9'5"	5'1" / 9'5"	6'3" / 9'5"	2'6" / 6'0"	3'3" / 6'0"	4'8" / 11'0"	3'0" / 5'6"	3'4" / 5'6"	4'0" / 5'6"	4'8" / 6'3"
50	11'6" / 26'4"	7'11" / 18'10"	10'2" / 18'10"	12'6" / 18'10"	5'0" / 12'0"	6'6" / 12'0"	9'4" / 22'0"	5'11" / 11'0"	6'8" / 11'0"	8'0" / 11'0"	9'4" / 12'6"

SETUPS (Approximate Distance) — 105mm FIELD OF VIEW

	Full Aperture	Academy 1.33:1	Academy 1.66:1	Academy 1.85:1	Anamorphic 2.40:1	Super 35 1.85:1	Super 35 2.40:1	VistaVision	VistaVision 1.85:1	VistaVision 2.40:1	65mm
Ext Close Up	4' 3"	4' 11"	5' 11"	6' 7"	4' 3"	6' 1"	7' 10"	3' 2"	3' 10"	5' 0"	3' 3"
Close Up	6' 7"	7' 8"	9' 3"	10' 4"	6' 7"	9' 5"	12' 3"	4' 11"	6' 0"	7' 9"	5' 1"
Medium Shot	12' 2"	14' 2"	17' 2"	19' 2"	12' 3"	17' 6"	22' 9"	9' 2"	11' 2"	14' 5"	9' 5"
Full Figure	33' 9"	39' 4"	47' 6"	53' 0"	33' 11"	48' 6"	62' 11"	25' 3"	30' 11"	39' 11"	26' 1"
Angle of View	V 10.2° H 13.5°	V 8.3° H 11.4°	V 6.9° H 11.4°	V 6.2° H 11.4°		V 7.1° H 13.0°	V 5.5° H 13.0°	V 13.7° H 20.4°	V 11.1° H 20.4°	V 8.6° H 20.4°	
5	0' 11" / 1' 2"	0' 9" / 1' 1"	0' 8" / 1' 1"	0' 7" / 1' 1"	NA NA	0' 7" / 1' 2"	0' 6" / 1' 2"	1' 2" / 1' 10"	1' 0" / 1' 10"	0' 9" / 1' 10"	NA NA
5½	1' 0" / 1' 4"	0' 10" / 1' 2"	0' 8" / 1' 2"	0' 7" / 1' 2"	NA NA	0' 8" / 1' 3"	0' 6" / 1' 3"	1' 4" / 2' 0"	1' 1" / 2' 0"	0' 10" / 2' 0"	NA NA
6	1' 1" / 1' 5"	0' 11" / 1' 3"	0' 9" / 1' 3"	0' 8" / 1' 3"	NA NA	0' 9" / 1' 4"	0' 7" / 1' 4"	1' 5" / 2' 2"	1' 2" / 2' 2"	0' 11" / 2' 2"	NA NA
6½	1' 2" / 1' 7"	1' 0" / 1' 4"	0' 10" / 1' 4"	0' 9" / 1' 4"	NA NA	0' 10" / 1' 6"	0' 7" / 1' 6"	1' 7" / 2' 4"	1' 3" / 2' 4"	1' 0" / 2' 4"	NA NA
7	1' 3" / 1' 8"	1' 1" / 1' 6"	0' 11" / 1' 6"	0' 10" / 1' 6"	NA NA	0' 10" / 1' 7"	0' 8" / 1' 7"	1' 8" / 2' 6"	1' 4" / 2' 6"	1' 1" / 2' 6"	NA NA
8	1' 5" / 1' 11"	1' 3" / 1' 8"	1' 0" / 1' 8"	0' 11" / 1' 8"	NA NA	1' 0" / 1' 10"	0' 9" / 1' 10"	1' 11" / 2' 10"	1' 7" / 2' 10"	1' 2" / 2' 10"	NA NA
9	1' 7" / 2' 2"	1' 4" / 1' 11"	1' 2" / 1' 11"	1' 0" / 1' 11"	NA NA	1' 1" / 2' 1"	0' 10" / 2' 1"	2' 2" / 3' 3"	1' 9" / 3' 3"	1' 4" / 3' 3"	NA NA
10	1' 9" / 2' 4"	1' 6" / 2' 1"	1' 3" / 2' 1"	1' 2" / 2' 1"	NA NA	1' 3" / 2' 3"	0' 11" / 2' 3"	2' 4" / 3' 7"	1' 11" / 3' 7"	1' 6" / 3' 7"	NA NA

	1	2	3	4	5	6	7	8	9	10	11
12	2' 2" 2' 10"	1' 10" 2' 6"	1' 6" 2' 6"	1' 4" 2' 6"	NA NA	1' 6" 2' 9"	1' 2" 2' 9"	2' 10" 4' 4"	2' 4" 4' 4"	1' 10" 4' 4"	NA NA
14	2' 6" 3' 4"	2' 2" 2' 11"	1' 9" 2' 11"	1' 7" 2' 11"	NA NA	1' 9" 3' 2"	1' 4" 3' 2"	3' 4" 5' 0"	2' 9" 5' 0"	2' 1" 5' 0"	NA NA
16	2' 10" 3' 10"	2' 5" 3' 4"	2' 0" 3' 4"	1' 10" 3' 4"	NA NA	2' 0" 3' 8"	1' 6" 3' 8"	3' 10" 5' 9"	3' 1" 5' 9"	2' 5" 5' 9"	NA NA
18	3' 2" 4' 3"	2' 9" 3' 9"	2' 3" 3' 9"	2' 0" 3' 9"	NA NA	2' 3" 4' 1"	1' 9" 4' 1"	4' 3" 6' 6"	3' 6" 6' 6"	2' 8" 6' 6"	NA NA
20	3' 7" 4' 9"	3' 1" 4' 2"	2' 6" 4' 2"	2' 3" 4' 2"	NA NA	2' 6" 4' 7"	1' 11" 4' 7"	4' 9" 7' 2"	3' 11" 7' 2"	3' 0" 7' 2"	NA NA
25	4' 5" 5' 11"	3' 10" 5' 3"	3' 2" 5' 3"	2' 10" 5' 3"	NA NA	3' 1" 5' 9"	2' 5" 5' 9"	5' 11" 9' 0"	4' 10" 9' 0"	3' 9" 9' 0"	NA NA
50	8' 11" 11' 10"	7' 8" 10' 6"	6' 4" 10' 6"	5' 8" 10' 6"	NA NA	6' 2" 11' 5"	4' 9" 11' 5"	11' 10" 18' 0"	9' 9" 18' 0"	7' 6" 18' 0"	NA NA
75	13' 4" 17' 10"	11' 5" 15' 9"	9' 6" 15' 9"	8' 6" 15' 9"	NA NA	9' 3" 17' 2"	7' 2" 17' 2"	17' 10" 26' 11"	14' 7" 26' 11"	11' 3" 26' 11"	NA NA
100	17' 9" 23' 9"	15' 3" 20' 11"	12' 8" 20' 11"	11' 4" 20' 11"	NA NA	12' 4" 22' 10"	9' 6" 22' 10"	23' 9" 35' 11"	19' 5" 35' 11"	15' 0" 35' 11"	NA NA
125	22' 3" 29' 8"	19' 1" 26' 2"	15' 9" 26' 2"	14' 2" 26' 2"	NA NA	15' 5" 28' 7"	11' 11" 28' 7"	29' 8" 44' 11"	24' 3" 44' 11"	18' 9" 44' 11"	NA NA
150	26' 8" 35' 7"	22' 11" 31' 5"	18' 11" 31' 5"	17' 0" 31' 5"	NA NA	18' 7" 34' 3"	14' 4" 34' 3"	35' 7" 53' 11"	29' 2" 53' 11"	22' 6" 53' 11"	NA NA
175	31' 1" 41' 6"	26' 9" 36' 8"	22' 1" 36' 8"	19' 10" 36' 8"	NA NA	21' 8" 40' 0"	16' 8" 40' 0"	41' 6" 62' 10"	34' 0" 62' 10"	26' 3" 62' 10"	NA NA
200	35' 7" 47' 6"	30' 6" 41' 11"	25' 3" 41' 11"	22' 8" 41' 11"	NA NA	24' 9" 45' 9"	19' 1" 45' 9"	47' 6" 71' 10"	38' 10" 71' 10"	30' 1" 71' 10"	NA NA

SETUPS (Approximate Distance) — 135mm FIELD OF VIEW

	Full Aperture	Academy 1.33:1	Academy 1.66:1	Academy 1.85:1	Anamorphic 2.40:1	Super 35 1.85:1	Super 35 2.40:1	VistaVision	VistaVision 1.85:1	VistaVision 2.40:1	65mm
Ext Close Up	5' 5"	6' 4"	7' 8"	8' 6"	5' 5"	7' 10"	10' 1"	4' 1"	5' 0"	6' 5"	4' 5"
Close Up	8' 5"	9' 10"	11' 11"	13' 3"	8' 6"	12' 2"	15' 9"	6' 4"	7' 9"	10' 0"	6' 10"
Medium Shot	15' 8"	18' 3"	22' 1"	24' 7"	15' 9"	22' 6"	29' 3"	11' 9"	14' 4"	18' 7"	12' 9"
Full Figure	43' 5"	50' 6"	61' 1"	68' 2"	43' 7"	62' 5"	80' 11"	32' 6"	39' 9"	51' 4"	35' 2"
Angle of View	V 7.9° H 10.5°	V 6.5° H 8.9°	V 5.4° H 8.9°	V 4.8° H 8.9°	V 7.5° H 17.9°	V 5.5° H 10.2°	V 4.2° H 10.2°	V 10.7° H 15.9°	V 8.6° H 15.9°	V 6.7° H 15.9°	
5	0' 8" / 0' 11"	0' 7" / 0' 10"	0' 6" / 0' 10"	0' 5" / 0' 10"	0' 8" / 1' 8"	0' 6" / 0' 11"	0' 4" / 0' 11"	0' 11" / 1' 5"	0' 9" / 1' 5"	0' 7" / 1' 5"	NA / NA
5½	0' 9" / 1' 0"	0' 8" / 0' 11"	0' 6" / 0' 11"	0' 6" / 0' 11"	0' 9" / 1' 10"	0' 6" / 1' 0"	0' 5" / 1' 0"	1' 0" / 1' 6"	0' 10" / 1' 6"	0' 8" / 1' 6"	NA / NA
6	0' 10" / 1' 1"	0' 9" / 1' 0"	0' 7" / 1' 0"	0' 6" / 1' 0"	0' 10" / 1' 11"	0' 7" / 1' 1"	0' 5" / 1' 1"	1' 1" / 1' 8"	0' 11" / 1' 8"	0' 8" / 1' 8"	NA / NA
6½	0' 11" / 1' 2"	0' 9" / 1' 1"	0' 8" / 1' 1"	0' 7" / 1' 1"	0' 11" / 2' 1"	0' 7" / 1' 2"	0' 6" / 1' 2"	1' 2" / 1' 10"	1' 0" / 1' 10"	0' 9" / 1' 10"	NA / NA
7	1' 0" / 1' 4"	0' 10" / 1' 2"	0' 8" / 1' 2"	0' 7" / 1' 2"	1' 0" / 2' 3"	0' 8" / 1' 3"	0' 6" / 1' 3"	1' 4" / 1' 11"	1' 1" / 1' 11"	0' 10" / 1' 11"	NA / NA
8	1' 1" / 1' 6"	0' 11" / 1' 4"	0' 9" / 1' 4"	0' 8" / 1' 4"	1' 1" / 2' 7"	0' 9" / 1' 5"	0' 7" / 1' 5"	1' 6" / 2' 3"	1' 3" / 2' 3"	0' 11" / 2' 3"	NA / NA
9	1' 3" / 1' 8"	1' 1" / 1' 6"	0' 11" / 1' 6"	0' 10" / 1' 6"	1' 3" / 2' 11"	0' 10" / 1' 7"	0' 8" / 1' 7"	1' 8" / 2' 6"	1' 4" / 2' 6"	1' 1" / 2' 6"	NA / NA
10	1' 5" / 1' 10"	1' 2" / 1' 8"	1' 0" / 1' 8"	0' 11" / 1' 8"	1' 5" / 3' 3"	1' 0" / 1' 9"	0' 9" / 1' 9"	1' 10" / 2' 10"	1' 6" / 2' 10"	1' 2" / 2' 10"	NA / NA

12	1' 8" 2' 3"	1' 5" 1' 11"	1' 2" 1' 11"	1' 1" 1' 11"	1' 8" 3' 11"	1' 2" 2' 2"	0' 11" 2' 2"	2' 3" 3' 4"	1' 10" 3' 4"	1' 5" 3' 4"	NA NA
14	1' 11" 2' 7"	1' 8" 2' 3"	1' 4" 2' 3"	1' 3" 2' 3"	1' 11" 4' 7"	1' 4" 2' 6"	1' 0" 2' 6"	2' 7" 3' 11"	2' 1" 3' 11"	1' 8" 3' 11"	NA NA
16	2' 3" 2' 11"	1' 11" 2' 7"	1' 7" 2' 7"	1' 5" 2' 7"	2' 2" 5' 3"	1' 6" 2' 10"	1' 2" 2' 10"	2' 11" 4' 6"	2' 5" 4' 6"	1' 10" 4' 6"	NA NA
18	2' 6" 3' 4"	2' 2" 2' 11"	1' 9" 2' 11"	1' 7" 2' 11"	2' 6" 5' 10"	1' 9" 3' 2"	1' 4" 3' 2"	3' 4" 5' 0"	2' 9" 5' 0"	2' 1" 5' 0"	NA NA
20	2' 9" 3' 8"	2' 4" 3' 3"	2' 0" 3' 3"	1' 9" 3' 3"	2' 9" 6' 6"	1' 11" 3' 7"	1' 6" 3' 7"	3' 8" 5' 7"	3' 0" 5' 7"	2' 4" 5' 7"	NA NA
25	3' 5" 4' 7"	3' 0" 4' 1"	2' 5" 4' 1"	2' 2" 4' 1"	3' 5" 8' 2"	2' 5" 4' 5"	1' 10" 4' 5"	4' 7" 7' 0"	3' 9" 7' 0"	2' 11" 7' 0"	NA NA
50	6' 11" 9' 3"	5' 11" 8' 2"	4' 11" 8' 2"	4' 5" 8' 2"	6' 11" 16' 4"	4' 10" 8' 11"	3' 8" 8' 11"	9' 3" 14' 0"	7' 7" 14' 0"	5' 10" 14' 0"	NA NA
75	10' 4" 13' 10"	8' 11" 12' 3"	7' 4" 12' 3"	6' 7" 12' 3"	10' 4" 24' 5"	7' 3" 13' 4"	5' 7" 13' 4"	13' 10" 20' 11"	11' 4" 20' 11"	8' 9" 20' 11"	NA NA
100	13' 10" 18' 5"	11' 10" 16' 4"	9' 10" 16' 4"	8' 10" 16' 4"	13' 9" 32' 7"	9' 7" 17' 9"	7' 5" 17' 9"	18' 5" 27' 11"	15' 1" 27' 11"	11' 8" 27' 11"	NA NA
125	17' 3" 23' 1"	14' 10" 20' 4"	12' 3" 20' 4"	11' 0" 20' 4"	17' 3" 40' 9"	12' 0" 22' 3"	9' 3" 22' 3"	23' 1" 34' 11"	18' 11" 34' 11"	14' 7" 34' 11"	NA NA
150	20' 9" 27' 8"	17' 10" 24' 5"	14' 9" 24' 5"	13' 2" 24' 5"	20' 8" 48' 11"	14' 5" 26' 8"	11' 1" 26' 8"	27' 8" 41' 11"	22' 8" 41' 11"	17' 6" 41' 11"	NA NA
175	24' 2" 32' 4"	20' 9" 28' 6"	17' 2" 28' 6"	15' 5" 28' 6"	24' 1" 57' 0"	16' 10" 31' 1"	13' 0" 31' 1"	32' 4" 48' 11"	26' 5" 48' 11"	20' 5" 48' 11"	NA NA
200	27' 8" 36' 11"	23' 9" 32' 7"	19' 8" 32' 7"	17' 7" 32' 7"	27' 7" 65' 2"	19' 3" 35' 7"	14' 10" 35' 7"	36' 11" 55' 11"	30' 3" 55' 11"	23' 4" 55' 11"	NA NA

SETUPS (Approximate Distance) — 150mm FIELD OF VIEW

	Full Aperture	Academy 1.33:1	Academy 1.66:1	Academy 1.85:1	Anamorphic 2.40:1	Super 35 1.85:1	Super 35 2.40:1	VistaVision	VistaVision 1.85:1	VistaVision 2.40:1	65mm
Ext Close Up	6' 0"	7' 0"	8' 6"	9' 6"	6' 1"	8' 8"	11' 3"	4' 6"	5' 6"	7' 2"	4' 11"
Close Up	9' 4"	10' 11"	13' 2"	14' 9"	9' 5"	13' 6"	17' 6"	7' 0"	8' 7"	11' 1"	7' 7"
Medium Shot	17' 5"	20' 3"	24' 6"	27' 4"	17' 6"	25' 0"	32' 6"	13' 1"	15' 11"	20' 7"	14' 1"
Full Figure	48' 2"	56' 2"	67' 11"	75' 9"	48' 5"	69' 4"	89' 11"	36' 1"	44' 2"	57' 1"	39' 1"
Angle of View	V 7.1° H 9.5°	V 5.8° H 8.0°	V 4.8° H 8.0°	V 4.3° H 8.0°	V 6.8° H 16.2°	V 5.0° H 9.1°	V 3.8° H 9.1°	V 9.6° H 14.3°	V 7.8° H 14.3°	V 6.0° H 14.3°	V 8.4° H 18.4°
5	0' 7" / 0' 10"	0' 6" / 0' 9"	0' 5" / 0' 9"	0' 5" / 0' 9"	0' 7" / 1' 6"	0' 5" / 0' 10"	0' 4" / 0' 10"	0' 10" / 1' 3"	0' 8" / 1' 3"	0' 6" / 1' 3"	0' 9" / 1' 9"
5½	0' 8" / 0' 11"	0' 7" / 0' 10"	0' 6" / 0' 10"	0' 5" / 0' 10"	0' 8" / 1' 7"	0' 6" / 0' 11"	0' 4" / 0' 11"	0' 11" / 1' 5"	0' 9" / 1' 5"	0' 7" / 1' 5"	0' 10" / 1' 11"
6	0' 9" / 1' 0"	0' 8" / 0' 11"	0' 6" / 0' 11"	0' 6" / 0' 11"	0' 9" / 1' 9"	0' 6" / 1' 0"	0' 5" / 1' 0"	1' 0" / 1' 6"	0' 10" / 1' 6"	0' 8" / 1' 6"	0' 11" / 2' 1"
6½	0' 10" / 1' 1"	0' 8" / 0' 11"	0' 7" / 0' 11"	0' 6" / 0' 11"	0' 10" / 1' 11"	0' 7" / 1' 0"	0' 5" / 1' 0"	1' 1" / 1' 8"	0' 11" / 1' 8"	0' 8" / 1' 8"	1' 0" / 2' 3"
7	0' 10" / 1' 2"	0' 9" / 1' 0"	0' 7" / 1' 0"	0' 7" / 1' 0"	0' 10" / 2' 1"	0' 7" / 1' 1"	0' 6" / 1' 1"	1' 2" / 1' 9"	0' 11" / 1' 9"	0' 9" / 1' 9"	1' 1" / 2' 5"
8	1' 0" / 1' 4"	0' 10" / 1' 2"	0' 8" / 1' 2"	0' 8" / 1' 2"	1' 0" / 2' 4"	0' 8" / 1' 3"	0' 6" / 1' 3"	1' 4" / 2' 0"	1' 1" / 2' 0"	0' 10" / 2' 0"	1' 3" / 2' 10"
9	1' 1" / 1' 6"	1' 0" / 1' 4"	0' 10" / 1' 4"	0' 9" / 1' 4"	1' 1" / 2' 8"	0' 9" / 1' 5"	0' 7" / 1' 5"	1' 6" / 2' 3"	1' 3" / 2' 3"	0' 11" / 2' 3"	1' 5" / 3' 2"
10	1' 3" / 1' 8"	1' 1" / 1' 6"	0' 11" / 1' 6"	0' 10" / 1' 6"	1' 3" / 2' 11"	0' 10" / 1' 7"	0' 8" / 1' 7"	1' 8" / 2' 6"	1' 4" / 2' 6"	1' 1" / 2' 6"	1' 6" / 3' 6"

12	1'6" / 2'0"	1'3" / 1'9"	1'1" / 1'9"	0'11" / 1'9"	1'6" / 3'6"	1'0" / 1'11"	0'10" / 1'11"	2'0" / 3'0"	1'8" / 3'0"	1'3" / 3'0"	1'10" / 4'3"
14	1'9" / 2'4"	1'6" / 2'1"	1'3" / 2'1"	1'1" / 2'1"	1'9" / 4'1"	1'3" / 2'3"	0'11" / 2'3"	2'4" / 3'6"	1'11" / 3'6"	1'6" / 3'6"	2'2" / 4'11"
16	2'0" / 2'8"	1'9" / 2'4"	1'5" / 2'4"	1'3" / 2'4"	2'0" / 4'8"	1'5" / 2'7"	1'1" / 2'7"	2'8" / 4'0"	2'2" / 4'0"	1'8" / 4'0"	2'5" / 5'7"
18	2'3" / 3'0"	1'11" / 2'8"	1'7" / 2'8"	1'5" / 2'8"	2'3" / 5'3"	1'7" / 2'11"	1'2" / 2'11"	3'0" / 4'6"	2'5" / 4'6"	1'11" / 4'6"	2'9" / 6'4"
20	2'6" / 3'4"	2'2" / 2'11"	1'9" / 2'11"	1'7" / 2'11"	2'6" / 5'10"	1'9" / 3'2"	1'4" / 3'2"	3'4" / 5'0"	2'9" / 5'0"	2'1" / 5'0"	3'1" / 7'0"
25	3'1" / 4'2"	2'8" / 3'8"	2'3" / 3'8"	2'0" / 3'8"	3'1" / 7'4"	2'2" / 4'0"	1'8" / 4'0"	4'2" / 6'3"	3'5" / 6'3"	2'8" / 6'3"	3'10" / 8'9"
50	6'3" / 8'4"	5'4" / 7'4"	4'5" / 7'4"	4'0" / 7'4"	6'2" / 14'8"	4'4" / 8'0"	3'4" / 8'0"	8'4" / 12'7"	6'10" / 12'7"	5'3" / 12'7"	7'8" / 17'7"
75	9'4" / 12'6"	8'0" / 11'0"	6'8" / 11'0"	5'11" / 11'0"	9'4" / 22'0"	6'6" / 12'0"	5'0" / 12'0"	12'6" / 18'10"	10'2" / 18'10"	7'11" / 18'10"	11'6" / 26'4"
100	12'5" / 16'7"	10'8" / 14'8"	8'10" / 14'8"	7'11" / 14'8"	12'5" / 29'4"	8'8" / 16'0"	6'8" / 16'0"	16'7" / 25'2"	13'7" / 25'2"	10'6" / 25'2"	15'4" / 35'1"
125	15'7" / 20'9"	13'4" / 18'4"	11'1" / 18'4"	9'11" / 18'4"	15'6" / 36'8"	10'10" / 20'0"	8'4" / 20'0"	20'9" / 31'5"	17'0" / 31'5"	13'2" / 31'5"	19'2" / 43'10"
150	18'8" / 24'11"	16'0" / 22'0"	13'3" / 22'0"	11'11" / 22'0"	18'7" / 44'0"	13'0" / 24'0"	10'0" / 24'0"	24'11" / 37'9"	20'5" / 37'9"	15'9" / 37'9"	23'0" / 52'8"
175	21'9" / 29'1"	18'8" / 25'8"	15'6" / 25'8"	13'10" / 25'8"	21'8" / 51'4"	15'2" / 28'0"	11'8" / 28'0"	29'1" / 44'0"	23'10" / 44'0"	18'5" / 44'0"	26'10" / 61'5"
200	24'11" / 33'3"	21'4" / 29'4"	17'8" / 29'4"	15'10" / 29'4"	24'9" / 58'8"	17'4" / 32'0"	13'4" / 32'0"	33'3" / 50'4"	27'2" / 50'4"	21'0" / 50'4"	30'8" / 70'2"

SETUPS (Approximate Distance) — 200mm FIELD OF VIEW

	Full Aperture V 5.3° H 7.1°	Academy 1.33:1 V 4.4° H 6.0°	Academy 1.66:1 V 3.6° H 6.0°	Academy 1.85:1 V 3.2° H 6.0°	Anamorphic 2.40:1 V 5.1° H 12.2°	Super 35 1.85:1 V 3.7° H 6.9°	Super 35 2.40:1 V 2.9° H 6.9°	VistaVision V 7.2° H 10.8°	VistaVision 1.85:1 V 5.8° H 10.8°	VistaVision 2.40:1 V 4.5° H 10.8°	65mm V 6.6° H 15.0°
Ext Close Up	8' 0"	9' 4"	11' 4"	12' 7"	8' 1"	11' 7"	15' 0"	6' 0"	7' 4"	9' 6"	6' 6"
Close Up	12' 6"	14' 7"	17' 7"	19' 8"	12' 7"	18' 0"	23' 4"	9' 4"	11' 5"	14' 10"	10' 2"
Medium Shot	23' 3"	27' 0"	32' 8"	36' 5"	23' 4"	33' 5"	43' 4"	17' 5"	21' 3"	27' 6"	18' 10"
Full Figure	64' 3"	74' 10"	90' 6"	100' 11"	64' 6"	92' 5"	119' 11"	48' 2"	58' 10"	76' 1"	52' 2"
5	0' 6" / 0' 7"	0' 5" / 0' 7"	0' 4" / 0' 7"	0' 4" / 0' 7"	0' 6" / 1' 1"	0' 4" / 0' 7"	0' 3" / 0' 7"	0' 7" / 0' 11"	0' 6" / 0' 11"	0' 5" / 0' 11"	0' 7" / 1' 4"
5½	0' 6" / 0' 8"	0' 5" / 0' 7"	0' 4" / 0' 7"	0' 4" / 0' 7"	0' 6" / 1' 3"	0' 4" / 0' 8"	0' 3" / 0' 8"	0' 8" / 1' 0"	0' 7" / 1' 0"	0' 5" / 1' 0"	0' 8" / 1' 5"
6	0' 7" / 0' 9"	0' 6" / 0' 8"	0' 5" / 0' 8"	0' 4" / 0' 8"	0' 7" / 1' 4"	0' 5" / 0' 9"	0' 4" / 0' 9"	0' 9" / 1' 2"	0' 7" / 1' 2"	0' 6" / 1' 2"	0' 8" / 1' 7"
6½	0' 7" / 0' 10"	0' 6" / 0' 9"	0' 5" / 0' 9"	0' 5" / 0' 9"	0' 7" / 1' 5"	0' 5" / 0' 9"	0' 4" / 0' 9"	0' 10" / 1' 3"	0' 8" / 1' 3"	0' 6" / 1' 3"	0' 9" / 1' 9"
7	0' 8" / 0' 10"	0' 7" / 0' 9"	0' 6" / 0' 9"	0' 5" / 0' 9"	0' 8" / 1' 6"	0' 5" / 0' 10"	0' 4" / 0' 10"	0' 10" / 1' 4"	0' 9" / 1' 4"	0' 7" / 1' 4"	0' 10" / 1' 10"
8	0' 9" / 1' 0"	0' 8" / 0' 11"	0' 6" / 0' 11"	0' 6" / 0' 11"	0' 9" / 1' 9"	0' 6" / 1' 0"	0' 5" / 1' 0"	1' 0" / 1' 6"	0' 10" / 1' 6"	0' 8" / 1' 6"	0' 11" / 2' 1"
9	0' 10" / 1' 1"	0' 9" / 1' 0"	0' 7" / 1' 0"	0' 6" / 1' 0"	0' 10" / 2' 0"	0' 7" / 1' 1"	0' 5" / 1' 1"	1' 1" / 1' 8"	0' 11" / 1' 8"	0' 9" / 1' 8"	1' 0" / 2' 4"
10	0' 11" / 1' 3"	0' 10" / 1' 1"	0' 8" / 1' 1"	0' 7" / 1' 1"	0' 11" / 2' 2"	0' 8" / 1' 2"	0' 6" / 1' 2"	1' 3" / 1' 11"	1' 0" / 1' 11"	0' 9" / 1' 11"	1' 2" / 2' 8"

12	1' 1" / 1' 6"	1' 0" / 1' 4"	0' 10" / 1' 4"	0' 9" / 1' 4"	1' 1" / 2' 8"	0' 9" / 1' 5"	0' 7" / 1' 5"	1' 6" / 2' 3"	1' 3" / 2' 3"	0' 11" / 2' 3"	1' 5" / 3' 2"
14	1' 4" / 1' 9"	1' 1" / 1' 6"	0' 11" / 1' 6"	0' 10" / 1' 6"	1' 4" / 3' 1"	0' 11" / 1' 8"	0' 8" / 1' 8"	1' 9" / 2' 8"	1' 5" / 2' 8"	1' 1" / 2' 8"	1' 7" / 3' 8"
16	1' 6" / 2' 0"	1' 3" / 1' 9"	1' 1" / 1' 9"	0' 11" / 1' 9"	1' 6" / 3' 6"	1' 0" / 1' 11"	0' 10" / 1' 11"	2' 0" / 3' 0"	1' 8" / 3' 0"	1' 3" / 3' 0"	1' 10" / 4' 3"
18	1' 10" / 2' 3"	1' 5" / 2' 0"	1' 2" / 2' 0"	1' 1" / 2' 0"	1' 8" / 4' 0"	1' 2" / 2' 2"	0' 11" / 2' 2"	2' 3" / 3' 5"	1' 10" / 3' 5"	1' 5" / 3' 5"	2' 1" / 4' 9"
20	1' 10" / 2' 6"	1' 7" / 2' 2"	1' 4" / 2' 2"	1' 2" / 2' 2"	1' 10" / 4' 5"	1' 4" / 2' 5"	1' 0" / 2' 5"	2' 6" / 3' 9"	2' 0" / 3' 9"	1' 7" / 3' 9"	2' 4" / 5' 3"
25	2' 4" / 3' 1"	2' 0" / 2' 9"	1' 8" / 2' 9"	1' 6" / 2' 9"	2' 4" / 5' 6"	1' 7" / 3' 0"	1' 3" / 3' 0"	3' 1" / 4' 9"	2' 7" / 4' 9"	2' 0" / 4' 9"	2' 11" / 6' 7"
50	4' 8" / 6' 3"	4' 0" / 5' 6"	3' 4" / 5' 6"	3' 0" / 5' 6"	4' 8" / 11' 0"	3' 3" / 6' 0"	2' 6" / 6' 0"	6' 3" / 9' 5"	5' 1" / 9' 5"	3' 11" / 9' 5"	5' 9" / 13' 2"
75	7' 0" / 9' 4"	6' 0" / 8' 3"	5' 0" / 8' 3"	4' 5" / 8' 3"	7' 0" / 16' 6"	4' 10" / 9' 0"	3' 9" / 9' 0"	9' 4" / 14' 2"	7' 8" / 14' 2"	5' 11" / 14' 2"	8' 8" / 19' 9"
100	9' 4" / 12' 6"	8' 0" / 11' 0"	6' 8" / 11' 0"	5' 11" / 11' 0"	9' 4" / 22' 0"	6' 6" / 12' 0"	5' 0" / 12' 0"	12' 6" / 18' 10"	10' 2" / 18' 10"	7' 11" / 18' 10"	11' 6" / 26' 4"
125	11' 8" / 15' 7"	10' 0" / 13' 9"	8' 3" / 13' 9"	7' 5" / 13' 9"	11' 7" / 27' 6"	8' 1" / 15' 0"	6' 3" / 15' 0"	15' 7" / 23' 7"	12' 9" / 23' 7"	9' 10" / 23' 7"	14' 5" / 32' 11"
150	14' 0" / 18' 8"	12' 0" / 16' 6"	9' 11" / 16' 6"	8' 11" / 16' 6"	13' 11" / 33' 0"	9' 9" / 18' 0"	7' 6" / 18' 0"	18' 8" / 28' 3"	15' 4" / 28' 3"	11' 10" / 28' 3"	17' 3" / 39' 6"
175	16' 4" / 21' 10"	14' 0" / 19' 3"	11' 7" / 19' 3"	10' 5" / 19' 3"	16' 3" / 38' 6"	11' 4" / 21' 0"	8' 9" / 21' 0"	21' 10" / 33' 0"	17' 10" / 33' 0"	13' 10" / 33' 0"	20' 2" / 46' 1"
200	18' 8" / 24' 11"	16' 0" / 22' 0"	13' 3" / 22' 0"	11' 11" / 22' 0"	18' 7" / 44' 0"	13' 0" / 24' 0"	10' 0" / 24' 0"	24' 11" / 37' 9"	20' 5" / 37' 9"	15' 9" / 37' 9"	23' 0" / 52' 8"

SETUPS (Approximate Distance) — 300mm FIELD OF VIEW

	Full Aperture	Academy 1.33:1	Academy 1.66:1	Academy 1.85:1	Anamorphic 2.40:1	Super 35 1.85:1	Super 35 2.40:1	VistaVision	VistaVision 1.85:1	VistaVision 2.40:1	65mm
Ext Close Up	12'1"	14'0"	17'0"	18'11"	12'1"	17'4"	22'6"	9'0"	11'0"	14'3"	9'9"
Close Up	18'9"	21'10"	26'5"	29'5"	18'10"	27'0"	35'0"	14'1"	17'2"	22'2"	15'3"
Medium Shot	34'10"	40'7"	49'0"	54'8"	35'0"	50'1"	64'11"	26'1"	31'10"	41'3"	28'3"
Full Figure	96'5"	112'4"	135'9"	151'5"	96'10"	138'8"	179'10"	72'3"	88'3"	114'1"	78'3"
Angle of View	V 3.6° H 4.8°	V 2.9° H 4.0°	V 2.4° H 4.0°	V 2.2° H 4.0°	V 3.4° H 8.1°	V 2.5° H 4.6°	V 1.9° H 4.6°	V 4.8° H 7.2°	V 3.9° H 7.2°	V 3.0° H 7.2°	V 4.2° H 9.3°
5	0'4" / 0'5"	0'3" / 0'4"	0'3" / 0'4"	0'2" / 0'4"	0'4" / 0'9"	0'3" / 0'5"	0'2" / 0'5"	0'5" / 0'8"	0'4" / 0'8"	0'3" / 0'8"	0'5" / 0'11"
5½	0'4" / 0'5"	0'4" / 0'5"	0'3" / 0'5"	0'3" / 0'5"	0'4" / 0'10"	0'3" / 0'5"	0'2" / 0'5"	0'5" / 0'8"	0'4" / 0'8"	0'3" / 0'8"	0'5" / 1'0"
6	0'4" / 0'6"	0'4" / 0'5"	0'3" / 0'5"	0'3" / 0'5"	0'4" / 0'11"	0'3" / 0'6"	0'2" / 0'6"	0'6" / 0'9"	0'5" / 0'9"	0'4" / 0'9"	0'6" / 1'1"
6½	0'5" / 0'6"	0'4" / 0'6"	0'3" / 0'6"	0'3" / 0'6"	0'5" / 0'11"	0'3" / 0'6"	0'3" / 0'6"	0'6" / 0'10"	0'5" / 0'10"	0'4" / 0'10"	0'6" / 1'2"
7	0'5" / 0'7"	0'4" / 0'6"	0'4" / 0'6"	0'3" / 0'6"	0'5" / 1'0"	0'4" / 0'7"	0'3" / 0'7"	0'7" / 0'11"	0'6" / 0'11"	0'4" / 0'11"	0'7" / 1'3"
8	0'6" / 0'8"	0'5" / 0'7"	0'4" / 0'7"	0'4" / 0'7"	0'6" / 1'2"	0'4" / 0'8"	0'3" / 0'8"	0'8" / 1'0"	0'7" / 1'0"	0'5" / 1'0"	0'7" / 1'5"
9	0'7" / 0'9"	0'6" / 0'8"	0'5" / 0'8"	0'4" / 0'8"	0'7" / 1'4"	0'5" / 0'9"	0'4" / 0'9"	0'9" / 1'2"	0'7" / 1'2"	0'6" / 1'2"	0'8" / 1'7"
10	0'7" / 0'10"	0'6" / 0'9"	0'5" / 0'9"	0'5" / 0'9"	0'7" / 1'6"	0'5" / 0'10"	0'4" / 0'10"	0'10" / 1'3"	0'8" / 1'3"	0'6" / 1'3"	0'9" / 1'9"

12	0' 9" / 1' 0"	0' 8" / 0' 11"	0' 6" / 0' 11"	0' 6" / 0' 11"	0' 9" / 1' 9"	0' 6" / 1' 0"	0' 5" / 1' 0"	1' 0" / 1' 6"	0' 10" / 1' 6"	0' 8" / 1' 6"	0' 11" / 2' 1"
14	0' 10" / 1' 2"	0' 9" / 1' 0"	0' 7" / 1' 0"	0' 7" / 1' 0"	0' 10" / 2' 1"	0' 7" / 1' 1"	0' 6" / 1' 1"	1' 2" / 1' 9"	0' 11" / 1' 9"	0' 9" / 1' 9"	1' 1" / 2' 5"
16	1' 0" / 1' 4"	0' 10" / 1' 2"	0' 8" / 1' 2"	0' 8" / 1' 2"	1' 0" / 2' 4"	0' 8" / 1' 3"	0' 6" / 1' 3"	1' 4" / 2' 0"	1' 1" / 2' 0"	0' 10" / 2' 0"	1' 3" / 2' 10"
18	1' 1" / 1' 6"	1' 0" / 1' 4"	0' 10" / 1' 4"	0' 9" / 1' 4"	1' 1" / 2' 8"	0' 9" / 1' 5"	0' 7" / 1' 5"	1' 6" / 2' 3"	1' 3" / 2' 3"	0' 11" / 2' 3"	1' 5" / 3' 2"
20	1' 3" / 1' 8"	1' 1" / 1' 6"	0' 11" / 1' 6"	0' 10" / 1' 6"	1' 3" / 2' 11"	0' 10" / 1' 7"	0' 8" / 1' 7"	1' 8" / 2' 6"	1' 4" / 2' 6"	1' 1" / 2' 6"	1' 6" / 3' 6"
25	1' 7" / 2' 1"	1' 4" / 1' 10"	1' 1" / 1' 10"	1' 0" / 1' 10"	1' 7" / 3' 8"	1' 1" / 2' 0"	0' 10" / 2' 0"	2' 1" / 3' 2"	1' 8" / 3' 2"	1' 4" / 3' 2"	1' 11" / 4' 5"
50	3' 1" / 4' 2"	2' 8" / 3' 8"	2' 3" / 3' 8"	2' 0" / 3' 8"	3' 1" / 7' 4"	2' 2" / 4' 0"	1' 8" / 4' 0"	4' 2" / 6' 3"	3' 5" / 6' 3"	2' 8" / 6' 3"	3' 10" / 8' 9"
75	4' 8" / 6' 3"	4' 0" / 5' 6"	3' 4" / 5' 6"	3' 0" / 5' 6"	4' 8" / 11' 0"	3' 3" / 6' 0"	2' 6" / 6' 0"	6' 3" / 9' 5"	5' 1" / 9' 5"	3' 11" / 9' 5"	5' 9" / 13' 2"
100	6' 3" / 8' 4"	5' 4" / 7' 4"	4' 5" / 7' 4"	4' 0" / 7' 4"	6' 2" / 14' 8"	4' 4" / 8' 0"	3' 4" / 8' 0"	8' 4" / 12' 7"	6' 10" / 12' 7"	5' 3" / 12' 7"	7' 8" / 17' 7"
125	7' 9" / 10' 5"	6' 8" / 9' 2"	5' 6" / 9' 2"	4' 11" / 9' 2"	7' 9" / 18' 4"	5' 5" / 10' 0"	4' 2" / 10' 0"	10' 5" / 15' 9"	8' 6" / 15' 9"	6' 7" / 15' 9"	9' 7" / 21' 11"
150	9' 4" / 12' 6"	8' 0" / 11' 0"	6' 8" / 11' 0"	5' 11" / 11' 0"	9' 4" / 22' 0"	6' 6" / 12' 0"	5' 0" / 12' 0"	12' 6" / 18' 10"	10' 2" / 18' 10"	7' 11" / 18' 10"	11' 6" / 26' 4"
175	10' 11" / 14' 6"	9' 4" / 12' 10"	7' 9" / 12' 10"	6' 11" / 12' 10"	10' 10" / 25' 8"	7' 7" / 14' 0"	5' 10" / 14' 0"	14' 6" / 22' 0"	11' 11" / 22' 0"	9' 2" / 22' 0"	13' 5" / 30' 8"
200	12' 5" / 16' 7"	10' 8" / 14' 8"	8' 10" / 14' 8"	7' 11" / 14' 8"	12' 5" / 29' 4"	8' 8" / 16' 0"	6' 8" / 16' 0"	16' 7" / 25' 2"	13' 7" / 25' 2"	10' 6" / 25' 2"	15' 4" / 35' 1"

SETUPS (Approximate Distance) — 400mm FIELD OF VIEW

	Full Aperture	Academy 1.33:1	Academy 1.66:1	Academy 1.85:1	Anamorphic 2.40:1	Super 35 1.85:1	Super 35 2.40:1	VistaVision	VistaVision 1.85:1	VistaVision 2.40:1	65mm
Ext Close Up	16' 1"	18' 9"	22' 8"	25' 3"	16' 2"	23' 1"	30' 0"	12' 0"	14' 9"	19' 0"	13' 0"
Close Up	25' 0"	29' 1"	35' 2"	39' 3"	25' 1"	35' 11"	46' 8"	18' 9"	22' 11"	29' 7"	20' 3"
Medium Shot	46' 5"	54' 1"	65' 4"	72' 11"	46' 7"	66' 9"	86' 7"	34' 9"	42' 6"	54' 11"	37' 8"
Full Figure	128' 7"	149' 9"	181' 0"	201' 11"	129' 1"	184' 11"	239' 10"	96' 4"	117' 8"	152' 2"	104' 3"
Angle of View	V 2.7° H 3.6°	V 2.2° H 3.0°	V 1.8° H 3.0°	V 1.6° H 3.0°	V 2.5° H 6.1°	V 1.9° H 3.4°	V 1.4° H 3.4°	V 3.6° H 5.4°	V 2.9° H 5.4°	V 2.3° H 5.4°	V 3.2° H 6.9°
5	0' 3" / 0' 4"	0' 2" / 0' 3"	0' 2" / 0' 3"	0' 2" / 0' 3"	0' 3" / 0' 7"	0' 2" / 0' 4"	0' 2" / 0' 4"	0' 4" / 0' 6"	0' 3" / 0' 6"	0' 2" / 0' 6"	0' 3" / 0' 8"
5½	0' 3" / 0' 4"	0' 3" / 0' 4"	0' 2" / 0' 4"	0' 2" / 0' 4"	0' 3" / 0' 7"	0' 2" / 0' 4"	0' 2" / 0' 4"	0' 4" / 0' 6"	0' 3" / 0' 6"	0' 3" / 0' 6"	0' 4" / 0' 9"
6	0' 3" / 0' 4"	0' 3" / 0' 4"	0' 2" / 0' 4"	0' 2" / 0' 4"	0' 3" / 0' 8"	0' 2" / 0' 4"	0' 2" / 0' 4"	0' 4" / 0' 7"	0' 4" / 0' 7"	0' 3" / 0' 7"	0' 4" / 0' 9"
6½	0' 4" / 0' 5"	0' 3" / 0' 4"	0' 3" / 0' 5"	0' 2" / 0' 5"	0' 4" / 0' 9"	0' 3" / 0' 5"	0' 2" / 0' 5"	0' 5" / 0' 7"	0' 4" / 0' 7"	0' 3" / 0' 7"	0' 4" / 0' 10"
7	0' 4" / 0' 5"	0' 3" / 0' 5"	0' 3" / 0' 5"	0' 2" / 0' 5"	0' 4" / 0' 9"	0' 3" / 0' 5"	0' 2" / 0' 5"	0' 5" / 0' 8"	0' 4" / 0' 8"	0' 3" / 0' 8"	0' 5" / 0' 11"
8	0' 4" / 0' 6"	0' 4" / 0' 5"	0' 3" / 0' 5"	0' 3" / 0' 5"	0' 4" / 0' 11"	0' 3" / 0' 6"	0' 2" / 0' 6"	0' 6" / 0' 9"	0' 5" / 0' 9"	0' 4" / 0' 9"	0' 6" / 1' 1"
9	0' 5" / 0' 7"	0' 4" / 0' 6"	0' 4" / 0' 6"	0' 3" / 0' 6"	0' 5" / 1' 0"	0' 4" / 0' 6"	0' 3" / 0' 6"	0' 7" / 0' 10"	0' 6" / 0' 10"	0' 4" / 0' 10"	0' 6" / 1' 2"
10	0' 6" / 0' 7"	0' 5" / 0' 7"	0' 4" / 0' 7"	0' 4" / 0' 7"	0' 6" / 1' 1"	0' 4" / 0' 7"	0' 3" / 0' 7"	0' 7" / 0' 11"	0' 6" / 0' 11"	0' 5" / 0' 11"	0' 7" / 1' 4"

	1	2	3	4	5	6	7	8	9	10	11
12	0' 7" / 0' 9"	0' 6" / 0' 8"	0' 5" / 0' 8"	0' 4" / 0' 8"	0' 7" / 1' 4"	0' 5" / 0' 9"	0' 4" / 0' 9"	0' 9" / 1' 2"	0' 7" / 1' 2"	0' 6" / 1' 2"	0' 8" / 1' 7"
14	0' 8" / 0' 10"	0' 7" / 0' 9"	0' 6" / 0' 9"	0' 5" / 0' 9"	0' 8" / 1' 6"	0' 5" / 0' 10"	0' 4" / 0' 10"	0' 10" / 1' 4"	0' 9" / 1' 4"	0' 7" / 1' 4"	0' 10" / 1' 10"
16	0' 9" / 1' 0"	0' 8" / 0' 11"	0' 6" / 0' 11"	0' 6" / 0' 11"	0' 9" / 1' 9"	0' 6" / 1' 0"	0' 5" / 1' 0"	1' 0" / 1' 6"	0' 10" / 1' 6"	0' 8" / 1' 6"	0' 11" / 2' 1"
18	0' 10" / 1' 1"	0' 9" / 1' 0"	0' 7" / 1' 0"	0' 6" / 1' 0"	0' 10" / 2' 0"	0' 7" / 1' 1"	0' 5" / 1' 1"	1' 1" / 1' 8"	0' 11" / 1' 8"	0' 9" / 1' 8"	1' 0" / 2' 4"
20	0' 11" / 1' 3"	0' 10" / 1' 1"	0' 8" / 1' 1"	0' 7" / 1' 1"	0' 11" / 2' 2"	0' 8" / 1' 2"	0' 6" / 1' 2"	1' 3" / 1' 11"	1' 0" / 1' 11"	0' 9" / 1' 11"	1' 2" / 2' 8"
25	1' 2" / 1' 7"	1' 0" / 1' 4"	0' 10" / 1' 4"	0' 9" / 1' 4"	1' 2" / 2' 9"	0' 10" / 1' 6"	0' 8" / 1' 6"	1' 7" / 2' 4"	1' 3" / 2' 4"	1' 0" / 2' 4"	1' 5" / 3' 3"
50	2' 4" / 3' 1"	2' 0" / 2' 9"	1' 8" / 2' 9"	1' 6" / 2' 9"	2' 4" / 5' 6"	1' 7" / 3' 0"	1' 3" / 3' 0"	3' 1" / 4' 9"	2' 7" / 4' 9"	2' 0" / 4' 9"	2' 11" / 6' 7"
75	3' 6" / 4' 8"	3' 0" / 4' 1"	2' 6" / 4' 1"	2' 3" / 4' 1"	3' 6" / 8' 3"	2' 5" / 4' 6"	1' 11" / 4' 6"	4' 8" / 7' 1"	3' 10" / 7' 1"	2' 11" / 7' 1"	4' 4" / 9' 10"
100	4' 8" / 6' 3"	4' 0" / 5' 6"	3' 4" / 5' 6"	3' 0" / 5' 6"	4' 8" / 11' 0"	3' 3" / 6' 0"	2' 6" / 6' 0"	6' 3" / 9' 5"	5' 1" / 9' 5"	3' 11" / 9' 5"	5' 9" / 13' 2"
125	5' 10" / 7' 9"	5' 0" / 6' 10"	4' 2" / 6' 10"	3' 9" / 6' 10"	5' 10" / 13' 9"	4' 1" / 7' 6"	3' 2" / 7' 6"	7' 9" / 11' 9"	6' 4" / 11' 9"	4' 11" / 11' 9"	7' 2" / 16' 5"
150	7' 0" / 9' 4"	6' 0" / 8' 3"	5' 0" / 8' 3"	4' 5" / 8' 3"	7' 0" / 16' 6"	4' 10" / 9' 0"	3' 9" / 9' 0"	9' 4" / 14' 2"	7' 8" / 14' 2"	5' 11" / 14' 2"	8' 8" / 19' 9"
175	8' 2" / 10' 11"	7' 0" / 9' 7"	5' 10" / 9' 7"	5' 2" / 9' 7"	8' 2" / 19' 3"	5' 8" / 10' 6"	4' 5" / 10' 6"	10' 11" / 16' 6"	8' 11" / 16' 6"	6' 11" / 16' 6"	10' 1" / 23' 0"
200	9' 4" / 12' 6"	8' 0" / 11' 0"	6' 8" / 11' 0"	5' 11" / 11' 0"	9' 4" / 22' 0"	6' 6" / 12' 0"	5' 0" / 12' 0"	12' 6" / 18' 10"	10' 2" / 18' 10"	7' 11" / 18' 10"	11' 6" / 26' 4"

16mm/SUPER 16 — FIELD OF VIEW

LENS SIZE	5.9mm		8mm		10mm		12mm		16mm		25mm		37.5mm		50mm		85mm		100mm		150mm		200mm		300mm		400mm	
FORMAT	16mm	Super16	16mm	Super16	16mm	Super16	16mm	Super16	16mm	Super16	16mm	Super16	16mm	Super16	16mm	Super16	16mm	Super16	16mm	Super16	16mm	Super16	16mm	Super16	16mm	Super16	16mm	Super16
SETUPS (Approximate Distance)																												
Ext Cls Up	0'7"	0'8"	0'10"	0'11"	1'0"	1'2"	1'2"	1'5"	1'7"	1'11"	2'6"	2'11"	3'9"	4'5"	5'0"	5'11"	8'6"	10'0"	10'0"	11'9"	15'0"	17'8"	20'0"	23'6"	30'0"	35'4"	40'0"	47'1"
Close Up	0'11"	1'1"	1'3"	1'6"	1'7"	1'10"	1'10"	2'2"	2'6"	2'11"	3'11"	4'7"	5'10"	6'10"	7'9"	9'2"	13'3"	15'7"	15'7"	18'4"	23'4"	27'5"	31'2"	36'7"	46'9"	54'11"	62'3"	73'2"
Med Shot	1'8"	2'0"	2'4"	2'9"	2'11"	3'5"	3'6"	4'1"	4'8"	5'5"	7'3"	8'6"	10'10"	12'9"	14'5"	17'0"	24'7"	28'11"	28'11"	34'0"	43'4"	51'0"	57'10"	68'0"	86'9"	101'11"	115'8"	135'11"
Full Figure	4'9"	5'7"	6'5"	7'6"	8'0"	9'5"	9'7"	11'4"	12'10"	15'1"	20'0"	23'6"	30'0"	35'4"	40'0"	47'1"	68'1"	80'0"	80'1"	94'1"	120'1"	141'2"	160'2"	188'3"	240'3"	282'4"	320'4"	376'5"
ANGLE OF VIEW	V 63.2° / H 78.6°	V 56.8° / H 89.8°	V 48.8° / H 62.2°	V 43.5° / H 72.6°	V 39.9° / H 51.5°	V 35.4° / H 60.9°	V 33.7° / H 43.8°	V 29.8° / H 52.2°	V 25.6° / H 33.6°	V 22.5° / H 40.4°	V 16.5° / H 21.9°	V 14.5° / H 26.5°	V 11.1° / H 14.7°	V 9.7° / H 17.8°	V 8.3° / H 11.0°	V 7.3° / H 13.4°	V 4.9° / H 6.5°	V 4.3° / H 7.9°	V 4.2° / H 5.5°	V 3.7° / H 6.7°	V 2.8° / H 3.7°	V 2.4° / H 4.5°	V 2.1° / H 2.8°	V 1.8° / H 3.4°	V 1.4° / H 1.8°	V 1.2° / H 2.2°	V 1.0° / H 1.4°	V 0.9° / H 1.7°
FOCUS (feet)																												
2	2'6"	3'6"	1'10"	2'7"	1'6"	2'1"	1'3"	1'9"	0'11"	1'3"	0'7"	0'10"	0'5"	0'7"	0'4"	0'5"	0'2"	0'3"	0'2"	0'2"	0'1"	0'2"	NA	NA	NA	NA	NA	NA
2½	3'2"	4'4"	2'4"	3'2"	1'10"	2'7"	1'7"	2'2"	1'2"	1'7"	0'9"	1'0"	0'6"	0'8"	0'4"	0'6"	0'3"	0'4"	0'2"	0'3"	0'1"	0'2"	0'1"	0'2"	NA	NA	NA	NA

	3	3½	4	4½	5	5½	6	6½	7
	NA / NA	NA / NA	NA / NA	NA / NA	NA / NA	0'1" / 0'2"	0'1" / 0'2"	0'1" / 0'2"	0'1" / 0'2"
	NA / NA	NA / NA	NA / NA	NA / NA	0'1" / 0'2"	0'1" / 0'2"	0'1" / 0'3"	0'2" / 0'3"	0'2" / 0'3"
	NA / NA	NA / NA	0'1" / 0'2"	0'1" / 0'2"	0'1" / 0'2"	0'1" / 0'2"	0'2" / 0'2"	0'2" / 0'3"	0'2" / 0'3"
	0'1" / 0'2"	0'1" / 0'2"	0'1" / 0'2"	0'2" / 0'3"	0'2" / 0'3"	0'2" / 0'4"	0'2" / 0'4"	0'2" / 0'5"	0'3" / 0'5"
	0'2" / 0'2"	0'2" / 0'3"	0'2" / 0'3"	0'2" / 0'4"	0'3" / 0'5"	0'3" / 0'5"	0'3" / 0'6"	0'3" / 0'6"	0'4" / 0'7"
	0'2" / 0'2"	0'2" / 0'3"	0'2" / 0'3"	0'3" / 0'4"	0'3" / 0'4"	0'3" / 0'5"	0'4" / 0'5"	0'4" / 0'6"	0'4" / 0'7"
	0'3" / 0'4"	0'3" / 0'4"	0'4" / 0'5"	0'4" / 0'6"	0'4" / 0'6"	0'5" / 0'7"	0'5" / 0'7"	0'5" / 0'8"	0'5" / 0'10"
	0'3" / 0'4"	0'4" / 0'5"	0'4" / 0'6"	0'5" / 0'7"	0'5" / 0'7"	0'6" / 0'8"	0'6" / 0'9"	0'6" / 0'11"	0'6" / 0'11"
	0'5" / 0'7"	0'5" / 0'8"	0'6" / 0'9"	0'7" / 0'10"	0'8" / 0'11"	0'9" / 1'0"	0'10" / 1'2"	0'11" / 1'3"	1'1" / 1'5"
	0'7" / 0'10"	0'8" / 0'11"	0'10" / 1'1"	0'11" / 1'3"	1'0" / 1'4"	1'1" / 1'6"	1'2" / 1'8"	1'4" / 1'9"	1'5" / 1'11"
	0'11" / 1'3"	1'0" / 1'5"	1'2" / 1'8"	1'4" / 1'10"	1'6" / 2'1"	1'8" / 2'3"	1'10" / 2'6"	1'11" / 2'8"	2'1" / 2'10"
	1'5" / 1'11"	1'8" / 2'3"	1'10" / 2'7"	2'1" / 2'11"	2'4" / 3'2"	2'7" / 3'6"	2'10" / 3'10"	3'1" / 4'2"	3'3" / 4'6"
	1'10" / 2'7"	2'2" / 3'0"	2'6" / 3'5"	2'10" / 3'10"	3'1" / 4'3"	3'5" / 4'8"	3'9" / 5'2"	4'1" / 5'7"	4'4" / 6'0"
	2'3" / 3'1"	2'7" / 3'7"	3'0" / 4'1"	3'4" / 4'7"	3'9" / 5'2"	4'1" / 5'8"	4'6" / 6'2"	4'10" / 6'8"	5'3" / 7'2"
	2'10" / 3'10"	3'3" / 4'6"	3'9" / 5'2"	4'3" / 5'9"	4'8" / 6'5"	5'2" / 7'1"	5'7" / 7'8"	6'1" / 8'4"	6'7" / 9'0"
	3'3" / 6'0"	3'9" / 7'0"	4'3" / 8'0"	4'10" / 9'0"	5'5" / 10'0"	5'11" / 11'0"	6'6" / 12'0"	7'0" / 12'11"	7'7" / 13'11"
	3'10" / 5'3"	4'5" / 6'1"	5'1" / 6'11"	5'9" / 7'10"	6'4" / 8'8"	7'0" / 9'7"	7'7" / 10'5"	8'3" / 11'4"	8'11" / 12'2"

16mm/SUPER 16 — FIELD OF VIEW (Continued)

Each cell gives the two field-of-view dimensions (stacked) for that lens and format at the indicated focus distance.

FOCUS (feet)	5.9mm 16mm	5.9mm Super16	8mm 16mm	8mm Super16	10mm 16mm	10mm Super16	12mm 16mm	12mm Super16	16mm 16mm	16mm Super16	25mm 16mm	25mm Super16	37.5mm 16mm	37.5mm Super16	50mm 16mm	50mm Super16	85mm 16mm	85mm Super16	100mm 16mm	100mm Super16	150mm 16mm	150mm Super16	200mm 16mm	200mm Super16	300mm 16mm	300mm Super16	400mm 16mm	400mm Super16
8	10' 2" / 13' 11"	8' 8" / 15' 11"	7' 6" / 10' 3"	6' 5" / 11' 9"	6' 0" / 8' 3"	5' 1" / 9' 5"	5' 0" / 6' 10"	4' 3" / 7' 10"	3' 9" / 5' 2"	3' 2" / 5' 11"	2' 5" / 3' 3"	2' 0" / 3' 9"	1' 7" / 2' 2"	1' 4" / 2' 6"	1' 2" / 1' 8"	1' 0" / 1' 11"	0' 8" / 1' 0"	0' 7" / 1' 1"	0' 7" / 0' 10"	0' 6" / 0' 11"	0' 5" / 0' 7"	0' 5" / 0' 8"	0' 4" / 0' 5"	0' 4" / 0' 6"	0' 2" / 0' 3"	0' 2" / 0' 4"	0' 2" / 0' 2"	0' 2" / 0' 3"
9	11' 5" / 15' 8"	9' 9" / 17' 11"	8' 5" / 11' 7"	7' 2" / 13' 3"	6' 9" / 9' 3"	5' 9" / 10' 7"	5' 7" / 7' 8"	4' 9" / 8' 10"	4' 3" / 5' 9"	3' 7" / 6' 7"	2' 8" / 3' 8"	2' 4" / 4' 3"	1' 10" / 2' 6"	1' 6" / 2' 10"	1' 4" / 1' 10"	1' 2" / 2' 1"	0' 10" / 1' 1"	0' 8" / 1' 3"	0' 8" / 0' 11"	0' 7" / 1' 1"	0' 5" / 0' 7"	0' 5" / 0' 7"	0' 4" / 0' 6"	0' 4" / 0' 6"	0' 3" / 0' 4"	0' 3" / 0' 6"	0' 2" / 0' 3"	0' 2" / 0' 3"
10	12' 8" / 17' 5"	10' 10" / 19' 11"	9' 4" / 12' 10"	8' 0" / 14' 8"	7' 6" / 10' 3"	6' 5" / 11' 9"	6' 3" / 8' 7"	5' 4" / 9' 10"	4' 8" / 6' 5"	4' 0" / 7' 4"	3' 0" / 4' 1"	2' 7" / 4' 8"	2' 0" / 2' 9"	1' 8" / 3' 2"	1' 6" / 2' 1"	1' 3" / 2' 4"	0' 11" / 1' 2"	0' 9" / 1' 5"	0' 9" / 1' 0"	0' 8" / 1' 2"	0' 6" / 0' 8"	0' 6" / 0' 9"	0' 4" / 0' 4"	0' 4" / 0' 7"	0' 3" / 0' 4"	0' 3" / 0' 5"	0' 2" / 0' 3"	0' 2" / 0' 3"
12	15' 3" / 20' 10"	13' 0" / 23' 11"	11' 3" / 15' 5"	9' 7" / 17' 8"	9' 0" / 12' 4"	7' 8" / 14' 1"	7' 6" / 10' 3"	6' 5" / 11' 9"	5' 7" / 7' 8"	4' 9" / 8' 10"	3' 7" / 4' 11"	3' 1" / 5' 8"	2' 5" / 3' 3"	2' 0" / 3' 9"	1' 10" / 2' 6"	1' 6" / 1' 10"	1' 1" / 1' 5"	0' 11" / 1' 8"	0' 11" / 1' 3"	0' 9" / 1' 5"	0' 7" / 0' 10"	0' 7" / 0' 11"	0' 5" / 0' 7"	0' 6" / 0' 8"	0' 4" / 0' 5"	0' 4" / 0' 6"	0' 3" / 0' 4"	0' 3" / 0' 4"
14	17' 9" / 24' 4"	15' 2" / 27' 11"	13' 1" / 17' 11"	11' 2" / 20' 7"	10' 6" / 14' 4"	8' 11" / 16' 6"	8' 9" / 12' 0"	7' 5" / 13' 9"	6' 7" / 9' 0"	5' 7" / 10' 3"	4' 2" / 5' 9"	3' 7" / 6' 7"	2' 10" / 3' 10"	2' 5" / 4' 5"	2' 1" / 2' 10"	1' 9" / 3' 4"	1' 3" / 1' 8"	1' 1" / 1' 11"	1' 1" / 1' 5"	0' 11" / 1' 8"	0' 8" / 0' 11"	0' 8" / 1' 1"	0' 6" / 0' 9"	0' 7" / 0' 10"	0' 4" / 0' 6"	0' 4" / 0' 8"	0' 3" / 0' 4"	0' 3" / 0' 5"
16	20' 4" / 27' 10"	17' 3" / 31' 11"	15' 0" / 20' 6"	12' 9" / 23' 6"	12' 0" / 16' 5"	10' 2" / 18' 10"	10' 0" / 13' 8"	8' 6" / 15' 8"	7' 6" / 10' 3"	6' 5" / 11' 9"	4' 10" / 6' 7"	4' 1" / 7' 6"	3' 2" / 4' 5"	2' 9" / 5' 0"	2' 5" / 3' 3"	2' 0" / 3' 9"	1' 5" / 1' 11"	1' 3" / 2' 3"	1' 2" / 1' 8"	1' 0" / 1' 11"	0' 10" / 1' 1"	0' 8" / 1' 3"	0' 7" / 0' 10"	0' 6" / 0' 11"	0' 5" / 0' 7"	0' 4" / 0' 8"	0' 4" / 0' 5"	0' 3" / 0' 6"
18	22' 10" / 31' 4"	19' 5" / 35' 11"	16' 10" / 23' 1"	14' 4" / 26' 6"	13' 6" / 18' 6"	11' 6" / 21' 2"	11' 3" / 15' 5"	9' 7" / 17' 8"	8' 5" / 11' 7"	7' 2" / 13' 3"	5' 5" / 7' 5"	4' 7" / 8' 6"	3' 7" / 4' 11"	3' 1" / 5' 8"	2' 8" / 3' 8"	2' 4" / 4' 3"	1' 7" / 2' 2"	1' 4" / 2' 6"	1' 4" / 1' 10"	1' 2" / 2' 1"	0' 11" / 1' 3"	0' 9" / 1' 5"	0' 8" / 0' 11"	0' 7" / 1' 1"	0' 5" / 0' 7"	0' 5" / 0' 7"	0' 4" / 0' 6"	0' 3" / 0' 6"

20	25' 5"/34' 9"	21' 7"/39' 10"	18' 9"/25' 8"	15' 0"/20' 6"	12' 6"/17' 1"	9' 4"/12' 10"	6' 0"/8' 3"	4' 0"/5' 6"	3' 0"/4' 1"	1' 9"/2' 5"	1' 6"/2' 1"	1' 0"/1' 4"	0' 9"/1' 0"	0' 6"/0' 8"	0' 4"/0' 6"	0' 4"/0' 7"
25	31' 9"/43' 6"	15' 11"/29' 5"	23' 5"/32' 1"	18' 9"/25' 8"	15' 7"/21' 5"	11' 8"/16' 0"	7' 6"/10' 3"	5' 0"/6' 10"	3' 9"/5' 2"	2' 2"/3' 0"	1' 10"/2' 7"	1' 3"/1' 9"	0' 11"/1' 3"	0' 7"/0' 10"	0' 6"/0' 8"	0' 5"/0' 9"
50	63' 6"/87' 0"	27' 0"/49' 10"	19' 11"/36' 9"	15' 11"/29' 5"	13' 3"/24' 6"	10' 0"/18' 5"	12' 9"/20' 6"	10' 0"/13' 8"	7' 6"/10' 3"	4' 5"/6' 0"	3' 9"/5' 2"	2' 6"/3' 5"	1' 10"/2' 7"	1' 3"/1' 9"	0' 11"/1' 3"	0' 10"/1' 6"
75	95' 3"/130' 5"	54' 0"/99' 8"	39' 10"/73' 6"	31' 11"/58' 10"	26' 7"/49' 0"	19' 11"/36' 9"	22' 6"/30' 9"	15' 0"/20' 6"	11' 3"/15' 5"	6' 7"/9' 1"	5' 7"/7' 8"	3' 9"/5' 2"	2' 10"/3' 10"	2' 2"/3' 11"	1' 5"/1' 11"	1' 2"/2' 2"
100	127' 0"/173' 11"	81' 1"/149' 6"	74' 11"/102' 7"	46' 10"/64' 2"	39' 10"/73' 6"	29' 11"/55' 2"	30' 0"/41' 1"	20' 0"/27' 4"	15' 0"/20' 6"	8' 10"/12' 1"	7' 6"/10' 3"	5' 0"/6' 10"	3' 9"/5' 2"	2' 6"/3' 5"	1' 10"/2' 7"	1' 7"/2' 11"
125	158' 9"/217' 5"	135' 1"/249' 2"	93' 8"/128' 3"	63' 9"/117' 7"	53' 2"/98' 0"	49' 10"/91' 11"	37' 6"/51' 4"	25' 0"/34' 2"	21' 3"/39' 2"	11' 0"/12' 1"	9' 5"/17' 4"	6' 3"/8' 7"	4' 8"/6' 5"	3' 2"/4' 11"	2' 4"/3' 2"	2' 0"/3' 8"
150	190' 6"/260' 11"	162' 1"/299' 0"	119' 6"/220' 6"	95' 8"/176' 5"	79' 8"/147' 6"	59' 9"/110' 3"	44' 11"/61' 7"	35' 0"/47' 11"	25' 6"/47' 0"	15' 5"/21' 2"	11' 3"/20' 9"	8' 9"/12' 0"	6' 7"/9' 0"	4' 9"/8' 10"	3' 3"/4' 6"	2' 5"/4' 5"
175	222' 3"/304' 4"	139' 6"/257' 3"	131' 2"/179' 7"	109' 3"/149' 8"	93' 0"/171' 6"	69' 9"/128' 8"	52' 5"/71' 10"	44' 8"/82' 4"	29' 9"/54' 11"	17' 8"/24' 2"	13' 2"/24' 3"	10' 0"/13' 8"	7' 6"/10' 3"	5' 7"/10' 3"	4' 4"/6' 0"	2' 9"/5' 2"
200	254' 0"/347' 10"	187' 4"/256' 6"	159' 5"/294' 0"	127' 6"/235' 2"	106' 3"/196' 0"	93' 8"/128' 3"	59' 8"/147' 0"	51' 0"/94' 1"	34' 0"/62' 9"	25' 6"/47' 0"	15' 0"/27' 8"	10' 8"/13' 8"	7' 6"/10' 3"	6' 5"/11' 9"	3' 9"/5' 2"	3' 2"/5' 11"

SUPER 8mm/6.5mm — CAMERA DEPTH-OF-FIELD, HYPERFOCAL DISTANCE, AND FIELD OF VIEW

CAMERA APERTURE: 0.224 x 0.166 inches

CIRCLE OF CONFUSION=0.0020 inches

Hyperfocal Distance	f/1.4	f/2.0	f/2.8	f/4.0	f/5.6	f/8.0	f/11.0	f/16.0	f/22.0	ANGLE OF VIEW H 47.3° / V 35.9°
	1' 11"	1' 4"	1' 0"	0' 8"	0' 6"	0' 4	0' 3"	0' 2"	0' 1"	
FOCUS	NEAR FAR	NEAR FAR	NEAR FAR	NEAR FAR	NEAR FAR	NEAR FAR	NEAR FAR	NEAR FAR	NEAR FAR	FIELD OF VIEW
2	1' 0" INF	0' 10" INF	0' 8" INF	0' 6" INF	0' 5" INF	0' 4" INF	0' 3" INF	0' 2" INF	0' 1" INF	1' 9" x 1' 3"
4	1' 4" INF	1' 0" INF	0' 9" INF	0' 7" INF	0' 5" INF	0' 4" INF	0' 3" INF	0' 2" INF	0' 1" INF	3' 6" x 2' 7"
6	1' 6" INF	1' 1" INF	0' 10" INF	0' 7" INF	0' 5" INF	0' 4" INF	0' 3" INF	0' 2" INF	0' 1" INF	5' 3" x 3' 11"
8	1' 7" INF	1' 2" INF	0' 10" INF	0' 8" INF	0' 6" INF	0' 4" INF	0' 3" INF	0' 2" INF	0' 1" INF	7' 0" x 5' 2"
10	1' 8" INF	1' 2" INF	0' 11" INF	0' 8" INF	0' 6" INF	0' 4" INF	0' 3" INF	0' 2" INF	0' 1" INF	8' 9" x 6' 6"
12	1' 8" INF	1' 3" INF	0' 11" INF	0' 8" INF	0' 6" INF	0' 4" INF	0' 3" INF	0' 2" INF	0' 1" INF	10' 6" x 7' 9"
16	1' 9" INF	1' 3" INF	0' 11" INF	0' 8" INF	0' 6" INF	0' 4" INF	0' 3" INF	0' 2" INF	0' 1" INF	14' 0" x 10' 4"
25	1' 10" INF	1' 4" INF	0' 11" INF	0' 8" INF	0' 6" INF	0' 4" INF	0' 3" INF	0' 2" INF	0' 1" INF	21' 10" x 16' 2"

SUPER 8mm/13mm — CAMERA DEPTH-OF-FIELD, HYPERFOCAL DISTANCE, AND FIELD OF VIEW

CAMERA APERTURE: 0.224 x 0.166 inches
CIRCLE OF CONFUSION=0.0020 inches

FOCUS	Hyperfocal Distance	f/1.4 NEAR FAR	f/2.0 NEAR FAR	f/2.8 NEAR FAR	f/4.0 NEAR FAR	f/5.6 NEAR FAR	f/8.0 NEAR FAR	f/11.0 NEAR FAR	f/16.0 NEAR FAR	f/22.0 NEAR FAR	ANGLE OF VIEW H 27.7° / V 18.4° — FIELD OF VIEW
		7' 10"	5' 5"	3' 11"	2' 9"	1' 11"	1' 4"	1' 0"	0' 8"	0' 6"	
2		1' 7" / 2' 8"	1' 6" / 3' 1"	1' 4" / 4' 0"	1' 2" / 7' 1"	1' 0" / INF	0' 10" / INF	0' 8" / INF	0' 6" / INF	0' 5" / INF	0' 10" x 0' 8"
4		2' 8" / 8' 1"	2' 4" / 14' 7"	2' 0" / INF	1' 8" / INF	1' 4" / INF	1' 0" / INF	0' 10" / INF	0' 7" / INF	0' 5" / INF	1' 9" x 1' 3.5"
6		3' 5" / 25' 5"	2' 10" / INF	2' 4" / INF	1' 11" / INF	1' 6" / INF	1' 1" / INF	0' 10" / INF	0' 7" / INF	0' 6" / INF	2' 7" x 1' 11"
8		4' 0" / INF	3' 3" / INF	2' 8" / INF	2' 1" / INF	1' 7" / INF	1' 2" / INF	0' 11" / INF	0' 8" / INF	0' 6" / INF	3' 6" x 2' 7"
10		4' 5" / INF	3' 6" / INF	2' 10" / INF	2' 2" / INF	1' 8" / INF	1' 2" / INF	0' 11" / INF	0' 8" / INF	0' 6" / INF	4' 4" x 3' 3"
12		4' 9" / INF	3' 9" / INF	2' 11" / INF	2' 3" / INF	1' 8" / INF	1' 3" / INF	0' 11" / INF	0' 8" / INF	0' 6" / INF	5' 3" x 3' 11"
16		5' 3" / INF	4' 1" / INF	3' 2" / INF	2' 4" / INF	1' 9" / INF	1' 3" / INF	0' 11" / INF	0' 8" / INF	0' 6" / INF	7' 0" x 5' 2"
25		5' 11" / INF	4' 6" / INF	3' 5" / INF	2' 6" / INF	1' 10" / INF	1' 4" / INF	0' 11" / INF	0' 8" / INF	0' 6" / INF	10' 11" x 8' 1"

SUPER 8mm/38mm — CAMERA DEPTH-OF-FIELD, HYPERFOCAL DISTANCE, AND FIELD OF VIEW

CAMERA APERTURE: 0.224 x 0.166 inches — CIRCLE OF CONFUSION=0.0020 inches

FOCUS		f/1.4	f/2.0	f/2.8	f/4.0	f/5.6	f/8.0	f/11.0	f/16.0	f/22.0	ANGLE OF VIEW H 8.5° / V 6.3°
Hyperfocal Distance		66' 7"	46' 8"	33' 4"	23' 4"	16' 8"	11' 8"	8' 6"	5' 10"	4' 3"	FIELD OF VIEW
2	NEAR	1' 11"	1' 11"	1' 11"	1' 10"	1' 10"	1' 9"	1' 8"	1' 6"	1' 5"	0' 4" x 0' 2.6"
	FAR	2' 1"	2' 1"	2' 1"	2' 2"	2' 3"	2' 5"	2' 7"	2' 11"	3' 7"	
4	NEAR	3' 9"	3' 8"	3' 7"	3' 5"	3' 3"	3' 0"	2' 9"	2' 5"	2' 1"	0' 5" x 0' 5.3"
	FAR	4' 3"	4' 4"	4' 6"	4' 10"	5' 3"	6' 0"	7' 4"	11' 11"	INF	
6	NEAR	5' 6"	5' 4"	5' 1"	4' 10"	4' 5"	4' 0"	3' 7"	3' 0"	2' 6"	0' 11" x 0' 8"
	FAR	6' 7"	6' 10"	7' 3"	8' 0"	9' 3"	12' 1"	19' 7"	INF	INF	
8	NEAR	7' 2"	6' 10"	6' 6"	6' 0"	5' 5"	4' 9"	4' 2"	3' 5"	2' 10"	1' 2" x 0' 11"
	FAR	9' 1"	9' 8"	10' 6"	12' 1"	15' 2"	24' 8"	INF	INF	INF	
10	NEAR	8' 9"	8' 3"	7' 9"	7' 0"	6' 3"	5' 5"	4' 7"	3' 9"	3' 0"	1' 6" x 1' 1"
	FAR	11' 9"	12' 8"	14' 3"	17' 4"	24' 7"	65' 5"	INF	INF	INF	
12	NEAR	10' 2"	9' 7"	8' 10"	7' 11"	7' 0"	5' 11"	5' 0"	3' 11"	3' 2"	1' 9" x 1' 4"
	FAR	14' 7"	16' 1"	18' 8"	24' 5"	41' 10"	INF	INF	INF	INF	
16	NEAR	12' 11"	11' 11"	10' 10"	9' 6"	8' 2"	6' 9"	5' 7"	4' 4"	3' 4"	2' 5" x 1' 9"
	FAR	21' 0"	24' 3"	30' 7"	50' 2"	INF	INF	INF	INF	INF	
25	NEAR	18' 2"	16' 4"	14' 4"	12' 1"	10' 0"	8' 0"	6' 4"	4' 9"	3' 8"	3' 9" x 2' 9"
	FAR	39' 11"	53' 7"	98' 9"	INF	INF	INF	INF	INF	INF	

SUPER 8mm/50mm — CAMERA DEPTH-OF-FIELD, HYPERFOCAL DISTANCE, AND FIELD OF VIEW

CAMERA APERTURE: 0.224 x 0.166 inches — CIRCLE OF CONFUSION=0.0020 inches

FOCUS	f/1.4	f/2.0	f/2.8	f/4.0	f/5.6	f/8.0	f/11.0	f/16.0	f/22.0	FIELD OF VIEW
Hyperfocal Distance	115' 4"	80' 9"	57' 8"	40' 4"	28' 10"	20' 2"	14' 8"	10' 1"	7' 4"	**ANGLE OF VIEW** H 6.5° / V 4.8°
	NEAR FAR	NEAR FAR	NEAR FAR	NEAR FAR	NEAR FAR	NEAR FAR	NEAR FAR	NEAR FAR	NEAR FAR	
2	NA NA	1' 11" 2' 1"	1' 11" 2' 1"	1' 11" 2' 1"	1' 11" 2' 2"	1' 10" 2' 2"	1' 9" 2' 3"	1' 8" 2' 5"	1' 7" 2' 8"	0' 2.7" x 0' 2"
4	3' 10" 4' 2"	3' 10" 4' 2"	3' 9" 4' 3"	3' 8" 4' 5"	3' 6" 4' 7"	3' 4" 4' 11"	3' 2" 5' 5"	2' 11" 6' 5"	2' 8" 8' 5"	0'5.5" x 0' 4"
6	5' 9" 6' 4"	5' 7" 6' 6"	5' 5" 6' 8"	5' 3" 7' 0"	5' 0" 7' 6"	4' 8" 8' 5"	4' 4" 10' 0"	3' 10" 14' 3"	3' 4" 29' 4"	0' 8" x 0' 6"
8	7' 6" 8' 7"	7' 4" 8' 10"	7' 1" 9' 3"	6' 8" 9' 11"	6' 3" 11' 0"	5' 9" 13' 1"	5' 3" 17' 2"	4' 6" 35' 10"	3' 10" INF	0' 11" x 0' 8"
10	9' 3" 10' 11"	8' 11" 11' 5"	8' 7" 12' 1"	8' 0" 13' 3"	7' 5" 15' 2"	6' 9" 19' 6"	6' 0" 30' 4"	5' 1" INF	4' 3" INF	1' 2.6" x 0' 10"
12	10' 11" 13' 4"	10' 6" 14' 1"	9' 11" 15' 1"	9' 3" 17' 0"	8' 6" 20' 4"	7' 7" 29' 0"	6' 8" 62' 0"	5' 6" INF	4' 7" INF	1' 4" x 1' 0"
16	14' 1" 18' 7"	13' 5" 19' 11"	12' 7" 22' 1"	11' 6" 26' 4"	10' 4" 35' 6"	9' 0" 74' 4"	7' 8" INF	6' 3" INF	5' 1" INF	1' 10" x 1' 4"
25	20' 7" 31' 10"	19' 1" 36' 1"	17' 6" 43' 11"	15' 6" 65' 0"	13' 5" 180' 5"	11' 2" INF	9' 3" INF	7' 3" INF	5' 8" INF	2' 10" x 2' 1"

VERTICAL ANGLE VS. EFFECTIVE FOCAL LENGTH
(Focal Length In Millimeters)

TRANSMITTED OR PROJECTED IMAGE	0.189"	0.260"	0.375"	0.500"	0.158"	0.286"	0.251"	0.446"	0.594"	0.700"	0.991"	0.870"
ANGLE (DEGREES)	TV 1/2" CCD	TV 2/3" CCD	TV 1" CCD	TV 1 2/3" CCD	SUPER -8	16mm	SUPER -16 1.85:1 AR	35mm 1.85:1 AR	35mm TV TRANS	35mm ANA	35mm VISTA	65mm
0.5	550	757	1091	1445	460	832	731	1298	1729	2037	2884	2532
0.7	393	541	780	1039	328	595	522	927	1235	1455	2060	1809
1	275	378	546	728	230	416	365	649	864	1019	1442	1266
1.5	183	252	364	485	153	277	244	433	576	679	961	844
2	138	189	273	364	115	280	183	325	432	509	721	633
2.5	110	151	218	291	92	166	146	260	346	407	577	506
3	92	126	182	242	77	139	122	216	288	339	481	422
3.5	79	108	156	208	66	119	104	185	247	291	412	362
4	69	95	136	182	57	104	91	162	216	256	360	316
4.5	61	84	121	162	51	92	81	144	192	226	320	281
5	55	76	109	145	46	83	73	130	173	204	288	253
6	46	63	91	121	38	69	61	108	144	170	240	211
7	39	54	78	104	33	59	52	93	123	145	206	181
8	34	47	68	91	29	52	46	81	108	127	180	158
9	30	42	61	81	25	46	41	72	96	113	160	140
10	27	38	54	73	23	42	36	65	86	102	144	126
15	18	25	36	48	15	28	24	43	57	68	96	84
20	14	19	27	36	11	21	18	32	43	50	71	63
25	11	15	21	29	9	16	14	26	34	40	57	50
30	9	12	18	24	7	14	12	21	28	33	47	41
35	8	10	15	20	6	12	10	18	24	28	40	35
40	7	9	13	17	6	10	9	16	21	24	35	30
45	6	8	11	15	5	9	8	14	18	21	30	27
50	5	7	10	14	4	8	7	12	16	19	27	24
55	5	6	9	12	4	7	6	11	15	17	24	21
60	4	6	8	11	3	6	6	10	13	15	22	19
65	4	5	7	10	3	6	5	9	12	14	20	17
70	3	5	7	9	3	5	5	8	11	13	18	16
75	3	4	6	8	3	5	4	7	10	12	16	14
80	3	4	6	8	2	4	4	7	9	11	15	13
85	3	4	5	7	2	4	3	6	8	10	14	12
90	2	3	5	6	2	4	3	6	8	9	13	11
95	2	3	4	6	2	3	3	5	7	8	12	10
100	2	3	4	5	2	3	3	5	6	7	11	9

HORIZONTAL ANGLE VS. EFFECTIVE FOCAL LENGTH
(Focal Length In Millimeters)

TRANSMITTED OR PROJECTED IMAGE	0.252"	0.346"	0.5"	0.667"	0.209"	0.380"	0.463"	0.825"	1.676"	1.485"	1.912"
ANGLE (DEGREES)	TV 1/2" CCD	TV ⅔" CCD	TV 1" CCD	TV 1 ⅔" CCD	SUPER -8	16mm	SUPER -16 1.85:1 AR	35mm 1.85:1 AR	35mm ANA	35mm VISTA	65mm
0.5	733	1007	1455	1941	608	1106	1348	2401	4878	4322	5565
0.7	524	719	1039	1387	435	790	963	1715	3484	3087	3975
1	367	504	728	971	304	553	674	1201	2439	2161	2782
1.5	244	336	485	647	203	369	449	800	1626	1441	1855
2	183	252	364	485	152	276	337	600	1219	1081	1391
2.5	147	201	291	388	122	221	269	480	975	864	1113
3	122	168	242	323	101	184	225	400	813	720	927
3.5	105	144	208	277	87	158	192	343	697	617	795
4	92	126	182	243	76	138	168	300	610	540	695
4.5	81	112	162	216	68	123	150	267	542	480	618
5	73	101	145	194	61	111	135	240	488	432	556
6	61	84	121	162	51	92	112	200	406	360	463
7	52	72	104	138	43	79	96	171	348	308	397
8	46	63	91	121	38	69	84	150	304	270	347
9	41	56	81	108	34	61	75	133	270	240	309
10	37	50	73	97	30	55	67	120	243	216	278
15	24	33	45	64	20	37	45	80	162	143	184
20	18	25	36	48	15	27	33	59	121	107	138
25	14	20	29	38	12	22	27	47	96	85	110
30	12	16	24	32	10	18	22	39	79	70	91
35	10	14	20	27	8	15	19	33	68	60	77
40	9	12	17	23	7	13	16	29	58	52	67
45	8	11	15	20	6	12	14	25	51	46	59
50	7	9	14	18	6	10	13	22	46	40	52
55	6	8	12	16	5	9	11	20	41	36	47
60	6	8	11	15	5	8	10	18	37	33	42
65	5	7	10	13	4	8	9	16	33	30	38
70	5	6	9	12	4	7	8	15	30	27	35
75	4	6	8	11	3	6	8	14	28	25	32
80	4	5	8	10	3	6	7	12	25	22	29
85	3	5	7	9	3	5	6	11	23	21	26
90	3	4	6	8	3	5	6	10	21	19	24
95	3	4	6	8	2	4	5	10	20	17	22
100	3	4	5	7	2	4	5	9	18	16	20

35mm DEPTH OF FIELD and EXPOSURE FACTOR vs. MAGNIFICATION or FIELD OF VIEW
Extreme Close-Up — CIRCLE OF CONFUSION=0.001 inches

Magnification Ratio		Field of View 1.85:1 AR	DEPTH OF FIELD (Total: front + back, in inches)									Exposure Increase Factor	T-Stop Increase
Dec.	Frac		f/1.4	f/2	f/2.8	f/4	f/5.6	f/8	f/11	f/16	f/22		
0.100	1/10	4.46" x 8.25"	0.31"	0.44"	0.62"	0.88"	0.1.23"	1.76"	2.42"	3.52"	4.84"	1.21	.27
0.111	1/9	4.01" x 7.43"	0.25"	0.36"	0.51"	0.72"	1.01"	1.44"	1.98"	2.89"	3.97"	1.23	.30
0.125	1/8	3.57" x 6.6"	0.20"	0.29"	0.40"	0.58"	0.81"	1.15"	1.58"	2.30"	3.17"	1.27	1/3
0.143	1/7	3.12" x 5.78"	0.16"	0.22"	0.31"	0.45"	0.63"	0.89"	1.23"	1.79"	2.46"	1.31	.39
0.167	1/6	2.68" x 4.95"	0.12"	0.17"	0.23"	0.34"	0.47"	0.67"	0.92"	1.34"	1.84"	1.36	.45
0.200	1/5	2.23" x 4.12"	0.08"	0.12"	0.17"	0.24"	0.34"	0.48"	0.66"	0.96"	1.32"	1.44	.53
0.250	1/4	1.78" x 3.3"	0.06"	0.08"	0.11"	0.16"	0.22"	0.32"	0.44"	0.64"	0.88"	1.56	2/3
0.333	1/3	1.34" x 2.48"	0.03"	0.05"	0.07"	0.09"	0.14"	0.19"	0.26"	0.38"	0.53"	1.78	.83
0.500	1/2	.89" x 1.65"	0.017"	0.02"	0.03"	0.05"	0.07"	0.10"	0.13"	0.19"	0.26"	2.25	1 1/3
0.667	2/3	067" x 1.24"	0.010"	0.015"	0.02"	0.03"	0.04"	0.06"	0.08"	0.12"	0.17"	2.78	1.47
0.750	3/4	.59" x 1.10"	0.009"	0.012"	0.017"	0.03"	0.04"	0.05"	0.07"	0.10"	0.14"	3.06	1 2/3
0.875	7/8	.50" x .94"	0.007"	0.010"	0.014"	0.02"	0.03"	0.04"	0.05"	0.08"	0.11"	3.52	1.81
1.0	1/1	.45" x .83"	0.006"	0.008"	0.011"	0.016"	0.03"	0.03"	0.04"	0.06"	0.09"	4.0	2.0

16mm Extreme Close Up — DEPTH OF FIELD and EXPOSURE FACTOR vs. MAGNIFICATION or FIELD OF VIEW
CIRCLE OF CONFUSION=0.006 inches

| Magnification Ration | | FOV (projected image) | | DEPTH OF FIELD (Total: front + back, in inches) | | | | | | | | | Exposure Increase Factor | T-Stop Increase |
Dec.	Frac.	16mm .286" x .380"	SUPER 16 .251" x .463"	f/1.4	f/2	f/2.8	f/4	f/5.6	f/8	f/11	f/16	f/22		
0.100	1/10	2.86" x 3.80"	2.51" x 4.63"	0.19"	0.26"	0.37"	0.53"	0.74"	1.06"	1.45"	2.11"	2.90"	1.21	.27
0.111	1/9	2.58" x 3.42"	2.26" x 4.17"	0.15"	0.22"	0.30"	0.43"	0.61"	0.87"	1.19"	1.73"	2.38"	1.23	.30
0.125	1/8	2.9" x3.04"	2.01" x 3.70"	0.12"	0.17"	0.24"	0.35"	0.48"	0.69"	0.95"	1.38"	1.90"	1.27	1/3
0.143	1/7	2.0" x 2.66"	1.76" x 3.24"	0.09"	0.13"	0.19"	0.27"	0.38"	0.54"	0.74"	1.07"	1.48"	1.31	.39
0.167	1/6	1.71" x 2.28"	1.50" x 2.78"	0.07"	0.10"	0.14"	0.20"	0.28"	0.40"	0.55"	0.80"	1.11"	1.36	.45
0.200	1/5	1.43" x 1.90"	1.26" x 2.32"	0.05"	0.07"	0.10"	0.14"	0.20"	0.29"	0.40"	0.58"	0.79"	1.44	.53
0.250	1/4	1.14" x 1.52"	1.00" x 1.85"	0.03"	0.05"	0.07"	0.10"	0.13"	0.19"	0.26"	0.38"	0.53"	1.53	2/3
0.333	1/3	.859" x 1.14"	.754" x 1.39"	0.02"	0.03"	0.04"	0.06"	0.08"	0.12"	0.16"	0.23"	0.32"	1.78	.83
0.500	1/2	.572" x .760"	.502" x .926"	0.010"	0.014"	0.02"	0.03"	0.04"	0.06"	0.08"	0.12"	0.16"	2.25	1 1/3
0.667	2/3	.429" x .570"	.376" x .694"	0.006"	0.009"	0.013"	0.018"	0.03"	0.04"	0.05"	0.07"	0.10"	2.78	1.47
0.750	3/4	.381" x .507"	.335" x .617"	0.005"	0.007"	0.010"	0.015"	0.02"	0.03"	0.04"	0.06"	0.08"	3.06	1 2/3
0.875	7/8	.327" x .434"	.286" x .529"	0.004"	0.006"	0.008"	0.012"	0.016"	0.02"	0.03"	0.05"	0.07"	3.52	1.81
1.0	1/1	.286" x.380"	.251" x .463"	0.003"	0.005"	0.007"	0.010"	0.013"	0.019"	0.03"	0.04"	0.05"	4.0	2.0

APERTURE COMPENSATOR FOR EXTREME CLOSE-UPS
2 INCH LENS (16mm OR 35mm CAMERAS)

EXAMPLE: A 2 inch lens photographing an object at a distance of 4 inches would require an f/8 light level to film it with the lens set at f/4.

| DISTANCES IN INCHES | | ACTUAL LENS APERTURE SETTINGS | | | | | | | |
LENS DIAPHRAGM TO FILM	LENS DIAPHRAGM TO OBJECT	f/2	f/2.8	f/4	f/5.6	f/8	f/11	f/16	f/22
		EFFECTIVE f/STOP (LIGHT REQUIRED FOR ABOVE f/STOPS)							
2 ¼	18	f/2.2	f/3.2	f/4.5	f/6.3	f/9	f/12.7	f/18	f/25
2 ½	10	f/2.5	f/3.5	f/5	f/7	f/10	f/14	f/20	f/28
2 ¾	7	f/2.8	f/4	f/5.6	f/8	f/11	f/16	f/22	f/32
3	6	f/3.2	f/4.5	f/6.3	f/9	f/12.7	f/18	f/25	f/36
4	4	f/4	f/5.6	f/8	f/11	f/16	f/22	f/32	f/45
5	3 ½	f/4.5	f/6.3	f/9	f/12.7	f/18	f/25	f/36	f/50
6	3	f/6.3	f/9	f/12.7	f/18	f/25	f/36	f/50	f/72

PLUS DIOPTER LENSES FOCAL LENGTH CONVERSION TABLE
For 50mm, 75mm, 100mm and 150mm Lenses, 16mm or 35mm

Example: A 75mm lens with +3 diopter lens is converted to a focal length of 61.21mm. It will be in focus at 13.11 inches when set at infinity.

Power of Supplementary Lens in Diopters	Focal Length in Meters	Focal Length in mm	Lens in Focus at This Distance When Set at Infinity — Focal Length in inches	ACTUAL FOCAL LENGTH in mm — Focal Length of Lens in Combination with Diopter Lens			
				50	75	100	150
+1	1	1000	39.37	47.62	69.77	90.91	130.43
+2	1/2	500	19.68	45.45	65.22	83.33	115.38
+3 (2+1)	1/3	333	13.11	43.47	61.21	76.91	103.42
+4 (3+1)	1/4	250	9.84	41.67	57.69	71.43	93.75
+5 (3+2)	1/5	200	7.87	40.00	54.55	66.66	85.71
+6 (3+3)	1/6	166.6	6.53	38.48	51.76	62.55	79.02
+7	1/7	142.8	5.62	37.05	49.20	58.85	73.21
+8	1/8	125	4.92	35.71	46.88	55.55	68.18
+9	1/9	111.1	4.37	34.47	44.76	52.61	63.79
+10	1/10	100	3.93	33.33	42.85	50.00	60.00

EXPOSURE COMPENSATION FOR EXTREME CLOSE-UP CINEMATOGRAPHY (16mm or 35mm)

This table Shows the Light Level Required for Filming Close-Ups of Objects from 1/10th to 5X Actual Size
EXAMPLE: Shooting an Object at 2X Magnification an Actual Lens Setting of f/4 Requires an f/12 Light Level

Reduction or Magnification	Image to Object Ratio	Exposure Factor	ACTUAL LENS APERTURE SETTING													
			f/2	f/2.3	f/2.8	f/3.2	f/4	f/4.5	f/5.6	f/6.3	f/8	f/9	f/11	f/12.7	f/16	f/18
			Light levels shown below must be employed for above lens aperture settings when using various image to object ratios shown at left.													
1/10	1:10	1.2	2.2	2.5	3.1	3.5	4.4	5	6.1	7	8.8	10	12.1	13.8	17.6	19.8
1/8	1:8	1.3	2.3	2.6	3.2	3.6	4.5	5.1	6.3	7.1	9	10.2	12.4	14	18	20
1/6	1:6	1.4	2.4	2.7	3.3	3.7	4.7	5.3	6.6	7.4	9.4	10.6	12.8	14.6	18.7	21
1/5	1:5	1.5	2.4	2.8	3.4	3.8	4.8	5.5	6.8	7.6	9.7	11	13.2	15	19.2	21.5
1/4	1:4	1.6	2.5	2.9	3.5	4	5	5.6	7	7.9	10	11.3	13.8	15.6	20	22
1/3	1:3	1.8	2.7	3.1	3.8	4.3	5.4	6	7.6	8.4	11	12.1	14.6	16.7	21.6	24
1/2	1:2	2.3	3	3.5	4.2	4.8	6	6.8	8.4	9.5	12	13.7	16.5	18.8	24	27
1	1:1	4	4	4.5	5.6	6.3	8	9	11	12.7	16	18	22	25	32	36
1 1/3X	1.33:1	5.4	4.7	5.4	6.6	7.5	9.4	10.5	13	14.7	19	21	26	29	38	42
1 1/2X	1.5:1	6.3	5	5.8	7	8	10	11.3	14	15.8	20	23	28	31	40	45
1 3/4X	1.75:1	8	5.6	6.3	8	9	11	12.7	16	18	22	25	32	36	45	48
2X	2:1	9	6	6.9	8.4	9.6	12	13.5	18	19	24	27	33	38	48	54
3X	3:1	16	8	9.1	11	12.5	16	18	22	25	32	36	44	50	64	72
4X	4:1	25	10	11	14	16	20	22	28	32	40	46	55	63	80	90
	5:1	36	12	13.8	16	19	24	27	34	38	48	55	66	75	96	—

EXTREME CLOSE-UP FOCUSING CHART FOR 2, 3, 4, & 6 INCH LENSES (16mm or 35mm Cameras)
(EXTENSION TUBES OR BELLOWS REQUIRED)

Distances from lens diaphragm to object and lens diaphragm to film in inches
Magnification ratio (Number of times object is enlarged on film) • Exposure factor (and number of f/stops increase required)
(Note: These values are approximate since lens focal length will vary slightly.
Many lenses will deliver a better quality image if reversed in their mounts at high magnification.)

Number of f/Stops Increase	Exposure Factor	Magnification Ratio	2 INCH LENS		3 INCH LENS		4 INCH LENS		6 INCH LENS	
			Diaphragm to Object	Diaphragm to Film	Diaphragm to Object	Diaphragm to Film	Diaphragm to Object	Diaphragm to Film	Diaphragm to Object	Diaphragm to Film
2	4	1:1	4	4	6	6	8	8	12	12
3$\frac{1}{6}$	9	2:1	3	6	4$\frac{1}{2}$	9	6	12	9	18
4	16	3:1	2$\frac{5}{8}$	8	4	12	5$\frac{3}{8}$	16	8	24
4$\frac{2}{3}$	25	4:1	2$\frac{1}{2}$	10	3$\frac{3}{4}$	15	5	20	7$\frac{1}{2}$	30
5$\frac{1}{6}$	36	5:1	2$\frac{7}{16}$	12	3$\frac{5}{8}$	18	4$\frac{3}{4}$	24	7$\frac{3}{8}$	36
5$\frac{2}{3}$	49	6:1	2$\frac{3}{8}$	14	3$\frac{1}{2}$	21	4$\frac{5}{8}$	28	7	42
6	64	7:1	2$\frac{5}{16}$	16	3$\frac{7}{16}$	24	4$\frac{9}{16}$	32	6$\frac{7}{8}$	48
6$\frac{1}{3}$	81	8:1	2$\frac{1}{4}$	18	3$\frac{3}{8}$	27	4$\frac{1}{2}$	36	6$\frac{3}{4}$	54
6$\frac{2}{3}$	100	9:1	2$\frac{3}{16}$	20	3$\frac{5}{16}$	30	4$\frac{7}{16}$	40	6$\frac{5}{8}$	60
7	121	10:1	2$\frac{1}{8}$	22	3$\frac{1}{4}$	33	4$\frac{3}{8}$	44	6$\frac{1}{2}$	66

LENS FOCAL LENGTH CONVERSION TABLE
(16mm or 35mm CAMERAS)

The table on the following page supplies the multiplying factor required for obtaining same size images with lenses of different focal length at different distances. Lenses being compared must be used with the same size film. Although perspective will vary with camera distance, the table will prove handy for matching image sizes with cameras having different focal length lenses.

It is also useful for obtaining same size images when the camera must be set at a different distance because of space limitations and physical obstructions.

EXAMPLE: How far must a 28mm lens be positioned to obtain the same size image as a 32mm lens 15 feet from the subject? Pick out 32mm in the left column, cross the row horizontally to the 28mm column to find the number .88. Multiply .88 by 15 feet to obtain 13.2 feet.

NEW FOCAL LENGTH (MM)

ORIGINAL FOCAL LENGTH (MM)	9	10	12.5	13	14.5	15	16	18	20	25	28	30	32	35	37.5	40	50	75	85	100	150	200	250
9	1.0	1.1	1.4	1.4	1.6	1.7	1.8	2.0	2.2	2.8	3.1	3.3	3.6	3.9	4.2	4.4	5.6	8.3	9.4	11.1	16.7	22.2	27.8
10	.90	1.0	1.3	1.3	1.5	1.5	1.6	1.8	2.0	2.5	2.8	3.0	3.2	3.5	3.8	4.0	5.0	7.5	8.5	10.0	15.0	20.0	25.0
12.5	.72	.80	1.0	1.0	1.2	1.2	1.3	1.4	1.6	2.0	2.2	2.4	2.6	2.8	3.0	3.2	4.0	6.0	6.8	8.0	12.0	16.0	20.0
13	.69	.77	.96	1.0	1.1	1.2	1.2	1.4	1.5	1.9	2.2	2.3	2.5	2.7	2.9	3.1	3.8	5.8	6.5	7.7	11.5	15.4	19.2
14.5	.62	.69	.86	.90	1.0	1.0	1.1	1.2	1.4	1.7	1.9	2.1	2.2	2.4	2.6	2.8	3.4	5.2	5.9	6.9	10.3	13.8	17.2
15	.60	.67	.83	.87	.97	1.0	1.1	1.2	1.3	1.7	1.9	2.0	2.1	2.3	2.5	2.7	3.3	5.0	5.7	6.7	10.0	13.3	16.7
16	.56	.63	.78	.81	.91	.94	1.0	1.1	1.3	1.6	1.8	1.9	2.0	2.2	2.3	2.5	3.1	4.7	5.3	6.3	9.4	12.5	15.6
18	.50	.56	.69	.72	.81	.83	.89	1.0	1.1	1.4	1.6	1.7	1.8	1.9	2.1	2.2	2.8	4.2	4.7	5.6	8.3	11.1	13.9
20	.45	.50	.63	.65	.73	.75	.80	.90	1.0	1.3	1.4	1.5	1.6	1.8	1.9	2.0	2.5	3.8	4.3	5.0	7.5	10.0	12.5
25	.36	.40	.50	.52	.58	.60	.64	.72	.80	1.0	1.1	1.2	1.3	1.4	1.5	1.6	2.0	3.0	3.4	4.0	6.0	8.0	10.0
28	.32	.36	.45	.46	.52	.54	.57	.64	.71	.89	1.0	1.1	1.1	1.3	1.3	1.4	1.8	2.7	3.0	3.6	5.4	7.1	8.9
30	.30	.33	.42	.43	.48	.50	.53	.60	.67	.83	.93	1.0	1.1	1.2	1.3	1.3	1.7	2.5	2.8	3.3	5.0	6.7	8.3
32	.28	.31	.39	.41	.45	.47	.50	.56	.63	.78	.88	.94	1.0	1.1	1.2	1.3	1.6	2.3	2.7	3.1	4.7	6.3	7.8
35	.26	.29	.36	.37	.41	.43	.46	.51	.57	.71	.80	.86	.91	1.0	1.1	1.1	1.4	2.1	2.4	2.9	4.3	5.7	7.1
37.5	.24	.27	.33	.35	.39	.40	.43	.48	.53	.67	.75	.80	.85	.93	1.0	1.1	1.3	2.0	2.3	2.7	4.0	5.3	6.7
40	.23	.25	.31	.33	.36	.38	.40	.45	.50	.63	.70	.75	.80	.88	.94	1.0	1.3	1.9	2.1	2.5	3.8	5.0	6.3
50	.18	.20	.25	.26	.29	.30	.32	.36	.40	.50	.56	.60	.64	.70	.75	.80	1.0	1.5	1.7	2.0	3.0	4.0	5.0
75	.12	.13	.17	.17	.19	.20	.21	.24	.27	.33	.37	.40	.43	.47	.50	.53	.67	1.0	1.1	1.3	2.0	2.7	3.3
85	.11	.12	.15	.15	.17	.18	.19	.21	.24	.29	.33	.35	.38	.41	.44	.47	.59	.88	1.0	1.2	1.8	2.4	2.9
100	.09	.10	.13	.13	.15	.15	.16	.18	.20	.25	.28	.30	.32	.35	.38	.40	.50	.75	.85	1.0	1.5	2.0	2.5
150	.06	.07	.08	.09	.10	.10	.11	.12	.13	.17	.19	.20	.21	.23	.25	.27	.33	.50	.57	.67	1.0	1.3	1.7
200	.05	.05	.06	.07	.07	.08	.08	.09	.10	.13	.14	.15	.16	.18	.19	.20	.25	.38	.43	.50	.75	1.0	1.3
250	.04	.04	.05	.05	.06	.06	.06	.07	.08	.10	.11	.12	.13	.14	.15	.16	.20	.30	.34	.40	.60	.80	1.0

PLUS DIOPTER LENSES
FOCUS CONVERSION TABLE
16mm or 35mm Camera
(MAY BE USED WITH ANY FOCAL LENGTH LENS)

NOTE: Position diopter lens in front of camera lens so that arrow (if inscribed on rim) points toward subject., or with convex (outward) curve toward subject. When two diopters are used in combination, place highest power nearest camera lens. The acutual field size photographed depends slightly on the separation between diopter and camera lens.

Power of Supplementary Lens in Diopters	Focusing Distance on Lens Mount in FEET	Actual Distance Focused on in INCHES From Diopter Lens
+¼	Inf.	157$\frac{1}{3}$
	25	139
	15	129$\frac{1}{2}$
	10	118$\frac{1}{2}$
	6	102
	4	86$\frac{1}{2}$
+½	Inf.	78$\frac{3}{4}$
	25	69$\frac{1}{2}$
	15	64$\frac{3}{4}$
	10	59$\frac{1}{4}$
	6	51
	4	43$\frac{1}{4}$
+1	Inf.	39$\frac{3}{8}$
	25	34$\frac{3}{4}$
	15	32$\frac{3}{8}$
	10	29$\frac{5}{8}$
	6	25$\frac{1}{2}$
	4	21$\frac{5}{8}$
+2	Inf.	19$\frac{5}{8}$
	25	18$\frac{1}{2}$
	15	17$\frac{3}{4}$
	10	16$\frac{7}{8}$
	6	15$\frac{1}{2}$
	4	14
+3 (2+1)	Inf.	13$\frac{1}{8}$
	25	12$\frac{1}{2}$
	15	12$\frac{1}{4}$
	10	11$\frac{7}{8}$
	6	11$\frac{1}{8}$
	4	10$\frac{3}{8}$
+4	Inf.	9$\frac{7}{8}$
+5	Inf.	7$\frac{7}{8}$
+6	Inf.	6$\frac{1}{2}$
+8	Inf.	5
+10	Inf.	4

			Selected Color Filters for B&W Cinematography Daylight Exteriors		
Kodak Wratten #	**Color**	**From From 3 to 29 — renders blue skies increasingly darker and increasingly penetrates haze. Yellow & Red will not darken a misty sky.**	**Effect/Use**	**Average Exposure**	
				Factor	**T/Stop Increase**
3	Light Yellow		Slight Correction	1.5	2/3
8	Yellow		Corrects color rendition to visual appearance as gray	2	1
12	Deep Yellow		Slight over correction. Useful in aerial cinematography	2.5 (Reversal Film 2)	1 1/3 (1)
15	Deep Yellow		Greater contrast. Useful with the tele lenses and for aerial cinematography	3	1 2/3
21	Orange		Same but stronger than#15. Makes blue water dark	3.5 (Reversal Film 3)	1 5/6 (1 2/3)
23A	Light Red		Moderate over correction. Not for close ups– whitens faces	5	2 1/3
25	Red		Very dark sky. Day-for-Night. (complete red separation). No faces!	8 (Reversal film 10)	3 (3 1/3)
29	Deep Red		Black sky, greenery. Day-for-Night. No faces!	25 (Reversal film 40)	4 2/3 (5 1/3)
11	Yellowish Green		Similar to #8 but better flesh tones and flower colors	2	1
56	Light Green		Darkens Sky, lightens foliage	4	2
58	Green		(Complete green separation) Lightens dark foliage, darkens sky	6	2 2/3
47	Blue		(Complete blue separation) Accentuates haze. Darkens reds, Lightens blues	5	2 1/3
23A + 56			Helps flesh renditions for Day-for-Night. Darkens sky	Day-for-Night 6	2 2/3
POLA	Gray		Darkens sky, removes reflections	2.5 to 4	1 1/3 to 2

Color Filters for Altering B&W Contrast of Colored Subjects

Kodak Wratten #	Color of Subject				Tungsten Exposure	
	Blue	Green	Yellow	Red	Factor	T/Stop Increase
3	Very Slightly Darker	Very Slightly Lighter	Very Slightly Lighter	Very Slightly Lighter	NR	NR
8	Slightly Darker	Very Slightly Lighter	Slightly Lighter	Very Slightly Lighter	1.5	$^2/_3$
12	Fairly Dark	Fairly Light	Light	Fairly Light	1.5	$^2/_3$
15	Dark	Light	Very Light	Light	2	1
21	Dark	Very Slightly Darker	Very Light	Very Light	4	2
23A	Very Dark	Dark	Slightly Lighter	Very Light	3	1 $^2/_3$
25	Black	Very Dark	Fairly Light	Very Light	6	2 $^2/_3$
29	Black	Black	Very Light	White	4	2
11	Fairly Dark	Light	Fairly Light	Medium Dark	3	1 $^2/_3$
56	Fairly Dark	Fairly Light	Slightly Light	Fairly Dark	6	2 $^2/_3$
58	Very Dark	Very Light	Light	Very Dark	8	3
47	White	Dark	Very Dark	Black	8	3
23A+56	Very Dark	Very Dark	White	Light	NR	NR

Note: Relative to a neutral gray subject, any given filter will render its own color lighter and its complimentary color darker.

Correlated Color Temperature of Typical Light Sources

Artificial Light

Source		Mireds
Match flame	1700°K	588
Candle flame	1850°K	541
Tungsten-gas filled lamps		
40–100W	2650–2900°K	317–345
200–500W	2980°K	336
1000W	2990°K	334

Daylight

Source		Mireds
Sunlight		
Sunrise or sunset	2000°K	500
One hour after sunrise	3500°K	286
Early morning, late afternoon	4300°K	233
Average noon, (Wash. D.C.)	5400°K	185
Midsummer	5800°K	172
Overcast sky	6000°K	167
Average summer daylight	6500°K	154
Light summer shade	7100°K	141
Average summer shade	8000°K	125
Partly cloudy sky	8000–10000°K	125–100
Summer skylight	9500–30000°K	105–33

Sunlight should not be confused with daylight. Sunlight is the light of the sun only. Daylight is a combination of sunlight and skylight. These values are approximate since many factors affect the correlated color temperature. For consistency, 5500°K is considered to be nominal photographic daylight. The difference between 5000°K and 6000°K is only 33 mireds, the same photographic or visual difference as that between household tungsten lights and 3200°K photolamps (the approximate equivalent of ¼ Blue or 1/8 Orange lighting filters).

Kodak Conversion Filters for Color Films

Filter Color	Filter Number	Exposure Increase in Stops*	Conversion In Degrees °K	Mired Shift Value
Blue	80A	2	3200 to 5500°K	-131
	80B	1⅔	3400 to 5500°K	-112
	80C	1	3800 to 5500°K	-81
	80D	⅓	4200 to 5500°K	-56
Amber	85C	⅓	5500 to 3800°K	+81
	85	⅔	5500 to 3400°K	+112
	85N3	1⅔	5500 to 3400°K	+112
	85N6	2⅔	5500 to 3400°K	+112
	85N9	3⅔	5500 to 3400°K	+112
	85B	⅔	5500 to 3200°K	+131

*These values are approximate. For critical work,
they should be checked by practical test, especially if more than one filter is used.

Kodak Light Balancing Filters

Filter Color	Filter Number	Exposure Increase in Stops*	To Obtain 3200 °K From:	To Obtain 3400 °K From:	Mired Shift Value
Bluish	82C + 82C	1⅓	2490°K	2610°K	-89
	82C + 82B	1⅓	2570°K	2700°K	-77
	82C + 82A	1	2650°K	2780°K	-65
	82C + 82	1	2720°K	2870°K	-55
	82C	⅔	2800°K	2950°K	-45
	82B	⅔	2900°K	3060°K	-32
	82A	⅓	3000°K	3180°K	-21
	82	⅓	3100°K	3290°K	-10
	No Filter Necessary		3200 °K	3400 °K	
Yellowish	81	⅓	3300°K	3510°K	+9
	81A	⅓	3400°K	3630°K	+18
	81B	⅓	3500°K	3740°K	+27
	81C	⅓	3600°K	3850°K	+35
	81D	⅔	3700°K	3970°K	+42
	81EF	⅔	3850°K	4140°K	+52

*These values are approximate. For critical work,
they should be checked by practical test, especially if more than one filter is used.

Kodak Color Compensating Filters for Color Films

Peak Density	Yellow (Absorbs Blue)	Exposure Increase in Stops*	Magenta (Absorbs Green)	Exposure Increase in Stops*	Cyan (Absorbs Red)	Exposure Increase in Stops*
.05	CC-05Y	$\frac{1}{6}$	CC-05M	$\frac{1}{3}$	CC-05C	$\frac{2}{3}$
.10	CC-10Y	$\frac{1}{3}$	CC-10M	$\frac{1}{3}$	CC-10C	$\frac{1}{3}$
.20	CC-20Y	$\frac{1}{3}$	CC-20M	$\frac{1}{3}$	CC-20C	$\frac{1}{3}$
.30	CC-30Y	$\frac{1}{3}$	CC-30M	$\frac{2}{3}$	CC-30C	$\frac{2}{3}$
.40	CC-40Y	$\frac{1}{3}$	CC-40M	$\frac{2}{3}$	CC-40C	$\frac{2}{3}$
.50	CC-50Y	$\frac{2}{3}$	CC-50M	$\frac{2}{3}$	CC-50C	1

Peak Density	Yellow (Absorbs Blue)	Exposure Increase in Stops*	Magenta (Absorbs Green)	Exposure Increase in Stops*	Cyan (Absorbs Red)	Exposure Increase in Stops*
.05	CC-05R	$\frac{1}{3}$	CC-05G	$\frac{1}{3}$	CC-05B	$\frac{1}{3}$
.10	CC-10R	$\frac{1}{3}$	CC-10G	$\frac{1}{3}$	CC-10B	$\frac{1}{3}$
.20	CC-20R	$\frac{1}{3}$	CC-20G	$\frac{1}{3}$	CC-20B	$\frac{2}{3}$
.30	CC-30R	$\frac{2}{3}$	CC-30G	$\frac{2}{3}$	CC-30B	$\frac{2}{3}$
.40	CC-40R	$\frac{2}{3}$	CC-40G	$\frac{2}{3}$	CC-40B	1
.50	CC-50R	1	CC-50G	1	CC-50B	$1\frac{1}{3}$

* These values are approximate. For critical work, they should be checked by practical test, especially if more than one filter is used.

Kodak Ultraviolet and Haze Cutting Filters

Kodak Wratten #	Color	Effect/Use (no exposure increase required)
1A (skylight)	Pale Pink	Absorbs ultraviolet for color film. To reduce blue outdoors in open shade under clear blue sky.
2A	Pale Yellow	Absorbs ultraviolet below 405nm. Reduces haze in black-and-white film.
2B	Pale Yellow	Absorbs ultraviolet below 390nm. More effective than 2A in haze reduction.
2C	Pale Yellow	Absorbs ultraviolet below 385nm. Less effective than 2B in haze reduction.
2E	Pale Yellow	Absorbs ultaviolet below 415nm. Similar to 2B, but absorbs more violet.
HF-3	Light Yellow	Haze cutting filter for aerial photography.
HF-4	Very Light Yellow	Haze cutting filter. Always used in combination with HF-3 filter. For color balancing of different sky conditions and altitudes.
HF-5	Very Light Yellow	Haze cutting filter. Always used in combination with HF-3 filter. For color balancing of different sky conditions and altitudes.

ND Filter Selector Chart

				Stop for correct exposure															
Stops	Factor	% Trans	ND Filter	1.4	2	2.8	4	5.6	8	11	16	22	32	45	64	90	128	180	256
⅓	1.25	80	.10	1.3	1.8	2.5	3.5	5	7	10	14	20	28	40					
⅔	1.5	63	.20	1.1	1.6	2.2	3.2	4.5	6.3	9	12.7	18	25	35					
1	2	50	.30	1	1.4	2	2.8	4	5.6	8	11	16	22	32	45				
1⅓	2.5	40	.40	.9	1.3	1.8	2.5	3.5	5	7	10	14	20	28	40				
1⅔	3	32	.50	.8	1.1	1.6	2.2	3.2	4.5	6.3	9	12.7	18	25	35				
2	4	25	.60	.7	1	1.4	2	2.8	4	5.6	8	11	16	22	32	45			
3	8	12.5	.90		.7	1	1.4	2	2.8	4	5.6	8	11	16	22	32	45		
4	16	6.25	1.2			.7	1	1.4	2	2.8	4	5.6	8	11	16	22	32	45	
5	32	3	1.5				.7	1	1.4	2	2.8	4	5.6	8	11	16	22	32	45
6	64	1.6	1.8					.7	1	1.4	2	2.8	4	5.6	8	11	16	22	32
7	128	0.8	2.1						.7	1	1.4	2	2.8	4	5.6	8	11	16	22
8	256	0.4	2.4							.7	1	1.4	2	2.8	4	5.6	8	11	16

Left groupings: ⅓ Stops Steps (rows ⅓ through 2), One Stop Steps (rows 3 through 8).

The columns to the left of the "ND Filter" show the filter factor both numerically and in the lens stops and the percent transmission of each. Up to 0.6ND, increments are in 1/3 stop steps. From 0.6ND to 2.4ND the increments are in full stops. Densities may be added: (0.6ND plus 0.9ND equals 1.5ND). If correct exposure indicates a very small stop beyond the calibration of the lens AND/OR: If it is desired to open the lens to a wide aperture to throw the background out of focus: Select the desired lens stop in the column under indicated stop, and use the corresponding ND Filter from the left shaded column. (For B&W photography, account for the factor of any color filter also.)

Filter Compensator / Filter Factors

Lens stop no filter	1.25	1.5	2	2.5	3	4	5	6	8	10	12	16	20	25
22	20	18	16	14	12.7	11	10	9	8	7	6.3	5.6	5	4.5
20	18	16	14	12.7	11	10	9	8	7	6.3	5.6	5	4.5	4
18	16	14	12.7	11	10	9	8	7	6.3	5.6	5	4.5	4	3.5
16	14	12.7	11	10	9	8	7	6.3	5.6	5	4.5	4	3.5	3.2
14	12.7	11	10	9	8	7	6.3	5.6	5	4.5	4	3.5	3.2	2.8
12.7	11	10	9	8	7	6.3	5.6	5	4.5	4	3.5	3.2	2.8	2.5
11	10	9	8	7	6.3	5.6	5	4.5	4	3.5	3.2	2.8	2.5	2.2
10	9	8	7	6.3	5.6	5	4.5	4	3.5	3.2	2.8	2.5	2.2	2
9	8	7	6.3	5.6	5	4.5	4	3.5	3.2	2.8	2.5	2.2	2	1.8
8	7	6.3	5.6	5	4.5	4	3.5	3.2	2.8	2.5	2.2	2	1.8	1.6
7	6.3	5.6	5	4.5	4	3.5	3.2	2.8	2.5	2.2	2	1.8	1.6	1.4
6.3	5.6	5	4.5	4	3.5	3.2	2.8	2.5	2.2	2	1.8	1.6	1.4	1.3
5.6	5	4.5	4	3.5	3.2	2.8	2.5	2.2	2	1.8	1.6	1.4	1.3	1.1
5	4.5	4	3.5	3.2	2.8	2.5	2.2	2	1.8	1.6	1.4	1.3	1.1	1
4.5	4	3.5	3.2	2.8	2.5	2.2	2	1.8	1.6	1.4	1.3	1.1	1	.9
4	3.5	3.2	2.8	2.5	2.2	2	1.8	1.6	1.4	1.3	1.1	1	.9	.8
3.5	3.2	2.8	2.5	2.2	2	1.8	1.6	1.4	1.3	1.1	1	.9	.8	.7
3.2	2.8	2.5	2.2	2	1.8	1.6	1.4	1.3	1.1	1	.9	.8	.7	
2.8	2.5	2.2	2	1.8	1.6	1.4	1.3	1.1	1	.9	.8	.7		
2.5	2.2	2	1.8	1.6	1.4	1.3	1.1	1	.9	.8	.7			
2.2	2	1.8	1.6	1.4	1.3	1.1	1	.9	.8	.7				
2	1.8	1.6	1.4	1.3	1.1	1	.9	.8	.7					
1.8	1.6	1.4	1.3	1.1	1	.9	.8	.7						
1.6	1.4	1.3	1.1	1	.9	.8	.7							
1.4	1.3	1.1	1	.9	.8	.7								
1.3	1.1	1	.9	.8	.7									
1.1	1	.9	.8	.7										
1	.9	.8	.7											
.9	.8	.7												

COLOR FILTER SELECTION CHART
FOR UNDERWATER PHOTOGRAPHY
Filter Density/Depth-Distance

Depth (feet)	Subject Distance from Camera (feet)	Total Distance from Surface to Subject to Camera (feet)	C.C. Filter Density		
			CC-Y (yellow)	CC-M (magenta)	CC-R (red)
Surface to 5	0–10	0–15	none to .05	none to .05	none to .05
	10–20	10–25	.10	.10–.20	.10
	20–40	20–45	.10–.20	.10–.30	.10–.20
	40–	40–	.30–.40*	.30–.40*	.30–.40*
5-15	0–10	5-25	.05–.10	.10–.20	.05–.10
	10–20	15-35	.10–.20	.10–.30	.10–.20
	20–40	25-55	.20–.30	.20–.40*	.20–.30
	40–	45–	.30–.40*	.20–.40*	.30–.40*
15-30	0–10	15–40	.10–.20	.20–.30	.10–.20
	10–20	25–50	.20–.30	.20–.40*	.20–.30
	20–40	35–70	.20–.40	.20–.40*	.20–.40*
	40–	55–	.30–.40*	.20–.40*	.30–.40*
30-50	0–10	30–60	.20–.30	.20–.40*	.20–.30
	10–20	40–70	.20–.30	.20–.40*	.20–.30
	20–40	50–90	.30–.40*	.20–.40*	.30–.40*
50	0–10	50–60	.30	.30–.40*	.30
	10-	60-	.30–.40*	.30–.40*	.30–.40*

*Use only when absolutely certain of high enough light level.

Comparison of Filter System Names

Wratten	Mired	European	Mired	Hasselblad	Mired	Fuji	Mired	Nikon
80A	-131	KB 15	-150	CB	-150	LBB-12	-120	
80B	-112	KB 12	-120	CB	-120			B12
80C	-81	KB 12	-90	CB	-90	LBB-8	-80	B8
80D	-56	KB 6	-60	CB	-60	LBB-6	-60	
82	-10					LBB-1	-10	
82A	-21	KB 1.5	-15	CB	-15	LBB-2	-20	B2
82B	-32	KB 3	-30	CB	-30	LBB-3	-30	
82C	-45	KB 6	-60	CB	-60	LBB-4	-40	
81	+9					LBA-1	+10	
81A	+18	KR 1.5	+15	CR	+15	LBA-2	+20	A2
81B	+27					LBA-3	+30	
81C	+35	KR 3	+30	CR	+30			
81D	+42					LBA-4	+40	
81EF	+52	KR6	+60	CR	+60	LBA-6	+60	
85	+112	KR 12	+120	CR	+120			A12
85B	+131	KR15	+150	CR	+150	LBA-12	+120	
85C	+81	KR 9	+90	CR	+90	LBA-8	+80	

MOST COMMON FILTER SIZES FOR MOTION PICTURES

40.5mm	2" x 2"
48mm	3" x 3"
Series 9 (82.55mm)	4" x 4"
4.5" round	4" x 5.650" (Panavision)
138mm	6" x 6" 6.6" x 6.6"

TYPICAL COMMERCIAL/INDUSTRIAL LIGHT SOURCE CHARACTERISTICS

Description	Correlated Color Temperature (°Kelvin)	Color Rendering Index	Efficacy (Lumens/ Watt)
Fluorescent Types			
Daylight	6500°K	79	60
Design White	5200°K	82	50
Cool White	4300°K	67	70
Deluxe Cool White	4100°K	86	50
Natural White	3700°K	81	45
White	3500°K	62	70
Warm White	3050°K	55	70
Deluxe Warm White	2950°K	73	45
Incandescent	2700°K	90	35
Mercury Vapor Types			
Clear Mercury	5900°K	17	50
White Deluxe	4000°K	45	55
Warm Deluxe	3500°K	62	70
Metal Halide Additive Types			
Muti-arc ™; Metal Vapor ™	5900°K	65	80-115
Metalarc C ™	3800°K	70	80-115
High Pressure Sodium			
Lucalox ™ Lumalox ™	2100°K	25	80-140

CHARACTERISTICS OF PHOTOGRAPHIC LIGHT SOURCES

Description	Correlated Color Temperature (at rated voltage)	Mired Value	Efficacy (Lumens/Watt)
Incandescent			
Standard and Tungsten/halogen	3200°K	312	26
CP gas filled	3350°K	299	32
Photoflood	3400°K	294	34
Daylight blue photoflood	4800°K	208	
Carbon arc (225A Brute)			
White Flame, Y-1 filter	5100°K	196	24
White Flame, no filter	5800°K	172	
Yellow flame YF 101 filter	3350°K	299	
*Xenon, high pressure			
DC short arc	6000°K	167	35-50
*Metal halide additive AC Arc			
HMI	5600°K	179	80-102
CID	5600°K	179	80
CSI	4200°K	238	85
*Need filtering for color photography			

Filters for Daylight Correction

Neutral Density and Combinations (for Windows)

Neutral Density	N.D. Value	Stops Loss
Rosco #3415	.15	½
Lee #29B	.15	½
GAM #1514	.15	½
Formatt #298	.15	½
Rosco #3402	.30	1
Lee #209	.30	1
GAM #1515	.30	1
Formatt #209	.30	1
Rosco #3403	.60	2
Lee #210	.60	2
GAM #1516	.60	1.7
Formatt #210	.60	2
Rosco #3404	.90	3
Lee #211	.90	3
GAM #1517	.90	2½
Formatt #211	.90	3
Lee # 299	1.20	4
GAM #1518	1.20	2.7
Formatt #299	1.20	4

Combinations	Mired Shift Value	Effect On: 5500°K (182 Mireds)	6000°K (167 Mireds)
Lee #207 Full CTO + .3ND	+159	2930°K	3070°K
Lee #208 Full CTO + .6ND	+159	2930°K	3070°K
Rosco #3405 Roscosun 85N.3	+131	3200°K	3360°K
Rosco #3406 Roscosun 85N.6	+131	3200°K	3360°K
GAM #1556 Full CTO + .3ND	+96	3540°K	4040°K
GAM #1557 Full CTO + .6ND	+89	3650°K	4150°K
GAM #1558 Full CTO + .9ND	+13	5100°K	5600°K
Formatt #207 Full CTO + .3ND	+159	2930°K	3070°K
Formatt #208 Full CTO + .6ND	+159	2930°K	3070°K

Acrylic Panels

	Mired Shift Value	Effect On: 5500°K	6000°K
Lee #A204 Full CTO*	+159	2930°K	3070°K
Roscolex #85 3761**	+131	3200°K	3360°K
Lee #A205 Half CTO	+109	3440°K	3629°K
Roscolex #3751 1⁄2 CTO	+ 81	3800°K	4030°K
Lee #A207 Full CTO + .3ND	+159	2930°K	3070°K
Lee #A208 Full CTO + .6ND	+159	2930°K	3070°K
Lee #A209 .3 ND	Notes:		
Roscolex #3762 .3 ND	* Lee Acrylic Panels are available		
Lee #A210 .6 ND	5 x 8 feet (152 x 244 cm)		
Roscolex #3763 .3 ND	** Rosco Acrylic Panels are available		
Lee #A211 .9 ND	in either 4 x 8 feet (122 x 244 cm)		
Roscolex #3764 .9 ND	or 5 x 8 feet (152 x 244 cm)		

Lighting Filters for Color Temperature Adjustment

This Table, listing the most commonly used filters for adjusting color temperature, are presented along with their primary characteristics and the effect that they have on light sources at 2900°K and 3200°K, along with the Mired Shift value for each.

Increase Color Temperature (Blue)	Mired Shift Value	Effect on: 3200°K (312 Mired)	2900°K (345 Mired)
Lee #200 Double C.T. Blue	-274	26,000°K	14,000°K
Rosco #3220 Double C.T. Blue	-274	26,000°K	14,000°K
GAM #1520 Extra C.T. Blue	-190	8150°K	7850°K
Formatt #200 Double C.T. Blue	-274	26,000°K	14,000°K
Lee #201 Full C.T. Blue	-137	5700°K	4800°K
Rosco #3202 Full Blue	-131	5500°K	4670°K
GAM #1523 Full C.T. Blue	-141	5500°K	5200°K
Formatt #201 Full C.T. Blure	-137	5700°K	4910°K
Lee #281 Three Quarter C.T. Blue	-112	5000°K	4290°K
Rosco #3203 Three Quarter Blue	-100	4720°K	4080°K
GAM #1526 Three Quarter C.T. Blue	-108	4750°K	4450°K
Formatt #281 Three Quarter C.T. Blue	-112	5000°K	4290°K
Lee #202 Half C.T. Blue	- 78	4270°K	3750°K
Rosco #3204 Half Blue	- 68	4100°K	3610°K
GAM #1529 Half C.T. Blue	-75	4100°K	3800°K
Formatt #202 Half C.T. Blue	-78	4270°K	3750°K
Rosco #3206 Third Blue	- 49	3800°K	3380°K
Lee #203 Quarter C.T. Blue	- 35	3610°K	3230°K
Rosco #3208 Quarter Blue	- 30	3550°K	3180°K
GAM #1532 Quarter C.T. Blue	-38	3600°K	3300°K
GAM #1534 Sixth C.T. Blue	-28	3520°K	3220°K
Lee #218 Eighth C.T. Blue	- 18	3400°K	3060°K
Rosco #3216 Eighth Blue	- 12	3330°K	3000°K
GAM #1535 Eighth Blue	- 20	3400°K	3100°K
Formatt #218 Eighth C.T. Blue	-18	3400°K	3060°K

Lighting Filters for Color Temperature Adjustment

This Table, listing the most commonly used filters for adjusting color temperature, are presented along with their primary characteristics and the effect that they have on light sources at 5500°K and 6000°K, along with the Mired Shift value for each.

Decrease Color Temperature (Amber)	Mired Shift Value	Effect on: 5500°K (182 Mireds)	6000°K (167 Mireds)
Rosco #3407 Roscosun CTO	+167	2865°K	3000°K
Rosco #3441 Full Straw (CTS)	+167	2865°K	3000°K
Rosco #3420 Double CTO	+334	2900°K	3400°K
GAM #1540 Extra CTO	+240	2290°K	2690°K
		+30G	+30G
Lee #204 Full C.T. Orange	+159	2930°K	3070°K
Lee #441 Full Straw	+160	2925°K	3060°K
Formatt #204 Full C.T. Orange	+159	2930°K	3070°K
Formatt #441 Full C.T. Straw	+160	3061°K	2925°K
GAM #1543 Full CTO	+146	2990°K	3390°K
Rosco #3401 Roscosun 85	+131	3200°K	3360°K
Rosco #3411 Three-Quarters CTO	+131	3200°K	3360°K
Lee #285 Three-Quarters C.T. Orange	+124	3270°K	3440°K
GAM #1546 Three-Quarters CTO	+125	3200°K	3600°K
Formatt #285 Three-Quarters C.T. Orange	+124	3436°K	3268°K
Lee #205 Half C.T. Orange	+109	3440°K	3620°K
GAM #1549 Half CTO	+ 79	3800°K	4200°K
Formatt #205 Half C.T. Orange	+109	3440°K	3629°K
Rosco #3408 Roscosun 1/2 CTO	+ 81	3800°K	4030°K
Rosco #3442 Half Straw (1/2 CTS)	+ 81	3800°K	4030°K
Lee #442 Half Straw	+ 81	3800°K	4030°K
Formatt #442 Half C.T. Straw	+ 81	3800°K	4030°K
Lee #206 Quarter C.T. Orange	+ 64	4060°K	4330°K
GAM #1552 Quarter CTO	+ 40	4480°K	4880°K
Formatt #206 Quarter C.T. Orange	+ 64	4060°K	4330°K
Rosco #3409 Roscosun 1/4 CTO	+ 42	4460°K	4800°K
Rosco #3443 Quarter Straw (1/4 CTS)	+ 42	4460°K	4800°K
Lee #443 Quarter C.T. Straw	+ 42	4460°K	4780°K
Formatt #443 Quarter C.T. Straw	+ 42	4460°K	4800°K
Lee #223 Eighth C.T. Orange	+ 26	4810°K	5180°K
Formatt #223 Eighth C.T. Orange	+ 26	4680°K	5180°K
GAM #1555 Eighth CTO	+ 20	4950°K	5350°K
Rosco #3410 Roscosun 1/8 CTO	+ 20	4950°K	5350°K
Rosco #3444 Eighth Straw (1/8 CTS)	+ 20	4950°K	5350°K
Lee #444 Eighth C.T. Straw	+ 20	4950°K	5350°K
Formatt #444 Eighth C.T. Straw	+20	4950°K	5350°K
Rosco #3414 UV Filter	+ 8	5260°K	5710°K
Lee UV	+ 2	5430°K	5920°K
Decrease Color Temperature (Red-Amber)	Mired Shift Value	Effect on: 5500°K (182 Mireds)	6000°K (167 Mireds)
Lee #236 HMI (To Tungsten)	+134	3160°K	3320°K
Rosco #3106 Tough MTY	+131	3200°K	3360°K
Lee #237 CID (To Tungsten)	+131	3200°K	3360°K
Rosco 3102 Tough MT2	+110	3425°K	3790°K
Lee #238 CSI (To Tungsten)	+ 49	4330°K	4630°K

Filters for Arc Discharge and Fluorescent Lamps

Green/Magenta Adjusting Filters for Arc Discharge and Fluorescent
(May be Used with Blue/Amber Color Temperature Filters)

Green Filters (Decrease Red/Blue (Magenta))	CC Equivalent
Rosco #3304 Tough Plusgreen	CC30G
Lee #244 Plus Green	CC30G
GAM #1585 Plus Green	CC15G
Formatt #244 Plus Green	CC30G
Rosco #3315 Tough ½ Plusgreen	CC15G
Lee #245 Half Plus Green	CC15G
GAM #1587 Half Plus Green	CC10G
Formatt #245 Half Plus Green	CC15G
Rosco # 3316 Tough ¼ Plusgreen	CC075G
Lee #246 Quarter Plus Green	CC075G
GAM #1588 Quarter Plus Green	CC05G
Formatt #246 Quarter Plus Green	CC075G
Lee #278 Eighth Plus Green	CC035G
Rosco #3317 ⅛ Plusgreen	CC035G
GAM #1589 Eighth Plus Green	CC05G
Formatt #278 Eighth Plus Green	CC035G
Lee #241 Fluorescent 5700° K	CC30G + 80A
Formatt #241 Fluorescent 5700° K	
Lee #242 Fluorescent 4300° K	CC30G + 80C
Formatt #242 Fluorescent 4300° K	
Lee #243 Fluorescent 3600° K	CC30G + 82B
Formatt #243 Fluorescent 3600° K	
Formatt #219 Fluorescent Green	

Magenta Filters (Decrease Green)	
GAM #1578 Extra Minus Green	CC90M
Rosco #3308 Tough Minusgreen	CC30M
Lee # 247 Minus Green	CC30M
GAM #1580 Minus Green	CC55M
Formatt #247 Minus Green	CC30M
GAM #1581 Three Quarter Minus Green	CC45M
Rosco #3313 Tough ½ Minusgreen	CC15M
Lee #248 Half Minus Green	CC15M
GAM #1582 Half Minus Green	CC25M
Formatt #248 Half Minus Green	CC15M
Rosco #3314 Tough ¼ Minusgreen	CC075M
Lee #249 Quarter Minus Green	CC075M
GAM #1583 Quarter Minus Green	CC15M
Formatt #249 Quarter Minus Green	CC075M
Rosco #3318 Tough ⅛ Minusgreen	CC035M
Lee #279 Eighth Minus Green	CC035M
GAM #1584 Eighth Minus Green	CC10M
Formatt #279 Eighth Minus Green	CC035M
Rosco #3310 Fluorofilter	CC30M + 85B
GAM #1590 Fluorofilter CW	CC30M +85

Color Correction for Carbon Arcs

LEE

Arc Correction (Carbon-Regular)

212	LC.T. Yellow (Y1)	Reduces color temperature of low carbon arcs to 3200°K
213	White Flame Green	Corrects white flame carbon arcs by absorbing ultra violet.

Arc Correction (Carbon-Color Balanced)

230	Super Correction LC. T.Yellow	Converts yellow carbon arc (of low color temperature) to tungsten.
232	Super Correction W.F. Green to Tungsten	Converts white flame arc to 3200°K, for use with tungsten film.

ROSCO

3107	Tough Y1	Pale straw filter for use on white flame arcs to absorb UV and provide daylight balance.
3106	Tough MTY	A single filter for correcting white flame arcs to 3200°K tungsten.
3102	Tough MT2	When used with Y1 converts white flame arcs to 3200°K tungsten.
3134	Tough MT54	A pale straw, gentle warming filter for arcs and HMI.
3114	Tough UV Filter	A slightly warm filter that absorbs 90% of UV output below 390 nm. Eliminates fluorescing of dyes and pigments caused by arcs.

GAM Color Cinefilters

1560	Y-1 LGT Yellow	
1565	MTY	SAME EFFECTS AS ABOVE
1570	MT2	
1575	1⁄3 MT2	

FORMATT

Arc Correction (Carbon-Regular)

212	LC.T. Yellow (Y1)	Reduces color temperature of low carbon arcs to 3200°K
213	White Flame Green	Corrects white flame carbon arcs by absorbing ultra violet.

Arc Correction (Carbon-Color Balanced)

230	Super Correction LC. T. Yellow	Converts yellow carbon arc (of low color temperature) to tungsten.
232	Super Correction W.F. Green to Tungsten	Converts white flame arc to 3200°K, for use with tungsten film.

Arc Correction (Compact Source)

236	HMI (To Tungsten)	Converts HMI to 3200°K, use with tungsten film
237	CID (To Tungsten)	Converts CID to 3200°K, use with tungsten film
238	CSI (To Tungsten)	Converts CSI to 3200°K, use with tungsten film

Ultra Violet Absorbtion

226	UV	Transmission of less than 50% at 410nms

CalColor

Calibrated Color by Rosco is a series of color effects lighting filters designed specifically to the spectral sensitivity of color film. The series includes the primary colors Blue, Green and Red, along with the secondary colors Yellow, Magenta and Cyan and the intermediary colors Pink and Lavender. Each color is designed in four densities: 15, 30, 60 and 90, corresponding to the familiar ½, 1, 2 and 3 stop calibrations.

4215	15 Blue (½ stop)	4615	15 Red (½ stop)
4230	30 Blue (1 stop)	4630	30 Red (1 stop)
4260	60 Blue (2 stop)	4660	60 Red (2 stop)
4290	90 Blue (3 stop)	4690	90 Red (3 stop)
4307	07 Cyan (¼ stop)	4715	15 Magenta (½ stop)
4315	15 Cyan (½ stop)	4730	30 Magenta (1 stop)
4330	30 Cyan (1 stop)	4760	60 Magenta (2 stop)
4360	60 Cyan (2 stop)	4790	90 Magenta (3 stop)
4390	90 Cyan (3 stop)		
4415	15 Green (½ stop)	4815	15 Pink (½ stop)
4430	30 Green (1 stop)	4830	30 Pink (1 stop)
4460	60 Green (2 stop)	4860	60 Pink (2 stop)
4490	90 Green (3 stop)	4890	90 Pink (3 stop)
4515	15 Yellow (½ stop)	4915	15 Lavender (½ stop)
4530	30 Yellow (1 stop)	4930	30 Lavender (1 stop)
4560	60 Yellow (2 stop)	4960	60 Lavender (2 stop)
4590	90 Yellow (3 stop)	4990	90 Lavender (3 stop)

Tiffen Decamired Filters

	Filter	Mired Shift	Exposure Increase
Blue	B1.5	-15	⅓
	B3	-30	⅔
	B6	-60	1
	B12	-120	1½
Red	R1.5	+15	⅓
	R3	+30	½
	R6	+60	⅔
	R12	+120	1⅓

* These values are approximate. For critical work, they should be checked by practical test, especially if more than one filter is used.

Examples of Mired Shift Value (Filter) Effects

Initial Source		Filter Mired Shift	Filtered Source		° Kelvin Changes
°K	Mireds		Mireds	°K	
10,000	100	+112	212	4720	5280
6,000	167	+112	279	3600	2400
5,000	200	+112	312	3200	1800
2,600	385	-21	364	2750	150
2,900	345	-21	324	3090	190
3,200	312	-21	291	3440	240

Mired Values of Color Temperatures from 2000°K – 10,000°K

°K	+0	100	200	300	400	500	600	700	800	900
2000	500	476	455	435	417	400	385	370	357	345
3000	333	323	312	303	294	286	278	270	263	256
4000	250	244	238	233	227	222	217	213	208	204
5000	200	196	192	189	185	182	179	175	172	169
6000	167	164	161	159	156	154	152	149	147	145
7000	143	140	139	137	135	133	132	130	128	126
8000	125	123	122	120	119	118	116	115	114	112
9000	111	110	109	108	106	105	104	103	102	101
10,000	100									

HMI LAMPS — Summary of Electrical and Physical Characteristics								
Lamp Power Rating (Watts)	200	575	1200	2500	4000	6000	12000	18000
Minimum Open Circuit A.C. Voltage to the lamp for Ignition (Volts)	198	198	198	209	360	220	380	380
Lamp Operating Voltage (Volts)	80	95	100	115	200	135	160	225
Lamp Operating Current (Amperes)	3.1	7.0	13.8	25.6	24.0	55	65.0	88
Luminous Flux (Light output in Lumens)	16,000	49,000	110,000	240,000	410,000	630,000	1,008,000	1,700,000
Luminous Efficacy (Lumens/Watt)	80	85	92	96	102	105	84	94.4
Average Life (Hours)	300	750	750	500	500	350	300	300
Burning Position	Horizontal 15°	Any	Any	Horizontal 15°	Horizontal 15°	Horizontal 15°	Horizontal 15°	Horizontal 15°

Characteristics of Typical Photographic Light Sources

Type	Range (Watts)	Temperature (°Kelvin)	Efficacy (lm/Watt)	Luminance (cd/cm2)	Current	Life (Hours)
HMI	125–18,000	6000 °K	70–96	3000–30,000	AC	150–1,000
Tungsten-Halogen	5–24,000	3000–3400 °K	Max. 37	200–5,000	AC/DC	15–2,000
Xenon-Short Arc	10,000 max.	6000 °K	15–20	20,000–500,000	DC	500–2000
Lo-Pressure Xenon	1100–15,000	5400 °K	18–50	Not Available	DC	200
Lo-Pressure Xenon	10K–50K	5400 °K	18–50	Not Available	AC	100–200
Fluorescent	35–50	various	45–80	0.3–2	AC	10,000

National Carbons for Studio Lighting						
Fixture Type	Car-bon No.	Positive Description	Car-bon No.	Negative Description	Arc D.C. Electri-cal Am-peres	Rat-ing Volts
Duarc 40	1	8mm x 12 in. CC MP Studio	8	7mm x 9 in. CC MP Studio	40	36
M.R. 90	2	13.6mm x 22 in. H.I. Studio	9	$7/16$ in. x $8\frac{1}{2}$ in. CC MP Studio	120	58
M.R. 170	3	16mm x 20 in. H.I. Studio	10	$1/2$ in. x $8\frac{1}{4}$ in. CC MP Studio	150	68
M.R. Brute 4691 4661	4	16mm x 22 in. Super H.I. Studio Positive-White Flame	11	$17/32$ in. x 9 in. Special CC	225	73
	5	16mm x 22 in. Super H.I. Studio Positive-Yellow Flame				
M.R. Titan	6	16mm x 25 in. Ultrex HIWF Studio	12	$11/16$ in. x 9 in. CC MP Studio	350	79
	7	16mm x 25 in. HIYF Special Studio			300	73

Color Balancing for Existing Non-Photographic Lighting

Common Fluorescent and AC Discharge Commercial Lighting	Using existing fluorescent lighting unfiltered — Camera filters (Kodak or equivalent)				Photo lamp filters to match Fluorescent Lamps (Rosco, Lee, Gam or Format)				Filtering fluorescent lights to match photo lamps			
	3200°K film (Tungsten)	S.I.*	5500°K film (Daylight)	S.I.*	3200°K	L.L.*	5500°K	L.L.*	Camera filter: none (Tungsten negative or reversal) To match 3200°K	L.L.*	Camera filter: Tungsten Negative #85 Daylight film: none To match 5500°K	L.L.*
Cool white	CC10M +#85	1⅓	CC20M	⅓	Full blue CTB Plusgreen +Quarter Blue +1/4 Plusgreen	3	Plusgreen +Third blue	1	Fluorofilter +½ Minusgreen	1	Minusgreen	⅔
Cool white deluxe	CC10R +#85C	⅔	#82C	⅔	Half blue +¼ Plusgreen +Eighth Blue	1⅓	MT54 +Eighth Blue +UV Filter	1	Sun 1/2 CTO +¼ Minusgreen +Quarter Blue	1⅓	Quarter Blue +1/4 Minusgreen +Eighth Blue	1
Warm white	CC30M +#81EF	1⅓	CC50B +CC15M	1⅔	Half Blue +Plusgreen +Quarter blue	2	Plusgreen +½ Plusgreen +Sun 1/8 CTO	1	Minusgreen +1/4 Minusgreen +Sun 1/4 CTO	1½	Half blue +Minusgreen +Eighth blue	2
Warm white deluxe	CC10M +#81	⅔	#80B +CC05G	2	¼ Plusgreen +Quarter blue +UV Filter	⅔	Sun ½ CTO +UV Filter	⅓	¼ Minusgreen	⅓	Full blue CTB +1/2 Minusgreen	2⅓
Mercury vapor	CC50M +#85	1⅓	CC50M +#81A	1	½ to Full CTO +2x to 3x Minusgreen	3⅔ to 2⅓	Full CTB +2x to 3x Plusgreen	3 to 2⅓	NR		NR	
Sodium vapor	CC30 to 50M +#80A	2⅔	CC30M +#80A	2⅔	3/4 CTO +101 Yellow	1⅓	1½ to 2x Full CTO +101 Yellow	2½ to 1⅔	NR		NR	

Check with color temperature meter.   *S. I. = Stop Increase   *L.L. = Light Loss in stops

COLOR BALANCING TO MATCH DAYLIGHT OR AMBIENT LIGHT ON LOCATION INTERIORS

Emulsion Balance	Exposure Balance	Camera Filter	Photographic Lights/Filters	Practical Existing Lights/Filters	Window Filters
Balancing Interior to Daylight from Windows					
3200°K	Daylight	85Neg 85B Rev.	3200°K Tungsten/Full Blue CTB or Dichroic	Household Tungsten/ Full Blue + 1/4 CTB	ND as required
			White flame Arc/Y-1	See p 839 for Fluorescent, Mercury and Sodium Vapor Lamps	
			HMI, CID/Y-1		
			5500°K Kino Flo GE Cinema55/ None		
Daylight	Daylight	None	Use same filters as above		
Balancing Color of Ambient Lighting to 3200°K					
3200°K	3200°K	None	3200°K Tungsten/None	Household Tungsten/ 1/4 CTB	Full or 3/4 CTO or Sun 85 plus ND as required
			3200°K HMI/ None		
			3200°K Kino Flo, GE Cinema32/ None	See p 839 for Flourescent, Mercury and Sodium Vapor Lamps	
			Yellow Flame Arc/YF 101		
			HMI, CID, White Flame Arc/ Y-1+MT2* or MTY or 3/4 CTO		
Daylight	3200°K	80A	Use same filters as above		

Exact conversion requires both source and filter to be precise.

Artificial daylight sources vary greatly in their ability to replicate photographic daylight (5500°K). White-Flame Carbon Arcs and Xenon lamps are very stable and excellent continuous-spectrum photographic daylight sources.

HMI and CID sources are problematic. There can be variations in green output and they tend to lose one degree of Kelvin per hour of lamp life. The consistency in manufacturing of these globes is a factor that requires checking.

Even so-called "full-spectrum color-correct" fluorescents will have excess green when they overheat. 3200°K Tungsten-Halogen photographic globes are very stable and have excellent color rendering when operated at 117–120V throughout their life.

Filtering systems vary by manufacturer. They must be checked by a color-temperature meter for accuracy.

Color Balancing for Existing Fluorescent Lighting

| Typical Fluorescent Lights | Using existing fluorescent lighting unfiltered — Camera filters (Kodak or equivalent) | | | | Filtering fluorescent lights to match photo lights — Photo lamp filters (Rosco, Lee, GAM or Formatt) | | | | Camera filter: none (Tungsten negative or reversal) | | Camera filter: Tungsten Negative: #85 Daylight film: none | |
	3200°K film	S.I.*	5500°K	S.I.*	3200°K film	L.L.*	5500°K	L.L.*	To match 3200°K	L.L.*	To match 5500°K	L.L.*
Durotest Optima 50	+#85	2/3	#82A +CC05M	2/3	Full blue (CTB) +Sun 1/4 (CTO)	2	1/4 Plusgreen	1/3	Sun 1/2 (CTO)	1/2	1/4 Minusgreen +1/4 blue	1
Durotest Optima 32	#81 +CC05M	11/3	#80C +#82A	11/3	1/4 blue +UV Filter	1/2	Sun 1/2 (CTO) +Sun 1/4 (CTO)	1	1/4 Minusgreen +Sun 1/4 (CTO)	2/3	Half blue +1/4 blue	11/2
General Electric Chroma 50	CC05M +#81 +#85	11/3	CC10M +#82A	2/3	Full blue (CTB) +1/4 Plusgreen +Sun 1/8 (CTO)	2	1/4 Plusgreen	1/3	Sun 1/2(CTO) +1/4 Minusgreen	1	Minusgreen +1/4 blue	11/3
General Electric SPX-35	CC40R +#81A	1	CC15M +CC30B	1	Half blue Plusgreen +1/3 blue	2	Plusgreen +1/2 Plusgreen	2/3	1/2 Minusgreen +Sun 1/4 (CTO) +1/4 Minusgreen +Sun 1/4 (CTO)	11/2	Half blue +1/2 Minusgreen +1/4 Minusgreen	12/3

Check with color temperature meter.   S.I.* = Stop Increase   L.L.* = Light Loss in Stops

Handheld Apps For Production Use

by Taz Goldstein

As smart phone and portable computer technology has grown more sophisticated, the use of apps either designed or adapted for motion imaging use has expanded at a rapid rate. In production, these tools have become a standard part of the cinematographer's kit, as valuable as a light meter or a reference book. Below are some of the most prominent apps currently in use.

ACCESSORY
fStop Wireless WiFi Receiver
PLC Electronic Solutions Ltd.
http://www.plcelectronicsolutions.com/
The fStop Wireless Receiver and Wireless iris iOS application allows users to move around the set without any additional hardware, and wirelessly control the focus, iris or zoom of each camera from an iPhone, iPod Touch or iPad. The receiver creates its own WiFi access point, and has an approximate range of 150 meters/492 feet (depending on the site).

Cube
Teradek
http://www.teradek.com/
A camera-top encoder, capable of streaming HD video over WiFi or wired ethernet. As the camera records to it's primary medium, the Cube can record proxy movies (dailies) directly to a wirelessly networked computer. These proxy movies can then be viewed instantly on a wirelessly connected iPad running Air Video (or a similar application). This translates into instant wireless dailies.

ANDROID
Film Utility
ADibu
http://www.fatslimmer.com/
Helps filmmakers convert frames, feet, and time code and see the result of all three simultaneously. The film counter calculator can be used as a stopwatch that counts time (precision milliseconds), length in feet and total frames.

Photo Tools
ADibu
http://www.fatslimmer.com/

The app contains 15 calculators, good for any format, digital or film SLR camera. Calculations include exposure, circle of confusion, depth of field, magnification, angle of view, field of view, flash guide number and aperture, camera pixels, aperture average, stops difference, and an exposure unit converter.

Acacia
Ephemerald Creative Arts
http://www.ephemerald.com/

Provides a depth of field calculator, equipment management, shot logging and a rudimentary slate.

CamCalc
Go Visual, Inc.
http://www.govisualinc.com/

Multifunction app that provides calculator for depth of field, field of view, focal length equivalents, flash exposure calculations, color temperature conversion, miniature photography, and solar calculations (including sun path).

Depth of Field Calculator
Allen Zhong

Photographer's depth of field calculator.

On The Level 4
Stephen Lebed
http://apps.mechnology.com/my-apps/

A combination digital inclinometer and bubble level. Measurements are calibrated to a hundredths of a degree accuracy.

SL DigiSlate
Stephen Lebed
http://apps.mechnology.com/my-apps/

A digital movie slate (clapper board) with integrated shot logging. Logs can be edited and emailed. Slate information can be entered manually, and advanced with simple controls.

SL Director's Viewfinder
Stephen Lebed
http://apps.mechnology.com/my-apps/

A virtual director's viewfinder that uses the Android's built-in camera to simulate multiple cameras, formats and lenses.

IOS

LightMeter
Ambertation
http://iphone.ambertation.de/lightmeter/
Turns an iPhone's camera into a exposure meter. The app allows you to change the f-stop, shutter or iOS values after you've measured the scene without altering the exposure. Also allows users to include filter parameters.

Panascout
Panavision
http://www.panascout.com
Allows filmmakers to capture images of a given location, while recording GPS data, compass heading, the current date, and sunrise/sunset times. You can then share the images and data in a variety of ways.

Catchlight
Ben Syverson
http://bensyverson.com/software/catchlight/
Turns your mobile iOS device into a color programmable light source. It can be used as a catchlight/eye light, or as a mini softbox for low-light photography.

Cinemek Storyboard Composer HD
Cinemek Inc.
http://www.cinemek.com/storyboard/
A mobile storyboarding and previsualization app that allows users to acquire photos with their phones, and then add traditional storyboarding markups such as dolly, track, zoom and pan. Users can reorder panels, add stand-ins, set panel durations, enter text notes, record audio, and then play it all back to get real time feedback on pacing and framing. Storyboards can be exported as animated movies or as PDF files.

Clinometer
Peter Breitling
http://www.plaincode.com/
A professional angle/slope measurement app for mobile iOS devices. This virtual clinometer offers many manual and automatic features as well as a variety of informational displays.

Focalware
Spiral Development Inc.
http://spiraldev.com/focalware/

Focalware calculates sun and moon position for a given location and date. Use the interactive compass to determine the path and height of the sun or moon.

Gel Swatch Library
Wybron, Inc.
http://www.wybron.com

Lets lighting production personnel browse, search, and compare more than 1,000 gel color filters made by the following manufacturers: Apollo, GAM, Lee, and Rosco. Users can compare similar and complementary colors, as well as examine each color's detailed Spectral Energy Distribution graphs.

Helios Sun Position Calculator
Chemical Wedding
http://www.chemicalwedding.tv/helios.html

Helios is a sun position calculator and compass that graphically represents the position of the sun from dusk to dawn, on any given day, in any given place, without the need for complex tables or graphs. Four modes of operation allow users to view graphical representations of the sun's predicted position, elevation, and path in the sky. It can also calculate the proportional lengths of the shadows being cast.

Light Calc
D!HV Lighting
http://www.dhvproductions.com/

Light Calc is a photometric calculation tool featuring a database of commonly used theatrical lighting fixtures. Users can select a type of lighting fixture, choose one of several lamp types, and set a throw distance. The calculator will then return a beam diameter and field diameter, in feet, as well as center field illumination, in footcandles.

MatchLens
Indelible Pictures, Inc.
http://web.me.com/donmatthewsmith/Site/MatchLens.html

This calculator computes the equivalent lens focal length to produce the same field of view between two cameras with different aperture/sensor sizes. It will do a "Match Lens" calculation, and produce the closest equivalent angle of view lens, in millimeters, for both vertical and horizontal frames, between the original camera's focal length and the current camera's focal length.

pCAM Film/Digital Calculator
David Eubank
http://www.davideubank.com

A well-known film and video tool that performs a wide variety of calculations including: depth of field, hyperfocal, splits/aperture finder, field of view, field of view preview, angle of view, focal length matching, exposure, running time to length, shooting to screen time, HMI flicker-free, color correction (choosing filters), diopter, macro, time lapse, underwater distance, scene illumination (beam intensity), light coverage (width/distance), mired shift (with suggested color correction gels), and more.

Photo fx
The Tiffen Company
http://www.tiffen.com/photofx_homepage.html

Lets users apply multiple effects to still photos. Filters include simulations of many popular Tiffen glass filters, specialized lenses, optical lab processes, film grain, color corrections, natural light and photographic effects.

Pocket DIT
Clifton Production Services
http://www.cliftonpost.com

A multifunction app that provides a RED ONE virtual menu navigator, a depth of field calculator (with near focus, far focus, and hyperfocal distances for 16mm, 35mm, and RED formats), a transfer time calculator, a storage calculator, a time calculator that lets users determine the maximum frame-rate/timebase that can be recorded given a particular RED configuration,and a maximum fps indicator that helps users determine the maximum frame rate/time base that can be recorded given a particular RED configuration.

PocketLD
Michael Zinman
http://www.lightingiphoneapps.com

Pocket LD is a photometric database and calculation tool for lighting professionals. It's large, searchable, user-expandable fixture database can be referenced while organizing easy-to-manage lists of commonly used items. Additionally, users can enter any throw distance to determine beam/field diameter and footcandles/lux for any selected fixture and lamp.

PowerCalc
West Side Systems
http://westsidesystems.com/iphone/

PowerCalc performs basic electrical power calculations with watts, volts, amps, and motor power factor. It has three modes: DC mode, AC Resistive mode, and AC Inductive mode. It works for any voltage, in any country.

Wrap Time Lite
RedPipe Media
http://redpipemedia.com

Can help crew members keep track of hours, pay, and job information. Users can save their call, meal, and wrap times. The app will then calculate a users pay, overtime, and meal penalties according to the provided job information. Various options allow users to customize the experience, and include additional expenses and discounts.

mRelease
being MEdia, LLC
http://www.mReleaseApp.com/

mRelease helps users obtain appearance releases, property releases, location release, and crew releases. After setting up the app, users can add details about their subject, import an image from the built-in camera or photo library, and capture a signatures via their device's touch screen. The app creates, stores, and emails PDF files of the signed releases.

Toland ASC Digital Assistant
Chemical Wedding in Partnership with the ASC
http://www.chemicalwedding.tv

A full featured, multi-tasking, photographic and camera calculation system. Unlike single-function calculators that answer specific questions, Toland is designed to track your photographic choices as you make them. It serves as a reflection of your entire photographic system. As you change the camera speed, you get feedback on how it affects running time and exposure; when you change lenses, depth of field and field of view automatically updates. The app will also log information and build comprehensive camera reports.

Camera Order
Practical Applications
http://www.practical-applications.com/

This app offers cinematographers and camera assistants the ability to create complete camera package lists and email them straight from the app to production or the rental house. It features a complete list of cameras, lenses, accessories, filters, support, film and media.

Bento
FileMaker, Inc.
http://www.filemaker.com/products/bento/
A simple database application that easily syncs with its Mac-based counter-part. Since most databases are user generated, the app can be used to track just about anything (i.e., equipment, supplies, crew, locations, camera logs, etc.). Since all user data lives on the device (and possibly on a synched Mac computer), and not in the cloud, no Internet connection is required to view or edit a database.

GoodReader for iPhone
Good.iWare Ltd.
http://www.goodreader.net/goodreader.html
A very popular document reader for iOS devices that allows for easy reviewing, bookmarking, and annotating of PDF files (i.e., scripts, call sheets, camera logs, etc.). Documents can be imported and exported in a wide variety of ways.

TechScout Touch
LiteGear Inc.
http://www.litegear.com/techscout
This app helps lighting professionals create rental orders intended to be submitted to rental houses or to studio set lighting departments. Users enter basic info about the job, and then being adding items to their list. The app includes over 1000 lighting equipment items separated into categories and sorted by type and wattage. New items can also be entered manually. The resulting equipment list can be e-mailed directly from the app.

Movie*Slate
PureBlend Software
http://www.pureblendsoftware.com/movieslate
A powerful, multifunction digital slate (clapper board) that can sync to camera time code, generate new time code, playback synced music, log shots with extensive notes, and export those logs to editing systems like Final Cut Pro and Avid. The app can also wirelessly sync with other iOS devices running Movie*Slate. The base price does not include certain time-code features.

Easy Release
ApplicationGap
http://www.applicationgap.com
Easy Release helps users obtain a variety of releases (i.e., talent, location, etc.) using customizable forms. After setting up the app, users can add details about their subject, import an image from the built-in camera or photo library, and capture a signatures via their device's touch screen. Model and witness information can be imported directly from your device's contact list. The app creates, stores, and e-mails PDF files of the signed releases.

PDF Expert for iPad
Readdle
http://readdle.com

A very popular document reader for iOS devices that allows for easy reviewing, bookmarking, and annotating of PDF files (i.e., scripts, call sheets, camera logs, etc.). Documents can be imported and exported in a wide variety of ways.

Artemis Remote for iPad
Chemical Wedding
http://www.chemicalwedding.tv/artemis.hml

Artemis Remote for iPad can wirelessly receive streaming video from an iPhone (or iPod Touch) running Artemis Director's Viewfinder. This allows many people to remotely view whatever the iPhone (or iPod Touch) user is seeing. Artemis Remote users can also change lenses, and capture pictures to their iPad's image gallery.

OmniGraffle
The Omni Group
http://www.omnigroup.com/products/omnigraffle-ipad/

Helps people create diagrams and charts using pre-existing or original graphic elements. There are collections of film and video related elements available for free online. Omnigraffle is very useful when blocking camera and actor movements, designing lighting grids, or creating wiring diagrams.

TouchDraw
Elevenworks, LLC
http://elevenworks.com/touchdraw

TouchDraw is a powerful, easy to use, illustration and drawing application for iPad that can help users create diagrams for camera blocking, actor blocking, and lighting setups. Like Omnigraffle but with fewer features at a lower cost.

AJA DataCalc
AJA Video Systems, Inc.
http://www.aja.com/

Computes storage requirements for professional video and audio media. The app works with all the most popular industry video formats and compression methods, including Apple ProRes, DVCProHD, HDV, XDCAM, DV, CineForm, REDCODE, Avid DNxHD, Apple Intermediate, 16-bit RGB and RGBA, uncompressed, and more. Video standards supported include NTSC, PAL, 1080i, 1080p, 720p, 2K and 4K.

Almost DSLR
Rainbow Silo
http://www.rainbowsilo.com/
Gives more control to users shooting HD video with their iPhone or iPod Touch. Unlike the built-in camera app, almost DSLR lets users lock focus, lock iris, and lock white balance. Users can also monitor audio levels, show/hide grids, and control the built-in camera light.

BigStopWatch & BigStopWatch HD
Objective-Audio
http://objective-audio.jp/apps/
A large, graphic stopwatch that features an easy to control and read interface. The app also provides a lap timer and countdown timer.

Electrical Toolkit
Niranjan Kumar
http://iappsworld.com/site/iApps.html
Calculates circuit values, and instantly updates when users edit data.

Sun Seeker: 3D Augmented Reality Viewer
ozPDA
http://www.ozpda.com/
Reports the sun's position and path on a flat compass view, and on an augmented reality view which displays the app's data over a live view from the device's camera (as a user moves the device, the app updates the overlaid information).

WeatherBug for iPad
WeatherBug
http://weather.weatherbug.com/
Displays current local weather conditions, as well as extended forecasts, severe weather alerts, an animated Doppler radar, and live weather camera images.

IOS & ANDROID

Artemis Directors Viewfinder
Chemical Wedding
http://www.chemicalwedding.tv/artemis.html
Artemis is a digital director's viewfinder that works much the same way as a traditional director's viewfinder, though much more accurately. Users can select camera format, aspect ratio, and lens types. Using your device's built-in camera, Artemis will simulate the lens views you can expect when ready to shoot. Users can switch between virtual lenses, save shots, and wirelessly transmit video to Artemis Remote for iPad (wireless transmission not available on Android).

KODAK Cinema Tools
Eastman Kodak Co.
http://motion.kodak.com/US/en/motion/Tools/Mobile/index.html
The app features a Depth of Field Calculator (works any film format, including Super 8, 16mm, 35mm and 65mm), a film calculator that helps with footage computations, and broad film/video glossary. The included contact tool lets users quickly contact a Kodak representative online to get their technical questions answered.

WEB APP

Video Storage Calculator
Digital Rebellion LLC
http://www.digitalrebellion.com
http://www.digitalrebellion.com/webapps/video_calc_mobile.html
Calculates the hard-drive space necessary for a given video format and duration. The actual space taken up may differ slightly due to embedded audio, differing frame sizes and aspect ratios, and interframe compression/pull-down.

Film Rate Calculator
Digital Rebellion LLC
http://www.digitalrebellion.com
http://www.digitalrebellion.com/webapps/film_calc_mobile.html
Gives an indication of the number of film rolls needed to shoot a given amount of footage. The actual results may differ slightly due to the rounding system used for this tool.

Lens Angle Calculator
Digital Rebellion LLC
http://www.digitalrebellion.com
http://www.digitalrebellion.com/webapps/lens_calc_mobile.html
Helps you calculate the lens angle for a given sensor size and focal length.

Power Load Calculator
Digital Rebellion LLC
http://www.digitalrebellion.com
http://www.digitalrebellion.com/webapps/power_calc_mobile.html
Helps users calculate the load on a circuit to see if it is excessive. You can also calculate the minimum circuit breaker size for the given load. This is very useful when you are in preproduction as you will easily be able to calculate in advance whether or not you will need an external generator, and how many.

Arri Alexa Camera Simulator
ARRI Digital Camera Systems
http://www.arridigital.com/technical/simulator
http://www.arridigital.com/technical/simulator

An interactive training tool to familiarize yourself with the menu navigation of the new ARRI ALEXA digital camera. The ACS-1 Main User Interface shows an identical simulation of the ALEXA with software version 2.0.

Depth of Field Calculator
Digital Rebellion LLC
http://www.digitalrebellion.com
http://www.digitalrebellion.com/webapps/dof_calc_mobile.html

Lets users calculate the depth of field for a given sensor or film type, aperture, focal length and subject distance.

Sunrise & Sunset
Piet Jonas
http://www.speedymarks.com/
http://sun.speedymarks.com/

Helps to calculate the sunrise and sunset times for any location on any day of the year.

VideoSpace
Digital Heaven Ltd
http://www.digital-heaven.co.uk/
http://www.videospaceonline.com/

Disk space calculator for Final Cut Pro editors. Users can choose their codec, frame rate, audio settings, and duration. The app will then calculate the required disk space. VideoSpace can also calculate how much footage users can store by choosing the same settings, but entering their available drive space instead of a duration.

Weather Underground
Weather Underground
http://www.wund.com/
http://i.wund.com/

View current weather conditions, animated radar, forecasts, and severe weather alerts.

WINDOWS & ANDROID

Filmcalculator

Zebra Films

http://www.zebrafilm.com/products/filmcalculator/
filmcalculator-for-windows-mobile
http://www.zebrafilm.com/products/filmcalculator/
filmcalculator-for-windows-mobile

Contains over thirty-two calculations, as well as a film stock and camera database. The app also contains a large lamp database with full details and calculations.

Sunpath Computer Software

One of the most difficult parts of cinematography is scouting specific locations for a film that actually will be shot at another time of the year. A valuable tool used by many cinematographers is Sunpath computer software. Cinematographers using Sunpath can accurately predict the sun's position at virtually any location at any time of the year. This ensures that a production company can forecast on the actual day of photography how much available light will be "available." The software also plots out the location of the sun at each hour of the day, enabling you to predict when or if the sun will be obscured by landscape features or buildings. Sunpath contains a comprehensive, worldwide database of over 39,000 locations. The database includes coordinates, time zone, daylight saving's time and magnetic declination information for each location. The filmmaker simply selects the location and date range. Sunpath will display the sun's information on the screen and in a detailed printed report. The report contains a daily summary of sunrise, sunset, day length, estimated "magic hour" times, and the sun's position in 15-minute intervals with shadow-length information and a graphical plot of the sun's path during the day. Filmmakers take the printed report to locations, leaving the computer behind.

The size of the sun as seen from earth is 0° 32' 35" or about ½°. The sun moves 15° every hour; 1° every four minutes
In the northern hemisphere, the longest day is June 21, the shortest is December 22. The reverse is true in the south.

sunPATH™ ©1991-2000, Wide Screen Software (www.wide-screen.com)
Cities with the approx. Latitudes.
The first are cities in the US followed by Cities outside the US.
The format is City, State/Country

USA

City	Lat	City	Lat
Anchorage, AK	61°N	Boston, MA	42°N
Los Angeles, CA	34°N	Detroit, MI	42°N
San Francisco, CA	38°N	Atlantic City, NJ	39°N
Denver, CO	40°N	Las Vegas, NV	36°N
Washington, DC	39°N	New York, NY	41°N
Miami, FL	26°N	Portland, OR	46°N
Orlando, FL	29°N	Philadelphia, PA	40°N
Atlanta, GA	34°N	Sioux Falls, SD	44°N
Honolulu, HI	21°N	Memphis, TN	35°N
Des Moines, IA	42°N	Dallas, TX	33°N
Boise, ID	44°N	Houston, TX	30°N
Chicago, IL	42°N	Seattle, WA	48°N

Outside USA			
Algiers, Algeria	37°N	New Delhi, India	29°N
Buenos Aires, Argentina	35°S	Jakarta, Indonesia	6°S
Melbourne, Australia	38°S	Dublin, Ireland	53°N
Sydney, Australia	34°S	Jerusalem, Israel	32°N
Vienna, Austria	48°N	Rome, Italy	42°N
Nassau, Bahamas	25°N	Venice, Italy	45°N
Brasilia, Brazil	16°S	Kingston, Jamaica	18°N
Rio De Janeiro, Brazil	23°S	Tokyo, Japan	36°N
Sofia, Bulgaria	43°N	Amman, Jordan	32°N
Rangoon, Burma	17°N	Nairobi, Kenya	1°S
Phnom Penh, Cambodia	12°N	Acapulco, Mexico	17°N
Montreal, Canada	46°N	Mexico City, Mexico	19°N
Toronto, Canada	44°N	Amsterdam, Netherlands	52°N
Vancouver, Canada	49°N	Auckland, New Zealand	37°S
Santiago, Chile	34°S	Wellington, New Zealand	41°S
Beijing, China	40°N	Islamabad, Pakistan	34°N
Hong Kong, China	22°N	Manila, Philippines	15°N
Shanghai, China	31°N	Warsaw, Poland	52°N
Bogota, Colombia	5°N	Lisbon, Portugal	39°N
Prague, Czech Republic	50°N	Moscow, Russia	56°N
Copenhagen, Denmark	56°N	Vladivostok, Russia	43°N
Cairo, Egypt	30°N	Riyadh, Saudi Arabia	25°N
Helsinki, Finland	60°N	Singapore City, Singapore	1°N
Nice, France	44°N	Cape Town, South Africa	34°S
Paris, France	49°N	Johannesburg, South Africa	26°S
Berlin, Germany	53°N	Seoul, South Korea	38°N
Munich, Germany	48°N	Madrid, Spain	40°N
Athens, Greece	38°N	Stockholm, Sweden	59°N
Budapest, Hungary	48°N	Geneva, Switzerland	46°N
Reykjavik, Iceland	64°N	Bangkok, Thailand	14°N
Bombay, India	19°N	Edinburgh, United Kingdom	56°N
Calcutta, India	23°N	London, United Kingdom	52°N

Maximum Height of the Sun

Latitude	Jan	Feb	March	April	May	June	July	Aug	Sept	Oct	Nov	Dec
65°N	4°	12°	23°	35°	44°	48°	46°	39°	28°	16°	6°	2°
60°N	9°	17°	28°	40°	49°	53°	51°	44°	33°	21°	11°	7°
55°N	14°	22°	33°	45°	54°	58°	56°	49°	38°	26°	16°	12°
50°N	19°	27°	38°	50°	59°	63°	61°	54°	43°	31°	21°	17°
45°N	24°	32°	43°	55°	64°	68°	66°	59°	48°	36°	26°	22°
40°N	29°	37°	48°	60°	69°	73°	71°	64°	53°	41°	31°	27°
35°N	34°	42°	53°	65°	74°	78°	76°	69°	58°	46°	36°	32°
30°N	39°	47°	58°	70°	79°	83°	81°	74°	63°	51°	41°	37°
25°N	44°	52°	63°	75°	84°	88°	86°	79°	68°	56°	46°	42°
20°N	49°	57°	68°	80°	89°	87°	88°	84°	73°	61°	51°	47°
15°N	54°	62°	73°	85°	86°	82°	83°	89°	78°	66°	56°	52°
10°N	59°	67°	78°	90°	81°	77°	78°	86°	83°	71°	61°	57°
5°N	61°	72°	83°	85°	76°	72°	73°	81°	88°	76°	66°	60°
0°	69°	77°	87°	80°	71°	67°	68°	76°	87°	81°	71°	67°
5°S	74°	82°	87°	75°	66°	62°	63°	71°	82°	86°	76°	72°
10°S	79°	87°	82°	70°	61°	57°	58°	66°	77°	89°	81°	77°
15°S	84°	88°	77°	65°	56°	52°	53°	61°	72°	84°	86°	82°
20°S	88°	83°	72°	60°	51°	47°	48°	56°	67°	79°	89°	87°

Maximum Height of the Sun

Latitude	Jan	Feb	March	April	May	June	July	Aug	Sept	Oct	Nov	Dec
25°S	86°	78°	67°	55°	46°	42°	43°	51°	62°	74°	84°	88°
30°S	81°	73°	62°	50°	41°	37°	38°	46°	57°	69°	79°	83°
35°S	76°	68°	57°	45°	36°	32°	33°	41°	52°	64°	74°	78°
40°S	71°	63°	52°	40°	31°	27°	28°	36°	47°	59°	69°	73°
45°S	66°	58°	47°	35°	26°	22°	24°	31°	42°	54°	64°	68°
50°S	61°	53°	42°	30°	21°	17°	19°	26°	37°	49°	59°	63°
55°S	56°	48°	37°	25°	16°	12°	14°	21°	32°	44°	54°	58°
60°S	51°	43°	32°	20°	11°	7°	9°	16°	27°	39°	49°	53°

Hours of Daylight

Latitude	Jan	Feb	March	April	May	June	July	Aug	Sept	Oct	Nov	Dec
65°N	5.0	8.5	11.8	15.3	18.8	21.9	20.0	16.5	13.0	9.6	6.2	3.6
60°N	6.7	9.2	11.8	14.6	17.2	18.8	18.0	15.6	12.8	10.1	7.5	5.9
55°N	7.8	9.7	11.9	14.2	16.2	17.4	16.8	14.9	12.7	10.5	8.4	7.2
50°N	8.5	10.1	11.9	13.8	15.5	16.4	15.9	14.5	12.6	10.8	9.0	8.1
45°N	9.2	10.4	11.9	13.5	14.9	15.6	15.3	14.0	12.5	11.0	9.5	8.8
40°N	9.7	10.7	12.0	13.3	14.4	15.0	14.7	13.7	12.4	11.2	10.0	9.4
35°N	10.1	10.9	12.0	13.1	14.0	14.5	14.3	13.5	12.4	11.3	10.3	9.8

Hours of Daylight

Latitude	Jan	Feb	March	April	May	June	July	Aug	Sept	Oct	Nov	Dec
30°N	10.4	11.1	12.0	12.9	13.7	14.1	13.9	13.2	12.3	11.4	10.6	10.2
25°N	10.8	11.3	12.0	12.8	13.4	13.7	13.5	13.0	12.3	11.6	10.9	10.6
20°N	11.1	11.5	12.0	12.6	13.1	13.3	13.2	12.8	12.3	11.7	11.2	11.0
15°N	11.3	11.7	12.1	12.5	12.8	13.0	12.9	12.6	12.2	11.8	11.4	11.3
10°N	11.6	12.8	12.1	12.4	12.6	12.7	12.6	12.5	12.2	11.9	11.6	11.5
5°N	11.9	12.0	12.1	12.2	12.4	12.4	12.4	12.3	12.1	12.0	11.9	11.8
0°	12.0	12.0	12.1	12.0	12.0	12.0	12.0	12.0	12.1	12.0	12.0	12.0
5°S	12.4	12.3	12.1	12.0	11.9	11.8	11.9	12.0	12.1	12.2	12.4	12.4
10°S	12.7	12.4	12.2	11.9	11.7	11.6	11.6	11.8	12.0	12.3	12.6	12.7
15°S	12.9	12.6	12.2	11.8	11.4	11.3	11.3	11.6	12.0	12.4	12.8	13.0
20°S	13.2	12.8	12.2	11.6	11.2	10.9	11.0	11.4	12.0	12.6	13.1	13.3
25°S	13.5	12.9	12.3	11.5	10.9	10.6	10.7	11.3	11.9	12.7	13.4	13.7
30°S	13.9	13.1	12.3	11.3	10.6	10.2	10.4	11.1	11.9	12.8	13.7	14.1
35°S	14.3	13.4	12.3	11.2	10.3	9.8	10.0	10.8	11.9	13.0	14.0	14.5
40°S	14.7	13.6	12.3	11.0	9.9	9.3	9.6	10.6	11.9	13.2	14.4	15.0
45°S	15.2	13.9	12.4	10.8	9.5	8.8	9.1	10.3	11.8	13.4	14.8	15.6
50°S	15.9	14.3	12.5	10.5	9.0	8.1	8.5	9.9	11.8	13.6	15.4	16.4
55°S	16.7	14.7	12.5	10.2	8.3	7.2	7.7	9.5	11.7	13.9	16.1	17.3
60°S	18.0	15.3	12.6	9.8	7.4	5.9	6.6	8.9	11.6	14.3	17.1	18.8

Calculations were made for the 15th of each month using sunPATH

	Sunrise / Sunset at Sea Level (Azimuth Bearings from True North)					
Latitude	Jan Sunrise/Sunset	Feb Sunrise/Sunset	March Sunrise/Sunset	April Sunrise/Sunset	May Sunrise/Sunset	June Sunrise/Sunset
65°N	145°/215°	119°/241°	93°/268°	64°/297°	37°/324°	14°/346°
60°N	134°/226°	115°/246°	92°/268°	68°/292°	47°/313°	35°/325°
55°N	127°/233°	111°/249°	92°/268°	71°/289°	54°/306°	45°/315°
50°N	123°/237°	109°/251°	92°/268°	73°/287°	58°/302°	51°/309°
45°N	120°/240°	107°/253°	92°/268°	75°/285°	62°/298°	55°/305°
40°N	117°/243°	106°/254°	92°/268°	76°/284°	64°/296°	58°/302°
35°N	115°/245°	105°/255°	92°/268°	77°/283°	66°/294°	60°/300°
30°N	114°/246°	104°/256°	92°/268°	78°/282°	68°/293°	62°/298°
25°N	113°/247°	104°/257°	92°/268°	79°/281°	69°/292°	64°/296°
20°N	112°/248°	103°/257°	92°/268°	79°/281°	70°/291°	65°/295°
15°N	112°/248°	103°/257°	92°/268°	80°/281°	70°/290°	66°/294°
10°N	111°/249°	103°/257°	92°/268°	80°/280°	71°/289°	66°/294°
5°N	111°/249°	103°/258°	92°/268°	80°/280°	71°/289°	67°/294°
0°	111°/249°	103°/258°	92°/268°	80°/280°	71°/289°	67°/293°
5°S	111°/249°	103°/257°	92°/268°	80°/280°	71°/289°	67°/293°

Latitude	Jan Sunrise/Sunset	Feb Sunrise/Sunset	March Sunrise/Sunset	April Sunrise/Sunset	May Sunrise/Sunset	June Sunrise/Sunset
10°S	112°/248°	103°/257°	92°/268°	80°/280°	71°/289°	66°/294°
15°S	112°/248°	103°/257°	92°/268°	80°/280°	71°/289°	66°/294°
20°S	113°/247°	104°/256°	93°/268°	80°/280°	70°/290°	65°/295°
25°S	114°/246°	104°/256°	93°/268°	80°/281°	69°/291°	65°/295°
30°S	115°/245°	105°/255°	93°/267°	79°/281°	69°/292°	63°/297°
35°S	117°/243°	106°/254°	93°/267°	79°/282°	67°/293°	62°/298°
40°S	119°/241°	107°/253°	93°/267°	78°/282°	66°/294°	60°/300°
45°S	122°/239°	109°/251°	94°/267°	77°/283°	64°/294°	57°/303°
50°S	125°/235°	111°/249°	94°/266°	75°/285°	61°/299°	53°/307°
55°S	131°/230°	114°/246°	95°/266°	74°/287°	57°/303°	48°/312°
60°S	138°/222°	118°/243°	95°/265°	71°/289°	51°/309°	40°/320°

Sunrise / Sunset at Sea Level (Azimuth Bearings from True North)

Sunrise / Sunset at Sea Level (Azimuth Bearings from True North)

Latitude	July Sunrise/Sunset	Aug Sunrise/Sunset	Sept Sunrise/Sunset	Oct Sunrise/Sunset	Nov Sunrise/Sunset	Dec Sunrise/Sunset
65°N	26°/333°	53°/306°	81°/278°	109°/250°	137°/223°	155°/205°
60°N	41°/319°	60°/300°	83°/277°	106°/253°	128°/232°	140°/220°
55°N	49°/311°	64°/296°	84°/276°	104°/256°	122°/237°	!32°/228°
50°N	54°/306°	67°/293°	84°/275°	103°/257°	119°/241°	127°/233°
45°N	58°/302°	69°/291°	85°/275°	101°/258°	116°/244°	123°/237°
40°N	61°/299°	71°/289°	85°/274°	101°/259°	114°/246°	120°/240°
35°N	63°/297°	72°/288°	86°/274°	100°/260°	112°/248°	118°/242°
30°N	64°/295°	73°/287°	86°/274°	99°/260°	111°/249°	117°/243°
25°N	66°/294°	74°/286°	86°/273°	99°/261°	110°/250°	115°/245°
20°N	67°/293°	75°/285°	86°/273°	99°/261°	109°/250°	115°/245°
15°N	67°/292°	75°/285°	87°/273°	99°/261°	109°/251°	114°/246°
10°N	68°/292°	76°/284°	87°/273°	99°/261°	109°/251°	114°/246°
5°N	68°/292°	76°/284°	87°/273°	98°/261°	108°/251°	113°/247°
0°	68°/291°	76°/284°	87°/273°	99°/261°	108°/251°	113°/247°
5°S	68°/291°	76°/284°	87°/273°	99°/261°	109°/251°	113°/247°

Latitude	July Sunrise/Sunset	Aug Sunrise/Sunset	Sept Sunrise/Sunset	Oct Sunrise/Sunset	Nov Sunrise/Sunset	Dec Sunrise/Sunset
Sunrise / Sunset at Sea Level (Azimuth Bearings from True North)						
10°S	68°/292°	76°/284°	87°/273°	99°/261°	109°/251°	114°/246°
15°S	68°/292°	76°/284°	87°/273°	99°/261°	109°/250°	114°/246°
20°S	67°/293°	75°/284°	87°/273°	99°/260°	110°/250°	115°/245°
25°S	67°/293°	75°/285°	87°/273°	100°/260°	111°/249°	116°/244°
30°S	65°/294°	74°/286°	87°/273°	100°/259°	112°/248°	118°/242°
35°S	64°/296°	73°/286°	87°/273°	101°/259°	113°/246°	119°/240°
40°S	62°/298°	72°/287°	87°/273°	102°/258°	115°/244°	122°/238°
45°S	60°/300°	71°/289°	87°/273°	103°/257°	118°/242°	125°/235°
50°S	57°/303°	69°/291°	87°/273°	105°/255°	121°/239°	129°/231°
55°S	52°/308°	67°/293°	86°/273°	107°/253°	125°/234°	135°/225°
60°S	45°/315°	63°/297°	86°/274°	109°/250°	132°/228°	145°/215°

Calculations were made for the 15th of each month using sunPATH

EASTMAN KODAK — Color Negative Films

Color Negative	Balance	Emulsion Type 35mm/16mm	Edge	EI			
				T	filter	D	filter
Kodak Vision3 50D	D	5203/7203	ER	12	80A	50	—
Kodak Vision3 200T	T	5213/7213	EO	200	—	125	85
Kodak Vision3	T	5219/7219	EJ	500	—	320	85
Kodak Vision3 250D	D	5207/7207	EN	64	80A	250	—

All stocks also available in 65mm.
All print stocks are 70mm. All camera stocks are 65mm

EASTMAN KODAK — Black-and-White Negative Films

B&W Negative	Emulsion Type 35mm/16mm	Edge	EI	
			T	D
Eastman Double-X	5222/7222	E	200	250

EASTMAN KODAK — Black-and-White Reversal Films

B&W Reversal	Emulsion Type 16mm	Edge	EI	
			T	D
Kodak Tri-X Reversal	7266 (16mm only)	ED	160	200
	*in manually operated & automatic Super 8 cameras		160	160
	*for negative processing in motion picture negative developer		100	125

EASTMAN KODAK — Super 8 Films

Color Negative and Reversal	T	D
Kodak Vision3 (7213) 200T	200	125 (with an 85 filter)
Kodak Vision3 (7219) 500T	500	320 (with an 85 filter)
Kodak Vision3 (7203) 50D	12 (with an 80A filter)	50
Black and White Reversal	**T**	**D**
Tri-X Reversal (7266)	160	200

EASTMAN KODAK — Laboratory Films

Color Print Film	Emulsion Type 35mm/16mm
Kodak Vision Premier Color Print Film	2393 (35mm & 70mm only)
Kodak Vision Color Print Film	2383/3383

Black and White Print Film	Emulsion Type 35mm/16mm
Eastman Fine Grain Release Positive Film	5302/7302
Kodak Black and White Print Film	2302/3302

Color Intermediate Films	Emulsion Type 35mm/16mm
Kodak Vision Color Intermediate Film	2242/5242/7242/3242
Kodak Color Asset Protection Film	2232
Kodak Vision3 Color Digital Intermediate Film	5254/2254
Kodak Color Internegative Film	2273/3273/5273
Kodak Vision Color Internegative II Film	2272/5272/7272/3272

Black and White Intermediate Films	Emulsion Type 35mm/16mm
Kodak Vision Fine Grain Duplicating Positive Film	2366/3366
Kodak Vision Fine Grain Duplicating Panchromatic Negative Film	2234/5234/7234/3234
Kodak Vision3 Digital Separation Film	2237
Kodak Vision High Contrast Positive Film II	5363/7363
Kodak Vision Panchromatic Separation Film	2238 (35mm and 65mm only)

Sound Film	Emulsion Type 35mm/16mm
Kodak Panchromatic Sound Recording Film	2374/3374
Eastman EXR Sound Recording Film	2378/3378

Film Weight in Cans

16mm	35mm
100 ft. = 3¼ oz. (200 grams)	400 ft. = 2 lbs. 3 oz. (1 Kg.)
400 ft. = 1 lb. (500 grams)	1000 ft. = 5 lbs. 8 oz. (2.5 Kg.)

65mm
1000 ft. = 10 lbs. (4.54 Kg.)

Incident Key Light/T-Stop
(Foot Candles)

EI/ASA	2000	1600	1250	1000	800	640	500	400	320
T-stop 1.4	1.25	1.5	2	2.5	3	4	5	6	8
1.6	1.5	2	2.5	3	4	5	6	8	10
1.8	2	2.5	3	4	5	6	8	10	12
2	2.5	3	4	5	6	8	10	12	16
2.2	3	4	5	6	8	10	12	16	20
2.5	4	5	6	8	10	12	16	20	25
2.8	5	6	8	10	12	16	20	25	32
3.2	6	8	10	12	16	20	25	32	40
3.5	8	10	12	16	20	25	32	40	50
4	10	12	16	20	25	32	40	50	64
4.5	12	16	20	25	32	40	50	64	80
5	16	20	25	32	40	50	64	80	100
5.6	20	25	32	40	50	64	80	100	125
6.3	25	32	40	50	64	80	100	125	160
7	32	40	50	64	80	100	125	160	200
8	40	50	64	80	100	125	160	200	250
9	50	64	80	100	125	160	200	250	320
10	64	80	100	125	160	200	250	320	400
11	80	100	125	160	200	250	320	400	500
12.7	100	125	160	200	250	320	400	500	650
14	125	160	200	250	320	400	500	650	800
16	160	200	250	320	400	500	650	800	1000
18	200	250	320	400	500	650	800	1000	1290
20	250	320	400	500	650	800	1000	1290	1625
22	320	400	500	650	800	1000	1290	1625	2050

Most cinematography is at 24 frames per second.
The table is calculated for foot candles incident light on a fully lighted subject at 1/50 second exposure (172.8°precisely, but 170° to 180° varies from this by less than a printer point for normally processed color negative). For photography at 1/60 second (30 frames per second, 180° shutter; or 24 frames per second, 144° shutter), use one-third wider lens stop or one column to the right (one ASA step lower) on the incident light table.

Incident Key Light/T-Stop
(Foot Candles)

EI/ASA	250	200	160	125	100	80	64	50	40
T-stop 1.4	10	12	16	20	25	32	40	50	64
1.6	12	16	20	25	32	40	50	64	80
1.8	16	20	25	32	40	50	64	80	100
2	20	25	32	40	50	64	80	100	125
2.2	25	32	40	50	64	80	100	125	160
2.5	32	40	50	64	80	100	125	160	200
2.8	40	50	64	80	100	125	160	200	250
3.2	50	64	80	100	125	160	200	250	320
3.5	64	80	100	125	160	200	250	320	400
4	80	100	125	160	200	250	320	400	500
4.5	100	125	160	200	250	320	400	500	650
5	125	160	200	250	320	400	500	650	800
5.6	160	200	250	320	400	500	650	800	1000
6.3	200	250	320	400	500	650	800	1000	1290
7	250	320	400	500	650	800	1000	1290	1625
8	320	400	500	650	800	1000	1290	1625	2050
9	400	500	650	800	1000	1290	1625	2050	2580
10	500	650	800	1000	1290	1625	2050	2580	3250
11	650	800	1000	1290	1625	2050	2580	3250	4100
12.7	800	1000	1290	1625	2050	2580	3250	4100	5160
14	1000	1290	1625	2050	2580	3250	4100	5160	6500
16	1290	1625	2050	2580	3250	4100	5160	6500	8200
18	1625	2050	2580	3250	4100	5160	6500	8200	10000
20	2050	2580	3250	4100	5160	6500	8200	10000	
22	2580	3250	4100	5160	6500	8200	10000		

COMPARISON OF LIGHT VALUES
1 FOOTCANDLE = 10.764 LUX
1 LUX = .0929 FOOTCANDLES
1 FOOT LAMBERT = 3.426 CANDELAS PER SQUARE METER
1 CANDELA PER SQUARE METER = .292 FOOT LAMBERTS

Incident Key Light/T-Stop
(Foot Candles)

EI/ASA	32	25	20	16	12	10	8	6
T-stop 1.4	80	100	125	160	200	250	320	400
1.6	100	125	160	200	250	320	400	500
1.8	125	160	200	250	320	400	500	650
2	160	200	250	320	400	500	650	800
2.2	200	250	320	400	500	650	800	1000
2.5	250	320	400	500	650	800	1000	1290
2.8	320	400	500	650	800	1000	1290	1625
3.2	400	500	650	800	1000	1290	1625	2050
3.5	500	650	800	1000	1290	1625	2050	2580
4	650	800	1000	1290	1625	2050	2580	3250
4.5	800	1000	1290	1625	2050	2580	3250	4100
5	1000	1290	1625	2050	2580	3250	4100	5160
5.6	1290	1625	2050	2580	3250	4100	5160	6500
6.3	1625	2050	2580	3250	4100	5160	6500	8200
7	2050	2580	3250	4100	5160	6500	8200	10,000
8	2580	3250	4100	5160	6500	8200	10,000	
9	3250	4100	5160	6500	8200	10,000		
10	4100	5160	6500	8200	10,000			
11	5160	6500	8200	10,000				
12.7	6500	8200	10,000					
14	8200	10,000						
16	10,000							
18								
20								
22								

1 FOOT LAMBERT = .31831 CANDELAS PER SQUARE FOOT
1 FOOT LAMBERT = .0010764 LAMBERTS
1 FOOT LAMBERT = 1 LUMEN PER SQUARE FOOT
1 LUMEN = .07958 CANDLE POWER (SPHERICAL)
1 LUMEN = .00015 WATTS

EI/ASA Exposure Index Reduction Table

(Figures are rounded to nearest exposure index Example: ASA 200 with factor of 4 is reduced to ASA 50.)

ASA	\[Filter or Other Factor] 1.5	2	2.5	3	4	5	8	12	16	24	32
1000	640	500	400	320	250	200	125	80	64	40	32
800	500	400	320	250	200	160	100	64	50	32	25
640	400	320	250	200	160	125	80	50	40	25	20
500	320	250	200	160	125	100	64	40	32	20	16
400	250	200	160	125	100	80	50	32	25	16	12
320	200	160	125	100	80	64	40	24	20	12	10
250	160	125	100	80	64	50	32	20	16	10	8
200	125	100	80	64	50	40	25	16	12	8	6
160	100	80	64	50	40	32	20	12	10	6	5
125	80	64	50	40	32	25	16	10	8	5	4
100	64	50	40	32	25	20	12	8	6	4	3
80	50	40	32	25	20	16	10	6	5	3	2.5
64	40	32	24	20	16	12	8	5	4	2.5	2
50	32	25	20	16	12	10	6	4	3	2	1.6
40	25	20	16	12	10	8	5	3	2.5	1.6	1.2
32	20	16	12	10	8	6	4	2.5	2	1.2	1
25	16	12	10	8	6	5	3	2	1.6	1	
20	12	10	8	6	5	4	2.5	1.6	1.2		
16	10	8	6	5	4	3	2	1.2	1		
12	8	6	5	4	3	2.5	1.6	1			
10	6	5	4	3	2.5	2	1.2				
8	5	4	3	2.5	2	1.6	1				

T-Stop Compensation for Camera Speed
(constant shutter)

fps	6	7.5	9.5	12	15	19	24	30	38	48
ft/min	22.5	28	36	45	56	71	90	112	142	180
	2.8	2.5	2.2	2	1.8	1.6	1.4	1.3	1.1	1
	3.2	2.8	2.5	2.2	2	1.8	1.6	1.4	1.3	1.1
	3.5	3.2	2.8	2.5	2.2	2	1.8	1.6	1.4	1.3
	4	3.5	3.2	2.8	2.5	2.2	2	1.8	1.6	1.4
	4.5	4	3.5	3.2	2.8	2.5	2.2	2	1.8	1.6
	5	4.5	4	3.5	3.2	2.8	2.5	2.2	2	1.8
	5.6	5	4.5	4	3.5	3.2	2.8	2.5	2.2	2
	6.3	5.6	5	4.5	4	3.5	3.2	2.8	2.5	2.2
	7	6.3	5.6	5	4.5	4	3.5	3.2	2.8	2.5
	8	7	6.3	5.6	5	4.5	4	3.5	3.2	2.8
	9	8	7	6.3	5.6	5	4.5	4	3.5	3.2
	10	9	8	7	6.3	5.6	5	4.5	4	3.5
	11	10	9	8	7	6.3	5.6	5	4.5	4
	12.7	11	10	9	8	7	6.3	5.6	5	4.5
	14	12.7	11	10	9	8	7	6.3	5.6	5
	16	14	12.7	11	10	9	8	7	6.3	5.6
	18	16	14	12.7	11	10	9	8	7	6.3
	20	18	16	14	12.7	11	10	9	8	7
	22	20	18	16	14	12.7	11	10	9	8
	25	22	20	18	16	14	12.7	11	10	9
	28	25	22	20	18	16	14	12.7	11	10
	32	28	25	22	20	18	16	14	12.7	11
	35	32	28	25	22	20	18	16	14	12.7
	40	35	32	28	25	22	20	18	16	14
	45	40	35	32	28	25	22	20	18	16

T-Stop Compensation for Camera Speed (continued)
(constant shutter)

fps	60	76	96	120	150	192	240	300	384	484
ft/min	225	285	360	450	562	720	900	1125	1440	1815
	.9	.8	.7							
	1	.9	.8	.7						
	1.1	1	.9	.8	.7					
	1.3	1.1	1	.9	.8	.7				
	1.4	1.3	1.1	1	.9	.8	.7			
	1.6	1.4	1.3	1.1	1	.9	.8	.7		
	1.8	1.6	1.4	1.3	1.1	1	.9	.8	.7	
	2	1.8	1.6	1.4	1.3	1.1	1	.9	.8	.7
	2.2	2	1.8	1.6	1.4	1.3	1.1	1	.9	.8
	2.5	2.2	2	1.8	1.6	1.4	1.3	1.1	1	.9
	2.8	2.5	2.2	2	1.8	1.6	1.4	1.3	1.1	1
	3.2	2.8	2.5	2.2	2	1.8	1.6	1.4	1.3	1.1
	3.5	3.2	2.8	2.5	2.2	2	1.8	1.6	1.4	1.3
	4	3.5	3.2	2.8	2.5	2.2	2	1.8	1.6	1.4
	4.5	4	3.5	3.2	2.8	2.5	2.2	2	1.8	1.6
	5	4.5	4	3.5	3.2	2.8	2.5	2.2	2	1.8
	5.6	5	4.5	4	3.5	3.2	2.8	2.5	2.2	2
	6.3	5.6	5	4.5	4	3.5	3.2	2.8	2.5	2.2
	7	6.3	5.6	5	4.5	4	3.5	3.2	2.8	2.5
	8	7	6.3	5.6	5	4.5	4	3.5	3.2	2.8
	9	8	7	6.3	5.6	5	4.5	4	3.5	3.2
	10	9	8	7	6.3	5.6	5	4.5	4	3.5
	11	10	9	8	7	6.3	5.6	5	4.5	4
	12.7	11	10	9	8	7	6.3	5.6	5	4.5
	14	12.7	11	10	9	8	7	6.3	5.6	5

Shutter Angle / f.p.s. / T-stop change
(for 24 or 30 f.p.s. projection)

f.p.s.	24	22	20	19	18	16	15	14	12	9.5	7.6	6.	4.8(5)	3.8(4)	3	2.4
f.p.s.	30	27	25	24	22	20	19	17	15	12	9.5	7.6	6.	5(4.8)	4(3.8)	3
Exposure change in T-stops			1/3		2/3		1	1 1/3	1 2/3	2	2 1/3	2 2/3	3	3 1/3		
Maximum Shutter																
	235°	215°	196°	188°	176°	157°	147°	137°	118°	93°	74°	59°	47°	37°	29°	24°
	200°	183°	167°	158°	150°	133°	125°	117°	100°	79°	63°	50°	40°	32°	25°	20°
	180°	165°	150°	143°	135°	120°	113°	105°	90°	71°	57°	45°	36°	29°	23°	18°
	170°	156°	142°	135°	128°	113°	106°	99°	85°	67°	54°	43°	34°	27°	21°	17°
	150°	138°	125°	119°	113°	100°	94°	88°	75°	59°	48°	38°	30°	24°	19°	15°
	140°	128°	117°	111°	105°	93°	88°	82°	70°	55°	44°	35°	28°	22°	18°	14°
	135°	124°	113°	107°	101°	90°	84°	79°	68°	53°	43°	34°	27°	21°	17°	14°

If it is desired to slow the camera without varying the lens stop but maintain constant exposure:

If it is desired to reduce exposure without varying the lens stop:

If it is desired to reduce the exposure time per frame without reducing exposure:

This table gives shutter angles in one-third T-stop exposure intervals (bold columns), as well as for some camera speeds in less than one-third stop intervals.

SHUTTER ANGLE COMPENSATOR FOR CONSTANT EXPOSURE
(Below 24 F.P.S.)

Choose any shutter angle in left column,
then read across to find reduced angle at lower speeds.
(These are exact shutter angles for perfectly constant exposure.
In practice it may be necessary to use the nearest calibrated angle.)
(Constant Lens Aperture)

FRAMES PER SECOND							
24	22	20	18	16	14	12	8
235°	215°	196°	176°	153°	134°	118°	77°
200°	183°	167°	150°	133°	117°	100°	67°
180°	165°	150°	135°	120°	105°	90°	60°
175°	160°	146°	131°	117°	102°	88°	58°
170°	156°	142°	128°	113°	99°	85°	57°
165°	151°	138°	124°	110°	96°	83°	55°
160°	147°	133°	120°	107°	93°	80°	53°
145°	133°	121°	109°	97°	85°	73°	48°
130°	119°	108°	98°	87°	76°	65°	43°
115°	105°	96°	86°	77°	67°	58°	38°
100°	92°	83°	75°	67°	58°	50°	33°
90°	83°	75°	68°	60°	53°	45°	30°
80°	73°	67°	60°	53°	47°	40°	27°
75°	69°	63°	56°	50°	44°	38°	25°
65°	60°	54°	49°	43°	38°	33°	22°
60°	55°	50°	45°	40°	35°	30°	20°
50°	46°	42°	38°	33°	29°	25°	17°
45°	41°	38°	34°	30°	26°	23°	15°

CAMERA SPEED EXPOSURE COMPENSATOR
Exposure Increase and Decrease
Above And Below Normal 24 F.P.S.

ABOVE NORMAL SPEED

Frames Per Second	Factor	Stops Increase (open up)
24	0	0
30	1.25	1/3
38	1.5	2/3
48	2	1
60	2.5	1 1/3
76	3	1 2/3
96	4	2
120	5	2 1/3
150	6	2 2/3
192	8	3
240	10	3 1/3
300	12	3 2/3
384	16	4
484	20	4 1/3

BELOW NORMAL SPEED

Frames Per Second	Factor	Stops Decrease (close down)
24	0	0
19	1.25	1/3
15	1.5	2/3
12	2	1
9 ½	2.5	1 1/3
7 ½	3	1 2/3
6	4	2
3	8	3

REDUCED SHUTTER ANGLE EXPOSURE COMPENSATOR
(May be used at any constant camera speed)

Max. shutter exposure time at 24 F.P.S.		Max.	A 1/3 stop exposure is required for each column of reduced shutter angles.								
1/37	(.0272)	235°	188°	147°	118°	93°	74°	59°	47°	37°	29°
1/42	(.0236)	204°	162°	128°	102°	81°	64°	51°	40°	32°	25°
1/43	(.0231)	200°	158°	125°	100°	79°	63°	50°	40°	32°	25°
1/44	(.0226)	195°	155°	123°	97°	77°	61°	49°	39°	31°	24°
1/48	(.0208)	180°	143°	113°	90°	71°	57°	45°	36°	28°	22°
1/49	(.0203)	175°	139°	110°	87°	69°	55°	44°	35°	28°	22°
1/50	(.0200)	173°	137°	109°	86°	68°	54°	43°	34°	27°	22°
1/51	(.0197)	170°	135°	106°	85°	67°	54°	43°	34°	27°	21°
1/52	(.0190)	165°	131°	104°	82°	65°	52°	41°	33°	26°	21°
1/54	(.0185)	160°	127°	101°	80°	63°	50°	40°	32°	25°	20°
1/60	(.0167)	144°	114°	91°	72°	57°	45°	36°	29°	23°	18°
1/66	(.0150)	130°	103°	82°	65°	52°	41°	32°	26°	20°	16°
1/72	(.0139)	120°	95°	76°	60°	48°	38°	30°	24°	19°	15°

(These are exact shutter angles relating to 1/3 stop exposure intervals. In practice it may be necessary to use the nearest calibrated angle.) The maximum shutter angles listed are from actual cameras in use.

Exposure at Various Speeds and Shutter Openings

Shutter Angle	Frames per Second									
	2	4	6	8	10	12	14	16	18	20
280°	2/5	1/5	1/7	1/10	1/13	1/15	1/18	1/21	1/23	1/26
235°	1/3	1/6	1/9	1/12	1/15	1/18	1/21	1/25	1/27	1/31
200°	2/7	1/7	1/11	1/14	1/18	1/22	1/25	1/29	1/32	1/36
180°	1/4	1/8	1/12	1/16	1/20	1/24	1/28	1/32	1/36	1/40
175°	1/4	1/8	1/12	1/16	1/20	1/25	1/29	1/33	1/37	1/42
170°	2/9	1/9	1/13	1/17	1/21	1/26	1/30	1/34	1/38	1/42
160°	2/9	1/9	1/13	1/18	1/22	1/27	1/32	1/36	1/40	1/45
150°	1/5	1/10	1/14	1/19	1/24	1/29	1/33	1/38	1/42	1/48
140°	1/5	1/11	1/15	1/21	1/25	1/31	1/36	1/42	1/45	1/51
135°	1/5	1/11	1/16	1/21	1/26	1/32	1/37	1/43	1/47	1/53
120°	1/6	1/12	1/18	1/24	1/30	1/36	1/42	1/48	1/54	1/60
100°	1/7	1/15	1/21	1/29	1/36	1/43	1/51	1/58	1/65	1/72
90°	1/8	1/16	1/24	1/32	1/40	1/48	1/56	1/64	1/72	1/80
80°	1/9	1/18	1/27	1/36	1/45	1/54	1/63	1/72	1/81	1/90
75°	1/10	1/19	1/28	1/38	1/48	1/57	1/66	1/77	1/84	1/96
60°	1/12	1/24	1/36	1/48	1/60	1/72	1/84	1/96	1/111	1/120
45°	1/16	1/32	1/48	1/64	1/80	1/96	1/112	1/128	1/144	1/160
22.5°	1/32	1/64	1/96	1/128	1/160	1/192	1/224	1/256	1/288	1/320
10°	1/72	1/144	1/216	1/288	1/360	1/432	1/504	1/576	1/648	1/720
5°	1/144	1/288	1/432	1/576	1/720	1/864	1/1008	1/1152	1/1296	1/1440

Exposure at Various Speeds and Shutter Openings — continued

Shutter Angle	Frames per Second									
	22	24	32	40	48	64	72	96	120	128
280°	1/28	1/31	1/41	1/52	1/62	1/82	1/93	1/123	1/154	1/165
235°	1/34	1/37	1/49	1/62	1/77	1/98	1/110	1/147	1/184	1/196
200°	1/38	1/43	1/58	1/72	1/86	1/115	1/130	1/173	1/216	1/230
180°	1/44	1/48	1/64	1/80	1/96	1/128	1/144	1/192	1/240	1/256
175°	1/45	1/49	1/66	1/82	1/99	1/132	1/148	1/197	1/247	1/263
170°	1/47	1/51	1/68	1/84	1/102	1/136	1/152	1/204	1/254	1/271
160°	1/50	1/54	1/72	1/90	1/108	1/144	1/162	1/216	1/270	1/288
150°	1/53	1/58	1/77	1/96	1/115	1/154	1/173	1/230	1/288	1/307
140°	1/56	1/62	1/82	1/102	1/123	1/164	1/185	1/247	1/309	1/329
135°	1/58	1/64	1/85	1/106	1/128	1/171	1/192	1/260	1/320	1/341
120°	1/66	1/72	1/96	1/120	1/144	1/192	1/216	1/288	1/360	1/384
100°	1/76	1/86	1/115	1/144	1/173	1/230	1/259	1/346	1/432	1/461
90°	1/88	1/96	1/128	1/160	1/192	1/256	1/288	1/384	1/480	1/512
80°	1/99	1/108	1/144	1/180	1/216	1/288	1/324	1/432	1/540	1/576
75°	1/106	1/115	1/154	1/192	1/230	1/307	1/346	1/461	1/576	1/614
60°	1/132	1/144	1/192	1/240	1/288	1/384	1/432	1/576	1/720	1/768
45°	1/176	1/192	1/256	1/320	1/384	1/512	1/576	1/768	1/960	1/1024
22.5°	1/352	1/384	1/512	1/640	1/768	1/1024	1/1152	1/1536	1/1920	1/2048
10°	1/792	1/864	1/1152	1/1440	1/1728	1/2304	1/2592	1/3456	1/4320	1/4608
5°	1/1584	1/1728	1/2304	1/2880	1/3456	1/4608	1/5184	1/6912	1/8640	1/9216

Super 8mm Footage Table
Running Times and Film Lengths for Common Projection Speeds

		Super 8 (72 frames per foot)			
Projection speed in frames per second		**18**		**24**	
Running time and film length		**Feet + Frames**		**Feet + Frames**	
Seconds	1	0	18	0	24
	2	0	36	0	48
	3	0	54	1	0
	4	1	0	1	24
	5	1	18	1	48
	6	1	36	2	0
	7	1	54	2	24
	8	2	0	2	48
	9	2	18	3	0
	10	2	36	3	24
	20	5	0	6	48
	30	7	36	10	0
	40	10	0	13	24
	50	12	36	16	48
Minutes	1	15	0	20	0
	2	30	0	40	0
	3	45	0	60	0
	4	60	0	80	0
	5	75	0	100	0
	6	90	0	120	0
	7	105	0	140	0
	8	120	0	160	0
	9	135	0	180	0
	10	150	0	200	0
	15	225	0	300	0
	20	300	0	400	0
	30	450	0	600	0

Super 8mm Footage/Time Table
Typical Running Times

	Super 8 (72 frames per foot)			
Projection speed in frames per second	18		24	
Inches per second	3.0		4.0	
Film length and screen time	Minutes	Seconds	Minutes	Seconds
Feet 50	3	20	2	30
100	6	40	5	0
150	10	0	7	30
200	13	20	10	0
300	20	0	15	0
400	26	40	20	0
500	33	20	25	0
600	40	0	30	0
700	46	40	35	0
800	53	20	40	0
900	60	0	45	0
1000	66	40	50	0
1100	73	20	55	0
1200	80	0	60	0
2000	133	20	100	0
3000	200	0	150	0
4000	266	40	200	0
5000	333	20	250	0
6000	400	0	300	0
7000	466	40	350	0
8000	533	20	400	0
9000	600	0	450	0
10,000	666	40	500	0

16mm FOOTAGE TABLE — 24 F.P.S.
24 F.P.S. Sound Speed (1 foot = 40 frames)

Seconds			Seconds			Minutes		Minutes	
SECONDS	FEET	FRAMES	SECONDS	FEET	FRAMES	MINUTES	FEET	MINUTES	FEET
1		24	31	18	24	1	36	31	1116
2	1	8	32	19	8	2	72	32	1152
3	1	32	33	19	32	3	108	33	1188
4	2	16	34	20	16	4	144	34	1224
5	3		35	21		5	180	35	1260
6	3	24	36	21	24	6	216	36	1296
7	4	8	37	22	8	7	252	37	1332
8	4	32	38	22	32	8	288	38	1368
9	5	16	39	23	16	9	324	39	1404
10	6	10	40	24		10	360	40	1440
11	6	24	41	24	24	11	396	41	1476
12	7	8	42	25	8	12	432	42	1512
13	7	32	43	25	32	13	468	43	1548
14	8	16	44	26	16	14	504	44	1584
15	9		45	27		15	540	45	1620
16	9	24	46	27	24	16	576	46	1656
17	10	8	47	28	8	17	612	47	1692
18	10	32	48	28	32	18	648	48	1728
19	11	16	49	29	16	19	684	49	1764
20	12		50	30		20	720	50	1800
21	12	24	51	30	24	21	756	51	1836
22	13	8	52	31	8	22	792	52	1872
23	13	32	53	31	32	23	828	53	1908
24	14	16	54	32	16	24	864	54	1944
25	15		55	33		25	900	55	1980
26	15	24	56	33	24	26	936	56	2016
27	16	8	57	34	8	27	972	57	2052
28	16	32	58	34	32	28	1008	58	2088
29	17	16	59	35	16	29	1044	59	2124
30	18		60	36		30	1080	60	2160

16mm FOOTAGE TABLE — 25 F.P.S.

25 F.P.S. European Television Film Sound Speed (1 foot = 40 frames)

	Seconds						Minutes				
SECONDS	FEET	FRAMES	SECONDS	FEET	FRAMES	MINUTES	FEET	FRAMES	MINUTES	FEET	FRAMES
1		25	31	19	15	1	37	20	31	1162	20
2	1	10	32	20		2	75		32	1200	
3	1	35	33	20	25	3	112	20	33	1237	20
4	2	20	34	21	10	4	150		34	1275	
5	3	5	35	21	35	5	187	20	35	1312	20
6	3	30	36	22	20	6	225		36	1350	
7	4	15	37	23	5	7	262	20	37	1387	20
8	5		38	23	30	8	300		38	1425	
9	5	25	39	24	15	9	337	20	39	1462	20
10	6	10	40	25		10	375		40	1500	
11	6	35	41	25	25	11	412	20	41	1537	20
12	7	20	42	26	10	12	450		42	1575	
13	8	5	43	26	35	13	487	20	43	1612	20
14	8	30	44	27	20	14	525		44	1650	
15	9	15	45	28	5	15	562	20	45	1687	20
16	10		46	28	30	16	600		46	1725	
17	10	25	47	29	15	17	637	20	47	1762	20
18	11	10	48	30		18	675		48	1800	
19	11	35	49	30	25	19	712	20	49	1837	20
20	12	20	50	31	10	20	750		50	1875	
21	13	5	51	31	35	21	787	20	51	1912	20
22	13	30	52	32	20	22	825		52	1950	
23	14	15	53	33	5	23	862	20	53	1987	20
24	15		54	33	30	24	900		54	2025	
25	15	25	55	34	15	25	937	20	55	2062	20
26	16	10	56	35		26	975		56	2100	
27	16	35	57	35	25	27	1012	20	57	2137	20
28	17	20	58	36	10	28	1050		58	2175	
29	18	5	59	36	35	29	1087	20	59	2212	20
30	18	30	60	37	20	30	1125		60	2250	

16mm FOOTAGE TABLE — 29.97 F.P.S.

29.97 F.P.S. U.S. Television Film Sound Speed (1 foot = 40 frames)

Seconds			Seconds			Minutes			Minutes		
SECONDS	FEET	FRAMES	SECONDS	FEET	FRAMES	MINUTES	FEET	FRAMES	MINUTES	FEET	FRAMES
1	0	30	31	23	9	1	44	38	31	1393	24
2	1	20	32	23	39	2	89	36	32	1438	22
3	2	10	33	24	29	3	134	35	33	1483	21
4	3	0	34	25	19	4	179	33	34	1528	19
5	3	30	35	26	9	5	224	31	35	1573	17
6	4	20	36	26	39	6	269	29	36	1618	15
7	5	10	37	27	29	7	314	27	37	1663	13
8	6	0	38	28	9	8	359	26	38	1708	12
9	6	30	39	29	39	9	404	24	39	1753	10
10	7	20	40	29	39	10	449	22	40	1798	8
11	8	10	41	30	29	11	494	20	41	1843	6
12	9	0	42	31	19	12	539	18	42	1888	4
13	9	30	43	32	9	13	584	17	43	1933	3
14	10	20	44	32	39	14	629	15	44	1978	1
15	11	10	45	33	29	15	674	13	45	2022	39
16	12	0	46	34	19	16	719	11	46	2067	37
17	12	29	47	35	9	17	764	9	47	2112	35
18	13	19	48	35	39	18	809	8	48	2157	34
19	14	9	49	36	29	19	854	6	49	2202	32
20	14	39	50	37	19	20	899	4	50	2247	30
21	15	29	51	38	8	21	944	2	51	2292	28
22	16	19	52	38	38	22	989	0	52	2337	26
23	17	9	53	39	28	23	1033	39	53	2382	25
24	17	39	54	40	18	24	1078	37	54	2427	23
25	18	29	55	41	8	25	1123	35	55	2472	21
26	19	19	56	41	38	26	1168	33	56	2517	19
27	20	9	57	42	28	27	1213	31	57	2562	17
28	20	39	58	43	18	28	1258	30	58	2607	16
29	21	29	59	44	8	29	1303	28	59	2652	14
30	22	19	60	44	38	30	1338	26	60	2697	12

35mm FOOTAGE TABLE — 24 F.P.S.
24 F.P.S. Sound Speed (1 foot = 16 frames)

	Seconds						Minutes		
SECONDS	FEET	FRAMES	SECONDS	FEET	FRAMES	MINUTES	FEET	MINUTES	FEET
1	1	8	31	46	8	1	90	31	2790
2	3		32	48		2	180	32	2880
3	4	8	33	49	8	3	270	33	2970
4	6		34	51		4	360	34	3060
5	7	8	35	52	8	5	450	35	3150
6	9		36	54		6	540	36	3240
7	10	8	37	55	8	7	630	37	3330
8	12		38	57		8	720	38	3420
9	13	8	39	58	8	9	810	39	3510
10	15		40	60		10	900	40	3600
11	16	8	41	61	8	11	990	41	3690
12	18		42	63		12	1080	42	3780
13	19	8	43	64	8	13	1170	43	3870
14	21		44	66		14	1260	44	3960
15	22	8	45	67	8	15	1350	45	4050
16	24		46	69		16	1440	46	4140
17	25	8	47	70	8	17	1530	47	4230
18	27		48	72		18	1620	48	4320
19	28	8	49	73	8	19	1710	49	4410
20	30		50	75		20	1800	50	4500
21	31	8	51	76	8	21	1890	51	4590
22	33		52	78		22	1980	52	4680
23	34	8	53	79	8	23	2070	53	4770
24	36		54	81		24	2160	54	4860
25	37	8	55	82	8	25	2250	55	4950
26	39		56	84		26	2340	56	5040
27	40	8	57	85	8	27	2430	57	5130
28	42		58	87		28	2520	58	5220
29	43	8	59	88	8	29	2610	59	5310
30	45		60	90		30	2700	60	5400

35mm FOOTAGE TABLE — 25 F.P.S.

25 F.P.S. European Television Film Sound Speed (1 foot = 16 frames)

	Seconds						Minutes				
SECONDS	FEET	FRAMES	SECONDS	FEET	FRAMES	MINUTES	FEET	FRAMES	MINUTES	FEET	FRAMES
1	1	9	31	48	7	1	93	12	31	2906	4
2	3	2	32	50		2	187	8	32	3000	
3	4	11	33	51	9	3	281	4	33	3093	12
4	6	4	34	53	2	4	375		34	3187	8
5	7	13	35	54	11	5	468	12	35	3281	4
6	9	6	36	56	4	6	562	8	36	3375	
7	10	15	37	57	13	7	656	4	37	3468	12
8	12	8	38	59	6	8	750		38	3562	8
9	14	1	39	60	15	9	843	12	39	3656	4
10	15	10	40	62	8	10	937	8	40	3750	
11	17	3	41	64	1	11	1031	4	41	3843	12
12	18	12	42	65	10	12	1125		42	3937	8
13	20	5	43	67	3	13	1218	12	43	4031	4
14	21	14	44	68	12	14	1312	8	44	4125	
15	23	7	45	70	5	15	1406	4	45	4218	12
16	25		46	71	14	16	1500		46	4312	8
17	26	9	47	73	7	17	1593	12	47	4406	4
18	28	2	48	75		18	1687	8	48	4500	
19	29	11	49	76	9	19	1781	4	49	4593	12
20	31	4	50	78	2	20	1875		50	4687	8
21	32	13	51	79	11	21	1968	12	51	4781	4
22	34	6	52	81	4	22	2062	8	52	4875	
23	35	15	53	82	13	23	2156	4	53	4968	12
24	37	8	54	84	6	24	2250		54	5062	8
25	39	1	55	85	15	25	2343	12	55	5156	4
26	40	10	56	87	8	26	2437	8	56	5250	
27	42	3	57	89	1	27	2531	4	57	5343	12
28	43	12	58	90	10	28	2625		58	5437	8
29	45	5	59	92	3	29	2718	12	59	5531	4
30	46	14	60	93	12	30	2812	8	60	5625	

35mm FOOTAGE TABLE — 29.97 F.P.S.

29.97 F.P.S. U.S. Television Film Sound Speed (1 foot = 16 frames)

	Seconds					Minutes				
SECONDS	FEET	FRAMES	SECONDS	FEET	FRAMES	MINUTES	FEET	FRAMES	MINUTES	FEET	FRAMES
1	1	14	31	58	1	1	112	6	31	3484	0
2	3	12	32	59	15	2	224	12	32	3596	6
3	5	10	33	61	13	3	337	3	33	3708	13
4	7	8	34	63	11	4	449	9	34	3821	3
5	9	6	35	65	9	5	561	15	35	3933	9
6	11	4	36	67	7	6	674	5	36	4045	15
7	13	2	37	69	5	7	786	11	37	4158	5
8	15	0	38	71	3	8	899	2	38	4270	12
9	16	14	39	73	1	9	1011	8	39	4383	2
10	18	12	40	74	15	310	1123	14	40	4495	8
11	20	10	41	76	13	11	1236	4	41	4607	14
12	22	8	42	78	11	12	1348	10	42	4720	4
13	24	6	43	80	9	13	1461	1	43	4832	11
14	26	4	44	82	7	14	1573	7	44	4945	1
15	28	2	45	84	5	15	1685	13	45	5057	7
16	30	0	46	86	3	16	1798	3	46	5169	13
17	31	13	47	88	1	17	1910	9	47	5282	3
18	33	11	48	89	15	18	2023	0	48	5394	10
19	35	9	49	91	13	19	2135	6	49	5507	0
20	37	7	50	93	11	20	2247	12	50	5619	6
21	39	5	51	95	8	21	2360	2	51	5731	12
22	41	3	52	97	6	22	2472	8	52	5844	2
23	43	1	53	99	4	23	2584	15	53	5956	9
24	44	15	54	101	2	24	2697	5	54	6068	15
25	46	13	55	103	0	25	2809	11	55	6181	5
26	48	11	56	104	14	26	2922	1	56	6293	11
27	50	9	57	106	12	27	3034	7	57	6406	1
28	52	7	58	108	10	28	3146	14	58	6518	8
29	54	5	59	110	8	29	3259	4	59	6630	14
30	56	3	60	112	6	30	3371	10	60	6743	4

65/70mm FOOTAGE TABLE — 24 F.P.S.
24 F.P.S. SOUND SPEED (1 foot = 12.8 frames)

	Seconds						Minutes				
SECONDS	FEET	FRAMES	SECONDS	FEET	FRAMES	MINUTES	FEET	FRAMES	MINUTES	FEET	FRAMES
1	1	11.2	31	58	1.6	1	112	6.4	31	3487	6.4
2	3	9.6	32	60	0	2	225	0	32	3600	0
3	5	8.0	33	61	11.2	3	337	6.4	33	3712	6.4
4	7	6.4	34	63	9.6	4	450	0	34	3825	0
5	9	4.8	35	65	8.0	5	562	6.4	35	3937	6.4
6	11	3.2	36	67	6.4	6	675	0	36	4050	0
7	13	1.6	37	69	4.8	7	787	6.4	37	4162	6.4
8	15	0	38	71	3.2	8	900	0	38	4275	0
9	16	11.2	39	73	1.6	9	1012	6.4	39	4387	6.4
10	18	9.6	40	75	0	10	1125	0	40	4500	0
11	20	8.0	41	76	11.2	11	1237	6.4	41	4612	6.4
12	22	6.4	42	78	9.6	12	1350	0	42	4725	0
13	24	4.8	43	80	8.0	13	1462	6.4	43	4837	6.4
14	26	3.2	44	82	6.4	14	1575	0	44	4950	0
15	28	1.6	45	84	4.8	15	1687	6.4	45	5062	6.4
16	30	0	46	86	3.2	16	1800	0	46	5175	0
17	31	11.2	47	88	1.6	17	1912	6.4	47	5287	6.4
18	33	9.6	48	90	0	18	2025	0	48	5400	0
19	35	8.0	49	91	11.2	19	2137	6.4	49	5512	6.4
20	37	6.4	50	93	9.6	20	2250	0	50	5625	0
21	39	4.8	51	95	8.0	21	2362	6.4	51	5737	6.4
22	41	3.2	52	97	6.4	22	2475	0	52	5850	0
23	43	1.6	53	99	4.8	23	2587	6.4	53	5962	6.4
24	45	0	54	101	3.2	24	2700	0	54	6075	0
25	46	11.2	55	103	1.6	25	2812	6.4	55	6187	6.4
26	48	9.6	56	105	0	26	2925	0	56	6300	0
27	50	8.0	57	106	11.2	27	3037	6.4	57	6412	6.4
28	52	6.4	58	108	9.6	28	3150	0	58	6525	0
29	54	4.8	59	110	8.0	29	3262	6.4	59	6637	6.4
30	56	3.2	60	112	6.4	30	3375	0	60	6750	0

16mm Film
FOOTAGE OBTAINED AT VARIOUS CAMERA SPEEDS

Frames per second

Sec	1	2	4	8	12	16	20	22	24	32	48	64	96	120	128
5	⅛	¼	½	1	1½	2	2½	2¾	3	4	6	8	12	15	16
10	¼	½	1	2	3	4	5	5½	6	8	12	16	24	30	32
15	⅜	¾	1½	3	4½	6	7½	8¼	9	12	18	24	36	45	48
20	½	1	2	4	6	8	10	11	12	16	24	32	48	60	64
30	¾	1½	3	6	9	12	15	16½	18	24	36	48	72	90	96
60	1½	3	6	12	18	24	30	33	36	48	72	96	144	180	192

1 Foot = 40 Frames

⅘ Foot = 32 Frames

⅗ Foot = 24 Frames

½ Foot = 20 Frames

⅖ Foot = 16 Frames

⅕ Foot = 8 Frames

35mm FILM FOOTAGE + FRAMES OBTAINED AT VARIOUS CAMERA SPEEDS (1 Ft = 16 frames)

Frames Per Sec	1	2	4	8	12	16	20	22	24	32	48	64	96	120	128
Sec															
5	0'+5	0+10	1+4	2+8	3+12	5+0	6+4	6+14	7+8	10+0	15+0	20+0	30+0	37+8	40+0
10	0+10	1+4	2+8	5+0	7+8	10+0	12+8	13+4	15+0	20+0	30+0	40+0	60+0	75+0	80+0
15	0+15	1+14	3+12	7+8	11+4	15+0	18+12	20+10	22+8	30+0	45+0	60+0	90+0	112+8	120+0
20	1+4	2+8	5+0	10+0	15+0	20+0	25+0	27+8	30+0	40+0	60+0	80+0	120+0	150+0	160+0
30	1+14	3+12	7+8	15+0	22+8	30+0	37+8	41+4	45+0	60+0	90+0	120+0	180+0	225+0	240+0
60	3+12	7+8	15+0	30+0	45+0	60+0	75+0	82+8	90+0	120+0	180+0	240+0	360+0	450+0	480+0

65mm FILM FOOTAGE OBTAINED AT VARIOUS CAMERA SPEEDS (1 Ft = 12-4/5 frames)

Frames Per Sec	1	2	4	8	12	16	20	22	24	32	48	64	96	120	128
Sec															
5	0'+5fr.	0+10	1+7	3+2	4+9	6+3	7+10	8+8	9+5	12+6	18+10	25+0	37+6	46+12	50+0
10	0+10	1+7	3+2	6+3	9+5	12+6	15+8	17+2	18+10	25+0	37+6	50+0	75+0	94+2	100+0
15	1+2	2+4	4+9	9+5	14+1	18+10	23+6	25+10	28+4	37+6	56+3	75+0	112+6	141+7	150+0
20	1+7	3+2	6+3	12+6	18+10	25+0	31+3	34+5	37+6	50+0	75+0	100+0	150+0	187+4	200+0
30	2+4	4+9	9+5	18+10	28+4	37+6	46+11	51+7	56+3	75+0	112+6	150+0	225+0	281+2	300+0
60	4+9	9+5	18+10	37+6	56+3	75+0	93+10	103+2	112+6	150+0	225+0	300+0	450+0	562+4	600+0

1 Foot = 12⅘ Frames   5/8 Foot = 8 Frames   1/16 Foot = 4 Frames   3/4 Foot = 10 Frames   1/2 Foot = 6⅖ Frames   1/8 Foot = 1⅗ Frames

16mm Frame Totalizer
Showing Amount of Frames in Various Footage Totals of 16mm Film

1/20 foot = 2 frames	3/10 foot = 12 frames	7/10 foot = 28 frames
1/10 foot = 4 frames	3/8 foot = 15 frames	3/4 foot = 30 frames
1/8 foot = 5 frames	2/5 foot = 16 frames	4/5 foot = 32 frames
1/5 foot = 8 frames	1/2 foot = 20 frames	9/10 foot = 36 frames
1/4 foot = 10 frames	3/5 foot = 24 frames	1 foot = 40 frames

Feet Frames	Feet Frames	Feet Frames	Feet Frames	Feet Frames
1 = 40	21 = 840	41 = 1640	61 = 2440	81 = 3240
2 = 80	22 = 880	42 = 1680	62 = 2480	82 = 3280
3 = 120	23 = 920	43 = 1720	63 = 2520	83 = 3320
4 = 160	24 = 960	44 = 1760	64 = 2560	84 = 3360
5 = 200	25 = 1000	45 = 1800	65 = 2600	85 = 3400
6 = 240	26 = 1040	46 = 1840	66 = 2640	86 = 3440
7 = 280	27 = 1080	47 = 1880	67 = 2680	87 = 3480
8 = 320	28 = 1120	48 = 1920	68 = 2720	88 = 3520
9 = 360	29 = 1160	49 = 1960	69 = 2760	89 = 3560
10 = 400	30 = 1200	50 = 2000	70 = 2800	90 = 3600
11 = 440	31 = 1240	51 = 2040	71 = 2840	91 = 3640
12 = 480	32 = 1280	52 = 2080	72 = 2880	92 = 3680
13 = 520	33 = 1320	53 = 2120	73 = 2920	93 = 3720
14 = 560	34 = 1360	54 = 2160	74 = 2960	94 = 3760
15 = 600	35 = 1400	55 = 2200	75 = 3000	95 = 3800
16 = 640	36 = 1440	56 = 2240	76 = 3040	96 = 3840
17 = 680	37 = 1480	57 = 2280	77 = 3080	97 = 3880
18 = 720	38 = 1520	58 = 2320	78 = 3120	98 = 3920
19 = 760	39 = 1560	59 = 2360	79 = 3160	99 = 3960
20 = 800	40 = 1600	60 = 2400	80 = 3200	100 = 4000

35mm Frame Totalizer
Showing Amount of Frames in Various Footage Totals of 35mm Film

$\frac{1}{8}$ foot = 2 frames	$\frac{5}{8}$ foot = 10 frames
$\frac{1}{4}$ foot = 4 frames	$\frac{3}{4}$ foot = 12 frames
$\frac{3}{8}$ foot = 6 frames	$\frac{7}{8}$ foot = 14 frames
$\frac{1}{2}$ foot = 8 frames	1 foot = 16 frames

Feet Frames	Feet Frames	Feet Frames	Feet Frames	Feet Frames
1 = 16	23 = 368	45 = 720	67 = 1072	89 = 1424
2 = 32	24 = 368	46 = 736	68 = 1088	90 = 1440
3 = 48	25 = 400	47 = 752	69 = 1104	91 = 1456
4 = 64	26 = 416	48 = 768	70 = 1120	92 = 1472
5 = 80	27 = 432	49 = 784	71 = 1136	93 = 1488
6 = 96	28 = 448	50 = 800	72 = 1152	94 = 1504
7 = 112	29 = 464	51 = 816	73 = 1168	95 = 1520
8 = 128	30 = 480	52 = 832	74 = 1184	96 = 1536
9 = 144	31 = 496	53 = 848	75 = 1200	97 = 1552
10 = 160	32 = 512	54 = 864	76 = 1216	98 = 1568
11 = 176	33 = 528	55 = 880	77 = 1232	99 = 1584
12 = 192	34 = 544	56 = 896	78 = 1248	100 = 1600
13 = 208	35 = 560	57 = 912	79 = 1264	200 = 3200
14 = 224	36 = 576	58 = 928	80 = 1280	300 = 4800
15 = 240	37 = 592	59 = 944	81 = 1296	400 = 6400
16 = 256	38 = 608	60 = 960	82 = 1312	500 = 8000
17 = 272	39 = 624	61 = 976	83 = 1328	600 = 9600
18 = 288	40 = 640	62 = 992	84 = 1344	700 = 11200
19 = 304	41 = 656	63 = 1008	85 = 1360	800 = 12800
20 = 320	42 = 672	64 = 1024	86 = 1376	900 = 14400
21 = 336	43 = 688	65 = 1040	87 = 1392	1000 = 16000
22 = 352	44 = 704	66 = 1056	88 = 1408	2000 = 32000

35mm CAMERA RECOMMENDED PANNING SPEEDS AT VARIOUS FRAME RATES
Approximately 180° shutter — for static scenes

For 90° Sweep With Various Camera Speeds and Different Focal Length Lenses
EXAMPLE: 24 f.p.s. with 50mm Lens Should Take 23 Seconds to Pan 90° Sweep

FOCAL LENGTH OF LENS IN MM

PANNING SPEED

Unshaded Numbers: Seconds — Shaded Numbers: Minutes

CAMERA SPEED FRAMES PER/ SEC.	18 to 20	25 to 28	35	40	50	75	85	100	150	180	300
8	27	45	55	60	1.5	2.0	2.5	3.0	4.0	5.0	7.0
12	18	30	36	42	54	70	1.5	2.0	2.5	3.5	5.0
16	13	23	27	32	41	55	70	1.5	2.0	2.5	3.5
20	11	18	22	25	27	43	60	70	1.5	2.0	3.0
24	9	15	18	21	23	36	50	60	80	1.5	2.5
32	7	11	14	16	20	27	38	45	60	75	2.0
48	4.5	7.5	9	11	13	18	25	30	40	55	75
60	3.5	6	7	8	11	14	20	24	32	40	60
75	3	5	6	7	9	12	17	19	26	35	50
90	2.4	4	5	6	7	10	14	16	21	29	40
120	1.8	3	4	4	5	7	10	12	16	22	30
150	1.4	2.4	3	3.5	4	6	8	10	13	17	25

35mm CAMERA RECOMMENDED PANNING SPEEDS IN DEGREES PER SECOND
Approximately 180° shutter — for static scenes

For Various Camera Speeds and Different Focal Length Lenses
Example: 24 f.p.s. with 50mm Lens Should Be Panned 3.6° Per Second or 36° in 10 Seconds, etc.

Lens Focal Length: mm	24 f.p.s.	60 f.p.s.	80 f.p.s.	100 f.p.s.	120 f.p.s.
17	9.9°	25.0°	33.3°	41.6°	49.9°
25	7.0°	17.5°	23.3°	29.1°	34.9°
28	6.3°	15.7°	20.9°	26.1°	31.3°
32	5.5°	13.7°	28.2°	22.9°	27.4°
35	5.0°	12.7°	26.9°	21.1°	25.4°
50	3.6°	8.7°	11.7°	14.6°	17.5°
75	2.4°	6.0°	8.0°	9.9°	12.0°
85	1.7°	4.3°	5.8°	7.2°	8.7°
100	1.5°	3.9°	5.2°	6.4°	7.7°
125	1.3°	3.3°	4.3°	5.4°	6.5°
150	1.1°	2.8°	3.7°	4.6°	5.5°
180	0.95°	2.4°	3.2°	4.0°	4.7°
300	0.58°	1.5°	1.9°	2.4°	2.9°
500	0.36°	0.64°	0.9°	1.07°	1.3°

35mm CAMERA RECOMMENDED PANNING SPEEDS
180° Shutter & Various Degrees of Sweep — For Static Scenes

EXAMPLE: 60° Pan with 75mm Lens Should Take 24 Seconds

FOCAL LENGTH OF LENS IN MM
PANNING SPEED

PANNING ANGLE IN DEGREES	18 to 20	25 to 28	35	40	50	75	85	100	150	180	300	500
	Unshaded Numbers: SECONDS									Shaded Numbers: MINUTES		
30°	3	5	6	7	9	12	18	20	27	32	50	80
60°	6	10	12	14	18	24	36	40	55	60	95	2.5
90°	9	15	18	21	23	36	50	60	80	90	2.5	4.0
120°	12	20	24	28	36	48	65	80	100	2.0	3.5	5.0
150°	15	25	30	35	41	60	86	100	2.0	2.5	4.0	6.5
180°	18	30	36	42	56	72	100	2.0	2.5	3.0	5.0	8.0

Camera Speed To Auto

	Shutter Openings									
	175°	161°	146°	131°	117°	102°	88°	73°	58°	44°
	24	22	20	18	16	14	12	10	8	6

Pictures Per Second

Desired Onscreen Effective Speed

ACTUAL AUTO SPEED PER HOUR										
6	7	8	9	10	11	12	15	18	24
8	9	10	12	14	15	16	20	24	32
10	11	12	15	17	18	20	25	30	40
12	13	15	18	21	22	24	30	36	48
15	16	18	22	25	27	30	37	45	60
20	22	25	30	35	37	40	50	60	80
25	28	31	37	43	47	50	62	75	100
30	34	37	45	52	56	60	75	90	120
35	39	43	52	59	65	70	87	105	140
40	45	50	60	70	75	80	100	120	160
45	51	56	72	79	85	90	113	135	180
50	56	62	75	87	94	100	125	150	200
55	62	69	82	96	103	110	137	165	220
60	67	75	90	105	112	120	150	180	240

Example: An auto traveling 30mph can be made to appear as if it is traveling 60mph, by using a shutter speed of 12 fps with an 88° shutter opening.

Time-Lapse Chart

ONE FRAME EXPOSURE INTERVALS	LENGTH OF SCENE IN SECONDS AT 24 FPS							
	5	10	15	20	25	30	45	60
SECONDS	TIME OF ACTION (HOURS AND MINUTES)							
2	0:04	0:08	0:12	0:16	0:20	0:24	0:36	0:48
3	0:06	0:12	0:18	0:24	0:30	0:36	0:54	1:12
4	0:08	0:16	0:24	0:32	0:40	0:48	1:12	1:36
5	0:10	0:20	0:30	0:40	0:50	1:00	1:30	2:00
6	0:12	0:24	0:36	0:48	1:00	1:12	1:48	2:24
7	0:14	0:28	0:42	0:56	1:10	1:24	2:06	2:48
8	0:16	0:32	0:48	1:04	1:20	1:36	2:24	3:12
9	0:18	0:36	0:54	1:12	1:30	1:48	2:42	3:36
10	0:20	0:40	1:00	1:20	1:40	2:00	3:00	4:00
12	0:24	0:48	1:12	1:36	2:00	2:24	3:36	4:48
14	0:28	0:56	1:24	1:52	2:20	2:48	4:12	5:36
16	0:32	1:04	1:36	2:08	2:40	3:12	4:48	6:24
18	0:36	1:12	1:48	2:24	3:00	3:36	5:24	7:12
20	0:40	1:20	2:00	2:40	3:20	4:00	6:00	8:00
25	0:50	1:40	2:30	3:20	4:10	5:00	7:30	10:00
30	1:00	2:00	3:00	4:00	5:00	6:00	9:00	12:00
35	1:10	2:20	3:30	4:40	5:50	7:00	10:30	14:00
40	1:20	2:40	4:00	5:20	6:40	8:00	12:00	16:00
45	1:30	3:00	4:30	6:00	7:30	9:00	13:30	18:00
50	1:40	3:20	5:00	6:40	8:20	10:00	15:00	20:00
55	1:50	3:40	5:30	7:20	9:10	11:00	16:30	22:00
MINUTES								
1	2:00	4:00	6:00	8:00	10:00	12:00	18:00	24:00
1.5	3:00	6:00	9:00	12:00	15:00	18:00	27:00	36:00
2	4:00	8:00	12:00	16:00	20:00	24:00	36:00	48:00
2.5	5:00	10:00	15:00	20:00	25:00	30:00	45:00	60:00
3	6:00	12:00	18:00	24:00	30:00	36:00	54:00	72:00
3.5	7:00	14:00	21:00	28:00	35:00	42:00	63:00	84:00
4	8:00	16:00	24:00	32:00	40:00	48:00	72:00	96:00
5	10:00	20:00	30:00	40:00	50:00	60:00	90:00	120:00
6	12:00	24:00	36:00	48:00	60:00	72:00	108:00	144:00
7	14:00	28:00	42:00	56:00	70:00	84:00	126:00	168:00
8	16:00	32:00	48:00	64:00	80:00	96:00	144:00	192:00
9	18:00	36:00	54:00	72:00	90:00	108:00	162:00	216:00
10	20:00	40:00	60:00	80:00	100:00	120:00	180:00	240:00
12	24:00	48:00	72:00	96:00	120:00	144:00	216:00	288:00
14	28:00	56:00	84:00	112:00	140:00	168:00	252:00	336:00
16	32:00	64:00	96:00	128:00	160:00	192:00	288:00	384:00
18	36:00	72:00	108:00	144:00	180:00	216:00	324:00	432:00
20	40:00	80:00	120:00	160:00	200:00	240:00	360:00	480:00
22	44:00	88:00	132:00	176:00	220:00	264:00	396:00	528:00
25	50:00	100:00	150:00	200:00	250:00	300:00	450:00	600:00
30	60:00	120:00	180:00	240:00	300:00	360:00	540:00	720:00
35	70:00	140:00	210:00	280:00	350:00	420:00	630:00	840:00
40	80:00	160:00	240:00	320:00	400:00	480:00	720:00	960:00
45	90:00	180:00	270:00	360:00	450:00	540:00	810:00	1080:00
50	100:00	200:00	300:00	400:00	500:00	600:00	900:00	1200:00
55	110:00	220:00	330:00	440:00	550:00	660:00	990:00	1320:00
HOURS								
1	120:00	240:00	360:00	480:00	600:00	720:00	1080:00	1440:00
1.5	180:00	360:00	540:00	720:00	900:00	1080:00	1620:00	2160:00
2	240:00	480:00	720:00	960:00	1200:00	1440:00	2160:00	2880:00
2.5	300:00	600:00	900:00	1200:00	1500:00	1800:00	2700:00	3600:00
3	360:00	720:00	1080:00	1440:00	1800:00	2160:00	3240:00	4320:00

Example: 20 second scene over four hours equals one exposure every 30 seconds.

Miniatures: Camera speed, model speed, exposure factors vs. miniature scale

Scale: inches per foot	3	2	1½	1	¾	3/8	¼	1/8
fraction of full size	¼	1/6	1/8	1/12	1/16	1/32	1/48	1/96
Frames per second	48	59	68	84	96	136	166	235
Exposure factor	2x	2.5x	2.8x	3.5x	4x	5.7x	6.9x	9.8x
Exposure increase, lens T-stops	1	1⅓	1½	1¾	2	2½	2¾	3⅓

Model Speed-Feet per second (Explanation and formula on pages 365, 682 and 683.)

Portrayed Speed miles per hour								
60	44	36	31.1	25.4	22	15.6	12.7	9
40	29.3	24	20.7	16.9	14.7	10.4	8.5	6
30	22	18	15.6	12.7	11	7.8	6.4	4.5
20	14.7	12	10.4	8.5	7.3	5.2	4.2	3
10	7.3	6	5.2	4.2	3.7	2.6	2.1	1.5
5	3.7	3	2.6	2.1	1.8	1.3	1.1	.7

PROJECTION CHART FOR PROCESS BACKGROUNDS
SIZE OF PICTURE OBTAINED WITH VARIOUS LENSES / DISTANCE FROM LENS TO SCREEN

Based on Projection Aperture .906 x .679 — SIZE OF PICTURE

Lens Size inches	Dim	20 FEET	25 FEET	30 FEET	40 FEET	50 FEET	60 FEET	70 FEET	80 FEET	90 FEET	100 FEET	110 FEET	120 FEET	130 FEET	140 FEET	150 FEET	160 FEET	170 FEET	180 FEET
3	W	6'0"	7'6"	9'1"	12'1"	15'0"	18'1"	21'1"	24'2"	27'2"	30'1"	33'1"	36'3"	39'2"	42'3"	45'2"	48'4"	52'2"	56'6"
3	H	4'5"	5'7"	6'8"	9'0"	11'4"	13'6"	15'8"	18'1"	20'3"	22'7"	24'8"	27'2"	29'5"	31'8"	33'8"	35'9"	38'3"	42'2"
4	W	4'5"	5'8"	6'8"	9'0"	11'3"	13'6"	15'7"	18'1"	20'2"	22'6"	24'7"	27'3"	29'4"	31'6"	33'9"	36'3"	38'6"	40'8"
4	H	3'4"	4'4"	5'1"	6'8"	8'5"	10'1"	11'9"	13'6"	15'1"	16'9"	18'7"	20'4"	22'1"	23'7"	25'4"	27'1"	28'6"	41'0"
4½	W	4'1"	5'1"	6'0"	8'1"	10'1"	12'1"	14'1"	16'2"	18'1"	20'1"	22'0"	24'1"	26'2"	23'8"	30'3"	32'2"	34'3"	36'0"
4½	H	3'1"	3'9"	4'5"	6'1"	7'7"	9'2"	10'7"	12'2"	13'6"	15'2"	16'7"	18'3"	19'7"	21'1"	22'5"	24'0"	25'7"	27'2"
5	W	3'6"	4'6"	5'4"	7'3"	9'1"	10'9"	12'7"	14'5"	16'3"	18'3"	19'7"	21'3"	23'4"	25'5"	27'2"	28'6"	30'6"	32'5"
5	H	2'7"	3'5"	4'1"	5'5"	6'8"	8'2"	9'5"	10'8"	12'1"	13'4"	14'8"	16'4"	17'5"	19'1"	20'2"	21'8"	23'4"	24'4"
5½	W	3'3"	4'2"	4'9"	6'7"	8'2"	9'9"	11'5"	13'2"	14'7"	16'4"	18'2"	19'6"	21'4"	23'2"	24'6"	26'3"	27'8"	29'8"
5½	H	2'6"	3'2"	3'7"	5'1"	6'1"	7'5"	8'4"	9'9"	11'2"	12'3"	13'7"	14'9"	16'2"	17'2"	18'6"	19'8"	20'6"	22'4"
6	W	3'0"	3'8"	4'5"	6'1"	7'5"	9'1"	10'4"	12'2"	13'4"	15'2"	16'6"	18'2"	19'4"	21'1"	22'6"	24'2"	25'6"	27'1"
6	H	2'3"	2'9"	3'4"	4'7"	5'6"	6'8"	7'8"	9'1"	10'2"	11'4"	12'5"	13'4"	14'8"	15'9"	16'8"	18'2"	19'3"	20'4"
6½	W	2'8"	3'6"	4'3"	5'6"	6'9"	8'4"	10'1"	11'2"	12'6"	13'9"	15'4"	16'6"	18'2"	19'4"	20'6"	22'4"	23'6"	25'2"
6½	H	2'1"	2'7"	3'3"	4'2"	5'3"	6'2"	7'6"	8'2"	9'5"	10'4"	11'4"	12'6"	13'6"	14'6"	15'8"	16'4"	17'8"	18'8"
7	W	2'6"	3'3"	3'9"	5'2"	6'4"	7'1"	9'1"	10'2"	11'5"	12'9"	14'3"	15'5"	16'8"	18'4"	19'6"	20'6"	21'8"	23'2"
7	H	1'9"	2'5"	2'9"	3'9"	4'9"	5'4"	6'8"	7'6"	8'8"	9'7"	10'7"	11'6"	12'8"	13'2"	14'6"	15'4"	16'4"	17'4"
8	W		2'9"	3'4"	4'5"	5'6"	6'8"	7'9"	9'1"	10'1"	11'2"	12'3"	13'5"	14'6"	15'8"	16'8"	18'1"	19'2"	20'3"
8	H		2'2"	2'6"	3'4"	4'3"	5'1"	5'9"	6'8"	7'7"	8'4"	9'4"	10'2"	11'2"	11'7"	12'8"	13'5"	14'2"	15'2"
9	W			3'3"	4'1"	5'0"	6'0"	7'0"	8'1"	9'1"	10'1"	11'2"	12'1"	13'1"	14'2"	15'2"	16'1"	17'2"	18'0"
9	H			3'0"	3'11"	3'9"	4'5"	5'3"	6'1"	6'8"	7'6"	8'3"	9'1"	9'9"	10'6"	11'4"	12'0"	12'8"	13'6"

Quick Picture Monitor Set-Up

by Lou Levinson
ASC Associate Member

Sometimes it is necessary to do a quick "eyeball" setup of a television monitor in the field. The only tool necessary is a SMPTE color bar feed, either from a live source or from tape. SMPTE bars can be differentiated from other types of color bars by the small "reverse" patches of color under some of the main vertical color bars, and a "plunge" signal in the lower right-hand corner of the test pattern for setting brightness/black level.

The reverse patches should appear as follows: blue under white, magenta under cyan, cyan under magenta and white under blue. Having a signal that is known to be truly monochromatic is a plus, as is having a waveform monitor and vectorscope to verify the SMPTE bars are at the correct levels.

In a given operating environment, only one person should set up all the monitors. As no two people will see things exactly alike, this will help achieve consistency.

BRIGHTNESS AND CONTRAST

Locate the brightness and contrast controls on the monitor. In this context, brightness refers to black level and contrast refers to white level. Put the contrast control about ⅔ of the way up. Look for the plunge signal in the lower right corner to adjust brightness. The plunge signal is a series of three vertical gray bars whose brightness increases from left to right. The brightness may have to be turned up to see the signal at all. Brightness is correctly set when the two left-hand bars are black and the right-hand bar is just visible above black.

It should be noted that the brightness adjustment is very sensitive to ambient viewing conditions and should be done in lighting conditions that will be the actual conditions used for monitoring. After setting the brightness, check the brightest white square (bottom, left of center) to be sure it appears white enough or that it is free from blooming or flare. If it seems gray, turn the contrast up, and if there is blooming or flare, turn it down until it seems there is a clean, white square. As brightness and contrast interact, it may take a number of passes through setting the brightness and contrast adjustments to get both ends correct. If you have access to a light meter that can make reasonably accurate measurements of flickering light sources, the white square should be 30 and 35 foot-lamberts.

If there is a monochrome signal available, put it up on the monitor. If it does not look reasonably black and white, call for help, because a more sophisticated setup is required. If the monitors are not needed to match exactly or needed for critical color decisions, proceed at your own risk.

HUE AND CHROMA

In this context, hue is the overall hue of the picture and chroma is the color-saturation level. With SMPTE bars going into the monitor, locate the switches that turn the red, green and blue components of the picture on and off. They may be hidden behind a door or panel. There may also be a switch labeled "blue only," which can also be used for setting chroma and hue. Turn off the red and green components of the picture, or turn on the blue only switch. Either way, you should see the second, fourth and sixth bars (from left) disappear. If green and red have been shut down, there will only be blue bars showing. If blue only has been used, the bars may be monochrome.

At the bottom of each vertical bar will be a small segment. The object of this setup is to make all the small bottom segments match the bigger counterparts above. The hue control will mainly affect the two inside bar pairs, and the chroma control will affect the two outside pairs. Because the adjustments interact it may take several passes to get both right at the same time.

Try not to take more than 30 seconds to match the bar pairs, because your brain tries to "normalize" things after a bit. If necessary look away at a reasonably neutral area for a minute or so, then return to the setup. When you have all four bar pairs matched, put the monitor back into operating mode (turn green and red back on). Note that monitors getting digital input signals may not let hue be adjusted. If this is so, and hue is not correct, call for help.

The above setup procedure will yield reasonably matched monitors, and if the monochrome pictures look black-and-white, reasonably accurate pictures.

Lou Levinson has spent more than a quarter century as a top feature-film colorist. Levinson is the chair of the DI subcommittee of the ASC Technology Committee. He took four years off to do HD research for MLA/MEI at Universal Studios. Since 1998, he has been the senior colorist for feature masters and digital intermediates at Post Logic. He holds a MFA from the Art Institute of Chicago.

Open Face and Softlights

Lighting Charts

The values in these charts are generic. They may vary by ± 5% depending on the condition and design of luminaire.

Softlights

Size	Watts	Feet	FC	Beam	Feet	FC	Beam	Feet	FC	Beam
6.25"	600	4'	150	5.0'	8'	38	10.0'	12'	17	15.3'
8.0"	650	4'	200	5.6'	8'	50	11.2'	12'	20	16.8'
8" x 17"	2000	4'	540	5.3' x 5.3'	8'	70	17.4' x 15.5'	12'	25	29.0' x 25.8'
18"	4000	4'	1030	5.6'	8'	270	11.2'	12'	125	16.8'
6.25"	600	6'	67	7.6'	10'	24	12.7'	20'		
8.0"	650	6'	90	8.4'	10'	30	14.0'	20'		
8" x 17"	2000	6'	150	11.6' x 10.3'	10'	40	23.2' x 20.7'	20'	45	28'
18"	4000	6'			10'			20'		

Open Face

Watts	Feet	FC FL	Beam Size	FC SP	Beam Size	Feet	FC FL	Beam Size	FC SP	Beam Size	Feet	FC FL	Beam Size	FC SP	Beam Size
600	4'	940	3.5'	3020	1.6	8'	215	7.9'	785	3.3'	12'	95	12.3'	345	5.0'
650	4'	640	4.4' x 5.6'	4800	1.3' x 1.3'	8'	135	8.8' x 11.2'	1200	2.6' x 2.6'	12'	60	13.2' x 16.8'	540	4.0' x 4.0'
1000	4'	1000	3.2' x 4.2'	7330	1.2' x 1.1'	8'	250	7.0' x 9.8'	1900	2.4' x 2.3'	12'				
2000	4'					8'					12'				
600	6'	400	5.7'	1380	2.5'	10'	135	10.2'	500	4.2'	20'	35	5.0	125	8.4'
650	6'	265	6.6' x 8.4'	2160	2.0' x 1.3'	10'	85	11.2' x 14.0'	780	3.3' x 3.3'	20'	20	4' x 4'	195	6.6' x 6.6'
1000	6'	450	5.2' x 7.4'	3350	1.8' x 1.7'	10'	160	8.8' x 12.5'	1220	3.0' x 2.9'	20'	40	22.0' x 28.0'	305	6.0' x 5.9'
2000	6'					10'	330	9.8' x 12.5'	2500	3.2' x 3.2'	20'	85	19.5' x 25.0'	625	6.4' x 6.4'

Tungsten Fresnels

	Watts	Lens	Field Angle	Feet	FC FL	Beam Size	FC SP	Beam Size	Feet	FC FL	Beam Size	FC SP	Beam Size	Feet	FC FL	Beam Size	FC SP	Beam Size
Fresnel 120 V	250	2"	22° to 57°	10'	28	8.1'	57	2.4'	20'					30'				
	300	3"	12° to 58°	10'	45	8.8'	248	1.5'	20'					30'				
	650	4.5"	17° to 70°	10'	78	11.3'	660	1.4'	20'	18	22.7'	180	3.0'	30'				6.0'
	1000	4.5"	21° to 70°	10'	140	11.2'	980	2.0'	20'	35	22.4'	250	4.0'	30'	15	33.6'	110	7.8'
	1000	6"	15° to 58°	10'	130	10.5'	600	2.5'	20'	30	21.1'	165	5.1'	30'	15	31.7'	70	7.8'
	2000	6"	27° to 55°	10'	400	8.5'	1500	2.8'	20'	100	16.9'	375	5.3'	30'	45	25.2'	165	7.9'
	2000	8"	15° to 65°	10'	490	8.8'	3920	1.6'	20'	130	17.4'	1000	3.4'	30'	55	26.1'	445	5.1'
	2000	10"	20° to 55°	10'	440	13.3'	3920	1.6'	20'	110	26.5'	1000	3.4'	30'	49	39.8'	445	5.1'
	5000	10"	17° to 61°	10'	950	9.3'	5800	1.9'	20'	240	18.3'	1470	3.7'	30'	110	27.5'	655	5.5'
	5000	14"	18° to 70°	10'	875	13.0'	5812	1.5'	20'	219	26.0'	1453	3.0'	30'	97	39.0'	646	4.4'
	10000	14"	15° to 63°	10'	1600	10.0'	12100	1.6'	20'	420	20.0'	3200	3.3'	30'	185	30.0'	1430	4.9'
	10000	20"	17° to 43°	10'	2440	10.5'	21200	2.1'	20'	610	20.3'	5300	4.1'	30'	271	30.5'	2358	6.2'
	12000	17"	13° to 54°	10'					20'	813	20.4'	3875	4.6'	30'	361	30.6'	1722	6.8'
	12000	20"	17° to 43°	10'	2440	10.5'	21200	2.1'	20'	610	20.3'	5300	4.1'	30'	271	30.5'	2356	6.2'
	10000	25"	21.8° to 66.5°	10'	3400	9.5'	22000	1.5'	20'	850	19.0'	5500	3.0'	30'	378	28.5'	2444	4.5'
	12000	25"	21.8° to 66.5°	10'	3800	9.5'	23600	1.5'	20'	950	19.0'	5900	3.0'	30'	422	28.5'	2622	4.5'
Fresnel 240 V	20000	25"	21.8° to 66.5°	10'	4275	9.9'	21900	2.1'	20'	1070	19.8'	6975	4.3'	30'	474	29.7'	3100	6.4'
	24000	25"	21.8° to 66.5°	10'	11700	9.9'	47700	2.1'	20'	2925	19.8'	11925	4.3'	30'	1300	29.7'	5300	6.4'

Tungsten Fresnels

	Watts	Lens	Field Angle	Feet	FC FL	Beam Size	FC SP	Beam Size	Feet	FC FL	Beam Size	FC SP	Beam Size	Feet	FC FL	Beam Size	FC SP	Beam Size
Fresnel 120 V	250	2"	22° to 57°	40'					50'					100'				
	300	3"	12° to 58°	40'					50'					100'				
	650	4.5"	17° to 70°	40'					50'					100'				
	1000	4.5"	21° to 70°	40'					50'					100'				
	1000	6"	15° to 58°	40'					50'					100'				
	2000	6"	27° to 55°	40'	20	33.6'	95	10.5'	50'					100'				
	2000	8"	15° to 65°	40'	30	34.8'	250	6.8'	50'					100'				
	2000	10"	20° to 55°	40'	28	53.0'	250	6.8'	50'					100'				
	5000	10"	17° to 61°	40'	60	36.6'	370	7.3'	50'	40	45.8'	235	9.2'	100'				
	5000	14"	18° to 70°	40'	55	52.0'	363	5.9'	50'	35	65.0'	233	7.4'	100'				
	10000	14"	15° to 63°	40'	105	40.0'	805	6.5'	50'	70	50.0'	515	8.2'	100'				
	10000	20"	17° to 43°	40'	153	40.8'	1325	8.2'	50'	98	50.8'	848	10.3'	100'				
	12000	17"	13° to 54°	40'	203	40.8'	969	9.1'	50'	130	51.0'	620	11.4'	100'	24	101.5'	212	20.5'
	12000	20"	17° to 43°	40'	153	40.6'	1325	8.2'	50'	98	50.8'	848	10.3'	100'	24	101.5'	212	20.5'
	10000	25"	21.8° to 66.5°	40'	212	38.0'	1375	6.0'	50'	136	47.5'	880	7.5'	100'	34	95.0'	220	15.0'
	12000	25"	21.8° to 66.5°	40'	238	38.0'	1475	6.0'	50'	152	47.5'	944	7.5'	100'	38	95.0'	236	15.0'
	20000	25"	21.8° to 66.5°	40'	265	39.6'	1745	8.5'	50'	170	49.5'	1115	10.7'	100'	43	99.0'	280	21.3'
240 V Fresnel	24000	25"	21.8° to 66.5°	40'	731	39.6'	2981	8.5'	50'	468	49.5'	1908	10.7'	100'	117	99.0'	477	21.3'

HMI Fresnels

HMI Fresnel — 10', 15', 20'

Watts	Lens	Field Angle	Feet	FC FL	Beam Size	FC SP	Beam Size
575	6"	15° to 58°	10'	160	8.4'	2160	1.2'
1200	8"	11° to 46°	10'	645	6.9'	7100	1.0'
2500	10"	17° to 61°	10'	1600	11.6'	16400	1.0'
6000	14"	14° to 64°	10'	2700	11.5'	40500	.9'
12000	25"	17° to 74°	10'	4050	10.9'	59980	1.3'
18000	25"	17° to 74°	10'	6800	11.2'	83400	1.5'
575	6"	15° to 58°	15'	70	12.6'	960	1.8'
1200	8"	11° to 46°	15'	285	10.3'	3150	1.5'
2500	10"	17° to 61°	15'	711	17.4'	7288	1.5'
6000	14"	14° to 64°	15'	1200	17.3'	18000	1.4'
12000	25"	17° to 74°	15'	1800	16.3'	30350	1.9'
18000	25"	17° to 74°	15'	3040	16.8'	41975	2.2'
575	6"	15° to °58	20'	40	17.1'	540	2.4'
1200	8"	11° to 46°	20'	160	13.7'	1770	2.0'
2500	10"	17° to 61°	20'	400	23.2'	4100	2.0'
6000	14"	14° to 64°	20'	675	23.1'	10125	1.9'
12000	25"	17° to 74°	20'	1012	21.7'	18400	2.5'
18000	25"	17° to 74°	20'	1710	22.4'	21850	2.9'

25', 30'

Feet	FC FL	Beam Size	FC SP	Beam Size
25'	25	21.1'	345	3.0'
25'	105	17.2'	1130	2.5'
25'	256	29.0'	2624	2.5'
25'	432	28.8'	6480	2.3'
25'	650	27.2'	12096	3.2'
25'	1095	28.0'	15265	3.7'
30'	18	25.2'	240	3.6'
30'	70	20.6'	785	3.0'
30'	177	34.8'	1822	3.0'
30'	300	34.6'	4500	2.8'
30'	450	32.6'	8400	3.8'
30'	760	33.6'	10600	4.4'

40', 50'

Feet	FC FL	Beam Size	FC SP	Beam Size
40'	40	27.5'	445	4.0'
40'	100	46.4'	1025	4.0'
40'	169	46.1'	2531	3.7'
40'	255	43.5'	4725	5.1'
40'	428	44.8'	5963	5.9'
50'	25	34.4'	280	5.0'
50'	64	58.0'	656	5.0'
50'	108	57.7'	1620	4.7'
50'	162	54.3'	3025	6.3'
50'	275	56.0'	3816	7.3'

100', 150', 200'

Watts	Lens	Field Angle	Feet	FC FL	Beam	FC SP	Beam
1200	25"	17° to 74°	100'	40	108.7'	756	12.7'
1800	25"	17° to 74°	100'	68	112.0'	954	14.7'
1200	25"	17° to 74°	150'	18	163.0'	335	19.0'
1800	25"	17° to 74°	150'	30	168.0'	424	22.0'
1200	25"	17° to 74°	200'	10	217.3'	190	25.3'
1800	25"	17° to 74°	200'	17	224.0'	239	29.3'

HMI and Quartz Beam Projectors

HMI Beam Projector

Watts	Lens	Feet	FC FL	Beam Size	FC SP	Beam Size	Feet	FC FL	Beam Size	FC SP	Beam Size	Feet	FC FL	Beam Size	FC SP	Beam Size
1200	18"	25'	720	5.0'	5760	1.5'	125'	29	26.0'	230	1.5'	225'	9	47.0'	71	1.5'
2500	24"	25'	2016	6.0'	17280	2.0'	125'	806	31.0'	691	2.0'	225'	25	56.0'	213	2.0'
4000	24"	25'	2016	6.0'	23673	2.0'	125'	806	31.0'	947	2.0'	225'	25	56.0'	292	2.0'
12000	36"	25'	6912	7.4'	89120	N/A	125'	278	32.0'	2784	N/A	225'	85	66.7'	853	N/A
1200	18"	75'	80	15.0'	640	1.5'	175'	15	36.0'	118	1.5'	300'	5	63.0'	40	1.5'
2500	24"	75'	224	18.0'	1920	2.0'	175'	41	43.0'	353	2.0'	300'	14	75.0'	120	2.0'
4000	24"	75'	224	18.0'	2630	2.0'	175'	41	43.0'	843	2.0'	300'	14	75.0'	300	2.0'
12000	36"	75'	788	22.2'	7680	N/A	175'					300'	48	89.0'	480	N/A

Quartz Beam Projector

Watts	Lens	Feet	FC FL	Beam Size	FC SP	Beam Size	Feet	FC FL	Beam Size	FC SP	Beam Size	Feet	FC FL	Beam Size	FC SP	Beam Size
2000	18"	25'	576	5.0'	5472	1.5'	125'	23	26.0'	219	1.5'	225'	7	47.0'	68	1.5'
5000	24"	25'	1152	6.0'	4032	2.0'	125'	46	30.0'	161	10.0'	225'	14	55.0'	50	1.9'
10000	24"	25'	1120	10.74'	4800	3.25'	125'	45	53.7'	192	16.25'	225'	14	96.6'	59	29.25'
20000	36"	25'	3600	7.4'	13880	N/A	125'	144	37.0'	547	N/A	225'	44	66.7'	168	N/A
2000	18"	75'	64	15.0'	608	1.5'	175'	12	36.0'	112	1.5'	300'	4	63.0'	38	1.5'
5000	24"	75'	128	18.0'	448	6.0'	175'	24	42.0'	82	15.0'	300'	8	73.0'	28	25.0'
10000	24"	75'	124	32.23'	533	9.75'	175'	23	75.2'	96	22.75'	300'	6	128.9'	33	39.0'
20000	36"	75'	400	22.2'	1520	N/A	175'					300'	18	103.8'	70	N/A

HMI PAR

575 W HMI PAR — 7 amps Max

Lens	Feet	FC	Beam	Lens	Feet	FC	Beam	Lens	Feet	FC	Beam	Lens	Feet	FC	Beam
NONE	20'	3216	2.4'	NONE	40'	804	4.8'	NONE	75'	229	9.1'	NONE	150'	57	18.3'
VNS	20'	1103	4.1'	VNS	40'	275	8.1'	VNS	75'	78	15.2'	VNS	150'	20	30.4'
NS	20'	613	5.2'	NS	40'	153	10.5'	NS	75'	44	19.7'	NS	150'	11	39.4'
W	20'	245	16.7'	W	40'	61	33.5'	W	75'	17	62.9'	W	150'	4	125.8'
XW	20'	92	28.6'	XW	40'	23	57.1'	XW	75'	7	107.0'	XW	150'	2	214.0'
NONE	30'	1429	3.7'	NONE	50'	515	6.1'	NONE	100'	129	12.2'	NONE	200'	32	24.5'
VNS	30'	490	6.1'	VNS	50'	176	10.1'	VNS	100'	44	20.3'	VNS	200'	11	40.5'
NS	30'	272	7.8'	NS	50'	98	13.1'	NS	100'	25	26.3'	NS	200'	6	52.7'
W	30'	109	25.2'	W	50'	39	42.0'	W	100'	9.8	83.9'	W	200'	3	168.0'
XW	30'	41	42.8'	XW	50'	15	71.4'	XW	100'	4	143.0'	XW	200'	1	285.0'

1200 W HMI PAR — 15.6 amps Max

Lens	Feet	FC	Beam	Lens	Feet	FC	Beam	Lens	Feet	FC	Beam	Lens	Feet	FC	Beam
NONE	20'	4000	2.1'	NONE	40'	1000	4.2'	NONE	75'	284	7.9'	NONE	150'	71	15.8'
VNS	20'	2200	3.3'	VNS	40'	550	6.6'	VNS	75'	156	12.4'	VNS	150'	39	24.8'
NS	20'	1000	6.5'	NS	40'	250	13.0'	NS	75'	71	24.4'	NS	150'	18	48.8'
W	20'	300	17.2'	W	40'	75	34.4'	W	75'	21	64.5'	W	150'	5	129.0'
XW	20'	100	26.4'	XW	40'	25	52.8'	XW	75'	7	99.0'	XW	150'	2	198.0'
NONE	30'	1777	3.2'	NONE	50'	640	5.3'	NONE	100'	160	10.5'	NONE	200'		
VNS	30'	978	5.0'	VNS	50'	352	8.3'	VNS	100'	88	16.5'	VNS	200'		
NS	30'	444	9.8'	NS	50'	160	16.3'	NS	100'	40	32.5'	NS	200'		
W	30'	133	25.8'	W	50'	48	43.0'	W	100'	12	86.0'	W	200'		
XW	30'	44	39.6'	XW	50'	16	66.0'	XW	100'	4	132.0'	XW	200'		

HMI PAR

2500 W HMI PAR — 25.6 amps Max

Lens	Feet	FC	Beam	Lens	Feet	FC	Beam	Lens	Feet	FC	Beam	Lens	Feet	FC	Beam
NONE	20'	11025	2.6'	NONE	40'	2755	5.2'	NONE	75'	784	9.8'	NONE	150'	195	19.5'
VNS	20'	5960	6.9'	VNS	40'	1490	13.9'	VNS	75'	425	26.0'	VNS	150'	105	52.0'
NS	20'	2025	11.3'	NS	40'	505	22.7'	NS	75'	145	42.5'	NS	150'	35	85.0'
W	20'	1015	21.7'	W	40'	255	43.5'	W	75'	70	81.5'	W	150'	20	163.0'
XW	20'	450	24.5'	XW	40'	115	49.1'	XW	75'	30	92.0'	XW	150'		
NONE	30'	4900	3.9'	NONE	50'	1765	6.5'	NONE	100'	440	13.0'	NONE	200'	110	26.0'
VNS	30'	2650	10.4'	VNS	50'	955	17.3'	VNS	100'	240	34.7'	VNS	200'	60	69.3'
NS	30'	900	17.0'	NS	50'	325	28.3'	NS	100'	80	56.7'	NS	200'	20	113.3'
W	30'	450	32.6'	W	50'	160	54.3'	W	100'	40	108.7'	W	200'		
XW	30'	200	36.8'	XW	50'	70	61.3'	XW	100'	18	122.7'	XW	200'		

4000 W HMI PAR — 24 amps Max

Lens	Feet	FC	Beam	Lens	Feet	FC	Beam	Lens	Feet	FC	Beam	Lens	Feet	FC	Beam
NONE	20'	19800	2.7'	NONE	40'	4950	5.3'	NONE	75'	1410	10.0'	NONE	150'	350	20.0'
VNS	20'	7650	3.9'	VNS	40'	1910	7.7'	VNS	75'	545	14.5'	VNS	150'	135	29.0'
NS	20'	2250	8.7'	NS	40'	560	17.3'	NS	75'	160	32.5'	NS	150'	40	65.0'
W	20'	1240	15.7'	W	40'	310	31.5'	W	75'	90	59.0'	W	150'	22	118.0'
XW	20'	675	19.5'	XW	40'	169	39.1'	XW	75'	50	73.3'	XW	150'		
NONE	30'	8800	4.0'	NONE	50'	3170	6.7'	NONE	100'	790	13.3'	NONE	200'	200	26.7'
VNS	30'	3400	5.8'	VNS	50'	1225	9.7'	VNS	100'	305	19.3'	VNS	200'	80	38.7'
NS	30'	1000	13.0'	NS	50'	360	21.7'	NS	100'	90	43.3'	NS	200'	20	86.7'
W	30'	550	23.6'	W	50'	200	39.3'	W	100'	50	78.7'	W	200'		
XW	30'	300	29.3'	XW	50'	110	48.8'	XW	100'	30	97.7'	XW	200'		

HMI PAR

6000W HMI PAR — 65 amps Max

Lens	Feet	FC	Beam	Lens	Feet	FC	Beam	Lens	Feet	FC	Beam	Lens	Feet	FC	Beam
NONE	20'	25200	2.9'	NONE	40'	6300	5.7'	NONE	75'	1792	10.7'	NONE	150'	448	21.5'
VNS	20'	8100	5.3'	VNS	40'	2025	10.6'	VNS	75'	576	20.0'	VNS	150'	144	40.0'
NS	20'	4950	10.0'	NS	40'	1238	20.0'	NS	75'	352	37.5'	NS	150'	88	75.0'
W	20'	2475	19.6'	W	40'	619	39.2'	W	75'	176	73.5'	W	150'	44	147.0'
XW	20'	900	22.7'	XW	40'	225	45.3'	XW	75'	64	85.0'	XW	150'	16	170.0'
NONE	30'	11200	4.3'	NONE	50'	4032	7.2'	NONE	100'	1008	14.3'	NONE	200'	252	28.7'
VNS	30'	3600	8.0'	VNS	50'	1296	13.3'	VNS	100'	324	26.4'	VNS	200'	81	53.3'
NS	30'	2200	15.0'	NS	50'	792	25.0'	NS	100'	198	50.0'	NS	200'	50	100.0'
W	30'	1100	29.4'	W	50'	396	49.0'	W	100'	99	98.0'	W	200'	25	196.0'
XW	30'	400	34.0'	XW	50'	144	56.7'	XW	100'	36	113.3'	XW	200'	9	226.7'

12000W HMI PAR — 78 amps Max

Lens	Feet	FC	Beam	Lens	Feet	FC	Beam	Lens	Feet	FC	Beam	Lens	Feet	FC	Beam
NONE	20'			NONE	40'	10718	6.9'	NONE	75'	3048	13.0'	NONE	150'	762	25.8'
VNS	20'			VNS	40'	6450	8.0'	VNS	75'	1830	15.0'	VNS	150'	458	30.0'
NS	20'			NS	40'	2290	9.4'	NS	75'	650	17.7'	NS	150'	163	35.4'
W	20'			W	40'	1182	27.5'	W	75'	336	51.6'	W	150'	84	103.2'
XW	20'			XW	40'	717	32.8'	XW	75'	204	61.5'	XW	150'	51	123.0'
NONE	30'	19055	5.2'	NONE	50'	6860	8.6'	NONE	100'	1715	17.2'	NONE	200'	430	34.4'
VNS	30'	11460	6.0'	VNS	50'	4125	10.0'	VNS	100'	1031	20.0'	VNS	200'	260	40.0'
NS	30'	4070	7.0'	NS	50'	1465	12.0'	NS	100'	366	23.6'	NS	200'	92	47.21'
W	30'	2100	20.6'	W	50'	456	34.4'	W	100'	189	68.8'	W	200'	47	137.6'
XW	30'	1275	24.6'	XW	50'	460	41.0'	XW	100'	118	82.0'	XW	200'	30	164.0'

HMI PAR

12000 W HMI PAR 78amps Max (focusable)

Lens	Feet	FC	Beam	Lens	Feet	FC	Beam	Lens	Feet	FC	Beam	Lens	Feet	FC	Beam
SPOT	20'			NONE	40'	4106	7.3'	NONE	75'	1168	13.7	NONE	150'	292	27.5'
FLOOD	20'			VNS	40'	1181	21.4'	VNS	75'	336	40.1'	VNS	150'	84	80.3'
SPOT	30'	7300	5.5'	NS	50'	2628	9.1'	NS	100'	657	18.3'	NS	200'	164	36.6'
FLOOD	30'	2100	16.0'	W	50'	756	26.7'	W	100'	189	56.6'	W	200'	47	107.1'

18000 W HMI PAR 78amps Max (focusable)

Lens	Feet	FC	Beam	Lens	Feet	FC	Beam	Lens	Feet	FC	Beam	Lens	Feet	FC	Beam
SPOT	20'			XW	40'	5338	7.3'	XW	75'	1518	13.7	XW	150'	380	27.5'
FLOOD	20'			NONE	40'	1535	21.4'	NONE	75'	437	40.1'	NONE	150'	109	80.3'
SPOT	30'	9490	5.5'	VNS	50'	3416	9.1'	VNS	100'	845	18.3'	VNS	200'	213	36.6'
FLOOD	30'	2730	16.0'	NS	50'	983	26.7'	NS	100'	246	56.6'	NS	200'	61	107.1'

225A Brute Arc

Using White Flame or Yellow Flame Carbons without Filters

Lens	Feet	FC	Beam	Feet	FC	Beam	Feet	FC	Beam	Feet	FC	Beam
SPOT	10'	62,300	1.0'	30'	9000	2.8'	75'	1440	6.9'	175'	265	16.1'
FLOOD	10'	10,000	5.5'	30'	1190	15.8'	75'	190	39.0'	175'	35	92.0'
SPOT	15'	34,200	1.4'	40'	5060	3.7'	100'	810	9.2'	200'	200	18.4'
FLOOD	15'	4750	7.9'	40'	670	21.0'	100'	110	53.0'	200'	30	105.0'
SPOT	20'	19,500	1.8'	50'	3240	4.6'	125'	520	11.5'			
FLOOD	20'	2650	10.5'	50'	430	26.0'	125'	70	66.0'			
SPOT	25'	12,950	2.3'	60'	2250	5.5'	150'	360	13.8'			
FLOOD	25'	1700	13.1'	60'	300	32.0'	150'	50	79.0'			

*Filter Light Losses: White Flame Carbon 10% with Y-1, 40% with MT-2 plus Y-1, Yellow Flame Carbon 15% with YF-101.

Courtesy of Mole-Richardson

1000 W PAR 64 Single 1000 W Globe

PAR 64 Fixtures

Color Temp	Lens	Feet	FC	Beam	Color Temp	Lens	Feet	FC	Beam	Color Temp	Lens	Feet	FC	Beam
3200°K	VNS	5'	5040	2.1' x 1.2'	3200°K	VNS	15'	560	6.4' x 3.7'	3200°K	VNS	30'	200	10.7' X 16.2'
3200°K	NS	5'	3600	2.6' x 1.4'	3200°K	NS	15'	400	7.7' x 4.2'	3200°K	NS	30'	145	12.8' x 7'
3200°K	MF	5'	1350	5.2' x 2.2'	3200°K	MF	15'	150	15.5' x 6.5'	3200°K	MF	30'	55	25.8' x 10.8'
3200°K	WF	5'	470	8.7' x 4.6'	3200°K	WF	15'	52	26' x 13.7'	3200°K	WF	30'	20	43.3' x 22.8'
DAYLIGHT	NS	5'	2700	2.5' x 1.3'	DAYLIGHT	NS	15'	300	7.5' x 3.9'	DAYLIGHT	NS	30'	110	12.5' x 6.5'
DAYLIGHT	MF	5'	900	5' x 2.2'	DAYLIGHT	MF	15'	100	15' x 6.5'	DAYLIGHT	MF	30'	35	25.6' x 10.8'
3200°K	VNS	10'	1260	4.3' x 2.5'	3200°K	VNS	20'	315	8.5' x 4.9'	3200°K	VNS	40'	150	16' x 9.2'
3200°K	NS	10'	900	5.1' x 2.8'	3200°K	NS	20'	225	10.3' x 5.6'	3200°K	NS	40'	65	19.2' x 10.5'
3200°K	MF	10'	340	10.3' x 4.3'	3200°K	MF	20'	85	20.7' x 8.7'	3200°K	MF	40'	25	38.7' x 16.3'
3200°K	WF	10'	120	17.3' x 9.1'	3200°K	WF	20'	30	34.7' x 18.3'	3200°K	WF	40'		
DAYLIGHT	NS	10'	675	5' x 2.6'	DAYLIGHT	NS	20'	170	10' x 5.2'	DAYLIGHT	NS	40'	50	18.8' x 9.8'
DAYLIGHT	MF	10'	225	10' x 4.3'	DAYLIGHT	MF	20'	55	20' x 8.7'	DAYLIGHT	MF	40'	15	37.5' x 16.2'

6000 W PAR 64 Six 1000 W Globe — PAR 64 Fixtures

Color Temp	Lens	Feet	FC	Beam	Color Temp	Lens	Feet	FC	Beam	Color Temp	Lens	Feet	FC	Beam
3200°K	VNS	20'	6300	4.7' x 2.8'	3200°K	MF	40'	505	20.7' x 9.2'	DAYLIGHT	NS	75'	225	19.8' x 11'
3200°K	NS	20'	5220	5.3' x 3.3'	3200°K	WF	40'	175	36' x 18.7'	DAYLIGHT	MF	75'	95	37.5' x 17.3'
3200°K	MF	20'	2025	10.3' x 4.6'	DAYLIGHT	NS	40'	900	10.5' x 5.9'	3200°K	VNS	100'	250	23.3' x 14'
3200°K	WF	20'	700	18' x 9.3'	DAYLIGHT	MF	40'	340	20' x 9.2'	3200°K	NS	100'	210	26.7' x 16.7'
DAYLIGHT	NS	20'	3600	5.3' x 2.9'	3200°K	VNS	50'	1010	11.7' x 7'	3200°K	MF	100'	80	51.7' x 23'
DAYLIGHT	MF	20'	1350	10' x 4.6'	3200°K	NS	50'	835	13.3' x 8.3'	3200°K	WF	100'	30	90' x 46.7'
3200°K	VNS	30'	2800	7' x 4.2'	3200°K	MF	50'	325	25.8' x 11.5'	DAYLIGHT	NS	100'	145	26.3' x 14.7'
3200°K	NS	30'	2320	8' x 5'	3200°K	WF	50'	110	45' x 23.3'	DAYLIGHT	MF	100'	55	50' x 23'
3200°K	MF	30'	900	15.5' x 6.9'	DAYLIGHT	NS	50'	575	13.2' x 7.3'	3200°K	VNS	150'	110	35' x 21'
3200°K	WF	30'	310	27' x 14'	DAYLIGHT	MF	50'	215	25' x 11.5'	3200°K	NS	150'	90	40' x 25'
DAYLIGHT	NS	30'	1600	7.9' x 4.4'	3200°K	VNS	75'	450	17.5' x 10.5'	3200°K	MF	150'	35	77.5' x 34.5'
DAYLIGHT	MF	30'	600	15' x 6.9'	3200°K	NS	75'	370	20' x 12.5'	3200°K	WF	150'		
3200°K	VNS	40'	1575	9.3' x 5.6'	3200°K	MF	75'	145	38.8' x 17.3'	DAYLIGHT	NS	150'	65	39.5' x 22'
3200°K	NS	40'	1305	10.7' x 6.7'	3200°K	WF	75'	50	67.5' x 35'	DAYLIGHT	MF	150'	25	75' x 34.5'

9000 W PAR 64 Nine 1000 W Globe

PAR 64 Fixtures

Color Temp	Lens	Feet	FC	Beam	Color Temp	Lens	Feet	FC	Beam	Color Temp	Lens	Feet	FC	Beam
3200°K	VNS	20'	10000	4.7' x 3'	3200°K	MF	40'	760	20.7' x 9.5'	DAYLIGHT	NS	75'	370	19.8' x 11.5'
3200°K	NS	20'	8100	5.3' x 3.4'	3200°K	WF	40'	255	36' x 18.8'	DAYLIGHT	MF	75'	130	37.5' x 17.8'
3200°K	MF	20'	3040	10.3' x 4.7'	DAYLIGHT	NS	40'	1295	10.5' x 6.1'	3200°K	VNS	100'	405	23.3' x 15'
3200°K	WF	20'	1010	18' x 9.4'	DAYLIGHT	MF	40'	450	20' x 9.5'	3200°K	NS	100'	325	26.7' x 17'
DAYLIGHT	NS	20'	5175	5.3' x 3.1'	3200°K	VNS	50'	1620	11.7' x 7.5'	3200°K	MF	100'	120	51.7' x 23.7'
DAYLIGHT	MF	20'	1800	10' x 4.7'	3200°K	NS	50'	1300	13.3' x 8.5'	3200°K	WF	100'	40	90' x 47'
3200°K	VNS	30'	4500	7' x 4.5'	3200°K	MF	50'	485	25.8' x 11.8'	DAYLIGHT	NS	100'	210	26.3' x 15.3'
3200°K	NS	30'	3600	8' x 5.1'	3200°K	WF	50'	160	45' x 23.5'	DAYLIGHT	MF	100'	70	50' x 23.7'
3200°K	MF	30'	1350	15.5' x 7.1'	DAYLIGHT	NS	50'	830	13.2' x 7.7'	3200°K	VNS	150'	180	35' x 22.5'
3200°K	WF	30'	450	27' x 14.1'	DAYLIGHT	MF	50'	290	25' x 11.8'	3200°K	NS	150'	145	40' x 25.5'
DAYLIGHT	NS	30'	2300	7.9' x 4.6'	3200°K	VNS	75'	720	17.5' x 11.3'	3200°K	MF	150'	55	77.5' x 35.5'
DAYLIGHT	MF	30'	800	15' x 7.1'	3200°K	NS	75'	575	20' x 12.8'	3200°K	WF	150'	20	135' x 70.5'
3200°K	VNS	40'	2530	9.3' x 6'	3200°K	MF	75'	215	38.8' x 17.8'	DAYLIGHT	NS	150'	90	39.5' x 23'
3200°K	NS	40'	2025	10.7' x 6.8'	3200°K	WF	75'	70	67.5' x 35.3'	DAYLIGHT	MF	150'	30	75' x 35.5'

Lighting Fixture Intensity | **913**

12000 W PAR 64 Twelve 1000 W Globe

PAR 64 Fixtures

Color Temp	Lens	Feet	FC	Beam	Color Temp	Lens	Feet	FC	Beam	Color Temp	Lens	Feet	FC	Beam
3200°K	VNS	20'	13300	4.7' x 3.1'	3200°K	MF	40'	1010	20.7' x 10'	DAYLIGHT	NS	75'	492	19.8' x 13.2'
3200°K	NS	20'	10773	5.3' x 3.5'	3200°K	WF	40'	340	36' x 19.5'	DAYLIGHT	MF	75'	172	37.5' x 18.8'
3200°K	MF	20'	4044	10.3' x 5'	DAYLIGHT	NS	40'	1795	10.5' x 17.1'	3200°K	VNS	100'	538	23.3' x 15.3'
3200°K	WF	20'	1343	18' x 9.7'	DAYLIGHT	MF	40'	598	20' x 10'	3200°K	NS	100'	432	26.7' x 17.7'
DAYLIGHT	NS	20'	6882	5.3' x 3.5'	3200°K	VNS	50'	2120	11.7' x 7.7'	3200°K	MF	100'	160	51.7' x 25'
DAYLIGHT	MF	20'	2394	10' x 5'	3200°K	NS	50'	1729	13.3' x 8.8'	3200°K	WF	100'	53	90' x 48.7'
3200°K	VNS	30'	5985	7' x 4.6'	3200°K	MF	50'	645	25.8' x 12.5'	DAYLIGHT	NS	100'	280	26.3' x 17.7'
3200°K	NS	30'	4788	8' x 5.3'	3200°K	WF	50'	212	45' x 24.3'	DAYLIGHT	MF	100'	93	50' x 25'
3200°K	MF	30'	1795	15.5' x 7.5'	DAYLIGHT	NS	50'	1104	13.2' x 8.8'	3200°K	VNS	150'	240	35' x 23'
3200°K	WF	30'	598	27' x 14.6'	DAYLIGHT	MF	50'	386	25' x 12.5'	3200°K	NS	150'	193	40' x 26.5'
DAYLIGHT	NS	30'	3059	7.9' x 5.3'	3200°K	VNS	75'	957	17.5' x 11.5'	3200°K	MF	150'	73	77.5' x 37.5'
DAYLIGHT	MF	30'	1064	15' x 7.5'	3200°K	NS	75'	765	20' x 13.2'	3200°K	WF	150'	27	
3200°K	VNS	40'	3364	9.3' x 6.1'	3200°K	MF	75'	285	38.8' x 18.8'	DAYLIGHT	NS	150'	120	39.5' x 26.5'
3200°K	NS	40'	2693	10.7' x 7.1'	3200°K	WF	75'	93	67.5' x 36.5'	DAYLIGHT	MF	150'	40	75' x 37.5'

24000 W PAR 64 Twenty Four 1000 W Globe — PAR 64 Fixtures

Color Temp	Lens	Feet	FC	Beam	Color Temp	Lens	Feet	FC	Beam	Color Temp	Lens	Feet	FC	Beam
3200°K	VNS	20'	16400	4.9' x 3.1'	3200°K	MF	40'	1155	21.5' x 10'	DAYLIGHT	NS	75'	599	21' x 13.2'
3200°K	NS	20'	13000	5.6' x 3.5'	3200°K	WF	40'	365	37.1' x 19.5'	DAYLIGHT	MF	75'	212	40.3' x 18.5'
3200°K	MF	20'	4620	10.7' x 5'	DAYLIGHT	NS	40'	2098	11.2' x 17.1'	3200°K	VNS	100'	660	24.3' x 15.3'
3200°K	WF	20'	1460	18.5' x 9.7'	DAYLIGHT	MF	40'	734	21.5' x 10'	3200°K	NS	100'	520	28' x 13.7'
DAYLIGHT	NS	20'	8332	5.6' x 3.5'	3200°K	VNS	50'	2630	12.2' x 7.7'	3200°K	MF	100'	185	53.7' x 25'
DAYLIGHT	MF	20'	2934	10.7' x 5'	3200°K	NS	50'	2090	14' x 8.8'	3200°K	WF	100'	58	92.7' x 48.7'
3200°K	VNS	30'	7300	7' x 4.6'	3200°K	MF	50'	740	26.8' x 12.5'	DAYLIGHT	NS	100'	340	28' x 17.7'
3200°K	NS	30'	5800	8.4' x 5.3'	3200°K	WF	50'	235	46.3' x 24.3'	DAYLIGHT	MF	100'	114	53.7' x 25'
3200°K	MF	30'	2055	16.1' x 17.5'	DAYLIGHT	NS	50'	1345	14' x 18.8'	3200°K	VNS	150'	290	36.5' x 23'
3200°K	WF	30'	650	27.8' x 14.6'	DAYLIGHT	MF	50'	473	26.8' x 12.5'	3200°K	NS	150'	232	42' x 26.5'
DAYLIGHT	NS	30'	3726	18.4' x 15.3'	3200°K	VNS	75'	1170	18.3' x 11.5'	3200°K	MF	150'	82	80.5' x 37.5'
DAYLIGHT	MF	30'	1304	16.1' x 17.5'	3200°K	NS	75'	930	21' x 13.2'	3200°K	WF	150'	26	139' x 73'
3200°K	VNS	40'	4100	9.7' x 6.1'	3200°K	MF	75'	330	40.3' x 18.8'	DAYLIGHT	NS	150'	146	42' x 26.5'
3200°K	NS	40'	3260	11.2' x 7.1'	3200°K	WF	75'	105	69.5' x 36.5'	DAYLIGHT	MF	150'	49	80.5' x 37.5'

36000 W PAR 64 Thirty-Six 1000 W Globe

PAR 64 Fixtures

Color Temp	Lens	Feet	FC	Beam	Color Temp	Lens	Feet	FC	Beam	Color Temp	Lens	Feet	FC	Beam
3200	VNS	20'	26650	5.1' x 3.3'	3200	MF	40'	1877	22' x 10.6'	DAYLIGHT	NS	75'	973	21.6' x 13.8'
3200	NS	20'	21125	6' x 4'	3200	WF	40'	593	37.8' x 20.2'	DAYLIGHT	MF	75'	344	41' x 19.3'
3200	MF	20'	7508	11.2' x 5.6'	DAYLIGHT	NS	40'	3410	11.7' x 7.6'	3200	VNS	100'	1072	74.7' x 15.8'
3200	WF	20'	2373	19.1' x 10.3'	DAYLIGHT	MF	40'	1192	22' x 10.6'	3200	NS	100'	845	28.8' x 18.3'
DAYLIGHT	NS	20'	13540	6' x 4'	3200	VNS	50'	4274	12.6' x 8'	3200	MF	100'	300	54.2' x 25.6'
DAYLIGHT	MF	20'	4767	11.2' x 5.6'	3200	NS	50'	3396	14.6' x 9.3'	3200	WF	100'	94	93.2' x 49.2'
3200	VNS	30'	11862	7.6' x 4.8'	3200	MF	50'	1202	27.4' x 13'	DAYLIGHT	NS	100'	552	28.8' x 18.3'
3200	NS	30'	9425	8.8' x 5.9'	3200	WF	50'	382	46.9' x 24.9'	DAYLIGHT	MF	100'	185	54.2' x 25.6'
3200	MF	30'	3340	16.7' x 8.2'	DAYLIGHT	NS	50'	2186	14.6' x 9.3'	3200	VNS	150'	471	37' x 23.8'
3200	WF	30'	1056	28.4' x 15.1'	DAYLIGHT	MF	50'	768	27.8' x 13'	3200	NS	150'	377	42.6' x 27.6'
DAYLIGHT	NS	30'	6054	8.8' x 5.9'	3200	VNS	75'	1901	18.6' x 12'	3200	MF	150'	133	81' x 38'
DAYLIGHT	MF	30'	2120	16.7' x 8.2'	3200	NS	75'	1511	21.6' x 13.8'	3200	WF	150'	42	139.7' x 73.8'
3200	VNS	40'	6662	10' x 6.5'	3200	MF	75'	536	41' x 19.3'	DAYLIGHT	NS	150'	273	42.6' x 27.2'
3200	NS	40'	5298	11.7' x 7.6'	3200	WF	75'	170	70.1' x 37'	DAYLIGHT	MF	150'	80	81' x 38'

Illumination Data for Source Four Ellipsoidal Spotlights

Lens Angle	Candle Power	Field Lumens	Beam Lumens	
5°	1,370,000	9,770	8,530	**Globe for all lamps: HpL 750/115 750 watts 115 volts Initial Lumens: 21, 900 3250°K**
10°	838,000	12,300	8,770	
19°	288,000	9,960	7,120	
26°	159,000	12,400	8,250	
36°	82,000	12,300	8,030	
50°	34,900	12,400	8,220	

For illumination in foot candles or LUX divide candle power by distance squared. (**Example: 34,900 ÷ 102 feet = 349fc.**)

To find field diameter, multiply distance by multiplying factor in chart below. (**Example: 10 feet x .95 = 9.5 foot field diameter.**)

To find beam diameter, multiply distance by multiplying factor in chart below. (**Example: 10 feet x .60 = 6 foot beam diameter.**)

Multiplying Factors as Supplied by Manufacturer

Lens Angle	Field Diameter	Beam Diameter	CONVERSIONS
5°	.12	.11	**For feet to meter, multiply by .305**
10°	.19	.16	
19°	.31	.27	**Meters to feet, multiply by 3.28**
26°	.45	.33	**For footcandles to Lux, multiply by 10.764**
36°	.63	.45	
50°	.95	.60	**Lux to footcandles, multiply by .0929**

Kino Flo Fixtures

Lamp	Globe	2'	4'	6'	8'	10'	12'	14'	16'	18'	20'
2' X 1	F20/T12	82	23	10	6	4	3				
2' X 2	F20/T12	141	41	19	11	7	5				
2' X 4	F20/T12	292	82	37	22	15	11				
4' X 1	F40/T12	101	35	17	10	7	5				
4' X 2	F40/T12	233	82	40	23	16	11				
4' X 4	F40/T12	432	140	70	41	28	20				
4' X 8	F40/T12		285	140	85	58	42			21	18
4' X 10	F40/T12		350	180	110	75	60				
6' X 1	F72/T12	130	49	26	16	11	8				
6' X 2	F72/T12		100	50	30	21	16				
6' X 16	F72/T12		550	306	200	137	100			53	46

Lamps are identified by length of globe then number of globes in the fixture as 4 foot 4 lamp or 4X4. The globes are KinoFlo TruMatch lamps. The units listed are the most common used. There are other units and globes available.

Kino Flo Fixtures

Lamp	Globe	2'	4'	6'	8'	10'	12'	14'	16'	18'	20'
ParaBeam 400	KF29	1050	367	186	112	77	54	40.3	31.3	25.5	21
ParaBeam 400	Studioline 32	1490	531	265	155	108	76	56	43.8	35	29.4
ParaBeam 200	KF29	525	184	93	56	39	27	20	15.6	13	11
ParaBeam 200	Studioline 32	745	266	133	77	54	38	28	22	18	14.7
Diva-Lite 400		540	153	75	45	30	25	10			
Diva-Lite 200		360	95	45	27	15					

Lamp	Globe	1'	2'	3'	4'	5'	6'	8'
Kamio		112	45	27	17		5	2.6
12V Single	15" lamp	95	30	14	8			
12V Single	24" lamp	112	45	27	17			
12V Single	48" lamp	165	75	40	25			
Mini-Flo	9" lamp	70	21	10	6			
Mini-Flo	12" lamp	82	27	13	7.2			

Lamp	Globe	2"	4"	6"	8"	10"	12"
Micro-Flo	100mm lamp	130	50	25	15	10	7
Micro-Flo	150mm lamp	146	60	30	17	13	9

NOTE:
The General Electric Studioline 32 globes, while more efficient, tend to have a green spike.

This is not a problem in video, but needs correction for film.

SoftSun 5400°K

Fixture		Beam Angle Vert	Horiz	Distance (data in Footcandles) 5'	10'	25'	50'	75'	100'	150'	200'
3.3 KW	Spot	15°	120°	5,500	2,200	88	22	10	4.5	N/A	N/A
3.3 KW	Flood	53°	120°	1,080	275	44	11	5	2.2	N/A	N/A
10 KW	Spot	14°	108°	20,000	5,600	940	244	107	58	N/A	N/A
10 KW	Flood	28°	108°	8,000	2,580	455	122	55	32	N/A	N/A
15 KW		80° Circular Beam		2,800	680	123	30	13	7	N/A	N/A
25 KW		30° Circular Beam		N/A	8,000	1,280	320	142	80	N/A	N/A
25 KW Linear	Flood	13°	100°	N/A	N/A	1,800	450	200	109	N/A	N/A
25 KW Linear	Flood	36°	100°	N/A	N/A	590	150	66	44	N/A	N/A
50 KW	Spot	11°	100°	N/A	N/A	3,800	1,040	472	267	116	68
50 KW	Flood	35°	100°	N/A	N/A	1,680	420	186	105	46	25
100 KW	Spot	16°	100°	N/A	N/A	8,330	2,400	1,111	630	278	151
100 KW	Flood	35°	100°	N/A	N/A	3,830	1,147	526	297	131	62

Courtesy of Lighting Strikes!

Further References

3-D
Spottiswood, Raymond, *Theory of Stereoscopic Transmission,* Berkeley, CA; University of California Press , 1953.

Aerial Cinematography
Wagtendonk, W.J., *Principles of Helicopter Flight, Aviation Supplies & Academics,* Newcastle, WA, 1996.

Crane, Dale, *Dictionary of Aeronatical Terms, Aviation Supplies & Academics,* Newcastle, WA, 1997.

Spence, Charles, *Aeronautical Information Manual and Federal Aviation Regulations,* McGraw-Hill, New York, NY, 2000.

Padfield, R., *Learning to Fly Helicopters,* McGraw-Hill, New York, NY, 1992.

Industry-Wide Labor-Management Safety Bulletins at: http://www.csatf.org/bulletintro.shtml

Arctic Cinematography
Eastman Kodak Publication: *Photography Under Artic Conditions.*

Fisher, Bob, "Cliffhanger's Effects were a Mountainous Task," *American Cinematographer,* Vol. 74, No. 6, pp. 66-74, 1993.

Miles, Hugh, "Filming in Extreme Climactic Conditions," *BKSTS Journal Image Technology,* February 1988.

Moritsugu, Louise, "Crew's Peak Performance Enhanced Alive," *American Cinematographer,* Vol. 74, No. 6, pp. 78-84, 1993.

Biographies and Interviews
Almendros, ASC, Nestor, *A Man With a Camera,* New York, Farrar, Straus, Giroux, 1984.

Bitzer, ASC, Billy, *Billy Bitzer – His Story: The Autobioagraphy of D.W. Griffith's Master Cameraman,* New York, Farrar, Straus, Giroux, 1973.

Brown, ASC, Karl, with Brownlow, Kevin, *Adventures With D.W. Griffith,* New York, Farrar, Straus, Giroux, 1973.

Cardiff, BSC, Jack, *Magic Hour,* London, Faber and Faber, 1996.

Challis, BSC, Christopher, *Are They Really So Awful?: A Cameraman's Chronicle,* Paul & Co. Publishing Consortium, 1995.

Clarke, ASC, Charles G., *Highlights and Shadows: The Memoirs of a Hollywood Cameraman,* Metuchen, NJ; Scarecrow Press, 1989.

Eyman, Scott, *Five American Cinematographers: Interviews with Karl Struss, Joseph Ruttenberg, James Wong Howe, Linwood Dunn and William H. Clothier,* Metuchen, NJ; Scarecrow Press, 1987.

Higham, Charles, *Hollywood Cameramen: Sources of Light,* Indiana University Press, 1970.

Kalmus, Herbert T. and Eleanor King, *Mr. Technicolor,* Abescon, NJ; Magic Image Filmbooks, 1993.

Lassally, BSC, Walter, *Itinerant Cameraman,* London, Murray, 1987.

Laszlo, ASC, Andrew, *Every Frame a Rembrandt: Art and Practice of Cinematography*, Boston, MA; Focal Press, 2000.

Laszlo, ASC, Andrew, *It's A Wrap!*, Hollywood, CA; ASC Press, 2004.

LoBrutto, Vincent, *Principal Photography: Interviews with Feature Film Cinematographers*, Westport, CT; Praeger, 1999.

Maltin, Leonard, *The Art of the Cinematographer: A Survey and Interviews with Five Masters*, New York, Dover Publications, 1978.

McCandless, Barbara, *New York to Hollywood: The Photography of Karl Struss, ASC*, Albuquerque, NM; University of New Mexico, 1995.

Miller, ASC, Virgil E., *Splinters From Hollywood Tripods: Memoirs of a Cameraman*, New York, Exposition Press, 1964.

Rainsberger, Todd, *James Wong Howe Cinematographer*, San Diego, CA; A.S. Barnes, 1981.

Rogers, Pauline B., *More Contemporary Cinematographers on Their Art*, Boston, MA; Focal Press, 2000.

Schaefer, Dennis and Salvato, Larry, *Masters of Light: Conversations with Contemporary Cinematographers*, Berkeley, CA; University of California Press, 1985.

Sterling, Anna Kate, *Cinematographers on the Art and Craft of Cinematography*, Metuchen, NJ; Scarecrow Press, 1987.

Walker, ASC, Joseph, *The Light On Her Face*, Hollywood, CA; ASC Press, 1984.

Young, BSC, Freddie, *Seventy Light Years: An Autobiography as told to Peter Busby*, London, Faber and Faber, 1999.

Camera

Adams, Ansel, *The Camera*, New York, Morgan and Morgan, Inc., 1975.

Fauer, ASC, Jon, *Arricam Book*, Hollywood, CA; ASC Press, 2002.

Fauer, ASC, Jon, *Arriflex 16 SR Book*, Boston, MA; Focal Press, 1999.

Fauer, ASC, Jon, *Arriflex 16 SR3 the Book*, Arriflex Corp., 1996.

Fauer, ASC, Jon, *Arriflex 35 Book*, Boston, MA; Focal Press, 1999.

Fauer, ASC, Jon, *Arriflex 435 Book*, Arriflex Corp., 2000.

Samuelson, David W., *Panaflex Users' Manual*, Boston, MA; Focal Press, 1990

Camera Manufacturers

Aaton, +33 47642 9550, www.aaton.com

ARRI, (818) 841-7070, www.arri.com

Fries Engineering, (818) 252-7700, www.frieseng.com

Ikonoskop AB, +46 8673 6288, info@ikonoskop.com

Panavision, (818) 316-1000, www.panavision.com

Photo-Sonics, (818) 842-2141, www.photosonics.com

Pro8mm, (818) 848-5522, www.pro8mm.com

Camera Supports

A + C Ltd., +44 (0) 208-427 5168, www.powerpod.co.uk

Aerocrane, (818) 785-5681, www.aerocrane.com

Akela: Shotmaker, (818) 623-1700, www.shotmaker.com

Aquapod, (818) 999-1411

Chapman/Leonard Studio Equipment, (888) 883-6559, www.chapman-leonard.com

Egripment B.V., +31 (0)2944-253.988, Egripment USA, (818) 787-4295, www.egripment.com

Fx-Motion, +32 (0)24.12.10.12, www.fx-motion.com

Grip Factory Munich (GFM), +49 (0)89 31901 29-0, www.g-f-m.net

Hot Gears, (818) 780-2708, www.hotgears.com

Hydroflex, (310) 301-8187, www.hydroflex.com

Isaia & Company, (818) 752-3104, www.isaia.com

J.L. Fisher, Inc., (818) 846-8366, www.jlfisher.com

Jimmy Fisher Co., (818) 769-2631

Libra, (310) 966-9089

Louma, +33 (0)1 48 13 25 60, www.loumasystems.biz

Megamount, +44 (0)1 932 592 348, www.mega3.tv

Movie Tech A.G., +49 0 89-43 68 913, Movie Tech L.P., (678) 417-6352, www.movietech.de

Nettman Systems International, (818) 623-1661, www.camerasystems.com

Orion Technocrane, +49 171-710-1834, www.technocrane.de

Pace Technologies, (818) 759-7322, www.pacetech.com

Panavision Remote Systems, (818) 316-1080, www.panavision.com

Panther, +49 89 61 39 00 01, www.panther-gmbh.de

Spacecam, (818) 889-6060, www.spacecam.com

Strada, (541) 549-4229, www.stradacranes.com

Straight Shoot'r, (818) 340-9376, www.straightshootr.com

Technovision, (818) 782-9051, www.technovision-global.com

Wescam, (818) 785-9282, www.wescam.com

Cinematography

Brown, Blain, *Cinematography,* Boston, MA; Focal Press, 2002.

Campbell, Russell, *Photographic Theory for the Motion Picture Cameraman,* London, Tantivy Press, 1970.

Campbell, Russell, *Practical Motion Picture Photography,* London, Tantivy Press, 1970.

Carlson, Verne and Sylvia, *Professional Cameraman's Handbook,* 4th edition, Boston, MA; Focal Press, 1994.

Clarke, ASC, Charles G., *Professional Cinematography,* Hollywood, CA; ASC Press, 2002.

Cornwell-Clyne, Major Adrian, *Color Cinematography,* 3rd edition, Chapman Hall LTD 1951.

Malkiewicz, Kris J. and Mullen, M. David, *Cinematography: A Guide for Filmmakers and Film Teachers,* New York, Fireside, 2005.

Mascelli, ASC, Joseph V., *The 5 C's of Cinematography,* Beverly Hills, CA, Silman-James Press, 1998 (c1965).

Wilson, Anton, *Anton Wilson's Cinema Workshop,* Hollywood, CA; ASC Press, 1983, 1994.

Color

Albers, J., *Interaction of Color,* New Haven and London; Yale University Press, 1963.

Eastman Kodak Publication H-12, *An Introduction to Color,* Rochester, 1972.

Eastman Kodak Publication E-74, *Color As Seen and Photographed,* Rochester, 1972.

Eastman Kodak Publication H-188, *Exploring the Color Image,* Rochester.

Evans, R. M., *An Introduction to Color,* New York, NY; John Wiley & Sons, 1948.

Evans, R. M., *Eye, Film, and Camera Color Photography,* New York, NY; John Wiley & Sons, 1959.

Evans, R. M., *The Perception of Color,* New York, NY; John Wiley & Sons, 1974.

Friedman, J. S., *History of Color Photography,* Boston, MA; American Photographic Publishing Company, 1944.

Hardy, A. C., *Handbook of Colorimetry,* MIT, Cambridge, MA; Technology Press, 1936.

Hunt, R. W. G., *The Reproduction of Colour,* Surrey, UK, Fountain Press, 1995.

Itten, J., *The Art of Color,* New York, Van Nostrand Reinhold, 1973.

National Bureau of Standards Circular 553, *The ISCC-NBS Method of Designating Colors and A Dictionary of Color Names,* Washington D. C., 1955.

Optical Society of America, *The Science of Color,* New York, NY; Thomas Y. Crowell Company, 1953.

Society of Motion Picture and Teclevision Engineers, *Elements of Color in Professional Motion Pictures,* New York, NY, 1957.

Wall, E. J., *History of Three-Color Photography,* New York and London, Boston, MA; American Photographic Publishing Company, 1925.

Film

Adams, Ansel, *The Negative,* New York, Little Brown, 1989.

Adams, Ansel, *The Print,* New York, Little Brown,1989.

Eastman Kodak Publication H-1: *Eastman Professional Motion Picture Films.*

Eastman Kodak Publication H-23: *The Book of Film Care.*

Eastman Kodak Publication H-188: *Exploring the Color Image.*

Eastman Kodak Publication N-17: *Infrared Films.*

Eastman Kodak Publication: *ISO vs EI Speed Ratings.*

Eastman Kodak Publication: *Ultraviolet and Fluorescence Photography.*

Hayball, Laurie White, *Advanced Infrared Photography Handbook,* Amherst Media, 2001.

Hayball, Laurie White, *Infrared Photography Handbook,* Amherst Media, 1997.

Film Design

Affron, Charles and Affron, Mirella Jona, *Sets in Motion,* Rutgers University Press, 1995.

Carrick, Edward, *Designing for Films,* The Studio LTD and the Studio Publications Inc, 1941, 1947.

Carter, Paul, *Backstage Handbook,* 3rd edition., Broadway Press, 1994.

Cruickshank, Dan, *Sir Banister Fletcher's A History of Architecture,* 20th edition,
New York, NY, Architectural Press, 1996.

Edwards, Betty, *Drawing on the Right Side of the Brain,* revised edition, Jeremy P. Tarcher, 1989.

de Vries, Jan Vredeman, *Perspective,* Dover Publications, 1968.

Heisner, Beverly, *Studios,* McFarland and Co., 1990.

Katz, Stephen D., *Shot by Shot – Visualizing from Concept to Screen,* Boston, MA;
Focal Press, 1991, pp. 337-356.

Preston, Ward, *What an Art Director Does,* Silman-James Press, 1994.

Raoul, Bill, *Stock Scenery Construction Handbook,* 2nd edition, Broadway Press, 1999.

St John Marner, Terrance, *Film Design,* The Tantivy Press, 1974.

Film History

The American Film Institute Catalog: *Feature Films 1911–1920,* Berkeley and Los Angeles,
University of California Press, 1989.

The American Film Institute Catalog: *Feature Films 1931–1940,* Berkeley and Los Angeles,
University of California Press, 1993.

The American Film Institute Catalog: *Feature Films 1921–1930,* Berkeley and Los Angeles,
University of California Press, 1997.

The American Film Institute Catalog: *Feature Films 1961–1970,* Berkeley and Los Angeles,
University of California Press, 1997.

The American Film Institute Catalog: *Within Our Gates: Ethnicity in American Feature Films
1911–1960,* Berkeley and Los Angeles, University of California Press, 1989.

The American Film Institute Catalog: *Feature Films 1941–1950,* Berkeley and Los Angeles,
University of California Press, 1999.

Belton, John, *Widescreen Cinema,* Cambridge, MA; Harvard University Press, 1992.

Brownlow, Kevin, *Hollywood the Pioneers,* New York, NY; Alfred A. Knopf, 1979.

Brownlow, Kevin, *The Parade's Gone By,* New York, Knopf, 1968.

Coe, Brian, *The History of Movie Photography,* New York, Zoetrope, 1982.

Fielding, Raymond, *A Technological History of Motion Pictures and Television,* University of California Press, 1967.

Finler, Joel W., *The Hollywood Story,* New York, Crown, 1988.

Ryan, R.T., *A History of Motion Picture Color Technology,* London, Focal Press, 1977.

MacGowan, Kenneth, *Behind the Screen: the History and Techniques of the Motion Picture,* New York, Delacorte Press, 1965.

Rotha, Paul and Griffith, Richard, *The Film Till Now: A Survey of World Cinema,* London, Spring Books, 1967. (New York, Funk & Wagnalls, 1951.)

Schatz, Thomas, *The Genius of the System: Hollywood Filmmaking in the Studio Era,* New York, Pantheon, 1988.

Turner, George E., *The Cinema of Adventure, Romance and Terror,* Hollywood, CA; ASC Press, 1989

Film Processing

ACVL Handbook, Association of Cinema and Video Laboratories.

Case, Dominic, *Motion Picture Film Processing,* London, Butterworth and Co. Ltd. (Focal Press), 1985.

Eastman Kodak publications: H-1, H-2, H-7, H-17, H-21, H-23, H-24.07, H-26, H-36, H-37, H-37A, H-44, H-61, H-61A, H-61B, H-61C, H-61D, H-61E, H-61F, H-807 and H-822.

Happe, L. Bernard, *Your Film and the Lab,* London, Focal Press, 1974.

Kisner, W.I., *Control Techniques in Film Processing,* New York, SMPTE, 1960.

Ryan, R.T., *Principles of Color Sensitometry,* New York, SMPTE, 1974.

Filters

Eastman Kodak Publication B-3: *Filters.*

Harrison, H.K., *Mystery of Filters-II,* Porterville, CA; Harrison & Harrison, 1981.

Hirschfeld, ASC, Gerald, *Image Control,* Boston, MA; Focal Press, 1993.

Hypia, Jorma, *The Complete Tiffen Filter Manual,* AmPhoto, New York, 1981.

Smith, Robb, *Tiffen Practical Filter Manual.*

Tiffen Manufacturing Corporation Publication T179: Tiffen Photar Filter Glass

Journals, Magazines and Associations

ANSI Standards, American National Standards Institute, www.ansi.org.

American Cinematographer, ASC Holding Corp.,www.cinematographer.com.

BKSTS Journal, "Image Technology," British Kinematograph, Sound and Television Society, www.bksts.com.

SMPTE Journal, Society Of Motion Picture and Television Engineers, www.smpte.org.

Lenses

Angenieux, P., "Variable focal length objectives," U.S. Patent No. 2,847,907, 1958.

Bergstein, L., "General theory of optically compensated varifocal systems," JOSA Vol. 48, No. 9, pp. 154-171, 1958.

Cook, G.H.,"Recent developments in television optics," *Royal Television Society Journal,* pp. 158-167, 1973.

Cox, Arthur, *Photographic Optics, A Modern Approach to the Technique of Definition,* expanded edition, London, Focal Press, 1971.

Kingslake, R. "The development of the zoom lens," *SMPTE* Vol. 69, pp. 534-544, 1960.

Mann, A., Ed., "Zoom lenses," *SPIE Milestone Series* Vol. MS 85, 1993.

Neil, I.A. and Betensky, E.I, "High performence, wide angle, macro focus, zoom lens for 35mm cinematography," *SPIE* Vol. 3482, pp. 213-228, Kona, Hawaii, U.S.A., 1998.

Neil, I.A., "First order principles of zoom optics explained via macro focus conditions of fixed focal length lenses," *SPIE* Vol. 2539, San Diego, California, U.S.A., 1995.

Neil, I.A., "Liquid optics create high performance zoom lens," *Laser Focus World,* Vol. 31, No. 11, 1995.

Neil, I.A., "Uses of special glasses in visual objective lenses," *SPIE* Vol. 766, pp. 69-74, Los Angeles, California, U.S. A., 1987.

Zuegge, H. and Moellr, B., "A complete set of cinematographic zoom lenses and their fundamental design considerations," Proceedings of the 22nd Optical Symposium, pp. 13-16, Tokyo, Japan, 1997.

Lighting

Adams, Ansel, *Artificial Light Photography,* New York, Morgan and Morgan, Inc., 1956.

Alton, John, *Painting With Light,* Berkeley and Los Angeles, University of California Press, 1995.

Bergery, Benjamin, *Reflections – 21 Cinematographers at Work,* Hollywood, CA; ASC Press, 2002.

Box, Harry, *Set Lighting Technician's Handbook,* Boston, MA, Focal Press, 2003.

Malkiewicz, Kris J., *Film Lighting: Talk with Hollywood's Cinematographers and Gaffers,* New York, Touchstone, a Division of Simon & Schuster, 2012.

Millerson, Gerald, *The Technique of Lighting for Television and Film,* Boston, Focal Press, 1991

Miscellaneous

Arnheim, Rudolf, *Art and Visual Perception,* Berkley, CA, University of California Press, 1974.

Darby, William, *Masters of Lens and Light: A Checklist of Major Cinematographers and Their Feature Films,* Metuchen, NJ, Scarecrow Press, 1991.

Houghton, Buck, *What a Producer Does,* Silman-James Press, 1991.

Kehoe, Vincent J. R., *The Technique of the Professional Makeup Artist,* Boston, MA, Focal Press, 1995.

Kepes, Gyorgy, *Language of Vision,* New York, MA, Dover Publications, 1995.

Moholy-Nagy, L., *Vision in Motion,* Wisconsin; Cuneo Press, 1997.

Nilsen, Vladimir, *The Cinema as a Graphic Art,* New York; Garland Pub., 1985.

Waner, John, *Hollywood's Conversion of All Production to Color Using Eastman Color Professional Motion Picture Films,* Newcastle, ME; Tobey Publishing, 2000.

Photography

Evans, R.M., W.T. Hanson Jr., and W.L. Brewer, *Principles of Color Photography,*
New York, John Wiley & Sons Inc., 1953.

Mees, C.E.K., *The Theory of the Photographic Process,* New York, Macmillan, 1977.

Thomas Jr., Woodlief, *SPSE Handbook of Photographic Science and Engineering,*
New York, John Wiley & Sons, 1973.

Woodbury, Walter E., *The Encyclopaedic Dictionary of Photography,*
New York, The Scovill and Adams Company, 1898.

Traveling Matte Composites

Composite Components Corp. (323) 257-1163, www.digitalgreenscreen.com

Curious Software (gFx roto)
UK: Tel: +44 (0)20 7428 0288   Fax: +44 (0)20 7428 5811
US: Tel: +1 505 988 7243, Fax: +1 505 988 1654
Email: info@curious-software.com
Web: www.curious-software.com

Dazian Theatrical Fabrics: East Coast (877) 232-9426 or East Coast Design Studio (212) 206-3515,
West Coast (877) 432-9426 or West Coast Design Studio (818) 841-6500.

Flo Co (818) 780-0039 or (661) 269-2065, www.flo-co.com

Keylight (650) 326-2656, www.thefoundry.com

Kino Flo (818) 767-6528, www.kinoflo.com

Pinnacle Systems, (Commotion, Primatte) www.pinnaclesys.com

Primatte: Phototron USA, Inc. (530) 677 9980, www.primatte.com or www.phototron.com

Red*D*Mix [Ray McMillan, Flo Co Distributor] (416) 879-3761
email: mcmillan20@cogeco.ca

RFX (compositing software and hardware) (323) 962-7400, www.rfx.com

The Science and Technology Council of the Motion Picture Acadamy
(310) 247 3000, www.oscars.org/council/index.html

Stewart Filmscreen Corp. (310) 784-5300, www.stewartfilm.com

Ultimatte Corp. (818) 993-8007, www.ultimatte.com

Underwater Cinematography

Mertens, Lawrence, *In Water Photography: Theory and Practice,* Wiley Interscience,
New York, John Wiley & Sons, 1970.

Ryan, R.T., *Underwater Photographic Applications – Introduction,* SMPTE Journal,
Vol. 82, No. 12, December 1973.

Industry-Wide Labor-Management Safety Bulletins at: http://www.csatf.org/bulletintro.shtml

Visual Effects

Abbott, ASC, L.B., *Special Effects with Wire, Tape and Rubber Bands,*
Hollywood, CA; ASC Press, 1984.

Bulleid, H.A.V. (Henry Anthony Vaughan), *Special Effects in Cinematography,*
London, Fountain Press, 1960.

Clark, Frank P., *Special Effects in Motion Pictures Some Methods for Producing Mechanical Effects,*
New York, SMPTE, 1966.

Dunn, ASC, Linwood, and Turner, George E., *ASC Treasury of Visual Effects,*
Hollywood, CA; ASC Press,1983.

Fielding, Raymond, *The Technique of Special Effects Cinematography,* Boston, MA;
Focal Press, 1985.

Glover, Thomas J., *Pocket Ref,* Littleton, CO, Sequoia Publishing, 1997.

Harryhausen, Ray, *Ray Harryhausen: An Animated Life,* New York, NY, Billboards Books, 2004.

Rogers, Pauline B., *The Art of Visual Effects: Interviews on the Tools of the Trade,*
Boston, MA; Focal Press, 1999.

The Nautical Almanac, commercial edition, Arcata, CA, Paradise Cay Publications (yearly).

Vaz, Matt Cotta and Barron, Craig, *The Invisible Art: The Legends of Movie Matte Painting,*
San Francisco, CA; Chronicle Books, 2002.

INDEX

Page numbers followed by an "f" refer to a figure or illustration

F

9 781467 568326